Learning VMware vSpheres

Lay the foundations for data center virtualization using VMware vSphere 6 and strengthen your understanding of its power

Abhilash G B
Rebecca Fitzhugh

Pack<t>

BIRMINGHAM - MUMBAI

Learning VMware vSphere

First published: September 2016

Production reference: 1270916

Published by Packt Publishing Ltd.
Livery Place
35 Livery Street
Birmingham
B3 2PB, UK.
ISBN 978-1-78217-415-8

www.packtpub.com

Credits

Authors
Abhilash G B

Rebecca Fitzhugh

Reviewers
Jason Dion

Kevin Elder

Commissioning Editor
Priya Singh

Acquisition Editor
Divya Poojari

Content Development Editor
Arun Nadar

Technical Editor
Rupali R. Shrawane

Copy Editor
Safis Editing

Project Coordinator
Ritika Manoj

Proofreader
Safis Editing

Indexer
Pratik Shirodkar

Graphics
Abhinash Sahu

Production Coordinator
Shantanu N. Zagade

About the Authors

Abhilash G B (@abhilashgb) is a virtualization specialist, author, designer, and VMware vExpert (2014, 2015, and 2016) specializing in the areas of data center virtualization and cloud computing.

He has been in the IT industry for more than a decade and has been working on VMware products and technologies since the start of 2007. He currently works as a senior VMware consultant for one of largest information technology and services company in the world.

He holds several VMware certifications, including VCP3, VCP4, VCP5-DCV, and VCP-Cloud. He also holds advanced certifications such as VCAP4-DCA and VCAP5-DCA.

He is also the author of three other books by Packt Publishing: *VMware vSphere 5.1 Cookbook* (ISBN 9781849684026) in July 2013, *Disaster Recovery using VMware vSphere Replication and vCenter Site Recovery Manager* (ISBN 9781782176442) in May 2014, and *VMware vSphere 5.5 Cookbook* (ISBN 9781782172857) in February 2015.

I dedicate this book to my family. Without their patience and support, this book would not have been possible. I would like to thank my co-author, Rebecca Fitzhugh (@RebeccaFitzhugh), who has done a wonderful job with all her chapters. Thanks to the technical reviewers Jason Dion (@virtualdion) and Kevin Elder for their valuable input. Special thanks to the entire Packt team for their support during the course of writing this book.

Rebecca Fitzhugh is an independent VMware consultant specializing in architecting vSphere, Horizon, and vCloud environments, along with delivering a variety of authorized VMware courses as VMware Certified Instructor (VCI). Prior to becoming a consultant and instructor, she served 5 years in the United States Marine Corps (2006-2011), where she assisted in the build out and administration of multiple enterprise networks residing on virtual infrastructure. Rebecca has written several white papers and articles for Global Knowledge and VMware Press, as along with previously authoring *vSphere Virtual Machine Management* (ISBN 9781782172185) for *Packt Publishing*.

Rebecca currently holds multiple IT industry certifications, including VMware Certified Advanced Professional (VCAP) in Data Center Design (DCD), Data Center Administration (DCA), and Cloud Infrastructure Administration (CIA). She has been selected as a vExpert three times (2014, 2015, and 2016). You can follow Rebecca on Twitter (@RebeccaFitzhugh) or contact her via LinkedIn (`www.linkedin.com/in/rmfitzhugh/`).

I would like to thank my amazing sister, Robyn, for her love and encouragement throughout all of my personal and professional endeavors. To my best friends, Lisa, Allie, and Josh, I appreciate you putting up with my crazy travel schedule and supporting me through all the ups and downs. Thanks to my VCDX wolf pack for keeping me inspired throughout this wild adventure. Lastly, thanks to Brett for getting me started on this path and Leann for your endless patience and humor.To the editors, technical editors, and reviewers who read through my writing, thank you for being stellar throughout the process.

About the Reviewers

Jason Dion is a systems engineering manager at VMware. He joined VMware in 2008 and was a staff systems engineer before being promoted to a manager in 2016. Jason has supported enterprise accounts in Florida for most of his career that has spanned over 20 years. He is a member of the CTO ambassador program at VMware, a vExpert, and is a certified VCP in vSphere versions 3, 4, 5, and 6.

In addition to reviewing Learning vSphere, Jason has also reviewed VMware vSphere Essentials for Packt Publishing.

You can read his blogs at `http://www.flcloudlabs.com` and `http://www.friendsofwalt.com` or follow him on Twitter at `@virtualdion` or on LinkedIn at `https://www.linkedin.com/in/dionjason`.

When not talking virtualization, he enjoys spending time with his wife, Amy, and two kids, Lauren and Nick.

Kevin Elder has worked in the IT space for the past 15 years. He currently works for a VAR based in Portland, Oregon and focuses on selling, installing, and supporting virtualization and storage technologies.

www.PacktPub.com

Mapt

https://www.packtpub.com/mapt

Get the most in-demand software skills with Mapt. Mapt gives you full access to all Packt books and video courses, as well as industry-leading tools to help you plan your personal development and advance your career.

Why subscribe?

- Fully searchable across every book published by Packt
- Copy and paste, print, and bookmark content
- On demand and accessible via a web browser

Table of Contents

Preface

What began as an attempt to virtualize x86 architecture has now grown beyond the limits of a server's hardware and has gone into the realm of storage and network virtualization. Today, most modern data centers aim to achieve a hundred percent virtualization. Although there are multiple players offering virtualization solutions, with its extensive portfolio of products and solutions, VMware is still the market leader in data center virtualization.

Learning VMware vSphere is written with an aim to help you understand the concepts behind server virtualization and act as a handy guide to creating a scalable and responsive virtualization platform for hosting the virtual machine workloads of any business. VMware vSphere is the platform with its core suite of products that helps you lay the foundation of a fully functional virtualized data center for your application workloads, cloud, and the business.

We begin by introducing you to the concepts of CPU, memory, and IO virtualization and delve deeper into the architecture of a hypervisor—more specifically, VMware's ESXi. You will be introduced to the concepts of a virtual machine and learn how to create and manage them. You will learn how to create a management layer for your vSphere environment by deploying VMware vCenter Server. The book further covers vSphere Storage and Networking concepts and configuration, monitoring the performance of a vSphere environment, securing a vSphere environment, and the life cycle management of a vSphere environment.

You will walk away with enough knowledge to plan, implement, manage, and monitor a VMware vSphere environment.

What this book covers

Chapter 1, *An Introduction to Server Virtualization Using VMware*, introduces you to the concepts of server virtualization. You will learn how the processor, memory, and storage resources are virtualized with the help of the Virtual Machine Monitor (VMM). You will also be introduced to the components of VMware vSphere. This sets the foundation for what you are about to learn in the subsequent chapters.

Chapter 2, *The Hypervisor - ESXi*, discusses the architecture of ESXi hypervisor. You will learn to install or deploy ESXi hosts and perform the initial configuration. You will also learn different methods of deploying ESXi onto bare metal servers.

Chapter 3, *The Management Layer – vCenter*, teaches you how to install and configure VMware vCenter Server. You will learn how to deploy both Windows and Linux versions of vCenter Server and also how to perform the post-installation configuration on them. You will learn how to configure identity sources on the SSO server and configure licenses for vSphere environment. Then, you will learn how to configure Enhanced Linked Mode for vCenters.

Chapter 4, *vSphere Networking Concepts and Management*, explores the networking concepts associated with a VMware infrastructure. You will learn how to create and manage virtual switches (standard or distributed). From there, you will learn more about virtual switch security settings, traffic shaping, load balancing, and failover. You will explore the network monitoring methods and bandwidth management using Network I/O Control.

Chapter 5, *vSphere Storage Concepts and Management*, explains how to plan, implement, and manage storage access to a vSphere infrastructure. You will explore the Pluggable Storage Architecture (PSA), a modular API framework that lets storage vendors build their own SATP or PSP plugins. You will learn how to configure access to Fiber Channel, iSCSI, and NFS storage. You will learn how to create and manage VMFS Datastores.

Chapter 6, *Advanced Infrastructure Management*, explores vSphere vMotion in detail. You will learn how to enable DRS on a cluster. Then, you will learn how to enable and configure vSphere HA. You will also learn about the VM Component Protection feature of vSphere HA, which enables recovery of virtual machines affected by storage connectivity issues.

Chapter 7, *Understanding Host Profiles, Image Profile and Auto Deploy*, discusses how to use and manage Host Profiles. You will learn how to customize and manage image profiles using Image Builder. You will also explore how Auto Deploy allows you to provision hundreds of ESXi hosts at a time.

Chapter 8, *Virtual Machine Concepts and Management*, explains the Virtual Machine components and introduces the new vSphere 6 Virtual Machine Features. You will learn to modify Virtual Machine settings. You will explore all about Fault Tolerance and configure it on a Virtual Machine.

Chapter 9, *Monitoring Performance of a vSphere Environment*, shows how to monitor the performance of a vSphere environment. You will explore the tools that are available within vSphere that assist VMware administrators to monitor resources and detect any potential bottlenecks. You will learn how to configure and use Alarms to alert administrators when specific events occur or when thresholds are exceeded.

Chapter 10, *Certificate Management for a vSphere Environment*, introduces vSphere 6's new VMware Certificate Authority (VMCA) and discusses how it could be used to alleviate some of the headaches surrounding certificate management. You will then explore certificate management in detail. You will look at multiple configurations, including using VMCA signed certificates, using VMCA as an intermediate certificate authority, using external certificate authority signed certificates, or a hybrid configuration.

Chapter 11, *Securing a vSphere Environment*, guides you through the importance of securing a vSphere environment. You will learn how to secure ESXi, vCenter Server, and virtual machines. You will also learn how to configure Single Sign-On and grant privileges to users in vSphere.

Chapter 12, *Life Cycle Management of a vSphere Environment*, discusses vSphere life cycle management. You will learn how to upgrade vSphere components from vSphere 5.x to vSphere 6.

What you need for this book

You will learn about the software requirements for every vSphere component covered in this book in their respective chapters, but to start with a basic lab setup, you will need at least two ESXi hosts, a vCenter Server instance, a Domain Controller, a DHCP server, a DNS server, and a TFTP Server. For learning purposes, you don't really need to run ESXi on physical machines.

You can use VMware Workstation or VMware Fusion to set up a hosted lab on your PC or Mac, provided the machine has adequate compute and storage capacity.

For shared storage, you can use any of the following free virtual storage applications:

- Celerra UBER 3.2: `http://nickapedia.com/21/1/4/play-it-again-sam-celer ra-uber-v3-2/`
- OpenFiler: `https://www.openfiler.com`
- HP StoreVirtual Storage: `http://www8.hp.com/in/en/products/data-storage/ storevirtual.html`

Who this book is for

This book is intended for experienced technologists who want to design and implement VMware solutions. This book will help the reader get a head start in learning how to design, implement, and manage a modern day Data Center. Infrastructure architects and system administrators will also find this book useful to aid them in their day-to-day activities. You can use this book as reference material for VCP and VCAP certification exams. Keep in mind, however, that the book is not written to follow the blueprint for either of the exams.

Conventions

In this book, you will find a number of text styles that distinguish between different kinds of information. Here are some examples of these styles and an explanation of their meaning.

Code words in text, database table names, folder names, filenames, file extensions, pathnames, dummy URLs, user input, and Twitter handles are shown as follows: "Mount the downloaded `WebStorm-10*.dmg` disk image file as another disk in your system."

New terms and **important words** are shown in bold. Words that you see on the screen, for example, in menus or dialog boxes, appear in the text like this: "The shortcuts in this book are based on the `Mac OS X 10.5+` scheme."

A block of code is set as follows:

```
.encoding = "UTF-8"
config.version = "8"
virtualHW.version = "11"
nvram = "ExampleVM.nvram"
pciBridge0.present = "TRUE"
```

Warnings or important notes appear in a box like this.

Tips and tricks appear like this.

Reader feedback

Feedback from our readers is always welcome. Let us know what you think about this book-what you liked or disliked. Reader feedback is important for us as it helps us develop titles that you will really get the most out of.

To send us general feedback, simply e-mail feedback@packtpub.com, and mention the book's title in the subject of your message. If there is a topic that you have expertise in and you are interested in either writing or contributing to a book, see our author guide at www.packtpub.com/authors.

Customer support

Now that you are the proud owner of a Packt book, we have a number of things to help you to get the most from your purchase.

Downloading the color images of this book

We also provide you with a PDF file that has color images of the screenshots/diagrams used in this book. The color images will help you better understand the changes in the output. You can download this file from http://www.packtpub.com/sites/default/files/downl oads/LearningVMwarevSphere_ColorImages.pdf.

Errata

Although we have taken every care to ensure the accuracy of our content, mistakes do happen. If you find a mistake in one of our books-maybe a mistake in the text or the code-we would be grateful if you could report this to us. By doing so, you can save other readers from frustration and help us improve subsequent versions of this book. If you find any errata, please report them by visiting http://www.packtpub.com/submit-errata, selecting your book, clicking on the **Errata Submission Form** link, and entering the details of your errata. Once your errata are verified, your submission will be accepted and the errata will be uploaded to our website or added to any list of existing errata under the Errata section of that title.

To view the previously submitted errata, go to https://www.packtpub.com/books/conten t/support and enter the name of the book in the search field. The required information will appear under the **Errata** section.

Piracy

Piracy of copyrighted material on the Internet is an ongoing problem across all media. At Packt, we take the protection of our copyright and licenses very seriously. If you come across any illegal copies of our works in any form on the Internet, please provide us with the location address or website name immediately so that we can pursue a remedy.

Please contact us at `copyright@packtpub.com` with a link to the suspected pirated material.

We appreciate your help in protecting our authors and our ability to bring you valuable content.

Questions

If you have a problem with any aspect of this book, you can contact us at `questions@packtpub.com`, and we will do our best to address the problem.

1
An Introduction to Server Virtualization Using VMware

Let's go back to a time when there wasn't a concept of server virtualization. We had data centers running a large number of machines; most of them were bought to run an application or a set of services. All those servers had enough CPU, memory, and storage capacity to host the application or the services that were running on it. The amount of compute and storage resources depended on what the application or the service would need during its peak load. However, the catch here is that not all servers execute peak load all the time. Research shows that more than 90% of hardware resources remain under-utilized. That is a huge number in terms of resource wastage. Running more than one application or service for the business always meant that there was a demand for additional hardware resources. Such a demand contributed to other factors such as power consumption, investment in cooling solutions, hardware maintenance, and the real estate space required to host all the hardware.

Now, a possible solution an administrator could have fantasized about would be to find a way to somehow magically connect all these servers together and present it as a large pool of resources to the applications or services. If that were possible, then you would probably be renting out 90% of your resources, that you have already invested in, to someone else to run their applications and you are paid for that service. Or, if you were in the planning phase of a new infrastructure, you could reduce the amount of server hardware needed for hosting the services. Unfortunately, such a conglomeration was far from reality due to two main reasons, the first one being the physical boundaries that separate these hardware resources and the second one being that not all services could run alongside each other without running into a conflict, affecting both the services. This is where the concept of server virtualization did its magic, on its introduction, like never perceived before.

In this chapter, we will learn the following:

- The magic of server virtualization
- What is a hypervisor?
- What is a virtual machine?
- An introduction to VMware vSphere

The magic of server virtualization

Server virtualization lets you run multiple conventional operating systems such as Windows and Linux, isolated from each other but sharing the same physical server hardware. This is achieved by creating an abstraction layer between the server hardware and the operating systems that run on them. The abstraction layer acts as the interface and the resource management layer, which enables the sharing of the resources between the operating systems:

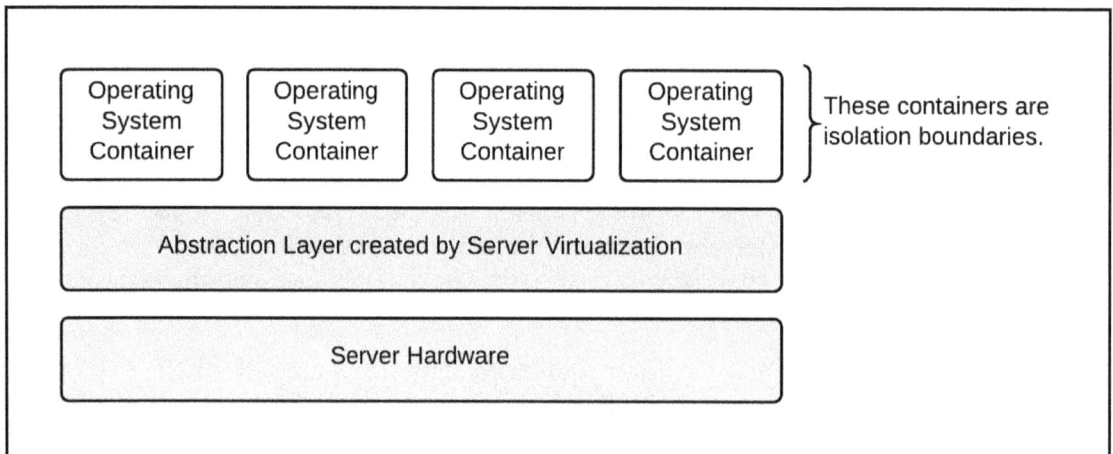

The operating systems remain completely unaware of the fact that they are running inside a virtual machine and that there are other operating systems running on the same hardware. This is because each of these operating systems live in their own *containers*, which isolates them from other operating systems. *This should not be confused with application containers such as Docker or Rocket.*

Although the server's hardware resources are shared, server virtualization requires you to assign resources to the operating system containers. The resources are assigned in terms of the number of virtual CPUs, amount of memory, amount of storage, and virtual network cards.

Server virtualization is enabled by a piece of code called the *hypervisor*, and the resource-assigned container for running the operating systems is called a *virtual machine*. We will discuss more on the concepts of hypervisors and virtual machines later in this chapter.

The benefits of server virtualization

Before we delve into the further details of virtualization, it is important to understand the benefits of virtualization:

- **Cost, energy, and real estate savings**: Virtualizing reduces the number of hardware servers required to host your applications. This is due to the fact that you no longer would need to buy separate physical servers to host conflicting applications. Instead, you could run them on separate virtual machines running on the same server hardware. A lesser number of physical servers will mean reduced power requirements and smaller data center real estate as well.
- **Easier management**: Unlike managing physical machines separately, you now can manage all your virtual machines from a single management interface. This greatly reduces the administrative effort, which would otherwise be required to manage a large number of physical machines.
- **Easier maintenance**: Performing hardware maintenance no longer requires application downtime since virtual machines can be migrated in their live state from the server which needs maintenance to another working server.

Although there are several benefits, we have covered the most salient ones in this section. *The Economics of Virtualization, Moving toward an application-based Cost Mode, WHITE PAPER* is a great read to understand the benefits that virtualization offers.

For more information, visit `https://www.vmware.com/files/pdf/Virtualization-application-based-cost-model-WP-EN.pdf`.

What is a hypervisor?

A hypervisor is a piece of software usually not very big in terms of compute or storage footprint, which makes server virtualization possible. It forms an abstraction layer between the server's hardware resources and the operating system containers. There are two types of hypervisors defining two different types of approaches:

- Type 1 hypervisor (bare-metal hypervisor)
- Type 2 hypervisor (hosted hypervisor)

A type 1 hypervisor is installed directly on the server hardware as you would install an operating system on any hardware. Hence it is referred to as a bare-metal hypervisor. It interfaces directly with the hardware. This empowers it to effectively manage sharing of the server hardware resources, among the virtual machines:

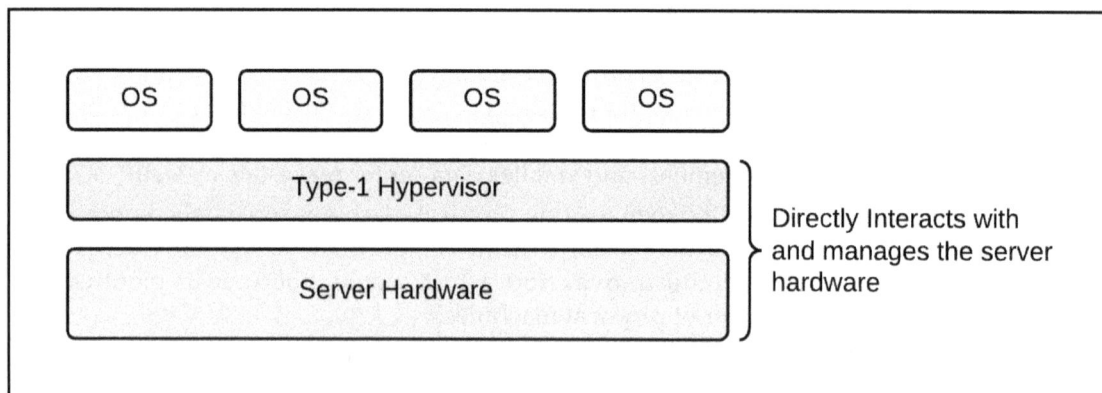

Examples of a type 1 hypervisor are VMware ESXi, Microsoft Hyper-V, and Citrix XenServer.

A type 2 hypervisor cannot be installed directly on server hardware. It is installed as a piece of software on any of the supported conventional operating systems such as Apple OS X, Microsoft Windows, or Linux. It leverages the underlying operating systems ability for resource management. The performance of a type 2 hypervisor is considered to be lower than that of a type 1 hypervisor. This is due to the fact that it cannot directly interface or manage the server's hardware resources:

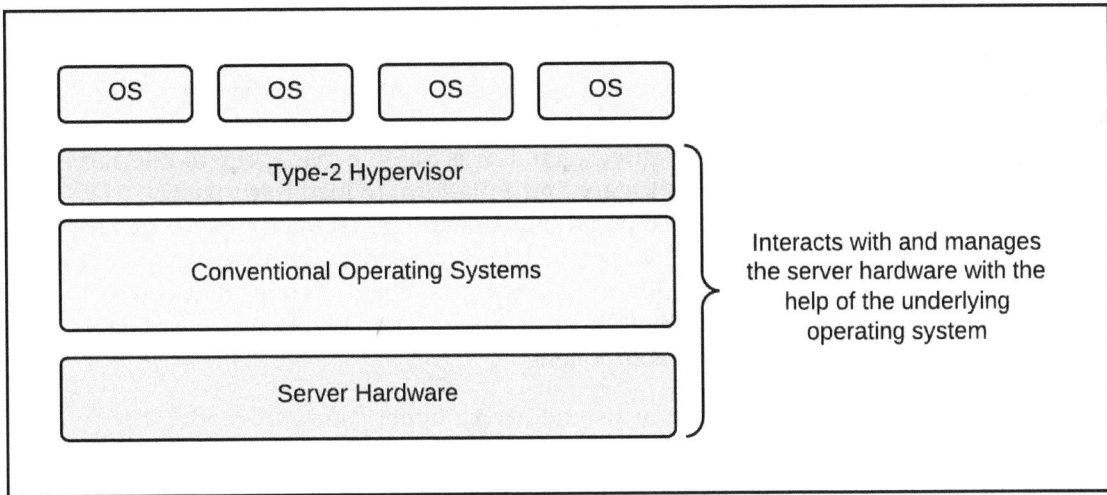

Examples of a type 2 hypervisor include VMware Workstation, VMware Fusion, Parallels Desktop, and Virtual Box.

VMware ESX hypervisor

ESX is VMware's proprietary hypervisor. It is the foundation that enables virtualization of your data center.

VMware released their first hypervisor in the year 2001 and it was simply called ESX. They did release a second version, ESX 1.1, the same year and ESX 1.5 in 2002. After that there were several major version releases â©© ESX 2.0 in 2003 and ESX 2.5 in 2004. In 2006 they released VMware Infrastructure 3, which was their first product suite that included ESX 3.0, followed by several product suite releases – VMware Infrastructure 3.5, VMware vSphere 4.0 in 2009, vSphere 4.1 in 2010, vSphere 5.0 in 2011, vSphere 5.1 in 2012, vSphere 5.5 in 2013, and vSphere 6 in 2015. All of the releases have seen new features and improvements that continue to revolutionize our modern day data centers.

Before the release of VMware ESX 3.5, VMware had a Linux-based Service Console packaged along with the hypervisor. The Service Console was VMware's Linux-based console operating system, which provided a management interface to the ESX server. Meaning that if you were to assign an IP address to the ESX server, then it was the Service Console that had the IP address configured on it. It was the sole management interface. It was also used as a command-line workspace and a platform to load third-party management agents. Since it was based on a Linux operating system, the Service Console brought with it all the bugs, security issues which that particular Linux release had. This is not to say that Linux is buggy, but it did bring in the most common bugs that you see in a conventional operating system into the ESXi package. VMware had to periodically release security fixes for the Service Console component.

With the release of version 3.5, VMware also released a hypervisor-only model. The hypervisor-only model no longer had the Linux-based Service Console packaged with it, making it considerably small in terms of both compute and storage footprint. It was small enough to be embedded into the server motherboards, by storing the ESXi in flash storage chips. It also allowed ESXi to be loaded onto a USB bootable device. One of the prime advantages of ESXi was that it exposed very little surface area for security attacks. VMware called the ESX with Service Console ESX and the hypervisor-only model, ESXi. The ESX version with the Service Console was commonly referred to as ESX Classic and the hypervisor-only model was embedded.

VMware hypervisor models

VMware's type-1 hypervisor or VMKernel had two different models. One of them is the older ESX classic model and the other is a subsequent hypervisor-only model (ESXi).

Although the *ESX Classic* model had the same VMKernel component, it also used an RHEL-based console operating system that ran in a privileged mode enabling the management of ESX. It was primarily used to provide a command-line interface for ESX, but was also used to run host management agents, third-party agents like that of a hardware monitoring or a system management agent, backup agents. VMware no longer makes the classic model of ESX, because it posed a larger surface area for security attacks. VMware had to frequently release patches to secure the console operating system, whilst only a few number of patches were required for the actual hypervisor component-VMKernel. The presence of the console operating system also meant a larger compute and storage footprint for ESX:

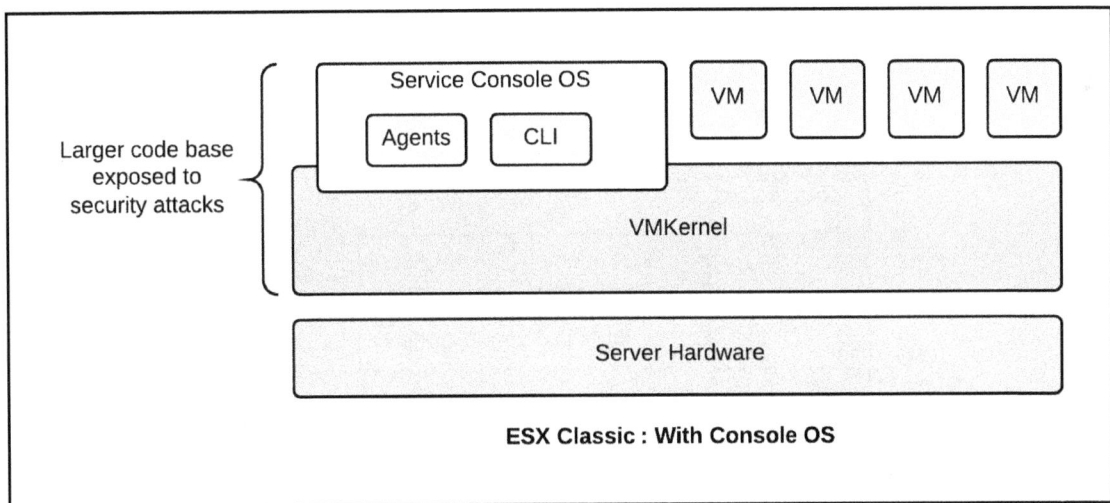

The *ESX Hypervisor-only* model (ESXi) does not have the console operating system, making it small enough to be embedded on motherboards or held in a USB thumb drive. And more importantly, it is more secure as it only exposed a very small surface area for security attacks. ESXi was first introduced with the release of ESX 3.5. It then had both the ESX classic and ESXi versions available. Starting with vSphere 5, VMware no longer makes the ESX classic version:

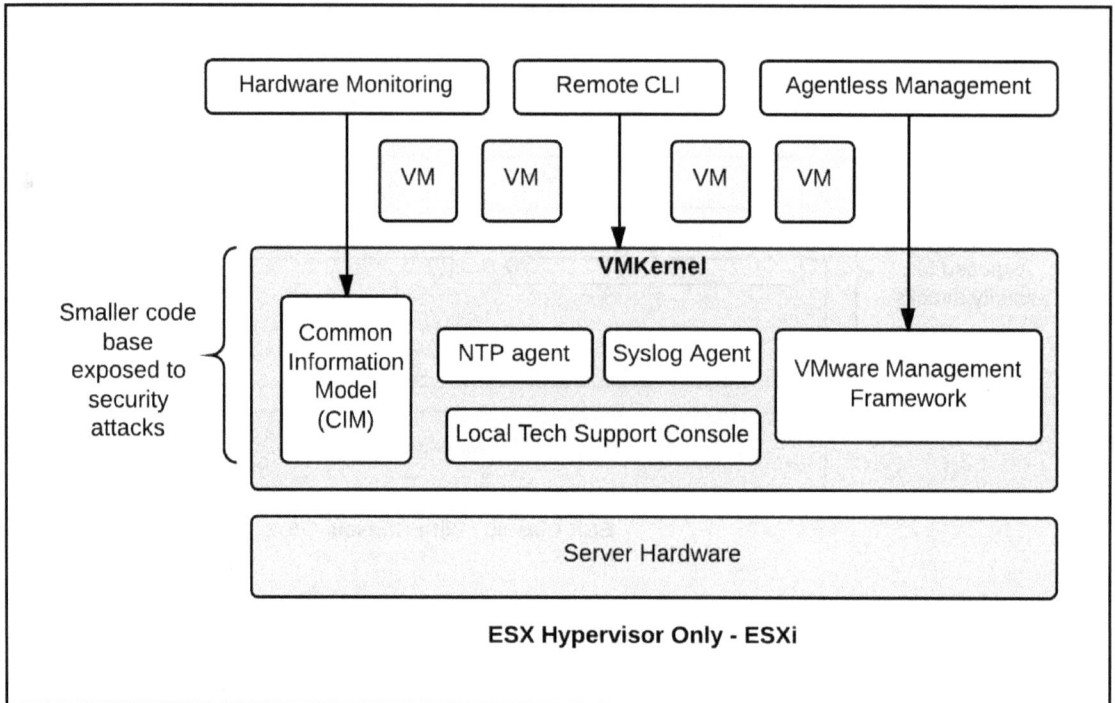

With ESXi, most of the functionalities that were available via agents running at the Console OS, have now been replaced with supporting frameworks built into VMKernel, making those functionalities agentless.

What is a virtual machine?

A virtual machine is a software construct that acts as a container for installing and running conventional operating systems on a server hardware managed by a hypervisor. It is an isolation boundary between the operating systems running on the shared hardware.

An operating system running on a virtual machine is completely unaware of the fact that it is indeed running on a virtual machine and resources assigned to it are also shared among other virtual machines. It assumes ownership of every resource that is assigned to it. Managing the sharing of resources among virtual machines is the duty of the hypervisor. The performance of the virtual machine is dependent on the hypervisor's ability to manage the shared resources.

When a virtual machine is created, it is assigned resources such as the CPU, memory, network interface, and storage. These resources are slices from a larger pool of resources that the server hardware can provide.

What makes up a virtual machine?

Now that we know the purpose of virtual machines, it is important to understand what components make up a virtual machine. Much like a physical machine, a virtual machine also has different components required for it to host a conventional operating system. The only difference being that the components and devices that become part of a virtual machine are behind an abstraction layer and hence don't have direct access to the hardware. Instead, every component such as the CPU, memory, and hard disks are slices from the physical server resources available. The operating system running on the virtual machine has an impression that it is running on physical hardware; indeed it is, but only the portion of the resources assigned to the virtual machine are exposed to the operating system:

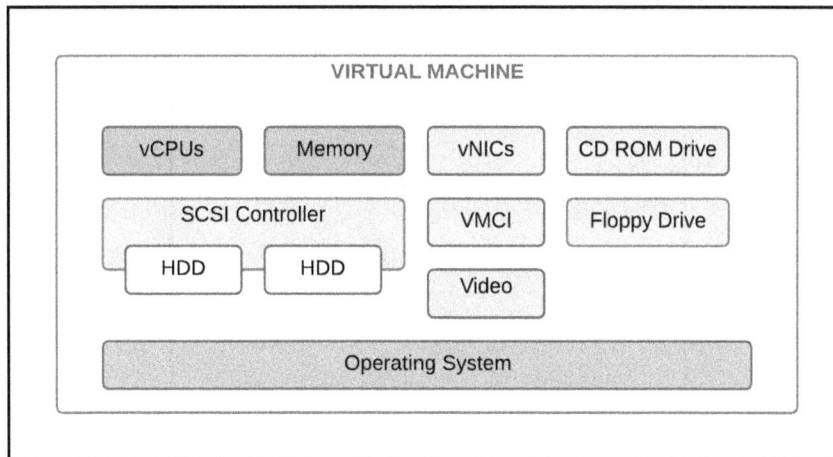

Virtual Machine Monitor

From the previous sections, we have a brief idea as to what components make up a virtual machine. We know that it is an isolation container to run an operating system and its code without intervening with any of the other operating systems running on the same server hardware.

However, what enables this isolation? Who manages the resources for each of the virtual machines? You might already have an answer in mindâ◦◦the VMKernel. Of course, it is the VMKernel, but VMKernel has several subfunctions. The kernel component that enables the concept of a virtual machine is called the **Virtual Machine Monitor** (**VMM**). Every virtual machine has an associated VMM providing virtual BIOS, virtual memory management, and other virtual devices.

The VMM has the following functions:

- Processor virtualization
- Memory virtualization
- I/O virtualization

Processor virtualization

Every x86 operating system is coded to run directly on hardware (bare metal), which means that the operating system will run in the ring with the highest privilegeâ◦◦**Ring 0**:

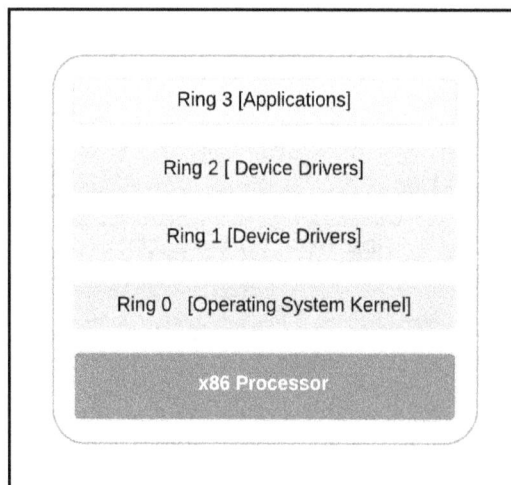

```
┌─────────────────────────────────────┐
│  ┌───────────────────────────────┐  │
│  │     Ring 3 [Applications]      │  │
│  │                               │  │
│  │    Ring 2 [ Device Drivers]    │  │
│  │                               │  │
│  │    Ring 1 [Device Drivers]     │  │
│  │                               │  │
│  │  Ring 0  [Operating System Kernel] │  │
│  │                               │  │
│  │        x86 Processor          │  │
│  └───────────────────────────────┘  │
└─────────────────────────────────────┘
```

Anything that runs at **Ring 0** will have direct access to the x86 processor hardware. Now, the challenge is the placement of the VMM. Much like an x86 operating system kernel, the VMM also needs to run at a privilege level that has direct access to the processor hardware. VMware achieved full virtualization by using BT and DE techniques or Hardware-assisted Virtualization.

Binary Translation (BT) and Direct Execution (DE)

Binary Translation (**BT**) translates the privileged instructions from the guest operating system and then executes it on the processor.

Every operating system has two types of instructions-*normal* instructions such as arithmetic instructions and *privileged* instructions such as initiating an I/O or system calls. System calls are nothing but a method to call a privileged instruction, which is hidden from the user mode.

When executing a user's program or application code, the processor goes about doing its job by executing the normal instructions in the user mode (**Ring 1, Ring 2,** and **Ring** 3).

During the execution, if the processor encounters a privileged instruction such as initiating an I/O or a system call, it generates a trap indicating an exception and would need to switch to the kernel mode. Switching to kernel mode is nothing but handing over the execution to the operating system's kernel running at **Ring 0**. A kernel that runs at **Ring 0** can execute every machine instruction and reference every memory location.

What is a trap?

A trap is generated by the CPU indicating that it has encountered a condition which it cannot handle and requires assistance from the operating system. Traps are used to invoke a system call.

Since x86 wasn't designed with virtualization in mind, not every instruction will have a corresponding trap facility. A trap is an operating system functionality that captures an exception and passes the control over to the operating system kernel, to be executed at **Ring 0**.

Full virtualization using BT and DE requires the VMM to run at **Ring 0** and the guest operating system at **Ring 1**:

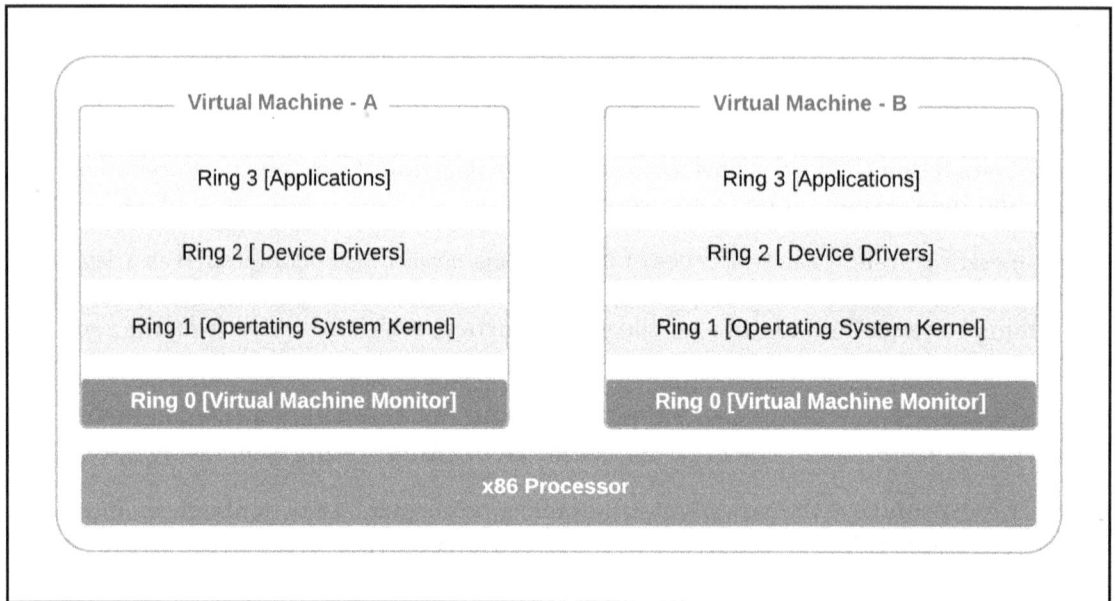

Since the x86 operating systems are not written to run at **Ring 1**, every privileged instruction that is handed over to it will now have to be translated and executed by the VMM, running at **Ring 0**.

The dilemma here is that not every x86 OS instruction will have a trap facility. This is where *binary translation* does its job. It doesn't wait for the processor to encounter an exception and generate a trap. Instead, it captures and reviews the instructions. On encountering an exception, it emulates a trap and takes control over the execution of that instruction.

Direct Execution (**DE**) is used to send the user mode instructions directly to the processor. Although the guest OS is now placed at **Ring 1**, it is still at that level with a much higher privilege than the user mode instructions. Hence there is no need to translate the user mode instructions, rather they can be sent directly to the processor.

Hardware-assisted Virtualization

Both Intel and AMD have added enhancements to their processor families to assist virtualization:

- Intel VT-x
- AMD-V

These enhancements allow VMM to run in a new higher-privileged mode than **Ring 0**.

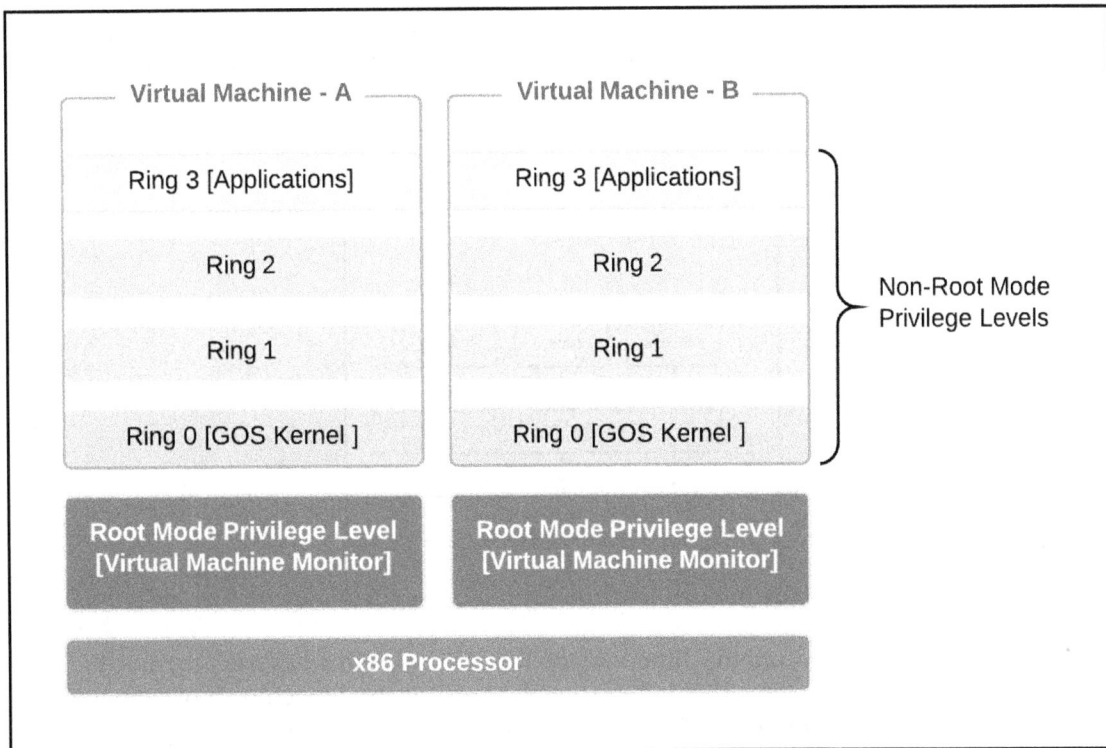

With Hardware-assisted Virtualization, privileged and sensitive instructions encountered can now be directly send to the VMM. Intel VT-x or AMD-V features should be enabled in BIOS of an ESXi host, to be able to run 64-bit virtual machines on it.

Memory virtualization

Like with the processor resources, the server's memory resource should also be shared among the virtual machines.

The processor has a mechanism to access every memory bit on a memory module by addressing those memory locations using physical addresses. The operating system maintains another contiguous address space called the virtual addresses for the processes that run on them. Every time a process tries to access memory, it uses the virtual address for that memory location. The operating system will then have to translate the virtual address to a physical address:

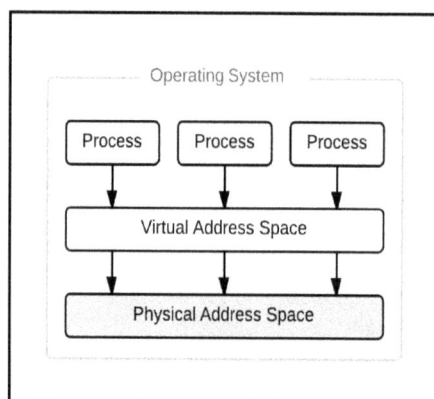

Now, when we throw a virtual machine into the mix, things take a different turn. All conventional operating systems that will be installed on a virtual machine have a memory management technique similar to what was alluded to in the previous paragraph. But since the whole idea behind virtualization is to let multiple such virtual machines, there has to be a mechanism to manage physical memory access or allocation to these virtual machines. On an ESXi host, the VMKernel does all the resource management. In this case, it has to find a way to manage the physical memory. It does so by adding another memory management layer called the machine address space:

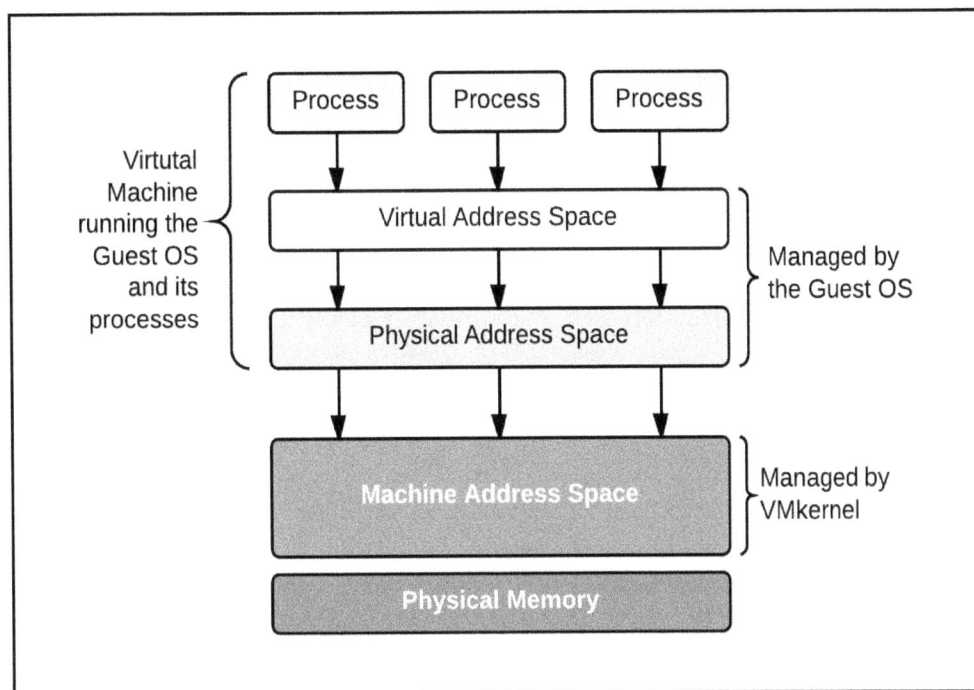

Now, when a process running inside of a guest operating system tries to access a memory location, it uses the virtual address space to do so. The virtual address requested will then have to translate to a physical address as seen by the operating system. The operating system will then have to translate the physical address to a machine address. The machine address eventually hits the physical memory. If this procedure were to be followed for every memory access, it would add a considerable overhead. Memory virtualization addresses this problem, by providing a mechanism to directly map the guest operating system's virtual address space to the machine address space by maintaining *Shadow page tables*.

Hardware-assisted memory virtualization eliminates the need for Shadow page tables by providing a mechanism to map the guest operating system's physical address space to the VMKernel machine address space.

Hardware-assisted memory virtualization technologies

The following are the examples of Hardware-assisted memory virtualization technologies:

- **Intel's Extended Page Tables (EPT)**.
- AMD's **Rapid Virtualization Index (RVI)** or **Nested Page Tables (NPT)**. Both RVI and NPT are different names for the same AMD MMU virtualization technology.

> For more information on how hardware-assisted memory virtualization works refer to the *Performance Best Practices for vSphere 5.5*: http://www.vmware.com/pdf/Perf_Best_Practices_vSphere5.5.pdf

I/O virtualization

I/O devices such as physical network interface cards and SCSI controllers will have to be made available to the virtual machines. But it wouldn't make sense if we allowed a virtual machine to own or control a device. If done so, it wouldn't allow other virtual machines to use the same resource. So, there is a compelling reason to virtualize I/O resources as well.

I/O virtualization is achieved by presenting emulated virtual devices or paravirtualized devices to the virtual machines. For emulated devices like that of an e1000 virtual network interface card, the guest operating system needs to have the required driver. For paravirtualized devices such as the VMXNET series of network interface cards you will need drivers supplied with VMware Tools. The driver corresponding to a device will interact with the I/O virtualization stack of VMkernel.

An introduction to VMware vSphere

VMware vSphere is a suite of core infrastructure solutions that help manage and monitor a virtual data center. The term vSphere was coined by VMware as a new name for their flagship virtual infrastructure in the year 2009 with the release of VMware Virtual Infrastructure 4. All the previous releases were called Virtual Infrastructure 3.x or 3.5 or 2.5, and backwards. The most recent version being *vSphere 6* is the sixth generation of VMware's vSphere product line. They are the most feature rich and probably the only virtualization suite on the market covering every aspect of the virtual infrastructure with their own products or solutions.

So what really makes up vSphere? vSphere is basically a set of software solutions which include the hypervisor (ESXi), the vCenter server, and its plugins, supporting databases and host management agents. The hypervisors create a platform to run virtual machines and the vCenter forms the management layer. vCenter enables the creation of virtual data centers. Every other solution will interface and interact with the vCenter to manage or utilize the virtual data center. Having said that, VMware does offer APIs which allow third-party software developers to build tools that help manage platforms or leverage the management layer formed by the vCenter servers in an environment.

However, there are several components, tools, and features that fall under the umbrella of the vSphere suite. Not all components are within the scope of this book, but we will make an effort to include their relevance wherever possible. Most of the components are covered in depth in different chapters, but it is critical to have a brief understanding of these components before we learn about them in detail.

We will go through a very basic introduction of the following components and features.

vSphere ESXi

If you have read through the chapter up to this point then you will already have an understanding of what ESXi is. With the latest version, ESXi 6.0, there are a few scalability and a number of security enhancements.

Each ESXi 6.0 host can now support up to 480 logical CPUs, 12 terabytes of memory, and 1024 virtual machines. Let's compare this with some of the earlier versions of the ESXi hypervisor:

Limits	ESXi 6.0	ESXi 5.5	ESXi 5.1	ESXi 5.0	ESXi 4.1	ESXi 4.0
Number of logical CPUs per ESXi host	480	320	160	160	160	64
Amount of memory per ESXi host	12 TB	4TB	2TB	2TB	ITB	ITB
Number of virtual machines per ESXi host	1024	512	512	512	320	320

There are a number of security enhancements with the new version, and these include:

- Managing the local accounts on an ESXi host either via vCenter or using new ESXCLI commands. With the earlier versions the local account management was performed via a direct vSphere Client connection to the ESXi host or using the Linux-like user management commands from the ESXi console.
- New host advanced system settings to manage account lockout and password complexity policies.
- Better auditability. User information in the logs for all actions initiated from the vCenter will now include the actual vCenter username along with `vxpuser`.
- There are two different lockdown modes with the release of ESXi 6.0-Normal mode and Strict mode.
- Enhanced graphics performance for VMware Horizon virtual desktops by leveraging NVIDIA GRID™ technology.

VMware vCenter Server

In the previous sections of this chapter, we learnt about ESXi and virtual machines. In a large infrastructure, these entities need to be centrally managed. The central management is achieved using VMware vCenter Server. It comes in the form of a Windows installable program and also as a Linux-based virtual appliance. Without the vCenter server, you cannot cluster the ESXi hosts, which is essential for the enablement of the VMware features such as vSphere HA, vSphere DRS, and vSphere DPM. Also, every other management solution that is out there will need to interface with the vCenter Server by means of a plugin.

vSphere desktop and web clients

Currently, there are two types of client available from VMware that can be used to connect and manage your vSphere infrastructure. One of them is a desktop client which can only be installed on a Windows machine. It can be used to connect directly to an ESXi host or a vCenter Server. This form of the client will reach its end of life very soon as VMware will transition every GUI action to be performed through their web client. The desktop client is C# based and it is currently available only for backward compatibility and to support a few plugins which haven't been completely transitioned to the vSphere Web Client. Unlike the desktop client, the *vSphere Web Client* is a server component installed and configured on a machine and the users willing to connect will rely on their web browsers to connect the web client server to access the vCenter GUI. The most critical difference is that the vSphere Web Client cannot be used to connect to an ESXi host directly. You need to rely on the vSphere C# based desktop client for that, and it is one of many reasons why the desktop client is still around.

vRealize Orchestrator

VMware vRealize Orchestrator, also known as the vCenter Orchestrator, is a GUI-based process automation tool that is installed along with your vCenter Server. It is primarily used to create workflows to automate repeatable IT processes. It has a plug-in framework which can be used by other solutions to perform actions. The vCenter Server, vRealize Automation, VROPS, VCM, and tools that can leverage the Orchestrator to perform actions.

vSphere Update Manager

It becomes necessary to upgrade or patch your vSphere environment to maintain a reliable platform for your virtual machines. Although the ESXi hosts can be patched or upgraded manually it becomes a very tedious process and would require many man-hours to perform the activity in a large environment. This is where VMware **vSphere Update Manager** (**VUM**) comes in handy. It provides a mechanism to patch and upgrade the ESXi hosts with reduced manual intervention. It can also be used to upgrade or patch third-party products such as the Cisco Nexus 1,000V.

VMware Power CLI

VMware Power CLI is a set of modules or snap-ins which include cmdlets based on Microsoft Power Shell. It is used as a scripting tool for managing or automating most of the vSphere actions. The latest version, 6.0, has more than 400 cmdlets for both vSphere and vCloud environments.

VMware VROPS

VMware **vRealize Operations** Manager (**VROPS**) is an infrastructure monitoring solution. It does provide greater insights into the performance, capacity, and health characteristics of your vSphere environment. It can present information in the form of dashboards, it can generate smart alerts, and can perform predictive analysis. It comes packaged with a vCenter plugin, but you can install several other third-party plugins to let VROPS gather information from other components as well. For instance, there are adapters for EMC Symmetrix, VNX storage systems, and many more.

vSphere Data Protection

vSphere Data Protection (**VDP**) is an EMC Avamar-based backup and recovery solution from VMware Inc. It is available in the form, a Linux virtual appliance and can support up to 8 terabytes of de-duplicated backup data per appliance and up to 20 such virtual appliances can be associated with a single vCenter Server.

vShield Endpoint

VMware vShield Endpoint is a security framework from VMware which enables hosting the load of performing antivirus or antimalware analysis on virtual machines onto a dedicated appliance. The framework utilizes a thin-agent included with VMware Tools and a heuristics engine running on a separate appliance provided by the security vendor. Every ESXi host will run such an appliance for the virtual machines running on it.

VMware vMotion and Storage vMotion

VMware vMotion will let you migrate the live state of a powered-on virtual machine from one ESXi host to another without affecting any of the applications or its services running on it. Whilst Storage vMotion can relocate all the files backing the virtual machine from one data store to another and also migrate its live state from one host to another, or it can migrate only the files backing the virtual machine and leave the live state on the same host.

vSphere High Availability

VMware vSphere **High Availability (HA)** is a functionality that is used to configure a cluster of ESXi hosts to respond to an unplanned downtime event and ensure the availability of the virtual machines that were running on them, with very minimal downtime possible. It has the ability to monitor the guest operating systems and the applications running inside of a virtual machine and then decide to restart the affected virtual machine in an effort to reduce the downtime of a service due to an affected guest operating system hosting the service or a nonresponsive application corresponding to the service. It is important to understand that even though HA is configured on a cluster of ESXi hosts, it only provides high availability for the virtual machines and not for the hosts. It cannot start up or restart an affected ESXi host.

vSphere Fault Tolerance

VMware vSphere **Fault Tolerance (FT)** is used to enable continuous availability of a virtual machine with zero downtime, maintaining an identical copy of the virtual machine in lock-step mode. We will learn more about this, in `Chapter 8`, *Virtual Machine Concepts and Management*. Unlike vSphere HA, FT is enabled on individual virtual machines. Although, FT had imposed a lot of restrictions on the scalability and the actions that can be performed on an FT-enabled virtual machine with the earlier versions of vSphere, with vSphere 6, it has been vastly improved and most of the restrictions don't exist anymore:

Features	vSphere 6.0 FT	vSphere 5.5 FT
Number of vCPUs	4-vCPU SMP	1-vCPU
Max. memory on the VM	64 GB	64 GB
Sync technology	Fast checkpointing	Record and replay
Virtual machine snapshots	Yes	No
VMDK types	All types	Eager-zeroed thick only

vSphere Distributed Resource Scheduler and Storage Distributed Resource Scheduler

VMware vSphere **Distributed Resource Scheduler** (**DRS**) is a series of algorithms devised to manage an aggregated pool of computing resources and distribute virtual machines among the ESXi hosts in a cluster in an effort to reduce any resource imbalance in the cluster. It also helps in reducing the power consumption in the data center using DRS's power management feature known as **Distributed Power Management** (**DPM**). VMware DPM can help reduce the energy consumption of a data center by vacating VMs from an underutilized host and putting that host in a power-off state.

Unlike DRS, which manages the compute resources, *Storage DRS* manages the storage resources. It is a mechanism to balance space utilization and the I/O load on data stores in a data store cluster by migrating (using Storage vMotion) the VMs. Storage DRS can only be enabled on a data store cluster. It also influences the initial placement of the VMs on the data stores, by generating placement recommendations. vSphere Storage DRS requires Enterprise Plus licensing.

> To understand how the vSphere licensing editions compare refer to: `https ://www.vmware.com/products/vsphere/compare`

vSphere Storage I/O Control and Network I/O Control

VMware **vSphere Storage I/O Control** (**SIOC**) is used to throttle the VMkernel device queue depth of a LUN, based on the shares set on the virtual machine disks contending for I/O bandwidth. SIOC can only be enabled on data stores (FC/ISCSI/NFS) and not on RDMs. It cannot be enabled on data stores with multiple extents. In this book, you will learn how to enable SIOC on a data store.

VMware vSphere **Network I/O Control** (**NIOC**) enables use and creation of Network Resource Pools. Much like with the compute resources of an ESXi cluster, you can use resource pools on a **vSphere Distributed Switch** (**VDS**) to configure Shares, Bandwidth Limitation, and **Quality of Service** (**QoS**) values. Such resource pools are referred to as **Network Resource Pools** (**NRP**). There are both System Defined and User Defined NRPs.

Both SIOC and NIOC requires vSphere Enterprise Plus licensing.

vSphere Standard Switch and Distributed Virtual Switches

VMware **vSphere Standard Switch** (**vSwitch**) is a software switching construct (*in other words, a software-based network switch*) local to each ESXi host. It provides a network infrastructure for the virtual machines running on that host. Unlike a physical switch, a vSphere Standard Switch is not a managed switch. It doesn't learn MAC addresses to build a MAC table, but it does know the MAC addresses of the virtual machine vNICs connected to it.

Unlike the standard switch, the **vSphere Distributed Switch** (**VDS**) spans across multiple ESXi hosts. It is not locally managed at the ESXi host. It requires VMware vCenter Server for configuration and management, though VDS is only available with the vSphere Enterprise Plus license. It has a control plane which resides at the vCenter Server and a data plane which resides on an ESXi host that is connected to the VDS.

vSphere Virtual Symmetric Multiprocessing

VMware vSphere Virtual **Symmetric Multiprocessing** (**SMP**) enables a virtual machine to use more than one logical processor simultaneously.

VMware Virtual Machine File System

Virtual Machine File System (**VMFS**) is VMware's proprietary cluster filesystem that can be used to format block storage units presented to an ESXi host. VMFS will let more than one host have simultaneous read/write access to the volume. To make sure that a virtual machine or its files are not simultaneously accessed by more than one ESXi host, VMFS uses an on-disk locking mechanism called distributed locking. The current version of VMFS is 5.

VMware Virtual Volumes

Virtual Volumes (**VVols**) is a newly introduced concept with vSphere 6.0. It is not intended to replace VMFS, but to take advantage of the hardware capabilities of the storage system. It requires a supported vSphere API for Storage Awareness (VASA) provider for its functioning. It is not a filesystem by any means. It is only a method to encapsulate files, backing a virtual machine into virtual volumes, and these are created automatically when you create or modify a virtual machine. ESXi does not have direct control over the VVols created, instead it interacts with a Protocol Endpoint, which again is provided by the storage vendor.

vSphere Storage APIs

VMware vSphere Storage API is an application programming interface framework from VMware that enables the storage and backup software vendors to enable or enhance integration with vSphere. The **vSphere Storage APIs-Data Protection** (**VADP**) is a framework that enables backup vendors to create backup and recovery solutions that integrate with vSphere. The **vSphere Storage APIs-Storage Awareness** (**VASA**) enables storage vendors to create storage providers which become an interface for vCenter to gather storage characteristics for the LUNs presented to the ESXi hosts. The **vSphere Storage APIs-Array Integration** (**VAAI**) enables ESXi to offload certain storage operations to a supported storage array. For instance, the process of zeroing the blocks of an eager-zeroed thick VMDK during its creation can be offloaded to the array to speed up the process. The availability of these APIs is dependent of the type of license in use. So, when you are designing an environment for performance it is important to understand what APIs are available with which VMware license editions.

VMware Virtual SAN

VMware Virtual SAN is a hyper-converged storage architecture that enables creating a shared storage platform using the local storage on the participating ESXi hosts. Since this ability is built into the hypervisor, there is no requirement to deploy appliances. All the management is from the vCenter Server. VSAN supports two types of configuration, an all-flash architecture and a hybrid architecture. In a hybrid-architecture, SSD and magnetic HDDs are mixed together to form the storage layer. The SSDs will be used for caching purposes to increase performance. In an all-flash architecture, both caching and storage are done on SDDs, hence delivering a very high performance storage platform.

Storage Thin Provisioning

vSphere Storage Thin Provisioning enables the creation of **Virtual Machine Disks** (**VMDKs**) that consume the space required for the data in it and not the actual size of the VMDK. Meaning, if the VMDK is of the size 50GB, but the data in it is only 15 GB, then only 15 GB worth of storage space is consumed from the data store. It is beneficial because not every disk created is fully consumed leading to wastage of storage space. Thin provisioning helps in over-allocation, but requires better reporting to manage the consumption of the storage resources.

vSphere Flash Read Cache

Flash storage (**Solid State Disks–SSDs**) disks offer higher I/O performance when comparted to the magnetic disks. Unfortunately, SSDs are far more expensive than the regular hard disks. With the vSphere Flash Read Cache mechanism, you can configure the available local SDD storage to act as a cache for virtual machines to use. VMkernel handles the assignment and allocation of the cache.

vSphere Content Library

With vSphere 6, VMware introduced a new feature called the *Content Library*. It is used to store templates and other files that can be shared across infrastructures, and it is backed by a data store. They can be local to a vCenter, published to be subscribed, or subscribed from a published library.

vSphere Auto Deploy

vSphere Auto Deploy is a web server component, which once configured can be used to quickly provision a large number of the ESXi hosts without the need to use the ESXi installation image to perform an installation on the physical machine. It can also be used to perform the upgrade or patching of the ESXi hosts without the need for VUM.

vSphere Host Profiles

A VMware vSphere Host Profile is a configuration template that is created from existing ESXi hosts. It could only be created using the vCenter GUI. Host Profiles can be attached to other ESXi hosts managed by the vCenter and can be used to track configuration changes by monitoring compliance of the attached hosts, or it can even be used to apply configuration changes to a large number of hosts, greatly reducing the amount of manual work which would otherwise be required.

vSphere Replication

vSphere Replication is a replication engine that can be leveraged to configure replication on individual virtual machines. It can replicate a virtual machine and its disks from one location to another without the need to incorporate an expensive array-based replication. What it really does is provide a mechanism to replicate a virtual machine using the existing Ethernet infrastructure and recover them when there is a need. It directly integrates with the vSphere platform and is available with Standard, Enterprise, and Enterprise Plus editions. It is storage agnostic, which means that a virtual machine or its disk files can be replicated to a data store, regardless of it being a VMFS volume or an NFS mount. You can learn more about vSphere Replication from the book *Disaster Recovery using VMware vSphere Replication and vCenter Site Recovery Manager, Abhilash GB, ISBN 9781782176442, Packt Publishing*.

Summary

This chapter provided you with a sneak peek into concepts around server virtualization. We learned how the processor, memory, and storage resources are virtualized. It also introduced you to the components of VMware vSphere. This sets the foundation for what you are about to learn in the subsequent chapters.

In the next chapter, we will discuss the architecture of ESXi. We will also learn how to install or deploy ESXi hosts and perform the initial configuration. We will discuss other deployment methods, such as unattended scripted installation or the deployment of stateless and stateful ESXi hosts using vSphere Auto Deploy.

2
The Hypervisor – ESXi

VMware's ESXi is a piece of software that you install on a bare-metal server. ESXi creates a layer of abstraction that allows for virtual machines to run by utilizing the server's hardware resources independently. In the previous chapter, we learned how the hardware resources such as the CPU, memory, and I/O are virtualized with the help of the **Virtual Machine Monitor** (**VMM**). In this chapter, we continue discussing the architecture of the ESXi hypervisor. We will also learn different methods of deploying ESXi onto bare-metal servers.

We will cover the following topics in this chapter:

- The architecture of ESXi
- Laying the groundwork for an ESXi installation
- Installing ESXi – the interactive method
- Using the vSphere Client
- Creating additional local users on an ESXi host
- Using an ESXi **Managed Object Browser** (**MOB**)
- Understanding other ESXi deployment methods

You can download ESXi for free if you register to evaluate the product at VMware's website. At the time of writing this book, vSphere 6 is the latest of their suite of vSphere products. We will learn how it can be downloaded and installed in this chapter. Before we begin installing ESXi, it is critical to understand the architecture of it. In the next section we will walk through the architecture of ESXi.

The architecture of ESXi

Chapter 1, *An Introduction to Server Virtualization using VMware*, introduced you to the architecture of a type-1 hypervisor and the differences between ESX Classic (no longer developed) and ESXi, in terms of their architecture.

The ESXi hypervisor is made up of the VMkernel, the **User World** layer and the Virtual Machine Monitors. What these components provide is the foundation for other processes to enable core functionalities.

The VMkernel layer

VMkernel is a Posix-like operating system which is primarily responsible for resource scheduling. In an effort to allocate a fair share of the hardware resources between all the hosted virtual machines, it creates a level of abstraction so that the guest operating systems on the virtual machines can consume resources like they would do on a physical machine, without interfering in the operations of the guest operating systems running on other virtual machines. VMkernel includes a storage stack which supports the use of a proprietary distributed file system called the **Virtual Machine File System** (**VMFS**), and a network stack that enables the creation of virtual switches.

User World APIs

The User World provides a set of APIs that help other processes to natively interact with VMkernel and those include:

- Management agents —hostd and vpxa
- The HA agent —FDM
- CIM Broker
- DCUI
- Syslog daemon
- Software iSCSI adapter
- NTP client
- SNMP
- VMX User World helper processes for every running virtual machine. The helper process will handle the device I/O, virtual machine snapshots, and so on.

The management agents, *hostd* and *vpxa*, help send commands to the hypervisor through a management interface such as the vSphere Client or the vCenter Server.

The *hostd* is commonly referred to as the host management agent and is involved in every user interaction with the hypervisor. When the vSphere Client is connected directly to ESXi, commands are sent to the *hostd* agent, which uses the vSphere API (User World API) to complete the requested actions. *hostd* also has an embedded SNMP agent than can be used to send traps or receive polling requests from an SNMP server.

The *vpxa* is an agent used for communication between the vCenter and the ESXi hosts it manages. It proxies the commands received from the vCenter Server to the *hostd* agent. Every ESXi host will have a *vpxa* agent when it is connected to a vCenter Server.

The *vSphere HA agent* or *Fault Domain Manager Agent* will be installed on an ESXi host when HA is enabled on it. It is the vCenter that will transfer and install the agent on the host.

The *CIM Broker* is a set of APIs that can be used by an application to fetch the status of the hardware devices on an ESXi host. Hardware vendors are allowed to develop their own CIM plugins to use the broker APIs to monitor and collect health information.

The **Direct Console User Interface** (**DCUI**) is a menu-driven console interface which is used to manage an ESXi host. It can be used to perform very basic management and configuration changes to an ESXi host. We will learn more about DCUI later in this chapter.

The *syslog daemon* is used to redirect the storing of logs onto a remote syslog server.

The *Software iSCSI adapter* can be used for iSCSI target discovery without the need for a hardware-based solution.

The *NTP Client* helps synchronize the ESXi host with an NTP server for accurate time keeping.

VMM worlds

The Virtual Machine Monitor worlds provide an execution environment for every running virtual machine. They are responsible for virtualizing CPU instructions issued by the guest operating systems and also manage the virtual machine's memory.

ESXi's in-memory filesystem

ESXi has a very minimal storage footprint when installed. It is so small that it can be loaded directly into the memory of the server without the need for secondary storage. ESXi maintains an in-memory filesystem which is used to store all the configuration files that enable ESXi's core functionalities. The in-memory filesystem forms a work desk for ESXi to operate. The work desk has several drawers for storing essential files of different types and which serve different purposes. So, the work desk here is a disk partition layout and the drawers are different partitions that are formed during the deployment and installation.

Here is a list of five partitions that ESXi uses:

- Bootloader partition
- Bootbank partition
- Alternative bootbank partition
- Store partition
- Core dump partition

The bootloader partition is where the bootloader is stored. This partition is *4 megabytes* in size. The bootloader is responsible for booting the system and handing over the control the VMkernel.

The bootbank is a *48-megabyte* partition that will hold the ESXi hypervisor code along with any of the vendor specific drivers and so on.

The alternative bootbank is the same size as the bootbank and holds an identical copy of the hypervisor code. This bank is used during hypervisor upgrades as a working partition, and the original bootbank will act as a failsafe during the first boot after the upgrade. We will learn more about what happens during the upgrade later in this book.

The store partition is a *540-megabyte* partition that acts as runtime storage for the VMkernel and also holds other essential binaries including VMware Tools packages for all supported guest operating system types and VMware vSphere Client binaries. The vSphere Client binaries are just Windows installation packages that are available for download from the ESXi host's web page.

The core dump partition is *110 megabytes* in size and used to store the VMkernel's memory dump in the event of an unrecoverable error affecting the running state of the ESXi hypervisor. The core dump partition can also be a remote partition.

Laying the groundwork for ESXi deployment

When you buy server hardware from a chosen vendor you must make sure that the hardware features of the server meet the infrastructure design requirements and ESXi's hardware requirements. It is important to make sure that the make and model of the server hardware is listed as compatible in the VMware Compatibility Guide. Once that decision is made, and the servers are procured, you will need to prepare them for the hypervisor (ESXi) installation. The preparation will include buying licenses, configuring BIOS, and planning the locale for the hypervisor.

> VMware Compatibility Guide URL: `http://www.vmware.com/go/hcl`

Licensing

VMware sells separate licenses for the hypervisor and the vCenter Server. Also, the Support and Subscription (Production or Basic) packages are sold separately. The vCenter Server is available in two editions, an Essential and a Standard Edition. Most of the features are licensed with the hypervisor. Hypervisor licenses are available in three different categories:

- The VMware vSphere Edition
- The VMware vSphere Remote Office Branch Office Edition
- The VMware vSphere Essentials Kit

The *vSphere Edition* is sold on a per-processor socket basis. There are three different editions, vSphere Standard, Enterprise, and Enterprise Plus.

The *Remote Office Branch Office Edition* is sold in packs of 25 virtual machines. There are two different editions, the Standard and the Advanced.

The *vSphere Essentials kit* supports up to three ESXi hosts with a minimum of two processor sockets on each host. A vCenter Server Essential license is sold with the kit. There are two different editions, the Essentials and the Essentials Plus.

> For a comprehensive comparison of all the editions from all three categories, visit the following
> URL: `http://www.vmware.com/in/products/vsphere/compare`

Configuring the server BIOS

It is essential to configure the BIOS of the server that will host the hypervisor to take advantage of the hardware features that the server offers, and also to disable devices, ports, or features that will not be used. For instance, if you don't plan on using the USB ports available on the server, then you can disable them. The same goes for serial ports. Not all vendors use the same BIOS and not all of them present the information in the same manner, hence it is important to refer to the vendor documentation before you set out to configure the BIOS settings. The most critical ones are the BIOS version, CPU, and memory features that ESXi can take advantage of, the Hardware-Assisted Virtualization features such as Intel VT-x, Intel **Extended Page Tables (EPT)**, AMD-V and **Rapid Virtualization Index (RVI)**, and Power Management. It is advised that you configure the BIOS in a manner as per the vendor documentation so that the power management is operating system controlled, in this case by the ESXi hypervisor. If your server is NUMA capable, it is advised to enable NUMA in the BIOS.

Planning the locale for the hypervisor

ESXi can be deployed on the local storage of the server or on remote storage accessible to the server. The decision will depend on your infrastructure design. For instance, if you have chosen to buy diskless servers for hosting the hypervisor then you will have to present some sort of remote storage for storing the hypervisor code. The hypervisor code can also remain fully operational while being only in the memory of the server. Such a diskless deployment can be achieved using vSphere Auto Deploy which will be covered in this chapter.

Meeting the hypervisor requirements

Hardware requirements for hosting ESXi may not change with every hypervisor version that VMware releases, but a major version release can have new requirements. For instance, ESXi 5.5 or ESXi 6.0 requires a minimum of 4 GB of memory for the hypervisor installation to proceed. Earlier versions required a minimum of 2 GB of memory. Hence it is important to refer to the ESXi installation guide for the hardware requirements.

There are a few common requirements though:

- ESXi will only run on 64-bit x86 based processors
- It requires a minimum of two processor cores
- Support for 64-bit virtual machines is only available if Intel VT-x or AMD-V is enabled in the server's BIOS
- A Gigabit or 10 Gigabit Ethernet controller

Most of the requirements, however, are considered when you plan for a server model during the design phase.

Downloading ESXi image from VMware

VMware ESXi is available in the form of an ISO image or a ZIP bundle from VMware's downloads page. The ISO image is available with or without VMware Tools packages bundled. The ZIP archive is nothing but an offline bundle that will be used by vSphere Auto Deploy to provision stateless or stateful ESXi hosts. To download VMware vSphere ESXi:

1. Visit www.vmware.com.
2. Go to **Downloads**.
3. Click on **vSphere** under **Product Downloads**.
4. In the **Download VMware vSphere** web page, select the version.
5. Scroll the web page down to locate the VMware ESXi listed under your license edition.
6. Click on the hyperlink **Go to Downloads** listed against the VMware ESXi listing.
7. On the Download VMware ESXi X.X page locate the form (ISO or ZIP) of ESXi image you intend to download.
8. Click on **Download** or **Download Manager** to initiate the download.

> At this stage, if you are not already logged in to your **My VMware** account you will be prompted for its credentials.

Reserving IP and creating DNS records

It is best practice to configure ESXi with a static IP address and also configure it with an FQDN. In most environments you would use an internal IP management tool to reserve IP addresses for the devices you deploy on your network. For the DNS records you might need to contact your Domain Services team for updating the DNS host records corresponding to the ESXi you deploy. They would need the IP address, the hostname, and the domain name to create the record.

> Make sure you have a PTR record created for every host record.

Installing ESXi – the interactive method

ESXi can be installed onto a bare-metal server by running it through the interactive installer bundled with the hypervisor image that you have downloaded. You will need the ISO bundle to perform the interactive installation. You can either mount it to the server through its IPMI interface (HP ILO, Cisco KVM, or Dell DRAC) or burn the image onto a DVD and load that into the server's DVD ROM drive if you are using tower servers. Before you begin, make sure to configure the server's BIOS to boot from the CD ROM. Now, let's walk through the interactive installation procedure:

1. When the server boots up from the ESXi image, you will be presented with the ESXi installer's standard boot menu, the first line item being the ESXi installer and the second being the option to boot from the local disk. Unless you want to boot from the local disk select the ESXi installer entry and hit Enter to load the installer into the memory. The process of loading the installer into the memory and scanning the server for hardware information will take some time to complete and the progress of the operation will be indicated on the screen. Once done, you will be presented with the welcome to ESXi installation screen:

```
                  ESXi-6.0.0-2494585-standard Boot Menu

  ESXi-6.0.0-2494585-standard Installer
  Boot from local disk












                    Press [Tab] to edit options
```

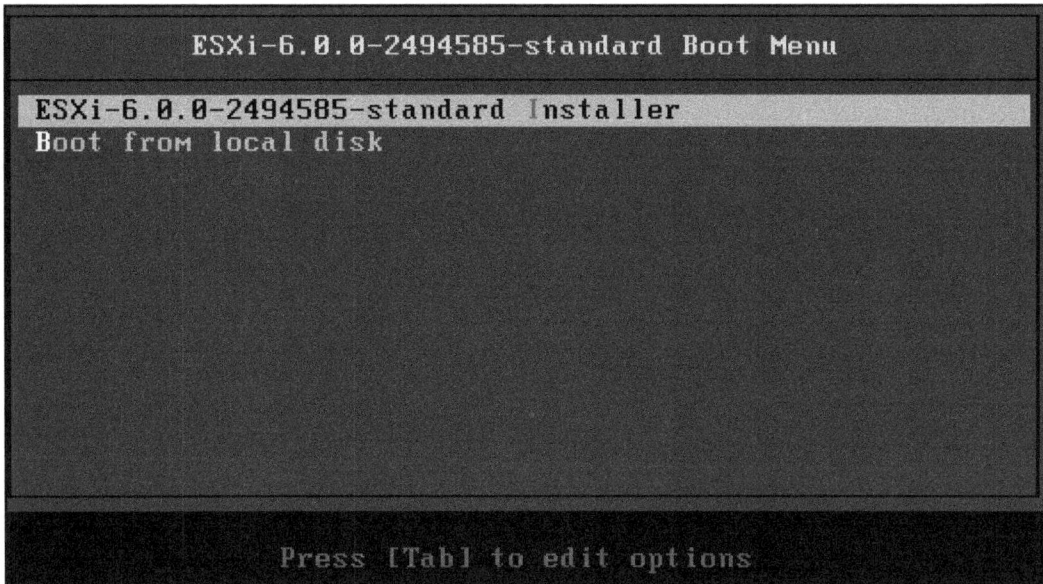

2. At the welcome to ESXi installation screen, hit *Enter* to continue or you can hit *Esc* at this stage to cancel the installation and reboot the server:

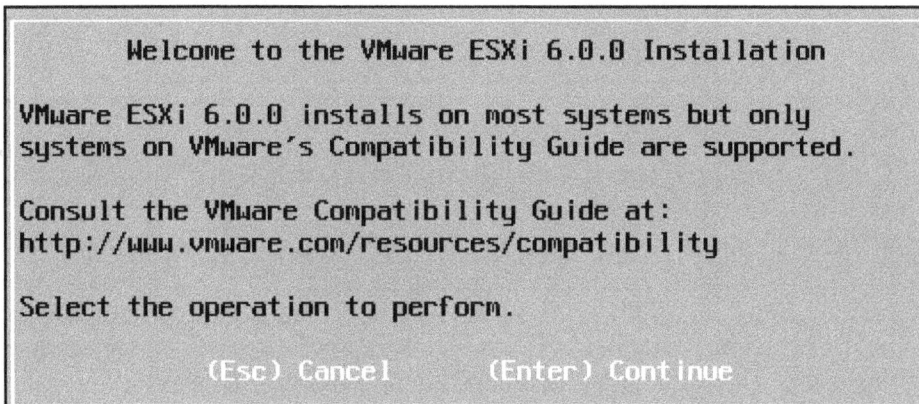

```
            Welcome to the VMware ESXi 6.0.0 Installation

  VMware ESXi 6.0.0 installs on most systems but only
  systems on VMware's Compatibility Guide are supported.

  Consult the VMware Compatibility Guide at:
  http://www.vmware.com/resources/compatibility

  Select the operation to perform.

            (Esc) Cancel         (Enter) Continue
```

3. You will then be presented with a customary EULA screen. Hit the function key *F11* to accept the EULA and proceed further.

4. It will now scan for available and accessible storage devices and present you with a list of storage devices available. The local and remote storage devices will be listed separately. Make a cautious effort to select the correct disk for the installation, as this will erase any data on the selected disk. The selection can be made using the Up/Down arrow keys. With the intended storage device selected you can optionally hit the function key *F1* to view the details of the storage device selected. This is another way to make sure that you have selected the correct disk for the installation. Once you are confident that you have selected the correct storage device, hit *Enter* to continue:

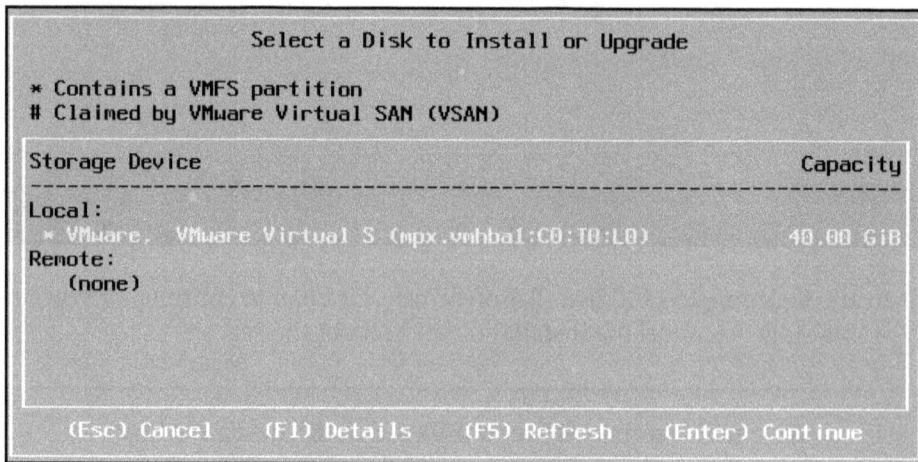

```
              Select a Disk to Install or Upgrade

 * Contains a VMFS partition
 # Claimed by VMware Virtual SAN (VSAN)

 Storage Device                                           Capacity
 ----------------------------------------------------------------------
 Local:
   * VMware,  VMware Virtual S (mpx.vmhba1:C0:T0:L0)       40.00 GiB
 Remote:
     (none)




    (Esc) Cancel      (F1) Details      (F5) Refresh    (Enter) Continue
```

5. Select a preferred keyboard layout and hit *Enter*.

6. You will now be prompted to set the root password. Supply the password, confirm it, then hit *Enter* to continue.

7. It will now take its time to scan the server for additional information or pre-checks that it would need to perform to proceed further. At this stage if any of the pre-checks fail, you will be warned accordingly. For instance, if you do not have Intel VT-x or AMD-V enabled in the BIOS, then it will warn you about the same. It can also warn you about unsupported devices detected during the scan. Most warnings will not stop you from proceeding further but will only indicate what will not be configured or supported. Hit *Enter* to continue.

8. You will now be prompted with a **Confirm Install** screen, showing you the storage device you selected for the installation, and also indicating that the device will be partitioned. This is an important verification because anything that is done to the storage device past this stage by the installer is irreversible. Hit the function key *F11* to confirm the installation:

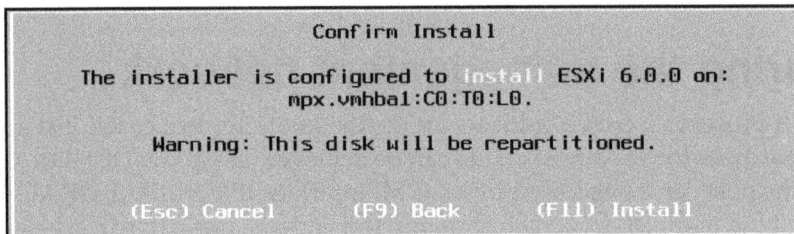

```
                        Confirm Install

        The installer is configured to install ESXi 6.0.0 on:
                        mpx.vmhba1:C0:T0:L0.

            Warning: This disk will be repartitioned.


        (Esc) Cancel        (F9) Back        (F11) Install
```

9. The installation takes a while to complete. The screen will indicate the progress of the installation.

10. Once the installation is complete, the installer will indicate the same and suggest a reboot after unmounting the installer image.

11. Unmount the ESXi image and hit *Enter* to reboot:

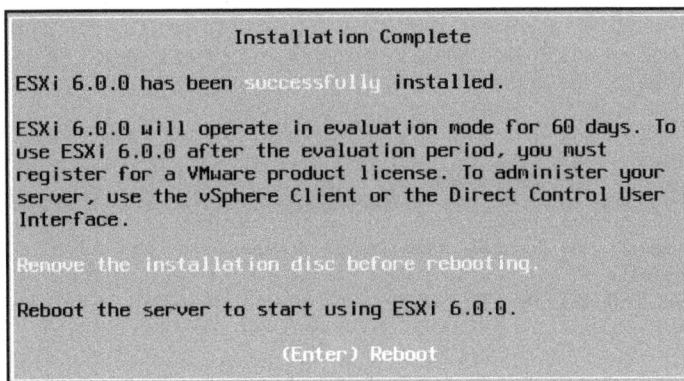

```
                    Installation Complete

ESXi 6.0.0 has been successfully installed.

ESXi 6.0.0 will operate in evaluation mode for 60 days. To
use ESXi 6.0.0 after the evaluation period, you must
register for a VMware product license. To administer your
server, use the vSphere Client or the Direct Control User
Interface.

Remove the installation disc before rebooting.

Reboot the server to start using ESXi 6.0.0.

                        (Enter) Reboot
```

12. On a successful reboot, you will be presented with the main **Direct Console User Interface** (**DCUI**) screen.

13. Now that the ESXi may or may not have procured a DHCP address, it is important to do the static IP configuration. This is achieved by accessing the DCUI.

Configuring the management network

ESXi by default procures a DHCP address on its first boot. In most cases, it is advisable to use a static IP address for ESXi hosts. This can be achieved using the DCUI of the ESXi host. The DCUI of the host can be accessed by its IPMI interface like the iLO, DRAC, or KVM. Once you are at the main DCUI screen showing the version, basic hardware details of the server, and its current IP configuration, hit the function key *F2* to enter the DCUI:

1. Hit *F2* to enter the DCUI. You will prompted for the root credentials to proceed further:

```
VMware ESXi 6.0.0 (VMKernel Release Build 2809209)

VMware, Inc. VMware Virtual Platform

2 x AMD Athlon(tm) Processor*
8 GiB Memory


Download tools to manage this host from:
http://esx601/
http://192.168.70.20/ (STATIC)




<F2> Customize System/View Logs                    <F12> Shut Down/Restart
```

If the credentials are successfully validated, then you are presented with the
System Customization screen:

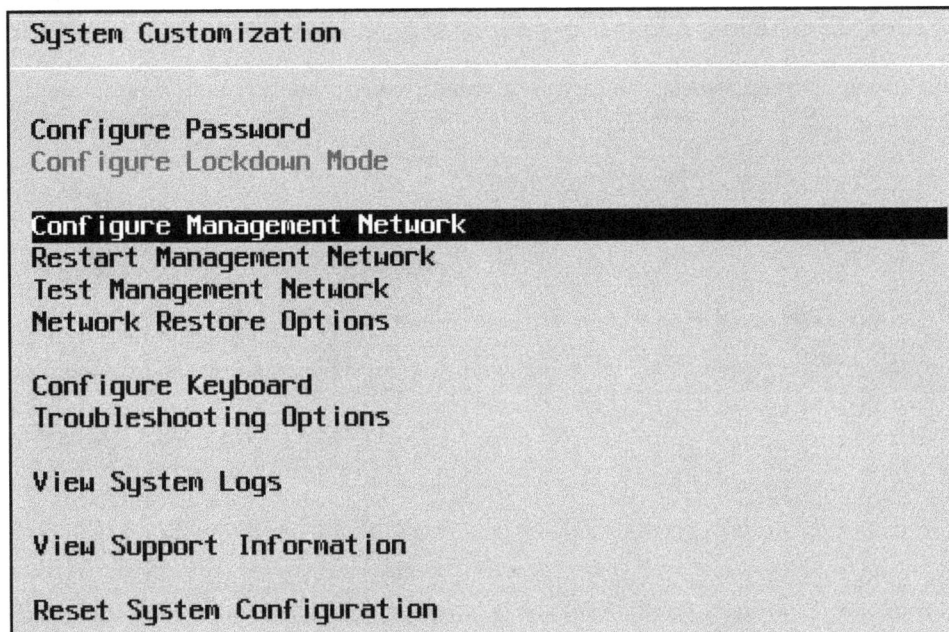

```
System Customization


Configure Password
Configure Lockdown Mode

Configure Management Network
Restart Management Network
Test Management Network
Network Restore Options

Configure Keyboard
Troubleshooting Options

View System Logs

View Support Information

Reset System Configuration
```

2. Select **Configure Management Network** and hit *Enter*. You will now be
   presented with options to select the **Network Adapters** for the management
   network, supply an optional VLAN, configure IPv4 and IPv6 settings, and DNS
   settings:

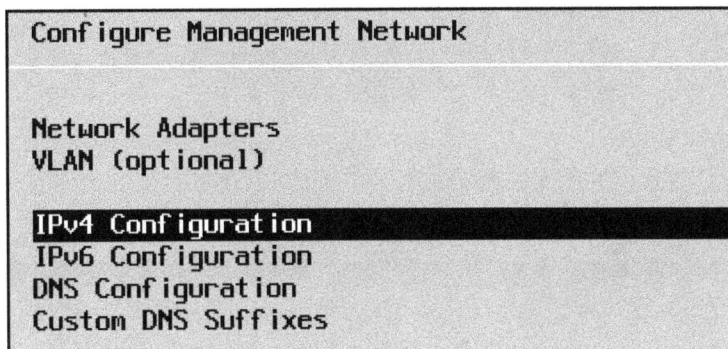

```
Configure Management Network


Network Adapters
VLAN (optional)

IPv4 Configuration
IPv6 Configuration
DNS Configuration
Custom DNS Suffixes
```

3. Select IPv4 Configuration and hit *Enter*. Use the keyboard arrow keys to select the **Set static IPv4 address and network configuration** option and hit the Space key to confirm the selection. Supply the static **IPv4 address**, **Subnet Mask**, the **Default Gateway**, hit *Enter* to save the setting, and return to the previous menu:

```
 IPv4 Configuration

 This host can obtain network settings automatically if your network
 includes a DHCP server. If it does not, the following settings must be
 specified:


 ( ) Disable IPv4 configuration for management network
 ( ) Use dynamic IPv4 address and network configuration
 (o) Set static IPv4 address and network configuration:

 IPv4 Address                                    [ 192.168.70.130   ]
 Subnet Mask                                     [ 255.255.255.0    ]
 Default Gateway                                 [ 192.168.70.2     ]


 <Up/Down> Select   <Space> Mark Selected        <Enter> OK  <Esc> Cancel
```

4. Select, **DNS Configuration**, hit *Enter* and supply the **Primary** and **Alternate DNS servers** and **hostname**. Hit *Enter* again to save the settings and return to the previous menu:

```
 DNS Configuration

 This host can only obtain DNS settings automatically if it also obtains
 its IP configuration automatically.


 ( ) Obtain DNS server addresses and a hostname automatically
 (o) Use the following DNS server addresses and hostname:

 Primary DNS Server     [ 192.168.70.2                              ]
 Alternate DNS Server   [                                          ]
 Hostname               [ esx601                                    ]


 <Up/Down> Select   <Space> Mark Selected        <Enter> OK  <Esc> Cancel
```

5. Use the **Custom DNS Suffixes** option to enter the suffixes:

```
Custom DNS Suffixes

DNS queries will attempt to locate hosts by appending the
suffixes specified here to short, unqualified names.

Use spaces or commas to separate multiple entries.

Suffixes:            [ vdescribed.lab                       ]

                              <Enter> OK   <Esc> Cancel
```

6. You can use the **VLAN** option if the management network is in a different VLAN and the cable is connected to the trunk port on the physical switch.

7. The **Network Adapters** option can be used to assign more adapters to the Management Network's port group:

```
Network Adapters

Select the adapters for this host's default management network
connection. Use two or more adapters for fault-tolerance and
load-balancing.

      Device Name   Hardware Label (MAC Address)   Status
 [X] vmnic0         Ethernet0 (...c:29:4d:a0:f5)   Connected (...)
 [X] vmnic1         Ethernet1 (...c:29:4d:a0:ff)   Connected (...)
 [ ] vmnic2         Ethernet2 (...c:29:4d:a0:09)   Connected
 [ ] vmnic3         Ethernet3 (...c:29:4d:a0:13)   Connected

 <D> View Details   <Space> Toggle Selected        <Enter> OK   <Esc> Cancel
```

8. Once you are done with all the network configuration, while on the **Configure Management Network** screen, hit *Esc* to be prompted to apply the changes by seeking consent for a restart of the management network. Hit *Y* to apply the settings:

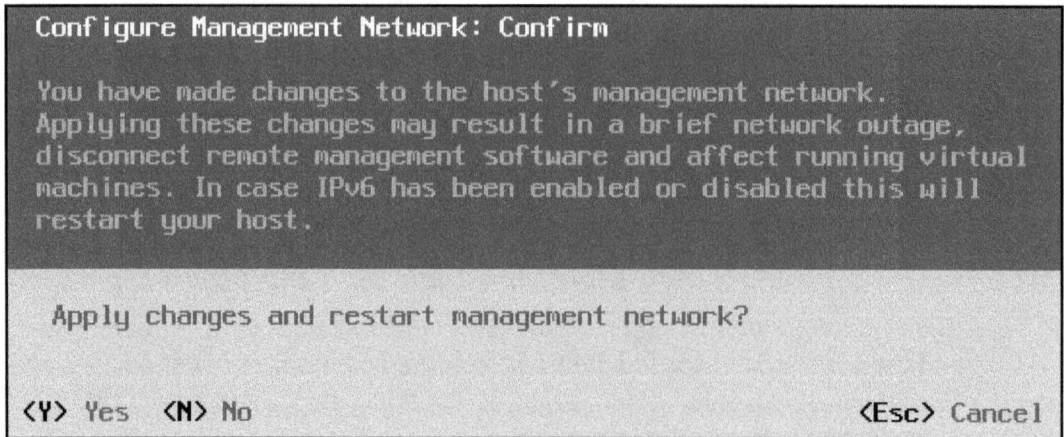

```
Configure Management Network: Confirm

You have made changes to the host's management network.
Applying these changes may result in a brief network outage,
disconnect remote management software and affect running virtual
machines. In case IPv6 has been enabled or disabled this will
restart your host.

    Apply changes and restart management network?


<Y> Yes   <N> No                                      <Esc> Cancel
```

With the networking configured you should now be able to connect to the ESXi host using the vSphere Client or add the host to a vCenter server. Both can be achieved only if the ESXi management IP is reachable from the machine where the vSphere Client is installed or from the vCenter machine.

Using the vSphere Client

The vSphere Client is a program used to connect to a supported version of an ESXi host or a vCenter Server. The client can only be installed on a Microsoft Windows machine. The client uses TCP port 443 to establish a connection either with the ESXi host or the vCenter Server.

The client can be downloaded from the ESXi **Getting Started** web page, which can be accessed using the hostname or the IP address of the host:

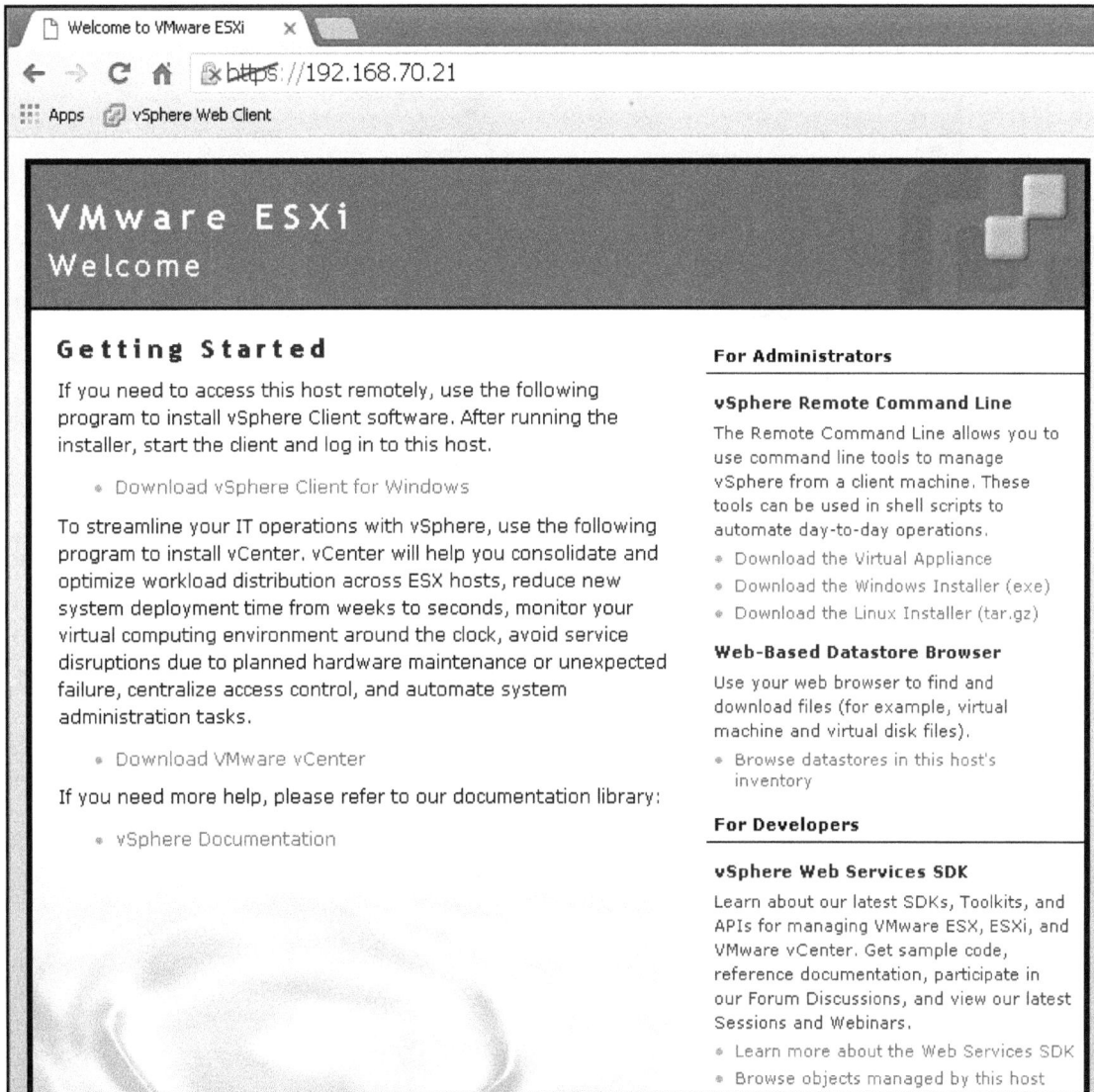

On the **Getting Started** page, click on the hyperlink **Download vSphere Client for Windows** to download the installer. Once downloaded, the installation is pretty straightforward and requires no special details. Make sure, though, that it is installed on a machine which can reach the ESXi host or vCenter over the network.

Once the client is installed it can simply be executed by double-clicking the shortcut corresponding to that to bring up the VMware vSphere Client window.

In the **VMware vSphere Client** window, supply the IP address or the hostname of the ESXi host, and the root credentials to log in:

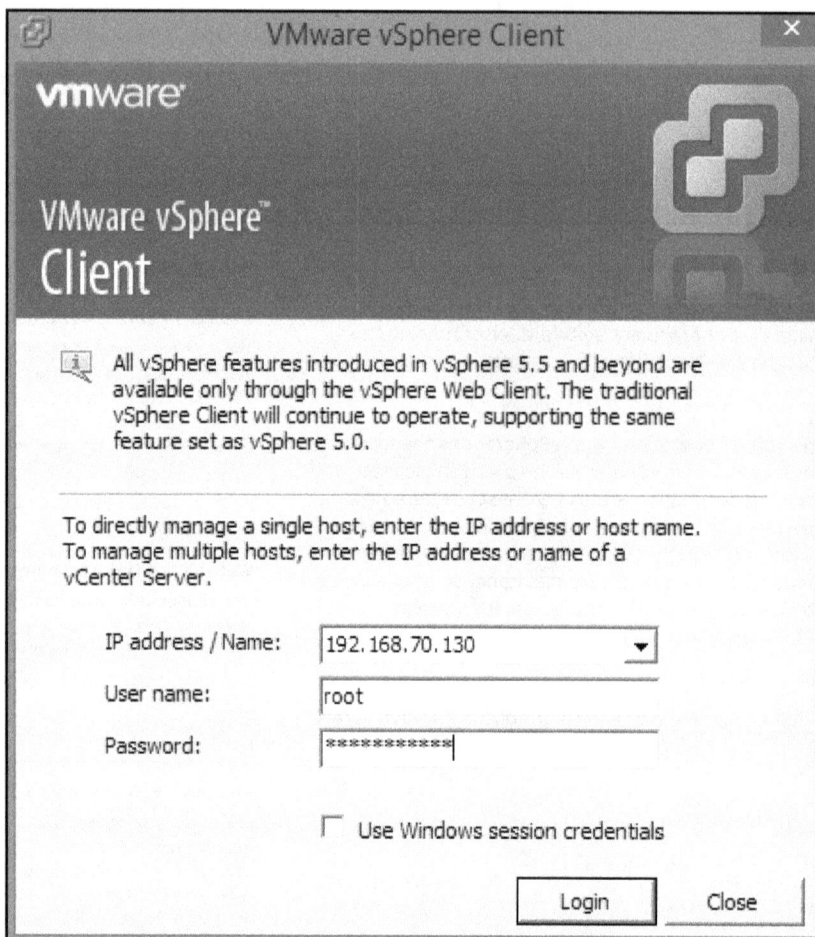

Creating additional local users on an ESXi host

It is not best practice to share the *root* credentials to users other than the administrator. You can either add users from the active directory, or create additional local users on an ESXi host using the vSphere Client, and assign the level of access the user will have on the ESXi host and its objects. In this topic, we will cover the procedure for creating additional local users.

By default, an ESXi host will have three default users created:

- **The vpx user**: The vCenter will have an administrator's role on every ESXi host that it is configured to manage. This is achieved by creating a user called the *vpxuser* with the administrator role assigned to it, and this is done automatically by the vCenter managing the host.
- **The dcui user**: The DCUI is severed by a process running on ESXi. The dcui user is used by DCUI to modify the locked down mode.
- **The root account**: This the mandatory root account on an ESXi host.

To create a new user:

1. Connect to the ESXi host using the vSphere Client using either the root account or an account with the administrator role.
2. Navigate to the **Users** tab, which will display the default users and any additional users if they were created.
3. Right-click on the vacant area and select **Add**:

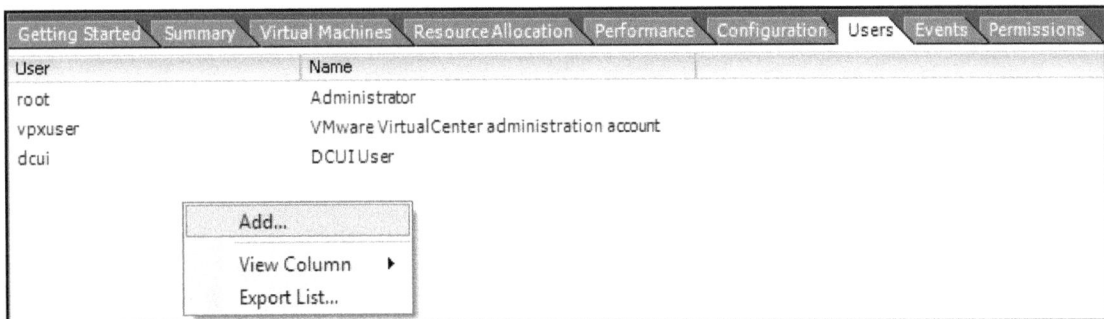

Getting Started	Summary	Virtual Machines	Resource Allocation	Performance	Configuration	Users	Events	Permissions

User	Name
root	Administrator
vpxuser	VMware VirtualCenter administration account
dcui	DCUI User

Add...
View Column ▶
Export List...

4. In the **Add New User** window, supply a login name, an optional username, and then the password. Click on **OK** to add the user.

5. Now, the Users tab should list the newly created user.

6. Navigate to the **Permissions** tab, right-click on the vacant area, and select **Add Permission…**:

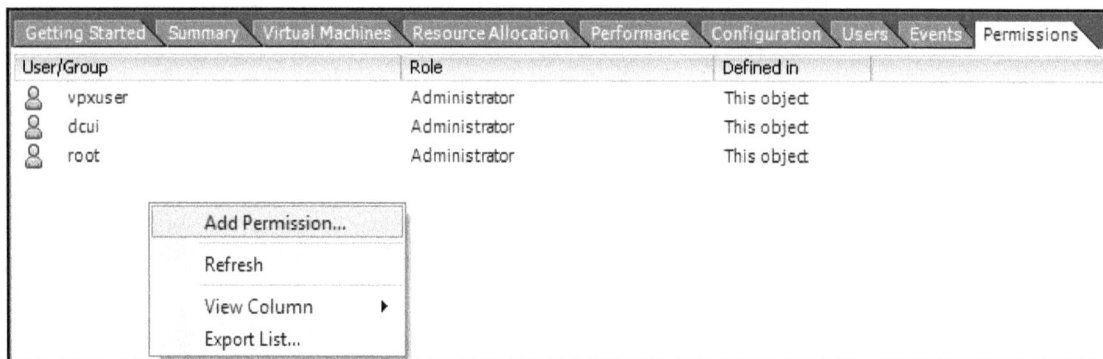

Getting Started	Summary	Virtual Machines	Resource Allocation	Performance	Configuration	Users	Events	Permissions

User/Group	Role	Defined in
vpxuser	Administrator	This object
dcui	Administrator	This object
root	Administrator	This object

Add Permission...
Refresh
View Column ▶
Export List...

7. In the **Add Permissions…** window, add the newly created user to the **User and Groups** pane.

8. Choose a role to assign to the user from the **Assigned Role** pane. The only options available are `Administrator`, `Read-only`, and `No Access`. Click on **OK** to confirm the changes:

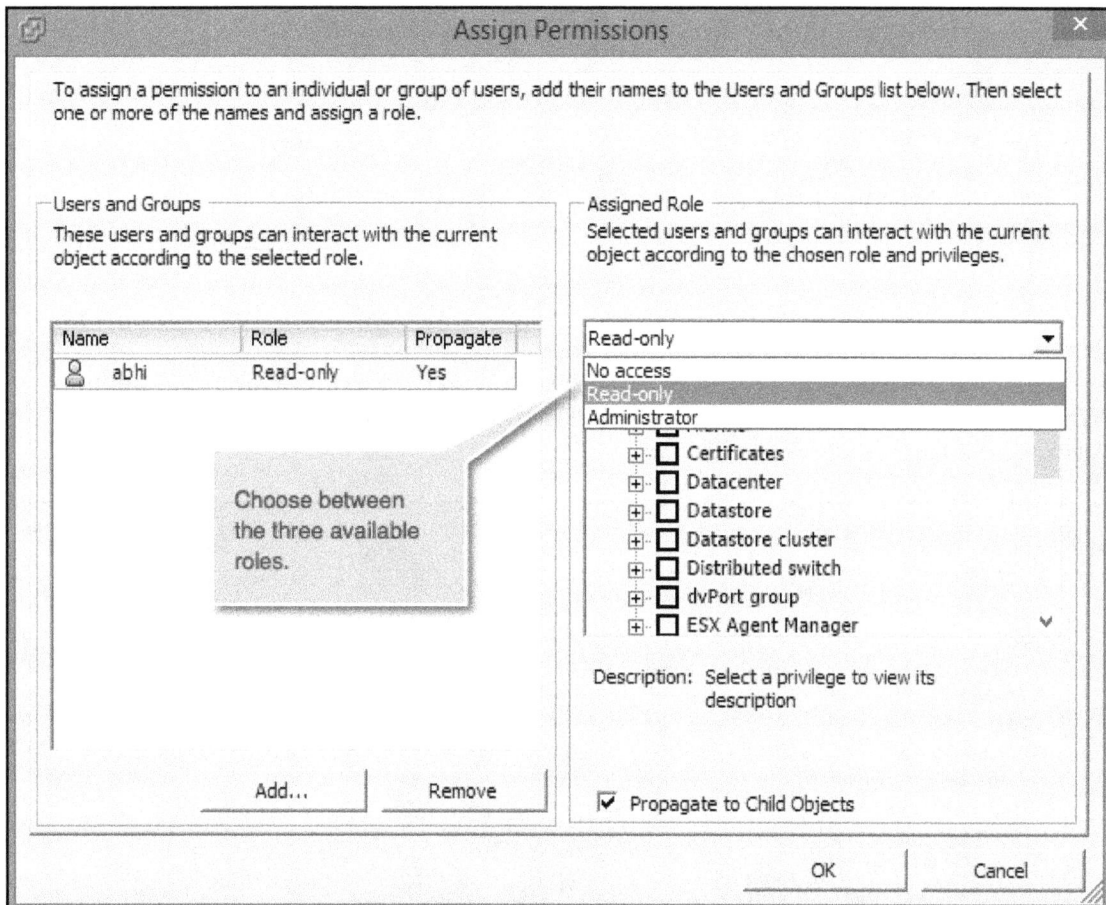

Unless you have not assigned a permission or assigned a `No  access` role to it, you should be able to log in to the ESXi host using the new user.

Using the ESXi Managed Object Browser

The **Managed Object Browser (MOB)** is a web-based server program that runs on an ESXi host to provide web-based access to all the objects managed by the ESXi host.

Starting with vSphere 6, MOB is disabled by default on ESXi.

Before you can access MOB, you will need to enable it through the **Advanced SettingsConfig.HostAgent.plugins.solo.enableMob** on the ESXi host. To bring up the **Advanced Settings** window, navigate to the **Configuration** tab and then click **AdvancedSettings** in the **Software** pane:

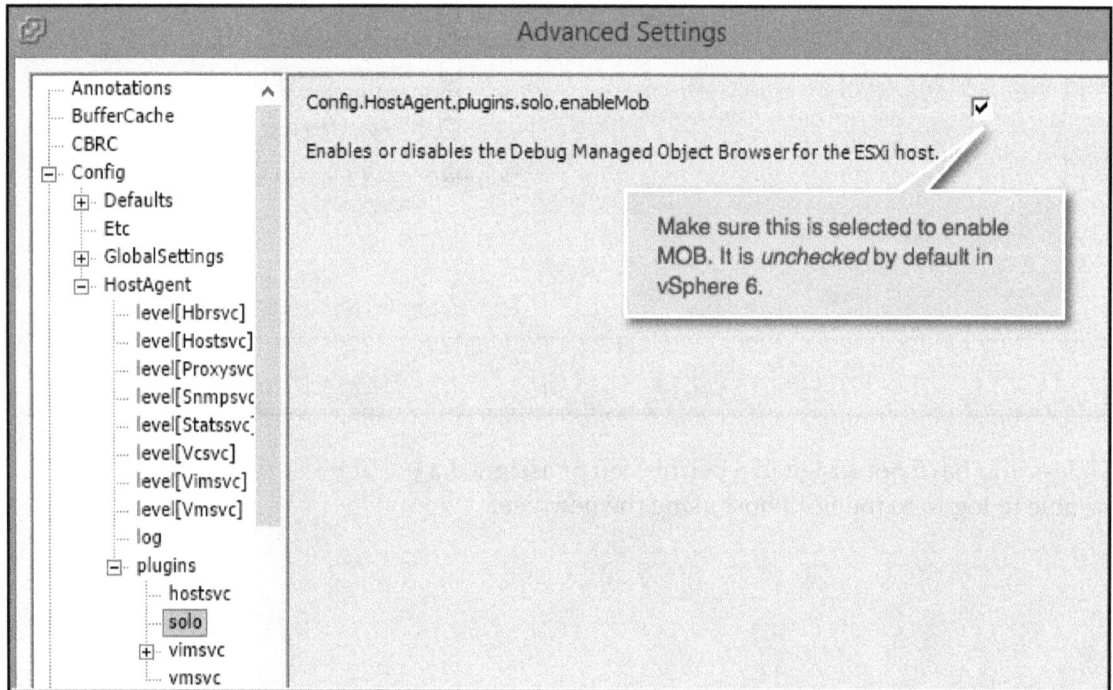

Once enabled, you should be able to get to the MOB of the ESXi host using the following URL syntax: `https://IP address or FQDN/mob`.

The MOB can be used to invoke commands on the objects managed by the ESXi host. For instance, you can invoke the method `CurrentTime` to retrieve the current date or time value from the host. Hence it requires an authenticated user to access the MOB interface. When you try to access the MOB URL of any ESXi host, you will be prompted for the credentials. The credentials supplied could be of any user with at least read-only permissions. Once you log in to the MOB, the home page will present you with the **Properties** and **Methods** that are available for use against the objects managed by the ESXi host:

Home			Logout

Managed Object Type: ManagedObjectReference:ServiceInstance
Managed Object ID: **ServiceInstance**

Properties

NAME	TYPE	VALUE
capability	Capability	capability
content	ServiceContent	content
serverClock	dateTime	"2015-05-17T15:20:49.780111Z"

Methods

RETURN TYPE	NAME
dateTime	CurrentTime
HostVMotionCompatibility[]	QueryVMotionCompatibility
ServiceContent	RetrieveServiceContent
ProductComponentInfo[]	RetrieveProductComponents
Event[]	ValidateMigration

Understanding other ESXi deployment methods

VMware ESXi can be installed and deployed using different methods. One of the most common methods is the interactive installation that can be performed by mounting the installation DVD, or its image, to the server chosen for hosting ESXi. The installation was covered in the previous section but there are two other deployment methods:

- The scripted-unattended installation
- vSphere Auto Deploy

> Since the use of vSphere Auto Deploy is dependent on vCenter and other features such as Host Profiles, we will be covering this topic in a later chapter.

Scripted-unattended ESXi installation

A scripted-unattended installation will require the use of an install script that is accessible to the server either via direct access (CD or USB) or via network access (HTTP, HTTPS, FTP, or NFS). The install script is referred to as a *kickstart file*. Kickstart is a Linux method to perform an unattended installation, hence the name. VMware supports the use of kickstart's syntax to perform an unattended ESXi installation.

Here is the default `ks.cfg` script located at `/etc/vmware/weasel`:

```
#
# Sample scripted installation file
#

# Accept the VMware End User License Agreement vmaccepteula

# Set the root password for the DCUI and Tech Support Mode
  rootpw mypassword

# Install on the first local disk available on machine
  install --firstdisk -overwritevmfs

# Set the network to DHCP on the first network adapter
  network --bootproto=dhcp --device=vmnic0

# A sample post-install script
```

```
%post --interpreter=python --ignorefailure=true
import time
stampFile = open('/finished.stamp', mode='w')
stampFile.write( time.asctime() )
```

Although it is the default script, the ESXi installer does not use it unless it is explicitly specified in the boot options using the `ks=` syntax:

```
ks=file://etc/vmware/weasel/ks.cfg
```

When you install using the default `ks.cfg` script, the default password will be set to `mypassword`.

There are many more commands than you see in the default script, and those commands can be used to create scripts to install ESXi hosts as per your requirements. Starting with ESXi 5.0, you can use the script to perform upgrades on the server. The following is a list of commands that can be included in scripts. The list may not cover every command available, but should cover the most common ones:

- `vmaccepteula`
- `clearpart`
- `dryrun`
- `install`
- `installorupgrade`
- `keyboard`
- `network`
- `paranoid`
- `part` or `partition`
- `reboot`
- `rootpw`
- `upgrade`
- `%include`
- `%pre`
- `%post`
- `%firstboot`

The commands prefixed with a percent (`%`) symbol are multi-line commands. Also, all the commands in the kickstart script should be in lower-case.

A single script can be used to install ESXi on multiple machines. Some modifications might be needed if you choose to install ESXi on a different hard drive, because by default it would install on the first local hard drive.

A scripted install has two procedural stages:

1. In the first stage, we create a custom script with the required commands, or edit the script if it needs to be unique for a specific host, and place it in a location accessible to the ESXi host
2. In the second stage we edit the boot options to redirect the installer to use the custom script file using the `ks=` option

If we do not specify the `ks=` boot option, then the standard-text installation will proceed.

The `ks=` boot option supports the following syntaxes:

- `ks=cdrom:/path`
- `ks=usb:/path`
- `ks=file://path`
- `ks=protocol://serverpath`

On successfully locating the configuration (`.cfg`) file, the installer will go through the following phases to finish the unattended installation:

- Preliminary checks
- Writing binary to the boot partition
- Partitioning the disk for ESXi
- Writing binary to the boot partition
- Writing GUIDs to the bootbanks
- Caching network settings
- Writing the first-boot scripts

Here is a sample procedure to perform an unattended installation of ESXi using the kickstart script. In this example, the kickstart script is located at an FTP location:

1. Boot the server with the ESXi installation CD in the CD/DVD ROM drive and at the ESXi installation standard boot menu select the ESXi installer and hit *Enter* to continue.

2. At the **Loading ESXi Installer** screen, press *Shift + O*. You have exactly 5 seconds to interrupt the loading screen:

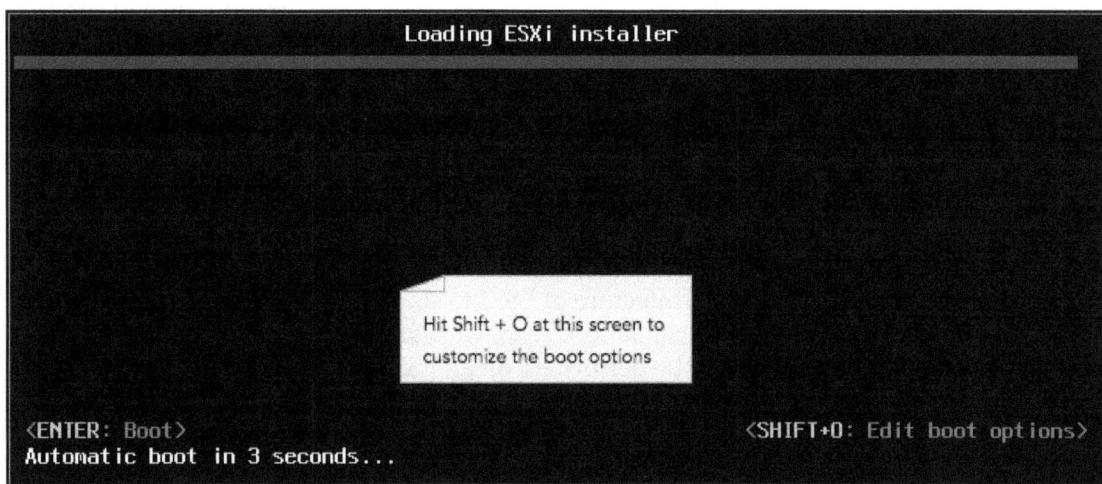

```
                      Loading ESXi installer




                              ┌──────────────────────────┐
                              │ Hit Shift + O at this screen to │
                              │ customize the boot options      │
                              └──────────────────────────┘

<ENTER: Boot>                              <SHIFT+O: Edit boot options>
Automatic boot in 3 seconds...
```

3. Pressing *Shift + O*, will reveal the default command, the `runweasel`. This will run weasel which is nothing but the ESXi installer:

```
<ENTER: Apply options and boot>        <ESC: Cancel>
> runweasel
```

4. At the `runweasel` prompt, specify the location of the install script. Local CD ROM, USB driver, HTTP/HTTPS, or NFS are other supported script locations:

```
<ENTER: Apply options and boot>
> runweasel ks=ftp://user01:pass346@192.168.70.222/ks.cfg
```

5. The installer will then locate and load the specified configuration file and proceed with the installation.
6. Once the installation is complete, it will prompt for a reboot. Press Enter to reboot.

Summary

In this chapter, we discussed the architecture of ESXi to start with. We also learned how to perform an interactive or scripted installation. Also, we learned about the post-installation configuration tasks that will ideally be performed on an ESXi host.

In the next chapter, we will learn about the installation and configuration of a vCenter Server.

3
The Management Layer – VMware vCenter

VMware vCenter Server is the management layer that helps manage hundreds of ESXi hosts under a single management plane. It helps cluster ESXi hosts and enable features such as vSphere HA and vSphere DRS which otherwise would not be possible.

In this chapter, we will cover the following topics:

- VMware vCenter Server concepts
- Laying the foundation for a vCenter installation or deployment
- Installing vCenter on a Windows platform
- Deploying the appliance based vCenter and its components
- Configuring identity sources on the Single Sign-On server.
- Configuring licensing for the vSphere infrastructure
- Adding ESXi to the vCenter
- Enhanced Linked Mode

VMware vCenter Server concepts

VMware vCenter Server is available in two formsâ®®â®®a Windows version and a Linux appliance. An appliance is nothing but a virtual machine running a **Just enough Operating System (JeOS)** version of SUSE Linux with all the vCenter components pre-installed on it.

> JeOS refers to a traditional operating system that has been customized to fit the needs of a particular application that will be installed on it.

There is no Linux installable version of vCenter. It is only available in the form of a Linux appliance. The Linux version of vCenter offers the same functionalities and performance as the Windows version. However, there are differences in how they can be installed, deployed, and configured. The Windows version will require you to run an installer on a virtual or physical machine running a supported version of Microsoft Windows; however, the Linux version is available in the form of an appliance, which can be deployed as a virtual machine.

The vCenter bundle contains the following components:

- vCenter server
- **Single Sign-On (SSO)**
- Inventory service
- vSphere web client
- Several other services such as content library, licensing, storage profile service, performance charts, and so on

The vCenter Server runs the core logic of managing the vSphere resources. It is responsible for sending commands to the ESXi host agent (hostd), retrieving configuration changes from the ESXi hosts using the vCenter Agent (vpxa), running on the host, and updating the vCenter database with the latest configuration data.

The authentication server is called the SSO. This service enables all the supported components to authenticate with vCenter without the need for the user to supply the credentials for every connection. Instead, it uses an authenticated token to serve this purpose. We will learn more about SSO in this chapter.

The database is the heart of the vCenter. The vCenter Server wouldn't function without an active connection to the database. Everything that you see and manipulate at the vCenter GUI is backed by its configuration saved in the database. VMware supports the use of Microsoft SQL Server, Oracle, and IBM DB2 as a database server for vCenter. The Linux version of vCenter comes with a bundled **PostgreSQL** database, which supports the use of an external Oracle Database, but with no support for Microsoft SQL Server.

Certificate management â⊚⊚ VMware products require a signed certificate for establishing a secure connection between components or products. Hence, the installation of any such components does come with a self-signed certificate. However, most enterprises would opt for **Certificate Authority** (**CA**) signed certificates. The management of certificates has always been the pain an administrator has endured. With vSphere 6, VMware have released a built-in certificate authority called the **vSphere Certificate Manager**, which uses **VMware Certificate Authority** (**VMCA**). We will learn more about the certificate manager and VMCA later in this chapter.

With vCenter Server being the management plane for virtual infrastructure management, there are a plethora of VMware and third-party tools that can be configured to integrate or interact with the vCenter to further sophisticate the management of your virtual infrastructure. Some of these tools include VMware Update Manager, VMware Horizon View, VMware vRealize Automation vCenter, and VMware vRealize Operations Manager.

VMware Platform Services Controller

One of the pain points with the installation and management of vCenter were the tools and services it depended on for its operation. Those tools included the SSO, inventory service, and the certificates. With versions prior to vCenter 6.0 for Windows all of these components had individual installers, making it possible to be either installed on the same machine as the vCenter or installed them onto separate machines. Hence it became necessary to protect and manage more than one virtual or physical machine running Windows. It also made upgrading and troubleshooting cumbersome. Starting with vSphere 6.0, VMware have bundled the essential services such as the SSO, Inventory Service, and Certificate Management into a single manageable solution called the **Platform Services Controller** (**PSC**). The PSC can be installed on the same machine as the vCenter, installed on a separate supported Windows machine, or a PSC running on the virtual appliance.

Here are the components of a PSC:

- VMCA
- VMware SSO
- VMware licensing service

VMCA

VMCA is an installable service that helps manage the certificates used by vCenter, its components, and the ESXi hosts it manages. It offers a command-line interface. It is a requirement that the certificates and the private keys are stored in VMCA's key store, with an exception of the ESXi host certificates which are stored locally on the hosts.

The VMCA has two main services:

- A built-in certificate authority that can be used within a vSphere environment to issue certificates to the vCenter components and the ESXi hosts
- A client-side key store for certificate information called the VMware Endpoint Certificate Services (VECS)

VMCA can operate in three modes:

- VMCA (Default)
- Custom Certificate Authority
- Thumbprint mode

In the *default* mode, the VMCA becomes the certificate authority and issues VMCA signed certificates to the VMware Components. Hence the root certificate belongs to the VMCA.

In the *enterprise* mode, the VMCA will act as a subordinate CA and the root CA as a public or enterprise-wide CA. In this case, the VMCA root certificate will be replaced with the third-party CA signed certificate. VMCA will continue to remain the tool to generate on-demand certificates. The generated certificate chain will include the VMCA as a subordinate CA.

In the *custom* mode the VMCA is bypassed and all the certificates are requested from a third-party CA. While in this mode, since VMCA does not handle any certificate management, you will have to manually replace the certificates of all the requested vCenter components and the ESXi hosts.

Unless in custom mode, it is necessary to store all the certificate information in the VECS.

> VMware Knowledge base article KB#2097936 has more information on how to use VMCA. URL-`http://kb.vmware.com/kb/297936`.

VMware SSO

VMware SSO is an authentication server released with vSphere 5.1. With version 5.5, it has been rearchitected so that it is simple to plan and deploy and easier to manage. With vSphere 6.0, it is now embedded into the PSC.

It is an authentication gateway, which takes the authentication requests from various registered components and validates the credential pair against the identity sources added to the SSO server. The components are registered to the SSO server during their installation. At the time of writing this book, the following are the components that could register and leverage SSO's ability:

- VMware vCenter Server
- VMware vCenter Inventory Service
- VMware vCenter Orchestrator
- VMware vShield Manager
- VMware vCloud Director (partial integration)
- VMware vSphere Web Client
- VMware vSphere Data Protection
- VMware Log Browser

SSO supports authenticating against the following identity sources:

- Active directory
- Active directory as an LDAP server
- Open LDAP
- Local OS

Once authenticated, the SSO client is provided with a token for further exchanges. The advantage here is that the user or administrator of the client service is not prompted for a credential pair (username and password) every time it needs to authenticate.

> Starting with vSphere 5.5, SSO no longer requires an external database.

SSO 5.1 had three deployment modesâ◉◉basic, high availability, and multisite. For the HA and Multisite modes, we had the concept of a **Primary Node** and only one **Primary Node** could exist in a particular SSO environment. You always had to plan and decide on the deployment mode before you installed SSO, because once deployed in a particular mode, changing to a different mode wasn't an easy job.

This is, however, changed with SSO 5.5, where-in there is only a single deployment mode and three placement methods:

- Method 1 â◉◉ First SSO server:

  This is used when deploying the first SSO server at the site. This can either be done during the Simple Installation or by running the SSO installer separately on a different machine.

- Method 2 â◉◉ Additional SSO server at the same site:

  This is used to spawn an additional SSO server at the same site. This additional instance will not be involved in any failover or load balancing with the first SSO server, unless you use a third-party load balancer to achieve this.

- Method 3 â◉◉ Additional SSO server at a different site:

  This is used to spawn an additional SSO server at a different (remote) site. The additional SSO servers deployed at the remote sites cannot be involved in a failover.

With vSphere 6.0, since the SSO component is a part of the Platform Services Controller, the deployment rules apply to the Platform Services Controller machine. The PSCs can be installed in two different modes, an *embedded* mode wherein the PSC is installed on the same machine along with the vCenter, or in an *external* mode wherein the PSC is installed on a different machine. It is recommended not to exceed connecting eight vCenters to a PSC for optimal performance. You can have up to eight PSCs per SSO site.

VMware Licensing Service

The VMware Licensing Service is designed to act as a repository that will host the licensing information of all VMware products that are compatible with the PSC. Now that licensing is managed by a separate service you will no longer have to perform license management on every vCenter server in your environment. Since every vCenter 6.0 will have a PSC associated to it, license management is no longer dependent on the availability of vCenter. License information is replicated between only those PSCs which are in the same SSO domain.

Laying the foundation for a vCenter deployment

VMware vCenter can be deployed as a Linux-based appliance or it can be installed on a machine running a supported version of Microsoft Windows. There are no real capacity or performance differentiators between both the deployment types. However, the Linux-based vCenter appliance does not support the use of an external Microsoft SQL database, owing to the fact that there are no supported Microsoft SQL drivers for Linux yet.

There is always a reason behind why an architect would choose either of the two deployment methods. Here, we will try to visit some of those aspects first before we delve deeper into the possible deployment models.

vCenter Appliance versus vCenter on Windows

We have categorized the design decisions into the following five categories:

- Ease of deployment
- Server management
- Choice of database
- Backup and recovery
- Cost of licensing

Ease of deployment

The **vCenter Server Appliance** (**VCSA**) comes packaged with all the services required for the vCenter to run. The Platform Services Controller is also embedded into the appliance. Hence the deployment is only a matter of a few clicks and your vCenter virtual machine will be up and running. The deployment of VCSA is quicker than the Windows-based installation, since all the services are already installed and ready to be configured. The Linux-based version of vCenter comes only in the form of an appliance and therefore cannot be installed on a physical machine:

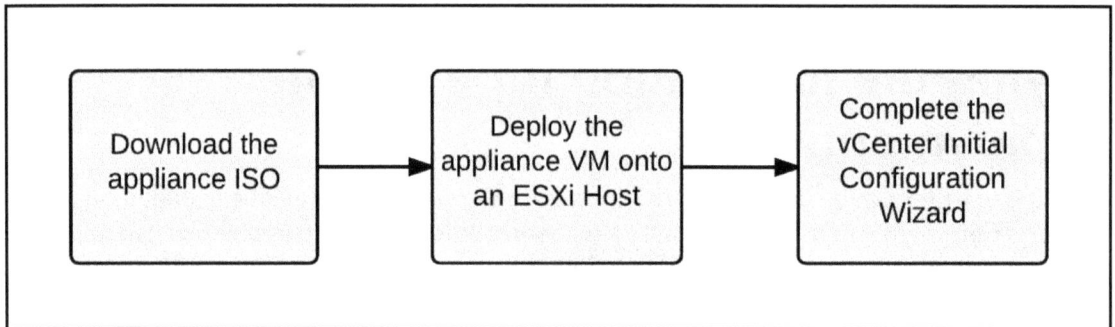

```
┌──────────────┐     ┌──────────────┐     ┌──────────────┐
│ Download the │     │  Deploy the  │     │ Complete the │
│ appliance ISO│ ──▶ │ appliance VM │ ──▶ │vCenter Initial│
│              │     │   onto an    │     │Configuration │
│              │     │  ESXi Host   │     │   Wizard     │
└──────────────┘     └──────────────┘     └──────────────┘
```

vCenter for Windows has to be installed on a machine (VM or physical) running a supported version of Microsoft Windows. In most environments, this requires identifying a supported hardware (if physical) and then installing a supported version on Windows. If the vCenter was intended to be running on a virtual machine, then you will need to create a new virtual machine and install a supported version of Windows on it. Once you have the machine (VM or physical) ready, you will then have to go through the process of running the Windows-based installer to finish the installation:

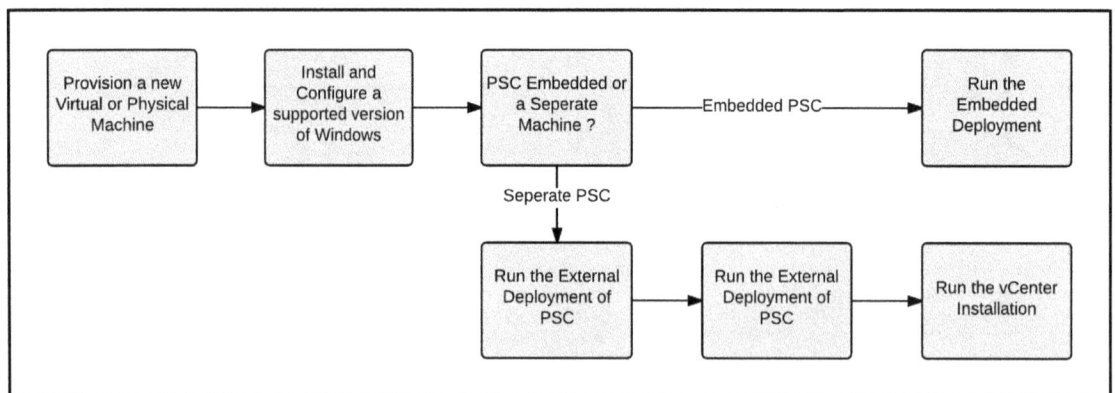

```
┌──────────┐   ┌──────────┐   ┌──────────┐                    ┌──────────┐
│Provision │   │Install and│   │PSC       │                    │ Run the  │
│a new     │   │Configure a│   │Embedded  │── Embedded PSC ──▶ │ Embedded │
│Virtual or│──▶│supported  │──▶│or a      │                    │Deployment│
│Physical  │   │version    │   │Seperate  │                    │          │
│Machine   │   │of Windows │   │Machine ? │                    │          │
└──────────┘   └──────────┘   └──────────┘                    └──────────┘
                                    │
                               Seperate PSC
                                    │
                                    ▼
                              ┌──────────┐   ┌──────────┐   ┌──────────┐
                              │Run the   │   │Run the   │   │ Run the  │
                              │External  │──▶│External  │──▶│ vCenter  │
                              │Deployment│   │Deployment│   │Installation│
                              │of PSC    │   │of PSC    │   │          │
                              └──────────┘   └──────────┘   └──────────┘
```

The Windows-based install is expectedly time consuming when compared to a VCSA deployment because every required service will be have to be installed and configured for the installation to complete.

Server management

Like with any asset hosting a service in a modern day data center, the vCenter machine will also have to be managed and monitored for stability and optimal performance. Ease of server management is a debatable topic and is very dependent on the type of environment and the technical staff managing the environment. For instance, a data center with most of its services hosted on Windows would prefer vCenter installed on Windows. Likewise, a data center with a predominant Linux footprint would prefer deployment of the Linux-based appliance. Therefore, the decision to choose between the VCSA and a Windows-based installation can only be an outcome of a discussion with the stakeholders.

Backup and recovery

Like with any other business application, the vCenter server and its data should be backed up.

The Windows version of vCenter will require you to backup the database separately. If vCenter is running in a VM then it can also be backed up like any other virtual machine in the environment.

The backup of VCSA will depend on factors such as the PSC deployment mode, use of embedded vPostgres, or an External Oracle database. If you have deployed VCSA with an embedded database and embedded PSC, then either full VM backup will help. If you are using an external PSC then they should be backed up separately.

You can also backup and restore the embedded vPostgres database. The VMware knowledge base article 2091961 covers the backup and restore of the vPostgres database. Here is the URL: `https://kb.vmware.com/kb/291961`.

The vCenter appliance also has built-in integration with**VMware vStorage APIs for Data Protection** (**VADP**). So you could even use**vSphere Data Protection** (**VDP**) or any other backup product that uses VADP to backup and restore VCSA.

The choice of database

The choice of database will again depend on the current organizational standards and the size of the environment. If the design were to be for a smaller environment you could choose to use the default embedded vPostgres database which is limited to 1000 ESXi hosts and 10000 virtual machines. Larger environments would require the use of an external Oracle or Microsoft SQL database.

If an organization uses Oracle to host databases for all their applications, then they may choose not to spend on licenses for a Microsoft SQL server. The Oracle database can be used with either the VCSA or vCenter's Windows version.

However, if the organization uses Microsoft SQL for all its applications then they could decide not to spend on the license required to host an Oracle database, hence leaving them with no choice other than the use of vCenter for Windows. VCSA does not support the use of Microsoft SQL server for hosting its database, hence it cannot be used in such an environment.

Cost of licensing

The main cost advantage of using VCSA is that it does not require operating system licensing. All Windows machines hosting VMware products or solutions need to be licensed. The cost of licensing would still be debatable and the choices can vary. For instance, in a large enterprise, the cost of Windows server licensing may not be significant since Windows Server Datacenter licensing may be used for the hosts.

Deploying vCenter and its components

Once a design decision regarding the type of vCenter to be used in the environment has been made, it is important to plan how vCenter and its components are laid out for better management and performance. Some design decisions play a major role in how flexible or scalable the resultant infrastructure can be. In this section, we will try to understand the possible deployment methods and the rationale behind the choice of a particular method.

With vSphere 5.1 and 5.5, the Single Sign-On component played a major role in design decisions. With vSphere 6.0, it is still the SSO, but since it is now embedded into the Platform Services Controller, the PSC now dictates the deployment methods and optimal and recommended limits.

vCenter 6.0 can now be deployed in two modes:

- vCenter with an embedded PSC, wherein both the vCenter server software and the PSC are installed on the same machine. This mode is possible with both vCenter for Windows and the VCSA:

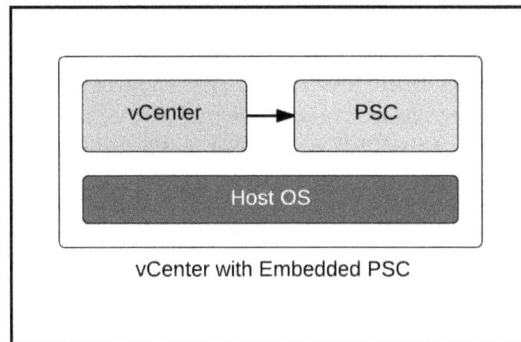

vCenter with Embedded PSC

- While in, embedded mode, the PSC can still be joined to existing the PSC domain.

- vCenter with an external PSC, wherein the Platform Services Controller is installed onto a separate machine. Again, this is possible with both vCenter for Windows and VCSA:

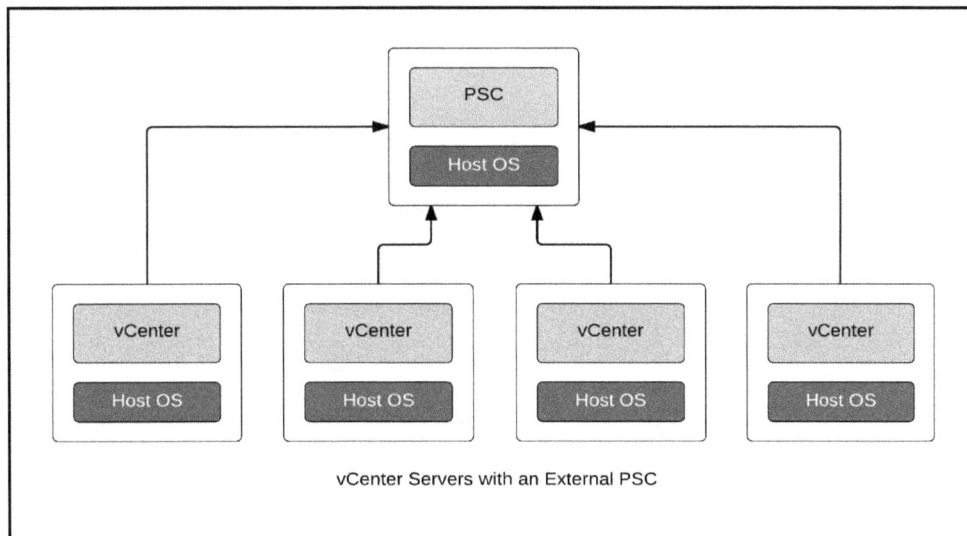

vCenter Servers with an External PSC

The PSC can become a single point of failure if it is not protected. If a PSC becomes unavailable, then the vCenter or the components which were using the PSC would not be able to allow new connections or user sessions. Already active connections or sessions would continue to remain active. The same applies to the vCenter service as well. If for any reason the vCenter service is stopped then you would not be able to restart it without the PSC being available.

You can have more than one PSC deployed for a set of vCenters, they sync data between them, but high availability is not built into them. This means that, if one of the PSCs fail for any reason, the existing ones would not take over the role of the failed PSC. To achieve high availability, you will need to put the PSC nodes behind a network load balancer. The PSC VMs should be in an HA-enabled cluster for increased resiliency:

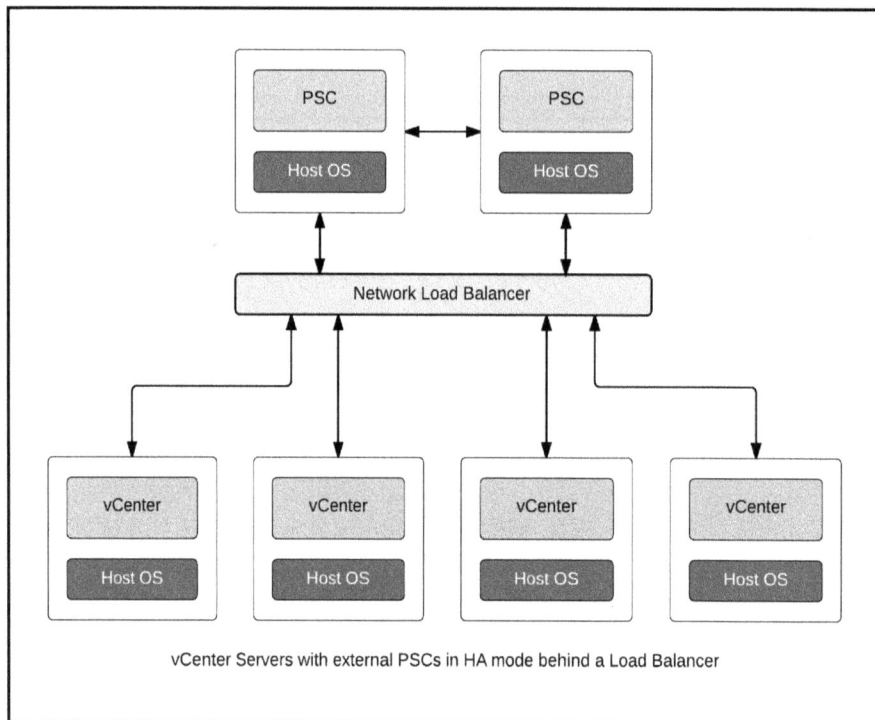

vCenter Servers with external PSCs in HA mode behind a Load Balancer

Keep in mind though, that when you pair the PSCs for high availability, it should be of the same type: VCSA-based or Windows-based.

Here is a list of some of the configuration maximums:

Item	Configuration maximum
PSCs per SSO domain	8
PSCs per SSO site, behind a load balancer	4
VMware solutions connected to a single PSC	4
VMware solutions in a single SSO domain	10
Number of user or group objects within an SSO domain	1000000

Understanding the hardware and software requirements

The hardware requirement for both vCenter-Windows or the vCenter appliance will change based on the deployment type. The following table shows the CPU and memory requirements per deployment type:

Deployment Type	Windows-based		Linux-appliance Based	
CPUs	Memory (GB)	CPUs		Memory (GB)
PSC Only	2	2	2	2
10 ESXi hosts, 100 VMs	2	8	2	8
100 ESXi hosts, 1000 VMs	4	16	4	16
400 ESXi hosts, 4000 VMs	8	24	8	24
1000 ESXi hosts, 10000 VMs	16	32	16	32

The vCenter or the Platform Services Controller can be installed on a machine running 64-bit Windows 2008 R2 or later.

Here is a list of supported Windows operating systems:

- Microsoft Windows Server 2008 Service Pack 1 64-bit
- Microsoft Windows Server 2008 R2 64-bit
- Microsoft Windows Server 2008 R2 – Service Pack 1 64-bit
- Microsoft Windows Server 2012 64-bit
- Microsoft Windows Server 2012 R2 64-bit

The Linux-based appliance does not require OS level life cycle management by the customer. VMware manages all the updates and compatibility. So, every time VMware makes a Linux appliance, it will certainly be running a supported and compatible version of Linux. The appliance is based on SUSE Linux Enterprise 11.

Installing vCenter on a Windows platform

vCenter and all its components can be installed on a supported Microsoft Windows operating system. In the previous section *Laying the foundation for a vCenter deployment* we learnt about the different deployment models and system requirements for a vCenter installation. In this section, we will cover the installation of vCenter and PSC separately. The installer can handle the installation of PSC and vCenter if you choose to deploy a PSC-embedded deployment model. But in most enterprise data centers customers would choose to deploy PSC separately. Hence, we will cover the installation of the PSC first and then install vCenter Server.

Installing PSC on a Windows machine

VMware PSC can be installed on a machine (physical or VM) running a supported version of Windows Server 2008 or 2012 64-bit operating system. The PSC installer is located on the ISO image for vCenter. The ISO downloaded can either be mounted to a virtual machine or burned to a DVD if you intend to install PSC onto a physical machine. If Windows does autoplay the ISO image, then you should be presented with the VMware vCenter installer screen.

The installer screen gives you options to start the following installers:

- vCenter Server for Windows
- vSphere Client
- vSphere Update Manager Server
- vSphere Update Manager Download Service
- vSphere Authentication Proxy

To install the PSC you will need to initiate the vCenter Server installer:

1. Select **vCenter Server for Windows** and click **Install** to start the vCenter installer.
2. On the installer's welcome screen, click **Next** to continue.
3. Accept VMware's End User License Agreement and click **Next** to continue.
4. In the **Select deployment type** screen, select the **Platform Services Controller** option under **External Deployment**. Click **Next** to continue:

- Doing so, will only install the Platform Services Controller component onto the Windows machine the installer is being run on.
- On the next screen, supply the FQDN of the machine you are installing the PSC on as the system name. Click **Next** to continue.
- Now, you will be prompted to create or join an SSO domain:

    - If you choose to create a new domain, then supply a domain name (default: `vsphere.local`), a password for the SSO administrator, and an SSO Site name:

Create a new vCenter Single Sign-On domain	
Domain name:	vsphere.local
vCenter Single Sign-On user name:	administrator
vCenter Single Sign-On password:	••••••••••••
Confirm password:	••••••••••••
Site name:	Site-A

    - If you choose to join an existing SSO domain, then supply the FQDN or IP address of a PSC belonging to the domain you intend to join and its SSO administrator password:

Join a vCenter Single Sign-On domain	
Platform Services Controller FQDN or IP address:	pscfirst01
vCenter Single Sign-On HTTPS port:	443
vCenter Single Sign-On user name:	administrator
vCenter Single Sign-On password:	••••••••••••

5. On the next screen, you will be allowed to configure common ports such as HTTP/HTTPs, Syslog service and TLS ports, and the PSC's STS ports. It is not mandatory to modify these port numbers unless they are already blocked in your environment for a reason. The screen also informs you about a set of ports that aren't configurable and have to be unblocked in your infrastructure:

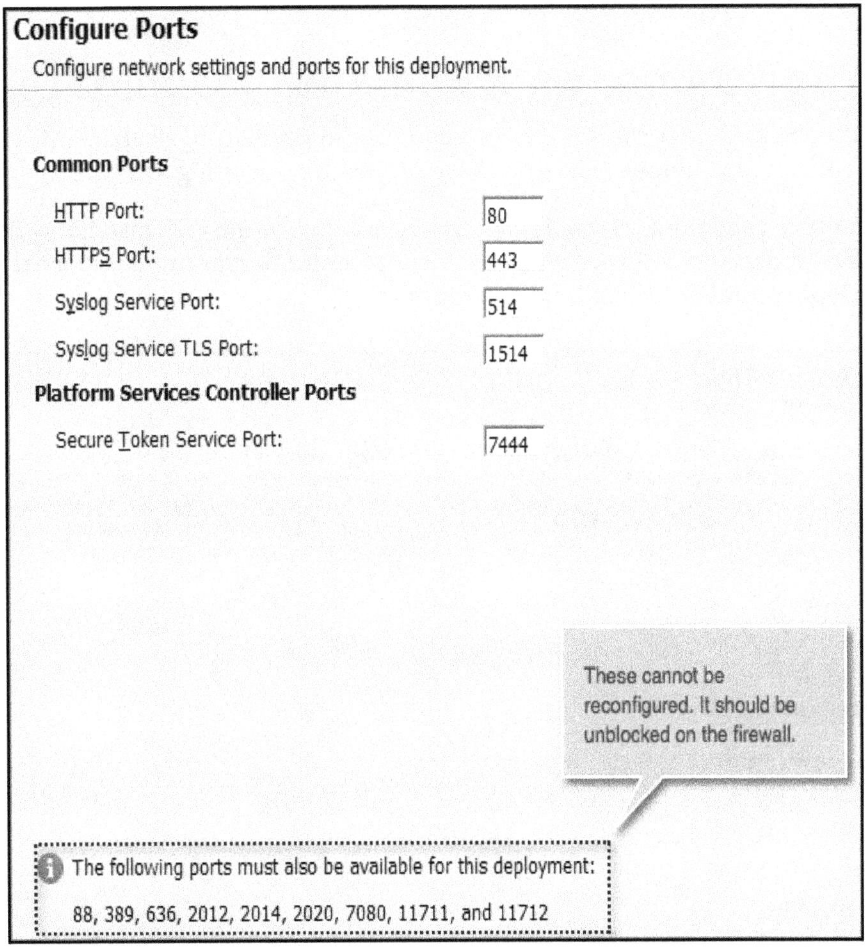

Configure Ports

Configure network settings and ports for this deployment.

Common Ports

HTTP Port:	80
HTTPS Port:	443
Syslog Service Port:	514
Syslog Service TLS Port:	1514

Platform Services Controller Ports

Secure Token Service Port:	7444

These cannot be reconfigured. It should be unblocked on the firewall.

ⓘ The following ports must also be available for this deployment:

88, 389, 636, 2012, 2014, 2020, 7080, 11711, and 11712

6. The next screen will allow you to modify the storage location for the PSC. It is not required to modify though. Click **Next** to continue.

7. On the **Ready to Install** screen, click **Install** to begin the installation.

8. If the installation completes successfully, you will be presented with a **Setup Complete** screen. Click **Finish** to exit the installer's wizard.

Installing vCenter on a Windows machine

Much like the PSC, vCenter can also be installed on a machine (physical or VM) running a supported version of Windows Server 2008 or 2012 64-bit operating system:

1. Launch the vCenter Installer much like you do for the PSC installation and in the **Select deployment type** screen, choose **vCenter Server** under **External Deployment** and click **Next** to continue:

Select deployment type

Select the component to deploy.

vCenter Server 6.0.0 requires a Platform Services Controller, which contains shared services such as vCenter Single Sign-On, Licensing, and Certificate Management. An embedded Platform Services Controller is deployed on the same Windows Host as vCenter Server. An external Platform Services Controllers is deployed in a separate Windows Host. For smaller installations, consider vCenter Server with an embedded Platform Services Controller. For larger installations with multiple vCenter Servers, consider one or more Platform Services Controllers. Refer to product documentation for more information.

Note: Once you deploy vCenter Server, you can only change from an embedded to an external Platform Services Controller with a fresh install.

Embedded Deployment

○ vCenter Server and Embedded Platform Services Controller

VM or Host

Platform Services Controller

vCenter Server

External Deployment

○ Platform Services Controller

◉ vCenter Server

A previously installed Platform Services Controller is required

VM or Host

Platform Services Controller

VM or Host

vCenter Server

VM or Host

vCenter Server

2. Supply the FQDN of the vCenter machine as the System Name and Click **Next** to continue.

3. Supply the PSC's FQDN or IP address, its SSO password and Click **Next** to continue:

---

vCenter Single Sign-On registration

Connect vCenter Server to a vCenter Single Sign-On domain in an existing Platform Services Controller.

Platform Services Controller FQDN or IP address: | psc601.vdescribed.lab

Note: This is the external Platform Services Controller with the vCenter Single Sign-On you want to register with.

vCenter Single Sign-On HTTPS port: | 443

vCenter Single Sign-On user name: | administrator

vCenter Single Sign-On password: | ••••••••••••

---

4. You will be prompted for the PSC's certificate validation. Click **OK** to proceed.

5. Choose a service Account for the vCenter Windows service to use and click **Next** to continue. The service account should have the *Log on as a service* privilege on the machine. The service accounts are user accounts that have the minimum required permissions to run the service and that would be its sole purpose. Most organizations maintain separate service accounts as a security practice. Note that you could also use the local administrator account as a service account, but it is not a recommended practice:

◉ Specify a user service account

Account user name: | vdescribed\vcentersvc

Account password: | •••••••••••

---

6. In the **Database settings** screen you could choose between an embedded vPostgres database or specify the DNS name of an external database.

> Keep in mind though that the embedded database supports only up to 1000 ESXi hosts and 10,000 virtual machines.

7. On the **Configure Ports** screen review the ports in use. A change here is not mandatory unless otherwise required in your infrastructure to meet organizational standards. Some of the ports are not configurable though and should be unblocked in the firewall.
8. Change the destination directory only if necessary and click Next to continue.
9. In the **Ready to Install** screen, click **Install** to begin the installation.
10. If the installation completes successfully, you will be presented with a Setup Completed screen. Click **Finish** to exit the wizard.

With both the PSC and the vCenter Server installed, you should now be able to use the vSphere Web Client to log in and view the vCenter Server using the SSO administrator credentials.

Deploying the appliance-based vCenter and its components

The appliance-based vCenter and PSC can also be deployed separately. We will be deploying the PSC first and then the vCenter Server as separate virtual machines. The appliance based vCenter or it components cannot be installed onto a physical machine.

Deploying a PSC appliance

Unlike the previous version wherein the appliance was deployed from an OVA, with vSphere 6.0, the appliance is deployed onto an ESXi host without the need to connect to an ESXi host using the vSphere client. This would require you to install the VMware Client Integration plugin before the appliance is deployed.

To install the Client Integration plugin, navigate to the `vcsa` folder of the DVD drive and double-click on **VMware-ClientIntegrationPlugin-6.0.0.msi** to start the installer. The installation is pretty straightforward, click through the wizard and finish the installation.

Once the Client Integration plugin is installed, you can begin the process of deploying the VCSA-PSC appliance:

1. Double-click the HTML file, `vcsa-setup.html` at the root of the VCSA ISO image, to bring up the setup web page which presents you with two options, **Install** or **Upgrade**. Click **Install**.
2. Accept the VMware EULA and click **Next** to continue.
3. Supply the FQDN or IP address and the root credentials of the ESXi host onto which you would like to deploy the PSC appliance VM. Click **Next** to continue:

Connect to target server
Specify the ESXi host on which to deploy the vCenter Server Appliance.

FQDN or IP Address:	host005.vdescribed.lab
User name:	root
Password:	••••••••••••••

FQDN of the
target ESXi host

⚠ Before proceeding:

*   Make sure the ESXi host is not in lock down mode or maintenance mode.
*   When deploying to a vSphere Distributed Switch (VDS), the appliance must be deployed to an ephemeral portgroup. After deployment, it can be moved to a static or dynamic portgroup.

4. An SSL Certificate Warning should prompt you to accept its SHA1 thumbprint. Click **Yes** to accept:

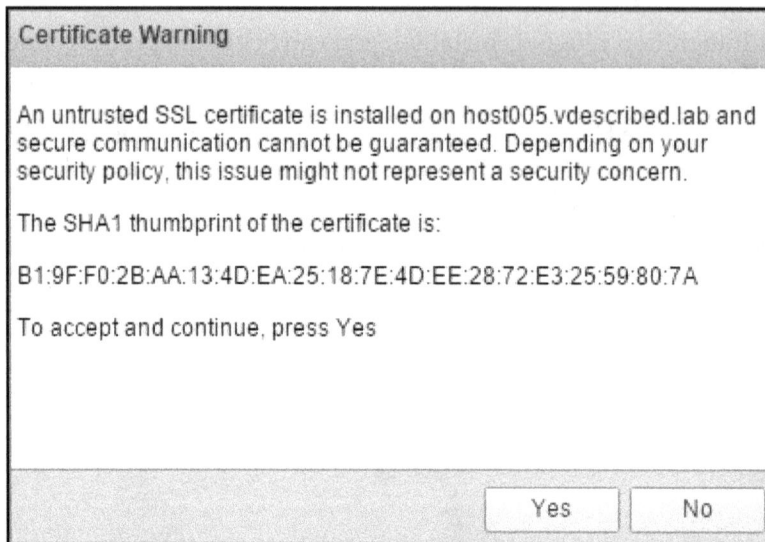

Certificate Warning

An untrusted SSL certificate is installed on host005.vdescribed.lab and secure communication cannot be guaranteed. Depending on your security policy, this issue might not represent a security concern.

The SHA1 thumbprint of the certificate is:

B1:9F:F0:2B:AA:13:4D:EA:25:18:7E:4D:EE:28:72:E3:25:59:80:7A

To accept and continue, press Yes

| Yes | No |

---

5. Supply a virtual machine name for the appliance and a password for its root user. Click **Next** to continue:

Set up virtual machine
Specify virtual machine settings for the vCenter Server Appliance to be deployed.

Appliance name:	pscapp01	
OS user name:	root	
OS password:	•••••••••••	
Confirm OS password:	•••••••••••	

---

6. In the **Select deployment type** screen, select the **Install Platform Services Controller** option under **External Platform Service Controller** and Click **Next** to continue:

Select deployment type
Select the services to deploy onto this appliance.

vCenter Server 6.0 requires a Platform Services Controller, which contains shared services such as Single Sign-On, Licensing, and Certificate Management. An embedded Platform Services Controller is deployed on the same Appliance VM as vCenter Server. An external Platform Services Controller is deployed in a separate Appliance VM. For smaller installations, consider vCenter Server with an embedded Platform Services Controller. For larger installations with multiple vCenter Servers, consider one or more external Platform Services Controllers. Refer to the vCenter Server documentation for more information.

Note: Once you install vCenter Server, you can only change from an embedded to an external Platform Services Controller with a fresh install.

Embedded Platform Services Controller

⬡ Install vCenter Server with an Embedded Platform Services Controller

VM or Host

Platform Services Controller

vCenter Server

External Platform Services Controller

◉ Install Platform Services Controller

⬡ Install vCenter Server (Requires External Platform Services Controller)

VM or Host

Platform Services Controller

VM or Host — vCenter Server

VM or Host — vCenter Server

7. You will now be prompted to create or join an SSO domain:

   - If you choose to create a new domain, then supply a password for the SSO administrator, a domain name (*default: vsphere.local*), and an SSO Site name
   - If you choose to join an existing SSO domain, then supply the FQDN or IP address of a PSC belonging to the domain you intend to join and its SSO administrator password

8. In the **Select appliance size** screen, no user input is needed as the installer will deploy the VM with a default size of 2 vCPUs, 2 GB Memory and 30 GB VMDK. Click **Next** to continue:

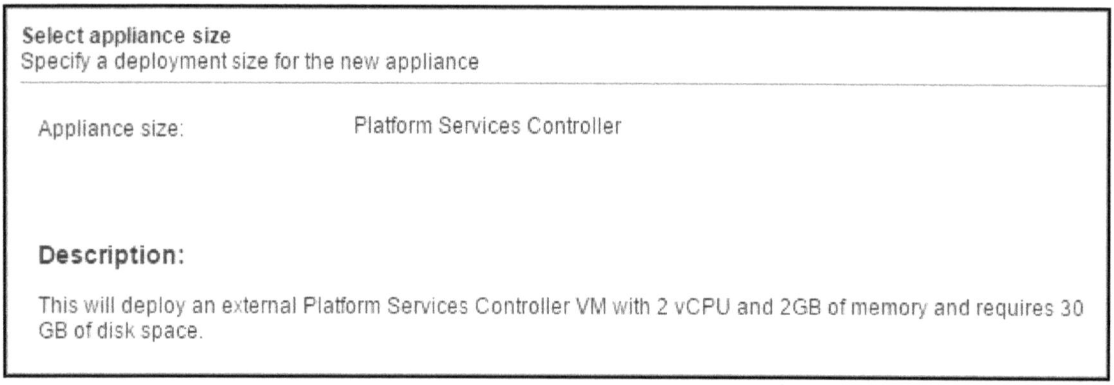

Select appliance size
Specify a deployment size for the new appliance

Appliance size: Platform Services Controller

Description:

This will deploy an external Platform Services Controller VM with 2 vCPU and 2GB of memory and requires 30 GB of disk space.

---

9. On the next screen, choose a data store to place the virtual machine files and click **Next** to continue. You also have the option to enable thin provisioning of the appliance's VMDK by selecting the option **Enable Thin Disk Mode**.

10. The Network Settings screen will require you to supply the following network details:

- Standard or distributed switch port group
- IP address version
- Network type-static/dynamic
- IP address
- System name â©© hostname/FQDN: Make sure the DNS A and PTR records are created for the chosen hostname
- Subnet mask
- Network gateway
- DNS Servers

- Time sync options âⓔⓔ sync with ESXi or sync with an NTP server:

Choose a network:	VM Network ▼ 🅘
IP address family:	IPv4 ▼
Network type:	static ▼
Network address:	192.168.70.134
System name [FQDN or IP address]:	pscapp01.vdescribed.lab 🅘
Subnet mask:	255.255.255.0
Network gateway:	192.168.70.2
Network DNS Servers (separated by commas)	192.168.70.3
Configure time sync:	◯ Synchronize appliance time with ESXi host ◉ Use NTP servers (Separated by commas) 192.168.70.3

11. On the **Ready to Complete** screen, click **Finish** to carry out the deployment.
12. If the installation completes successfully, you will be presented with an **Installation Complete** screen. Click **Close** to exit the wizard.

13. The console of the appliance VM should show the correct IP and hostname details:

```
VMware vCenter Server Appliance 6.0.0
Type: VMware Platform Services Controller

2 x Intel(R) Core(TM) i7 CPU 960 @ 3.20GHz
2 GiB Memory




Download support bundle from:
https://pscapp01.vdescribed.lab:443/appliance/support-bundle
https://192.168.70.134/ (STATIC)
```

Deploying VCSA vCenter

To deploy the VCSA bundled vCenter Server you will need to have the vSphere Client Integration plugin installed on the machine from where the installation will be initiated. If you were to use the same machine used to deploy the PSC then there is no need to install the Client Integration plugin again.

Here is how you can deploy the VCSA-vCenter Server:

1. Double-click the HTML file, **vcsa-setup.html** at the root of the VCSA ISO image.
2. The setup web page presents you with two options, **Install** or **Upgrade**. Click **Install**.
3. Accept the VMware EULA and Click **Next** to continue.
4. On the **Connect to target server** screen, supply the FQDN or IP address of the ESXi host onto which you would like to deploy the PSC appliance VM and the host's root credentials. Click **Next** to continue.
5. An SSL Certificate Warning should prompt you to accept its SHA1 thumbprint. Click **Yes** to accept.

6. Supply a virtual machine name for the vCenter appliance and a password for its root user. Click **Next** to continue:

Appliance name:	vcapp01 🛈
OS user name:	root
OS password:	•••••••••••• 🛈
Confirm OS password:	••••••••••••

7. In the **Select deployment type** screen, select the option **Install vCenter Server (Requires External Platform Services Controller)** under **External Platform Services Controller** and Click **Next** to continue:

8. Supply the external PSC's FQDN or IP address and its SSO administrator password to continue:

Configure Single Sign-On (SSO)
Connect vCenter Server to a SSO domain in an existing platform services controller. An SSO configuration cannot be changed after deployment.

Platform Services Controller FQDN or IP address:	pscapp01.vdescribed.lab
vCenter SSO User name:	administrator
vCenter SSO password:	••••••••••
vCenter Single Sign-On HTTPS Port:	443

⚠ Before proceeding, make sure you provide the password of the user 'administrator' in the existing vCenter Single Sign-On domain that you configured during Platform Services Controller deployment.

---

9. In the **Select appliance size** screen choose between **Tiny**, **Small**, **Medium**, or **Large** and the virtual machine will be sized accordingly:

Select appliance size
Specify a deployment size for the new appliance

Appliance size:

Tiny (up to 10 hosts, 100 VMs)

Tiny (up to 10 hosts, 100 VMs)
Small (up to 100 hosts, 1,000 VMs)
Medium (up to 400 hosts, 4,000 VMs)
Large (up to 1000 hosts, 10,000 VMs)

Description:

This will deploy a Tiny VM configured with 2 vCPUs and 8 GB of memory and requires 120 GB of disk space. These resources will be used by the vCenter Server services.

Appliance Size	Number of ESXi hosts	Number of VMs
Tiny	10	100
Small	100	1000
Medium	400	4000
Large	1000	10000

10. Choose a data store to put the virtual machine files on and click **Next** to continue.

11. On the **Configure database** screen, choose between the embedded vPostGres database or an external Oracle database:

> **Configure database**
> Configure the database for this deployment
>
> ⊙ Use an embedded database (vPostgres)
> ○ Use Oracle database

12. On the **Network Settings** screen supply the requested network details. These are similar to what is requested during the deployment of the PSC appliance:

Choose a network:	VM Network
IP address family:	IPv4
Network type:	static
Network address:	192.168.70.135
System name [FQDN or IP address]:	vcapp01.vdescribed.lab
Subnet mask:	255.255.255.0
Network gateway:	192.168.70.2
Network DNS Servers (separated by commas)	192.168.70.3
Configure time sync:	○ Synchronize appliance time with ESXi host ⊙ Use NTP servers (Separated by commas) 192.168.70.3

13. On the **Ready to complete** screen, review the settings and click **Finish** to begin the deployment.

14. If the deployment completes successfully you will be presented with an **Installation Complete** screen. Click **Close** to exit the wizard.

Configuring the identity sources on the SSO server

An identity source, as the name indicates, is a repository with information regarding the authentication domains that SSO should validate user credentials against and issue tokens using the **Secure Token Service (STS)**

SSO supports the following identity source types:

- **Active Directory (Integrated Windows Authentication)**: This can be used when your Active Directory is in Native mode. With this identity source type selected you could either use the current local machine account as the **Service Principal Name (SPN)** or choose to specify a different SPN.
- **Active Directory as an LDAP Server**: This is primarily used for backward compatibility.
- **Open LDAP**: This is used when you have an Open LDAP only based the directory service in your environment
- **Local OS**: This would become the source for the local operating system users on the machine where SSO is installed and not the vCenter Server.

Here is how you would add an identity source to the SSO server:

1. Use the vSphere Web Client to connect to the vCenter Server using the default SSO administrator and its domain (`administrator@vsphere.local`).

2. Click on **Administration** from the **Navigator** pane to bring up the **Administration** page:

3. Click on **Configuration** from the left pane and go to **Identity Sources** tab. The identity sources tab will show the current identity sources, one of them being the default. Click on the green + icon to bring up the **Add identity source** window:

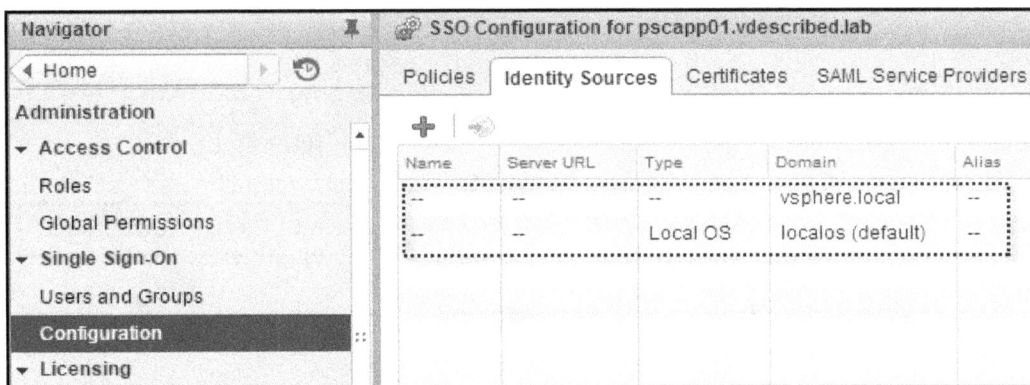

4. Select an **Identity source type**. The user inputs required will vary based on the type selected. In this case, we have selected **Active Directory as a LDAP Server**, supply the details requested, and click Test Connection to verify whether a connection can be established using the details provided. The following is a sample input set for a domain **vdescribed.lab**:

Name	`vdescried.lab`
Base DN for users	DC=vdescribed, DC=lab
Domain name	`vdescribed.lab`
Domain alias	VDESCRIBED
Base DN for groups	DC=vdescribed, DC=lab
Primary server URL	`ldap://dc2012.vdescribed.lab`
Username	`vcentersvc@vdescribed.lab`
Password	Password of domain user account

5. In the **Add identity source** window, click **OK** to begin adding the identity source. Once added, the new identity source will be listed in the **Identity Sources** tab:

Configuring licenses for the vSphere environment

As we learnt at the beginning of the chapter, the Platform Services Controller now has a stand alone service for the license management of vSphere products. Post installation of the vCenter, it is important to license your vSphere products including the vCenter server and ESXi hosts.

Here is how you would add licenses to the centralized license management system:

1. Use the vSphere Web Client to connect to the vCenter Server using the default SSO administrator and its domain (`administrator@vsphere.local`).
2. Click on **Administration** from the **Navigator** pane to bring up the **Administration** page.
3. Click on **Licenses** in the left pane to bring up the license management page. On this page, click on the green + icon to bring-up the **New Licenses** wizard:

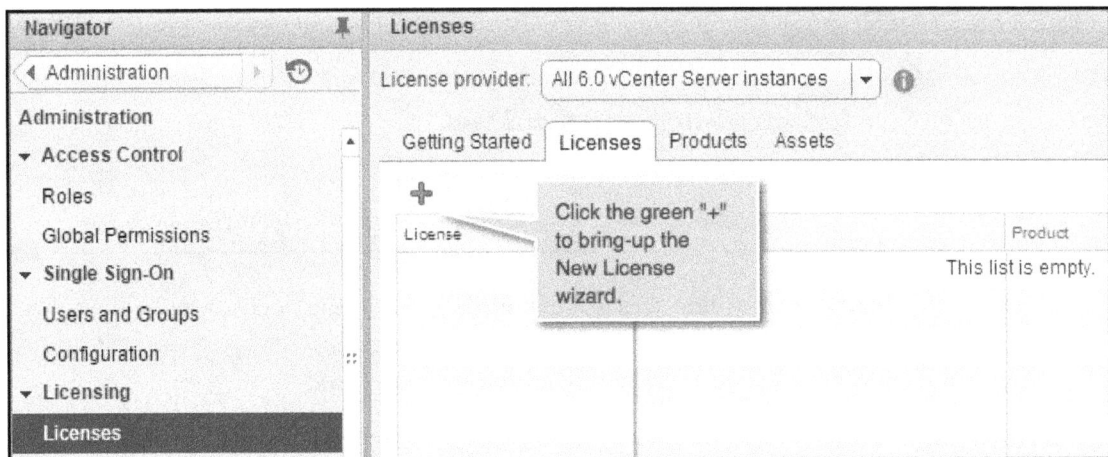

4. In the **New Licenses** wizard, enter the product license keys and click **Next** to continue:

5. The wizard will detect the products corresponding to the license keys entered and will prompt you to name them. Supply custom names if necessary and click **Next** to continue:

6. On the **Ready to complete** screen, click **Finish** to add the licenses to the inventory.
7. You should now see both the newly added licenses listed:

8. Now that you have the licenses added to the inventory, it is time to assign them to the vSphere assets in your infrastructure. To achieve that, navigate to the **Assets** tab:

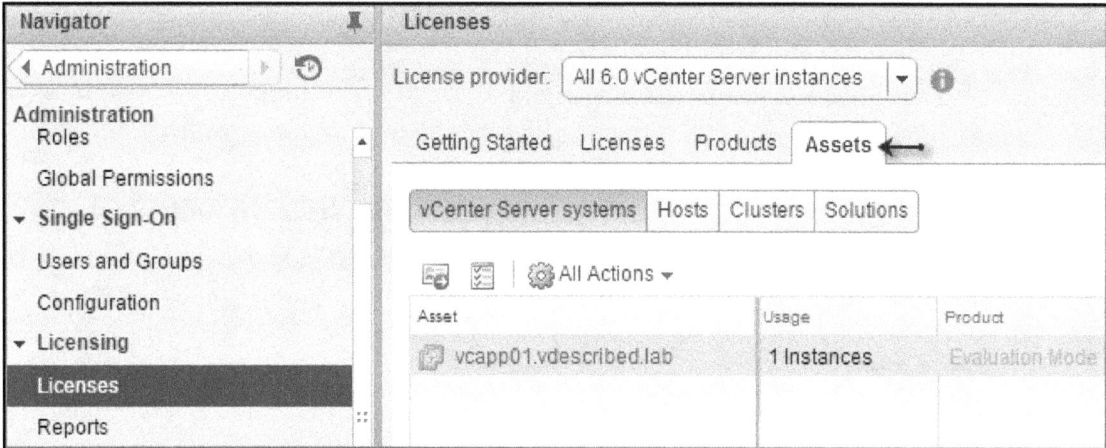

9. The **Assets tab** has four categories: **vCenter Server systems**, **Hosts**, **Clusters,** and **Solutions**. You could navigate to each of these categories and assign licenses to the assets under them. Right-click on the asset and click **Assign License** to bring up the Assign License window:

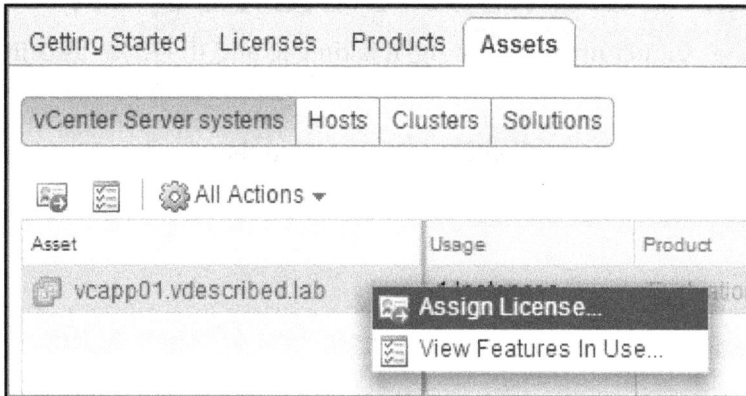

10. The **Assign Licenses** window shows the licenses corresponding to the asset's product type, in this case the vCenter. Select the license you intend to assign and click **OK**:

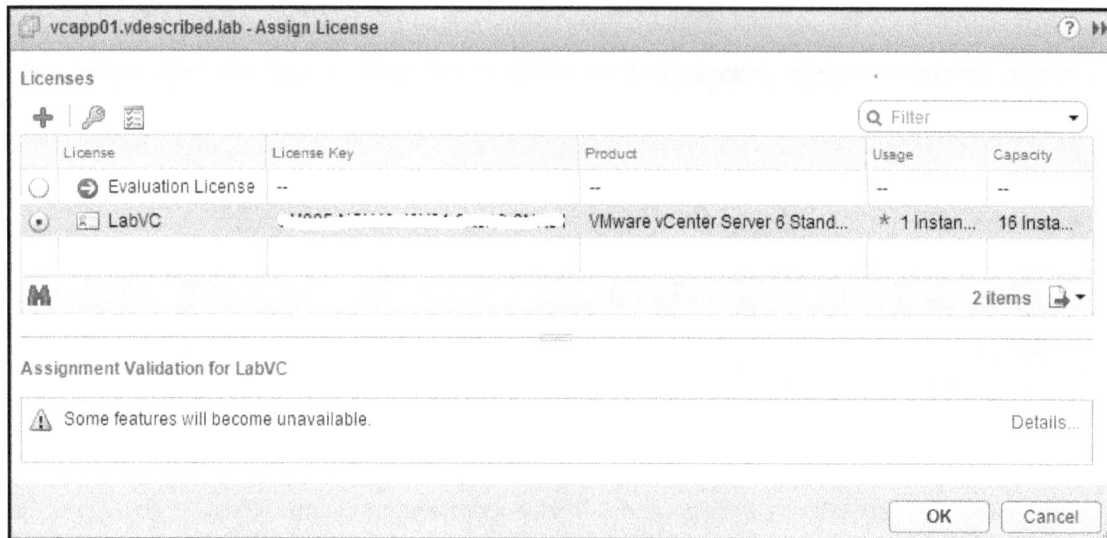

Adding an ESXi host to the vCenter

Now you have the vCenter up and running, it is time to add the ESXi hosts in your environment to the vCenter. vCenter maintains an inventory of objects it manages. There are seven main inventories: vCenter Inventory Lists, Hosts and Clusters, VMs and Templates, Storage, Networking, Content Libraries, and the vRealize Orchestrator:

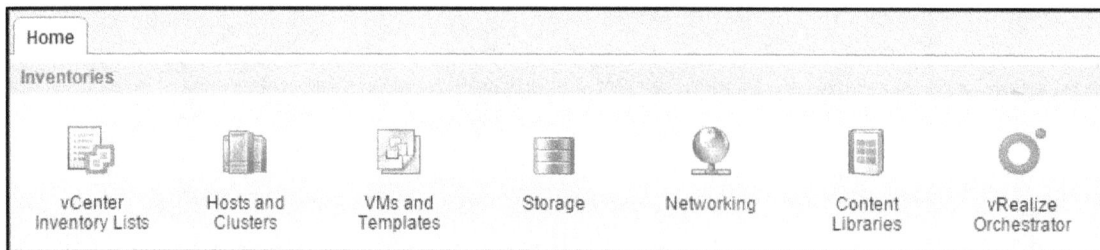

We will use the Host and Clusters inventory to add an ESXi host to the vCenter Server. Every vCenter inventory maintains an object hierarchy for easier management. Hence you would need to create a data center object before you could add a host to the vCenter server.

To create a data center:

1. Right-click on the vCenter and click **New Datacenter**.
2. In the New Datacenter window supply a name and click **OK**:

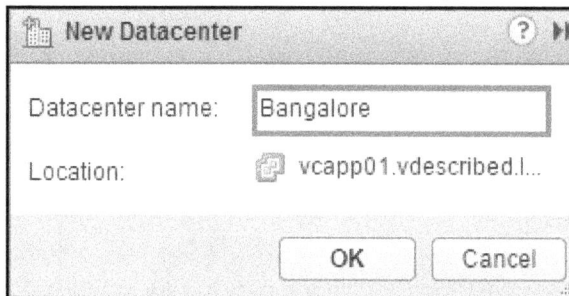

3. The new data center object should now be available in the inventory:

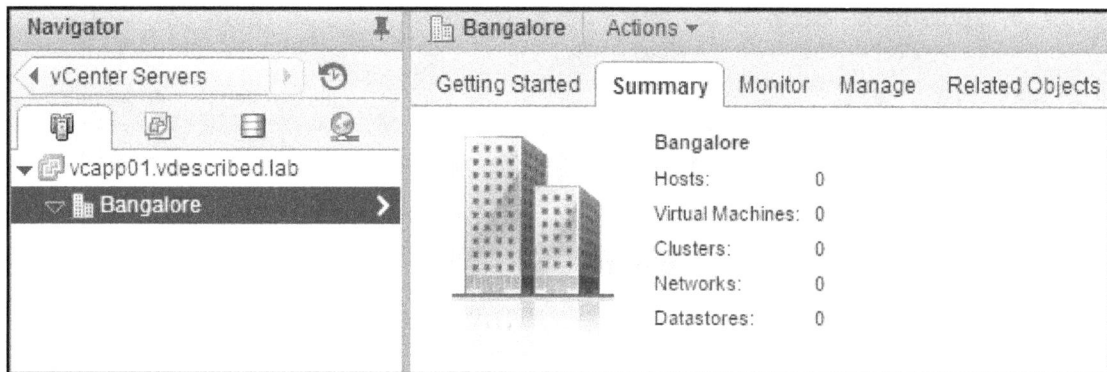

Now, to add a host to the vCenter:

1. Right-click on the data center and click **Add Host** to bring up the **Add Host** wizard:

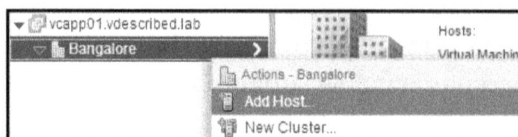

2. In the **Add Host** wizard, supply the hostname, FQDN, or IP address of the ESXi host and click **Next** to continue:

3. Supply the root credentials and click **Next**.

4. You will be prompted to replace the ESXi host's current certificate with a vCenter issued certificate. Click **Yes** to proceed:

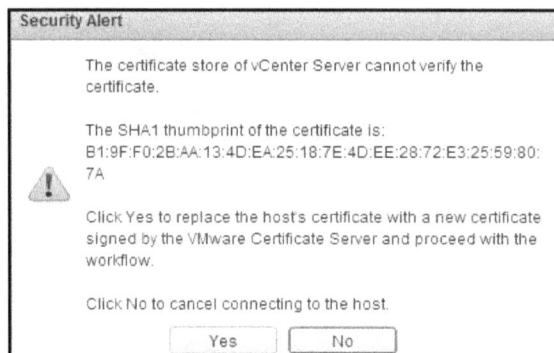

5. In the **Host summary** screen, click **Next** to continue.

6. In the **Assign License** screen, select the host license and click **Next**:

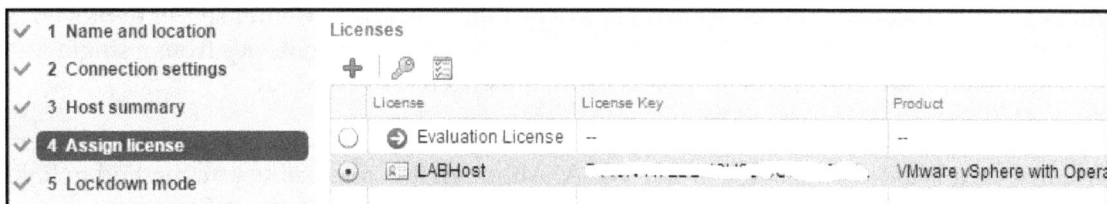

7. In the next screen, select the desired **Lockdown mode**. Leave it disabled if you do not want to make that decision at this point in time:

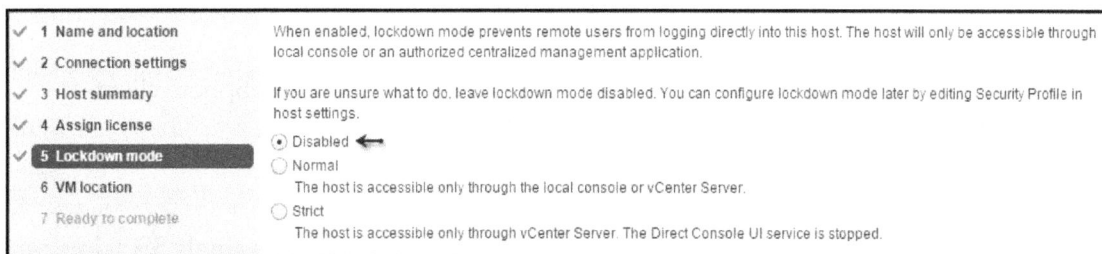

8. Select an inventory location for the virtual machines on this host. If you do not have any folders created, then the VMs will be directly under the data center object.

9. In the **Ready to complete** screen, review the settings and click **Finish** to add the ESXi host to the vCenter.

10. The Host and Clusters inventory should now show the newly added ESXi host and its virtual machines:

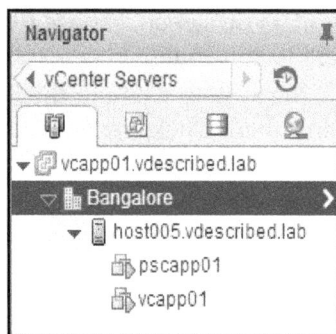

Enhanced Linked Mode

As you already know, vCenter enables centralized management of your core vSphere infrastructure. In large environments there can be more than one vCenter server deployed to manage the resources, it is beneficial to view all the vCenter inventories from a single management plane. This can be achieved using Enhanced Linked Mode.

Enhanced Linked Mode enables the linking of more than one vCenter Server, be it vCenter installed on a Windows machine or the VCSA. Although it is referred to as a method to link vCenter servers together, the actual linking happens between the Platform Service Controllers the vCenters are connected to. It is done so by making the PSCs join a single SSO domain. This is a requirement. The PSCs in the same SSO domain will replicate roles and permissions, licenses, and other details letting the administrator perform a single login into the vSphere Web Client to view and manage inventory objects of all the linked vCenter servers.

> Enhanced Linked Mode doesn't work with the standard vSphere client. It is only supported with the vSphere Web Client.

Enhanced Linked Mode will not be possible if the PSCs are not part of a single SSO domain. Furthermore, VMware does not support the linking of two embedded PSCs or a combination of embedded and external PSCs.

More importantly, you will only be able to link PSCs during the installation. Hence you need to plan the deployment method before the installation.

To join a PSC to an existing SSO domain during its installation, you should follow the following procedure:

1. Start the installation wizard and accept the license agreement.
2. In the **Select Deployment Type** screen, choose **Platform Services Controller** as the option and click **Next** to continue.
3. On the next screen, type the system name or the FQDN of the machine where PSC is currently being installed. Click **Next** to continue.

4. In the **vCenter Single Sign-On Configuration** screen, choose the option **Join a vCenter Single Sign-On domain** and supply the details of the external PSC to whose domain you would like the new PSC to join. Supply the FQDN and the SSO password of the external PSC and click **Next** to continue:

> **Join a vCenter Single Sign-On domain**
>
> Platform Services Controller FQDN or IP address: [psc01.vdescribed.lab]
>
> vCenter Single Sign-On HTTPS port: FDQN of an existing external PSC   [443]
>
> vCenter Single Sign-On user name: [administrator]
>
> vCenter Single Sign-On password: [••••••••••••]

5. You will be prompted for a certificate validation, click **OK** to continue.

6. In the **vCenter Single Sign-On Site** screen, you can choose between joining an existing site or creating a new site. For this demonstration, we have chosen the option **Create a new Site**, supply a site name, and click **Next** to continue:

> **vCenter Single Sign-On Site**
> Create or join a vCenter Single Sign-On site.
>
> Select an option to join an existing site or create a new site for this Platform Services Controller. For an existing site, VMware recommends a maximum of eight Platform Services Controllers per site. The site selection cannot be changed after install.
>
> ○ Join an existing site   [▾]
> Select this option for high availability at a single site.
>
> ● Create a new site   [Site-B ◁━●]
> Select this option for a multi-site deployment.

7. The remainder of the wizard screen is straightforward and similar to the PSC installation procedure. Refer to Steps 7 through 10 from the section Installing PSC on a Windows machine.

Once done, the vSphere Web Client will show both the linked vCenters and their inventory.

Summary

In this chapter, we covered VMware vCenter Server concepts such as the Platform Services Controller, Single Sign-On, VMware Licensing Service, and so on. We also covered the differences between the VCSA and vCenter running on a Windows machine. We learned how to deploy both Windows and Linux versions of the vCenter Server and also how to perform the post installation configuration on them. We learned how to configure identity sources on the SSO server and configure licenses for the vSphere environment. From there, we learned how to configure Enhanced Linked Mode for vCenters.

4
vSphere Networking Concepts and Management

A data center product/solution cannot be considered functional if it does not have the ability to network. Such is the case with the vSphere suite of products. In this chapter, we will learn a lot about the networking concepts associated with a VMware infrastructure and also learn how to configure them to meet our design needs.

This chapter will cover the following topics:

- The need for a software virtual switch
- The difference between a physical and virtual switch
- A virtual machine's network interface
- The VMkernel's network interface
- The standard virtual switch
- The distributed virtual switch
- Enabling VLANs on a virtual switch
- Configuring private VLANs on a virtual switch
- Switch security policies
- Switch load balancing policies
- Switch failover policies
- Linking status monitoring
- Port mirroring
- Enabling the use of Netflow monitoring

The need for a software virtual switch

Most physical machines will have one or more network cards that will not only enable them to communicate with other networked components but also provide a unique network identity in terms of a MAC address and an IP address. Now, when you use a single machine to host several virtual machines running the same traditional operating systems that were once run on a physical machine, there surfaces a challenge that needs to be addressed. The challenge is: how do we assign unique identities for each of the virtual machines and how do we make them part of our organization's network? Part of the answer introduces the concept of a **Virtual NIC** (**vNIC**): which is created on a virtual machine to let it connect to the network. The second part of the challenge is the fact that although you have multiple vNICs connected to a virtual machine, there should be a way to channel the vNIC traffic out of an ESXi host via its physical NICs. This challenge is addressed with the help of a *software switch*. The software switch is not a concept that was debuted with ESXi; a form of it was already included in VMware's hosted virtualization product called the VMware Workstation. However, it wasn't called a switch then. Since VMware Workstation is beyond the scope of this book, we will cover only the virtual switching constructs that are available in a vSphere environment. So, what exactly does a software switch do? It enables aggregating network connections from multiple vNICs, applies network configuration policies on them, and also pins them to the physical network adapters on the ESXi hosts for traffic flow. There is more to it than what I have tried to convey in the previous sentence. We will dive deeper into all of the virtual networking concepts in this chapter.

The difference between a physical and virtual switch

Now that we understand the need for a virtual switch, it is essential to understand how different a virtual switch is when compared to a physical switch. The fact that VMware calls it a virtual *switch* is indicative of the fact that it can switch frames between its virtual ports or physical uplinks. So, is it any different from a physical switch? The answer is yes, in a couple of ways. One of the differences is the manner in which the virtual switch handles frame transfers:

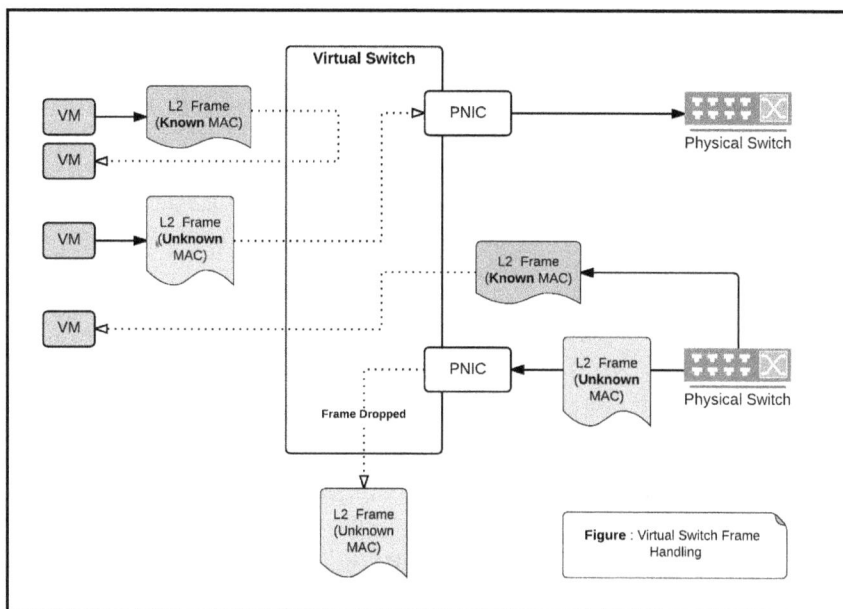

Figure : Virtual Switch Frame Handling

When a frame enters a physical switch, its destination is determined by the switch port number corresponding to its destination MAC address in the physical switch's MAC table. If it can't find an entry in the MAC table, it floods the frame out via every port other than the source port. Much like the physical switch, a virtual switch also maintains a MAC table, but there is no learning process for a virtual switch. A virtual switch will already have a list of MAC addresses and their virtual port numbers. If a frame with a destination MAC, which isn't present in the virtual switch's MAC table, enters a virtual switch, then it is sent out via physical NICs (active uplinks) connected to the virtual switch. This holds true only if a virtual machine or a vmkernel interface is the source of the flow, that is, only if that frame enters via a virtual port. If a frame with an unknown MAC enters the virtual switch via its physical uplinks, then that frame will be dropped by the virtual switch. The second difference is to do with the number of ports on the switch. Physical switches will have a fixed number of ports; however, a virtual switch will have a maximum limit but a large number of configurable ports. Currently, VMware supports up to 4,096 virtual switch ports per ESXi host. The third difference is that unlike some, or most, physical switches, it is not a manageable switch, per se, meaning, it doesn't have it is own management IP address or an operating system like the Cisco IOS. Instead, the virtual switches are managed at the hypervisor or the vCenter depending upon the type of virtual switch (standard vSwitch or VDS) in use.

Physical NIC enumeration

You can enable up to a maximum of 32 1 Gbps and 16 10 Gbps Ethernet ports on an ESXi host. The maximums are governed by the make/model/driver/feature of the NIC cards and their combinations. For instance, you have up to 32 Broadcom 1 GB Ethernet ports using a tg3 driver and NetQueue disabled, but the same NIC with NetQueue enabled can only present 16 ports. If you were to use a combination of 10 GB and 1 GB Ethernet ports, then only 16 10 GB and four 1 GB ports could be enabled.

Refer to the Networking maximums section on page 14 of the Configuration Maximums Guide for vSphere for more details: `https://www.vmware.com/pdf/vsphere6/r6/vsphere-6-configuration-maximums.pdf`.

Now that ESXi is capable of managing a large number of physical NICs, there should be a method to logically present these NICs to apply configuration policies on them. This is achieved by enumerating the physical NIC with a vmnicX pattern (vmnic0... vmnic32). Also, there is a logic behind the enumeration. The NICs are sequentially enumerated during the ESXi boot process by scanning the PCI bus, slot, and port number. The *PCI-id to vmnic* mapping can be found in the `/etc/vmware/esx.conf` configuration of an ESXi host:

```
/device/00000:000:07.1/vmkname = "vmhba0"
/device/00000:000:02.0/vmkname = "vmnic0"
/device/00000:000:03.0/vmkname = "vmnic1"
/device/00000:000:04.0/vmkname = "vmhba1"
```

A virtual machine network interface (vNIC)

Every virtual machine will need a network interface card that can connect and participate in a network. VMware calls it a vNIC. These entities can be created on each virtual machine. There are different types of vNICs that can be created on a virtual machine. The type of vNIC you choose will not only depend on the type of guest operating system that runs on a virtual machine but also on the purpose of the NIC card. VMware allows adding up to 10 vNICs per virtual machine. All the vNICs that you add to a virtual machine can be of any supported type or even a combination of multiple NIC types.

The available vNIC adapter types are:

- The **vla** adapter – this is the first version of vNIC and is an emulated version of *AMD's 79C970 PCNET32 LANCE* network adapters. Almost all traditional operating systems will have a driver bundle for this adapter. Hence, the installation of VMware tools is not necessary for the vNIC to function. The maximum speed supported by this adapter is 10 Mbps.
- The **e1000** series adapters – these are emulated versions of Intel's Gigabit Ethernet network adapters, **82**
- **545EM** and **82574,** as **e1000** and **e1000e** vNICs. The latter is only available from vSphere 5.0 onwards. Not all traditional operating systems bundle a driver for this adapter, nor does VMware tools. Hence, it is important to verify the compatibility before you add the vNIC to a virtual machine. From what we know, desktop operating systems – Windows XP (x64) or later, server operating systems – Windows Server 2003(x32) or later, and Linux Kernel version 2.4.19 or later, support the e1000 adapters.
- The **flexible** network adapter – this is an adapter type that has a dual personality. It, by default, presents itself as an emulated AMD lance (vlance) adapter. However, once VMware tools are installed, the VMXNET driver initializes the network adapter.

- **VMXNET** adapters – these are virtualization aware (*paravirtualized*) network adapters that can be added to a virtual machine. The adapters will only function if you have VMware tools installed as the drivers are bundled with it. This adapter type has seen a few generations, starting with **VMXNET**, followed by **VMXNET-Enhanced,** and the current version **VMXNET3**nce adapter – this is the first version of vNIC and is an emulated version of AMD's 79C970 PCNET32 LANCE network adapters. Almost all traditional operating systems will have a driver bundle for this adapter. Hence, the installation of VMware tools is not necessary for the vNIC to function. The maximum speed supported by this adapter is 10 Mbps. The e1000 series adapters – these are emulated versions of Intel's Gigabit Ethernet network adapters, 82 545EM and 82574, as e1000 and e1000e vNICs. The latter is only available from vSphere 5.0 onwards. Not all traditional operating systems bundle a driver for this adapter, nor does VMware tools. Hence, it is important to verify the compatibility before you add the vNIC to a virtual machine. From what we know, desktop operating systems – Windows XP (x64) or later, server operating systems – Windows Server 2003(x32) or later, and Linux Kernel version 2.4.19 or later, support the e1000 adapters. The flexible network adapter – this is an adapter type that has a dual personality. It, by default, presents itself as an emulated AMD lance (vlance) adapter. However, once VMware tools are installed, the VMXNET driver initializes the network adapter. VMXNET adapters – these are virtualization aware (paravirtualized) network adapters that can be added to a virtual machine. The adapters will only function if you have VMware tools installed as the drivers are bundled with it. This adapter type has seen a few generations, starting with VMXNET, followed by VMXNET-Enhanced, and the current version VMXNET3.

The VMkernel network interface (vmk)

Much like the virtual machines that run on the ESXi hosts, the vmkernel would also need to interface with the network for a variety of purposes. These interfaces act as network node points for the **vmkernel**. The very *first vmkernel interface – vmk0* is created during the installation of ESXi. This interface is the management interface for the ESXi host. VMware allows creating **a maximum of 256 (vmk0 – vmk255)** vmkernel interfaces on an ESXi host. The use cases include interfaces for management traffic, VMotion traffic, FT traffic, Virtual SAN traffic, iSCSI, and NAS interfaces. Since each interface is a network node point, it will need an IP configuration and a MAC address. The first vmkernel interface (vmk0) will procure the MAC address of the physical NIC it is connected to. The remaining interfaces pick up the VMware OUI MAC address generated by the ESXi host. We will learn more about how VMware handles the MAC address in the next section.

The VMware OUI MAC addresses

Every virtual machine and vmkernel interface that you create on an ESXi host will need a *layer-2 identity* to interface with the network. Much like in the physical world, MAC addresses provide this unique identity to all the virtual machines or interfaces that connect to a virtual switch. Every physical network interface will have a burned-in **48-bit MAC address** whose numbering is organizationally unique. This is because every vendor that makes the card will have a set of **Organizationally Unique Identifiers** (OUI) assigned to them by the **IEEE (Institute of Electrical and Electronics Engineers)**. In fact, the vendor purchases OUIs from IEEE's Registration Authority. VMware also has a set of OUIs assigned to it, and those are **00:50:56** and **00:0C:29**. Although both OUI are used differently, they can be assigned to virtual machine NICs and vmkernel interfaces. VMware also supports the use of **Locally Administered Addresses** (LAA) using the **prefix-based** and **range-based** allocation schemes. Both the allocation schemes require vCenter to be available to generate and manage the MAC addresses. With prefix-based allocation, each of the vCenters in the environment is given a unique 3-byte *LAA* prefix. With a range-based allocation scheme, a MAC address range is assigned to each vCenter and care should be taken to make sure that the range boundaries are unique to each vCenter. Default OUI based MAC addresses are referred to as **Universally Administered Addresses** (UAA).

How are MAC addresses generated?

Both ESXi and the vCenter can generate MAC addresses for the virtual machine interfaces. A MAC address is generated for a vNIC when the virtual machine is powered-on. The generated address will remain static unless there is a MAC address conflict in the environment.

If the virtual machine is not on an ESXi host that is managed by a vCenter it will be assigned a MAC with OUI – *00:0C:29*. If the host is managed by the vCenter then the virtual machine will be assigned a MAC address with the OUI – *00:56:54*.

All vmkernel interfaces except for vmk0 will receive a MAC address with OUI – *00:56:54*.

The vCenter/ESXi generated MAC address is referred to as the *initial MAC address*. The MAC used by the **Guest Operating System** (GOS) is called the *effective MAC address*. In almost all cases, the GOS will use the initial MAC as the effective MAC address, unless the GOS changes the effective MAC address for forged transmits, which wouldn't work unless the switch allows it. We will learn more about *forged transmits* and *MAC address changes* in a later section of this chapter.

The GOS is the traditional operating system that you install on a virtual machine.

The vSphere distributed switch will record what's called the runtime MAC address, which is the MAC as observed by the dvPort to which the vNIC is connected.

The standard virtual switch (vSwitch)

In previous sections, we covered the concepts that would help you understand how virtual switches work. There is lot more that a virtual switch offers in terms of features and configuration than just to switch layer-2 frames. We will cover the concepts and configuration of a standard vSwitch in this section.

We will cover the following in this section:

- Port groups
- Support for VLANs
- Creating and configuring standard vSwitches

The standard vSwitch is a core networking construct of the ESXi hypervisor. A vSwitch – **vSwitch0** is created during the installation to configure the management vmkernel interface (vmk0) on it. The following screenshot shows the default vSwitch created during the installation of ESXi:

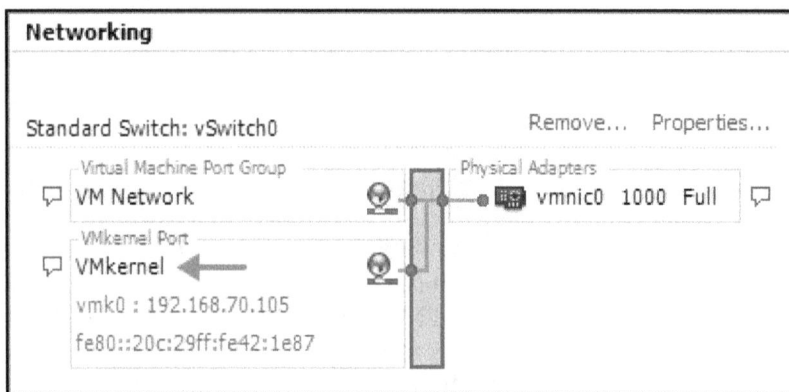

We will learn more about configuring a standard vSwitch in the section, *Creating and configuring standard vSwitches*.

Port groups

Port groups are logical constructs to group virtual ports on a vSwitch. The standard vSwitch does not expose individual ports in the user interface to apply policies on. Instead, we are allowed to use a port group to achieve the same. It is interesting to note that there is no set number or limit on the number of virtual ports that a port group can encompass. However, there are per vSwitch and per host limits. The Configuration Maximums guide is the absolute reference to understand the configuration limits.

Here is the URL to the Configuration Maximums guide: `https://www.vmware.com/pdf/vs phere6/r6/vsphere-6-configuration-maximums.pdf`:

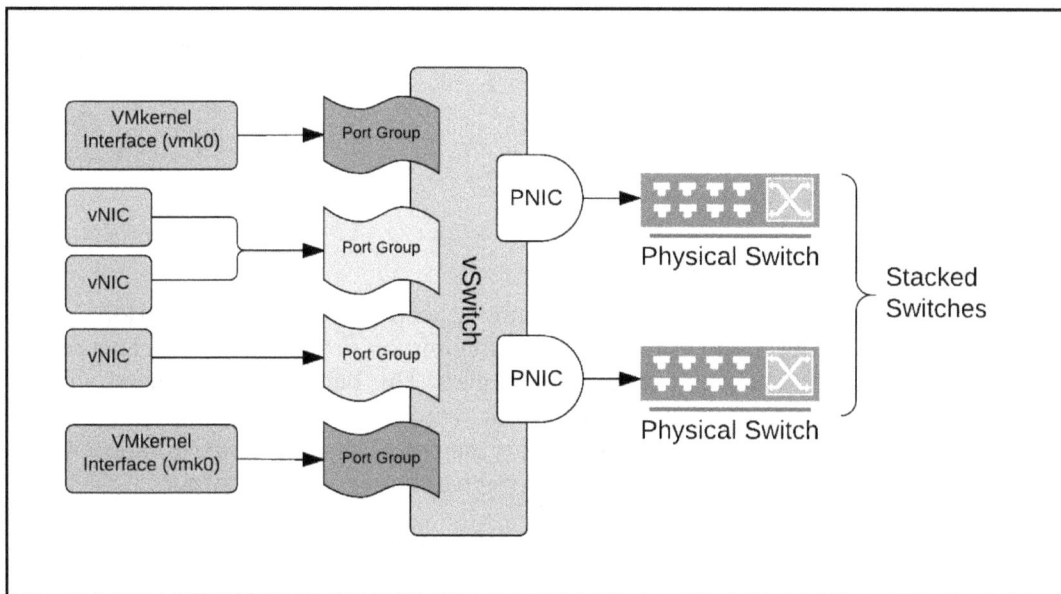

The ports are added under the umbrella of a port group as you connect more and more vNICs to it. A standard vSwitch by default would have 128 ports associated with it until vSphere 5.5. Since vSphere 5.5, there is no set number of ports on a vSwitch. If you were to view the same vSwitch properties using the vSphere web client, then the number of ports value will be shown as elastic, meaning the virtual ports are added/used on a vSwitch when you connect vNICs to a port group.

There are two basic types of port groups:

- A virtual machine port group
- A VMkernel port group

A **virtual machine port group** can only be used to connect virtual machines' vNICs to it. There can be more than one virtual machine port group on a standard vSwitch. A **VMkernel port group** can only be used to connect a Vmkernel interface. A number of virtual machines can connect to a single virtual machine port group, but each VMkernel port group requires a separate port group on a standard vSwitch. This behavior is slightly different on a distributed vSwitch. We will learn more about that in the section covering the vSphere distributed switch.

> You can configure a maximum of 512 port groups per standard vSwitch.

Support for VLANs

Now, let's assume that you have a large environment hosting workloads for various business units within your organization. It is not uncommon for business units to confine most of their workload into their own network subnets. This being a need, there should be a method to enable the use of VLANs in your virtual switching environment. Both the standard and distributed virtual switches support the use of VLANs. VLANs cannot be configured directly on a standard vSwitch; they have to be set on a port group.

There are three different ways by which VLANs are handled on a virtual switch:

- Physical/external switch tagging
- Virtual switch tagging
- Virtual guest tagging

External switch tagging

The physical switch to which the ESXi host's physical NIC are cabled will do the tagging/untagging of the layer-2 frames. The physical switch port will need to be configured as an access port for this to work. One of the major drawbacks to this type of implementation is that the entire vSwitch (*all the port groups on it*) will only handle traffic from a single layer-2 subnet:

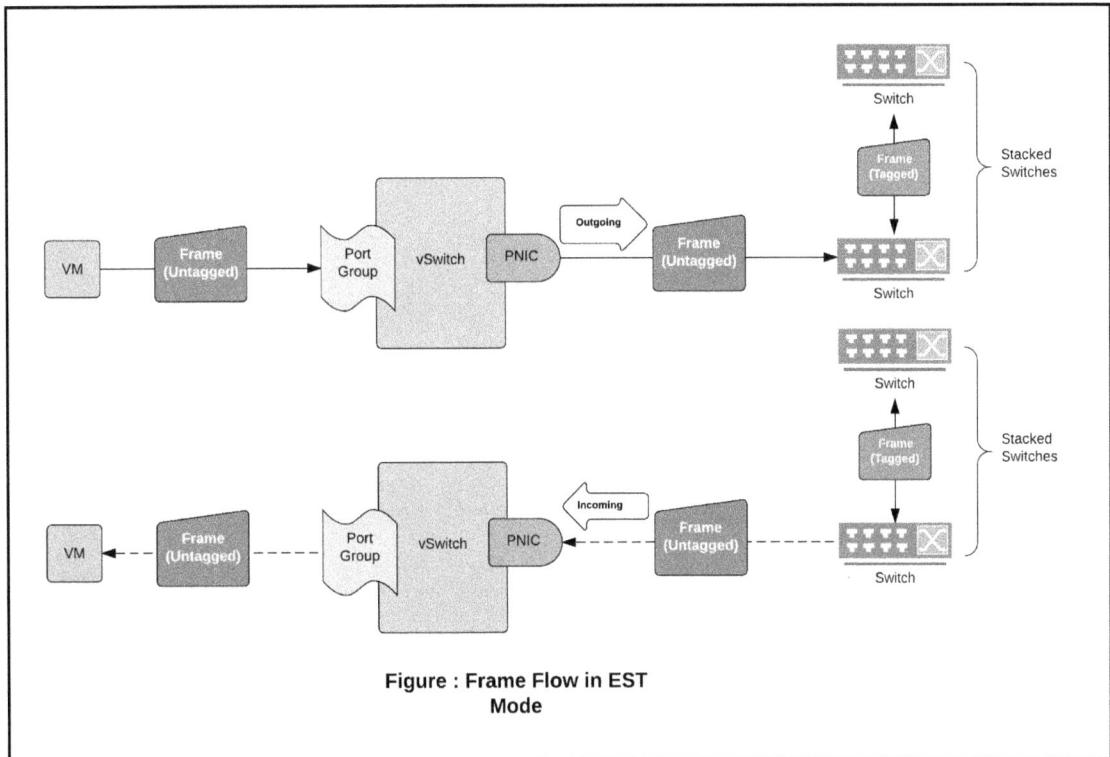

Figure : Frame Flow in EST Mode

In *EST mode*, when a virtual machine's layer-2 frame enters the vSwitch, it hits an active uplink, which then carries the frame onto the physical switch. The physical switch's access port will then assign a VLAN ID to it and handle the traffic switching. When a frame tries to flow back into the vSwitch, the access port will untag the frame and send the traffic into the vSwitch, then back to the virtual machine's vNIC.

Virtual switch tagging

The layer-2 frames are tagged at the virtual switch layer. For this implementation to work, the physical NIC carrying the traffic should be connected to a physical switch port, which is configured to trunk the necessary VLANs. The virtual machine or vmkernel port groups created on the vSwitch will then need to be configured with the VLAN IDs of their respective subnets. This is the most common and favored implementation in most large/medium/small environments, not just because of the flexibility it offers but also because of the fact the most modern day blade system environments have reduced the number of physical NIC ports on the server hardware, owing to the advent of the 10 Gbps ethernet:

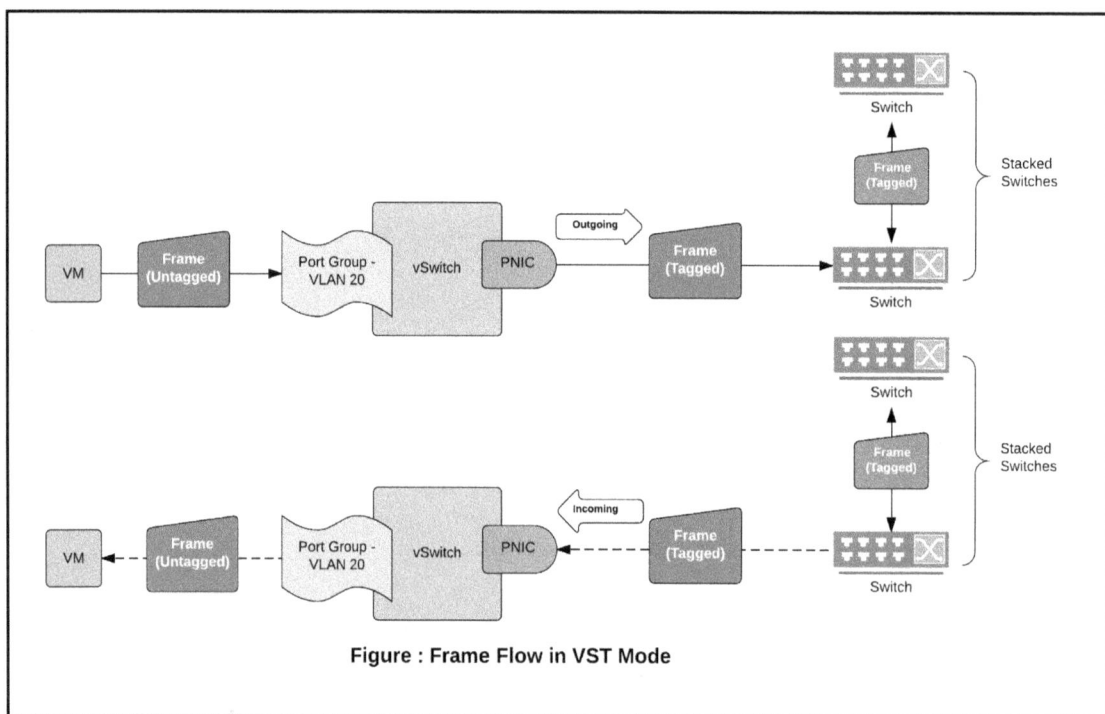

Figure : Frame Flow in VST Mode

In *VST mode*, when a frame from a virtual machine enters a virtual switch, it is assigned a VLAN number. The VLAN number should already be configured on the port group the virtual machine is connected to. The VLAN tag will then be carried over from the active physical NIC to the trunk port on the physical switch. When a frame enters a virtual switch from the physical switch, it will untag the frame and then switch the frame to the virtual machine.

Virtual guest tagging

Here, it becomes the guest operating system's responsibility to assign VLAN tags to its outbound traffic. The port group to which such a virtual machine is connected should be configured with **VLANID 4095** (meaning to trunk):

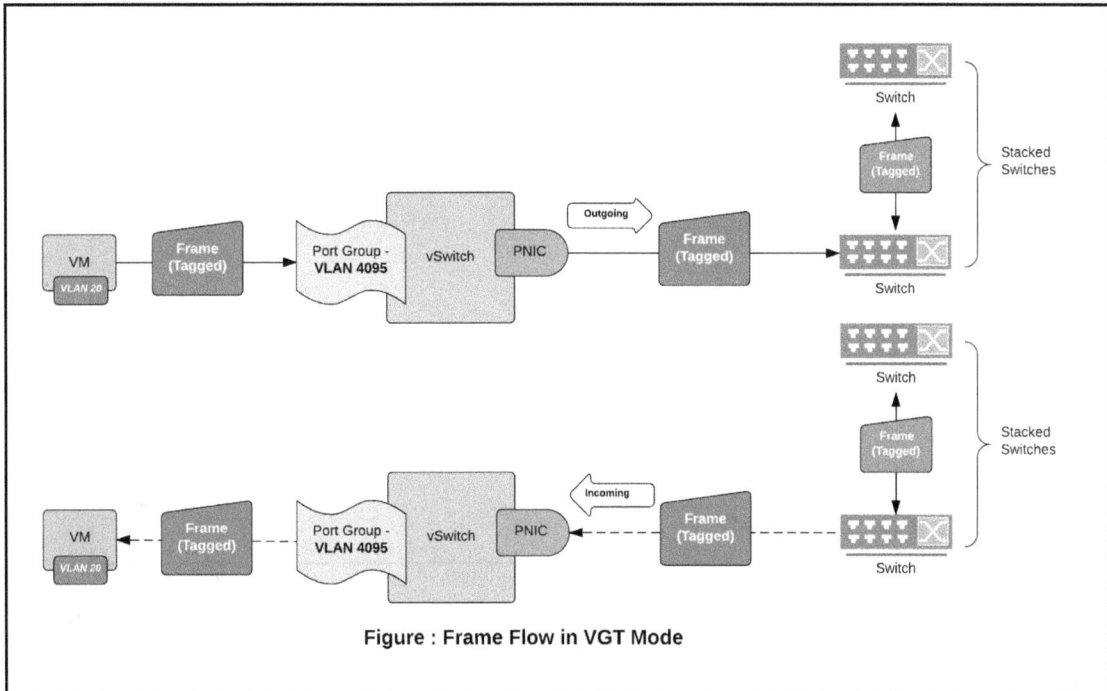

Figure : Frame Flow in VGT Mode

In *VGT mode*, the VLAN-tagged traffic will flow unmodified through the virtual switch and to the physical switch. The guest operating system is solely responsible for tagging and untagging on the frames.

Creating a standard vSwitch

To be able to create a standard vSwitch, you will either need access to a vCenter server managing the ESXi hosts or a direct vSphere client connection to the ESXi host. As I mentioned earlier, the ESXi installation will create the default **vSwitch0** so that it can create a management vmkernel interface on it. The IP configuration details that you supply post-installation correspond to the very first vmkernel interface (**vmk0**) that is created:

Device	Network Label	Switch	IP Address	TCP/IP Stack
vmk0	Management Netw...	vSwitch0	192.168.70.20	Default

VMkernel network adapter: vmk0

All   Properties   IP Settings   Policies

IPv4 settings

IPv4 address	192.168.70.20 (static)
Subnet mask	255.255.255.0
Default gateway for IPv4	192.168.70.1
DNS server addresses	192.168.70.2

To create a standard vSwitch, you will need to start the **Add Networking** wizard. There are several ways this wizard can be started. In this case, we are connected to vCenter 6.0 using the vSphere Web Client:

1. Drop down the **vCenter Inventory** menu and click on **Hosts and Clusters**:

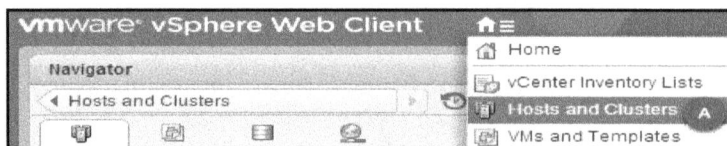

2. In the **Host and Cluster** view, select the ESXi host to create a standard vSwitch on, drop down the **Actions** menu and click on **Add Networking** to bring up the wizard:

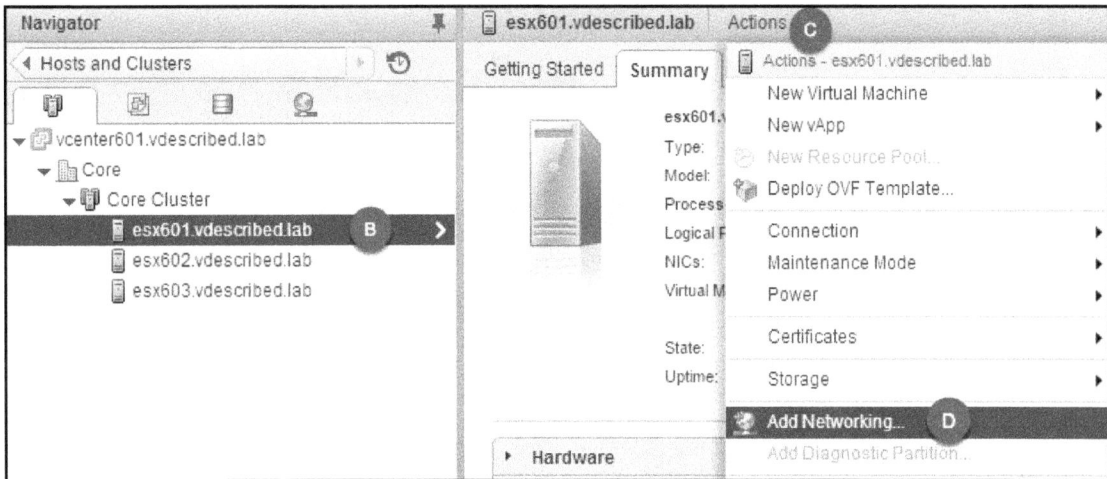

3. In the **Add Networking** wizard, select the connection type as **Virtual Machine Port Group for a Standard Switch**. It is interesting to note that whenever you create a vSwitch from the vSphere GUI, you will have to create a port group on it. This is in contrast to the CLI method, which will enable the creation of a vSwitch with no port groups:

4. In the subsequent screen, select **New standard switch** and click **Next** to continue:

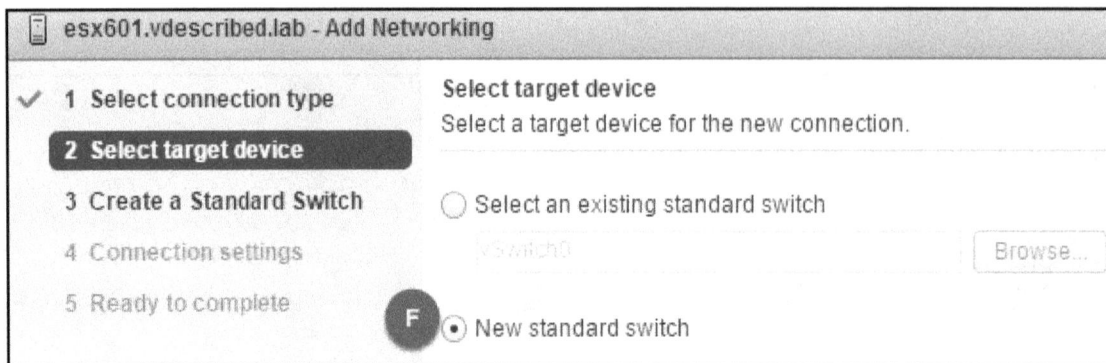

📱 **esx601.vdescribed.lab - Add Networking**

✓ **1 Select connection type**

2 Select target device

3 Create a Standard Switch

4 Connection settings

5 Ready to complete

Select target device
Select a target device for the new connection.

◯ Select an existing standard switch

vSwitch0   Browse...

F ◉ New standard switch

---

5. Now, assign active adapters to the standard vSwitch. To do this click on the ⊞ icon to bring up the **Add Physical Adapters to the Switch** window:

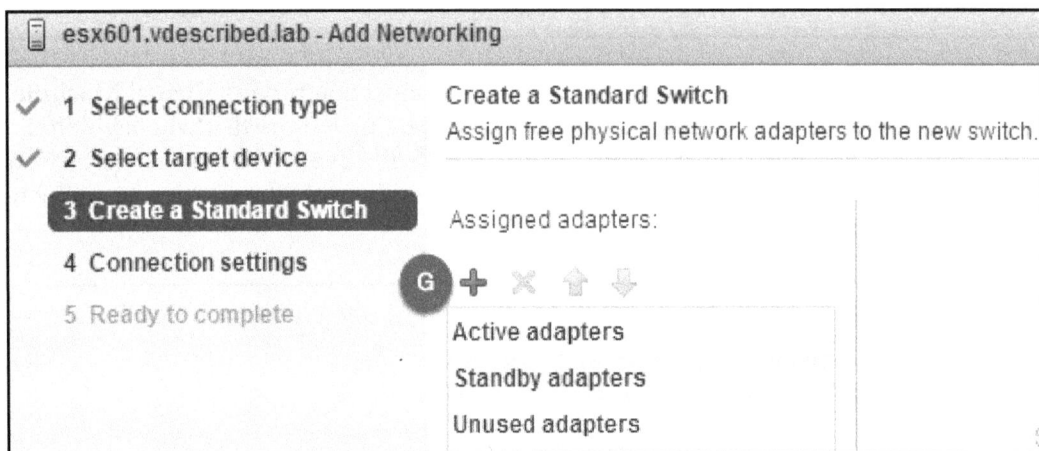

📱 **esx601.vdescribed.lab - Add Networking**

✓ **1 Select connection type**

✓ **2 Select target device**

3 Create a Standard Switch

4 Connection settings

5 Ready to complete

Create a Standard Switch
Assign free physical network adapters to the new switch.

Assigned adapters:

G ➕ ✕ ⬆ ⬇

Active adapters

Standby adapters

Unused adapters

In the **Add Physical Adapters to the Switch** window, select the network adapter to add and set the **Failover order group** to **Active Adapters** and click **OK**.

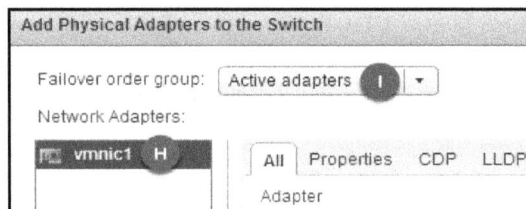

6. With NIC selected, click **Next** to proceed to the **Connection settings** screen.
7. In the **Connection settings** screen, assign a **Network label** for the virtual machine port group and an optional **VLAN ID** and click **Next** to continue.
8. In the **Ready to complete** screen, review the setting and click **Finish** to create the standard vSwitch.

In the **Recent Tasks** pane, you should see an **Update network configuration task** completed successfully. The **Manage | Networking** tab of the host will now show the new vSwitch with a new virtual machine port group. Have a look at the following image:

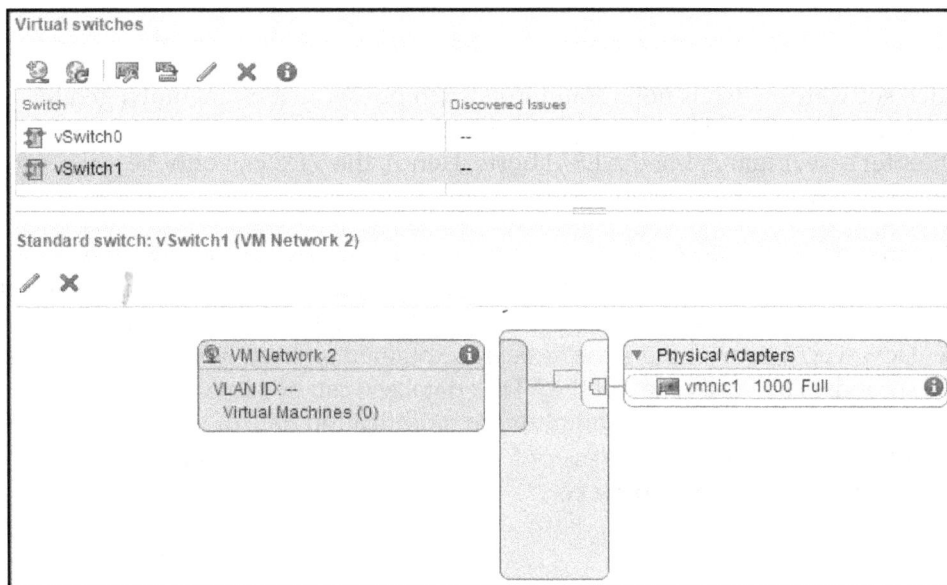

vSphere Distributed Virtual Switch (VDS)

A **vSphere distributed switch** (**VDS**) was primarily built to reduce the administrative overhead involved in maintaining the network configuration in a large environment. A very common misconception is that VDS is a single switch that spans over multiple ESXi hosts. The fact is that it is not. All it does is to offer a single management plane for all the host data planes (hidden software switches) distributed on the ESXi hosts, hence the name *distributed* switch:

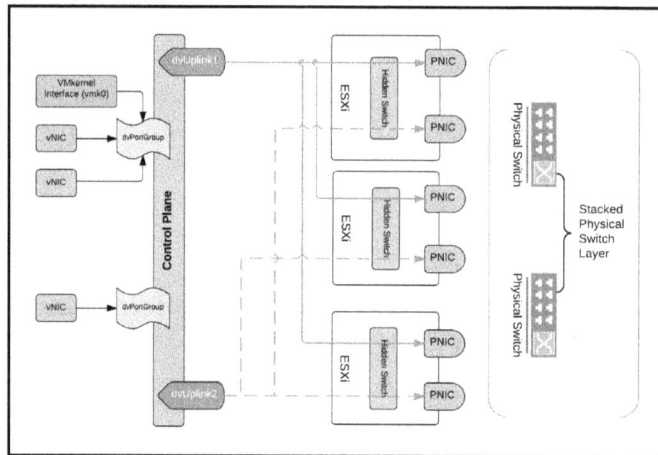

The hidden software switch is not a standard switch per se, as it offers much greater capabilities when compared to a vSphere standard switch. The management layer resides on the vCenter server managing the ESXi hosts. Hence, the VDS can only be created/managed using the vCenter server.

The Datacenter object in the vCenter inventory is the boundary for the VDS, meaning it can span across clusters but not across the data centers (from a vCenter inventory standpoint). As with every other object vCenter manages, the VDS data is also stored in the vCenter's database. However, a copy of the same data is maintained on each host and synchronized every 300 seconds. The host's copy of the VDS's database can be found at `/etc/vmware/dvsdata.db`. If you monitor the modification date of this file by just re-listing the file, you will see it change every 5 minutes (300 seconds). This is one way to tell if the host is in sync with the vCenter server:

```
[root@esx601:/etc/vmware]
[root@esx601:/etc/vmware] ls -ltrh dvs*
-rw-r--r--    1 root      root        29.5K Sep 17 18:38 dvsdata.db
[root@esx601:/etc/vmware]
```

It is a binary file; hence its contents cannot be viewed in plain text from the command line. Instead, you can use the command net-dvs to view the contents of the file.

The command syntax is as follows:

$ net-dvs | less

> The content of the file is not small enough to fit in one screen, so here we use the *less* command to display the content and scroll line by line.

```
[root@esx601:/etc/vmware]
[root@esx601:/etc/vmware] net-dvs | less
switch fa f7 28 50 f4 a9 9a f3-cf 58 3c 31 d5 2d 84 e4 (etherswitch)
        max ports: 1536
        global properties:
                com.vmware.common.alias = DSwitch01 ,    propType = CONFIG
                com.vmware.common.version = 0x 4. 0. 0. 0
                        propType = CONFIG
                com.vmware.common.opaqueDvs = false ,    propType = CONFIG
                com.vmware.etherswitch.ipfix:
                        idle timeout = 15 seconds
                        active timeout = 60 seconds
                        sampling rate = 0
                        collector = 0.0.0.0:0
                        internal flows only = false
                        propType = CONFIG
                        obsDomainID = 0
                com.vmware.etherswitch.mtu = 1500 ,       propType = CONFIG
                com.vmware.etherswitch.cdp = CDP, listen
                        propType = CONFIG
```

> As for vSphere 6, a vCenter server can manage up to a maximum of 128 VDS and the ESXi host can be connected to a maximum of 16 VDS.

We will cover the following topics in this section:

- Uplinks on a VDS
- Port groups on a VDS
- Private VLAN support on a VDS
- Network IO control
- Advanced network monitoring (port mirroring and NetFlow)
- Creating and configuring a VDS

Uplinks on a VDS

Uplinks on a VDS are called **dvUplinks**. They are software abstracts which have "1: many" relationships with the physical network adapters on the participating ESXi hosts, meaning a dvUplink can map to physical network adapters from multiple hosts but cannot map to more than one physical network adapter on a single host:

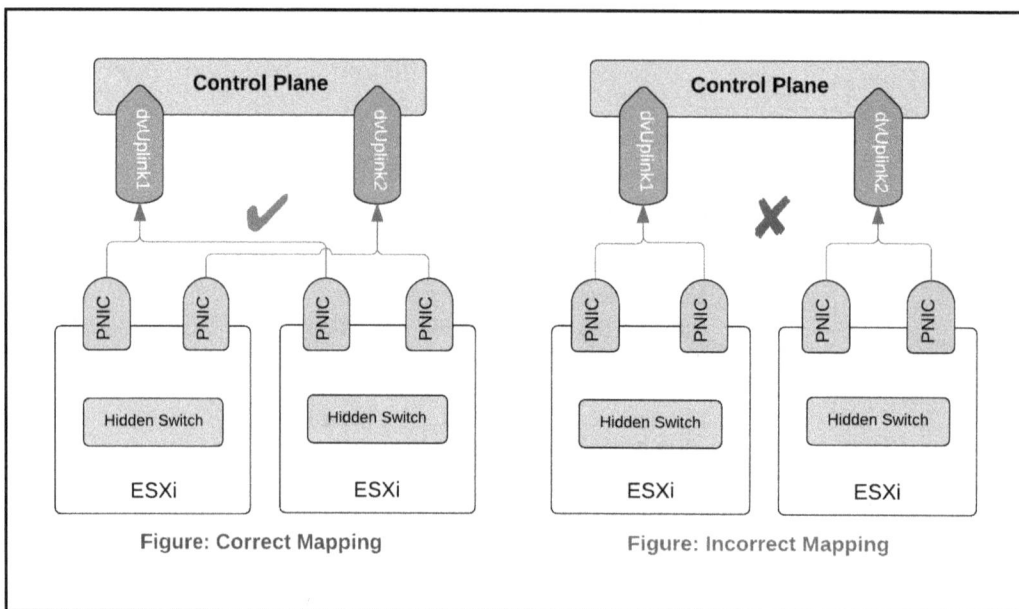

Figure: Correct Mapping   Figure: Incorrect Mapping

The number of dvUplinks on a VDS sets a limit on the number of physical NICs each ESXi host can connect to the VDS. For example, if you were to configure four dvUplinks on the VDS then each of the participating hosts can connect up to four physical NICs to the VDS.

You can configure up to a maximum of 32 dvUplinks per VDS, which is due to the fact that you cannot have more than 32 physical network interface ports on an ESXi host.

Port groups on a VDS

Unlike the port groups on a standard virtual switch, there is only a single common type of distributed port group. A distributed port group is sometimes referred to as a *dvPortGroup* and that will be the terminology that we will use throughout this book. A single dvPortGroup can serve both virtual machine and vmkernel traffic:

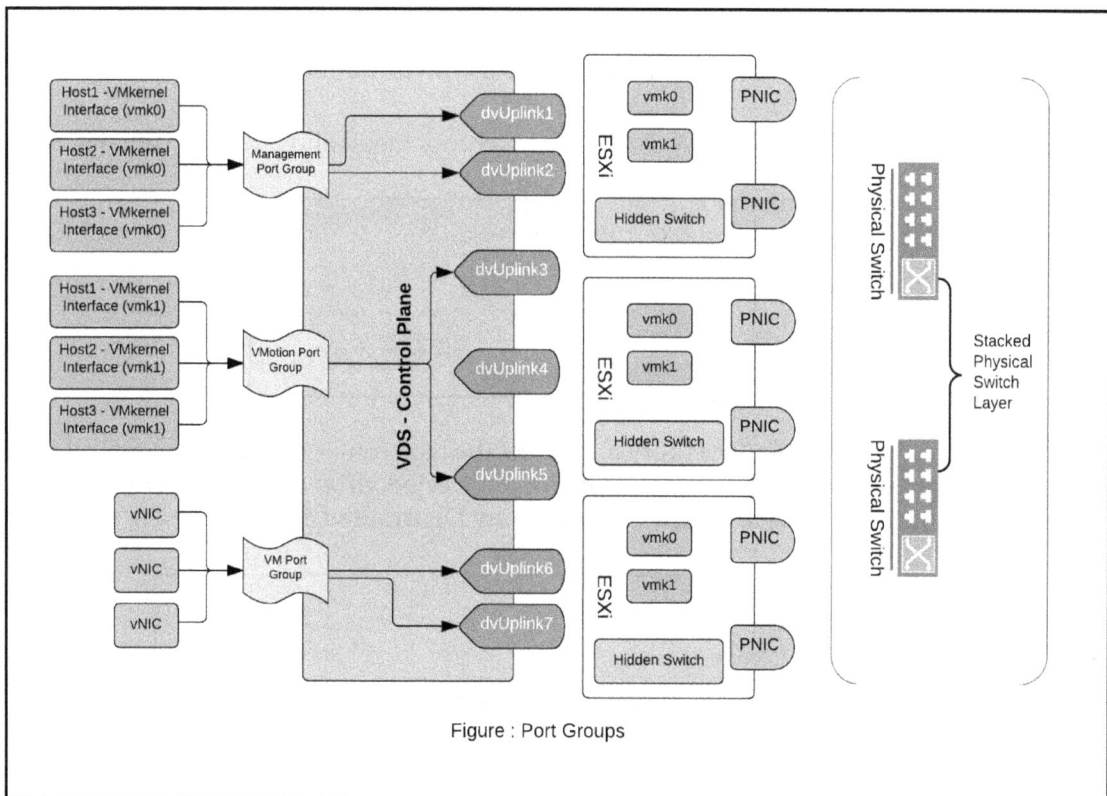

Figure : Port Groups

A good design practice is to form separate dvPortGroups for different traffic types as the failover and load balancing policies or the uplinks we use could be different.

The maximum number of dvPortGroups per VDS is 10,000 compared to a standard vSwitch which is 512.

Creating a VDS

To be able to create a VDS you will need access to a vCenter server managing ESXi hosts with an Enterprise Plus hypervisor license. A VDS is not available on lower hypervisor license models. Keep in mind that a VDS can only be created at the virtual data center level in the vCenter server.

The following procedure will guide you through the steps required to create a VDS:

1. Connect to the vCenter server using a user with an administrator role assigned to it.
2. Drop down the vSphere Web Client's inventory menu and click on **Networking**:

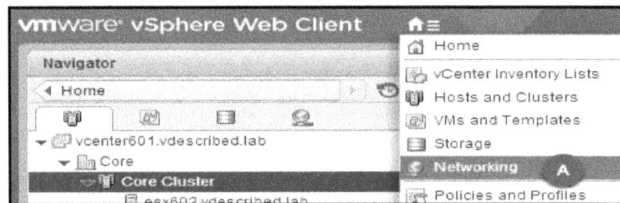

3. Expand the vCenter inventory and select the data center in which you intend to create the VDS. With the data center object elected, drop down the **Actions** menu and navigate to **Distributed Switch | New Distributed Switch**:

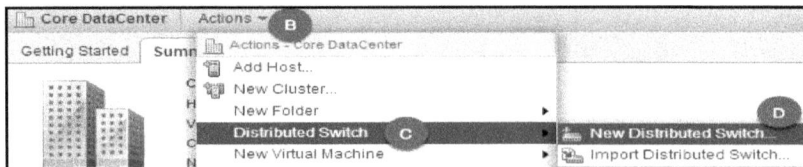

4. In the **New Distributed Switch** wizard, supply a name for the VDS and proceed to the next screen:

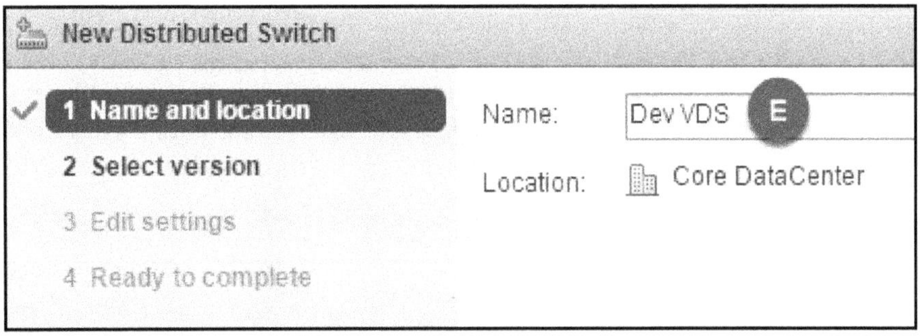

5. In the **Select version** screen, choose a VDS version depending on the ESXi version. For example, if your environment has mixed ESXi versions, let's say, ESXi 5.1, 5.5 and 6.0, then you have to choose a VDS version that supports ESXi 5.1 and above. If your current environment has only ESXi 6.0 hosts then select the VDS version 6.0:

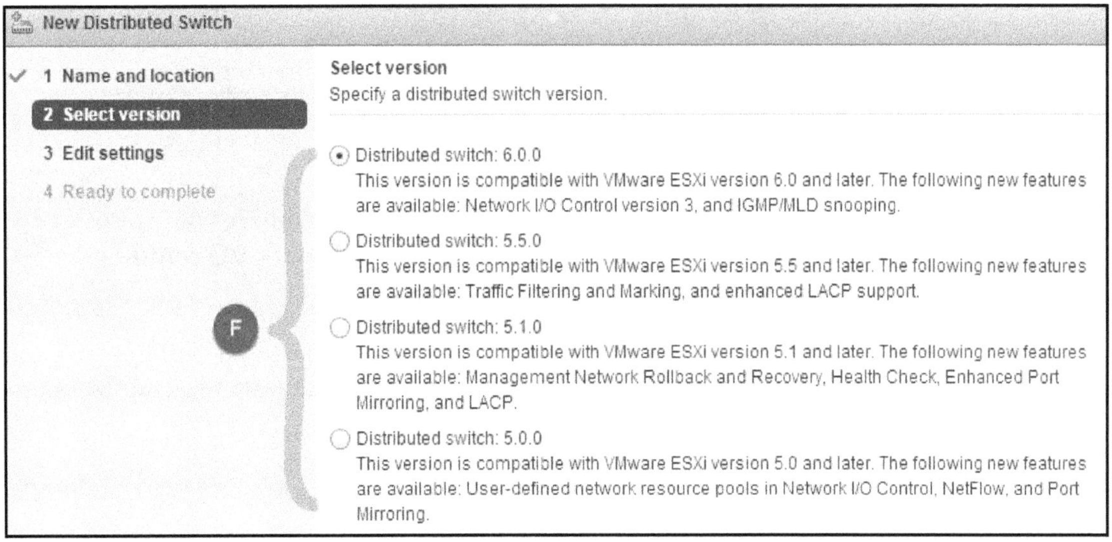

6. In the **Edit settings** screen, you could choose to change the default number of the uplinks, which is 4, to match the number of physical NICs you intend to map from each of the ESXi hosts to the VDS. NIOC (network I/O control) is enabled by default, and there is no logical reason to disable it at this point. What you can choose to change is whether to create a default port group on the VDS. Keep in mind that there is only one universal type of port group on a VDS, regardless of the traffic type you configure with it. If you intend to create a default port group though, you could supply a name for the port group and continue. We will learn about creating more dvPortGroups in the next section:

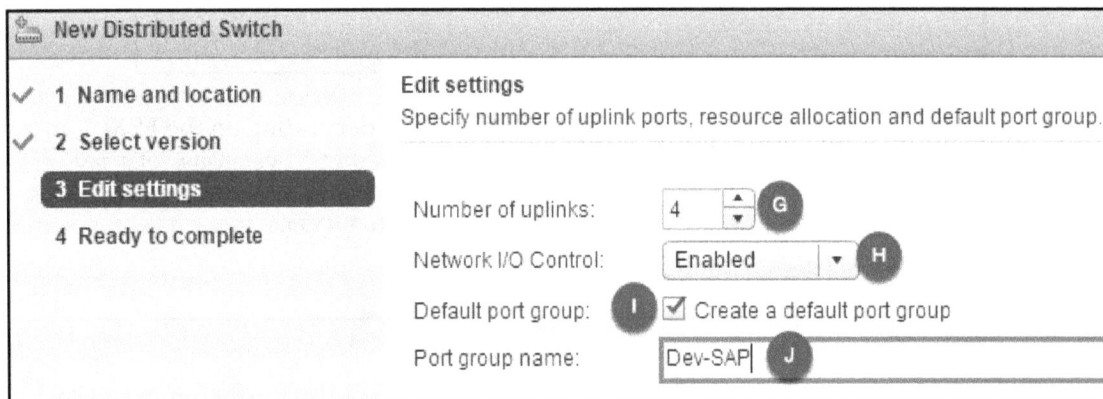

7. In the **Ready to complete** screen, review the settings and click **Finish** to create the VDS.

8. The Recent Tasks pane should show the tasks **Create a vSphere Distributed Switch**, **Add Distributed Port Groups**, and **Update network I/O control on vSphere Distributed Switch** completed successfully.

9. To review the properties of the newly created VDS, locate the VDS in the Networking inventory, select the VDS, navigate to the **Manage** tab, and then to **Settings** | **Properties**:

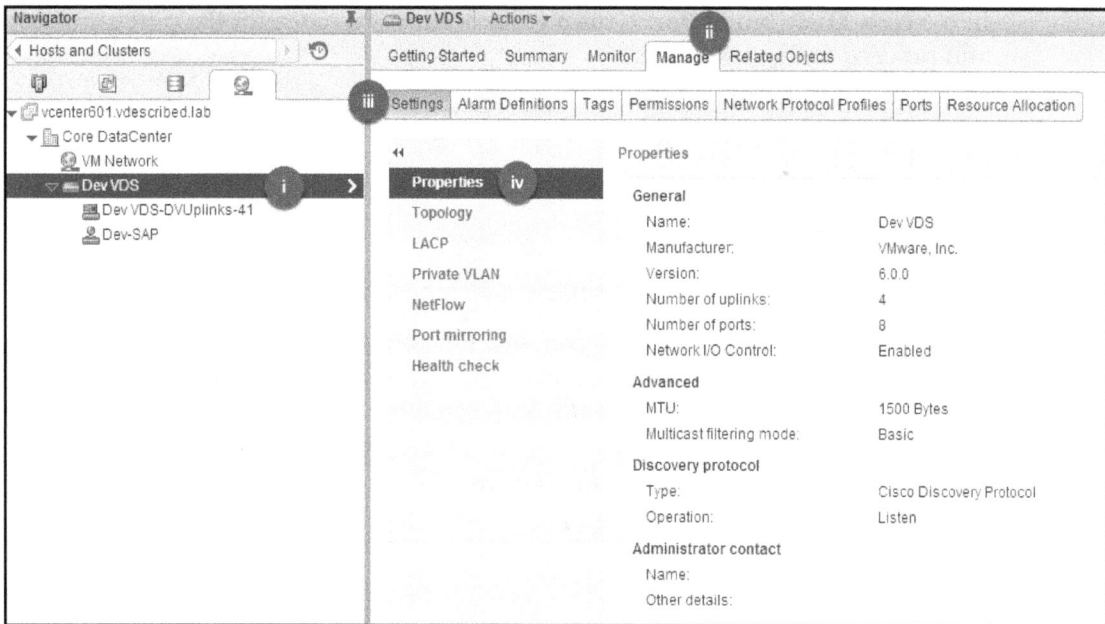

Creating dvPortGroups

When you create a VDS, the wizard includes an option to create a dvPortGroup along with it, but only one. However, there could always be a need to create more dvPortGroups. For instance, if you were to have virtual machines belonging to different VLANs, then there is a need to create a dvPortGroup with the VLAN ID set on it.

You can use the following procedure to create a dvPortGroup:

1. With the VDS selected from the Networking inventory, drop down the Actions menu and navigate to **Distributed Port Group** | **New Distributed Port Group**:

2. In the **New Distributed Port Group** wizard, supply a name for the port group and proceed to the next screen:

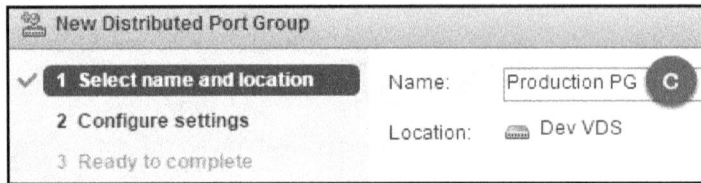

3. In the **Configure settings** screen, choose a **Port binding** (*Default* – **Static binding**) and **Port allocation** (*Default* – **Elastic**) method, the **Number of ports** (*Default* – **8**) the **Network resource pool** (*Default* – **default**), the **VLAN** (*Default* – **None**), and type (**VLAN**, **VLAN trunking** *and* **Private VLAN**). We will learn more about the settings and their effects later in this section:

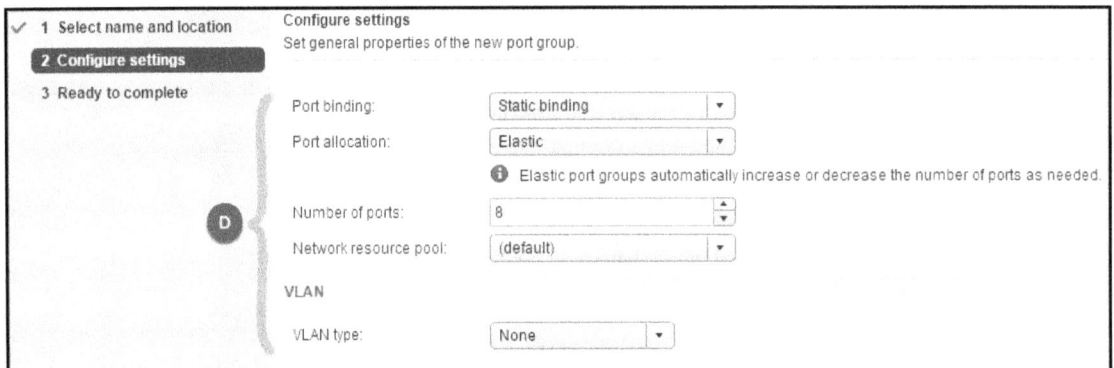

4. In the **Ready to complete** screen, review the settings and click **Finish** to create the dvPortGroup. The **Recent Tasks** pane should show an **Add Distributed Port Groups** task completed successfully.

5. To review the properties of the newly created dvPortGroup, locate the **dvPortGroup** from the Networking inventory and with it selected, navigate to **Manage** I **Settings** I **Properties**:

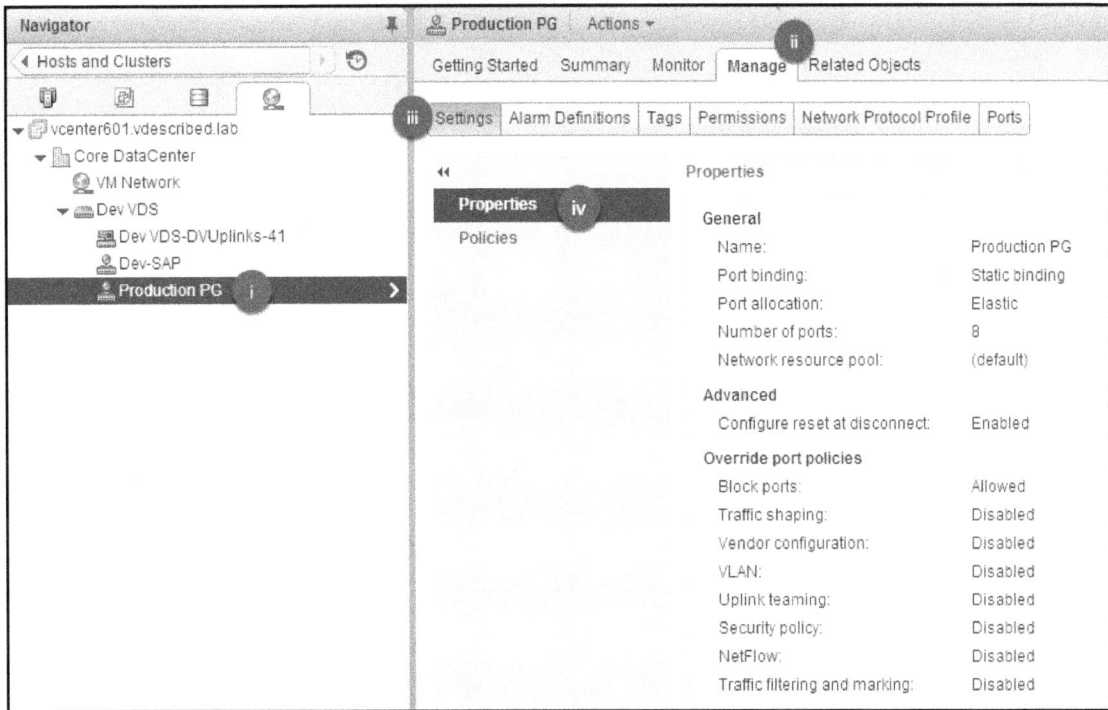

Port binding and port allocation

When we create a dvPortGroup, we chose the port binding and port allocation methods to be used. To make an appropriate choice, it is important to understand how they work.

Port binding

Port binding refers to the method of assigning a dvPort to a vNIC. There are three types of binding:

- Static binding
- Dynamic binding

- Ephemeral-no binding

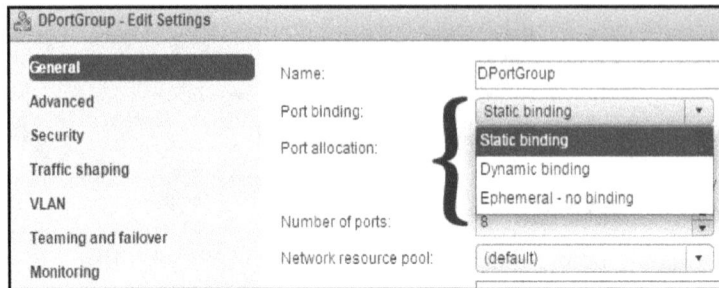

Let us have a look at each of them in brief:

- **Static binding** – assigns a dvPort to a vNIC when it is first configured to connect to a dvPortGroup. The dvPort ID that is assigned to a vNIC does not change unless the vNIC is configured not to use the same dvPortGroup. This is the default port binding method and is dependent on the vCenter server's availability for port assignments.

- **Dynamic binding** – assigns a dvPort Ephemeral-no binding Let us have a look at each of them in brief: Static binding – assigns a dvPort to a vNIC when it is first configured to connect to a dvPortGroup. The dvPort ID that is assigned to a vNIC does not change unless the vNIC is configured not to use the same dvPortGroup. This is the default port binding method and is dependent on the vCenter server's availability for port assignments. Dynamic binding – assigns a dvPort to a vNIC when it is configured to connect to a dvPortGroup and the virtual machine it belongs to is powered-on. The moment the virtual machine is powered-off, or the vNIC is disconnected from the port group, the dvPort is released back to the pool and it is not guaranteed that the vNIC will get the same dvPort again. Dynamic binding is fully dependent on the availability of the vCenter server to the extent that you will not be able to power-on virtual machines whose vNICs are connected to a dvPortGroup with dynamic binding enabled. Due to these limitations, dynamic binding is deprecated, starting with VDS 5.0, and Vmware does not recommend using it. However, it could be useful in environments where you have a limited static number of ports assigned to a dvPortGroup, but you have more virtual machines' vNICs than the ports available. In such a case, the assumption is that not all the virtual machines are powered-on at the same time.

> You can configure up to a maximum of 10,000 static/dynamic port groups per vCenter or VDS

- **Ephemeral binding** – behaves much like dynamic binding when it comes to port allocation/de-allocation. The only difference though is that the binding is *not* vCenter dependent, meaning, the ESXi hypervisor can also allocate or de-allocate dvPorts to vNICs.

> You can configure a maximum of 1,016 ephemeral port groups per vCenter or VDS

Both ephemeral and dynamic port binding have a performance impact, since they require the vCenter/ESXi to *assign/allocate/de-allocate* ports during virtual machine power state operations.

Port allocation

There are two types of port allocation methods – fixed and elastic.

DPortGroup - Edit Settings		
General	Name:	DPortGroup
Advanced	Port binding:	Static binding ▼
Security	Port allocation:	Elastic ▼
Traffic shaping		Fixed
VLAN		Elastic
Teaming and failover	Number of ports:	
Monitoring	Network resource pool:	(default) ▼
Traffic filtering and marking	Description:	
Miscellaneous		

The *elastic* allocation method will increase and decrease the number of available ports in a dvPortGroup as per requirements. It starts with a default of eight ports in the dvPortGroup. If you exhaust the available ports and if you are in need of additional ports to power-on virtual machines, then VDS will automatically add the required number of ports to the dvPortGroup. In the same manner, if the ports are no longer required then they are deleted from the dvPortGroup.

The *fixed* allocation method will let you set a limit on the number of ports available on a port group, the default being eight. Once you exhaust the available ports on a fixed allocation port group, you will no longer be able to connect any vNICs to it. If you try to power on a virtual machine it will complain about no free port being available in the dvPortGroup.

Connecting ESXi hosts to a VDS

The VDS created wouldn't be complete without the ESXi hosts connected to it. The number of physical NICs each ESXi host can connect to is dependent on the number of dvUplinks set on the VDS. For instance, if the VDS is configured to support eight dvUplinks then each of the ESXi hosts can connect up to a maximum of eight physical network adapters to the VDS.

In this section, we will learn how to connect ESXi hosts to the VDS. The procedure requires you to be connected to the vCenter server with a user that has the administrator role assigned to it:

1. Bring up the Networking inventory using the vSphere Web Client and select the VDS.
2. With the VDS selected, drop down the **Actions** menu to select **Add and Manage Hosts...**:

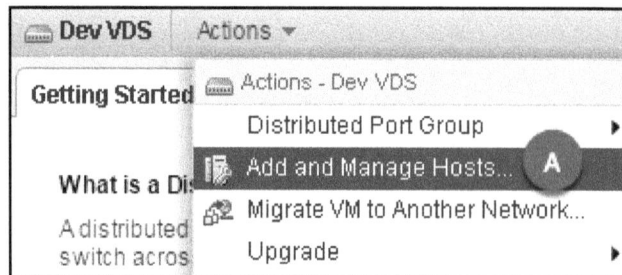

3. In the **Add and Manage Hosts** wizard, select the task as **Add hosts** and proceed:

4. In the **Select hosts** screen, click on **New hosts** to bring up a list of hosts managed by the vCenter server:

5. In the **Select new hosts** window, select the ESXi hosts you intend to add to the VDS and click **OK**:

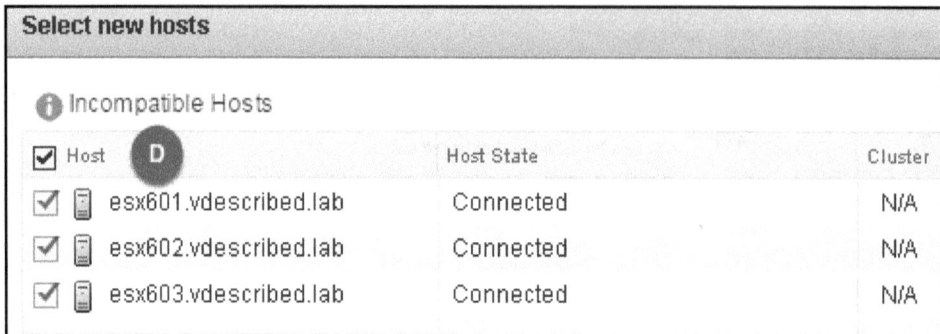

6. Back at the **Select hosts** wizard screen, select the check box **Configure identical network settings on multiple hosts (template mode)** and click **Next**. The *template mode will allow you to make the configuration on one of the ESXi hosts and the same will be applied to the remaining hosts. This is a very handy feature when you are dealing with many ESXi hosts:*

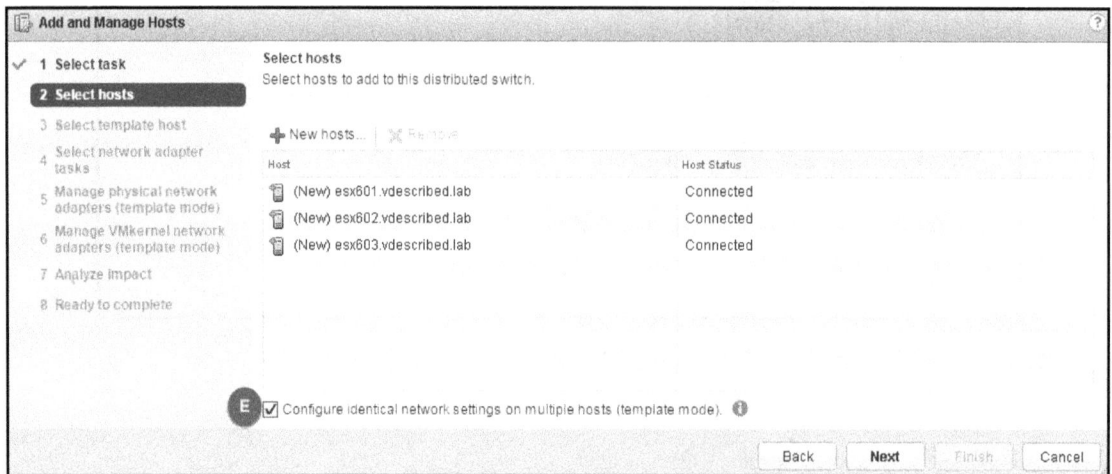

7. In the **Select template host** wizard, choose a host and click **Next** to continue.

Add and Manage Hosts

✓ 1 Select task
✓ 2 Select hosts
3 **Select template host**
4 Select network adapter tasks
5 Manage physical network adapters (template mode)
6 Manage VMkernel network adapters (template mode)
7 Analyze impact
8 Ready to complete

Select template host
Select a template host to apply its network configuration on this switch to the other hosts.

Host	1 ▲	Physical Adapters - On This Switch / All	VMkernel Adapters - On This Switch / All
esx601.vdescribed.lab (template)		**0 / 8**	**0 / 1**
esx602.vdescribed.lab		0 / 8	0 / 1
esx603.vdescribed.lab		0 / 8	0 / 1

Services (esx601.vdescribed.lab)

Fault Tolerance logging: --
Management traffic: vmk0
vSphere Replication traffic: --
vMotion traffic: --
Virtual SAN traffic: --

8. In the **Select network adapter tasks**, select the check-box **Manage physical adapters (template mode)** and click **Next** to continue:

Add and Manage Hosts

✓ 1 Select task
✓ 2 Select hosts
✓ 3 Select template host
4 **Select network adapter tasks**
5 Manage physical network adapters (template mode)
6 Analyze impact
7 Ready to complete

Select network adapter tasks
Select the network adapter tasks to perform.

☑ Manage physical adapters (template mode)
Add physical network adapters to the distributed switch, assign them to uplinks, or remove existing ones.

☐ Manage VMkernel adapters (template mode)
Add VMkernel network adapters to this distributed switch, migrate them from other switches, assign them to distributed port groups, configure their settings, or remove existing ones.

☐ Migrate virtual machine networking
Migrate VM network adapters by assigning them to distributed port groups on the distributed switch.

☐ Manage advanced host settings
Set the number of ports per legacy host proxy switch.

9. In the **Manage physical network adapters (template mode)** screen, use the top pane to assign **vmnics** to dvUplinks. This is done by selecting an unused vmnic and clicking the **Assign Uplink** option at the top left of the pane to bring up a list of dvUplinks on the VDS:

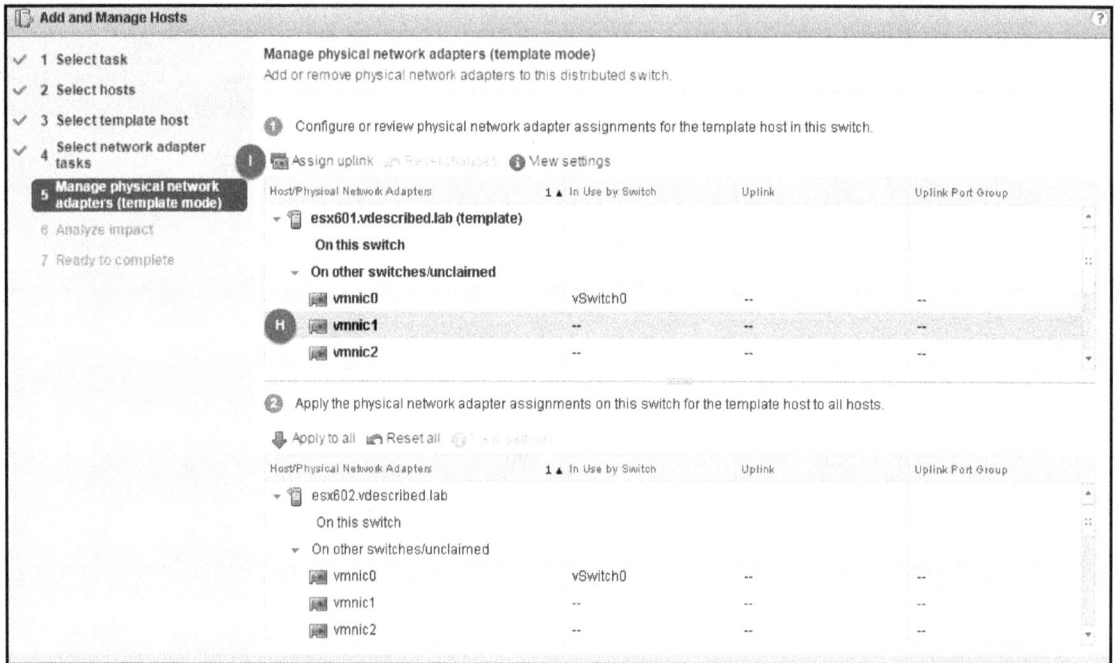

Choose an uplink and click on **OK** to return to the wizard screen:

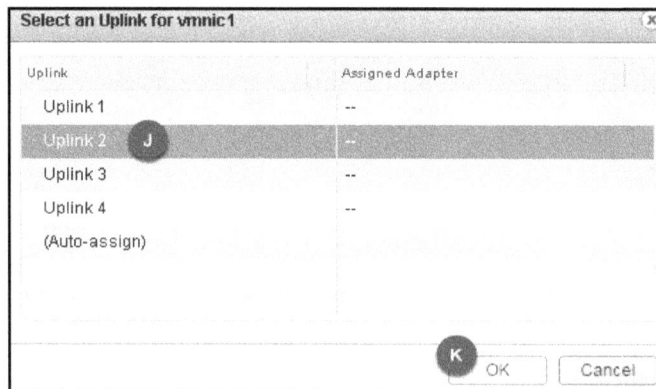

10. Repeat step-9 to map all the needed vmnics.

11. Once all the vmnics to uplink mapping have been done in the top pane, click on the **Apply to all** option in the bottom pane to push a similar configuration to the remaining hosts. It will use the exact vmnics to uplink mapping on all the hosts. Click **Next** to proceed:

Manage physical network adapters (template mode)
Add or remove physical network adapters to this distributed switch.

① Configure or review physical network adapter assignments for the template host in this switch.

🖥 Assign uplink   🔁 Reset changes   ℹ View settings

Host/Physical Network Adapters	1 ▲ In Use by Switch	Uplink	Uplink Port Group
▾ 🖥 esx601.vdescribed.lab (template)			
▾ On this switch			
🔲 vmnic1 (Assigned)	*Physical Adapter to dvUplink Mapping*	Uplink 2	Dev VDS-DVUplinks-21
🔲 vmnic2 (Assigned)		Uplink 3	Dev VDS-DVUplinks-21
▾ On other switches/unclaimed			
🔲 vmnic0	vSwitch0	--	--

Ⓛ Apply the physical network adapter assignments on this switch for the template host to all hosts.

⬇ Apply to all   🔁 Reset all   ⚙ View settings

Host/Physical Network Adapters	1 ▲ In Use by Switch	Uplink	Uplink Port Group
▾ 🖥 esx602.vdescribed.lab			
On this switch			
▾ On other switches/unclaimed			
🔲 vmnic0	vSwitch0	--	--
🔲 vmnic1	--	--	--
🔲 vmnic2	--	--	--

While in the template mode, you will not be allowed to proceed further without applying the settings to the remaining hosts that were selected to be connected to the VDS.

12. Review the **Analyze impact** screen for any possible impact detected by the wizard. Proceed further if there is no impact:

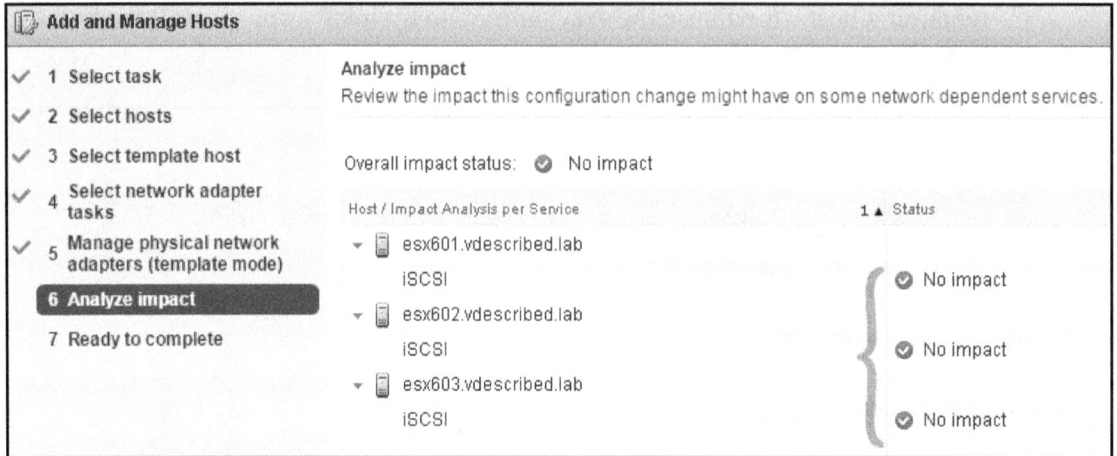

13. Review the summary of settings in the **Ready to complete** screen and click **Finish** to connect the ESXi hosts to the VDS.

Migrating from vSwitch to VDS

It is possible to unobtrusively migrate your infrastructure's virtual networking from a standard vSwitch to a VDS. In this section, we will learn how to perform such a migration in a manner that doesn't affect the functioning of the ESXi host or the virtual machines running on them. The migration includes two activities and those are:

- Migrating the VMkernel adapters
- Migrating virtual machine networking

While both the activities can be done separately, the wizard-driven method included in vSphere 6.0 enables achieving both the tasks unobtrusively at the same time. We will go through the procedure for the same in this section. To begin, much like the other networking configurations that we have performed so far, you will need access to the vCenter server managing the VDS as a user with the administrator role assigned to it:

1. With the VDS selected from the Networking inventory, drop down the **Actions** menu to select **Add and Manage Hosts**.

2. In the **Add and Manage Hosts** wizard, select the task **Manage host networking** and proceed:

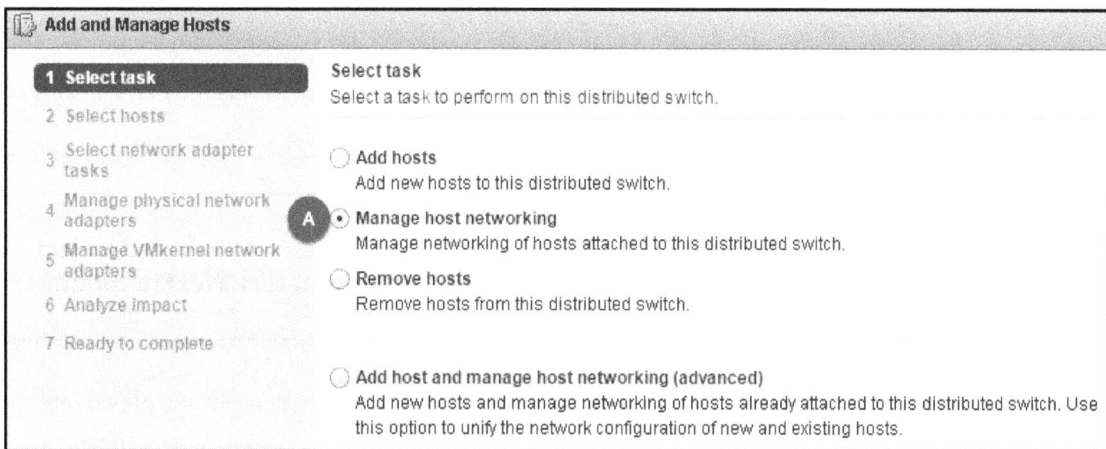

3. In the **Select hosts** screen, click on **Attached hosts** to bring up a list of ESXi hosts:

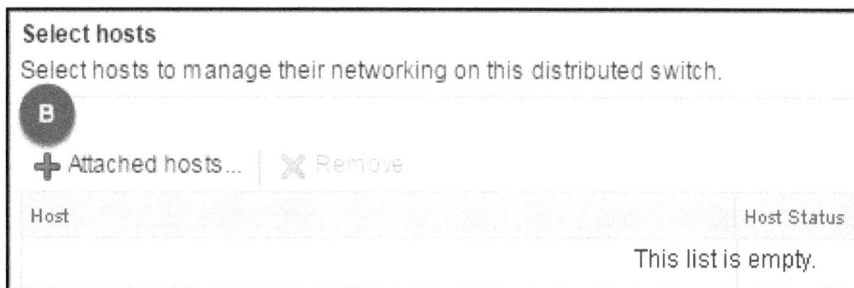

4. From the **Select member hosts** window, select the ESXi hosts to manage and click **OK** to return to the wizard screen:

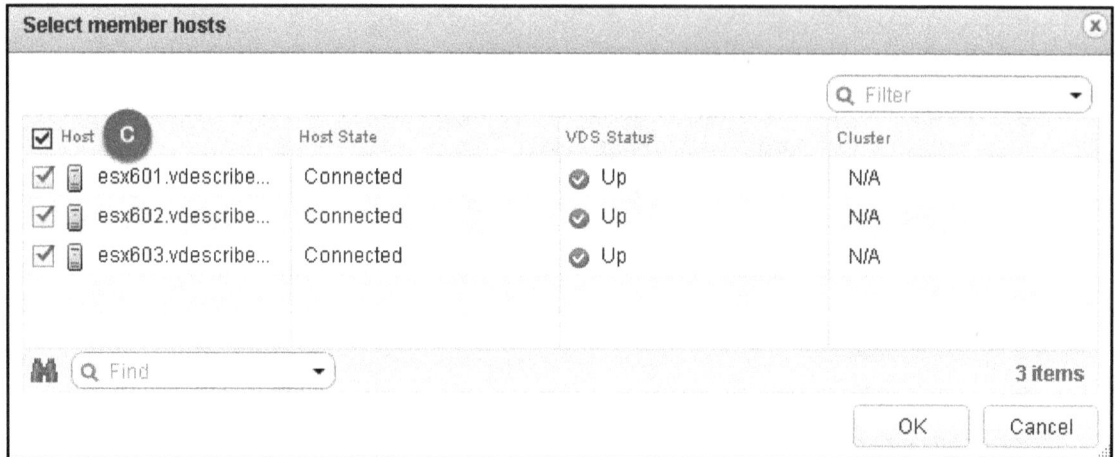

Select member hosts

Host C	Host State	VDS Status	Cluster
esx601.vdescribe...	Connected	Up	N/A
esx602.vdescribe...	Connected	Up	N/A
esx603.vdescribe...	Connected	Up	N/A

Q Find

3 items

OK   Cancel

5. Back at the wizard screen, select the template mode option **Configure identical network settings on multiple hosts (template mode)** and click **Next** to continue:

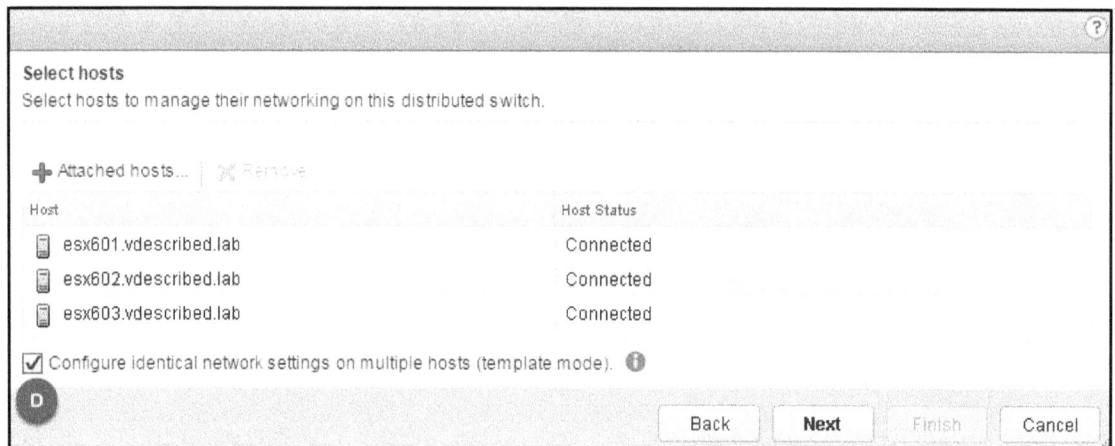

Select hosts
Select hosts to manage their networking on this distributed switch.

Attached hosts...   Remove

Host	Host Status
esx601.vdescribed.lab	Connected
esx602.vdescribed.lab	Connected
esx603.vdescribed.lab	Connected

☑ Configure identical network settings on multiple hosts (template mode).

Back   **Next**   Finish   Cancel

6. In the **Select template host** screen, select one of the ESXi hosts to be used as the template and click **Next** to continue:

Select template host
Select a template host to apply its network configuration on this switch to the other hosts.

Host	1 ▲ Physical Adapters - ...	VMkernel Adapters - On This Switch / All
⦿ 🗔 **esx601.vdescribed.lab (template)**	**2 / 8**	**0 / 1**
◯ 🗔 esx602.vdescribed.lab	2 / 8	0 / 1
◯ 🗔 esx603.vdescribed.lab	2 / 8	0 / 1

Services (esx601.vdescribed.lab)
Fault Tolerance logging: --
Management traffic: vmk0
vSphere Replication traffic: --
vMotion traffic: --
Virtual SAN traffic: --

7. In the **Select network adapter tasks** screen, choose the options **Manage Vmkernel adapters (template mode)** and **Migrate virtual machine networking** and click **Next** to continue:

Select network adapter tasks
Select the network adapter tasks to perform.

☐ Manage physical adapters (template mode)
  Add physical network adapters to the distributed switch, assign them to uplinks, or remove existing ones.

☑ Manage VMkernel adapters (template mode)
  Add VMkernel network adapters to this distributed switch, migrate them from other switches, assign them to distributed port groups, configure their settings, or remove existing ones.

☑ Migrate virtual machine networking
  Migrate VM network adapters by assigning them to distributed port groups on the distributed switch.

☐ Manage advanced host settings
  Set the number of ports per legacy host proxy switch.

8. In the **Manage Vmkernel network adapters (template mode)** screen, assign dvPortGroups to the vmkernel adapters. This is done by selecting a vmkernel interface listed in the top pane and clicking the **Assign port group** option:

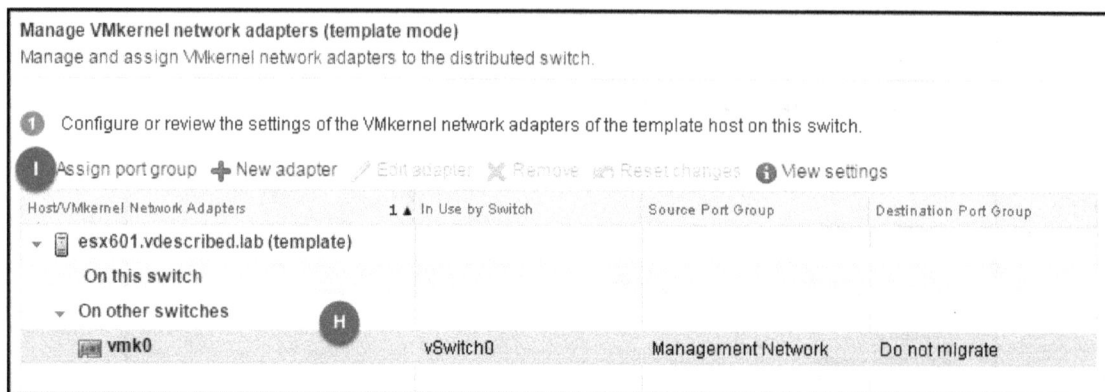

9. When you click on **Assign port group** it should bring up an **Assign destination port group** window with all the dvPortGroups listed. Choose a port group for the chosen adapter and click **OK** to confirm the selection and return to the wizard screen:

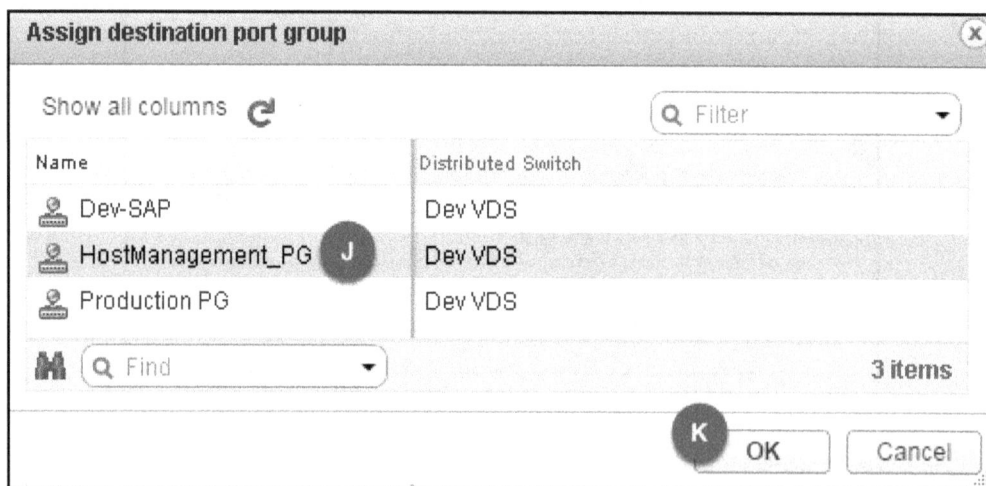

10. Back at the wizard screen, click on the **Apply to all** option to push the same mapping to the remaining hosts:

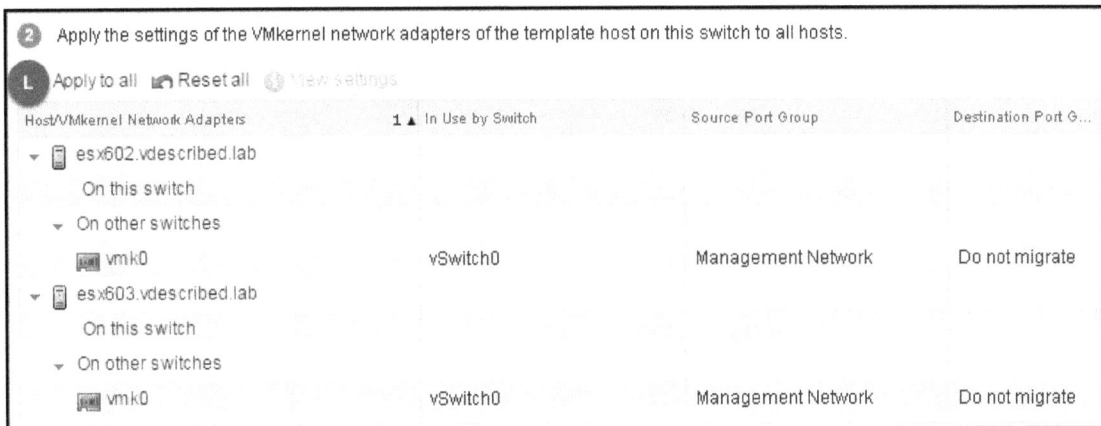

11. Doing so will bring up the **Apply Vmkernel network adapter configuration to other hosts** window. Supply the IP addresses for the **vmk** interfaces of the remaining hosts and click **OK**:

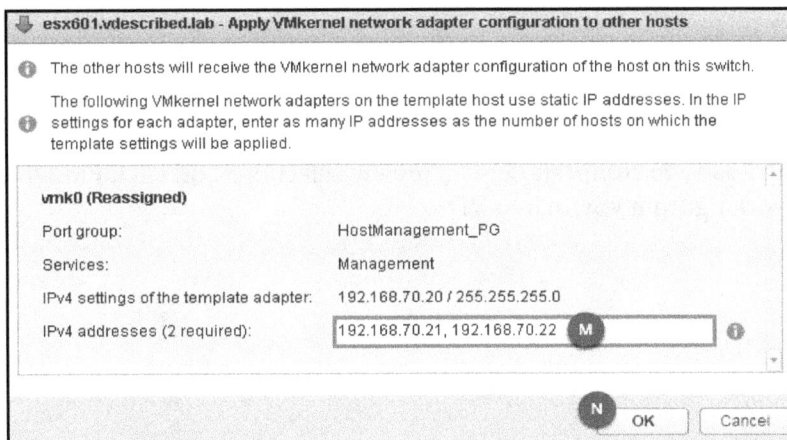

12. Back at the wizard screen, click Next to proceed to the **Analyze impact screen**. Review the impact status and click **Next** to proceed if there is no impact.

13. In the **Migrate VM networking** screen, select each of the VMs from the list (you can multi-select VMs, by using *control* + left-click). With the VMs selected, click on **Assign port group** to map the VM's networking to a dvPortGroup on the VDS. With the VMs assigned a dvPortGroup each, click **Next** to continue:

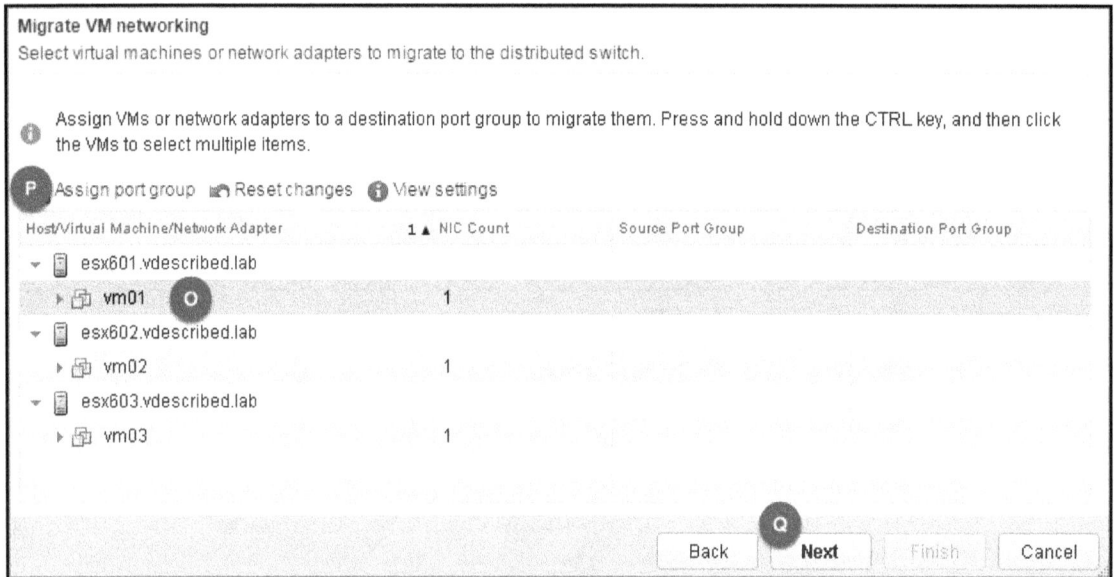

14. In the **Ready to complete** screen, review selections and click **Finish** to migrate the networking from vSwitch to VDS.

Private VLAN support on a VDS

Private VLAN support allows further segregation of VLAN subnets. It offers a level of flexibility with its intrinsic access boundary definitions. PVLAN is not a VMware concept, but a network concept that VMware supports on VDS. There are two types of PVLANs depending on their access boundary definitions – **isolated VLAN** and **community VLAN**:

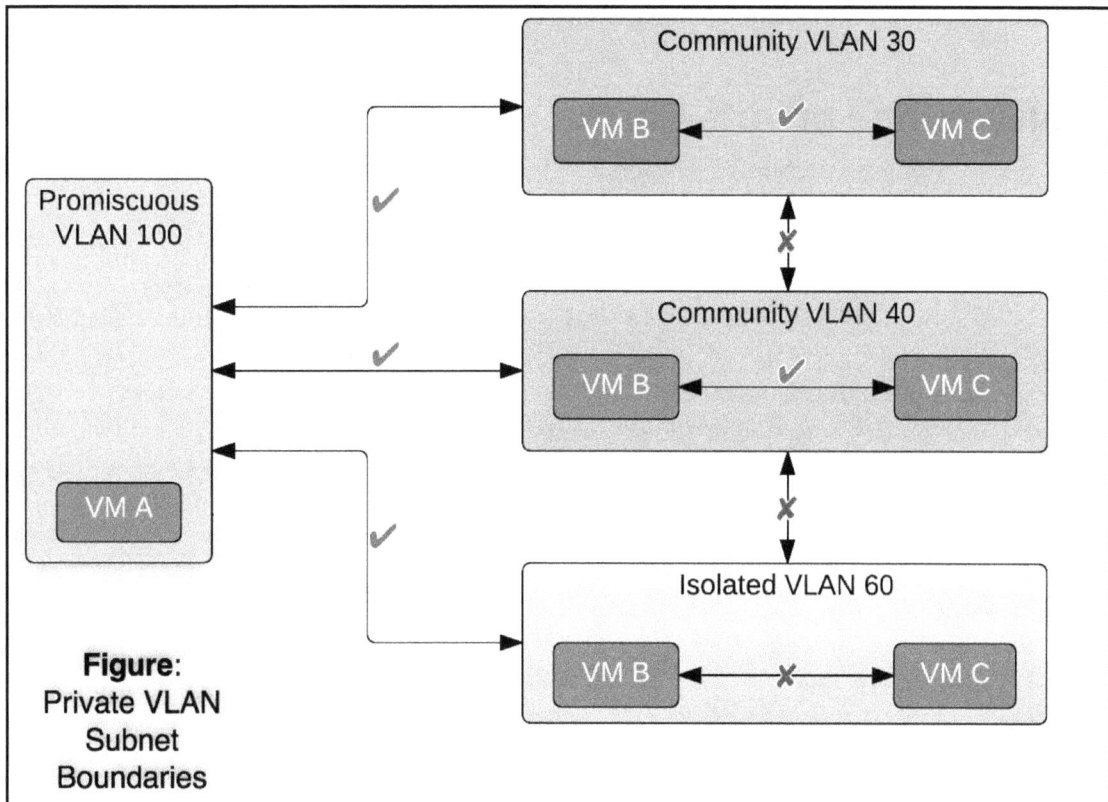

Figure:
Private VLAN
Subnet
Boundaries

Before, we delve deeper into each of the PVLAN types, it is important to understand what a **promiscuous VLAN** is. Although, most books or blogs categorize it as type of PVLAN, it really is not a type of VLAN, but a mode in which the primary (parent) VLAN of the PVLAN operates in. Anything that is a member of a promiscuous VLAN is not in a private VLAN. The nodes in a promiscuous VLAN are accessible to the private VLAN nodes regardless of the type of PVLAN they are a member of.

An **isolated VLAN** is a type of private VLAN used when there are nodes that should not be talking to each other or have access to each other's shared resources. In any private VLAN setup there can only be one isolated VLAN. Members of an isolated VLAN can however talk to the members of the promiscuous VLAN.

Members of a **community VLAN** are allowed to talk to each other, but not to members of another community or isolated VLAN. They are, however, allowed to communicate with the members of the promiscuous VLAN. There can be more than one community VLAN.

Implementing private VLANs using a VDS

To be able to configure private VLANs on a VDS you will need administrator role level access to the vCenter server managing the VDS.

Here is the step-by-step procedure:

1. Configure PVLANs on the physical switches and make a note of the VLAN IDs for use.
2. Connect to the vCenter server and navigate to the Networking inventory view and select the VDS you want to configure PVLANs on.
3. With the VDS selected, navigate to **Manage** | **Settings** | **Private VLAN** and click **Edit** to bring up the **Edit Private VLAN Settings** window:

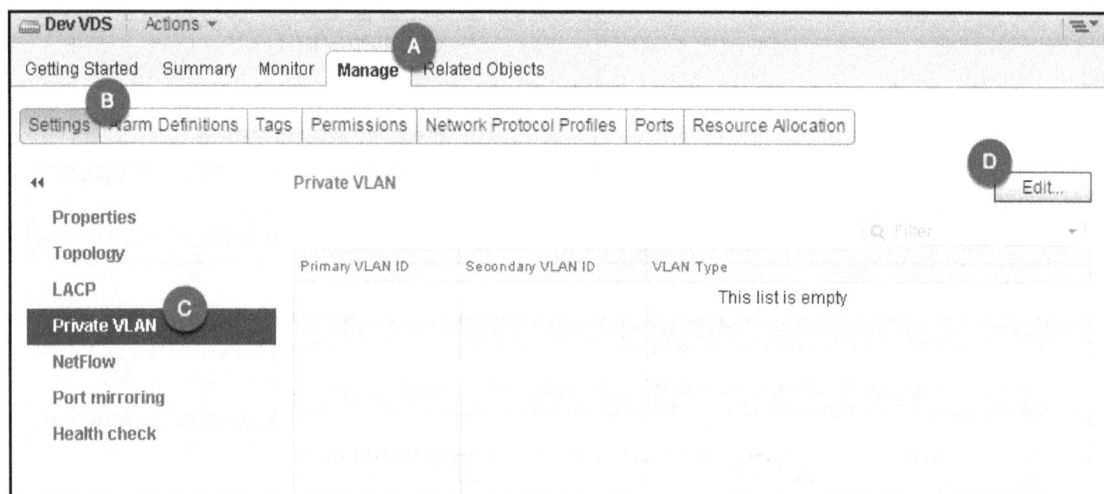

4. Add a **Primary VLAN** and the required **Secondary VLANs** of the type **Community** or **Isolated** and click **OK** to confirm the settings:

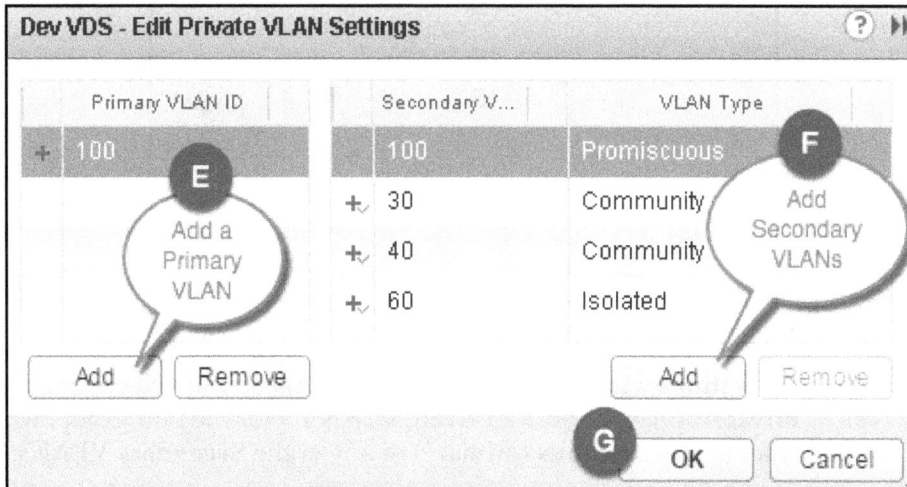

Once the private VLANs are configured, they can now be assigned to a dvPortGroup to allow the VMs in the port group to participate in the private VLAN subnet:

1. With the VDS selected, navigate to **Related Objects** | **Distributed Port Groups**:

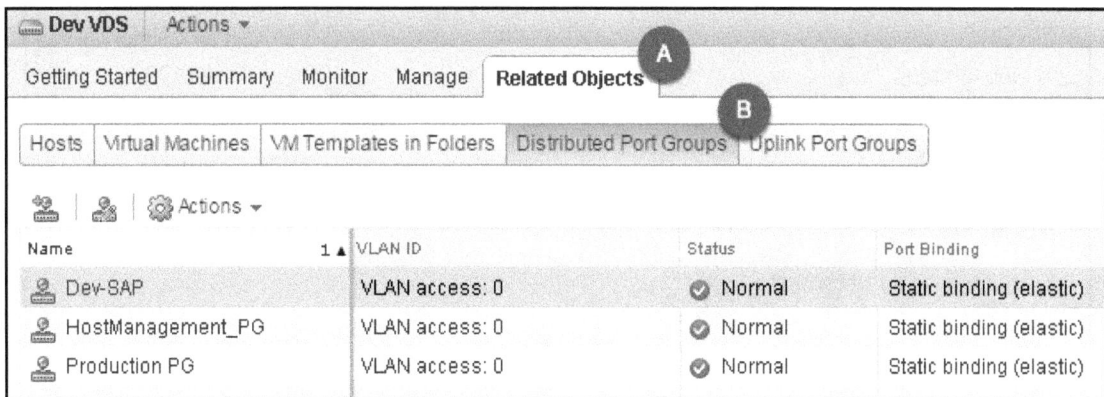

2. Right-click on the intended dvPortGroup from the list and click on **Edit Settings**:

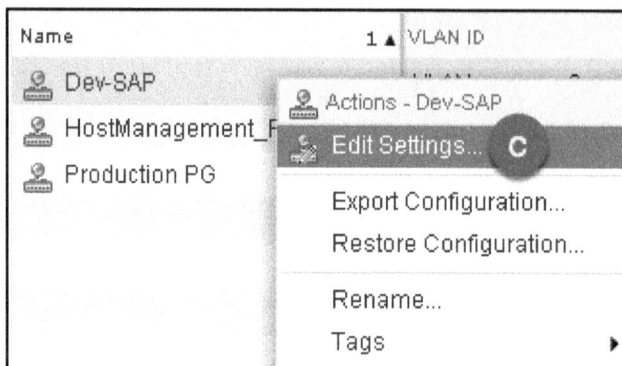

Name	1 ▲	VLAN ID
👤 Dev-SAP		
👤 HostManagement_F		
👤 Production PG		

- 👤 Actions - Dev-SAP
- 📝 Edit Settings... **C**
- Export Configuration...
- Restore Configuration...
- Rename...
- Tags ▶

3. In the **Edit Settings** window, navigate to the **VLAN** screen and choose the **VLAN type** as **Private VLAN**. Choose a **Private VLAN ID** for the port group, which would either be **Promiscuous (primary)** or any of the **Secondary VLANs**:

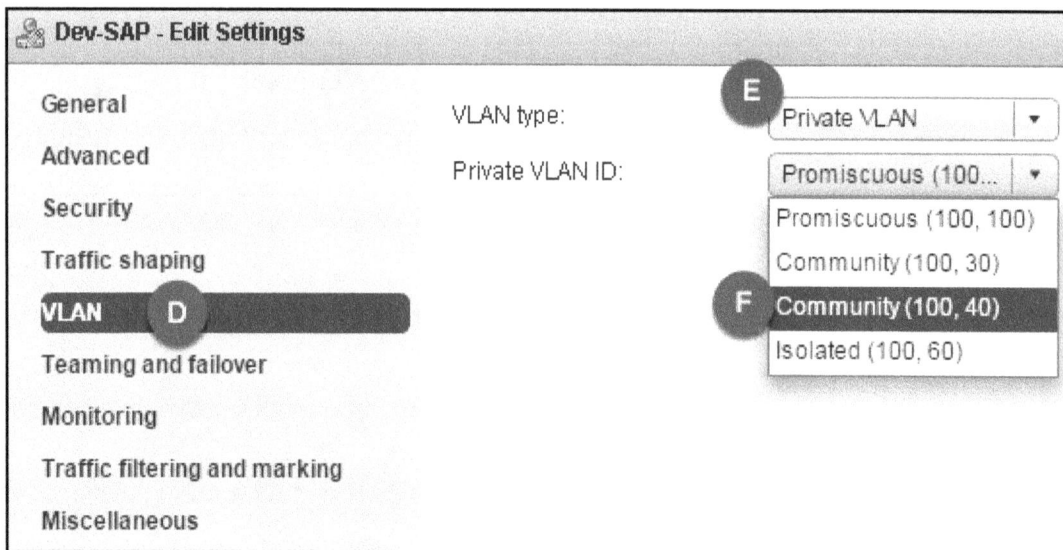

👤 **Dev-SAP - Edit Settings**

General		**E**
Advanced	VLAN type:	Private VLAN ▼
Security	Private VLAN ID:	Promiscuous (100... ▼
Traffic shaping		Promiscuous (100, 100)
VLAN D		Community (100, 30)
Teaming and failover		**F** Community (100, 40)
Monitoring		Isolated (100, 60)
Traffic filtering and marking		
Miscellaneous		

4. Click **OK** to confirm the settings.

Much like assigning a traditional VLAN ID, a dvPortGroup can only be associated with a single private VLAN ID.

Advanced network configuration

With virtual switches created in your environment, it becomes extremely important to configure them in a manner that enables performance and security like any other form of networking. Both the standard vSwitch and VDS have plenty of configuration options, making them flexible enough to meet the workload networking demands. In this section, we will cover the advanced settings that are available on both the standard vSwitch and the VDS. In most cases, both the switching constructs have the same settings, with VDS including a few unique capabilities.

We will cover the following advanced topics:

- Getting to the settings of a vSwitch, port group, dvPortGroup, and a dvPort
- Virtual switch security settings
- Traffic shaping
- Load balancing and failover
- Maximum transmission unit
- Link aggregation protocol support and configuration

Getting to the settings of a vSwitch, port group, dvPortGroup, and a dvPort

The goal of this section is to try to help you find the settings of a vSwitch, a port group on a standard vSwitch, a dvPortGroup, or a dvPort.

Standard vSwitch and port group settings

Here is how you could get to the settings of a standard vSwitch:

1. Select the ESXi host from the vCenter Inventory.
2. With the ESXi host selected, navigate to **Manage** | **Networking** | **Virtual Switches.**

3. Select the vSwitch and hit the pencil icon ![pencil] to bring up the **Edit Settings** of the vSwitch:

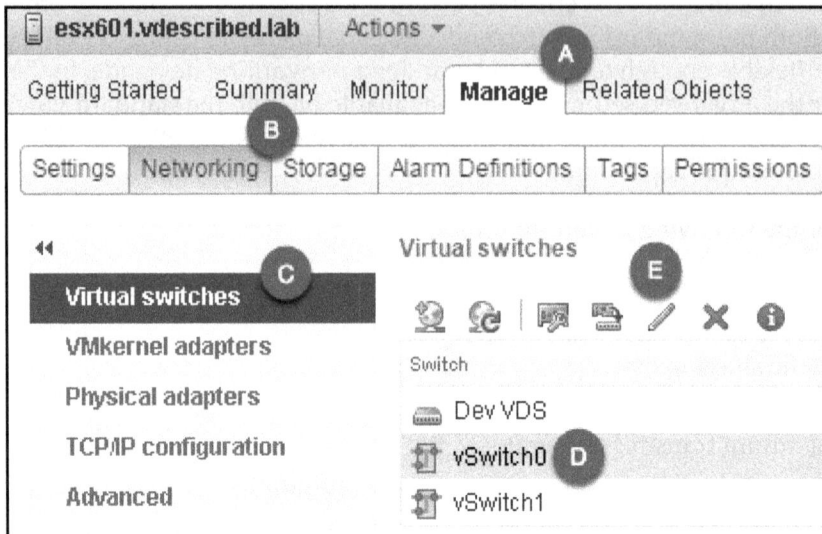

In the **Edit Settings** window, choose the setting you intend to modify from the left pane:

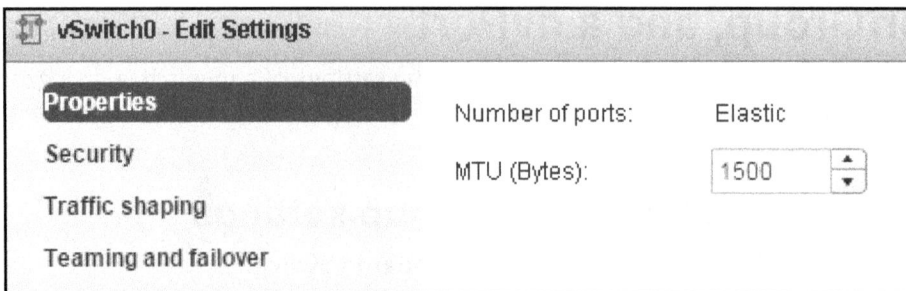

The procedure will remain the same for a *port group*, but you will need to make sure that you select the port group and click the **Edit Settings** icon of the port group:

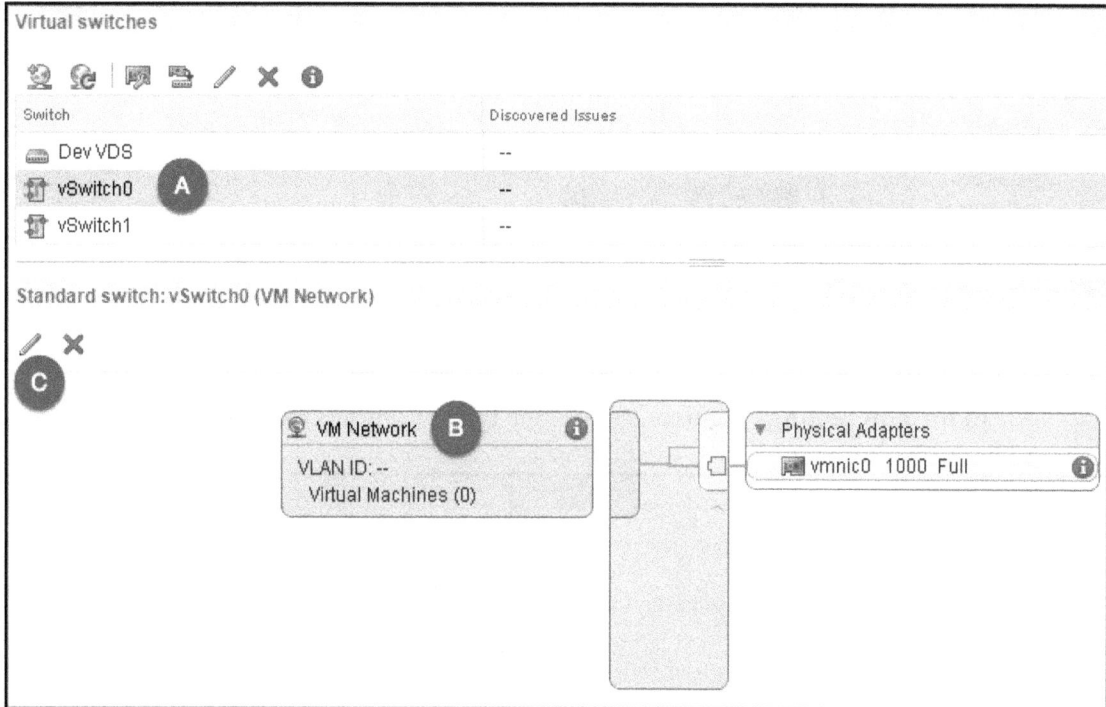

dvPortGroup and dvPort settings

This section will cover the procedures required to get to the settings page of a dvPortGroup or a dvPort:

1. Use the Networking inventory to find the desired VDS and expand its inventory tree to view all the dvPortGroup under it.

2. With a dvPortGroup selected, navigate to **Manage** | **Settings** and click on **Edit** to bring up the **Edit Settings** window:

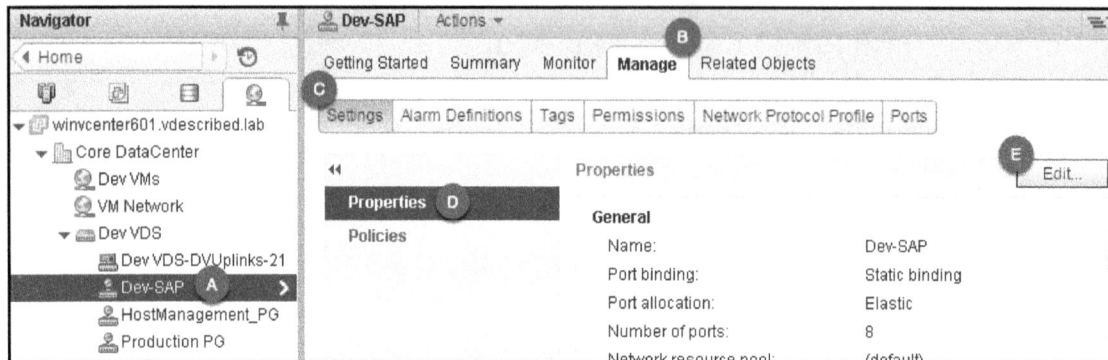

3. In the **Edit Settings** window, choose the type of settings from the left pane:

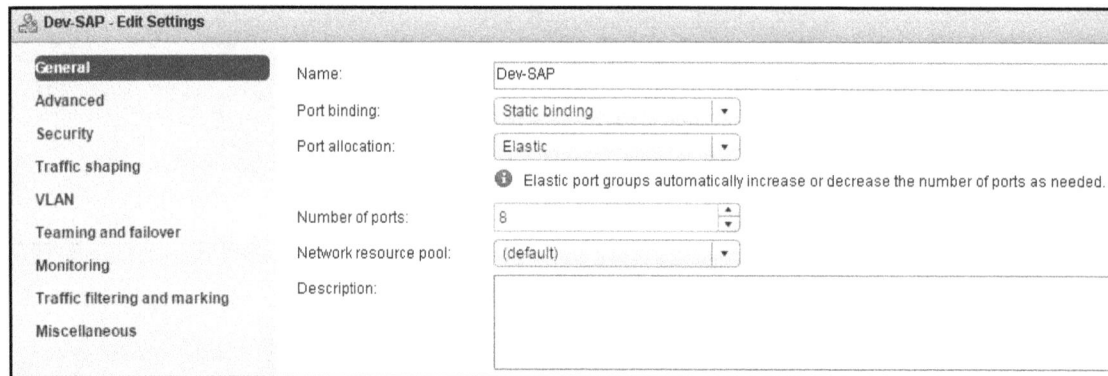

To achieve the same on a dvPort, follow these steps:

1. With the port group selected from the Networking inventory, navigate to **Manage | Ports.**
2. Under the **Port** tab, select the desired port and click on the pencil icon to bring up the **Edit Settings** window:

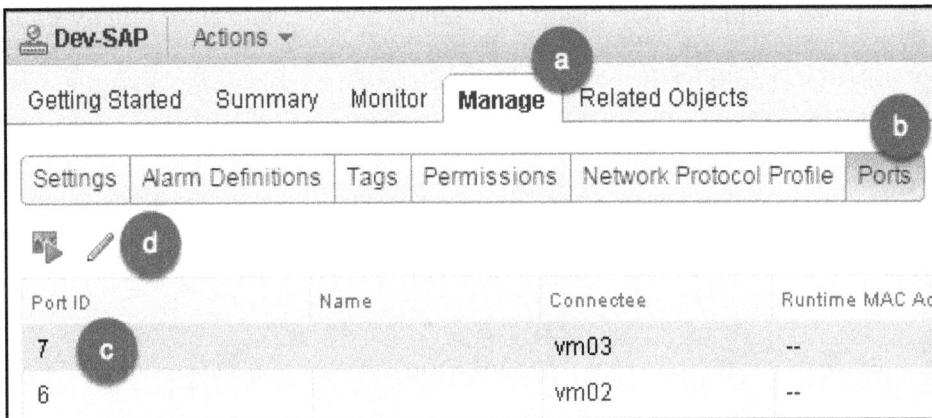

Virtual switch security settings

The virtual switch offers three distinct security settings:

- Promiscuous mode
- MAC address changes
- Forged transmits

All the three security settings that we have discussed operate identically on both the standard vSwitch and the VDS, with the VDS allowing an additional level of granularity by making the same settings at the dvPort level. This is, however, possible only if you configure the dvPortGroup to allow port level policy overrides. With a standard vSwitch, security settings can only be applied at the port group level.

Promiscuous mode

Much like any layer-2 switching device, a virtual switch (vSwitch or VDS) will unicast traffic to someone who is connected, unless the frame is marked for broadcast or multicast. However, let us assume that your business requires you to monitor every frame of a subnet that enters the virtual switch. This is where the promiscuous mode would come in handy. When a port group is configured with the promiscuous mode set to Accept instead of Reject every vNIC connected to that port group will receive frames destined to other vNICs on the same subnet (VLAN-ID). The VM that is configured to analyze the traffic from a particular subnet (VLAN-ID) should be the only member of a separate port group with the subnet's VLAN-ID and promiscuous mode enabled.

> With VDS, the need for a separated port group can be avoided by overriding the dvPortGroup settings at the dvPort to which the analyzer VM's vNIC is connected.

MAC address changes and forged transmits

MAC address spoofing is a common threat that most layer-2 switches in the real world are protected against. Both the standard vSwitch and the VDS do offer protection against MAC spoofing via two security settings:

- MAC address changes
- Forged transmits

Let us learn about both of them in some more depth:

- **MAC address changes** apply to the traffic entering a virtual machine from the virtual switch. If MAC address changes are set to **Accept**, then it would mean that you allow the virtual machine to receive traffic originally intended for another VM, by impersonating the other VM's MAC address. For example, if VM-A wanted to receive traffic intended for VM-B, then VM-A will need to present itself with a MAC address belonging to VM-B. This is usually achieved by changing the effective MAC address (OS level). Such a VM's initial MAC address will remain unchanged. With MAC address changes set to Accept, the virtual switch will allow the effective MAC address to be different from the initial MAC address. With **MAC Address Changes** set to **Reject**, the port/dvPort to which the vNIC is connected to will be blocked, consequently the VM will stop receiving any traffic.

- **Forged transmits** apply to the traffic leaving a virtual machine and entering a virtual switch. If set to **Accept**, it allows source MAC address spoofing, meaning, a virtual machine will be allowed to send out frames with a source MAC address that is different from the initial/effective MAC address. With the option set to Reject, the virtual switch will drop the frame with a MAC address that does not match the initial/effective MAC address.

> Note that all the security settings are set to **Reject** by default on both standard vSwitch and VDS.

Traffic shaping

Both the virtual switches (vSwitch or VDS) include a traffic shaper to help aid in controlling the network transfer rates. The only difference is that the traffic shaper on the standard vSwitch can only handle the Egress traffic, but the VDS can handle both **Ingress** and **Egress**. The most common confusion is in understanding what Ingress or Egress really refers to. From a traffic shaper's standpoint anything that leaves a virtual switch (standard or VDS) is called Egress, and anything that enters a virtual switch (standard or VDS) is Ingress. Now, the next question is: can the traffic enter/exit a virtual switch from the uplinks/virtual machine? So, among the directional flows, which one is considered by the traffic shaper? The answer is: VMware cannot control what happens beyond the host's physical network adapter boundaries. Hence, the flow that we refer to is the flow between the virtual machines and the virtual switch:

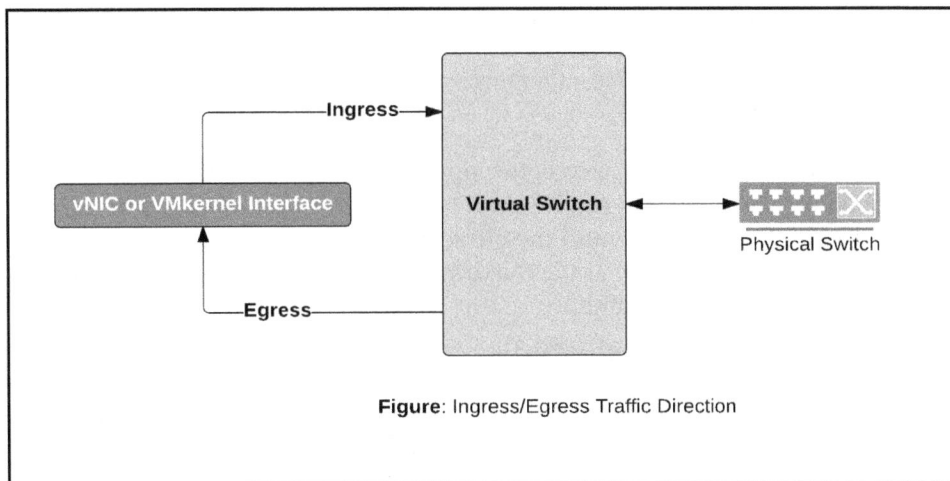

Figure: Ingress/Egress Traffic Direction

To simplify, traffic that enters a virtual switch from a virtual machine is referred to as **Ingress traffic** and the one that leaves a virtual switch towards a virtual machine is **Egress traffic**.

Traffic shaping transfer rates are expressed in kilobits per second (kbps).

The traffic shaper does its job by controlling three parameters that affect any network traffic:

- Average bandwidth
- Peak bandwidth
- Burst size

Now, let us go through each of the preceding points:

- The **average bandwidth** is the average transfer rate measured in kilobits per second (kbps) that the virtual switch can send traffic. It is a value that is normalized over time.
- The **peak bandwidth** is the maximum transfer rate measured in kilobits per second (kbps) that the virtual switch is allowed to perform at. This limit cannot be breached.
- **Burst size** is a tricky concept to understand. Although specified in kilobytes (KB), it is actually the effective amount of time measured in seconds that the virtual switch is allowed to perform at the maximum transfer rate.
- The effective amount of burst time is calculated using the following formula:

  Effective burst time = (burst size in kilobits) divided-by (peak bandwidth value in kbps)

- Let's take an example so as to better understand how the effective burst time is arrived at. If you were to set the peak bandwidth value to 4,000 kbps, the average bandwidth to 2,000 kbps, and the burst size to 2,000 KB then you are allowing the virtual switch to perform at the maximum transfer rate of 4,000 kbps lasting not more than 4 seconds in time.
- Here is how the value is arrived at:
  - Burst size in KB to be converted to kbits by multiplying the value by 8. In this case, it is 2,000 KB * 8 = 16,000 kbits.
  - Now, by applying the formula 16,000 kbits/4,000 kbps = 4 seconds

Configuring traffic shaping

Both the virtual switching constructs have made traffic shaping available at different levels within the construct. For instance, the vSwitch would let you configure it on both the vSwitch and the port groups. The settings on the port group will override the settings on the vSwitch though. However, with VDS you are not allowed to configure NIC teaming directly on the VDS; instead you can supply settings at the dvPortGroup and dvPort levels. The dvPort settings override the dvPortGroup settings.

Load balancing and failover

Now you know for a fact that workloads share not only the compute and storage resource on a server hardware but the network cards as well. There are limits on how well the network cards can serve the bandwidth needs of the virtual machines. More importantly, not every virtual machine has the same network workload characteristics. Hence, it becomes extremely critical for the virtual switches to have network load balancing and failover capabilities. Both the standard vSwitch and VDS offer several network load balancing and failover methods by letting you team up physical network adapters:

Load Balancing Method	Standard vSwitch	VDS
Route based on originating virtual port ID	Yes	Yes
Route based on source MAC hash	Yes	Yes
Route based on IP hash	Yes	Yes
Load based teaming	No	Yes
Failover method	*Standard vSwitch*	*VDS*
Use explicit failover order	Yes	Yes

Route based on virtual port ID

This is the default load balancing method for every vSwitch or VDS that is created. While this policy is set, the ports/dvPorts are assigned active physical adapters/dvUplinks in a round-robin fashion. The uplink assignment will not change unless the uplink itself becomes unavailable or if the VM is migrated/powered-off. The route based on the originating virtual port IP is known to be ideal for most workloads.

Route based on source MAC hash

This is a deprecated method of load balancing. An uplink is chosen based on the source MAC address of the frames that enter the virtual switch.

Route based on IP hash

This method uses the combined hash value of the source and destination IP addresses to choose an uplink. It is required to have the physical NICs in the same link aggregation group. If the physical NICs are cabled to different switches then those switches should be stacked. The route based on the IP hash is particularly useful if there are multiple source and destination IP addresses to calculate hashes from. For instance, if you have a web server virtual machine with clients from a different subnet then such a combination is an ideal candidate for the route based on the IP hash algorithm.

Load-based teaming (LBT)

This load balancing mechanism is only available on a VDS. Unlike the other methods, this offers true load balancing. The other methods only offer to distribute the physical adapter assignments based on their algorithms. With LBT, the initial assignment is done in a round-robin fashion, but thenceforth the physical adapters are monitored for load saturation. If any of the physical adapters hits a saturation threshold of 75%, then some of the traffic is relocated to another unsaturated physical adapter.

Use explicit failover order

This is not a load balancing or distribution method; instead it uses a pre-defined failover order to use active available physical adapters in the event of a failure. When you set load balancing to the use explicit failover order, all the traffic is traversed through a single physical adapter at any point in time. If there were to be more than one active physical adapter, then it would choose the adapter that is up and active the longest in time. For instance, if vmnic1, vmnic2, and vmnic3 are the three active uplinks, and have an uptime of 48 hours, 32 hours, and 5 minutes respectively, then vmnic1 with 48 hours of uptime is chosen. The logic behind such a choice is to select the most stable among the available adapters.

Maximum transmission unit (MTU)

Layer-2 frames have a maximum standard size of 1,500 bytes. This size is referred to as the maximum transmission unit or MTU. The MTU can be configured on both the virtual switches. Unlike the other settings that we have discussed so far, the MTU can only be configured on the virtual switches and not on their subconstructs like the port groups or ports:

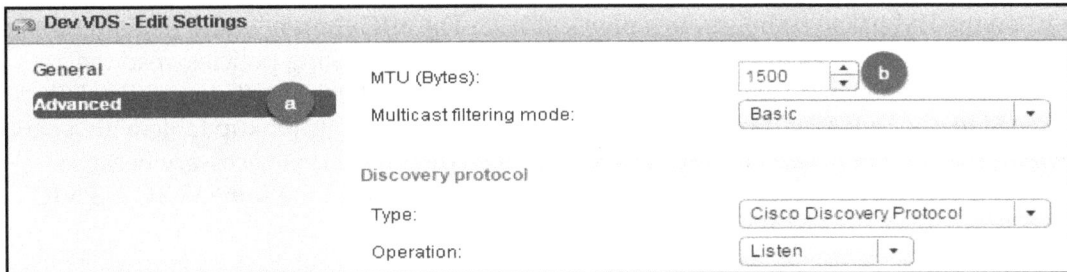

Unless you intend to enable the use of Jumbo frames in your environment there is no real need to modify this value. Jumbo frames are layer-2 frames with an MTU value that is more than *1,500 bytes*. When you configure a Jumbo frame it is critical to make sure every device along the path from the source and destination is configured to support the required MTU size.

Notify switches

Layer-2 physical switches have the ability to maintain a MAC address table, lookup table, or CAM table. The table maps MAC addresses to switch port numbers. If there is no corresponding entry for a frame's destination MAC address in the lookup table, the switch will flood the frame via every switch port, other than the source port. To reduce the occurrence of such flooding, the switch has a mechanism to learn the MAC addresses and maintain a mapping table. It does so by reading the source MAC address information from the frames that enter the switch. Now, when you cable the physical NICs of an ESXi host to the physical switch ports, the switch is expected to see the MAC addresses of a number of vNICs. The switch will only be able to add an entry into the lookup table if the VMs start to communicate. VMware, however, has the ability to proactively notify the physical switch of the virtual machine's MAC addresses so that its lookup table is up to date even before a VM begins to communicate. It achieves this by sending a gratuitous ARP (seen as a RARP frame by the switch) with vNIC's effective address as the source MAC of the RARP frame. The RARP will have the destination MAC address set to the broadcast address – *FF:FF:FF:FF:FF:FF*.

ESXi will send out an RARP under the following circumstances:

- When a virtual machine is powered-on
- When a virtual machine is migrated (VMotion) from one host to another.
- When there is an NIC failover
- When load-based teams rebind a vNIC to a different PNIC

Now, let's analyze each of the above circumstances. *When a virtual machine is powered- on*, the vNIC on the VM has to be bound to a physical NIC. The NIC chosen would depend on the load balancing policy used. To learn more about the load balancing policies, read the section, *Load balancing and failover*. When vSwitch assigns a physical NIC to a vNIC, ESXi will need to send a RARP frame to enable the switch to update its lookup table with a new physical port number mapping for the vNICs MAC address. This is necessary because every time a virtual machine is powered-on, it is not guaranteed the same vNIC to PNIC mapping.

When a virtual machine is migrated from one host to another, the vNICs of the corresponding VM will now be mapped to a physical NIC of the destination host. Hence, it becomes a proactive necessity to let the physical switch update its lookup table with a new port number for the vNIC's MAC address.

When a physical NIC failover occurs, the vNIC will be re-distributed amongst the available active adapters. Again, it becomes necessary for the physical switch to be notified of the new port numbers for the vNIC MAC addressees.

LBT automatically rebinds the vNICs to different PNICs based on the physical NIC load saturation levels. Since the vNIC to PNIC assignment is bound to change, the physical switch will need to be notified of the new port numbers of the vNIC MAC addresses.

The Notify Switches option is available in the Team and failover tab of the vSwitch, Standard Port Group, dvPortGroup, and dvPort settings:

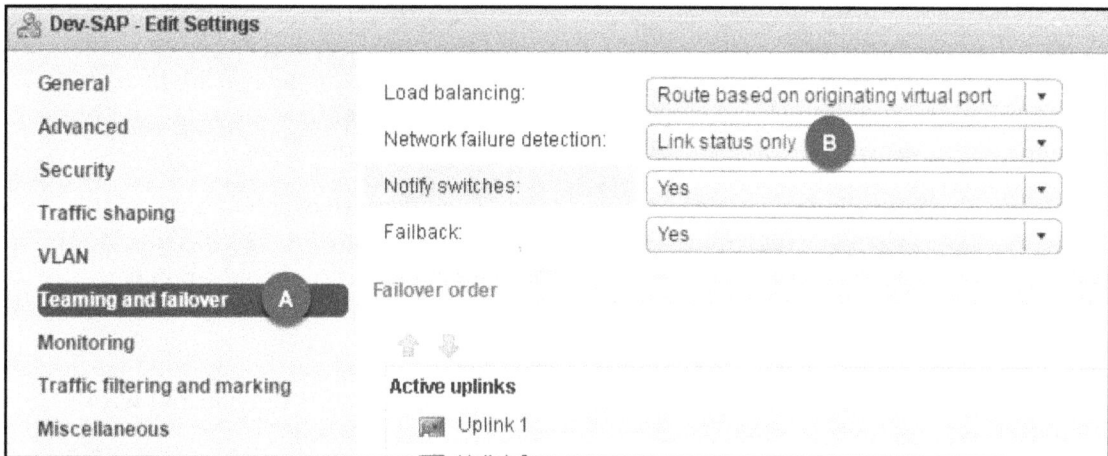

Failover order

Server hosts with a greater number of NICs can be teamed up to provide failover, performance, and redundancy. With both the virtual switches, we can control the participation of the physical adapters in different configurations. This is done by categorizing the available physical NIC into three categories:

- Active
- Standby
- Unused

Active adapters are available for use in any configuration and will carry traffic. **Standby adapters** act as backup to the active adapters and will be made active only if any of the active adapters fail. **Unused adapters** cannot be used in any of the configuration on the virtual switch construct (vSwitch, Standard port group, dvPortGroup, or dvPort).

Link aggregation protocol support and configuration

The link aggregation control protocol (LACP) allows the grouping of host physical adapters and physical switch ports to form a bigger communication pipeline increasing availability and bandwidth. Such a pipeline is referred to as an Etherchannel. The grouping of physical adapters or physical switch ports is called a link aggregation group (LAG).

LACP LAGs operates in two modes – active (dynamic) and passive (static). In **dynamic mode**, the LAG is in an active mode sending LACP PDUs negotiating LACP status and configuration. In **static mode**, the LAG is in a passive mode waiting on LACP PDUs from the active LAG. At least one of the LAGs in an Etherchannel should be in active mode for the LACP to work.

Prior to VDS 5.5, VMware supported the use of LACP (static mode), but starting with VDS 5.5 the support for the dynamic link aggregation group was enabled.

Configuring LACP is a five-step procedure:

1. Identify the NICs and ports to be part of the LAG and make sure that they have the same speed and duplex settings.
2. Create LAGs on the VDS.
3. Assign host physical NICs to the VDS LAG interfaces.
4. Configure the LAG at the physical switch in dynamic (active) mode.
5. Configure a dvPortGroup to use the LAG as the only active uplink.

> A LAG cannot be created on a standard vSwitch. It can be done only on a vSphere distributed switch.

The following figure is a logical depiction of what we will need to achieve for an Ether channel between an ESXi host and a physical switch:

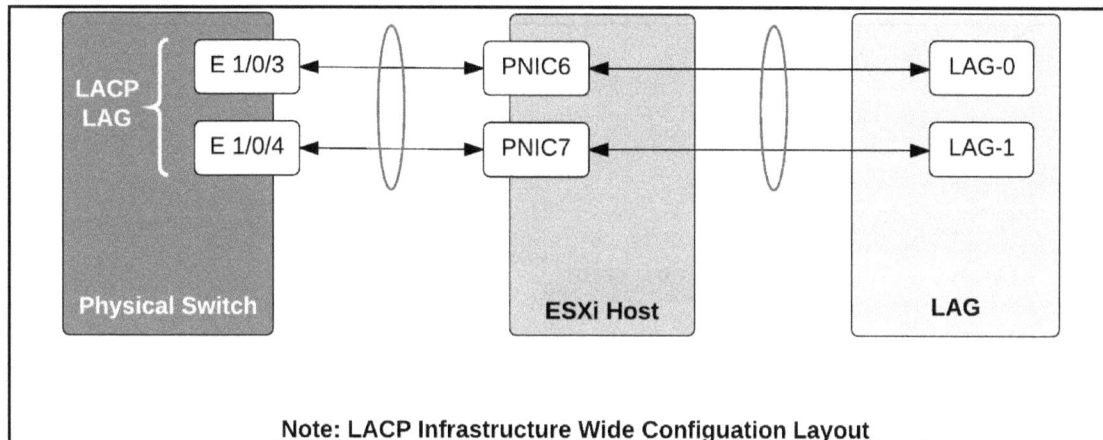

Note: LACP Infrastructure Wide Configuation Layout

Creating, configuring, and using LAGs on a VDS

This section covers the procedure involved in creating and using a LAG on a vSphere distributed switch. Keep in mind that configuring LAGs on the VDS alone will not create an Etherchannel. It would require you to configure LAGs on both the VDS and the physical switch to form an Etherchannel.

You can configure up to a maximum of 64 LAGs on a VDS of version 5.5 and above. Prior to VDS 5.5, we were allowed to create only a single LAG per VDS. Each LAG can have up to 24 LAG ports, meaning, from a VDS's perspective, every participating ESXi can map up to 24 physical NICs mapped to a single LAG.

The following procedure will guide you through the steps required to create, configure, and use LAGs on a VDS:

1. Use the Networking inventory to locate the desired VDS.
2. With the VDS selected, navigate to **Manage** I **Settings** I **LACP**.

3. At the **LACP** settings screen, click on the green plus ⊞ icon to bring up the **New Link Aggregation Group** window:

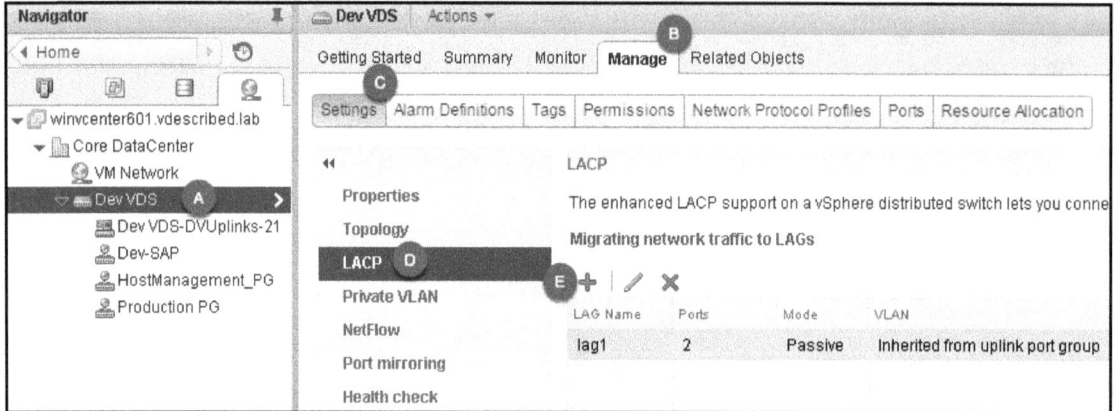

4. At the **New Link Aggregation Group** window, supply a name for the LAG, the number of ports needed, the mode (passive/active), and the load balancing mode. Once the desired selections have been made, click **OK** to confirm the settings:

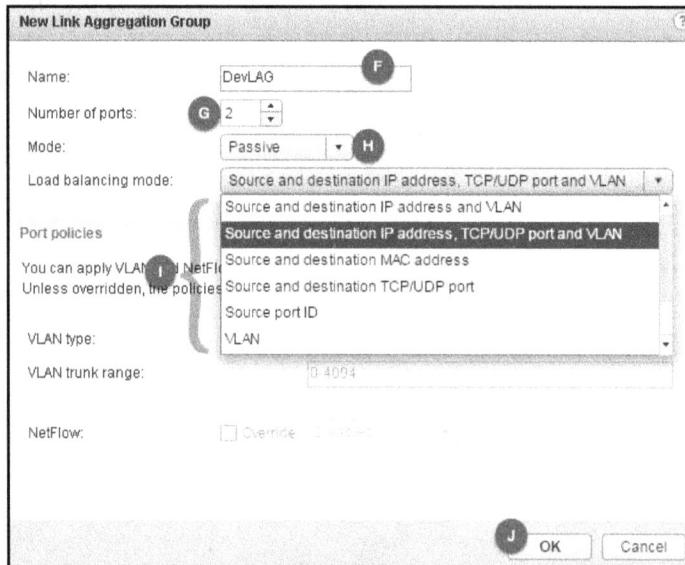

5. Back at the LACP settings screen, you should now see the new LACP listed:

6. Now, with the LAG created, the next step is to map physical NICs to the LAG ports. This can be done in an unobtrusive manner if the suggestions listed in the **Migrating Network Traffic to Link Aggregation Groups** is followed. To bring up the window click on the URL **Migrating network traffic to LAGs**:

7. The window offers direct links to the Manage Distributed Port Groups and the Add and Manage Hosts wizard. As per the recommendations:

a) Set the newly created LAG to Standby Uplink on the desired dvPortGroup. This is done by managing the **Teaming and failover** port group policy in the wizard:

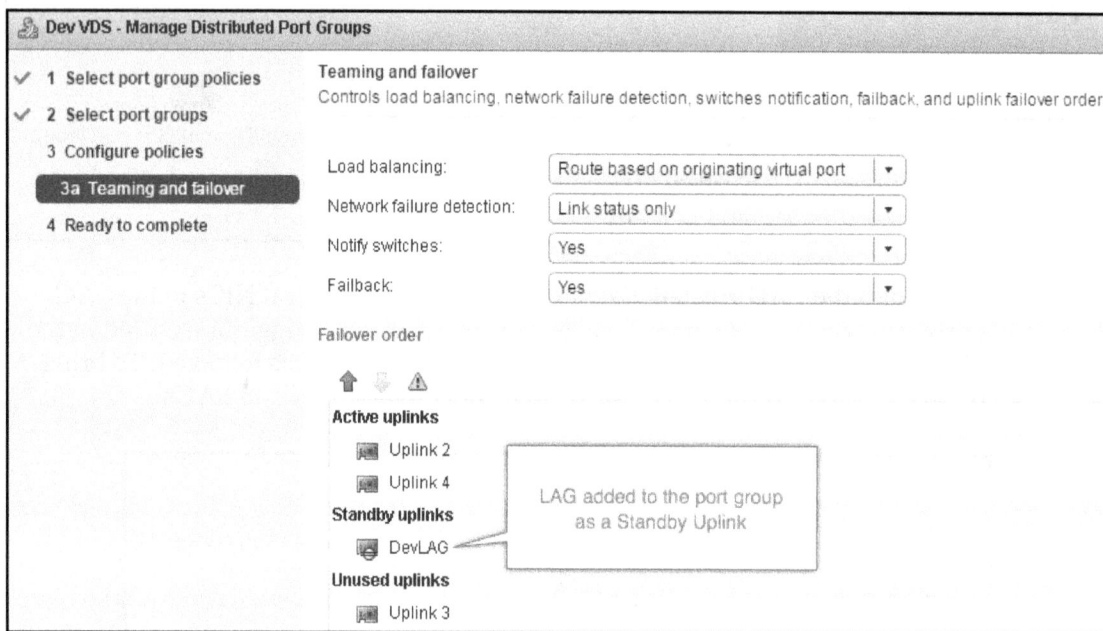

You will be warned about the use of a LAG as a standby uplink. This is expected, so click **OK** to ignore the warning:

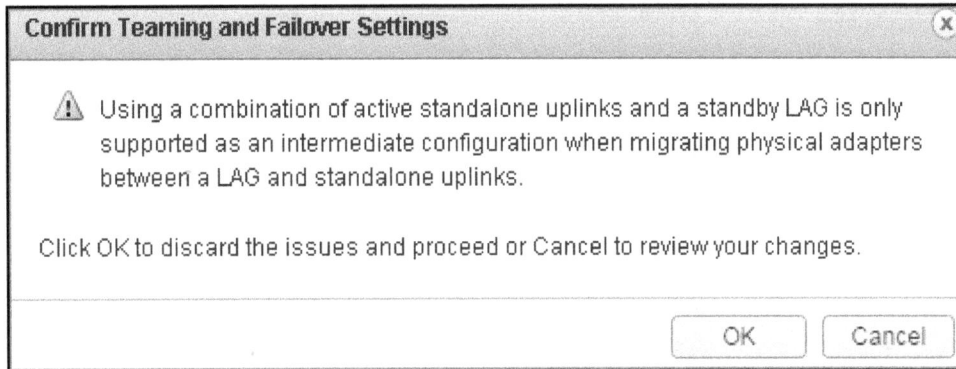

Confirm Teaming and Failover Settings ⊗

⚠ Using a combination of active standalone uplinks and a standby LAG is only supported as an intermediate configuration when migrating physical adapters between a LAG and standalone uplinks.

Click OK to discard the issues and proceed or Cancel to review your changes.

            OK   Cancel

---

b) Map the desired host physical adapters to the LAG ports. Use the **Manage physical adapters** option in the wizard to achieve this:

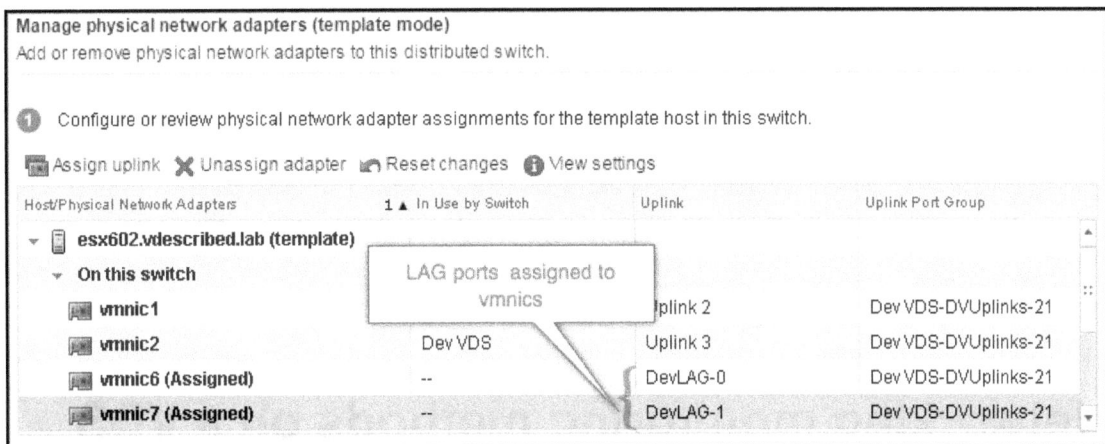

Manage physical network adapters (template mode)
Add or remove physical network adapters to this distributed switch.

① Configure or review physical network adapter assignments for the template host in this switch.

🔲 Assign uplink ✖ Unassign adapter ↩ Reset changes ① View settings

Host/Physical Network Adapters	1 ▲ In Use by Switch	Uplink	Uplink Port Group
▼ 🖥 esx602.vdescribed.lab (template)			
▼ On this switch			
🖼 vmnic1		Uplink 2	Dev VDS-DVUplinks-21
🖼 vmnic2	Dev VDS	Uplink 3	Dev VDS-DVUplinks-21
🖼 vmnic6 (Assigned)	--	DevLAG-0	Dev VDS-DVUplinks-21
🖼 vmnic7 (Assigned)	--	DevLAG-1	Dev VDS-DVUplinks-21

> LAG ports assigned to vmnics

---

c) Reconfigure the dvPortGroup and make the LAG the only active uplink and the other unused:

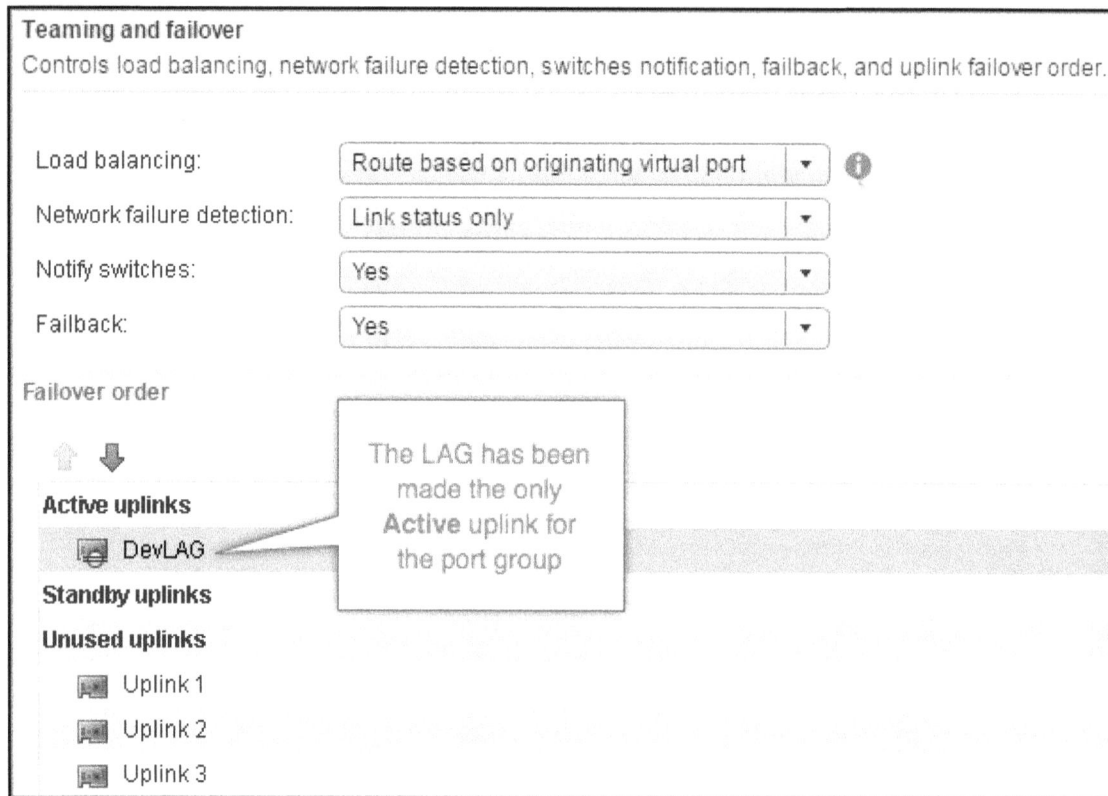

Teaming and failover
Controls load balancing, network failure detection, switches notification, failback, and uplink failover order.

Load balancing:	Route based on originating virtual port ▼ ⓘ
Network failure detection:	Link status only ▼
Notify switches:	Yes ▼
Failback:	Yes ▼

Failover order

⇧ ⇩

Active uplinks

   🖳 DevLAG ◄─── The LAG has been made the only **Active** uplink for the port group

Standby uplinks

Unused uplinks

   📺 Uplink 1

   📺 Uplink 2

   📺 Uplink 3

Networking monitoring methods on a VDS

Most environments will need a method to monitor the network traffic in one form or the other. Two of the common methods in real-world networking are SPAN (Switch Port Analyzer) and NetFlow. VMware employs both these concepts on the VDS:

- SPAN is simply referred to as port mirroring on a VDS
- NetFlow

Port mirroring

If there is a need to clone vNIC traffic for capturing or monitoring purposes, then that can be achieved by configuring port mirroring on a VDS. It supports four types of mirror sessions:

1. **Distributed port mirroring** – this is used to mirror traffic from vNIC-assigned dvPorts to other vNIC-assigned dvPorts across hosts.
2. **Remote mirroring source** – this is used to mirror traffic from vNIC-assigned dvPorts to an uplink or a set of uplinks on one or more hosts.
3. **Remote mirroring destination** – this is used to mirror traffic from one or more VLANs to one or more vNIC-assigned dvPorts on one or more hosts.
4. **Encapsulated remote mirroring (L3) source** – this is used to mirror traffic from one or more vNIC-assigned dvPorts to a packet capture or monitoring machine in the network. The mirror destination in this case is specified using the IP address of the monitoring machine.

Distributed port mirroring configuration options

To configure distributed port mirroring, identify the source and destination VM to establish a mirroring session and launch the **Add Port Mirroring Session** wizard:

1. Identify and select the desired VDS from the Networking inventory.
2. Navigate to **Manage** | **Settings** | **Port Mirroring**.
3. At the **Port Mirroring** settings screen, click **New** to bring up the **Add Port Mirroring Session** wizard:

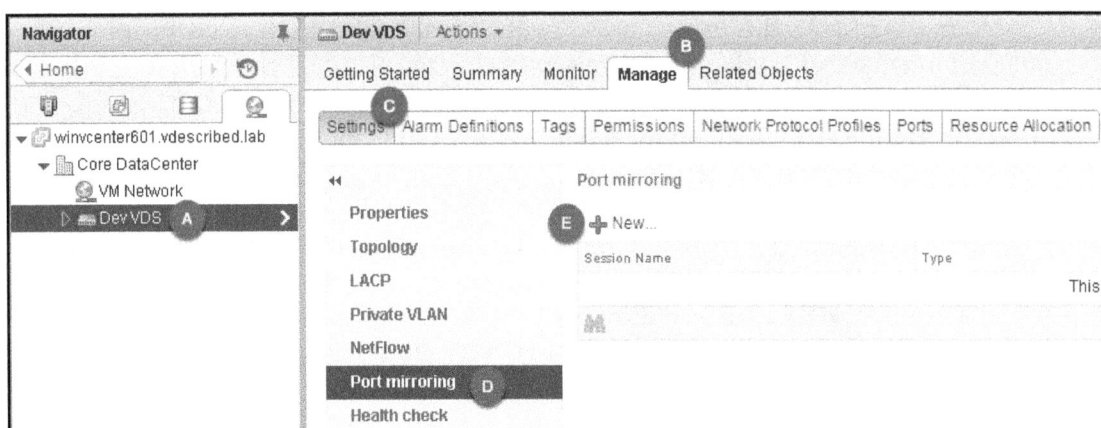

The options presented in the wizard can vary depending on the type of mirroring session you choose. The GUI operations are fairly straightforward, so, we will not be covering a step-by-step procedure for each of the session types. Instead, in this section, we will cover all the options available and their meaning, so that it will help you make a configuration decision while using the wizard.

Once you choose the session type, the wizard has three screens wherein you could supply session configuration details:

- Edit Properties
- Select Sources
- Select Destinations

We will categorize the configuration options available into those.

Edit properties

We have the following configuration entities under this category:

- **Name** – a string used to identify the session defined.
- **Status** – this can be set to either enabled/disabled.
- **Normal I/O on destination ports** – this will let you choose whether or not to allow regular traffic along with the mirrored traffic on the destination port. For instance, if the destination vNIC-assigned dvPort is the only port in use by the VM, then you might want to allow regular traffic on that as well.
- **Mirrored Packet Length (Bytes)** – this is used to set a limit of the mirror packet length in bytes. Leave this untouched unless you have not configured your destination monitoring tool to breakdown the packet per its requirement.
- **Sampling Rate** – this is used to define the number of packets to be mirrored. The default value of 1, will mirror every packet in the traffic. If you set it to 5, then every fifth packet is mirrored.
- **Description** – this is an optional field, unless you want to use it for notes.
- **Encapsulation VLAN ID** – this is made available only for the remote mirroring source session type. Since the destination of this mirroring type are uplinks, it is quite possible that the uplinks are trunked for a different VLAN. Therefore, it becomes necessary to encapsulate the frames in using the uplink's VLAN ID. If the source dvPorts are on a different VLAN themselves then you could choose the option **Preserve original VLAN** to double encapsulate the frames that are being mirrored.

Select sources and destination

The following table compares the select sources options available based on the mirror session types:

Mirroring Session Type	Available Sources type	Available Destination type
Distributed port mirroring	dvPorts	dvPorts
Remote mirroring source	dvPorts	Uplinks
Remote mirroring destination	VLAN ID	dvPorts
Encapsulated remote mirroring (L3) source	dvPorts	IP Address
Distributed port mirroring (legacy)	dvPorts	dvPorts and Uplinks

NetFlow

NetFlow is drastically different from port mirroring. NetFlow doesn't need a copy of the same traffic to be transferred somewhere else. Instead, it is used to let the NetFlow monitoring software gain insight into the metadata of the traffic on the VDS. VMware supports NetFlow version 10.

Assuming that there is already a NetFlow collection running in your environment, let's begin configuring the VDS for NetFlow:

1. Use the **Networking** inventory to locate and select the desired VDS.
2. With the VDS selected, navigate to **Manage** | **Settings** | **Netflow**.
3. In the **Netflow** settings page, click on **Edit**.
4. In the **Edit NetFlow Settings** screen, supply the following information:

   - **Collector IP Address** – this is the IP address of the NetFlow collector machine in your environment.
      - **Collector Port** – UDP port 2055 is the most widely used NetFlow collector port number.
      - **Observation Domain ID** – this is the observation ID of the NetFlow collector. This information can be obtained from the NetFlow collector machine.

- **Switch IP address** – this is just a representative IP address and not the real one. This doesn't make the VDS part of any network. It only provides a unique ID to the VDS in the NetFlow monitoring software.
- **Active flow export timeout** – the amount of time measured in seconds that the VDS will wait before it begins to fragment an active traffic flow and send the data to the NetFlow monitor.
- **Idle flow export timeout** – the amount of time measured in seconds that VDS will wait before it begins to fragment an idle flow and sends the data to the NetFlow monitor.
- **Sampling rate** – this value determines the number and frequency of the packet collection. The default 0 will collect every packet. If the value is set to 5, then it collects every fifth packet.
- **Process internal flows only** – this is used to collect data from traffic that never leave an ESXi host. For instance, traffic between two VMs in the same VLAN and same host does not have to leave the host:

Dev VDS - Edit NetFlow Settings		?
Collector IP address:	192.168.70.33	
Collector port:	2055	
Observation Domain ID:	0	
Switch IP address:	4.4.4.4	ⓘ
Advanced settings		
Active flow export timeout (Seconds):	60	
Idle flow export timeout (Seconds):	15	
Sampling rate:	0	
Process internal flows only:	Disabled	
	OK	Cancel

5. Once done, you can now enable NetFlow on individual dvPortGorups:

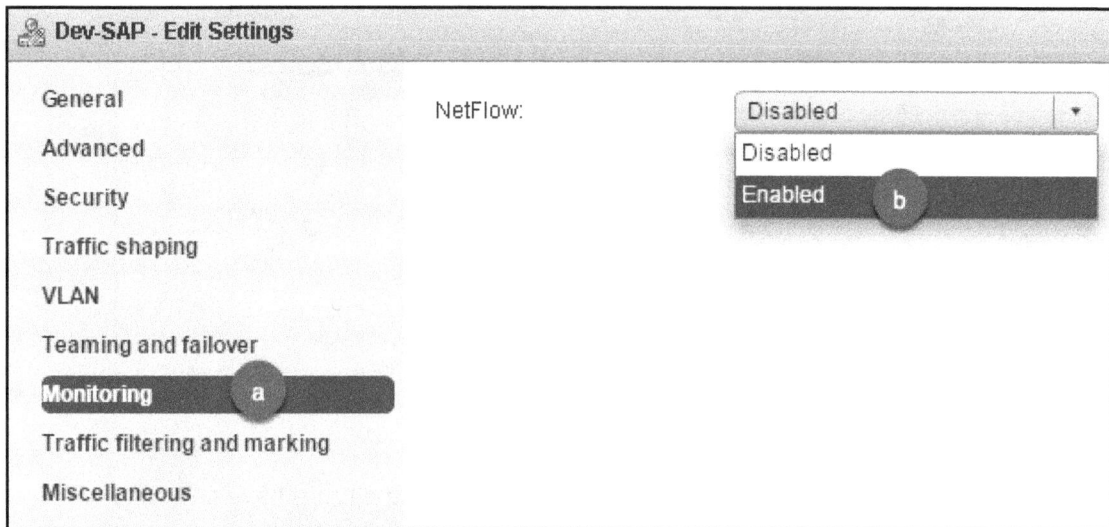

Bandwidth management using Network I/O Control (NetIOC)

Considering the fact that we now consolidate virtual machines with different workload characteristics less the number of hosts, the network I/O generated by these workloads can impose huge bandwidth requirements on the network adapters. Also, as the number of virtual machines increases, it takes some effort to monitor and control the bandwidth utilization of the workloads.

We did learn about using traffic shaping earlier in this chapter, but that has to be done as per the network construct level. NetIOC, however, operates at the vCenter level, giving it a bird's eye view of all the traffic types in a VDS. It can set bandwidth reservations, shares, limits, and so on to control the bandwidth utilization by controlling noisy neighbor situations.

NetIOC has this intrinsic ability to detect system traffic type and control its bandwidth usage based on shares, reservations, and limits. There are nine system traffic types as shown in the following screenshot:

Traffic Type	Shares	1 ▲ Shares Value	Reservation	Limit
Virtual Machine Traffic	High	100	0 Mbit/s	Unlimited
Fault Tolerance (FT) Traffic	Normal	50	0 Mbit/s	Unlimited
vMotion Traffic	Normal	50	0 Mbit/s	Unlimited
iSCSI Traffic	Normal	50	0 Mbit/s	Unlimited
Management Traffic	Normal	50	0 Mbit/s	Unlimited
NFS Traffic	Normal	50	0 Mbit/s	Unlimited
vSphere Replication (VR) Traffic	Normal	50	0 Mbit/s	Unlimited
Virtual SAN Traffic	Normal	50	0 Mbit/s	Unlimited
vSphere Data Protection Backup Traffic	Normal	50	0 Mbit/s	Unlimited

You might have already noticed that none of the system traffic types have any reservations on them yet. We are allowed to set a reservation on each of the traffic types by editing their settings:

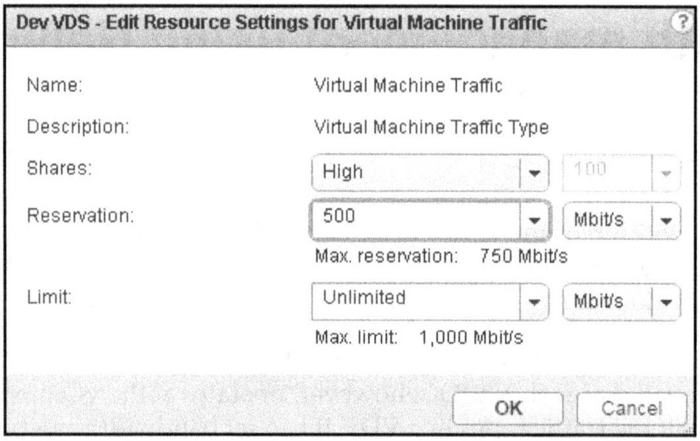

Dev VDS - Edit Resource Settings for Virtual Machine Traffic (?)

Name:	Virtual Machine Traffic
Description:	Virtual Machine Traffic Type
Shares:	High ▼	100 ▼
Reservation:	500 ▼	Mbit/s ▼
	Max. reservation: 750 Mbit/s
Limit:	Unlimited ▼	Mbit/s ▼
	Max. limit: 1,000 Mbit/s

OK   Cancel

In the preceding screenshot, I have set a reservation of 500 Mbps for the virtual machine traffic type. With such a reservation set regardless of the bandwidth requirements from other traffic types, all the virtual machine traffic is guaranteed a combined bandwidth of 500 Mbps. We are allowed to set similar reservations/limits or even modify shares of every system traffic type.

Creating network resource pools

We can also create custom network resource pools for virtual machines. These resource pools can be associated with any dvPortGroups with virtual machines mapped to them. Such custom resource pools can only be used to set bandwidth reservations in Mbps. Reservations are always met and any leftover bandwidth is allocated to different traffic types based on the relative share values:

1. With the VDS selected, navigate to **Manage** | **Resource Allocation** | **Network resource pools**. Before you can create your first network resource pools, you are required to reserve a certain amount of bandwidth for the virtual machine system traffic type. Click on **Reserve bandwidth for virtual machine system traffic**:

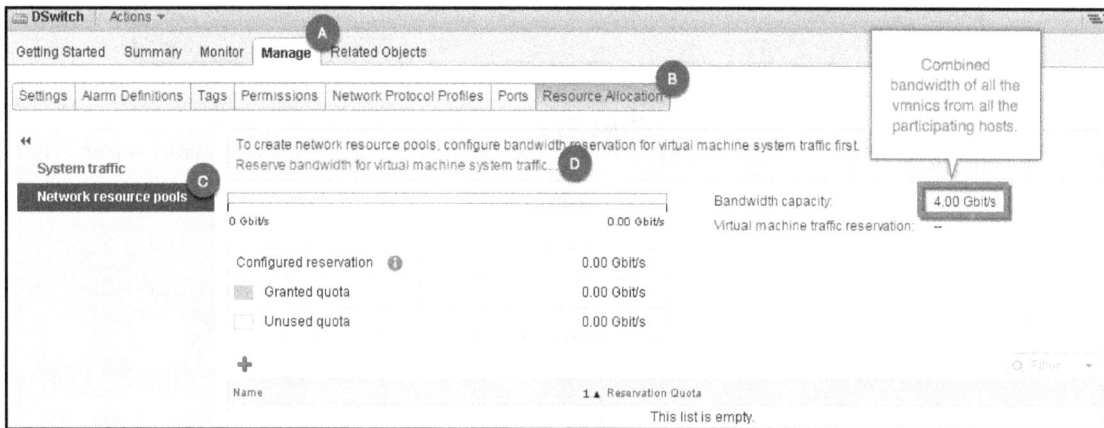

In the **Edit Resource Settings for Virtual Machine Traffic** window, leave the **Shares** value at **High** and set a **Reservation**. This reservation is a bandwidth reservation per physical NIC. In this case, I am setting it to **500** Mbps:

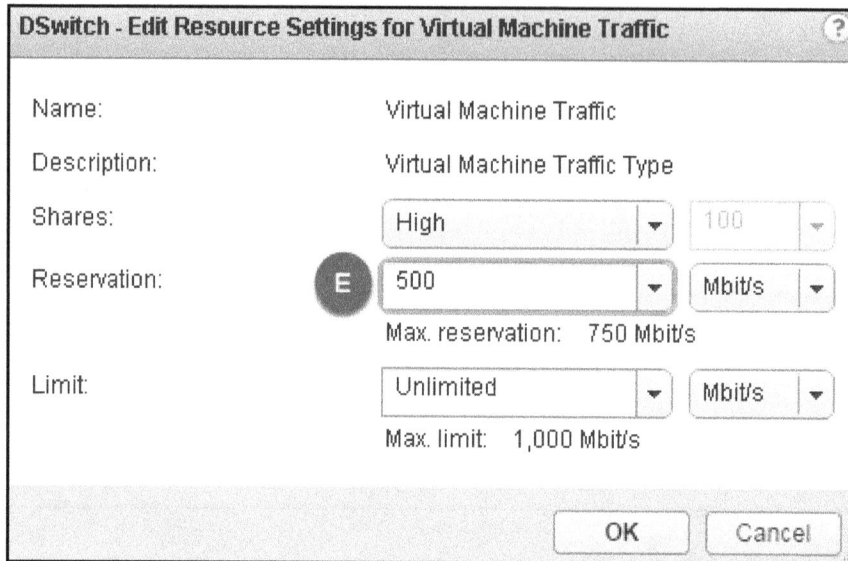

```
DSwitch - Edit Resource Settings for Virtual Machine Traffic        (?)

  Name:                          Virtual Machine Traffic

  Description:                   Virtual Machine Traffic Type

  Shares:                        High              ▼    100    ▼

  Reservation:         (E)       500               ▼    Mbit/s  ▼
                                 Max. reservation:  750 Mbit/s

  Limit:                         Unlimited         ▼    Mbit/s  ▼
                                 Max. limit:  1,000 Mbit/s

                                            OK        Cancel
```

2. Now you should see the **Configured reservation** equivalent to the total number of participating physical NICs multiplied by the bandwidth reservation per NIC:

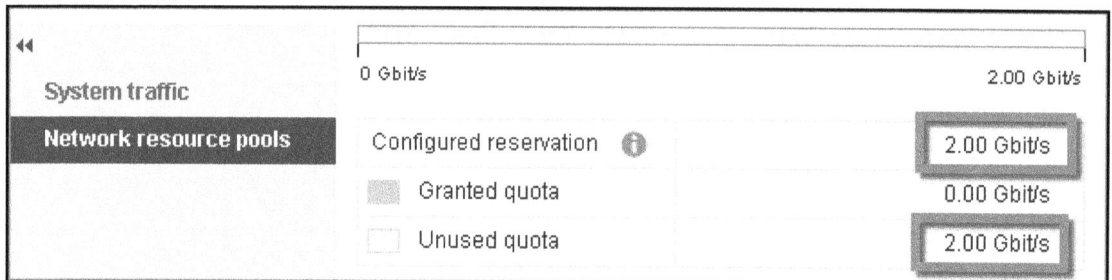

```
 ◀◀
                                0 Gbit/s                          2.00 Gbit/s
     System traffic

     Network resource pools     Configured reservation  ⓘ          2.00 Gbit/s

                                ▒ Granted quota                    0.00 Gbit/s

                                □ Unused quota                     2.00 Gbit/s
```

It is from this unused reservation quota that you could further divide the reservation among the network resource pools.

3. Click on the green plus ⊞ icon to bring up the **New Network Resource Pool** window. Supply a **Name** and the **Reservation quota** in Mbps/Gbps. In this case, I am reserving a bandwidth of 1 Gbps (1,000 Mbps) for the newly created network resource pool:

4. The next step is to assign the network resource pool to the desired dvPortGroup. This is done by editing the setting of the port group and under the **General** settings page, choosing the **Network Resource pool** to be assigned to the port group:

With the configuration, the port group is guaranteed to receive the reserved bandwidth regardless of the bandwidth requirement from other virtual machine traffic.

Understanding the use of shares

The configuration of NetIOC has been hugely simplified with the introduction of reservations. But shares also play a very critical role in allocating unreserved bandwidth amongst the contenders based on the share values. In this section, we will try to understand how shares work, with an example.

Let's take into account the default share value configuration of medium (50) for the traffic types vMotion, Management, and vSphere replication:

- Assume that all the three traffic types have to be configured to use an uplink that has a bandwidth of 10Gbps.
- Since each of the traffic types has a share value of 50, the cumulative share value for all the three traffic types is 150 on the uplink.
- During contention, each of the traffic types will get (50/150) *100 = 33% of the total bandwidth.
- That translates to 33% of 5,000 Mbps which is approximately 1.6 Gbps for each traffic type.

Summary

This chapter covered vSphere networking in detail. We covered the need for virtual switches in a vSphere environment and the differences between standard and distributed virtual switches. You learned how to create and manage the virtual switches (standard or distributed). From there you learned more about virtual switch security settings, traffic shaping, load balancing, and failover. Finally, you learned about the network monitoring methods and bandwidth management using network I/O control.

We are now all set to configure other services such as iSCSI or NFS, which will be discussed in the next chapter.

5

vSphere Storage Concepts and Management

A modern day virtual data center will need some sort of shared storage to hold all the virtual machine data or other files necessary to run the services that will be hosted on the infrastructure. It could be a direct attached or remote shared storage. Access to shared storage is required to enable most of the cluster features such as vSphere HA, DRS, and vSphere FT. In this chapter, you will learn how to plan, implement, and manage storage access to a vSphere infrastructure.

We shall cover the following topics in this chapter:

- Local versus remote storage
- Storage Protocols
- Pluggable storage architecture
- Storage Array types
- Configuring access to Fiber channel storage
- Configuring access to iSCSI Storage
- Configuring access to NFS storage
- Datastore management
- Storage I/O control
- Storage DRS

Local versus remote storage

ESXi supports the use of both local and remote storage. Local storage is a category that includes storage devices directly installed inside the server or any type of directly attached storage solution. Remote storage is a category that includes storage devices accessed over either the Ethernet or Fiber channel network:

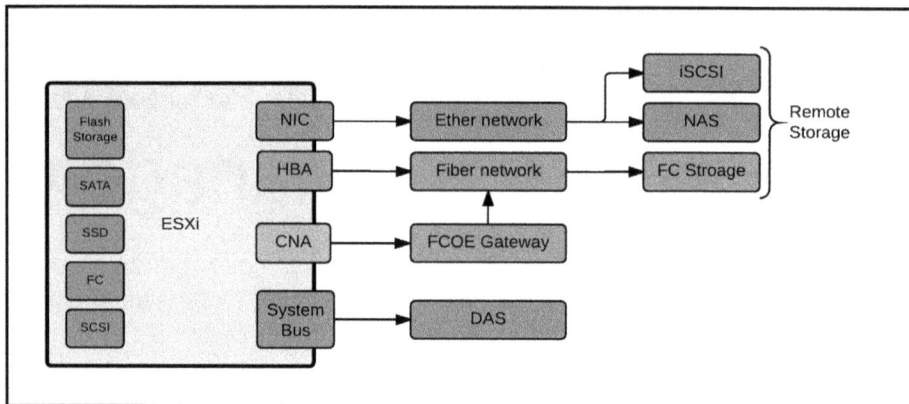

When you design an environment with no remote storage, special care should be taken to use supported hard disk types. VMware ESXi supports the following disk types:

- SATA
- SCSI
- IDE
- USB
- SAS

The type of hard disks used at the remote storage could be of any type supported by the storage array. This is because the remote storage is accessed over an already supported interface such as a network adapter (NIC) or a storage initiator (FC HBA).

Storage Protocols

When designing a vSphere infrastructure, it is important to understand that there is a variety of industry standard Storage Pprotocols to choose from. VMware supports the use of the most common ones that include **Fiber Channel (FC)**, **Internet SCSI (iSCSI)**, **Network File System (NFS)**, and **Fiber Channel Over Ethernet (FCoE)**.

The **Fiber Channel** (**FC**) protocol is used to encapsulate SCSI frames and send them natively over FC cables:

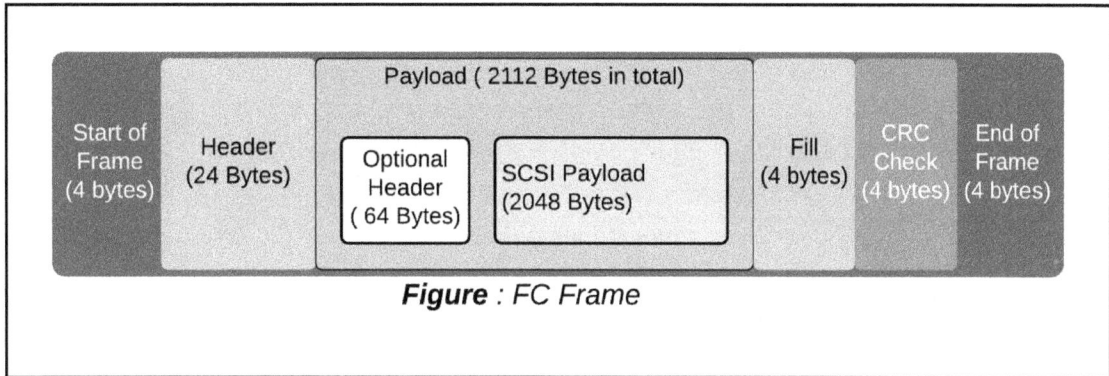

Figure : *FC Frame*

Any device that requires accessing data on an FC array will need a hardware initiator device called the **Host Bus Adapter** (**HBA**). The endpoint at the storage array is called storage processor, storage controller, or service processor. HBAs and the storage controllers connect to an **FC Switch**:

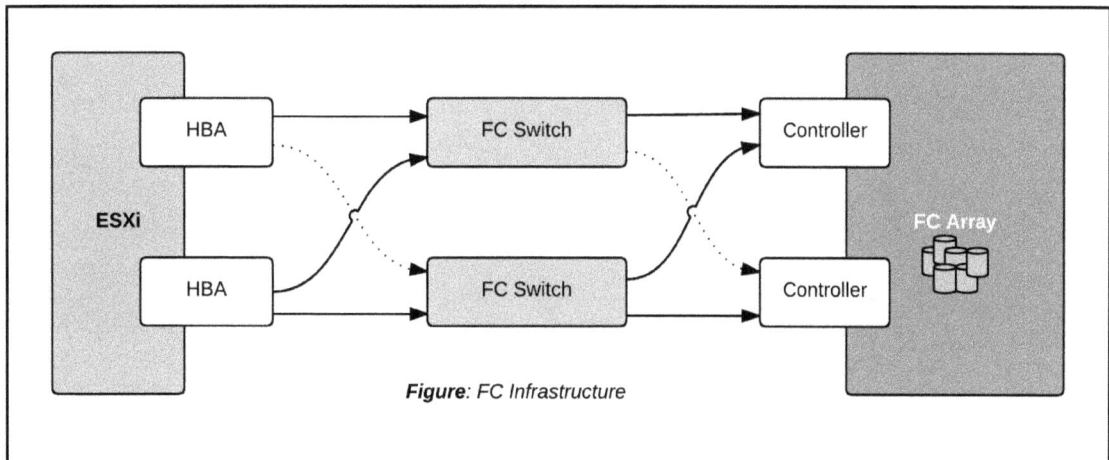

Figure: *FC Infrastructure*

The FC storage fabric management is performed at the Fabric Switches (**FC Switch**) by creating access zones or segments for the initiators accessing the storage array. Figure *FC Infrastructure* shows eight possible access paths to each of the array controllers. VMware maintains a list of compatible FC arrays, HBAs. This information can be fetched using various search filters using the VMware Compatibility Guide. You will learn about creating and managing FC datastores in the *Datastore Management* section of this chapter.

FCoE is a protocol that can be used to encapsulate an FC payload in an Ethernet frame. The FC payload includes the SCSI command in an FC frame:

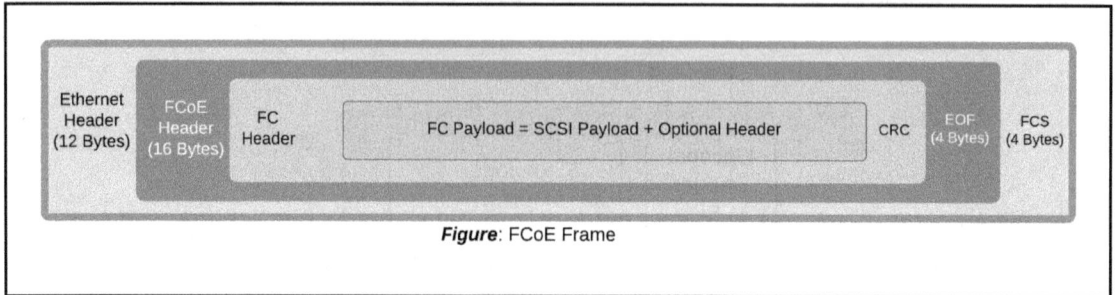

Figure: FCoE Frame

Setting up an FCoE infrastructure will require the procurement of **Converged Network Adapters (CNA)**, FCoE Switches, and a lossless Ethernet infrastructure. Keep in mind that the FCoE does not use TCP/IP for its communication:

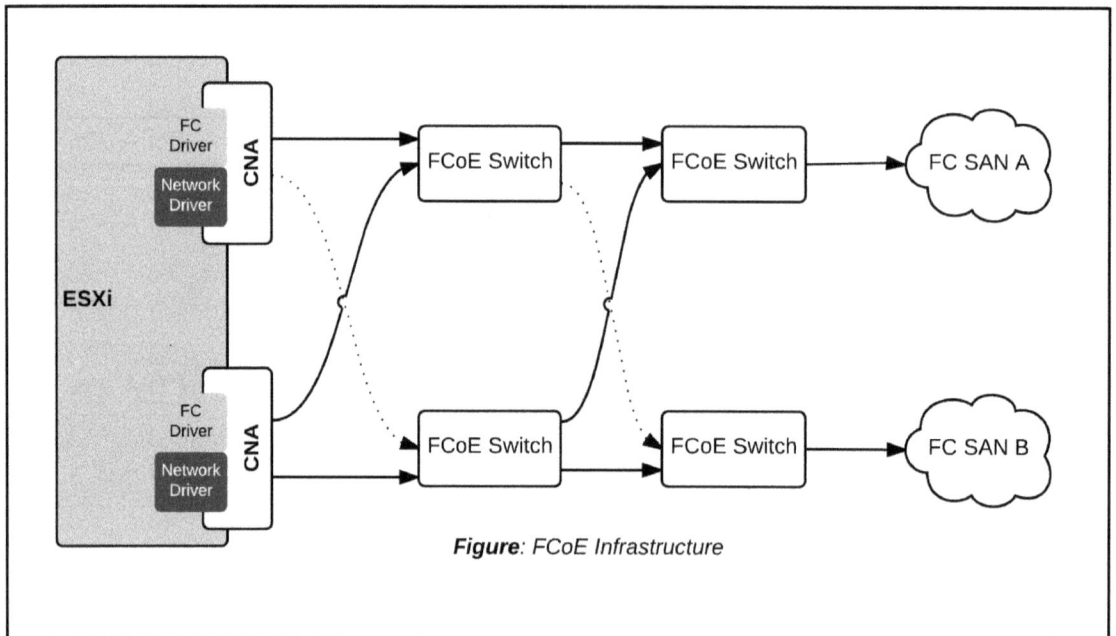

Figure: FCoE Infrastructure

Internet SCSI (iSCSI) is used to send SCSI commands over a TCP/IP infrastructure:

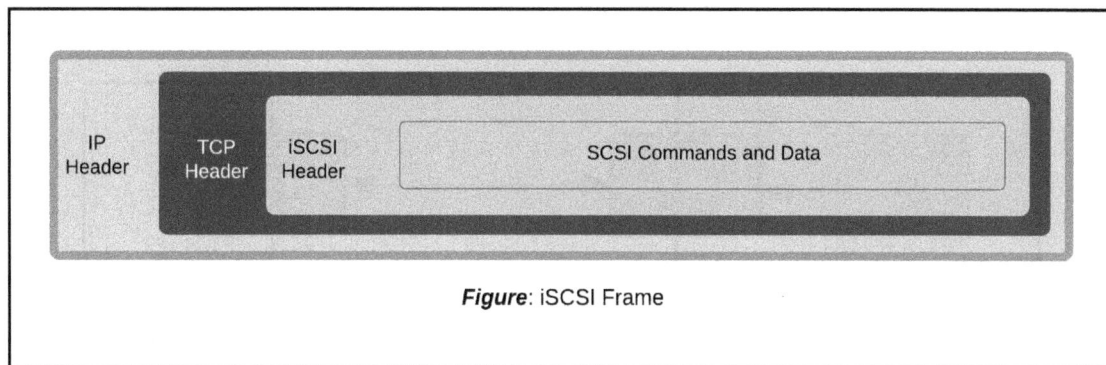

Figure: iSCSI Frame

One of the main benefits of iSCSI is that it does not enforce the need to procure special hardware to form a communication channel. It can simply use the existing TCP/IP infrastructure in the data center to communicate with the iSCSI storage array:

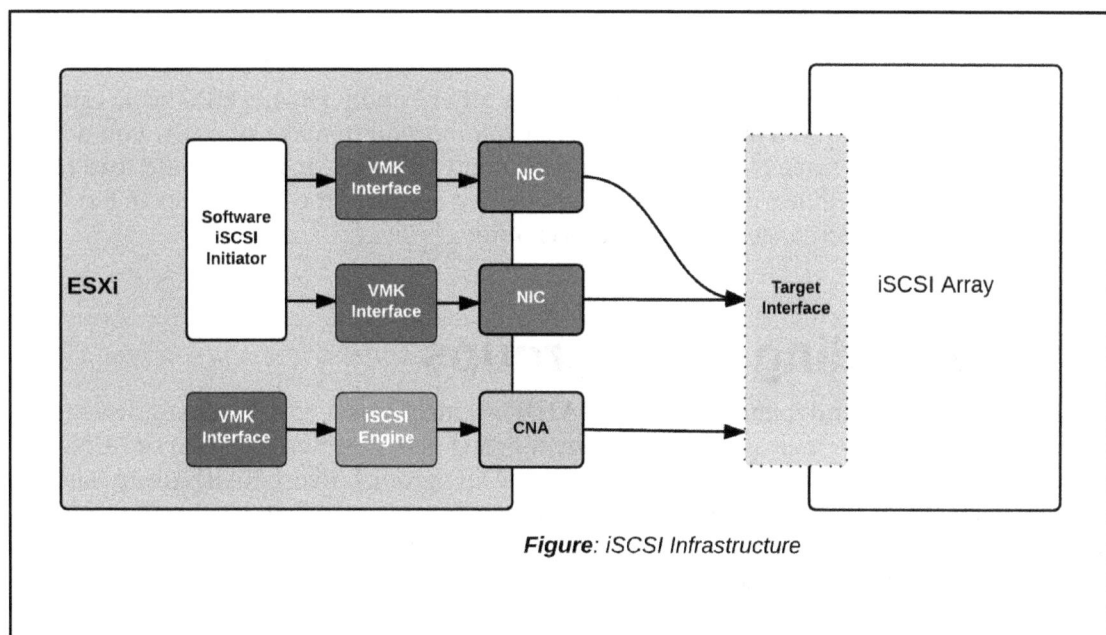

Figure: iSCSI Infrastructure

You will learn about configuring access to iSCSI LUNs in the *Configuring access to iSCSI storage* section of this chapter.

Network File System (**NFS**) is used to access filesystem shares over the TCP/IP network:

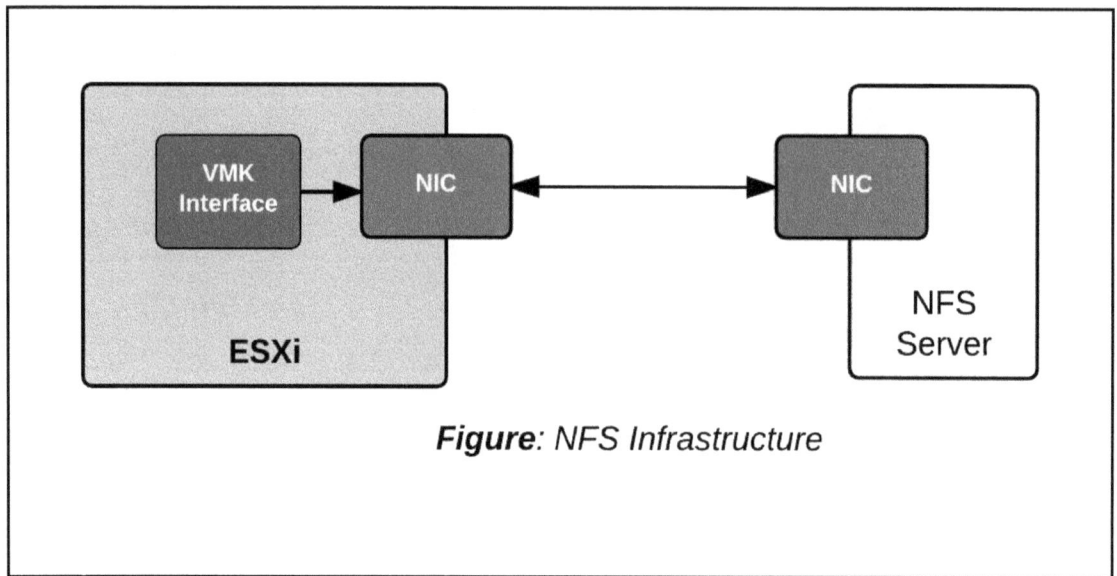

Figure: NFS Infrastructure

VMware vSphere 6 now supports the NFS versions NFSv3 and NFSv4.1. ESXi hosts can be configured to access the NFS mounts; however, it is important to make sure that you do not configure access to the same NFS mount using different NFS versions. This could lead to data corruption. You will learn more about configuring access to the NFS shares in the *Configuring access to NFS storage* section of this chapter.

Understanding RAID groups

Redundant Array Of Independent Disks (**RAID**) is a mechanism to group hard disks to form the foundation for logical units of storage. Logical disk partitions (drives) or LUNs with file systems or RAW LUNs can be hosted on RAID groups. Every RAID group has two main characteristics: performance and fault tolerance. Having said that, it is important to understand that there are different types of RAID groups based on two principles that dictate how the data destined to the disk group will be written, and they are striping and mirroring:

- **Striping** refers to the act of distributing the blocks of data to be written onto all the disks in the RAID group
- **Mirroring** refers to the act of writing identical copies of data to more than one disk

Striping and mirroring form the basis of all the other type of RAID groups that can be created. Although, understanding every possible RAID level is beyond the scope of this book, we will review a few that are commonly used in a modern day data center. With RAID space, utilization is at a maximum if you have identically sized hard disks, or else the size of the smallest disk will become the usable segment size from logical disk units (drives) using this RAID group. For example, if you have three hard disks with the sizes 50 GB, 100 GB, and 200 GB, then the usable segment size is reduced to 50 GB, therefore leaving unused space on the 100 GB (*50 GB unused*) and 150 GB (*100 GB unused*) hard disks.

RAID-0 or **striping** requires a minimum of two disks. The data blocks are sequentially distributed (written) onto the available disks. This is a performance-only setup and there is zero fault tolerance, as the loss of a single disk would make the data on the disk group unusable.

RAID-1 or **mirroring** requires a minimum of two disks. Identical copies of the data blocks are maintained on a disk pair. This RAID is fault tolerant; it delivers a doubled READ rate and a single hard disk's WRITE performance.

RAID-10 requires a minimum of four hard disks. This RAID level is a striped group of a mirrored set of disks. It is a RAID-0 (striped) grouping of RAID-1 (mirrored) disks. That is, if there are two mirrored sets of disks then the data is striped across the mirrored set and not within the mirrored set of disks. This RAID level offers excellent performance and data redundancy making it fault tolerant.

RAID-5 requires a minimum of three hard disks. It uses striping to distribute data blocks on to the hard disks in the group, but also distributes parity information across. This RAID level can sustain the failure of a single hard disk and offers good performance.

Logical Unit Number (LUN)

A **Logical Unit Number (LUN)** is a number assigned to a *logical disk unit* formed at a storage array. It is a unit of storage that can be uniquely identified regardless of the storage protocol (FC/iSCSI/FCoE). The logical disk unit is also referred to as a *LUN device*. A LUN device is also assigned a unique **NAA ID** (**Network Address Authority Identifier**).

A storage array is nothing but an array of hard disks either of the same type or of different types depending on the type, model, and the planned configuration of storage arrays. The disks are grouped into RAID groups to provide for performance and recoverability service level agreements. These RAID groups can cater storage space to one or more LUN devices:

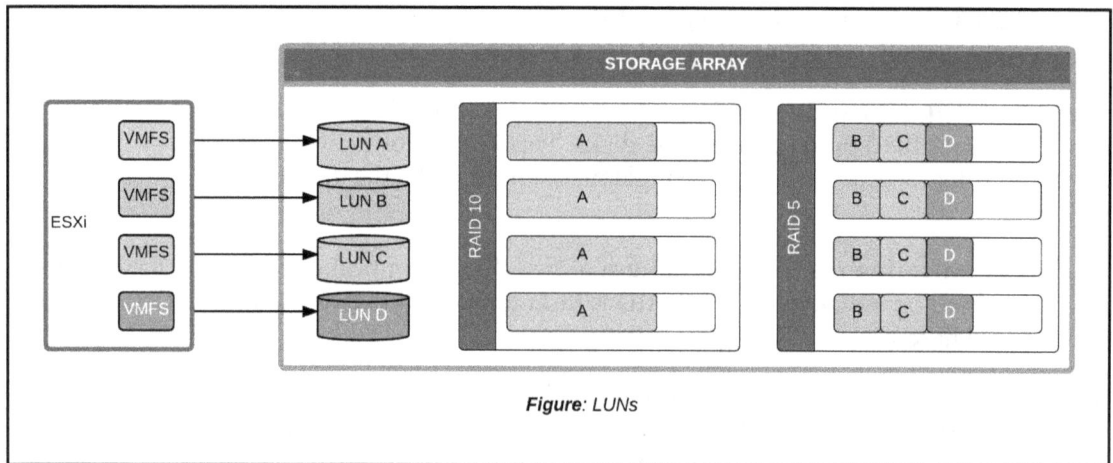

Figure: LUNs

In the diagram above, you will notice that the single RAID-10 group is catering storage space to a single LUN-A, whereas the RAID-5 group is catering to three LUNs – LUN-B, LUN-C, and LUN-D. An ESXi host can discover up to 256 LUN devices.

Pluggable Storage Architecture (PSA)

Pluggable Storage Architecture (PSA) is a modular storage management framework, which was introduced with VMware vSphere 5. It has a plugin framework, which can be used by third party vendors to create Multipathing plugins, which can leverage array-specific Multipathing, load balancing, or failover features. VMware has its own default Multipathing plugin called the **Native Multipathing Plugin** (**NMP**):

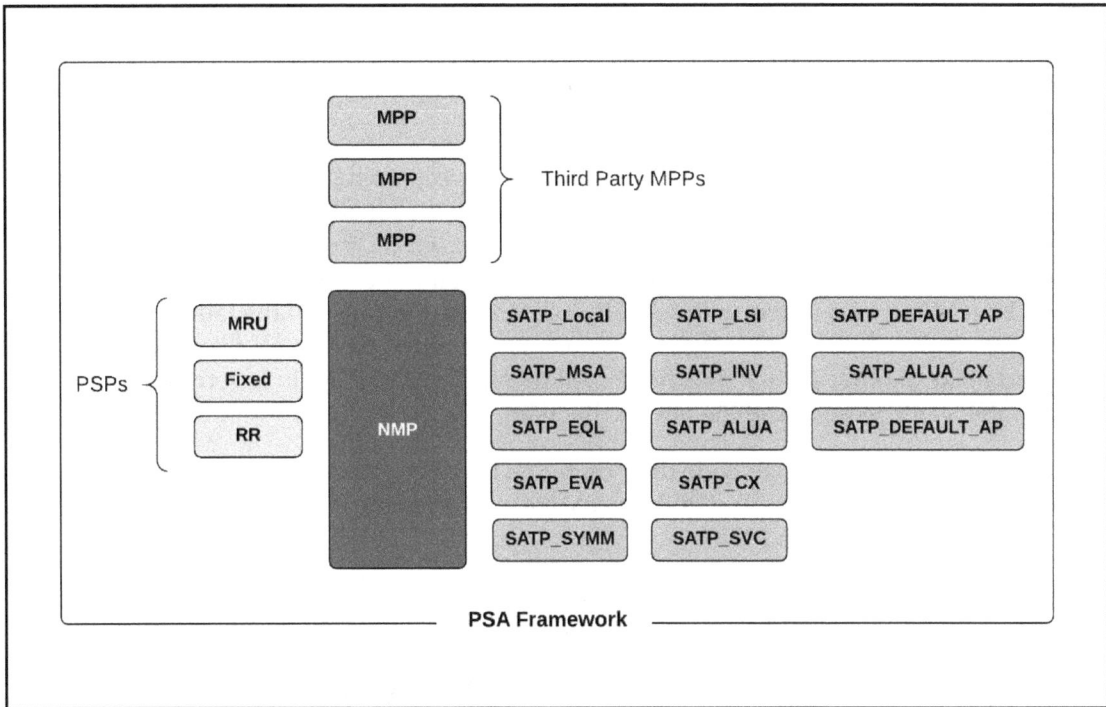

Since, third party plugins are beyond the scope of this book, we will delve deeper into the components and functions of VMware NMP.

Every storage device detected by the ESXi host will be associated with a **Multipathing plugin** (**MPP**). This is achieved with the help of a claim rule. If there aren't any claim rules for a third party MPP, then the VMware NMP will claim the device and associate an SATP and PSP to it.

VMware NMP has two main components:

- **Storage Array Type Plugin (SATP)**
- **Path Selection Plugin (PSP)**

SATP is responsible for keeping a tab on the status of every storage path it is associated with and capture details of a path failure, whereas PSP determines which physical path has to be chosen to send the I/O to the device. PSP relies on the path status information from the SATP.

VMware NMP uses both SATP and PSP to maintain access to the storage devices presented to the ESXi host. When I/O is issued to a storage device the NMP will instruct the PSP corresponding to the LUN to place the I/O on a path based on the policy (MRU/Fixed/RR) chosen. If for some reason the I/O operation failed to complete, it is reported back to the NMP. The NMP in turn instructs the SATP to determine the cause of the failure and take appropriate action. If the I/O had failed due to a path failure, SATP will mark that path as dead and make another path active. NMP will then call the PSP again to retry the I/O. This time the PSP can choose to use the new active path.

PSA allows storage vendors to code their own SATPs, PSPs, or an entire MPP itself. The vendor SATPs and PSPs can plug into the VMware NMP and be active alongside the VMware bundled SATPs and PSPs.

VMware NMP includes an SATP for every supported storage array. Depending on the array type, every SATP will have a default PSP.

> The following command can be issued to view a list of all STAPs and their associated PSPs:
> `# esxcli storage nmp satp list`

Although every array type will have an SATP associated with it, there can be only three PSPs associated with them, and they are:

- Most recently used
- Fixed
- Round robin

Each of these **Path Selection Policies** (**PSP**) function uniquely. VMware NMP uses the following names to represent them in the PSA framework:

- VMW_PSP_MRU
- VMW_PSP_Fixed
- VMW_PSP_RR

> The following command can be issued to view the list of PSPs supported by the framework:
> ```
> #esxcli storage nmp psp list
> ```

- The **Most Recently Used** (**MRU**) path selection policy will continue to use the new path after a failover even if the failed path subsequently becomes active. MRU is commonly used as a PSP for active/passive arrays.
- The **fixed** path selection policy will have a preferred path configured for data transport. In the event of a failed preferred path becoming active subsequent to a failover, the policy will failback to the preferred path. This policy is commonly used with active/active or ALUA arrays.

The **Round robin** (**RR**) path selection policy will distribute I/O over active or active optimized paths (*in case of ALUA array*) in a round robin fashion after every 1000 IOPS per path.

Storage Array types

We have learnt from the previous section that there are different types of arrays not just based on the protocol they support but also the type of load balancing and failover they support.

- There are three types of arrays based on their load balancing or failover abilities:
  - Active/active array
  - Active/passive array
  - ALUA (Asymmetric Logical Unit Access) array

- The *Active/Active* or Symmetric Active/Active array will have all the ports on its storage controllers to allow simultaneous processing of the I/O offering the same levels of performance and access to all LUNs:

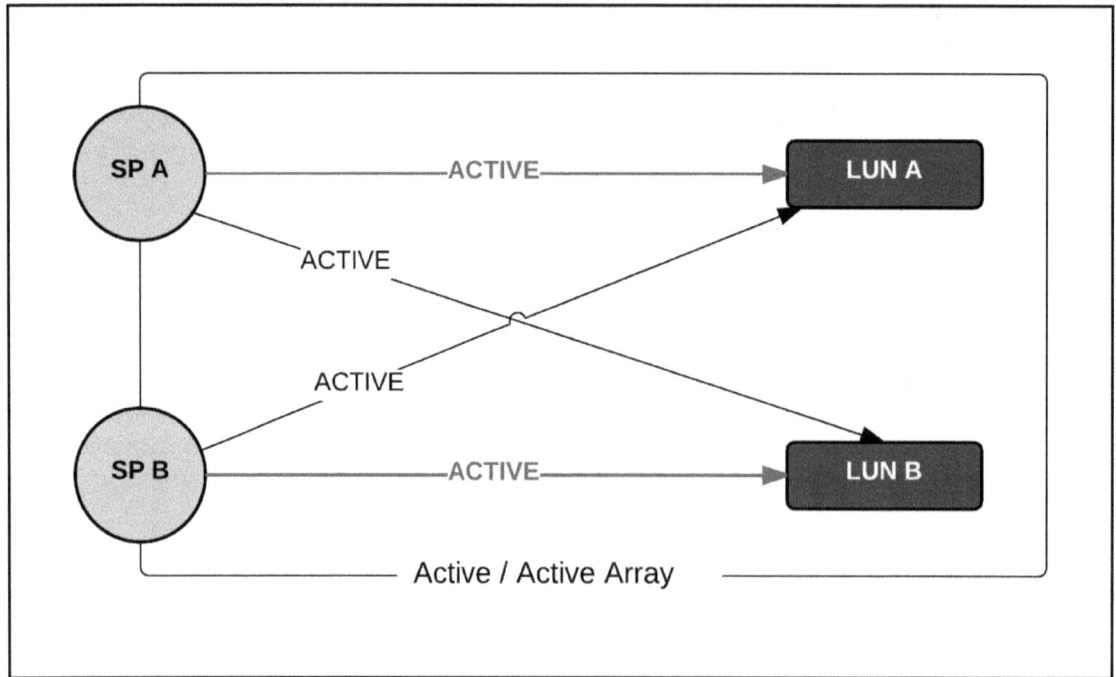

Active / Active Array

In a symmetric active/active array, there is no concept of a standby controller.

Design Tip: When designing a storage architecture with a symmetric active/active array, you can choose different preferred paths on different sets of ESXi hosts in a cluster/data center. For instance, if you have a 10 hosts cluster, then you could set five hosts to use a preferred path via controller-1 and a second set of five hosts to use a preferred path via controller-2. This is done to achieve I/O processing load distribution at the controller level.

Active/passive arrays will have active and standby storage controllers. A controller is referred to as active or passive relative to the LUNs they own. In an active/passive array an I/O to a set of LUNs can only be processed by a storage controller that owns them. The controller that owns a set of LUNs is referred to as an active controller for those LUNs:

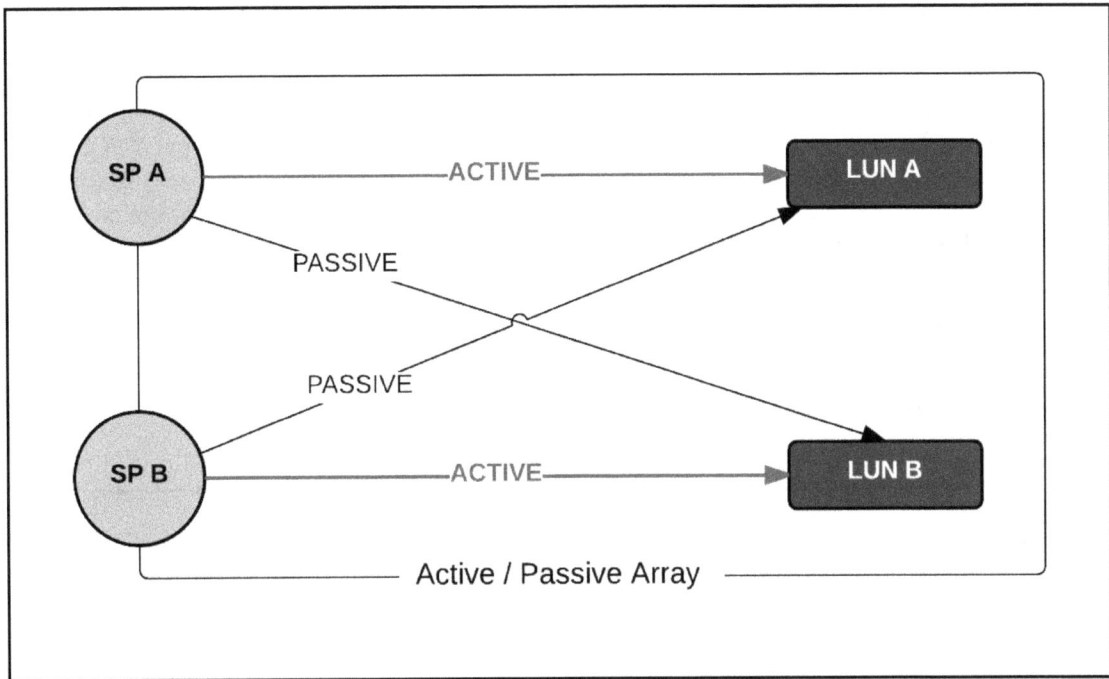

For instance, there are two LUNs created on an active/passive array with storage controllers SPA and SPB. SPA has been configured to own LUN A and SPB to own LUN B. Here SPA becomes an active and SPB becomes a passive controller for LUNs A. In the same manner, SPB becomes an Active and SPA becomes a passive controller for LUN B.

Design Tip: When designing an environment with active/passive arrays make sure that all ESXi hosts are configured to see the LUNs via their owning controllers. A misconfiguration will cause the array to trespass the LUN ownership, which may lead to path thrashing.

The **Asymmetric Logical Unit Access (ALUA)** array is a type of active/active array, which has the ability to concurrently use all its controllers to process I/O and also stand-in as failover partners of each other.

Much like in an active/passive array, a LUN or a set of LUNs can only be owned by a single controller. The owning controller will have symmetric (direct) access to the LUN, hence offering the best performance. The non-owning controller can process the I/O indirectly (asymmetric) for the LUN by transferring the I/O via the interconnect to the owning controller. Hence, there is a performance hit owing to time required to transfer the I/O to the owning controller.

Since the array presents a way to directly and indirectly process I/O for the LUNs presented, there has to be a way to let ESXi know about the direct and indirect paths to the LUN. This is achieved by an array feature called the TPGS (Target Port Groups). TPGS groups direct and indirect paths to a LUN separately. ESXi sees them as Active (Optimized) and Active (non-optimized) paths to the LUN. The active (non-optimized) storage controller ports could be active (optimized) ports for another set of LUN. ESXi will always place the I/O on the Active (optimized) paths:

Design Tip: The storage administrator should evenly distribute the LUNs among the controllers as necessary to achieve effective utilization of an ALUA array.

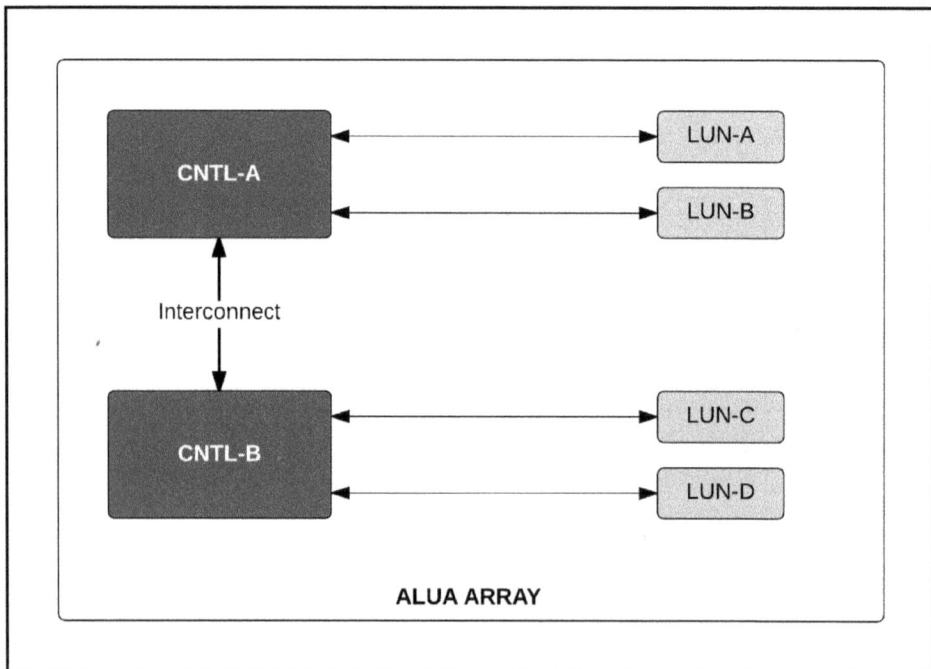

If you were to have an array configured as shown in the above diagram, then an I/O for LUN-A if issued via the controller CNTL-B, would result in CNTL-B passing the traffic via the interconnect to controller CNTL-A which would then process the I/O. This alternative path will be referred to as an active non-optimized path.

Configuring access to Fiber channel storage

It is not uncommon for an enterprise infrastructure to use Fiber channel storage to host their workloads. Though other technologies such as NFS and iSCSI offer enterprise class performance, FC still holds the reputation of being regarded as the best performing storage technology. VMware ESX supports access to FC storage from almost all key vendors. In this section, we will learn how to configure an ESXi host to access LUNs on FC storage.

We will cover the following topics in this section:

- Designing for redundancy
- Zoning and masking
- World Wide Names (WWN)

Designing for redundancy

Modern day data centers are filled with so many components that it is very easy to overlook single points of failure. Component failures are relatively common when you have a large infrastructure. Hence, it becomes necessary to design the infrastructure to survive such failures. Storage access is an integral part of any VMware infrastructure. Due to this reason mainly, it is critical to make sure that it is designed and implemented in a manner that not only achieves the desired level of performance, but also makes it resilient to failures.

Therefore, before we begin to understand how to design a failure resilient storage environment, it is beneficial to know the common types of failures that you would encounter:

- Faulty fabric cables
- HBA/port failures
- Fabric switch/port failures
- Storage array controller/port failures
- Hard disk failures

Avoiding single points of failure at the ESXi host

ESXi hosts that need to access FC storage will need to be equipped with FC Initiators or Host Bus Adapters (HBA). Some servers come with on-board adapters, some with an option to install cards, and some with a combination of both. HBAs are made with either single or multiple ports per card. Regardless of the number of ports, every single HBA is a point of failure, so it is important to make sure that you have at least two HBAs per server on which ESXi will be installed.

Avoiding single points of failure at the Fabric

The Fiber channel network is formed using a set of Fabric Switches. Such networks are referred to as Fabrics. It is recommended to use more than one fabric switch to support your fabric to eliminate single points of failure.

Avoiding single points of failure at the storage array

The storage array is the heart and soul of any data center. It stores most of the business's data. It is of prime importance to ensure that there are different levels of redundancy within a storage array to avoid single points of failure. To start with, all the LUNs that are created in the storage array are backed by multiple hard disks (HDD) in a RAID group to support the performance and recovery envisioned. If there are no RAID groups and if the LUNs are backed by a single large HDD, then the hard disk's components, such as the HDD controller, would become a single point of failure. Most arrays today will have more than one storage controller providing access to all the LUNs, eliminating single points of failure.

Zoning and masking

When you implement an infrastructure with FC storage, it is imperative to make sure that the storage presented to the ESXi hosts are done with an effort to make sure that only the intended ESXi hosts see the required LUNs. This is achieved by using two methods called zoning and masking.

Zoning is configured on the Fabric Switch that the ESXi HBAs and the storage controllers are cabled to. The zoning function is used to create logical segments within a fabric. Only the nodes within a zone can communicate with each other, with initiators (HBA) and targets (controllers) in it. There are two types of zoning:

- Hard zoning
- Soft zoning

Hard Zoning is done by grouping the F-ports into a zone. An F-port is the physical port on a fabric switch. Any device that connects to an F-port in the zone will have access to the other devices in the zone. Every F-port will have a dynamically assigned FC Address assigned to it when the port logs onto the fabric. This is considered to be the most secure type of zoning, but since the FC addresses can be affected due to a configuration change on the fabric, such an event will require you to redo the zoning with the newly assigned FC addresses of the F-ports:

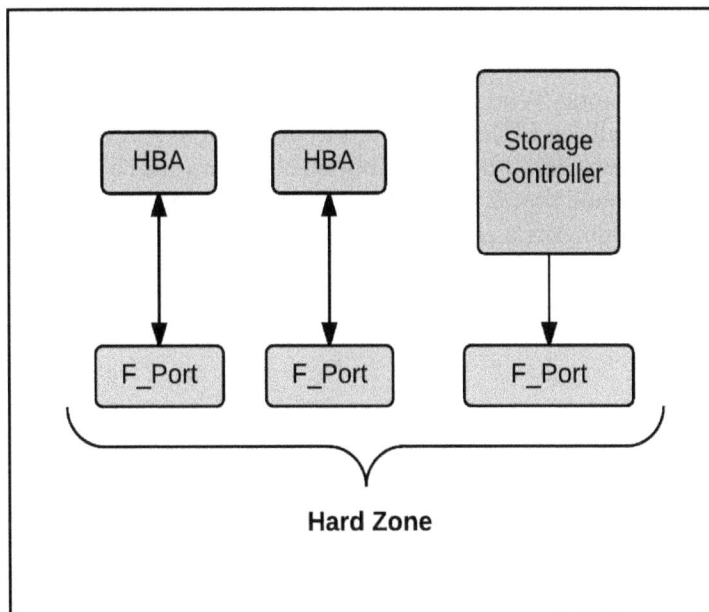

Soft Zoning is done using the **World Wide Names** (**WWN**) of the nodes that log onto the fabric. Since the WWNs are static and not bound to change, this is considered to be the most flexible type of zoning. You could even redo the cabling of the nodes to different F-ports on a Fabric Switch without affecting the zone configuration:

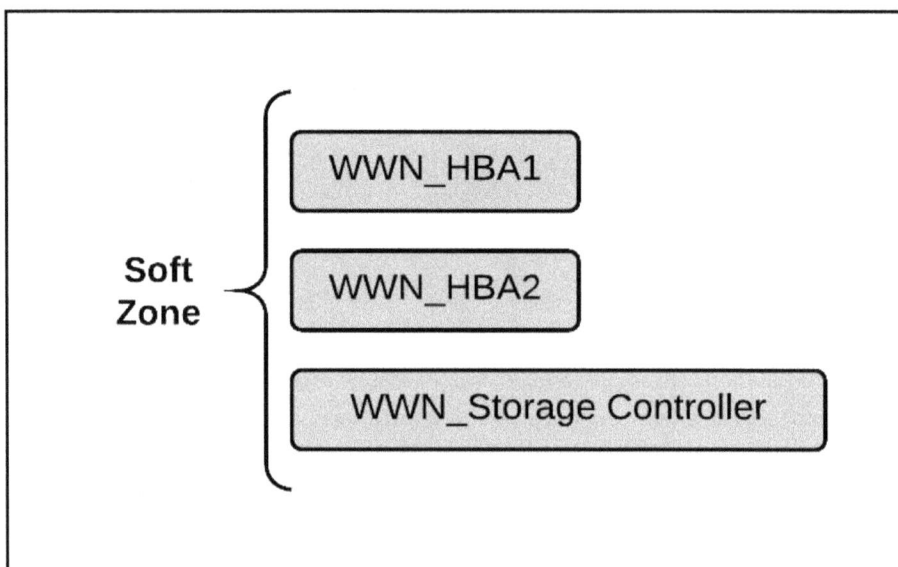

Masking can be done at either the storage array or the ESXi host. Zoning cannot go beyond the boundaries of the node ports that log onto the fabric. Masking is done to add a deeper level of security within a zone. When you zone HBAs and storage controllers into a zone, the HBAs have access to all the LUNs presented to the storage controllers. In a large environment, a storage array will host a number of LUNs and not all of them should be visible to every initiator node that is in the zone. This is where masking will come into the scene. Masking further segments a zone into access control lists by only allowing the intended hosts to see the required LUNs.

Let's consider the following example:

- With the zoning complete, we have two hosts [H1] and [H2] zoned to access storage controllers [A] and [B]
- Controller [A] has LUNs [L1] and [L2] mapped to it and Controller [B] has LUNs [L2] and [L3] mapped to it:

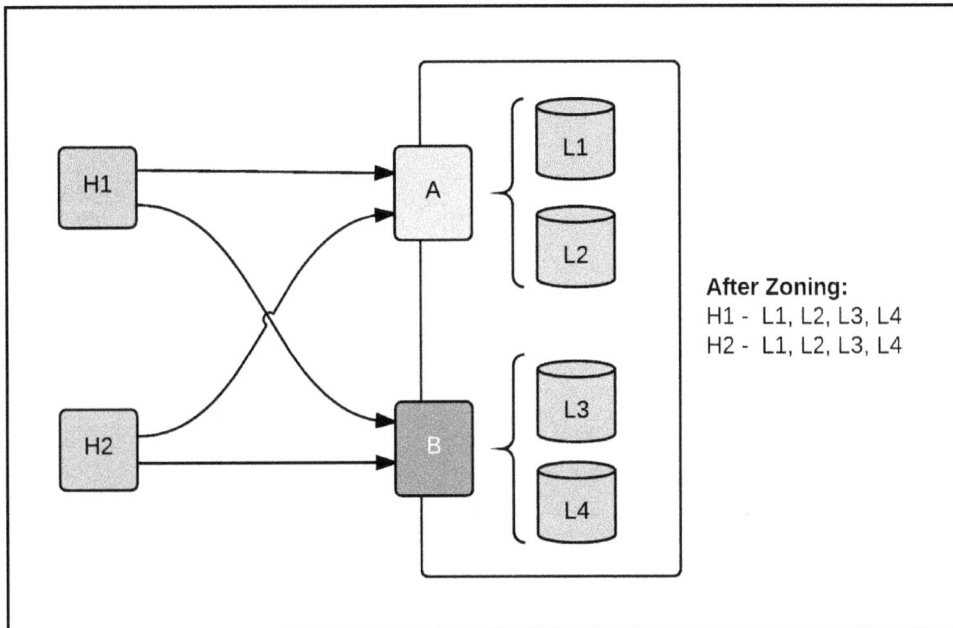

After Zoning:
H1 - L1, L2, L3, L4
H2 - L1, L2, L3, L4

- Now, let's assume that not all of the ESXi hosts in the zone should access all of the LUNs zoned. In this case, H1 needs access to LUNs 1 and 4 only and H2 needs access to LUNs 2 and 3 only. This can be achieved by creating Access Control Lists (ACLs) at controller ports A and B. Therefore, the controller at Port A will have an ACL entry for H1 and LUNs 1 and 4, and Port B will have an ACL entry for H2 and LUNs 2 and 3:

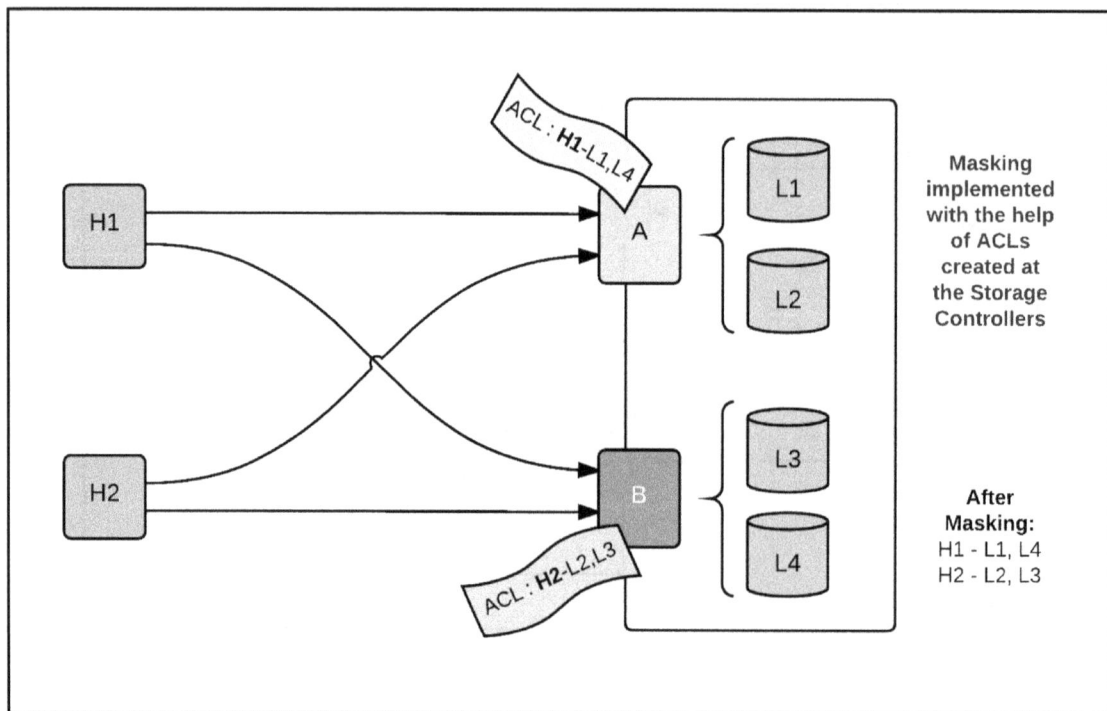

World Wide Names (WWN)

Much like what MAC addresses are meant for in an Ethernet infrastructure, in a Fiber Channel infrastructure every device is assigned with a 64-bit unique identifier called World Wide Names.

WWNs can be of two types: a **World Wide Node Name (WWNN)**, and a **World Wide Port Name (WWPN)**. WWPNs are also referred to as **Node Port IDs**.

For example, a dual port HBA adapter will have a WWPN assigned to each of its ports and a single WWNN for the HBA itself.

Configuring access to iSCSI storage

iSCSI, or SCSI over the Internet, is one of the top contenders for a place in an enterprise data center. The main benefit of iSCSI is that there is no need for an investment to support special switching hardware for you to enable access to the storage. Hence, all you need to make sure is that the iSCSI array is in a network that is reachable to a vmkernel interface on the ESXi host.

Design Tip: It is recommended to maintain separate switches for iSCSI traffic in a data center environment.

To learn more about vmkernel interfaces read `Chapter 4`, *vSphere Networking Concepts and Management*,.

We will cover the following topics in this section:

- How does iSCSI work?
- Types of iSCSI initiators
- Types of iSCSI arrays
- Configuring iSCSI initiators
- How to achieve multipathing?

How does iSCSI work?

- The **Internet Small Computer System Interface (iSCSI)** is a storage standard that enables access to non-local storage over an IP network infrastructure. The standard is detailed in the IETF **RFC document number 7143** (`https://tools.ie tf.org/html/rfc7143`).
- As per the standard, the source and destination involved in the data exchange should encapsulate SCSI commands in IP packets. Both the source and destination should have the ability to encapsulate and decapsulate the packets to read and interpret the SCSI commands embedded in them. The source is generally a hardware or software module present on a host machine and has the ability to embed SCSI frames into the IP packets. The source is referred to as an **iSCSI initiator**. Similarly, the destination will have a module referred to as an **iSCSI target**:

A communication channel established between an iSCSI initiator and an iSCSI target is called a **session**. Such a session could have several connections to the target's portal:

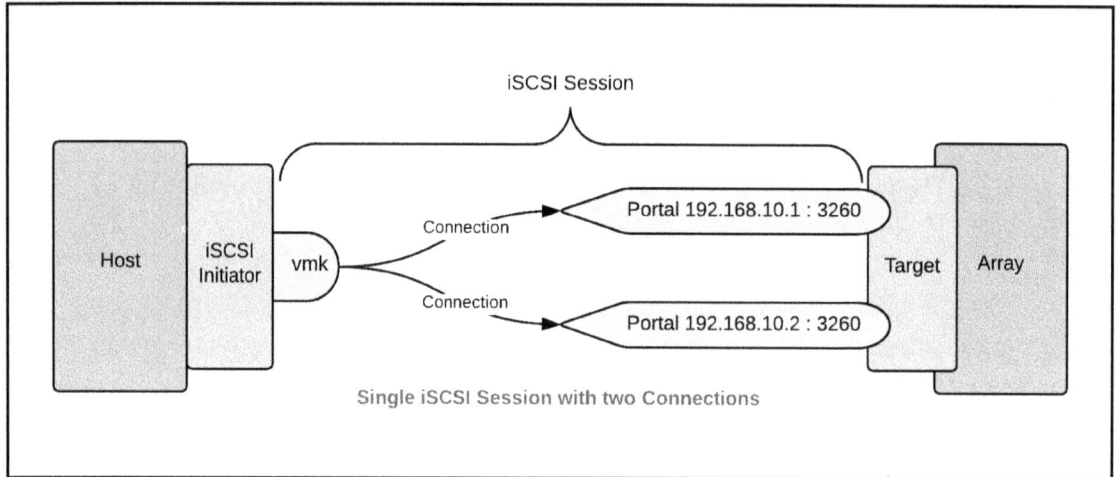

Single iSCSI Session with two Connections

A **target portal** is a combination of an IP address and a TCP port (*default 3260*) corresponding to a node at the iSCSI array. Whether a portal corresponds to a single target or there are multiple portals per target, would entirely depend on the vendor's design of the array. We will discuss more about the different types of iSCSI array in the topic *Types of iSCSI array:*

- Similar to a target portal, the initiator will also have a *network portal* denoted by the IP address of the initiator (*the vmkernel IP of the initiator unless it is an independent hardware iSCSI initiator*). We will learn more about the different types of iSCSI initiator in the topic *Types of iSCSI initiator.*

- Every iSCSI node should have a unique identifier associated with it. Such a naming convention is achieved with the help of naming schemes such as **IQN**, **EUI**, and **NAA**. The **iSCSI Qualified Name** (**IQN**) is a scheme that allows an identifier (*with a 255-character limit*) to be associated with every iSCSI node. The identifier starts with the string **iqn** followed by the year and month when the naming authority was established, the domain of the naming authority in reverse and a unique name for the storage node. Each of these strings is separated by a period (.):

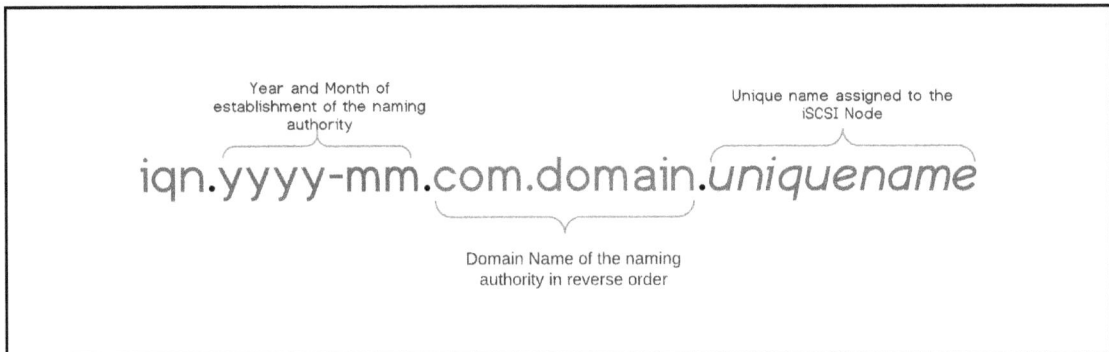

Year and Month of establishment of the naming authority

Unique name assigned to the iSCSI Node

iqn.yyyy-mm.com.domain.*uniquename*

Domain Name of the naming authority in reverse order

Examples:

- `iqn.2014-12.com.vdescribed.store1`
- `iqn.2014-12.com.vdescribed.store2`
- `iqn.1998-01.com.vmware:esx02-404f1ad6`

Types of iSCSI initiator

There are two main categories of iSCSI initiators, namely the *Software iSCSI initiator* and the *Hardware iSCSI initiator*:

- The **software iSCSI initiator** is a *vmkernel* component and can be enabled on an ESXi host. It requires a vmkernel port configured with an IP address to be associated with it, to establish a connection with the iSCSI array. Since it is a software construct, all the configuration and processing of the iSCSI packets is handled by vmkernel's network stack.

There can only be one Software iSCSI initiator on an ESXi host.

- The **Hardware iSCSI initiator** *offloads* some or all of the work to the hardware device. There are two types of hardware initiator, dependent and independent. A **dependent iSCSI hardware initiator** has the ability to offload the network packet processing to the **TCP Offload Engine** (**TOE**) on the hardware device. However, the configuration of the initiator should be done by associating a vmkernel port to the initiator. An **independent iSCSI hardware initiator** can handle both the configuration and the network packet processing. The configuration is done via the device's firmware, while the packet processing can be offloaded to the TOE on the device.

Types of iSCSI array

There are different types of iSCSI arrays based on the number of targets or target portals they present to the initiator. The key difference between a target and target portal is that an iSCSI target will have a unique IQN associated with it, whereas a portal is identified with a: *IP Address: Port Number* combination. A single target IQN can have more than one target portal associated with it.

Keeping these differences in mind, we could possibly categorize them into three categories:

- Single portal arrays
- Multi-portal arrays
- Multi-target arrays

With **single portal** arrays, the storage array exposes a single portal to be discovered by the source (initiator). Hence, the number of paths to such an array will depend on the number of **vmkernel** interfaces associated with the iSCSI initiator. The process of associating vmkernel interfaces with an iSCSI initiator is called **port binding**. We will learn more about port binding in the section *Configuring Multipathing for iSCSI* of this chapter. Arrays like the HP left hand and Dell Equalogic are examples of single portal arrays.

With **multi-portal** arrays, the storage array exposes multiple portals to be discovered by the iSCSI initiator. Therefore, the number of paths to array will not only depend on the number of vmkernel ports bound to the iSCSI initiator, but also the number of portals exposed. For instance, if two vmkernel ports are bound to the iSCSI initiator discovering four target portals, then the number of paths to the iSCSI target is eight.

With **multi-target** arrays, the storage array can have more than one iSCSI targets, with one or more portals associated with them.

The formula to calculate the number of paths possible is dependent on the number of sources (vmkernel port) and target portals and not the number of targets.

Number of paths = Number of Source Portal X Number of target portal.

Here, the Source Portal is nothing but the vmkernel interfaces bound to the iSCSI initiator.

When you view the Multipathing information for Single/Multi-portal arrays from the vCenter GUI, every discovery portal will be listed as a target. These targets will have the same IQN, but different portal IP addresses associated with them. However, for Multi-target arrays you will see targets with different IQNs as well.

Using Software iSCSI on an ESXi host

VMware ESXi has a built-in software iSCSI initiator module, which is disabled by default. Software iSCSI is dependent on vmkernel's network stack for interfacing with the iSCSI array. Enabling the software iSCSI on ESXi is a very simple procedure. You will need to access the ESXi host via the vSphere Client, or if the host is added to a vCenter Server then the task can be accomplished via the vCenter GUI as well. It is a design best practiced to form a separate network for iSCSI traffic alone to achieve performance and security. Hence, you will need to create a separate vmkernel interface for iSCSI before you begin:

1. Create a new **vmkernel** interface for use with iSCSI. Chapter 4, *vSphere Networking Concepts and Management* has sections covering the management of vmkernel interfaces.
2. Connect to the vCenter using vSphere Web Client and at the inventory **Home** page click on **Hosts and Clusters**.

3. Select the ESXi host you intend to enable iSCSI on and navigate to **Manage** | **Storage** | **Storage Adapters**:

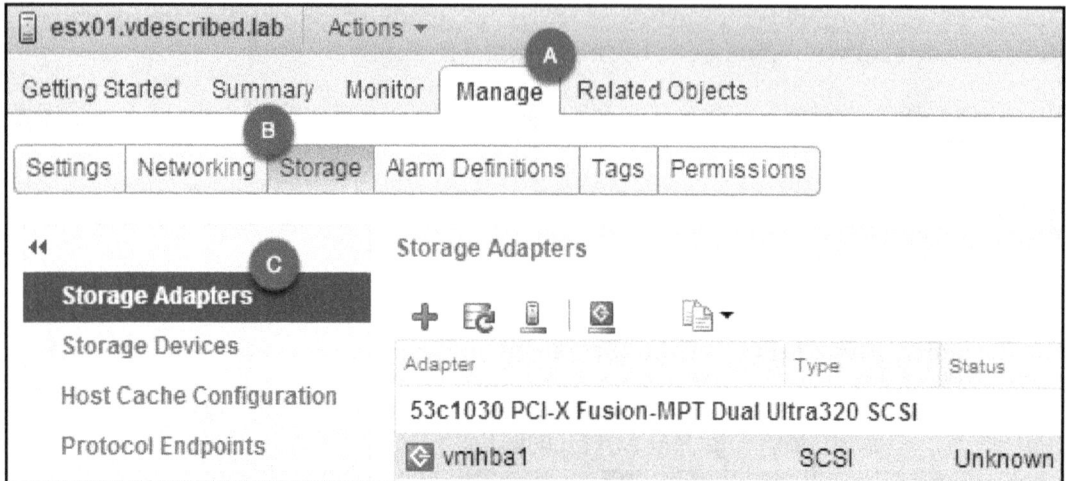

4. Click on the + icon and select **Software iSCSI adapter**:

5. In the **Add Software iSCSI Adapter** window, seeking your confirmation, click **OK** to confirm:

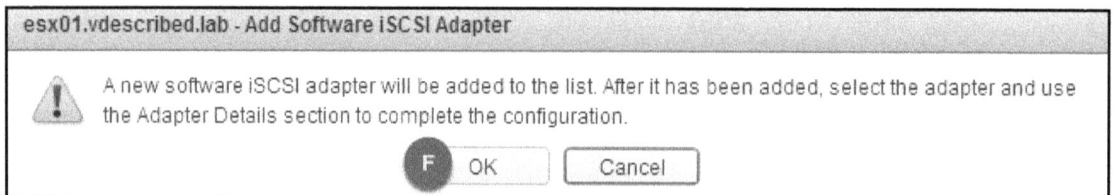

6. On doing so, the firewall TCP port 3260 will be opened for both ingress and egress traffic and then the iSCSI Client will be enabled on the host. Also, you should now see an **iSCSI Software Adapter** listed under **Storage Adapters**:

Storage Adapters			
Adapter	Type	1 ▲ Status	Identifier
53c1030 PCI-X Fusion-MPT Dual Ultra320 SCSI			
vmhba1	SCSI	Unknown	
PIIX4 for 430TX/440BX/MX IDE Controller			
vmhba32	Block SCSI	Unknown	
vmhba0	Block SCSI	Unknown	
iSCSI Software Adapter ←			
vmhba33	iSCSI	Online	iqn.1998-01.com.vmware:esx01-5391a76c

Configuring an iSCSI initiator to access storage

Once you have the iSCSI initiator enabled, it has to be configured to access the LUNs made available at the iSCSI array. Needless to say, the array has to be configured to allow the necessary LUNs to be discovered. This job is a pre-requisite and should be done by your array administrator. Since this activity differs from vendor to vendor, we aren't going to cover any examples in this section.

Now, assuming that the array has already been configured correctly, we need to go through the following information to proceed further:

- Discoverable IP address of the iSCSI target server and the port number.
- CHAP authentication details (if any).
- iSCSI Array configured to allow ESXi hosts access the LUNs. To configure access at the array, you will need the Software iSCSI Adapters IQN handy.

Once you have these details handy, on the ESXi host:

1. Navigate to **Manage** | **Storage** | **Storage Adapters** and select the iSCSI software adapter.
2. With the adapter selected, go to the **Targets** tab and then under **Dynamic Discovery**, click on **Add...**:

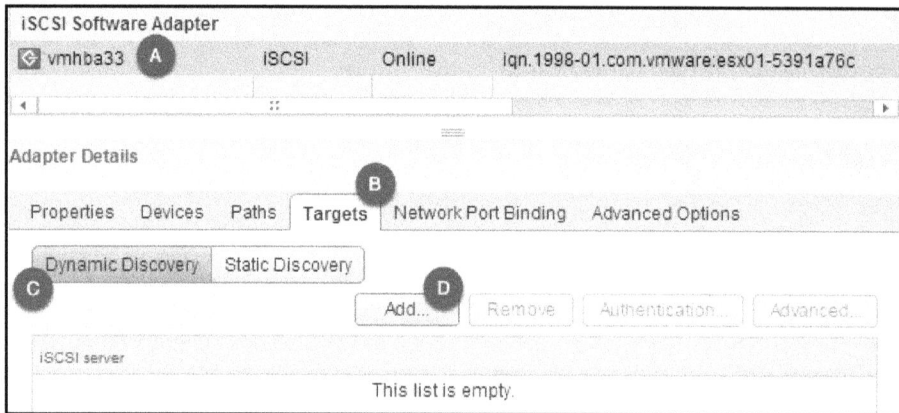

3. In the **Add Send Target Server** window, supply the IP address/FQDN of the iSCSI server and click on **OK** to finish adding the target:

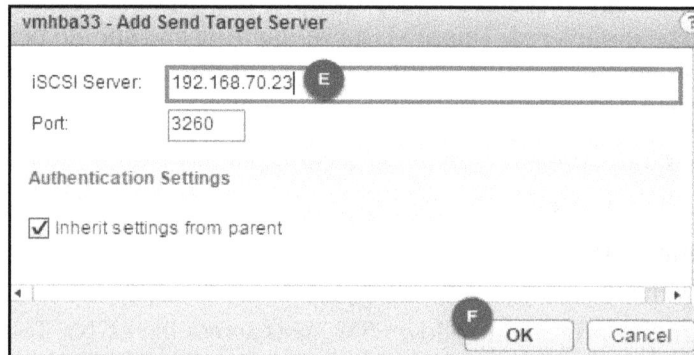

4. Once done, issue a rescan on the adapter to discover the LUNs available from the target. In fact, a rescan will be suggested by the UI:

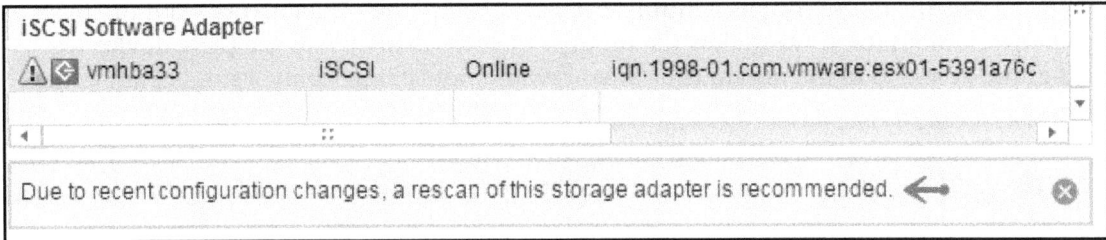

iSCSI Software Adapter			
⚠ 🔄 vmhba33	iSCSI	Online	iqn.1998-01.com.vmware:esx01-5391a76c

Due to recent configuration changes, a rescan of this storage adapter is recommended. ⬅● ⊗

5. To rescan the adapter, with the Software iSCSI adapter selected, click on the rescan adapter icon 🔄 in the Software Adapter pane.

6. Now, navigate to the **Devices** tab under the iSCSI adapter details pane. It should list the discovered storage devices:

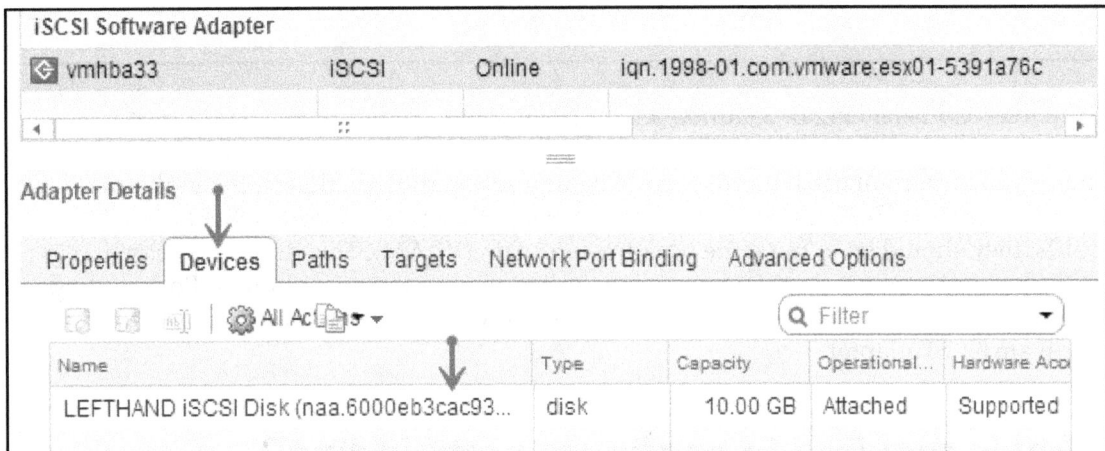

iSCSI Software Adapter			
🔄 vmhba33	iSCSI	Online	iqn.1998-01.com.vmware:esx01-5391a76c

Adapter Details

Properties | Devices | Paths | Targets | Network Port Binding | Advanced Options

⬚ ⬚ 📄 | ⚙ All Ac📋 ⬇ ▾   🔍 Filter ▾

Name	Type	Capacity	Operational...	Hardware Acc
LEFTHAND iSCSI Disk (naa.6000eb3cac93...	disk	10.00 GB	Attached	Supported

7. If you see all the devices you presented to the ESXi host at the array, then you have successfully configured access to the iSCSI array.

Configuring multipathing for iSCSI

By default, ESXi generates a single path between the software iSCSI adapter and the iSCSI targets, unless the iSCSI array is a multi-portal array allowing target access via more than one network interface. If we review the number of paths available to the LUN device we configured access to in the previous task, you would notice it has only a single path to the device:

| LEFTHAND iSCSI Disk (naa.... | disk | 10.00... | Attached | Supported | HDD | iSCSI | ▾ |

Device Details

Properties | Paths

Enable | Disable

Runtime Name	Status	Device	Target
vmhba33:C0:T0:L0	◆ Active (I/O)	LEFTHAND iSCSI Disk (naa.60...	iqn.2003-10.com.lefthand

To enable load balancing or redundancy for iSCSI traffic egressing an ESXi host, it is possible to bind more than one vmkernel adapter/interface to the Software iSCSI adapter. There is an important catch to this type of configuration though, that is, the vmkernel interfaces and the iSCSI target portals cannot be on disparate network subnets. In other words, they should be in the same broadcast domain (VLAN). This does not mean that iSCSI does not support routing; it is only a limitation with the port binding. Port binding is only done with the software iSCSI adapter. VMKernel adapters cannot be bound to a hardware iSCSI adapter.

What is required to configure port binding?

We will need to identify the vmnics/dvUplinks that have been connected to physical switch ports trunked to carry the desired VLAN traffic. We need IP addresses that can be assigned to the vmkernel interfaces, and of course, we need additional vmkernel interfaces created depending on the number of paths we plan to enable between the host and iSCSI array.

How do we go about configuring port binding?

To configure port binding, you will need to create two vmkernel interfaces with IP addresses in the same subnet as that of the iSCSI target portal. Then we use the Software iSCSI Initiator's Properties GUI to bind the vmkernel interfaces to it. We will not go through the procedure of creating the vmkernel interfaces, as Chapter 4, *vSphere Networking Concepts and Management* would have already helped you familiarize with the procedure. Instead, we will cover NIC teaming and the procedure to add the VMKernel interfaces to the Software iSCSI initiator. The following diagram depicts what we are trying to achieve:

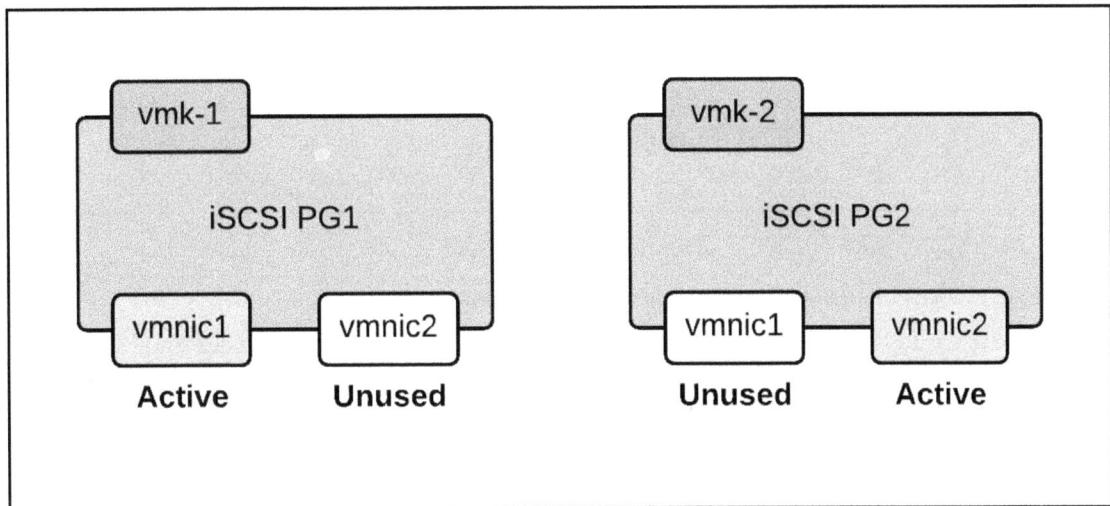

NIC teaming

While configuring NIC teaming for use with port binding, it is important to make sure that only the desired NIC is the active adapter. The remaining adapters should be configured as Unused. So, you might have already figured that we need a separate teaming configuration for each of the vmkernel ports. If you use vSphere Distributed Switches in your environment, then keep in mind that you need to manually create two separate Distributed Port Groups before you begin creating the vmkernel interfaces.

If you use the Standard vSwitch, every vmkernel interface you create, will intrinsically be housed in its own port group:

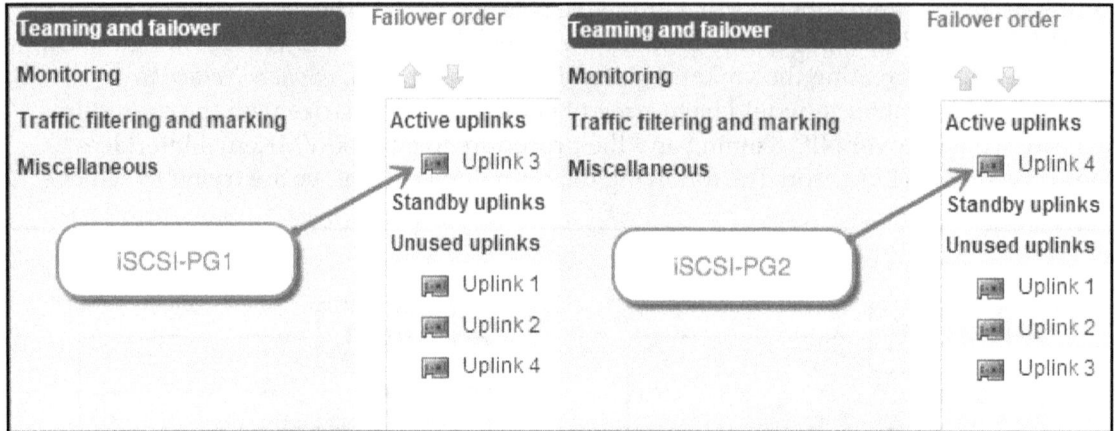

Binding vmkernel interfaces to the iSCSI adapter

Once we are done with the preparatory tasks of creating vmkernel interfaces and configuring NIC teaming on their respective port groups, the next step will be to map these interfaces to the iSCSI initiator. iSCSI network port binding is a process of mapping vmkernel network interfaces to the Software iSCSI adapter.

Here is how it is done:

1. Navigate to **Manage** | **Storage** | **Storage Adapters** to locate the **Software iSCSI Adapter**.
2. With the adapter selected, go to the **Network Port Binding** tab under **Adapter Details**.

3. In the **Network Port Binding** tab, click on the ⊞ icon to bring up a list of **VMkernel network adapters** to choose from:

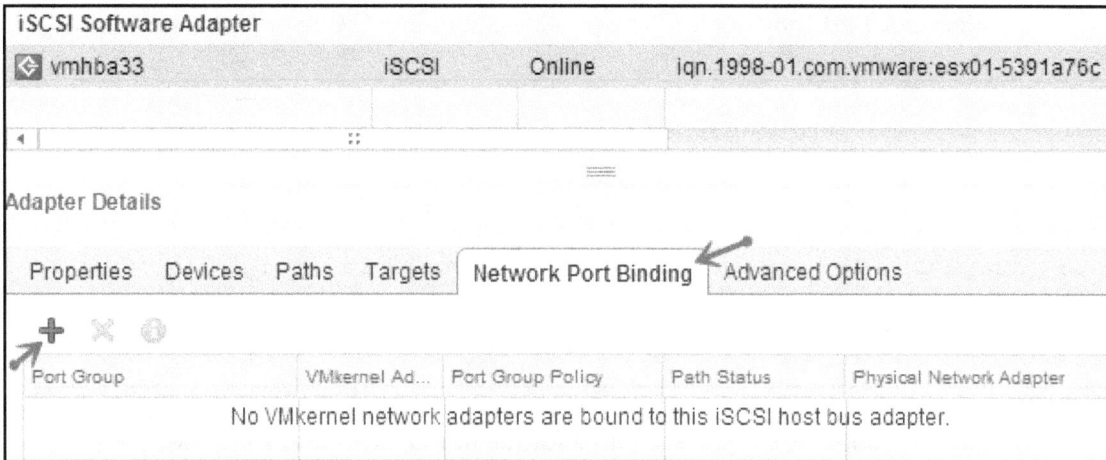

iSCSI Software Adapter			
⬙ vmhba33	iSCSI	Online	iqn.1998-01.com.vmware:esx01-5391a76c

Adapter Details

Properties   Devices   Paths   Targets   **Network Port Binding**   Advanced Options

➕ ✖ ⓘ

Port Group	VMkernel Ad...	Port Group Policy	Path Status	Physical Network Adapter
	No VMkernel network adapters are bound to this iSCSI host bus adapter.			

4. In the **Bind vmhbaXX with Vmkernel Adapter** window, select the port groups that were created for iSCSI and click **OK**:

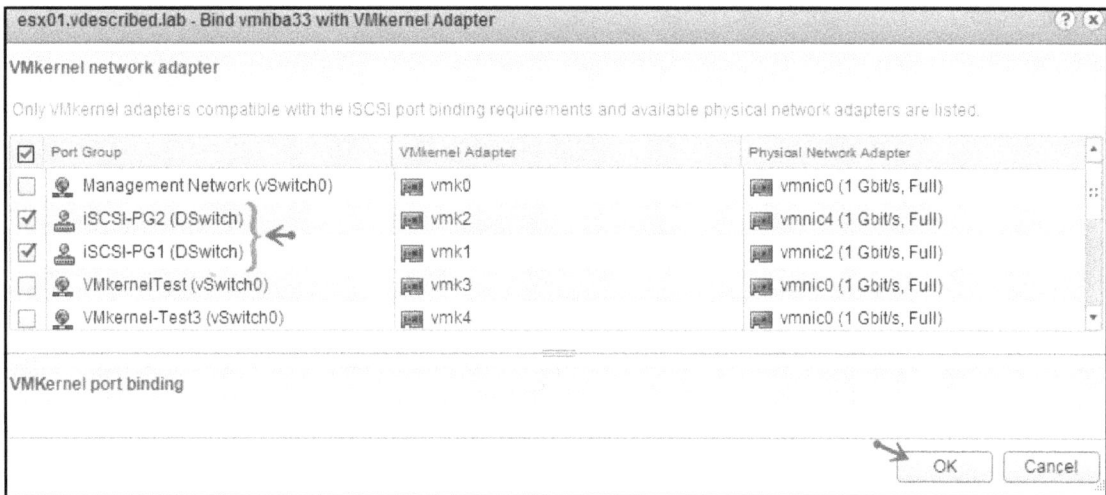

esx01.vdescribed.lab - Bind vmhba33 with VMkernel Adapter			

VMkernel network adapter

Only VMkernel adapters compatible with the iSCSI port binding requirements and available physical network adapters are listed.

☑	Port Group	VMkernel Adapter	Physical Network Adapter
☐	👤 Management Network (vSwitch0)	vmk0	vmnic0 (1 Gbit/s, Full)
☑	👤 iSCSI-PG2 (DSwitch)	vmk2	vmnic4 (1 Gbit/s, Full)
☑	👤 iSCSI-PG1 (DSwitch)	vmk1	vmnic2 (1 Gbit/s, Full)
☐	👤 VMkernelTest (vSwitch0)	vmk3	vmnic0 (1 Gbit/s, Full)
☐	👤 VMkernel-Test3 (vSwitch0)	vmk4	vmnic0 (1 Gbit/s, Full)

VMKernel port binding

OK   Cancel

5. Issue a rescan on the adapter for the new changes to take effect. It can be done by clicking the ⊡ icon.

6. Once the rescan is complete, you should see the status of the new paths under the **Network Port Binding** tab. The possible states are **Active** or **Not Used**:

Adapter Details				
Properties Devices Paths Targets	**Network Port Binding**	Advanced Options		
✚ ✖ ⓘ				
Port Group	VMkernel Ad...	Port Group Policy	Path Status	Physical Network Adapter
🖥 iSCSI-PG2 (DSwitch)	🖳 vmk2	✔ Compliant	◆ Active	🖳 vmnic4 (1 Gbit/s, Full)
🖥 iSCSI-PG1 (DSwitch)	🖳 vmk1	✔ Compliant	◇ Not used	🖳 vmnic2 (1 Gbit/s, Full)

7. Also, if you view the storage paths for the device, it should show two paths:

LEFTHAND iSCSI Disk (naa.600...	disk	10.00 ...	Attached	Supported	HDD	iSCSI

Device Details			
Properties	Paths		
Enable	Disable		
Runtime Name	Status	Device	Target
vmhba33:C1:T0:L0	◆ Active	LEFTHAND iSCSI Disk (naa.60...	iqn.2003-10.com.lefthandnetwo...
vmhba33:C0:T0:L0	◆ Active (I/O)	LEFTHAND iSCSI Disk (naa.60...	iqn.2003-10.com.lefthandnetwo...

8. If you see that the number of paths per device is equal to the number of vmkernel network interfaces you bound to the Software iSCSI Adapter, then you have successfully completed the task.

Configuring access to NFS storage

Like your iSCSI storage, NFS storage is also network attached and can easily be made a member of your data center infrastructure leveraging its current TCP/IP network. Unlike, iSCSI, NFS is not a block storage, meaning NFS runs and maintains its own file system. Hence, ESXi cannot format and form a new file system on the volumes presented to it from an NFS array. Instead, the NFS volumes, or rightly called *exports*, are just mount points on an ESXi host, to remote shares on an NFS storage array.

This section of the chapter will cover the procedures involved in configuring access to NFS shares on an NFS Storage.

What do we need?

The prerequisites needed for this task are:

- We need access to the network segment the NFS storage is on. Hence, the ESXi host will need a Vmkernel interface in the same subnet as the NFS storage. To learn how to create a Vmkernel interface, refer to `Chapter 4`, *vSphere Networking Concepts and Management*.
- NFS shares should have the `no_rootsquash` option configured.

How do you mount NFS shares?

NFS shares can be mounted using the **New Datastore** wizard. There is more than one method to start the wizard. We will discuss one of the easiest methods now:

1. Navigate to the `Host and Clusters` inventory view.

2. Right-click on the ESXi host on which you intend to enable access to the NFS share and navigate to **Storage** | **New Datastore**:

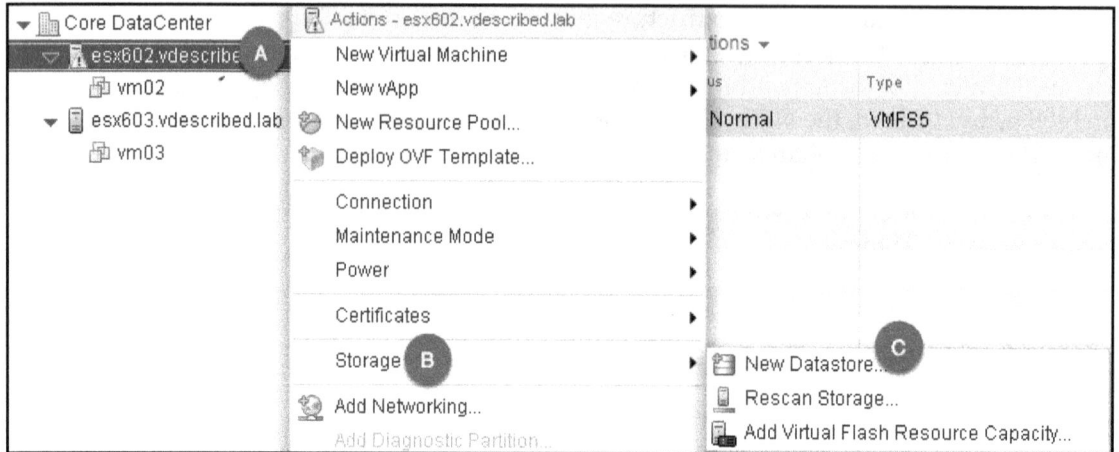

3. In the **New Datastore** wizard, select the **Type** as **NFS**. On the next screen select the **NFS version** and click **Next** to continue:

4. Supply a **Datastore name**, NFS Share's path, and the NFS Server's IP address and click **Next** to continue:

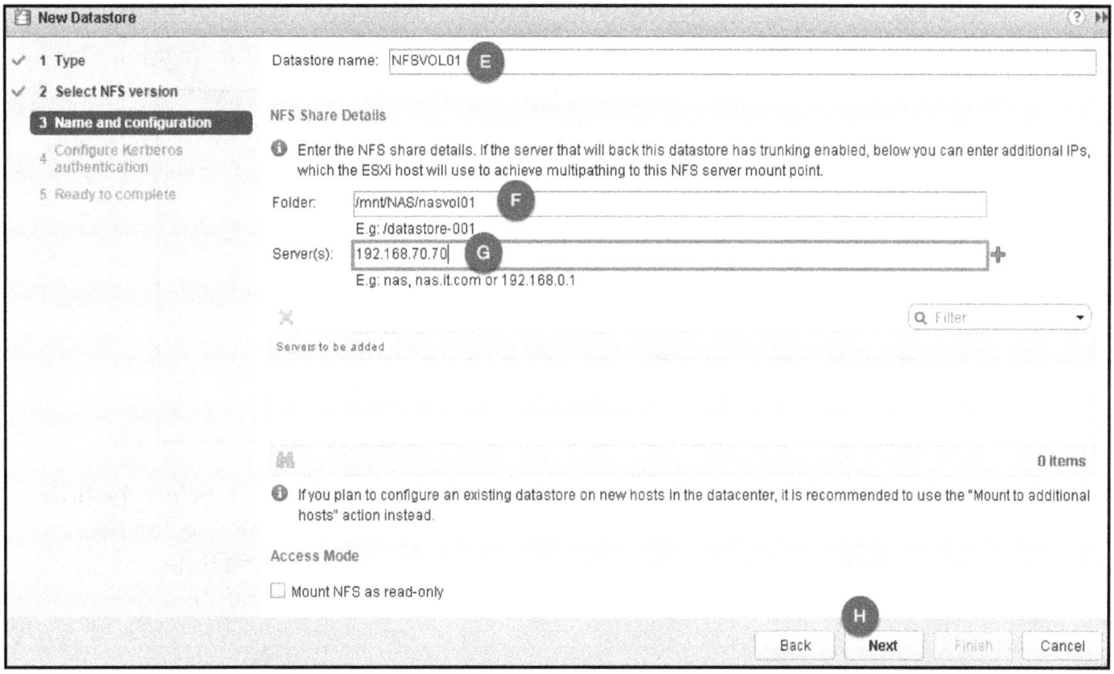

5. In the next screen you will be presented with an option to enable Kerberos authentication. The ESXi hosts should be a member of the Active Directory for this to be possible.
6. In the **Ready to Complete** screen, review the settings and click **Finish** to mount the NFS Share.

Mounting NFS onto multiple hosts

Once the NFS datastore is created, you could easily mount it on to other ESXi hosts. This can be done by right-clicking on the NFS datastore and selecting the option **Mount Datastore to Additional Hosts:**

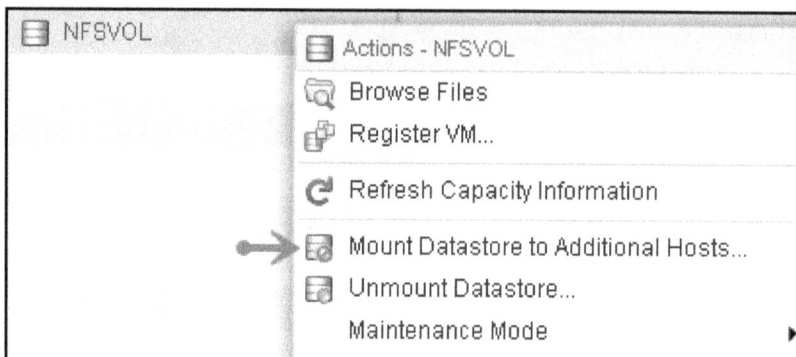

It should bring up a window with a list of all ESXi hosts in the data center. Select the hosts to mount the NFS on and click **OK**. This will mount the NFS share on the selected hosts using the same information that was provided to mount the share the first time.

Datastore management

Once we have configured access to the storage array, we will need to form file system containers on them. The LUNs presented to an ESXi host, unless they are NFS exports, do not have any filesystems on it. Such a LUN is called a Raw LUN. ESXi can create a distributed file system on it called the **Virtual Machine File System (VMFS).** Once formed, a logical data container called a datastore is presented to the user world on the ESXi. Datastore is however, a common term to refer to VMFS volumes and NFS mounts. In this section of the chapter, we will learn how to create and manage datastores.

We will cover the following topics:

- The virtual machine filesystem
- Creating VMFS datastores
- Managing the storage capacity of a datastore
- Managing VMFS snapshots

The Virtual Machine File System

A raw storage device presented to an ESXi host can be formatted to host VMware's propriety file system called the **Virtual Machine File System** (**VMFS**). It is a matured file system, which is currently at version 5 with vSphere 6, and it began its journey with the ESX 1.x version. It has seen several improvements since then and currently supports a maximum size of 64 TB, with the help of GPT (GUID Partition Table) partitioning scheme. VMFS-5 was introduced with vSphere 5, with several scalability improvements over the previous generation of Virtual Machine File Systems – VMFS-3.

With the support of GPT (GUID Partition Table), VMFS-5 can now support VMFS volumes that are greater than 2 terabytes in size. The current cap for the size of a VMFS volume is 64 terabytes.

Unlike VMFS-3, which had file-block sizes ranging from 1 megabyte to 8 megabytes, VMFS5 has a single block size of 1MB. It also maintains a smaller sub-lock size of 8KB unlike 64KB with VMFS-3. Smaller sub-blocks translate to reduced wastage of storage space if the VMFS volumes were to host a list of small files, such as virtual machine log files.

A VMFS volume can be created using the Add Storage wizard or from the ESXi host's command line. We will cover both the methods in this section of the chapter. To be able to create a VMFS volume you will need a LUN device smaller than 64 terabytes in size presented to the ESXi host. Having said that, it is not necessary that a volume can only reside within a single LUN's boundary. A VMFS volume can span over a maximum of 32 physical extents (LUNs). However, the size of the VMFS volume cannot exceed 64 terabytes.

Creating VMFS datastores

Once we have presented RAW LUNs to an ESXi host for it to be used as a storage container for virtual machine data, it needs to be formatted using VMFS. Creating a VMFS datastore is the process of formatting a LUN by creating a VMFS partition on it. A datastore (VMFS volume) can be created either by using the vSphere Web Clients' New Datastore wizard or by using ESXi's command-line interface. However, it is important that you have the NAA ID, LUN ID, and the size of the LUN handy to ensure that you don't end up using an unintended LUN. Perform a rescan on the HBAs to detect the presented LUNs.

The New Datastore wizard is available from the vSphere Web Clients' GUI. The following procedure will guide you through the steps required to achieve this:

1. Use the vSphere Web Client to connect to the vCenter Server.
2. Navigate to **Home** | **Storage**.
3. With the data center object selected, navigate to **Related Objects** | **Datastores**.
4. Click on the icon to bring up the **New Datastore** wizard.
5. In the wizard, select the Type as **VMFS** and click **Next** to continue.
6. Supply a Name for the datastore, and choose a host from the list to view the raw LUNs presented to it. Select the intended LUN and click **Next** to continue.
7. In the **Partition Configuration** screen, choose the datastore size and click **Next** to continue.
8. In the **Ready to Complete** screen, review the settings and click **Finish** to create the datastore.

Multipathing information of a LUN device

You can view or change the Multipathing configuration of a LUN device corresponding to a datastore:

1. Use the vSphere Web Client to connect to the vCenter Server.
2. Hit *Ctrl + Alt + 5* to bring up the `Datastore` inventory.
3. Select the datastore for whose multipathing configuration should be verified or modified.

5. Navigate to **Manage** | **Settings** | **Connectivity and Multipathing** to view a list of all the ESXi hosts that have access to the selected datastore.

6. Select the ESXi host to verify its current Multipathing policy and the paths.

6. You can change the path selection policy of the LUN by clicking on **Edit Multipathing**:

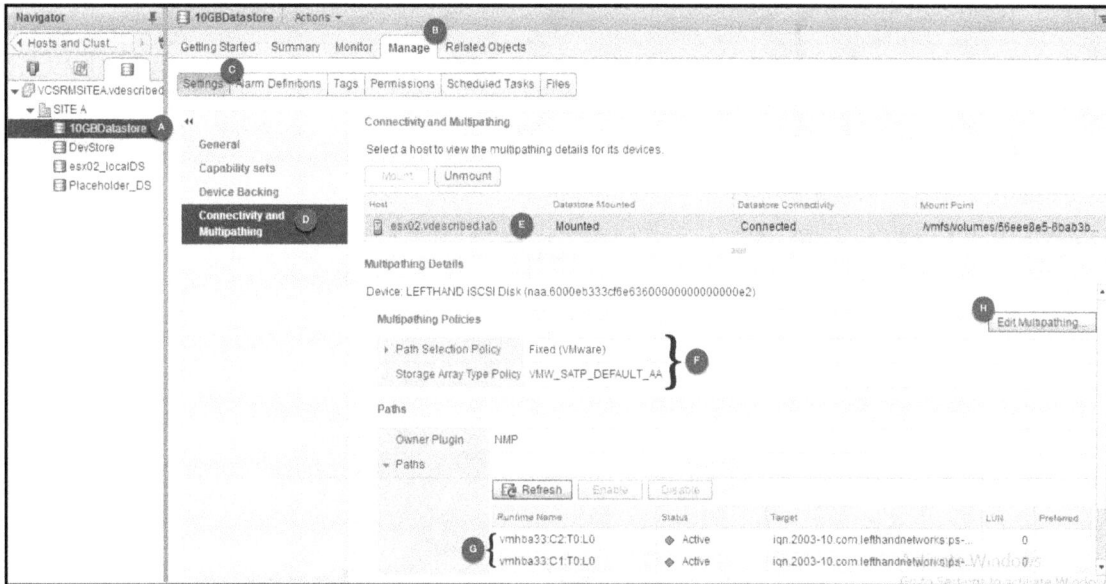

7. The **Edit Multipathing Policies** window will show the current Path selection policy selected and the number of paths to the LUN backing the datastore. You can use the drop-down menu to change the Multipathing policy:

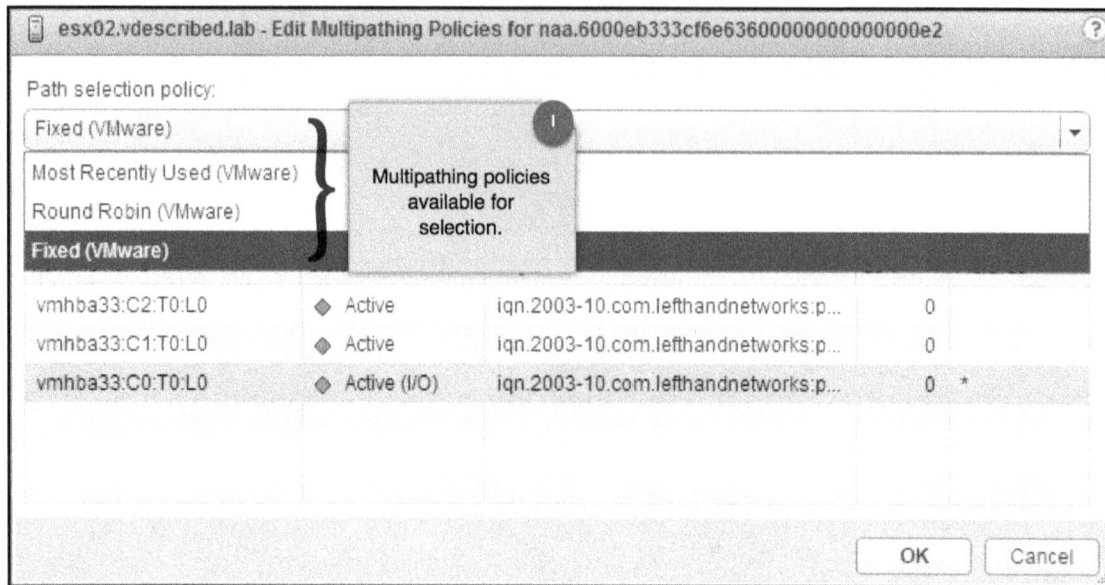

Managing storage capacity of a datastore

It is likely that you would run out of free space on a VMFS volume over time as you end up deploying more and more VMs on it, especially in a growing environment. Fortunately, accommodating additional free space on a VMFS volume is possible. However, this requires that either the LUN has free space left on it or it has been expanded/resized in the storage array. The procedure to resize/expand the LUN in the storage array differs from vendor to vendor, and as this is beyond the scope of this book, we assume that the LUN either has free space on it or has already been expanded.

Expanding/growing a VMFS datastore

Before attempting to grow the VMFS datastore, issue a rescan on the HBAs to ensure that the ESXi sees the increased size of the LUN. Also, make note of the NAA ID, LUN number, and the size of the LUN backing the VMFS datastore that you are trying to expand/grow.

We will go through the following process to expand an existing VMFS datastore using the vSphere Web Client's GUI:

1. Use the vSphere Web Client to connect to the vCenter Server.
2. Navigate to **Home** | **Storage**.
3. With the data center object selected, navigate to **Related Objects** | **Datastores**.

4. Right-click on the datastore you intend to expand and click on **Increase Datastore Capacity**.
5. Select the LUN backing the datastore and click on **Next**.
6. Use the **Partition Configuration** drop-down menu to select the free space left in DS01 to expand the datastore:

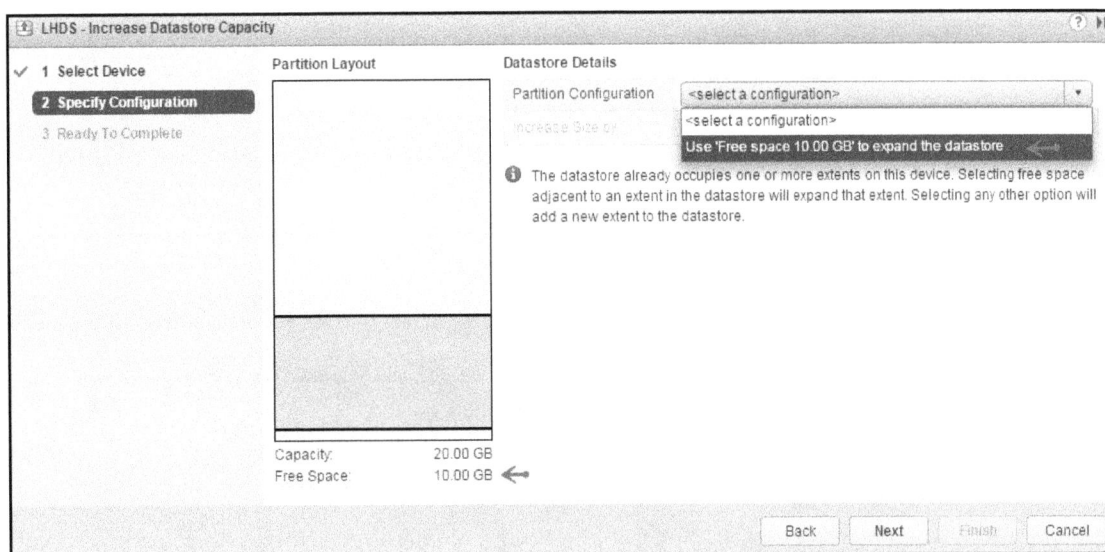

7. On the **Ready to Complete** screen, review the information and click on **Finish** to expand the datastore.

Expanding a VMFS datastore refers to the act of increasing its size within its own VMFS extent. Here, extent refers to a LUN backing the VMFS volume. This is possible only if there is free space available immediately after the extent. The maximum size of a LUN is 64 TB, so the maximum size of a VMFS volume is also 64 TB. The virtual machines hosted on this VMFS datastore will continue to be in the power-on state and remain uninterrupted, while this task is being accomplished.

Extending/spanning a VMFS datastore

You can run into a situation where there is no unused space on the LUN backing the VMFS volume, but your datastore runs out of space. Fortunately, vSphere supports the spanning of a VMFS volume onto multiple LUNs. This means you can span the VMFS volume onto a new LUN so that it can use the free space on it. *Such as a new LUN, which will be used to extend a VMFS volume, is referred to as an* **Extent**. This process of spanning a VMFS volume onto another LUN is called extending a VMFS datastore. The VMs running on the volume can still remain powered-on and will not be interrupted while this task is being accomplished:

1. Use the vSphere Web Client to connect to the vCenter Server.
2. Navigate to **Home** | **Storage**.
3. With the data center object selected, navigate to **Related Objects** | **Datastores**.
4. Right-click on the datastore you intend to expand and click on **Increase Datastore Capacity**.
5. Select the **RAW LUN** available to extend the datastore onto it.
6. Select **Use all available partitions** from the partition configuration drop-down box, choose a size to use, and click on **Next:**

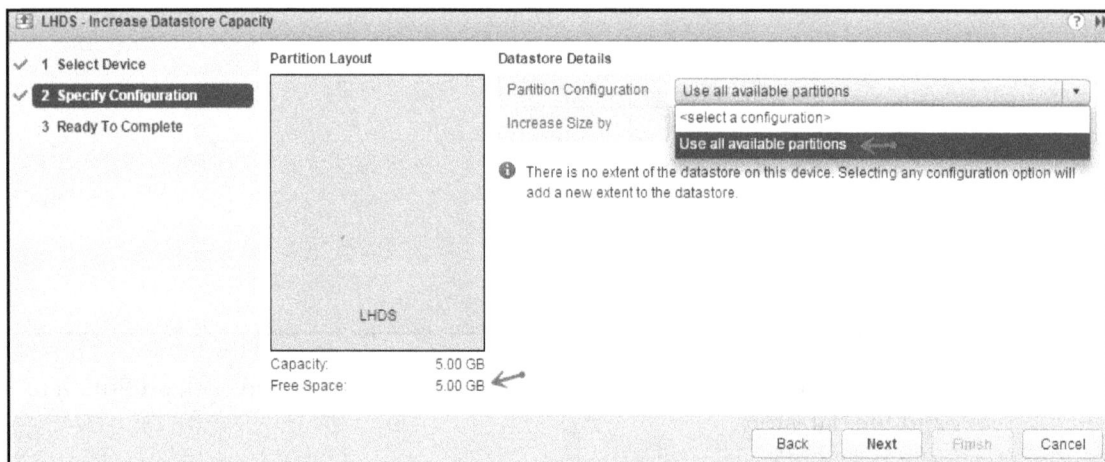

7. Review the details in the **Ready to Complete** screen and click on **Finish**.

Unlike expanding/growing a VMFS volume, extending a volume will make the volume span across multiple LUNs, and this is done by adding further extents to the VMFS volume. A VMFS datastore can span across a maximum of 32 LUN extents. The size of the extent can now be greater than 2 TB, the limit being the maximum VMFS volume size of 64 TB.

When you add extents to a datastore, the very first LUN that originally backed the datastore will become the head extent because it holds all the information regarding the other extents. If, for any reason, you lose the head extent, then that would make the entire VMFS datastore go offline. However, if you lose an extent that is not a head extent, then the datastore will still remain accessible, but only the virtual machines whose VMDKs depend on the lost extent will become inaccessible.

Removing access to a LUN

By now, you have a grasp on how VMFS Datastores are created and size-managed. However, anytime you might encounter a need to remove access to a particular or a bunch of Datastores from an ESXi host/cluster. There could be several reasons, one of them being maintenance or decommissioning. Regardless of the reason for the removal, it is recommended to gracefully remove access to the Datastore. This section of the chapter will walk you through the procedure:

1. Identify the datastore to be removed.
2. Verify whether any of the virtual machines are using the Datastore.
3. Unmount the datastore.
4. Detach the LUN device corresponding to the Datastore.
5. Un-present the LUN from the storage array.

This process can be achieved via either the vCenter GUI or the ESX's command -line interface. The VMware Knowledge base article 2004605 has the instructions for the same: `ht tp://kb.vmware.com/kb/2465`.

Managing VMFS snapshots

Storage array management tools allow us to clone/snapshot/replicate LUN/s backing VMFS datastore/s. The snapshots are created at the storage array using the array management interface. However, it is not possible to mount an identical copy of an existing VMFS datastore to the same ESXi host. This is deliberately disallowed to avoid data corruption, unless it is backed by a different device ID.

ESXi identifies each VMFS volume using its signature denoted by a **UUID** (**Universally Unique Identifier**). The UUID is generated when the volume is first created or resignatured and is stored in the LVM header of the VMFS volume.

The command `esxcli storage filesystem list` can be used to list all the VMFS datastores along with their details, which include the UUID, in columnar format as follows:

```
[root@esx02:~] esxcli storage filesystem list
Mount Point                                            Volume Name    UUID                                    Mounted  Type     Size         Free
-----------------------------------------------------  -------------  --------------------------------------  -------  -------  -----------  -----------
/vmfs/volumes/56782531-d69693c8-896e-000c29a1239a      ds03           56782531-d69693c8-896e-000c29a1239a     true     VMFS-5   21206401024  20238565376
/vmfs/volumes/56410901-0b4ff6d6-49b6-000c2922c8e8      esx02_localDS  56410901-0b4ff6d6-49b6-000c2922c8e8     true     VMFS-5   34896609280  23138926592
/vmfs/volumes/56440c24-fa2606eb-c539-000c29b5dab2      ds01           56440c24-fa2606eb-c539-000c29b5dab2     true     VMFS-5   10468982784  9543090176
/vmfs/volumes/56440c3a-41651ee4-5a1a-000c29b5dab2      ds02           56440c3a-41651ee4-5a1a-000c29b5dab2     true     VMFS-5   15837691904  14890827776
/vmfs/volumes/56dc9d97-e4f8e407-effa-000c2922c8e8                     56dc9d97-e4f8e407-effa-000c2922c8e8     true     vfat     4293591040   4279762944
/vmfs/volumes/3930df74-4d3c3f4b-4c67-143c89556f6a                     3930df74-4d3c3f4b-4c67-143c89556f6a     true     vfat     261853184    78577664
/vmfs/volumes/d8c58e7f-74951517-5557-b266ec76459a                     d8c58e7f-74951517-5557-b266ec76459a     true     vfat     261853184    91967488
/vmfs/volumes/56410901-b2b91637-093c-000c2922c8e8                     56410901-b2b91637-093c-000c2922c8e8     true     vfat     299712512    88342528
[root@esx02:~]
```

The following diagram shows the structure of a VMFS UUID:

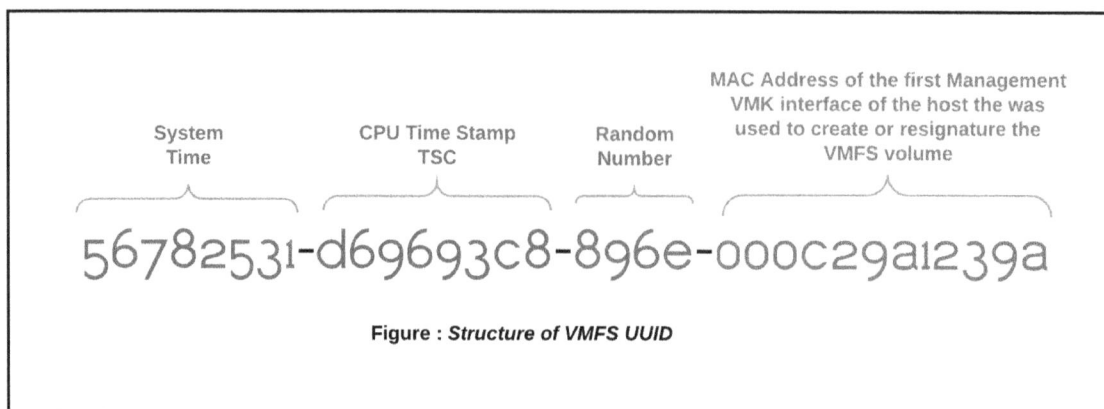

Figure : *Structure of VMFS UUID*

When an ESXi host scans for new LUN devices and VMFS volumes on it, it compares the physical device ID (NAA ID) of the LUN with the device ID (NAA ID) value stored in the VMFS volumes LVM header. If it finds a mismatch, then it flags the volume as a snapshot volume. Volumes detected as snapshots are not mounted by default.

There are two options to mount such volumes/datastores. These options are made available via the **New Datastore** wizard, only if you select a clone/snapshot/replica LUN with a VMFS volume on it:

New Datastore

✓ 1 Type

✓ 2 Name and device selection

✓ **3 Mount option**

4 Ready to complete

These are the two options for mounting a snapshot volume.

ⓘ An unresolved VMFS volume with signature 56440c24-fa2606eb-c539-000c29b5dab2 has been detected on this disk.

Specify whether you want to mount the detected VMFS volume with the same signature or with a new signature, or format the disk.

⦿ **Assign a new signature**

Data on the disk will be retained. A new signature will be assigned to the datastore and references to existing signature from VM configuration files will be updated.
Datastore will be mounted using the original name.

○ **Keep existing signature**

Data on the disk will be retained. The datastore will be mounted using the same signature.
Datastore will be mounted using the original name.

○ **Format the disk**

The current disk layout will be destroyed and all data will be lost permanently.

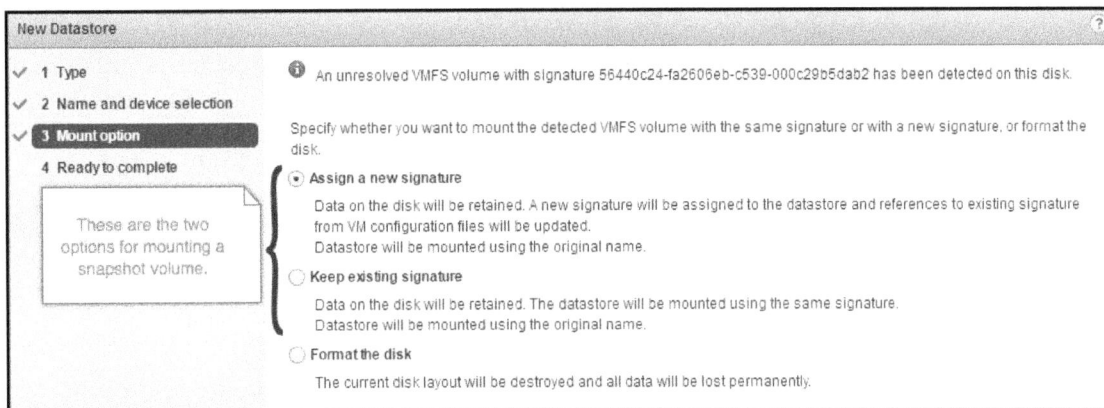

- The first option is to generate a new signature for the VMFS volume before mounting it. This has to be used if you are mounting a clone or a snapshot of an existing VMFS datastore to the same host/s. The option is presented as **Assign a new signature** in the **New Datastore** wizard. The process of assigning a new signature will not only update the LVM header with the newly generated UUID, but all the Physical Device ID (NAA ID) of the snapshot LUN. Here, the VMFS volume/datastore will be renamed by prefixing the word *snap* followed by a random number and the name of the original datastore:

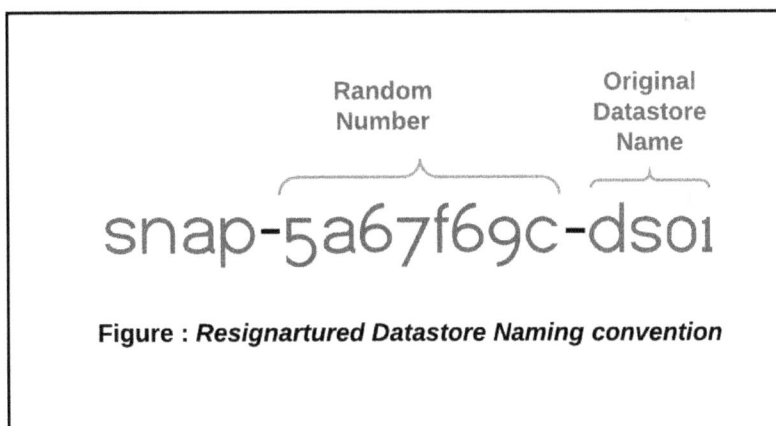

Random Number — **Original Datastore Name**

snap-5a67f69c-ds01

Figure : *Resignartured Datastore Naming convention*

- The second option is to mount the VMFS volume without generating a signature or updating the LVM header of the detected volume. The option is presented as **Keep existing signature** in the **New Datastore** wizard. This is used when you are attempting to temporarily mount the snapshot volume on an ESXi that doesn't see the original volume. If you were to attempt mounting the VMFS volume by keeping the existing signature and if the host sees the original volume, then you will not be allowed to mount the volume and will be warned about the presence of another VMFS volume with the same UUID:

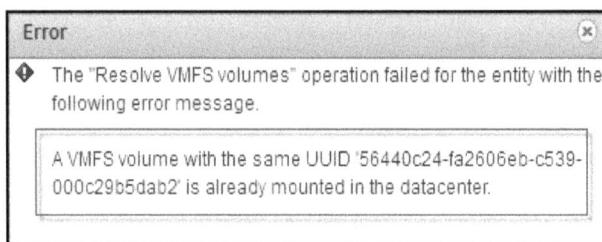

However, as mentioned before, the volume can be mounted onto an ESXi host that does not see the original datastore, with the same datastore name.

Storage I/O Control (SIOC)

Before we define or discuss what SIOC control is, there are a few concepts that form the basics and also explain the need for a mechanism like SIOC.

ESXi runs a local host scheduler to balance the I/O between the virtual machines. This means that if there are virtual machines churning a considerable amount of I/O (more than normal), then it is important to make sure that the other virtual machines residing on the same datastore remain unaffected, in a manner that they should be allowed to issue I/O to the device. This is achieved by controlling the volume of I/O each of the participating virtual machines can issue, with the help of per-vmdk shares. This works pretty much like the CPU or Memory shares. The default virtual disk share value is 1000, high being 2000 and low being – 500. The disk with a relatively higher share value will get to issue a larger volume of I/O operations to the device.

Now, all of this will work just fine as long as the datastore is seen by a single ESXi host. Unfortunately, that is not a common case. datastores are often shared among multiple ESXi hosts. When datastores are shared, you bring in more than one local host scheduler into the process of balancing the I/O among the virtual machines. Moreover, these lost host schedulers cannot talk to each other. Their visibility is limited to the ESXi hosts they are running on. This easily contributes to a serious problem called the *noisy neighbor* situation.

In the following example, since VM-C is the only virtual machine on ESX-02, it gets to consume the entire queue depth, which could starve virtual machines on the other two hosts. If VM-C indeed does a lot of IO consuming of the LUN's queue depth, then it will be referred to as a *noisy neighbor*:

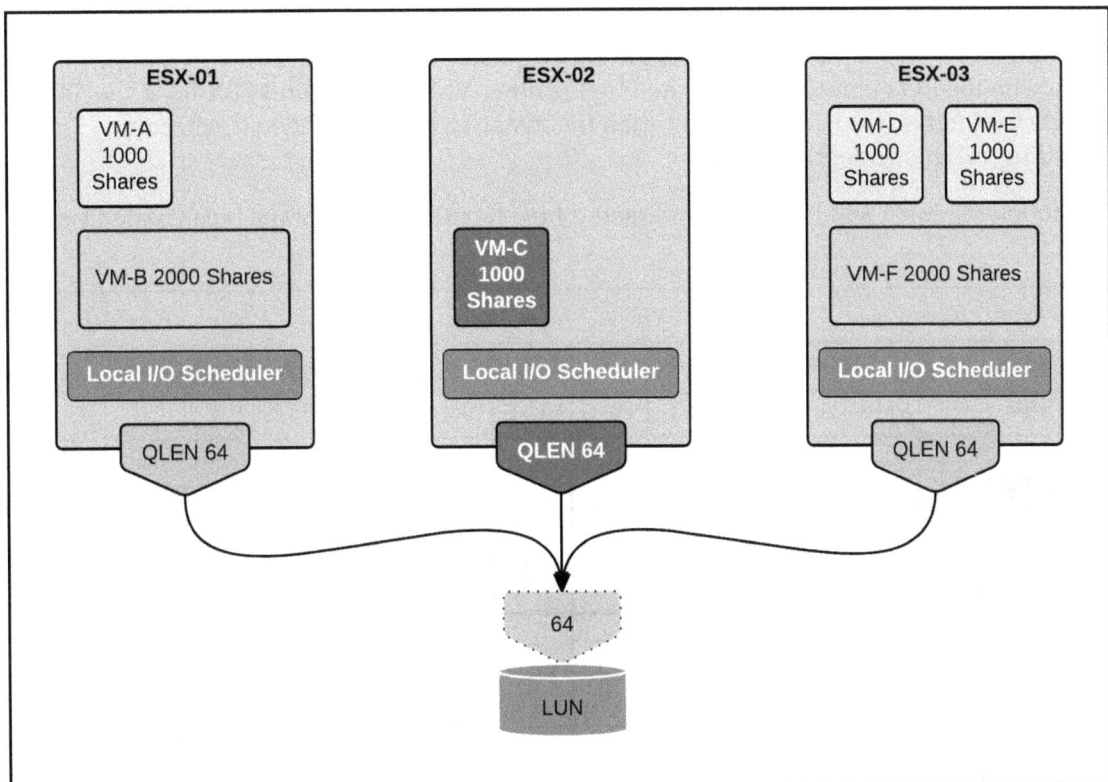

The job of SIOC is to enable some form of communication between these local host schedulers so that I/O can be balanced between virtual machines running on separate hosts. It does so by maintaining a shared file in the datastore that all hosts can read/write/update. When SIOC is enabled on a datastore, it starts monitoring the device latency on the LUN backing the datastore. If the latency crosses the threshold, it throttles the LUN's queue depth on each of the ESXi hosts in an attempt to distribute a fair share of access to the LUN for all the Virtual Machines issuing the I/O.

Let's consider the previous scenario, wherein there are six virtual machines running on three different ESXi hosts, accessing a single-shared LUN. Among the six VMs, four of them have a normal share value of 1000 and the remaining two have high (2000) disk share value sets on them. These virtual machines have only a single VMDK attached to them. VM-C on host ESX-02 is issuing a large number of I/O operations. Since that is the only VM accessing the shared LUN from that host, it gets the entire queue's bandwidth. This can induce latency on the I/O operations performed by the other VMs: ESX-01 and ESX-03. If the SIOC detects the latency value to be greater than the dynamic threshold, then it will start throttling the queue depth.

The following table will help you understand how fair share percentage is calculated by SIOC:

Hosts	ESX-01		ESX-02	ESX-03			How to arrive at the ratio (portion value) ?	
VMs	VM-A	VM-B	VM-C	VM-D	VM-E	VM-F		
Disk Shares	1000	2000	1000	1000	1000	2000	Ratio	(VM Share Value) / (Total Share Value)
VM's portion of the shares	1/8	1/4	1/8	1/4	1/8	1/8	1/8	1000/8000
							1/4	2000/8000
VM's Percent of Shares	12.5	25	12.5	25	12.5	12.5		
DQLEN for the VM	8	16	8	16	8	8		
DQLEN for the Host	24		8	32				

The throttled DQLEN for a VM is calculated as follows:

DQLEN for the VM = (VM's Percent of Shares) of (Queue Depth)

Example: 12.5 % of 64 à (12.5 * 64)/100 = 8

The throttled DQLEN per host is calculated as follows:

DQLEN of the Host = Sum of the DQLEN of the VMs on it

Example: VM-A (8) + VM-B(16) = 24

The following diagram shows the effect of SIOC throttling the queue depth:

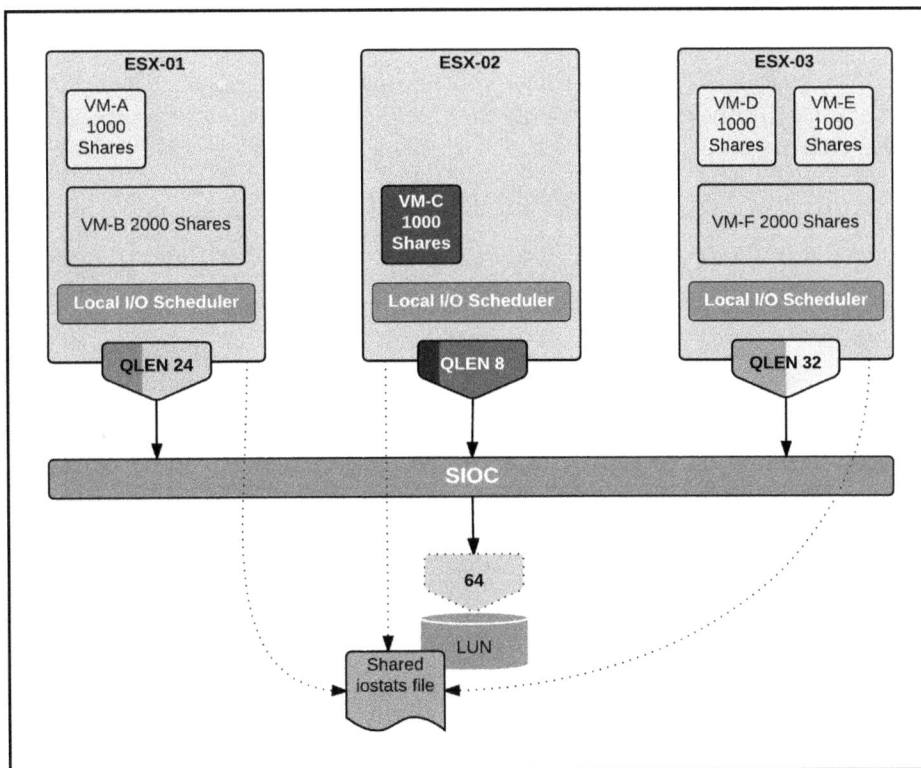

The local scheduler on each of the ESXi hosts uses the iostats file to keep its companion hosts aware of the device I/O statistics observed on the LUN. The file is placed in a directory (naa.xxxxxxxxx) on the same datastore:

Enabling SIOC

SIOC can only be enabled at the datastore level. You will need access to the vCenter Server managing the hosts to configure SIOC. Post that SIOC is not dependent on the vCenter for any of its operations.

The following procedure will guide you through the steps required to enable SIOC:

1. Connect to the vCenter Server and switch to the `Datastore` inventory view.
2. Select the datastore from the inventory and navigate to **Manage | Settings | General**.
3. In the **General** settings page, locate **Datastore Capabilities** and click on **Edit** to bring up the **Configure Storage I/O Control** window:

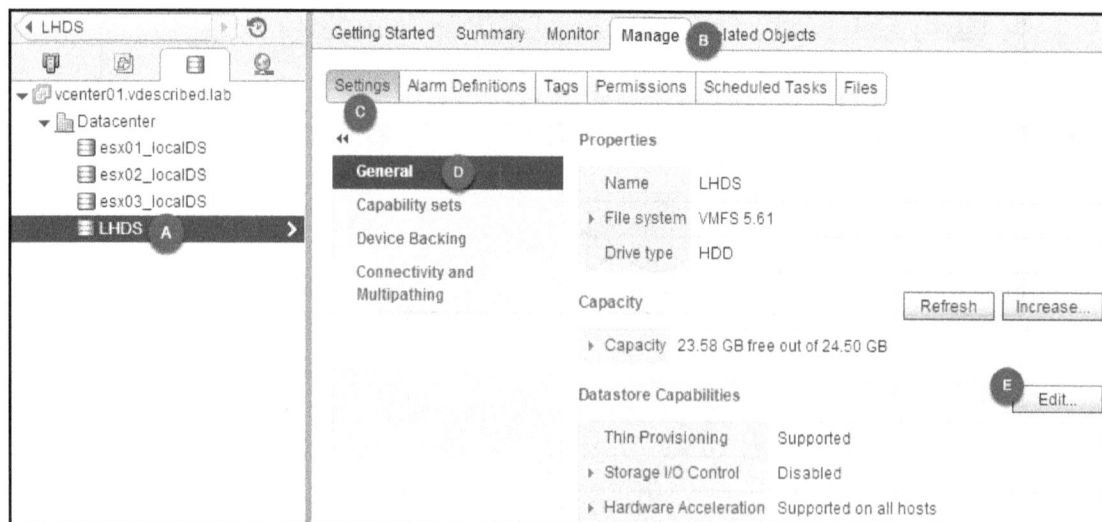

4. In the **Configure Storage I/O Control** window, select the checkbox **Enable Storage I/O Control**. Review the Congestion Threshold value and make sure it is ideal for your environment. By default, SIOC dynamically sets the latency value learnt while the datastore is operating at a peak throughput of 90%:

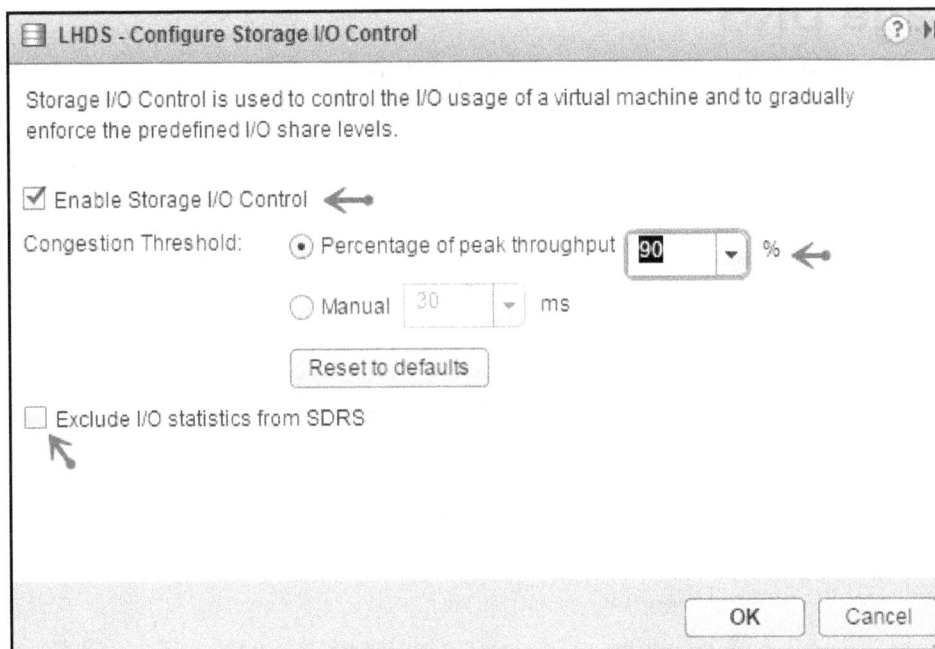

5. However, you can manually set the latency value based on your type and performance characteristics of the disk backing the LUN device.

6. Here is a chart that can help you arrive at an ideal Latency value:

Storage Media Type	Latency Threshold in milliseconds(ms)
Fiber Channel (FC)	20 – 30 ms
Serial Attached SCSI (SAS)	20 – 30 ms
Serial ATA (SATA)	30 – 50 ms
Solid State Device (SSD)	15 – 20 ms

7. You can also choose to exclude I/O statistics from SDRS at this point.
8. Select **Enable Storage I/O Control** and click **OK**.

Storage DRS

Much like ESXi hosts, the VMFS datastores can be grouped to form a datastore cluster. This helps in enabling the Storage Distributed Scheduler on it to ease datastore management.

Like with the clustering of the compute resource, datastore clusters will also need to meet certain requirements. Here are some of the most important ones:

- The datastores in a datastore cluster should only be accessible to ESXi hosts from a single data center (vCenter Data Center inventory object)
- A single datastore cluster cannot contain both VMFS and NFS volumes
- All the ESXi hosts accessing the datastores should be of version ESXi 5.0 or higher
- Additional requirements are listed in the vSphere 6 Resource Management Guide on page-91

Here is the URL to the guide: `http://bit.ly/vspherermg6`.

The following procedure will guide you through the steps required to create a datastore cluster and enable Storage DRS on it:

1. Connect to the vCenter Server and navigate to **Home** | **Storage**.
2. Right-click on the datacenter in which you intend to create the datastore cluster and click on **New Datastore Cluster...** to bring up the **New Datastore Cluster** wizard.
3. Supply a cluster name. Since the sole purpose of creating a datastore cluster is to enable Storage DRS on it, the option **Turn ON Storage DRS** is selected by default. Click **Next** to continue.
4. Choose a desired **Cluster automation level**. There are two automation levels:

- No Automation (Manual Mode) – *This is the default mode*
- Fully Automated

You can also set Space, I/O Imbalance, Affinity Rules enforcement, Storage/VM policy, and VM Evacuation automation levels at this point. By default, all the parameters are set to the **Use cluster settings** option:

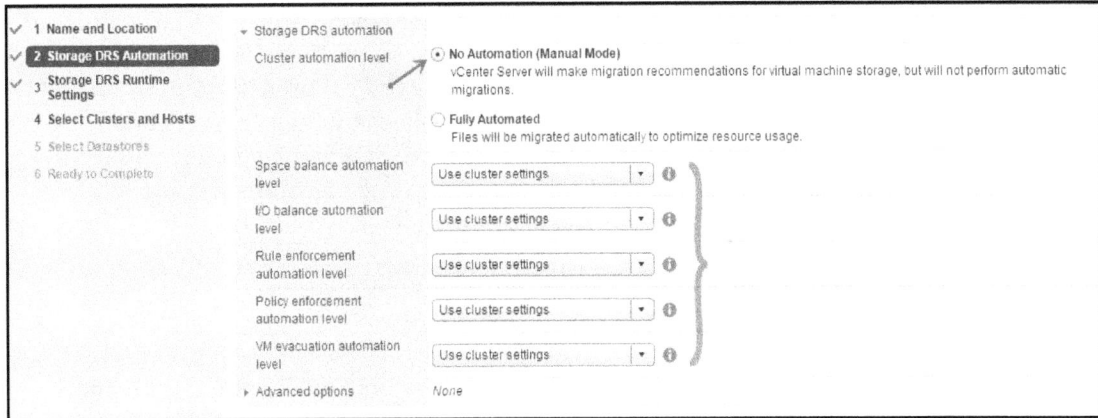

5. On the next screen set the **Storage DRS Runtime Settings**, which includes:

- Space threshold: 80% (default)
- I/O latency threshold: 15 ms (default)
- Default VM affinity: Keep VMDKs together by default
- Space difference threshold before recommendations are generated: 5%
- Frequency of the I/O imbalance check: 8 hours (default)
- I/O imbalance threshold: Aggressive+5 (default)

6. Once done, select the cluster to add the Datastores from.
7. Select the datastore that you intend to be part of the Datastore cluster.
8. Review the **Ready to Complete** screen and click **Finish** to create the datastore cluster with SDRS enabled on it.

Once Storage DRS is enabled, it generates storage migration recommendations based on the space utilization and latency threshold. Load balancing based on space utilization cannot be disabled, but load balancing based on the I/O congestion can be disabled.

Initial placement

When you deploy a VM onto a datastore cluster with SDRS enabled, SDRS will provide placement recommendations based on the space utilization and the I/O load on the datastores. This reduces the complexity in decision making when you have a large number of datastores in the environment, and of course, they must be part of a datastore cluster for this to work. SDRS provides placement recommendations and chooses one of the recommended datastores. However, the user can opt to select another recommended datastore. Although I/O load balancing can be disabled, the SDRS will still have access to the I/O statistics of the datastores. If SDRS finds more than one datastore suitable to place the virtual machine, then it will choose the datastore with the lowest I/O load.

Balancing space utilization

With Storage DRS not enabled, it is quite possible that over time, when you deploy more and more virtual machines, you end up saturating the free space on a set of datastores, while leaving a few other datastores underutilized. This could eventually cause "out-of-space" conditions, affecting the running VMs, but with Storage DRS enabled in a datastore cluster, the space utilization on the datastores and the growth rate of the VMDKs (if thin provisioned) is monitored. The default threshold for space utilization is 80 percent. Storage DRS will start generating Storage VMotion recommendations when the threshold is exceeded.

Balancing I/O load

The I/O load on a datastore is measured based on the current I/O latency, as seen by the virtual machines running on them. The default threshold for the latency is 15 milliseconds (15000 microseconds). If I/O load balancing is enabled, then the I/O latency statistics are evaluated every eight hours. SDRS uses 16 hours worth of data to generate Storage vMotion recommendations. The migrations based on I/O load imbalance occur only once a day.

Summary

In this chapter, we started with the basics of vSphere storage, understanding the difference between local and remote storage and also the different Storage Protocols supported by vSphere. We then learnt about the Pluggable Storage Architecture (PSA), a modular API framework that lets storage vendors build their own SATP or PSP plugins. We learnt how to configure access to Fiber Channel, iSCSI, and NFS storage. We learnt how to create and manage VMFS Datastores. Finally, we covered advanced topics such as Storage IO Control (SIOC) and Storage DRS. In the next chapter, we will cover some Advanced Infrastructure management topics.

6
Advanced vSphere Infrastructure Management

In the previous chapters, we learnt how to deploy and configure both ESXi hosts and the vCenter server. With vCenter being the management layer of your vSphere infrastructure, there is a plethora of management options available at this layer.

In this chapter, we will cover the following topics:

- Introducing vSphere vMotion
- Clustering ESXi hosts for compute aggregation and power management
- Clustering ESXi hosts for high availability

Introducing vSphere vMotion

vSphere vMotion is a VMware technology used to migrate a running virtual machine from one host to another without altering its power state. The beauty of the whole process is that it is transparent to the applications running inside the virtual machine. In this section, we will understand the inner workings of vMotion and learn how to configure it.

There are different types of vMotion:

- Compute vMotion
- Storage vMotion
- Unified vMotion
- Enhanced vMotion (X-vMotion)
- Cross vSwitch vMotion
- Cross vCenter vMotion
- Long Distance vMotion

Compute vMotion is the default vMotion method and is employed by other features such as DRS, FT, and maintenance mode. When you initiate a vMotion, it initiates an iterative copy of all the memory pages. After the first pass, all the dirtied memory pages are copied again by doing another pass and this is done iteratively until the amount of pages left over to be copied is small enough to be transferred, and to switch over the state of the VM to the destination host. During the switch over, the virtual machine's device states are transferred and resumed at the destination host. You can initiate up to eight simultaneous vMotion operations on a single host.

Storage vMotion is used to migrate the files backing a virtual machine (virtual disks, configuration files, and logs) from one datastore to another while the virtual machine is still running. When you initiate a storage vMotion, it starts a sequential copy of source disks in 64 MB chunks. While a region is being copied, all the writes issued to that region are deferred until the region is copied. An already copied source region is monitored for further writes. If there is a write I/O, then it will be mirrored to the destination disk as well. This process of mirror writes to the destination virtual disk continues until the sequential copy of the entire source virtual disk is complete. Once the sequential copy is complete, all subsequent reads/writes are issued to the destination virtual disk. Keep in mind though that while the sequential copy is still in progress all the reads are issued to the source virtual disk. Storage vMotion is used in the storage DRS. You initiate up to two simultaneous SvMotion operations on a single host.

Unified vMotion is used to migrate both the running state of a virtual machine and files backing it from one host and datastore to another. Unified vMotion uses a combination of both Compute and Storage vMotion to achieve the migration. First, the configuration files and the virtual disks are migrated and only then does the migration of live states of the virtual machine begin. You can initiate up to two simultaneous Unified vMotion operations on a single host.

Enhanced vMotion (X-vMotion) is used to migrate virtual machines between hosts that do not share storage. Both the virtual machine's running state and the files backing it are transferred over the network to the destination. The migration procedure is the same as the Compute and Storage vMotion. In fact, Enhanced vMotion uses Unified vMotion to achieve the migration. Since the memory and disk states are transferred over the vMotion network, ESXi hosts maintain a transmit buffer at the source and a receive buffer at the destination. The transmit buffer collects and places data on to the network, while the receive buffer will collect data received via the network and then flush it to the storage. You can initiate up to two simultaneous X-vMotion operations on a single host.

Cross vSwitch vMotion allows you to choose a destination port group for the virtual machine. It is important to note that unless the destination port group supports the same L2 network, the virtual machine will not be able to communicate over the network. Cross vSwitch vMotion allows changing from Standard vSwitch to a VDS, but not from a VDS to Standard vSwitch. vSwitch to vSwitch and VDS to VDS is supported.

Cross vCenter vMotion allows the migration of virtual machines beyond the vCenter's boundary. This is a new enhancement with vSphere 6.0. However, for this to be possible both the vCenters should be in the same SSO domain and should be in enhanced linked mode. Infrastructure requirements for Cross vCenter vMotion have been detailed in the VMware Knowledge Base article 2106952 at the following link: `http://kb.vmware.com/kb/216952`.

Long Distance vMotion allows migrating virtual machines over distances with a latency not exceeding 150 milliseconds. Prior to vSphere 6.0, the maximum supported network latency for vMotion was 10 milliseconds.

Using the provisioning interface

You can configure a provisioning interface to send all non-active data of the virtual machine being migrated. Prior to vSphere 6.0, vMotion used the vmkernel interface which has the default gateway configured on it (which in most cases is the management interface vmk0) to transfer non-performance impacting vMotion data. Non-performance impacting vMotion data includes the virtual machine's home directory, older delta in the snapshot chain, base disks, and so on. Only the live data will hit the vMotion interface. The provisioning interface is nothing but a vmkernel interface with provisioning traffic enabled on this. The procedure to do this is very similar to how you would configure a VMkernel interface for management or vMotion traffic. You will have to edit the settings of the intended **vmk** interface and set **Provisioning traffic** as the enabled service:

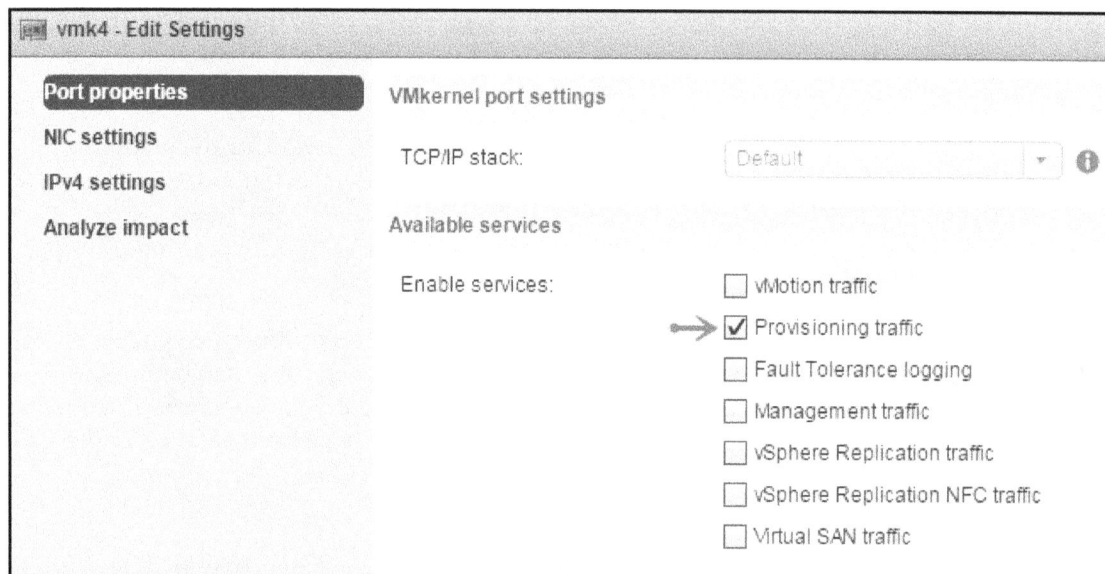

It is important to keep in mind that the provisioning interface is not just meant for VMotion data, but if enabled, it will be used for cold migrations, cloning operations, and virtual machine snapshots. The provisioning interface can be configured to use a different gateway other than VMkernel's default gateway.

Enabling vMotion

vMotion traffic should be enabled on a vmkernel interface to make an ESXi host vMotion capable.. The procedure is fairly straightforward. It can either be done using the vSphere Client or the vSphere Web Client. Although we will discuss how this can be done using the vCenter GU, it is not mandatory to use the vCenter to enable vMotion:

1. Connect to the vCenter using the vSphere Web Client
2. In the **Host and Clusters** inventory, select an ESXi, host, navigate to **Manage** | **Networking** | **VMkernel adapters,** and select the vmk interface to enable vMotion.
3. With the vmk interface selected, click on the pencil icon ![pencil icon] to bring-up the **Edit Settings** window.
4. In the **Edit Settings** window, select **vMotion traffic** as the **enabled service** and click **OK**:

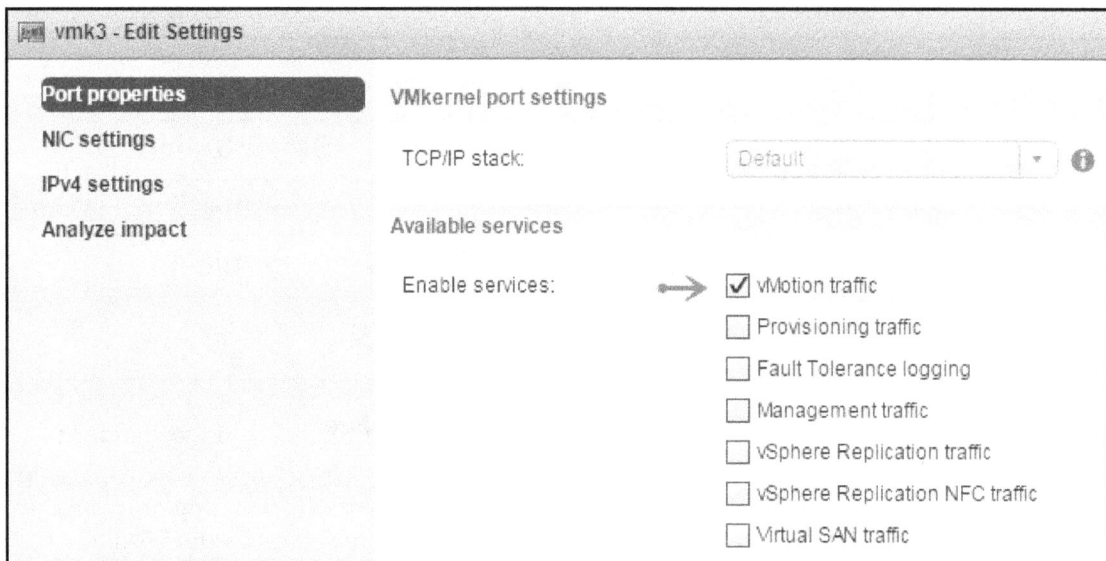

5. Repeat steps 2 through 4 to enable vMotion on all the hosts in the cluster.

Enabling Multi-NIC vMotion

vMotion can be configured to use more than one physical NIC for traffic. Regardless of whether this has been configured on a VDS or a standard vSwitch, multi-NIC vMotion is achieved by configuring two separate vmkernel interfaces with vMotion traffic enabled on them.

Here is how it is done:

1. Identify the physical adapters (vmnics) cabled to pass the vMotion traffic on.
2. Create two separate VMkernel interfaces with the vMotion traffic enabled on it.
3. Now, on the port groups corresponding to them, set the vmnics in active/standby mode configuration.

   For instance, if you were to use **vmnic4** and **vminc5,** then create two separate vmkernel interfaces, **vmk2** and **vmk3,** and configure the failover order as follows:

vmkernel interface	Active NIC	Standby NIC
vmk 2	vmnic 4	vmnic 5
vmk 3	vmnic 5	vmnic 4

4. You will have to repeat steps 1 through 3 on all the ESXi hosts, if the standard switch is being used.
5. If a VDS is being used, then you will have to configure NIC teaming only once at the dvPortGroup level. When you create vmkernel interfaces on the ESXi hosts, you will need to assign them to the dvPortGroup that was already created.

Performing a vMotion

vMotion can only be performed using the vCenter server. All the types of vMotion are achieved using the same migration wizard.

The migration wizard will present you with three migration types as options and those are:

- Change compute resource only
- Change storage only
- Change both compute resource and storage

Migrate Wizard Option	Achievable vMotion Type
Change compute resource only	vMotion
Change storage only	Storage vMotion
Change both compute resource and storage	Unified vMotion, Long Distance vMotion, Cross vCenter vMotion, Corss vSwitch vMotion

Any migration type that involves compute migration will be presented with a wizard option to choose the destination port group that the virtual machine will be connected to after a successful migration. Although, vCenter handles configuring to the VM to connect to a different port group, it doesn't deal with the changing of the IP address if the destination port group is a different layer-2 network. This should be manually done by the administrator.

You also get to set a priority for the vMotion operations, by choosing between high or normal priority. The priority determines the amount of CPU resources that will be allocated for the vMotion operation. The priority of each vMotion task is relative to the priority set on the other vMotion tasks.

The following walk-through will help you visualize how a migration is initiated for a virtual machine:

1. Connect to the vCenter server using the vSphere Web Client.
2. Select the virtual machine from the inventory, right-click on it, and select **Migrate**.
3. In the Migrate wizard screen, choose a migration type as per your requirement and click **Next** to continue:

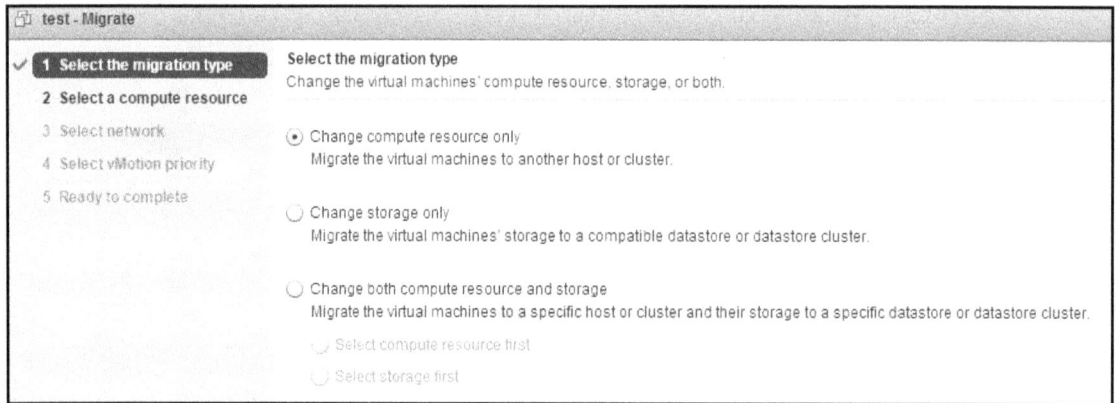

4. In the **Select a compute resource** screen, select a destination host or cluster (available from more than one vCenter if they are in enhanced linked mode) and click **Next**.
5. In the **Select network** screen, choose the destination port group for the virtual machine if required, and click **Next**.
6. In the **Select vMotion priority** screen, set a priority for the task and click **Next.**
7. In the **Ready to complete** screen, review the migration options selected and click **Finish** to start the migration.

Enhanced vMotion Capability

In a vSphere environment, as your clusters scale out, though it is imperative to have processors with the same make and model, you could end up having hosts in a cluster with uncommon processor feature sets. For Compute vMotion to work or for the migrated VM to function reliably on the destination host, it is important to guarantee that the processor feature set of all the ESXi hosts in the cluster are identical. With **Enhanced vMotion Capability** (**EVC**) you can present a common feature set to all the virtual machines in the cluster. VMware has made several baselines available to choose from, for both AMD and Intel processors. The baselines are generally categorized by their CPU generations.

The following table lists the available baselines with vSphere 6.x for both Intel and AMD:

Intel	AMD
Merom	Opteron Gen 1
Penryn	Opteron Gen 2
Nehalem	Opteron Gen 3 (with 3D Now)
Westmere	Opteron Gen 3
Sandy Bridge	Opteron Gen 4
Ivy Bridge	Opteron Piledriver
Haswell	Opteron Steamroller

Enabling EVC

Since EVC enables a common processor baseline, it is inevitable that some of the running virtual machines are using processor features that will become unavailable when you present a new baseline.

For the virtual machines to see the features available in a baseline, it requires a reboot. Also, you wouldn't be allowed to apply a lower EVC baseline than that of the current hardware processor generation until you evacuate the running/suspended virtual machines from the hosts.

Here is a sample warning message that prevents setting the chosen lower baseline:

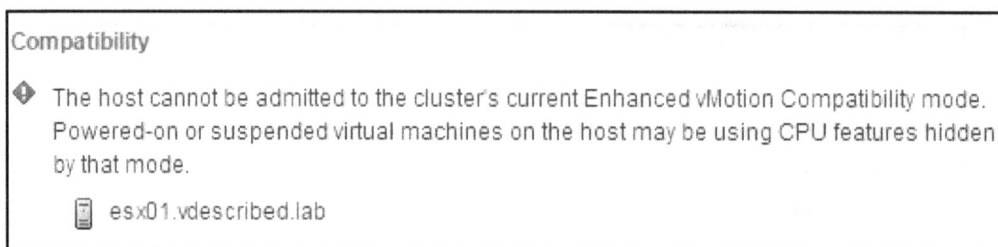

Compatibility

◆ The host cannot be admitted to the cluster's current Enhanced vMotion Compatibility mode. Powered-on or suspended virtual machines on the host may be using CPU features hidden by that mode.

     esx01.vdescribed.lab

To minimize the downtime, you could migrate the virtual machine to another cluster or a set of standby hosts before you enable the EVC baseline on the cluster. In cases where you do not have a cluster or standby hosts to migrate the virtual machines to, you will have to create a new EVC cluster and start moving evacuated (maintenance mode) hosts into the new cluster. As we progress, the moving host you can schedule downtime for sets off virtual machines and begins restarting them on the hosts in the new EVC cluster. If you are setting a processor baseline that has more features than the current processor, then it doesn't stipulate that the virtual machines should be evacuated. But, again, a reboot is necessary, if it has seen a new/differently represented feature.

The following walk-though will help you visualize the procedure involved in enabling EVC. The steps recommended in the walk-though will require a scheduled or an immediate downtime depending on the baseline level you choose to apply. Choosing a lower baseline would mean that you will have to plan for downtime at the same time as you plan to configure EVC. Choosing a higher baseline can allow you enough time to plan for a scheduled reboot at a later date. However, it is recommended to reboot the virtual machine once it has been moved to an EVC cluster:

1. Connect to the vCenter server using the vSphere Web Client and navigate to the Hosts and Clusters view.

2. Migrate all the virtual machines to another cluster, standalone hosts or shut them down.

3. Select the cluster to enable EVC on, navigate to **Manage** | **Settings** | **VMware EVC,** and click on **Edit** to bring up the **Change EVC Mode** window:

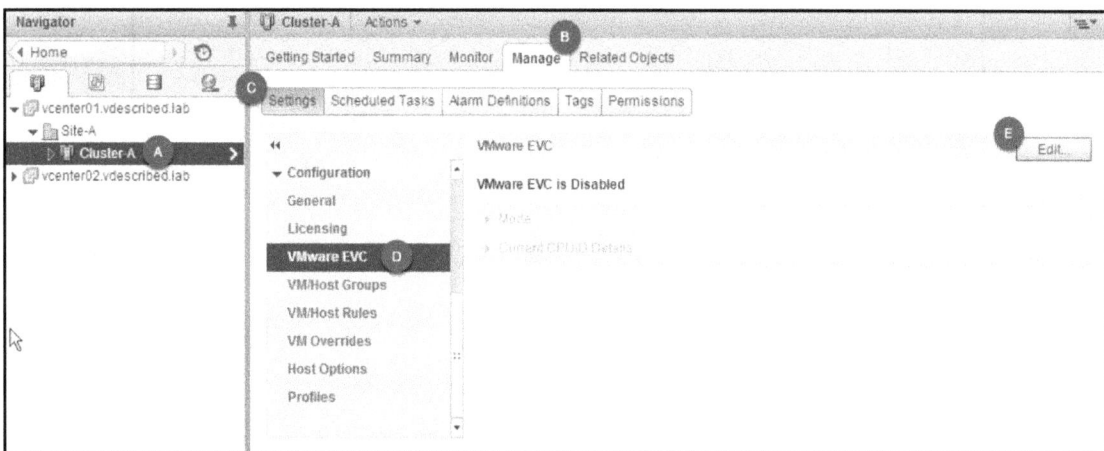

4. In the **Change EVC Mode** window, select an EVC baseline that matches the make of the host's processor hardware. You will be presented with three options:

   - **Disable EVC**
   - **Enable EVC for AMD Hosts**
   - **Enable EVC for Intel® Hosts**

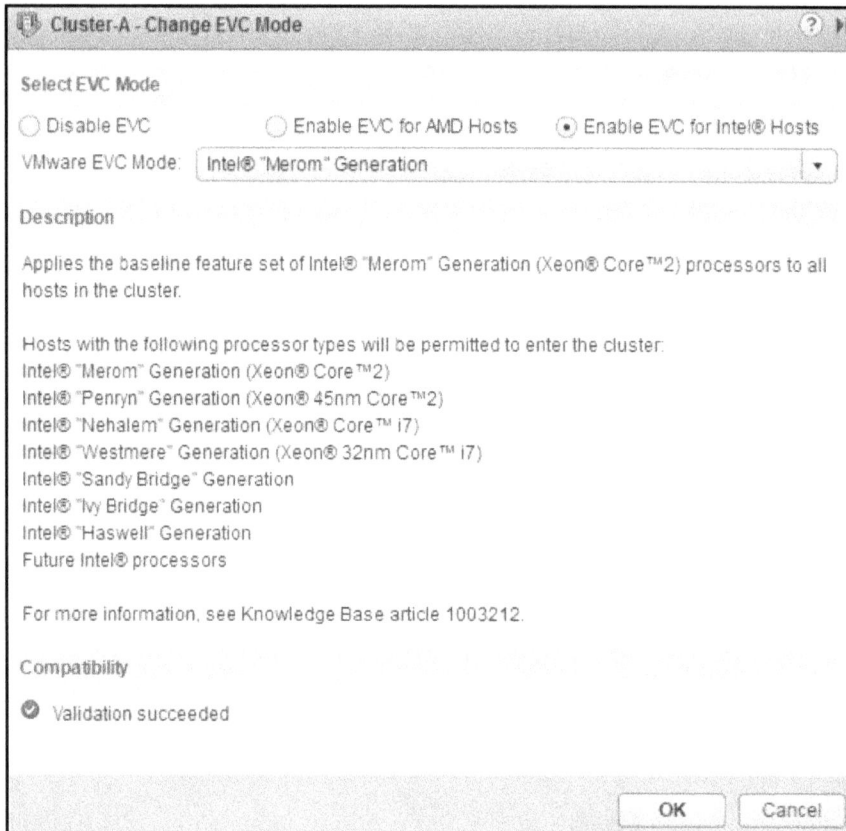

You cannot apply an AMD baseline to Intel or vice versa. Click **OK** if the validation succeeds.

5. Power-off the migrated VMs (if you have not already done so), move them back to the EVC cluster, and power them on.

Note that you cannot apply an EVC baseline if the underlying physical processor doesn't support the features in the baseline.

Clustering ESXi hosts for compute aggregation and power management

When you form an ESXi cluster, the compute resources, namely, the CPU and memory resources, can be managed as an aggregated pool of resources and load balanced. This is achieved by enabling vCenter's distributed resource scheduler or DRS. DRS is also used by other solutions like vSphere HA, vSphere Fault Tolerance, vCenter Update Manager, and so on. We will learn more about how these solutions leverage DRS later in this section.

Clustering of ESXi hosts also enables the ability to perform proactive power management of the hosts. This is achieved using the vCenter feature called distributed power management or DPM.

Distributed resource scheduler – DRS

DRS is vCenter's load balancing mechanism. It requires vCenter to be operational for it to work. DRS can only be enabled on a cluster of ESXi hosts. The vCenter server maintains a separate thread for every DRS cluster managed by it. DRS, once enabled, will have a holistic view of the cluster's compute resources, and hence has the ability to migrate virtual machines as per their changing runtime compute workload requirements. The so-called holistic view of a cluster's compute resources is referred to as a **root resource pool**. DRS uses vMotion to migrate virtual machines between the hosts to balance the workload on the hosts. This is an effort to reduce any compute resource imbalance in the cluster. Balancing the compute resources will ensure that the virtual machines in the cluster get the resources when they need it, thereby increasing the service levels. DRS monitors the resource utilization on the ESXi hosts, does an intelligent allocation of resources, balances the compute capacity, and also helps in reducing the power consumption in the data center using DRS's power management feature called distributed power management (DPM). VMware DPM can help reduce the energy consumption of a data center by vacating virtual machines from an underutilized host, putting that host in a power-off state and powering them back on when needed.

Another important benefit of using DRS is the ease by which virtual machines can be hosted on the ESXi host without being worried about verifying the resource utilization on ESXi hosts. In DRS terms, this is referred to as **initial placement**. When you choose a DRS enabled cluster as the destination for a virtual machine, DRS determines the best-suited host for the VM. DRS also lets you configure VM-to-VM **affinity** or **anti-affinity** rules. These rules help an administrator to create DRS placement definitions to force closeness or distance virtual machines as per their requirements. DRS is also used by another vCenter feature called the **host maintenance mode**. When you put an ESXi host into maintenance mode, vCenter leverages DRS to migrate virtual machines running on hosts to other suitable hosts in the cluster.

DRS resource pools

DRS resource pools are commonly referred to as consumers of cluster resources, but they really aren't consumers, since there is no workload associated with the resource pool itself. Instead, resource pools are workload load aggregators. Virtual machines that belong to a particular resource pool are the actual consumers. When DRS is enabled on a cluster, its compute resources are aggregated under a **root resource pool**. It becomes the parent resource pool for administrator-created DRS resource pools.

Enabling DRS on a cluster

vSphere DRS can only be enabled on an ESXi cluster via the vCenter managing that cluster. DRS can be enabled via the Cluster Creation wizard or by editing the settings of an already created cluster. Before you enable DRS on a cluster, you will need to enable vMotion on all ESXi hosts that will become a member of the cluster. Though this is not a mandatory initial step, it is a recommend practice.

The following walk-through will help you visualize the steps involved in enabling DRS on a cluster:

1. Connect to the vCenter using the vSphere Web Client and navigate to the **Hosts and Clusters inventory** view.

2. Select the cluster to enable DRS on, navigate to **Manage | Settings | vSphere DRS,** and click on **Edit.**

3. In the **Edit Cluster Settings** window, select the **Turn ON vSphere DRS** checkbox:

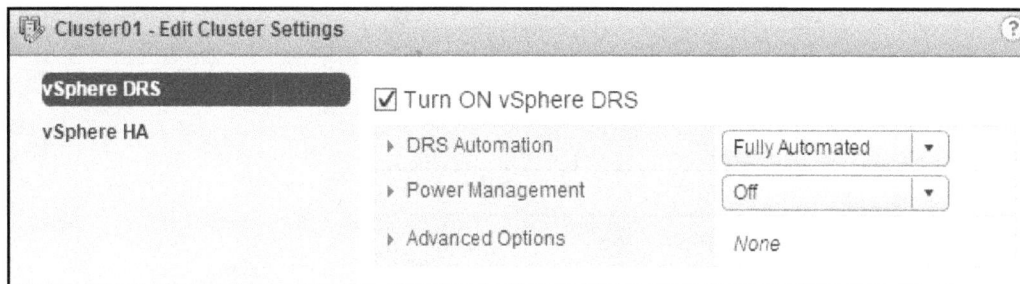

> You can jump to the last step (step 7) at this stage to enable DRS with all the defaults. If you wish to continue to customize DRS at this time, continue with step 4.

4. Click on **DRS Automation** to expand it and view the options available:

- **Automation Level**: choose one of the three automation levels (**Manual, Partial Automated,** or **Fully Automated**).
- **Migration Threshold**: use the slider to adjust the threshold to a desired level.
- **Virtual Machine Automation**: the checkbox to enable individual virtual machine automation levels is preselected by default. With this checkbox enabled, you can override DRS automation levels for individual virtual machines.

5. Click on **Power Management** to expand it and view the options available:

- **Automation Level**: it is off by default. You could choose between **Manual** or **Automatic** to enable it. You can set an host level DPM override from the **Host Options** configuration page. The procedure will be covered in a future section.

- **DPM Threshold**: use the slide to set a desired threshold level:

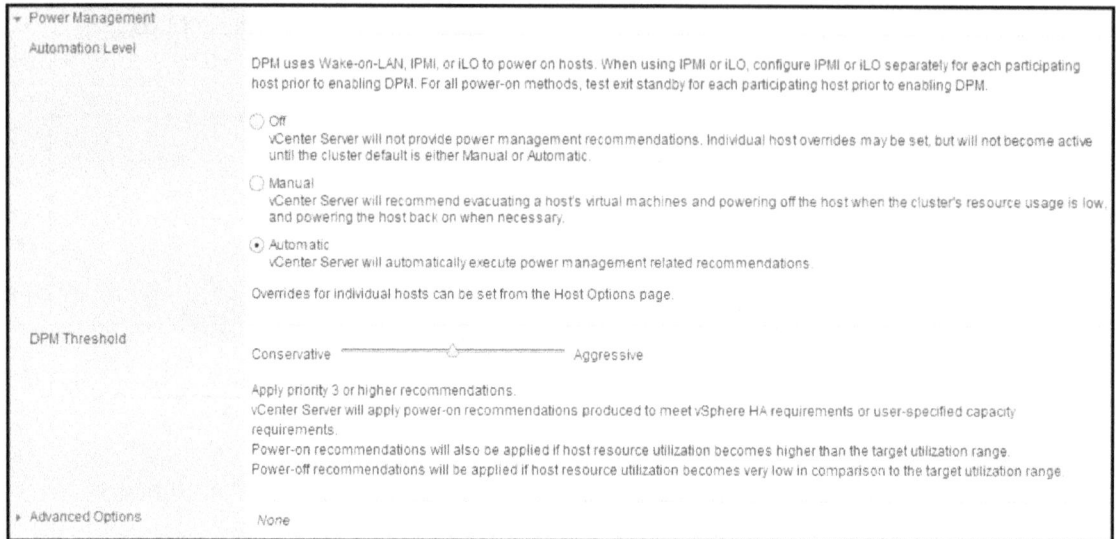

6. Click on **Advanced Options** to expand and set the **Configuration Parameters**.
7. Once done, click **OK** to enable DRS.

Once we have DRS enabled and active, its job is to load balance the DRS cluster for effective and fair utilization of the cluster resources. It does so by migrating or generating migration recommendations for virtual machines when needed. Migration recommendations will be generated by DRS only when it detects a resource imbalance in the cluster. A resource imbalance is determined on a per-ESXi hosts basis. It is done by comparing the resource reservations for all the virtual machines on the ESXi host against the total capacity of the host and then verifying whether the host can or cannot meet the cumulative resource reservation needs of the virtual machines.

The result of this verification will become a **deviation metric**, which is then compared against the **migration threshold** set on the cluster. This is referred to as an imbalance check. DRS does this imbalance check on each of the ESXi hosts in the cluster every 300 seconds (5 minutes). If DRS learns of an imbalance during the check, and if the deviation is more than the migration threshold set on the cluster, then DRS will generate a **migration recommendation**.

Migration recommendations are generated by simulating the Compute vMotion of each virtual machine on the ESXi host in order to recalculate cluster imbalance metrics. It will then choose to generate a migration recommendation for a virtual machine whose migration would best serve in reducing the resource crunch on the ESXi host.

DRS automation levels

DRS automation levels define how DRS will react to compute resource imbalances in a cluster and whether it requires little or no manual intervention. By default, DRS works in a fully-automated mode. You can, however, set it to manual or partially automated.

DRS can choose to apply the generated migration and initial placement recommendations or present them on the vCenter GUI for the administrator to take an action on them. If there is more than one migration recommendation, then the administrator is provided with a prioritized list of recommendations to choose from. Initial placement refers to the process of choosing an ESXi host from a DRS cluster to power on or resume a virtual machine. DRS generates initial placement recommendations by choosing an ESXi host that has enough resources to run the virtual machine being powered on or resumed.

The following table shows details on how migration and initial placement recommendations are actioned based on the DRS automation level configured on the cluster:

Automation Level	Compute vMotion	Initial Placement
Fully Automated	Virtual Machines migrations automatically initiated by DRS without the need for a manual intervention.	Virtual Machines are automatically registered and powered on /resumed on a suitable ESXi host.
Partially Automated	DRS generated migration recommendations are displayed in the vCenter GUI. The administration will have manually apply one of the recommendations.	Virtual Machines are automatically registered and powered on /resumed on a suitable ESXi host.
Manual	DRS generated migration recommendations are displayed in the vCenter GUI. The administration will have to manually apply one of the recommendations.	Initial placement recommendations are displayed in the vCenter GUI. The administrator will have to manually apply one of the recommendations

Setting virtual machine automation

You can configure DRS automation levels individually on every virtual machine that is managed by a DRS cluster. This is done by configuring **VM Overrides**. An override created for a virtual machine will allow that virtual machine to have an automation level different from the cluster level settings. A possible use case would be a need to have more control and awareness over the initial placement and migration activities corresponding to a virtual machine running a business-critical service or application. You can create a VM override for such a virtual machine and set the automation level to manual. From then on, all placement and migration recommendations specific to that virtual machine will be displayed in the vCenter GUI for the administrator's approval.

The following walk-through will help you visualize the steps involved in configuring VM overrides.

1. Connect to the vCenter using the vSphere Web Client and navigate to the **Hosts and Clusters** inventory view.
2. Select the DRS-enabled cluster and navigate to **Manage** | **Settings** | **VM Overrides**.

3. In the **VM Overrides** page, click on the **Add** button to bring up the **Add VM Overrides** window.
4. In the **Add VM Overrides** window, click on the ⊞ icon to bring up the **Select a VM** window. Select the virtual machine whose automation level needs to be overridden and click on **OK**. This should take you back to the **Add VM Overrides** window.
5. In the **Add VM Overrides** window, you should now see the added virtual machine. With the virtual machine selected, choose the required **Automation level** and click on **OK**.

6. The **VM Overrides** page should now show the virtual machine with its automation level listed against it.

DRS migration thresholds

Based on the level of compute load imbalance detected in a cluster, every migration recommendation generated by DRS will have a priority level associated with it. Setting migration thresholds is a way to tell DRS what priority level recommendation should be actioned or displayed. Setting a migration threshold (priority) does not stop DRS from working on generating recommendations. But before they are displayed (if manual/partially automated) or applied (if fully automated), the priority level associated with the generated recommendation will be compared against the migration threshold set on the cluster. If the migration threshold level is lower than the priority level of the recommendation, then it is ignored; otherwise, it is displayed or applied.

The following table will help you understand how migration recommendations are applied/displayed based on their priority values:

Migration Threshold	Priority Levels of the Recommendations that will be Applied or Displayed				
	Priority 1	Priority 2	Priority 3	Priority 4	Priority 5
Level 1 - Conservative	Yes	No	No	No	No
Level 2	Yes	Yes	No	No	No
Level 3 - Default	Yes	Yes	Yes	No	No
Level 4	Yes	Yes	Yes	Yes	No
Level 5 - Aggressive	Yes	Yes	Yes	Yes	Yes

DRS affinity rules

DRS lets you define affinity rules for hosts and virtual machines managed by it. These rules affect the migration and placement recommendation generated by DRS.

There are three types of affinity rules:

- Virtual machines to hosts
- Keep virtual machines together
- Separate virtual machines

Virtual machines to host rules

We can create DRS affinity rules for things that will affect the virtual machine migration recommendations and initial placement recommendation based on a virtual machine's affinity or anti-affinity rule with a group of hosts. This, however, requires the administrator to group ESXi hosts and virtual machines into DRS hosts and VMs groups before the rules can be applied. A virtual machine to host rule can either indicate a preference or a requirement. The requirements are classified as *must* rules and preferences as *should* rules as illustrated in the following table:

Must rules	Should rules
Must run on hosts in group	Should run on hosts in group
Must not run on hosts in group	Should not run on hosts in group

The *must* rules should be mandatorily met, whereas the *should* rules just state the preference, hence the virtual machines can run on other hosts if the *should* rules cannot be met. The VM/host affinity rules are generally used to meet specific requirements such as licensing and availability of hardware resources, for example a direct attached tape library, domain controllers, exchange servers, and so on. Keep in mind that vSphere HA, DRS, and DPM will not violate the *must* rules. Hence, the *must* rules should be defined very cautiously as they could even prevent vSphere HA from restarting virtual machines, thus affecting the availability of those virtual machines.

The *virtual machines to hosts* rules cannot be applied on individual hosts or virtual machines; hence, we will need to group them. The groups are created using the **DRS Groups Manager**.

The following walk-through will help you visualize the creation of **DRS host groups**:

1. Connect to the vCenter server using the vSphere Web Client and bring up the **Hosts and Clusters** view.
2. Select the DRS cluster, navigate to **Manage | Settings | VM/Hosts Groups,** and click on **Add** to bring up the **Create VM/Host Group** window.
3. In the **Create VM/Host Group** window, supply a name for the host group, choose the **Type** as **Host Group,** and click on the **Add** button to bring up the **Add VM/Host Group Member** window.
4. In the **Add VM/Host Group Member** window, select the ESXi hosts that should be added to the group and click **OK**.
5. The **Create VM/Host Group** should now list the hosts selected to be the members of this group. Click **OK** to create the group.

The following walk-through will help you visualize the creation of **DRS VM groups**:

1. Connect to the vCenter server using the vSphere Web Client and bring up the **Hosts and Clusters** view.
2. Select the DRS cluster, navigate to **Manage | Settings | VM/Hosts Groups,** and click on **Add** to bring up the **Create VM/Host Group** window.
3. In the **Create VM/Host Group** window, supply a name for the VM group, choose the **Type** as **VM Group,** and click on the **Add** button to bring up the **Add VM/Host Group Member** window.
4. In the **Add VM/Host Group Member** window, select the virtual machines that should be added to the group and click **OK**.
5. The **Create VM/Host Group** should now list the virtual machines selected to be the members of this group. Click **OK** to create the group.

Now that we know how to create DRS host and VM groups, let's review the steps required for creating virtual machines to hosts rules:

1. Connect to the vCenter server using the vSphere Web Client and bring up the **Hosts and Clusters** view.
2. Select the DRS cluster, navigate to **Manage | Settings | VM/Hosts Rules,** and click on the **Add** button to bring up the Create VM/Host Rule window.

3. In the **Create VM/Host Rule** window, supply a name for the rule and choose the rule **Type** as **Virtual Machines to Hosts**. Select a **VM Group**, a must/should rule, a **Host Group,** and then click **OK** to create the rule.

Virtual machine to virtual machine rules

The *keep virtual machines together* and *separate virtual machines* are the two VM-to-VM affinity rules that DRS will allow us to configure. These rules determine whether the virtual machines participating in the rule should or should not run on the same ESXi hosts. When there is a conflict between the rules, the oldest rule takes precedence and the others will be disabled by DRS. Let's have a look at the use cases for both these rules:

- Use case for *keep virtual machines together* – a two-tier application where both the virtual machines are in the same layer-2 subnet. Keeping these virtual machines together will cause the network traffic to not leave the host, hence increasing higher throughput and also reducing the traffic on the network switches.
- Use case for *separate virtual machines* – two active directories built for redundancy should run on two separate hosts to avoid a single point of failure.

The following procedure will guide you through the steps required to create a virtual machine to virtual machine rule:

1. Connect to the vCenter server using the vSphere Web Client and bring up the **Hosts and Clusters** view.
2. Select the DRS cluster, navigate to **Manage | Settings | VM/Hosts Rules,** and click on the **Add** button to bring up the **Create VM/Host Rule** window.
3. In the **Create VM/Host Rule** window, supply a name for the rule and choose the rule **type** as **Keep Virtual Machines Together or Separate Virtual Machines**.
4. Click the **Add** button to bring up the **Add Rule Member** window. Select more than one virtual machine from the list and click **OK** to return to the **Create VM/Host Rule** window.
5. Click **OK** to create the rule.

vSphere Distributed Power Management (DPM)

Although DPM will be discussed as a separate topic, keep in mind that DPM is a DRS feature. It can only be configured on a DRS-enabled cluster. DRS uses DPM to change the power state of underutilized ESXi hosts in order to reduce the data center power consumption by the cluster. DPM is disabled by default. It uses Intelligent Platform Management Interface (IPMI) for power management. ESXi hosts managed by DPM should have their corresponding **Baseboard Management Controller (BMC)** setting configured. Read the sub-section, *Configuring DPM host options,* for instructions.

Now that we have BMC details configured on all the ESXi hosts in the cluster, we can enable DPM on the cluster. Once enabled, DPM will analyze the cumulative resource requirement (current usage plus reservations), verify vSphere HA requirements, and determine the number of ESXi hosts required to meet them. DPM will then selectively put ESXi hosts into DPM **standby mode** (the host will actually be powered-off). Prior to putting an ESXi host into standby mode, DPM will leverage DRS to migrate all the virtual machines onto other ESXi hosts in the cluster.

DPM operates in three modes:

- **Off**: (default) DPM is disabled in this mode.
- **Manual**: DPM recommendations are displayed in the vCenter GUI for an administrator to take action.
- **Automatic**: DPM recommendations are automatically applied.

DPM requires hardware/firmware support for power management and can use the following protocols:

- **Intelligent Platform Management Interface (IPMI)**
- **Hewlett-Packard Integrated Lights-Out (HP ILO)**
- **Wake-On-LAN (WOL)**

> Keep in mind that DPM will power-on the hosts that are in the DPM standby mode, if needed.

Configuring DPM host options

The DPM automation level can be modified at a per hosts level using Host Options. Power management options specified here will override the cluster settings. The Host Options can also be used to supply the host's BMC details:

1. Connect to the vCenter server using the vSphere Web Client and bring up the **Hosts and Clusters** view.

2. To supply the BMC details, select the DRS cluster and navigate to **Manage** | **Settings** | **Host Options**.

3. In the **Host Options** page, select an ESXi host and click on **Edit** to bring up the **Edit Host Options** window. Choose a **Power Management** automation level, supply the BMC details requested, and click **OK**:

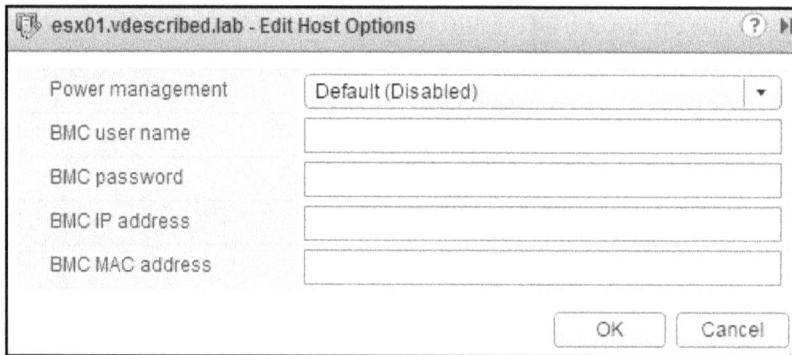

esx01.vdescribed.lab - Edit Host Options	? ▶▶
Power management	Default (Disabled) ▾
BMC user name	
BMC password	
BMC IP address	
BMC MAC address	
	OK Cancel

4. Repeat steps 1 through 3 for every host in the DRS-enabled cluster.

Clustering ESXi hosts for high availability

VMware **vSphere HA** (**high availability**) is a functionality that is used to configure a cluster of ESXi hosts to respond to an unplanned downtime event and ensure the availability of the virtual machines that were running on them, with very minimal downtime possible. Although that was a very simple definition, there is more to what vSphere HA can do in terms of providing high availability to the virtual machines running on the HA protected hosts. It can monitor the guest operating systems and the applications running inside of a virtual machine and then decide to restart the affected virtual machine in an effort to reduce the downtime of a service due to an affected guest operating system hosting the service, or a nonresponsive application corresponding to the service. Starting with vSphere 6.0, it can also detect APD and PDL events and choose to reset the virtual machines if necessary. However, it is important to understand that even though HA is configured on a cluster of ESXi hosts, it only provides high availability for the virtual machines and not for the hosts. It cannot start up or restart an affected ESXi host.

Enabling HA on a cluster

Since vSphere HA is enabled at the cluster level, you will need access to a vCenter server using the vSphere Web Client or the vSphere Client to accomplish the configuration. Although there is nothing more that you would need to enable HA, it is important to make sure that the ESXi hosts are participating in a HA cluster:

- Have access to the same shared storage
- Have access to the same virtual machine networks
- Have CPUs from the same family and feature set

If any of the preceding factors are not considered when designing an HA cluster, then it could either leave HA nonfunctional, increase the unplanned downtime, or even affect the performance of the guest operating system and the applications running inside the virtual machines.

The following steps will walk you through the procedure of enabling HA on an ESXi cluster:

1. From vCenter's Home inventory, navigate to the **Hosts and Clusters** view.

2. Select the cluster and navigate to **Manage** I **Settings** I **vSphereHA**, and click on **Edit**.

3. On the **Edit Cluster Settings** window, select the **Turn ON vSphere HA** checkbox, and click on **OK** to enable HA.

vSphere HA – behind the scenes

vSphere HA can only be enabled via the vCenter server managing the cluster. However, HA can continue to remain functional without the vCenter being available. When you enable HA on a cluster of ESXi hosts, the **Fault Domain Manager** (**FDM**) will install its agents on the hosts. Once done, one of the ESXi hosts in the cluster is elected as a master and the remainder as slaves. During the election process, an ESXi host with access to the largest number of datastores will be chosen as the master and the remainder of the hosts are flagged as slaves. The master node is responsible for restarting virtual machines, updating state information to the vCenter, and monitoring its slave nodes. Every set of slave nodes will have master node to exchange information with. If for any reason there is a network partition in a HA cluster, which means that a set of nodes in a HA cluster stop communicating with another set of nodes in the same cluster, then a network partition is said to have formed between the two sets of nodes. Now, if the nodes in each of those partitioned sets can talk to each other then they would participate in a HA election process again to choose a master node for that particular partition.

An election process is initiated even if the current master node fails. The election process will take approximately 15 seconds and will choose a host with the largest number of connected datastores. In the case that there is tie between hosts, then the host with the highest management object ID (MOB ID) is chosen as the master. The MOB IDs are compared lexically, which means that 9 will be higher than 10.

HA would remain functional only if every set of HA enabled hosts has a master node elected. One of the roles of the master is to monitor the slaves for their liveliness, which is done by sending and receiving network heartbeats between the master and the slaves over their management vmkernel interfaces. The network heartbeats are exchanged every second. If any of the slave hosts stop receiving heartbeats from the master, then it will begin determining whether it is network isolated with the master. This entire process can take up to a minute before it decides to execute the isolation response.

With vSphere HA, once enabled and configured correctly, in the event of a host failure or a network isolation, the virtual machines that were running on the failed host will be restarted on other hosts in the HA cluster.

Datastore heartbeating

The HA master uses network heartbeating to monitor the liveliness of the slave nodes. It is, however, sometimes possible that a slave node, though isolated from the heartbeat (management) network, could still be running and providing all necessary resources to the virtual machines running on them. To verify the occurrence of such a scenario, HA has another type of heartbeating called datastore heartbeating. Datastore heartbeating is enabled by default and chooses two heartbeat datastores per host. It does so by making sure that it selects the datastores that are not backed by the same NFS server or storage and are mapped to at least two ESXi hosts. Datastore heartbeating works by using VMFS's filesystem locking mechanism. It creates files, what VMware calls heartbeat files, which are kept open to keep a filesystem lock active on that file. Every host in the HA cluster gets a corresponding heartbeat file. In the event of a network isolation, the master checks the liveliness of the isolation host by checking if there is an active lock on its heartbeat file. The heartbeat files are stored in a directory called `.vSphere-HA` which can be located on the root of the heartbeat datastore.

The following procedure explains how to select a datastore for heartbeating:

1. From the vCenter's `Home` inventory, navigate to the **Hosts and Clusters** view.
2. Select the cluster, navigate to **Manage** | **Settings** | **vSphere HA,** and click on **Edit**. â☉¨
3. On the **Edit Cluster Settings** window, click on **Datastore Heartbeating** to expand and view its additional settings.
4. Choose between the **Automatically select Datastores accessible from the host**, **Use Datastores only from the specified list**, and **Use Datastores from the specified list and complement automatically if needed** options.
5. Click on **OK** to confirm the selection.

Host isolation response

The host isolation response setting is used by the ESXi host which detects itself as being network isolated form the heartbeat network, to decide whether to change the power state of the running virtual machines. If the master node is network isolated, it pings its isolation address and then within 5 seconds, since it was network isolated, it will action the configured isolation response. Things work a little different with slave nodes though.

If a slave node stops receiving heartbeats from the master, it elects itself as the master (*this is because it doesn't receive any election traffic*), pings the isolation address to determine the network isolation, and then actions the isolation response after approximately 60 seconds since it stopped receiving the heartbeats from the master.

HA offers three host isolation responses:

- **Leave powered on**: this setting will not change the power state of the running virtual machines. This is generally used in cases where you are aware that they could be network disconnected and if they are, then it wouldn't affect the iSCSI/NFS or the virtual machine network.
- **Power off then failover**: this will power-off the running virtual machines. Used in cases where the management network and the NFS or iSCSI storage are using the same physical NICs on the host, hence increasing the chances of the host losing access to storage when there is a network isolation. Powering off the virtual machines in response to an isolation will reduce the chances of more than one instance of the virtual machine running in the cluster. Also, if the virtual machines were to lose access to the storage then a graceful shutdown of the guest operating system would not be possible.
- **Shutdown then failover**: this will gracefully shutdown the virtual machines. This is useful in a case where both the management and virtual machine network could be affected but the storage connection will remain active. If the graceful shut down doesn't complete within 300 seconds, then a power-off is issued.

The following procedure explains how to set/modify the host isolation response settings on the cluster:

1. From the vCenter's Home inventory, navigate to the **Hosts and Clusters** view.
2. Select the cluster, navigate to **Manage | Settings | vSphereHA**, and â◉"click on **Edit**.
3. In the **Edit Cluster Settings** window, click on **Host Monitoring** to expand and view â◉"its additional settings.
4. Click on the **Host isolation response** drop-down box to select the required isolation response.
5. With a planned isolation response selected, click on **OK** to confirm the changes.

Virtual machine restart priority

Setting restart priorities for individual virtual machines will help HA to determine which VM should be restarted first when a host fails. The restart priorities set are relative. HA will restart the virtual machines with the highest priority first. If the priority is set to disabled for a VM, then in the event of host failure, that particular VM will not be restarted. The priorities set are only for HA to determine the restart order; they don't affect VM monitoring. Now, let's assume that we have set the failover capacity of an HA cluster to two hosts. With this configuration in place, if more than two ESXi hosts fail then you would want to make sure that even though your cluster capacity is reduced as compared to what the cluster was originally prepared for, the high priority VMs are started first. This can be achieved by setting VM restart priorities. It is a common practice to leave the cluster's restart priority at medium and set the required priorities on individual virtual machines.

The following procedure explains how to set/modify VM restart priority settings for an HA cluster:

1. From the vCenter's Home inventory, navigate to the **Hosts and Clusters** view. âⓞ¨
2. Select the cluster, navigate to **Manage | Settings | vSphere HA,** and click on **Edit**.
3. In the **Edit Cluster Settings** window, click on **Host Monitoring** to expand and view its additional settings.
4. Use the **VM restart priority** drop-down menu to choose the **Disabled, Low, Medium,** or **High** priority setting.
5. With the planned **VM restart priority** option selected, click on **OK** to confirm the changes.

vCenter admission control

A correctly configured HA cluster should have enough free resources to restart all the business-critical virtual machines in the cluster, in the event of host failures. The amount of free resources is referred to as the **failover capacity**. The failover capacity determines the number of ESXi hosts that can fail in an HA cluster and still leave enough usable resources to support all the running virtual machines in the cluster. vCenter admission control is used to monitor and maintain the necessary failover capacity:

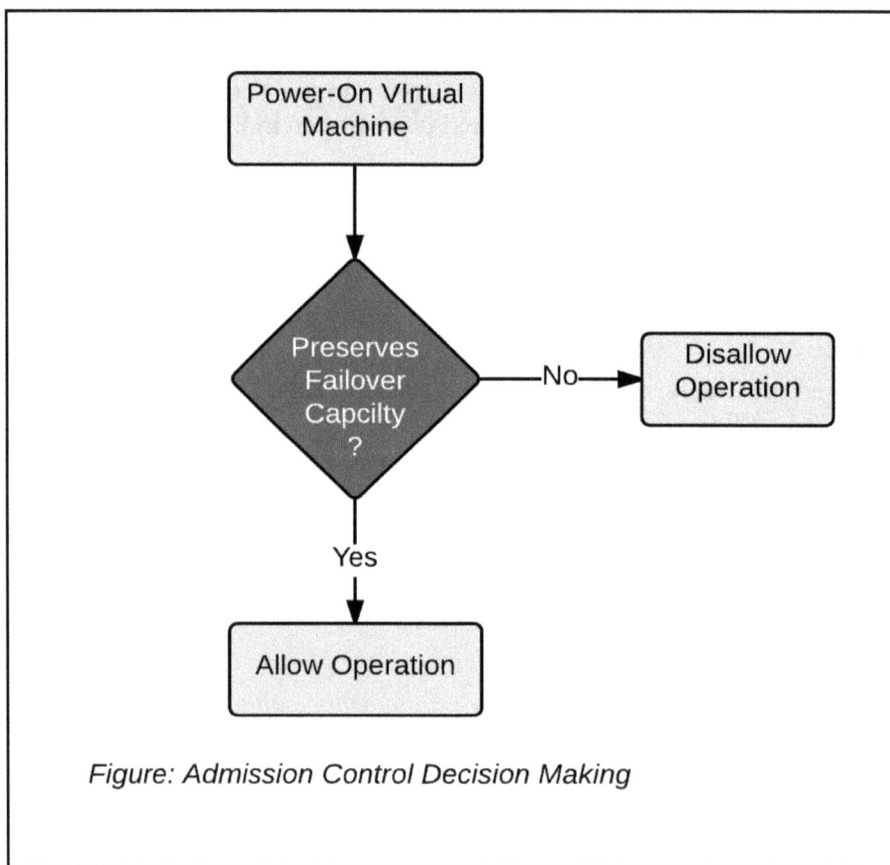

Figure: Admission Control Decision Making

vCenter admission control allows the use of three different methods to reserve HA failover capacity:

- Reserving a static number of hosts
- Reserving a percentage of cluster resources
- Specifying dedicated failover hosts.

Admission control is used to make sure that no operation will lower the failover capacity of the cluster, thereby preserving enough resources in the HA cluster to run VMs that are restarted in the event of a host(s) failure. Any operation that violates the resource constraints imposed by the admission control policy will not be permitted. Some of these operations include a virtual machine power-on operation, a vMotion operation, and a change in the CPU/memory reservation of the VM.

There are three admission control policies:

- Failover capacity by a static number of hosts
- Failover capacity by reserving a percentage of the cluster resources
- Using dedicated failover hosts

Failover capacity by a static number of hosts

This is used to specify resources worth a specific number of ESXi hosts as the failover capacity. For example, if you set the reserved failover capacity value to 2, then it means that 2 ESXi hosts should be reserved as the failover capacity. It also means that the cluster can be sustained with two ESXi hosts failing at the same time.

Here admission control uses slot sizes to calculate current failover capacity. A slot represents a combination of CPU and memory resources to be allocated to virtual machines. The number of slots a virtual machine would require depends on its resource requirements.

Now that we know what slots are, let's review how HA determines the slot sizes. HA picks the largest CPU and memory virtual machine reservation values as slot sizes. If no reservations are used, a value of 32 MHz and 100 MB is used. Once the slot sizes are determined, it determines the number of slots each of the ESXi hosts in the cluster can hold. It then picks the hosts with the largest number of slots as failover hosts and starts determining the current failover capacity of the cluster. If the current failover capacity of the cluster is less than the configured failover capacity, then it is considered as an admission control violation. This would be better understood with an example.

For instance, let's assume that your current cluster status in terms of the number of hosts, virtual machines, and their resource reservations, are as shown in the following diagram:

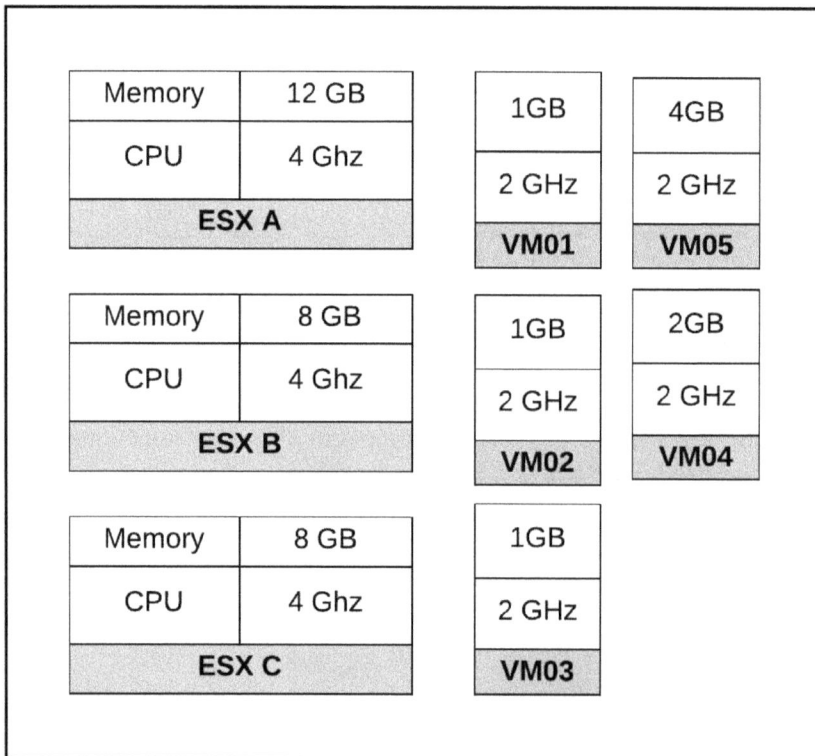

Memory	12 GB
CPU	4 Ghz
ESX A	

1GB
2 GHz
VM01

4GB
2 GHz
VM05

Memory	8 GB
CPU	4 Ghz
ESX B	

1GB
2 GHz
VM02

2GB
2 GHz
VM04

Memory	8 GB
CPU	4 Ghz
ESX C	

1GB
2 GHz
VM03

Here, the largest memory reservation by a virtual machine is 4GB and the vCPU is 2 GHz. The slot size is (4GB, 2Ghz).

Now let's calculate the slot capacity per host:

- Host A: three memory slots and two vCPU slots
- Host B: two memory slots and two vCPU slots
- Host C: two memory slots and two vCPU slots

Since Host A has the largest set of slots, it is taken out of the equation. So, with Host B and Host C we have four slots in total.

Now, let's take a look at the slot sizes required by the virtual machines:

- VM01: one slot
- VM02: one slot
- VM03: one slot
- VM04: one slot
- VM05: one slot

We need a total of five slots, but we have only four. Hence, the current failover capacity is less than the configured failover capacity of one. Therefore, you will need to power-off one of the VMs to enable admission control. Once admission control is enabled, if you try to power-on the VM then it won't let you do so since it violates the failover capacity requirement.

The following procedure explains how to specify a *static number of hosts for failover*:

1. From the vCenter's `Home` inventory, navigate to the **Hosts and Clusters** view.
2. Select the cluster, navigate to **Manage | Settings | vSphere HA**, and click on **Edit**.
3. In the **Edit Cluster Settings** window, click on **Admission Control** to expand and view its additional settings.

4. To define a reserved failover capacity in terms of the number of hosts that will be available to failover VMs, select the **Define failover capacity by static number of hosts** option. Also, choose a **Slot size policy** value for the VMs. The policy can either calculate the slot size based on the powered-on VMs, or you can specify a custom (fixed) slot size:

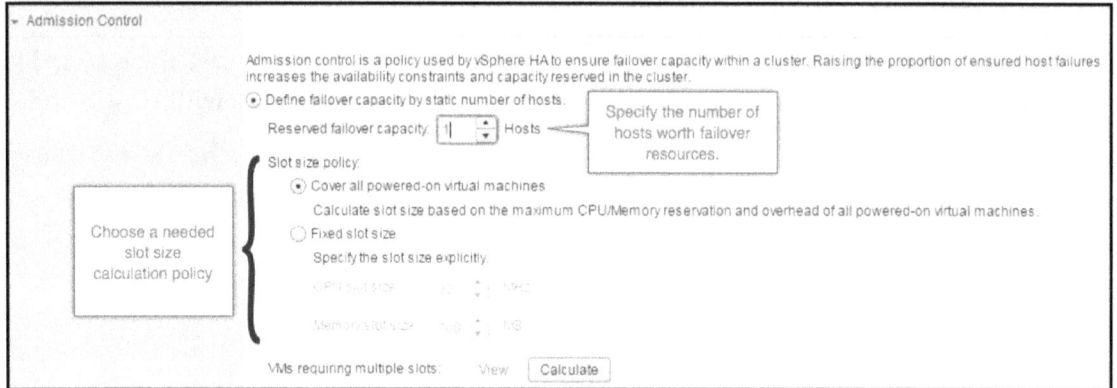

5. Click on **OK** to confirm the settings and reconfigure the cluster.

Failover capacity by reserving a percentage of the cluster resources

Here you define a percentage of cluster resources as the failover capacity. This is particularly useful if you have a very limited number of large virtual machines. Here HA uses a different formula to calculate the percentage of free resources in the cluster. It does so by using the following parameters:

- **Total available resources**: Actual capacity of the hosts
- **Cumulative amount of reserved resource**: Sum of all vCPU/memory reservations

The formula is as follows:

```
(Total available resources 'minus' Cumulative reserved resource) /
(Total available resources) = % of free resources
```

Let's review a scenario, and assume that you have reserved 25% CPU and 40% memory as failover resources:

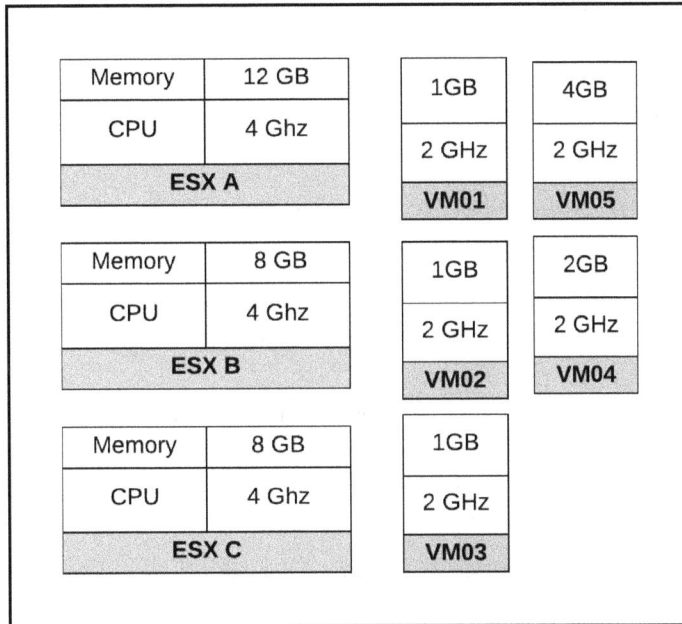

Memory	12 GB
CPU	4 Ghz
ESX A	

1GB
2 GHz
VM01

4GB
2 GHz
VM05

Memory	8 GB
CPU	4 Ghz
ESX B	

1GB
2 GHz
VM02

2GB
2 GHz
VM04

Memory	8 GB
CPU	4 Ghz
ESX C	

1GB
2 GHz
VM03

Here are the parameters for this cluster:

- Total available CPU resources: 12 GHz
- Total available memory resources: 28 GB
- Cumulative amount of reserved CPU resources: 10 Ghz
- Cumulative amount of reserved memory resources: 9 GB

The percent of free capacity is:

- CPU: (12 Ghz – 10 Ghz) / 12 Ghz: 16%
- Memory: (28 GB – 9GB) / 28 GB: 67%

In this case, it violates the CPU reservation for failover, but meets the memory reservation for failover. Since the failover requirement for one of the resources hasn't been met, it is considered to violate admission control.

The following procedure explains how to **reserve a percentage of the cluster resources (CPU and memory resources)** for failover:

1. From the vCenter's Home inventory, navigate to the **Hosts and Clusters** view. â◉¨
2. Select the cluster, navigate to **Manage | Settings | vSphere HA**, and click on **Edit**.
3. In the **Edit Cluster Settings** window, click on **Admission Control** to expand and view its additional settings.
4. Specify a failover capacity by reserving a percentage of CPU and memory resources from the cluster:

5. Click on **OK** to confirm the settings and reconfigure the cluster. â◉¨

Use dedicated failover hosts

Here you define a set of ESXi hosts to be used as failover hosts. These hosts will not be permitted to run any virtual machines on them, unless there is an HA event.

> **TIP**
> Admission control can be disabled by selecting the **Do not reserve failover capacity** option or by just unchecking the admission control checkbox.

The following procedure explains how to **specify the hosts that will be used as failover hosts**:

1. From the vCenter's Home inventory, navigate to the **Hosts and Clusters** view.
2. Select the cluster and navigate to **Manage** | **Settings** | **vSphere HA** and click on **Edit**.
3. In the **Edit Cluster Settings** window, click on **Admission Control** to expand and view its additional settings.
4. Select the **Use dedicated failover hosts** option, and click on the green ⊞ icon to bring up the **Add Failover Hosts** window.
5. On the **Add Failover Host** window, select the host(s) to be added as failover host(s), and then click on **OK**.
6. The **Settings** screen should now list the selected host as a failover host:

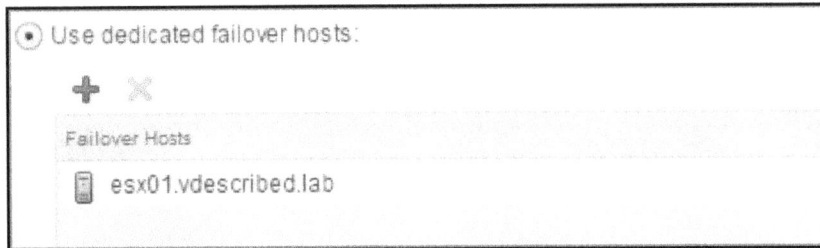

7. Click on **OK** to confirm the settings and reconfigure the cluster.

Virtual machine monitoring

vSphere HA can be configured to monitor virtual machines, so that unresponsive VMs can be restarted (*reset*). This can be achieved by enabling VM monitoring on the HA cluster. HA can further monitor the applications running inside the VM if application monitoring is enabled. However, this would mean that the application should be coded to use the necessary APIs. VM monitoring is very handy when you have VMs hosting services for which you can't afford longer downtime.

Once enabled, VM monitoring, with the help of VMware tools installed in the VMs, will monitor the heartbeats from the VMs. The intervals are governed by the monitoring sensitivity configured for the VM. The default monitoring sensitivity is set to high, in which case HA expects a heartbeat from the virtual machine every 30 seconds. If the heartbeat is not received, then VM monitoring will look for any storage or network I/O activity in the past 120 seconds (this is the default *das.iostatsInterval* value). If there are none, then the VM is reset, and more importantly it is reset only three times during an hour's reset-time window. Prior to issuing a reset, a screenshot of the virtual machine's console will be captured.

The following procedure describes how to configure VM monitoring on an HA cluster:

1. From the vCenter's Home inventory, navigate to the **Hosts and Clusters** view.
2. Select the cluster, navigate to **Manage | Settings | vSphere HA,** and click on **Edit**.
3. In the **Edit Cluster Settings** window, click on **VM Monitoring** to expand and view its additional settings.
4. To enable VM monitoring, you can choose between the **Disabled, VM Monitoring only**, and **VM and Application Monitoring** options:

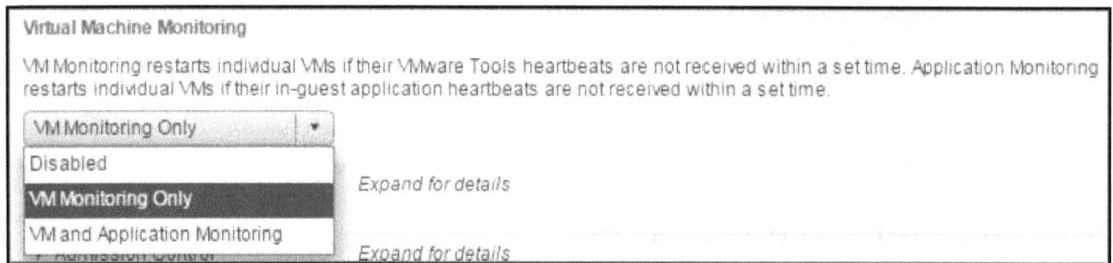

5. With the monitoring type selected, set a planned **Monitoring Sensitivity** value, and click on **OK**.

VM Component Protection(VMCP)

Apart from the ESXi host going down, taking all the virtual machines with it, it is quite possible that the storage access issues can render the virtual machine unusable. The VMware Component Protection feature of vSphere HA can recover VMs affected by storage access issues.

VMCP enables protection against two types of storage access issuesâ◎◎**All Paths Down (APD)** and **Permanent Device Loss (PDL).** Before we learn more about VCMP, it is important to understand what APD and PDL events are.

PDL occurs when an ESXi is notified about the fact that a LUN device is permanently unavailable. A PDL event can occur only when the ESXi can still communicate with the array. The array notifies the host by issuing a SCSI sense code to the ESXi host. On detecting a PDL state for a LUN the ESXi hosts will stop sending I/O requests to the LUN device.

APD occurs when the ESXi host loses access to a LUN device, but hasn't received a PDL SCSI sense code. This could happen if there is a failure at the fabric or HBA level. Since the ESXi host is unsure about the state of the LUN except for the fact that it has lost access to the LUN, it assumes the condition to be transient in nature and continues to retry the commands until it reaches the APD timeout value of 140 seconds. On reaching the timeout, ESXi will start failing the outstanding I/O to the device.

For more details on the SCSI sense codes and log events that indicate PDL or APD refer to VMware Knowledgebase Article number 2004684 at: `https://kb.vmware.com/kb/24684`.

Now that we know what APD and PDL events are, let's see how VMCP plays its part in recovering the virtual machines affected by such events. The first question to answer is, *Why do we need HA to recover these VMs?* The answer to the question is the fact that APD/PDL events may not affect all the ESXi hosts in the cluster. There can be hosts in the cluster that might still have access to the affected LUN device. Hence, HA can be used to restart the affected VMs onto ESXi hosts that have access to the LUN. This is an additional effort required by the uptime SLAs for the virtual machines.

Enabling VCMP

VCMP can only be enabled on an HA enabled cluster of ESXi hosts. The following procedure will guide you through the steps required to enable VM Component Protection on a HA cluster:

1. From the vCenter's `Home` inventory, navigate to the **Hosts and Clusters** view.
2. Select the cluster, navigate to **Manage | Settings | vSphere HA,** and click on **Edit**.

3. In the **Edit Cluster Settings** window, select the checkbox P**rotect against Storage Connectivity Loss** and click on it:

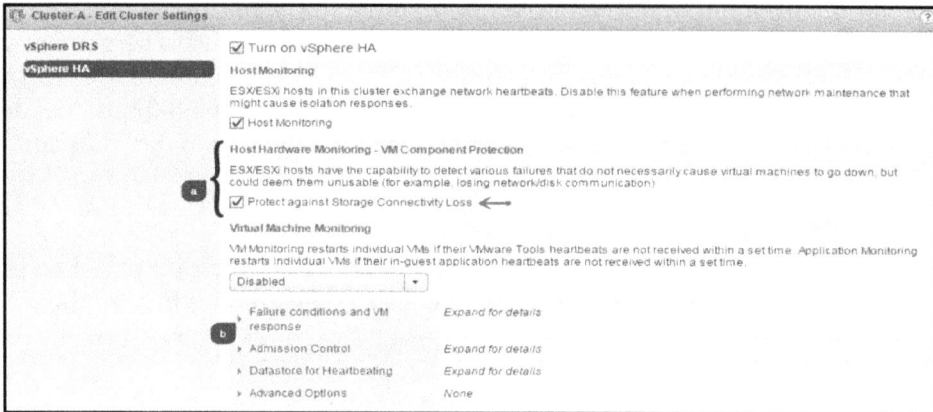

4. On expanding the failure conditions and VM response, you will find three options related to VM Component Protection:

- **Response for Datastore with Permanent Device Loss (PDL)**
- **Response for Datastore with All Paths Down (APD)**
- **Response for APD recovery after APD timeout**

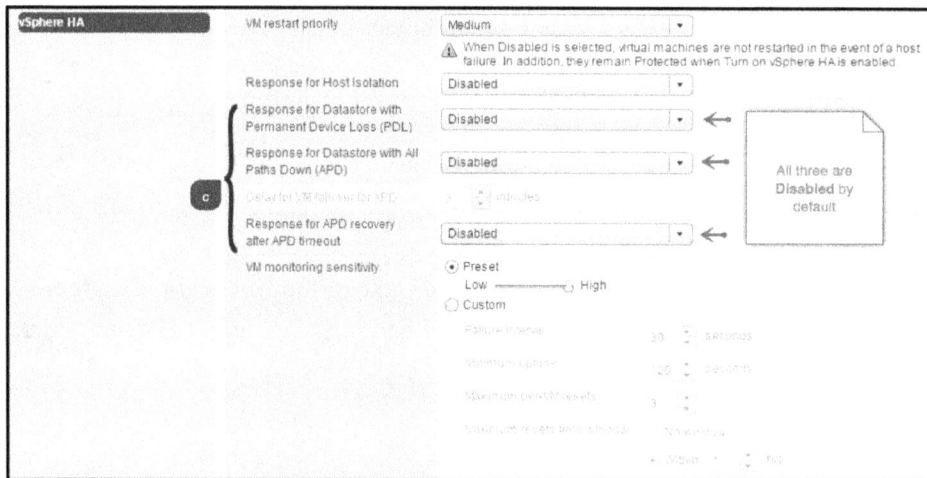

5. Once you have selected the designed responses for APD/PDL events, click on **OK** to confirm the settings.

Now that we know how to enable VMCP, let's explore each of the VMCP responses that can be configured:

- **Response for Datastore with Permanent Device Loss (PDL)** has three configurable responses – Disabled, Issue events, and Power off and restart VMs:

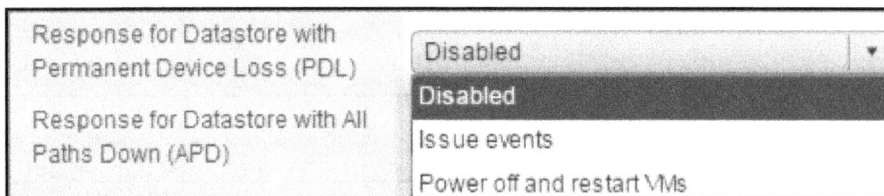

Response for Datastore with Permanent Device Loss (PDL)	Disabled ▼
	Disabled
Response for Datastore with All Paths Down (APD)	Issue events
	Power off and restart VMs

  - **Disabled**: HA will not respond to PDL events, thereby does not perform any action on the affected virtual machines.
  - **Issue events**: HA will notify the administrator of such events.
  - **Power off and restart VMs**: HA will power-off the virtual machines on the affected datastores and attempt restarting them on another ESXi host in the same cluster that has access to the datastore in question.
- **Response for Datastore with All Paths Down (APD)** has four options to choose from – **Disabled, Issue events, Power off and restart VMs (conservative)**, and **Power off and restart VMs (aggressive)**:

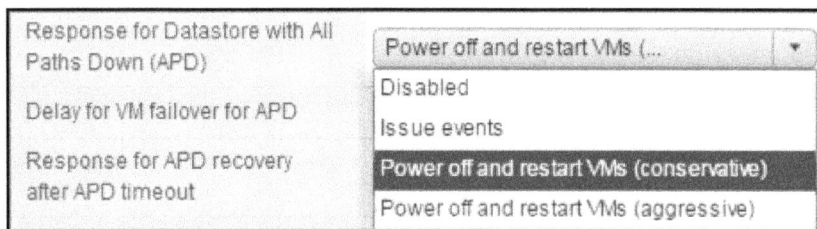

Response for Datastore with All Paths Down (APD)	Power off and restart VMs (... ▼
	Disabled
Delay for VM failover for APD	Issue events
Response for APD recovery after APD timeout	Power off and restart VMs (conservative)
	Power off and restart VMs (aggressive)

  - **Disabled**: HA will not respond to the APD events.
  - **Issue Events**: HA will notify the administration of such events.
  - **Power off and restart VMs (conservative):** HA will attempt power off and to restart the affected virtual machines on a host that has access to the affected datastore. However, it won't attempt the restart unless it finds a host that has access to the datastore. It also verifies whether the HA enabled cluster has enough resources to power-on the virtual machine/s. If the affected host is unable to reach the master HA node to determine the same, then the restart will not be attempted.

- **Power off and restart VMs (aggressive)**: unlike the conservative approach, with this option selected, HA will not wait to find an ESXi host that has access to the affected datastore. It will simply power-off the VMs so that they can be restarted. It would however attempt to determine whether there is enough free capacity in the cluster to power-on the virtual machines. But, in case it is unable to reach the master HA node, it would still attempt the restart. In this case, it is quite possible that vSphere HA might not be able to power-on all the affected virtual machines on another host.

- **Delay for VM failover for APD**: this option is enabled only if you choose a power off or restart action for the APD events. As explained earlier, at the start of this topic, since APD is considered as a transient condition, the ESXi host will retry the I/O commands to the LUN until the *APD time out of 140(default) seconds* is reached. The delay for VM failover for the APD option will make VCMP wait *for an additional 180 (default)* seconds before the VMs are powered-off:

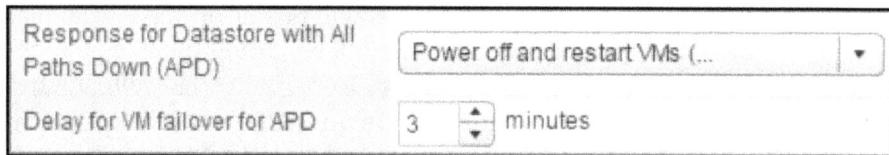

Response for Datastore with All Paths Down (APD)	Power off and restart VMs (... ▼
Delay for VM failover for APD	3 ▲▼ minutes

Keep in mind that the APD default time out value is 140 seconds and the VCMP timeout is 180 seconds. Hence, it waits for a cumulative of 320 seconds before it actions the configured response.

- **Response for APD recovery after APD timeout** has two options:
  - **Reset VMs**
  - **Disabled**

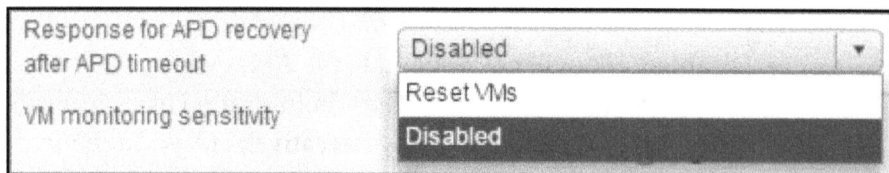

Response for APD recovery after APD timeout	Disabled ▼
VM monitoring sensitivity	Reset VMs
	Disabled

Since VCMP waits for another 180 seconds after the APD timeout, it is possible that the host might recover from the transient APD conditions, thereby restoring the connection to the affected LUN, before the VCMP timeout is reached. In such a scenario, you can choose to either reset the VMs or not to restart them by disabling the response.

Summary

In this chapter, we covered vSphere vMotion in detail. We learned about EVC and looked at some use cases. We learned how to enable DRS on a cluster, covered DRS resource pools, DRS automation levels, DRS migration thresholds, and DRS affinity.

We also learned how to enable and configure vSphere HA, covered admission control, and virtual machine monitoring. Finally, we learned about the VM Component Protection feature of vSphere HA, which enables recovery of virtual machines affected by storage connectivity issues.

7
Understanding Host Profiles, Image Profiles, and Auto Deploy

vSphere has many features that can make an administrator's life easier. Host profiles can be used quickly and easily to initially configure new ESXi hosts, and to determine configuration drifts. Image Builder can be used to customize ESXi image profiles in order to avoid having to install drivers or other components post-install. vSphere Auto Deploy allows you to quickly provision a large number of ESXi hosts in your datacenter infrastructure using a PXE infrastructure. vSphere host profile and Auto Deploy are vSphere Enterprise Plus features.

In this chapter, you will learn:

- Host profile overview and use cases
- How to create and edit a host profile
- How to import and export a host profile
- Image Builder use cases
- How to modify and export an image profile
- vSphere Auto Deploy use cases
- Configuring vSphere Auto Deploy rules

Host profiles

Host profiles are a vSphere Enterprise Plus feature that can greatly simplify the host configuration management required as your deployment scales out, by using configuration policies. Host profile policies can be used to eliminate per-host manual configuration, and to maintain configuration consistency across the entire datacenter. Host profiles are essentially blueprints or templates of known, validated *gold* ESXi configurations. These can be used to manage settings and monitor compliance for networking, storage, security, and other configurations for multiple ESXi hosts. Host profiles can be managed using the vSphere Web Client, PowerCLI, or vSphere APIs.

Overview of host profile workflow

The workflow for host profiles starts with the reference host. A reference host acts as the template from which the host profile is referenced and created. The process would go as follows:

1. Install ESXi and configure the reference host.
2. Create a host profile from reference host.
3. Modify host profile as needed.
4. Attach other ESXi hosts or clusters to the host profile.
5. Check compliance to the host profile.
6. Remediate (as needed).
7. Detach the ESXi hosts or cluster from the host profile.

As of vSphere 6.0, a dedicated reference host is no longer required for host profiles. Previously, vSphere required that a reference host was available for host profile tasks, like importing, exporting, and editing. However, there is now reference host independence.

Using host profiles

Host profiles are necessary when using vSphere Auto Deploy, a feature that will be discussed later in the chapter, but can be used independently. If you're new to vSphere management, host profiles are comparable to Group Policy Objects (GPO) in that there are many options that can be configured and applied to many ESXi hosts. Host profiles can be imported as well as created from scratch.

Let's have a look at the advantages of using host profiles:

- Elimination of per host configurations, giving simplified setup and change management for ESXi
- Maintaining configuration consistency and corrections
- Easy detection of non-compliance with a standard configuration
- Automated remediation

Creating a host profile

Before going through the process of creating a host profile, you want to configure an ESXi host to be the reference, or *golden* template, of how all similar ESXi hosts should be configured. You can have multiple host profiles which should be used for each different configuration. For example, you wouldn't configure the virtual networking settings the same for an ESXi host with six X 1 Gbps network adapters as you would an ESXi host with two X 10 Gbps network adapters. The same principle applies for blades versus rack mount servers or even different hardware vendors.

Once the reference host has been configured and you are ready to create the host profile, go to the Home area of the vSphere Web Client. Select **Host Profiles**:

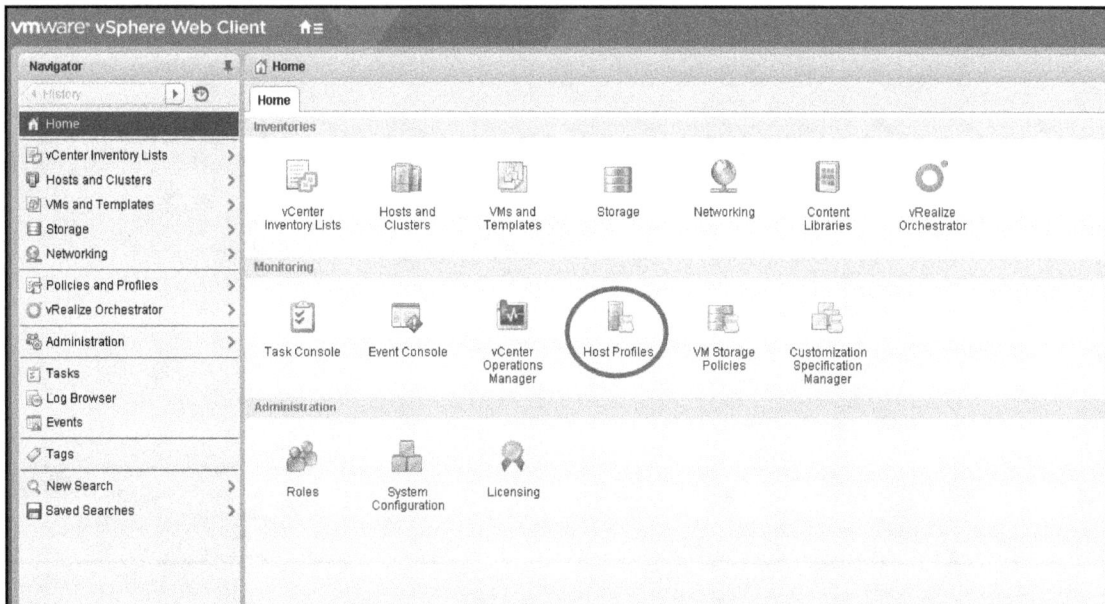

Once you have navigated to **Host Profiles**, then you will be able to press the + button to create a new host profile:

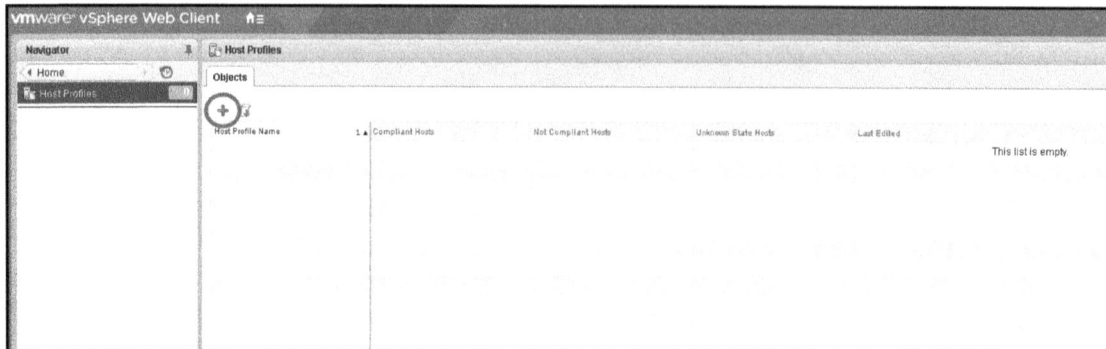

This will bring up the **Extract Host Profile** dialog; from here select the correct **vCenter Server** and which ESXi host the host profile should reference. Press the **Next** button once the options have been selected:

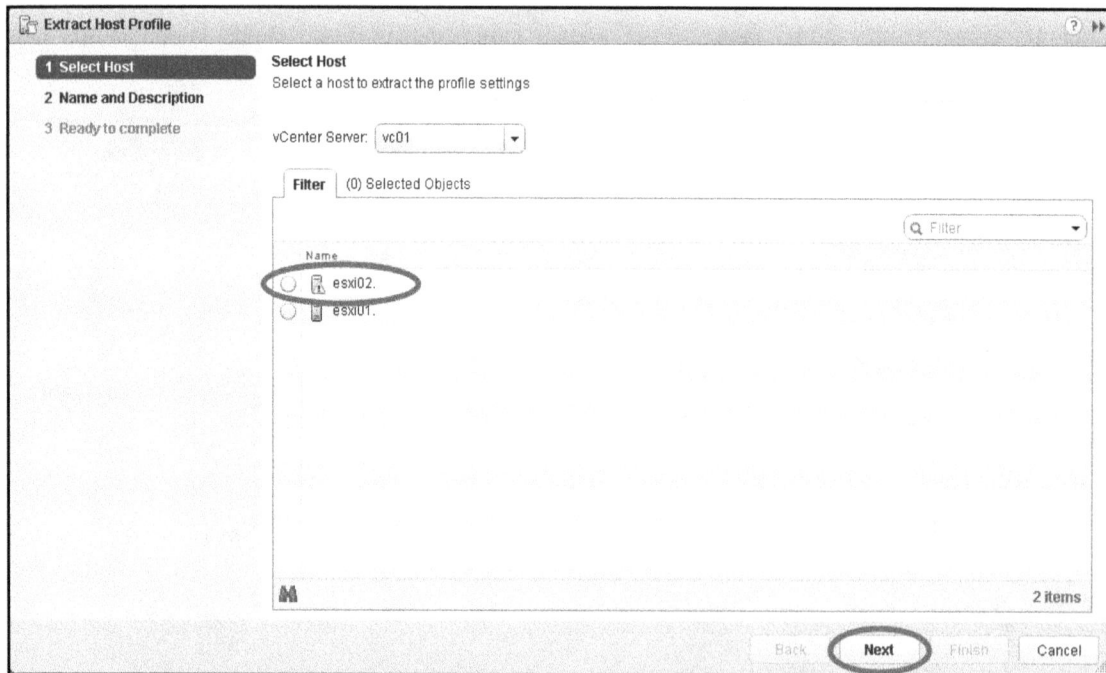

Specify a **Name** and optional **Description** for the profile. Press **Next**:

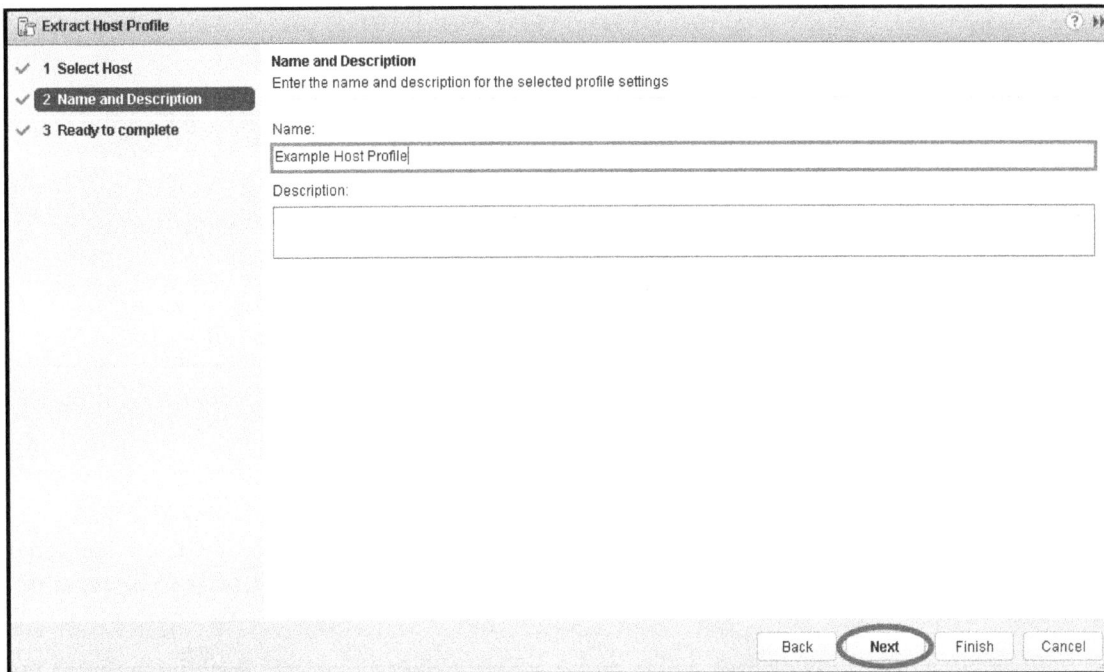

Review settings and press the **Finish** button:

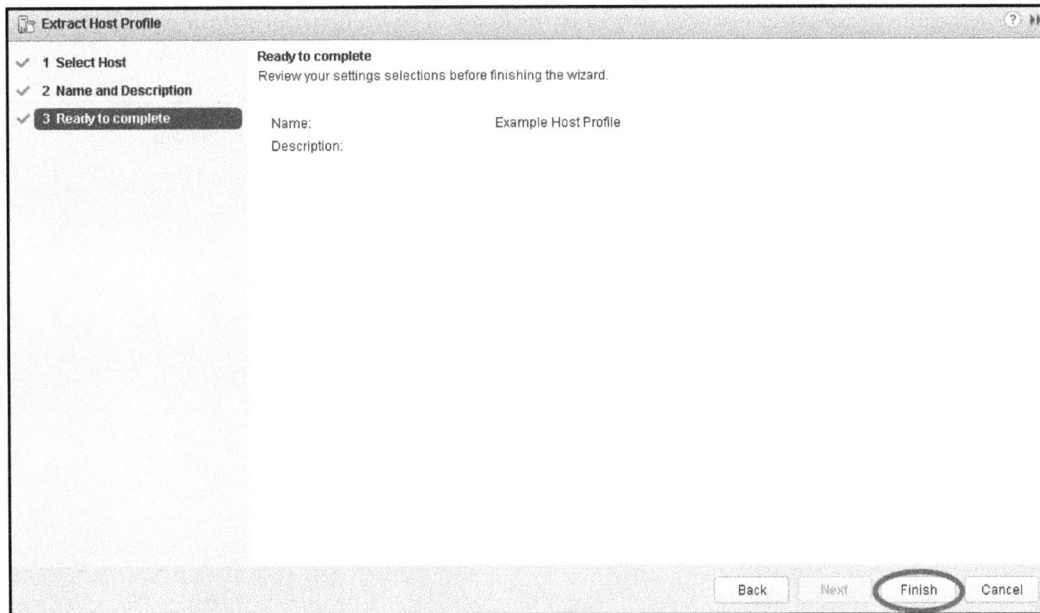

Once the creation process has completed, you should see the host profile you created under **Host Profiles** | **Objects** in the **Navigator** pane:

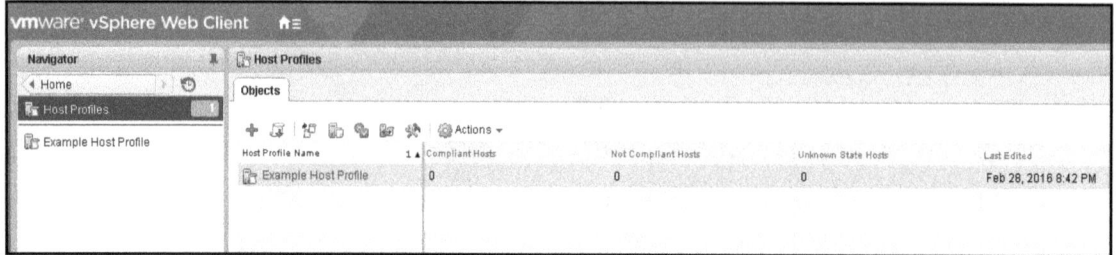

Attaching a host profile

In order to check the compliance of an ESXi host or cluster of ESXi hosts compared to a defined host profile, the host profile must be attached to the ESXi host or cluster. To attach a host profile, select the host profile and press the **Attach/Detach a host profile to hosts and clusters** button:

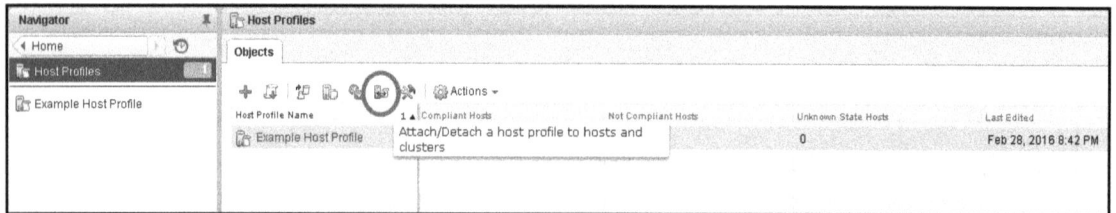

This will bring up a dialog box that allows you to select specific ESXi hosts or to attach an entire cluster. Select the desired objects in the left-hand pane and press the **Attach** button. Once the objects are located in the right-hand pane, press **Next**:

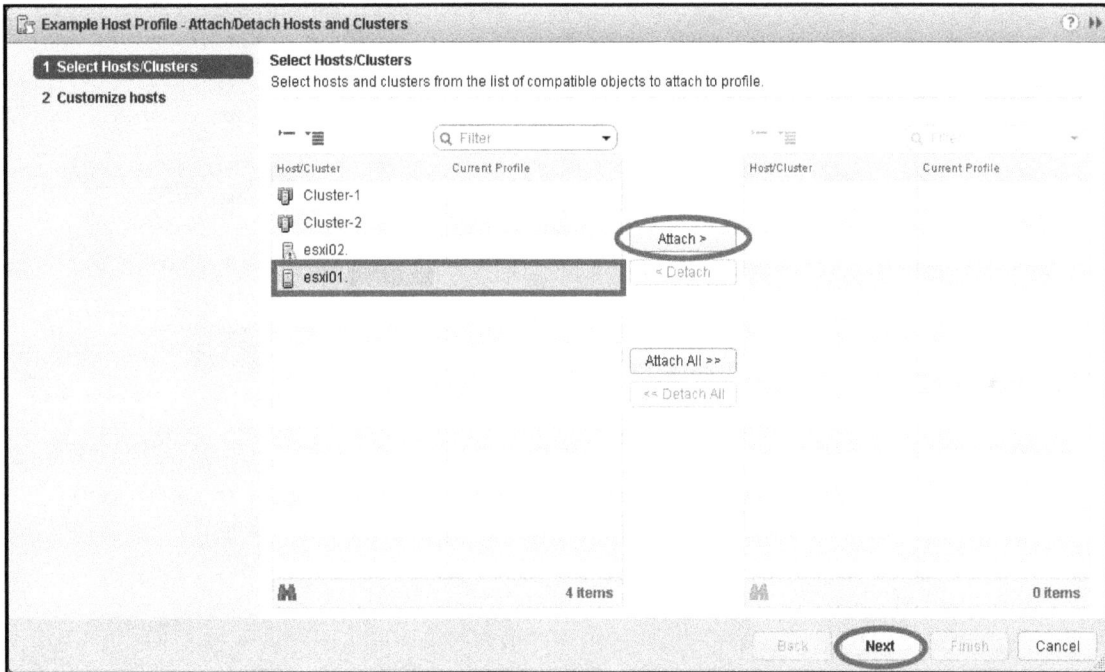

The **Customize hosts** screen will allow you to modify any property that may be unique per individual ESXi host, for example a VMkernel port for iSCSI traffic would be configured with a unique IP address for each ESXi host. Press **Finish**:

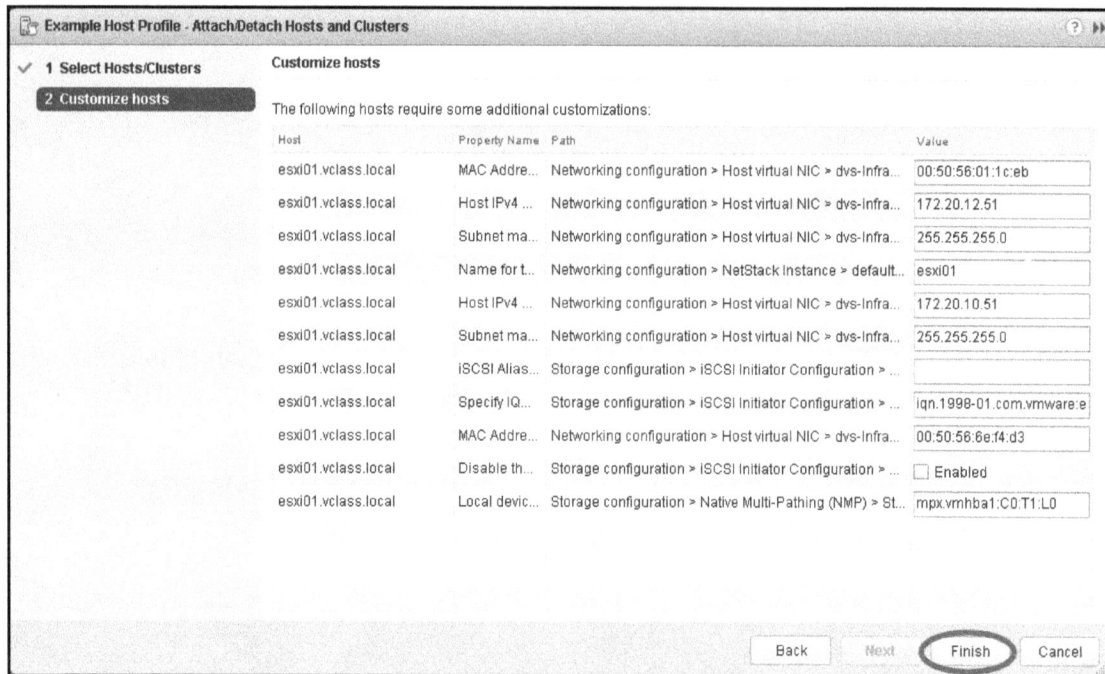

Checking for compliance and remediation

Once a host profile has been attached to an ESXi host and/or cluster, you will be able to check whether remediation is needed. To check compliance, press the **Check host profile compliance of associated entities** button:

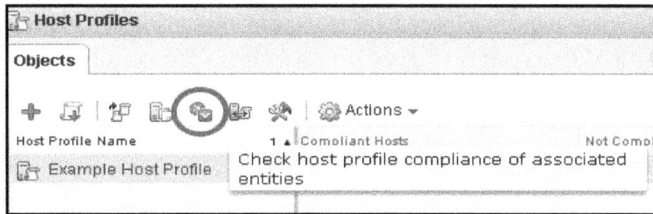

You may also check the compliance and get more detailed information by selecting the host profile in the left-hand navigation pane, then select the **Monitor** tab and finally press the **Compliance** button. You will be able to view each host's results independently and get more detailed information regarding compliance:

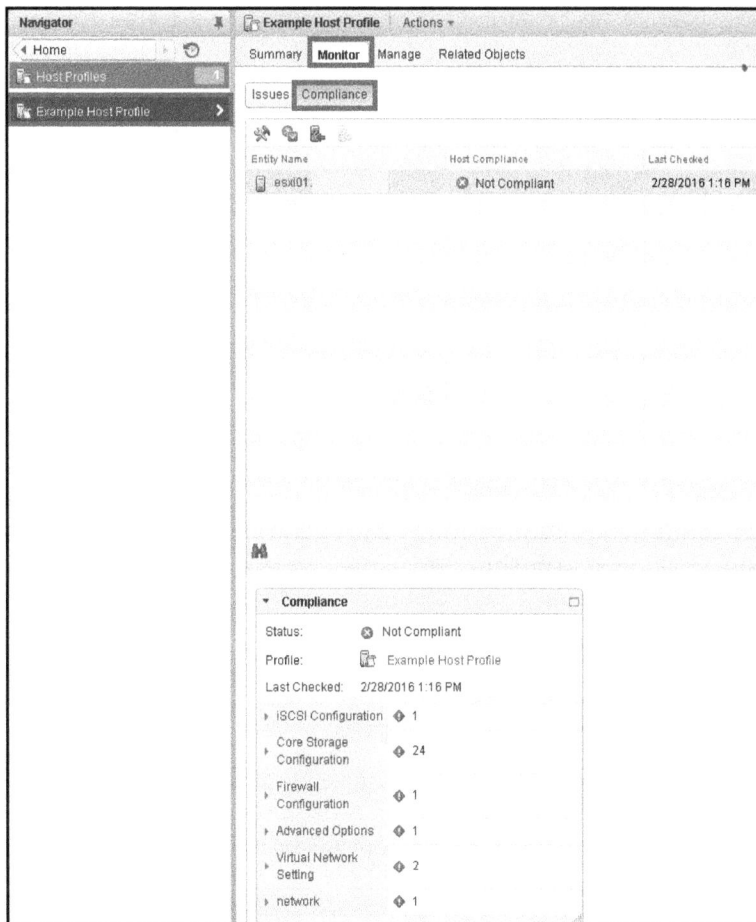

More detailed information can be viewed by pressing the triangle next to each section in the **Compliance** pane. This will expand to give you a better idea of what kind of misconfigurations there are and what amount of remediation is needed:

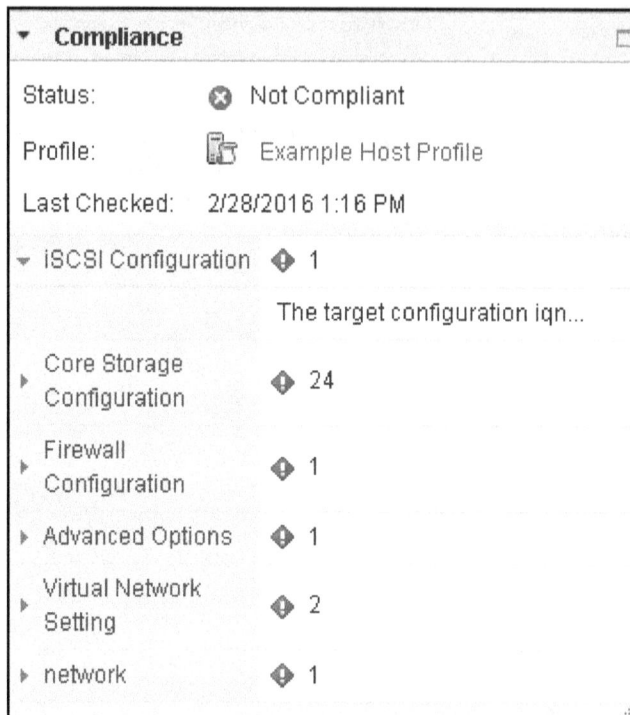

▼	Compliance		
Status:	⊗ Not Compliant		
Profile:	▣ Example Host Profile		
Last Checked:	2/28/2016 1:16 PM		
▼ iSCSI Configuration	◆ 1		
	The target configuration iqn...		
▸ Core Storage Configuration	◆ 24		
▸ Firewall Configuration	◆ 1		
▸ Advanced Options	◆ 1		
▸ Virtual Network Setting	◆ 2		
▸ network	◆ 1		

To remediate an ESXi host, it may need to be in maintenance mode. In order to successfully enter maintenance mode, there cannot be any actively running virtual machines on that host. You may suspend, power off/shut down, or evacuate (migrate off the virtual machines) the ESXi host.

Once there are no actively running virtual machines, you may press the **Enter Maintenance Mode** button:

> If vSphere DRS is enabled and fully automated, then DRS will automatically evacuate an ESXi host trying to enter maintenance mode.

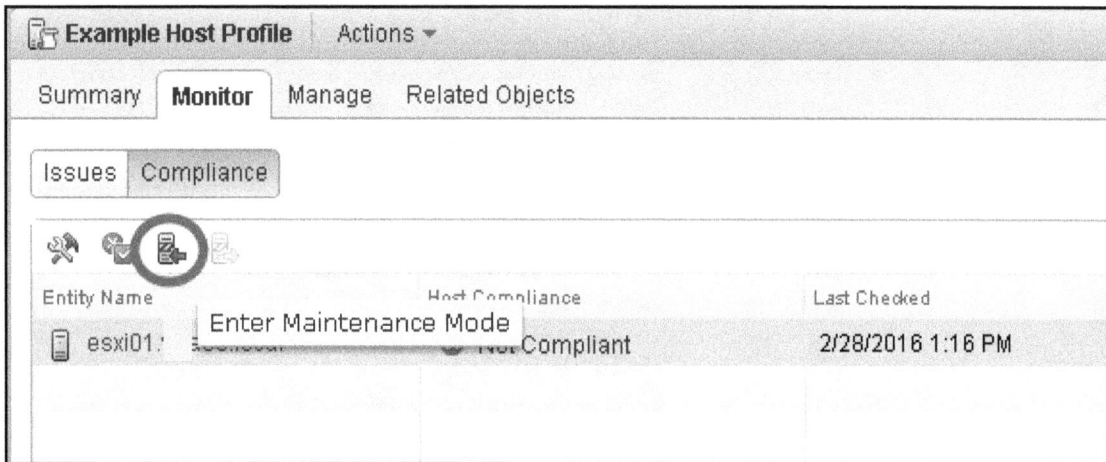

As demonstrated in the figure below, once the host is in maintenance mode, you may press the **Remediate host based on its host profile** button to begin the remediation process:

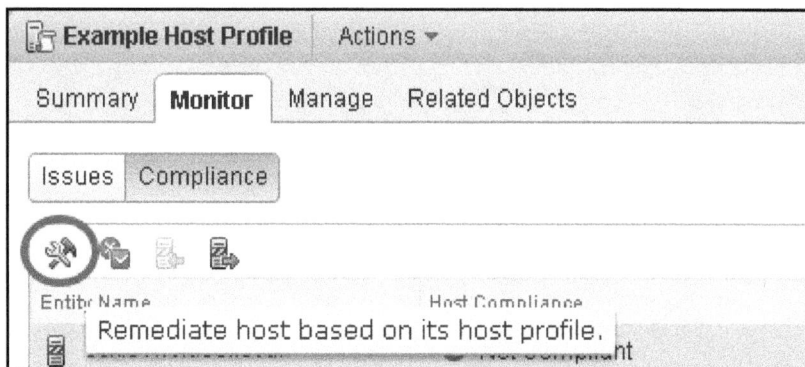

The remediation wizard will prompt you to validate or enter any unique values for the selected ESXi host(s). This effectively creates an answer file. An answer file simply contains the information that preserves the uniqueness across the different ESXi hosts. Press **Next** once the variables have been entered:

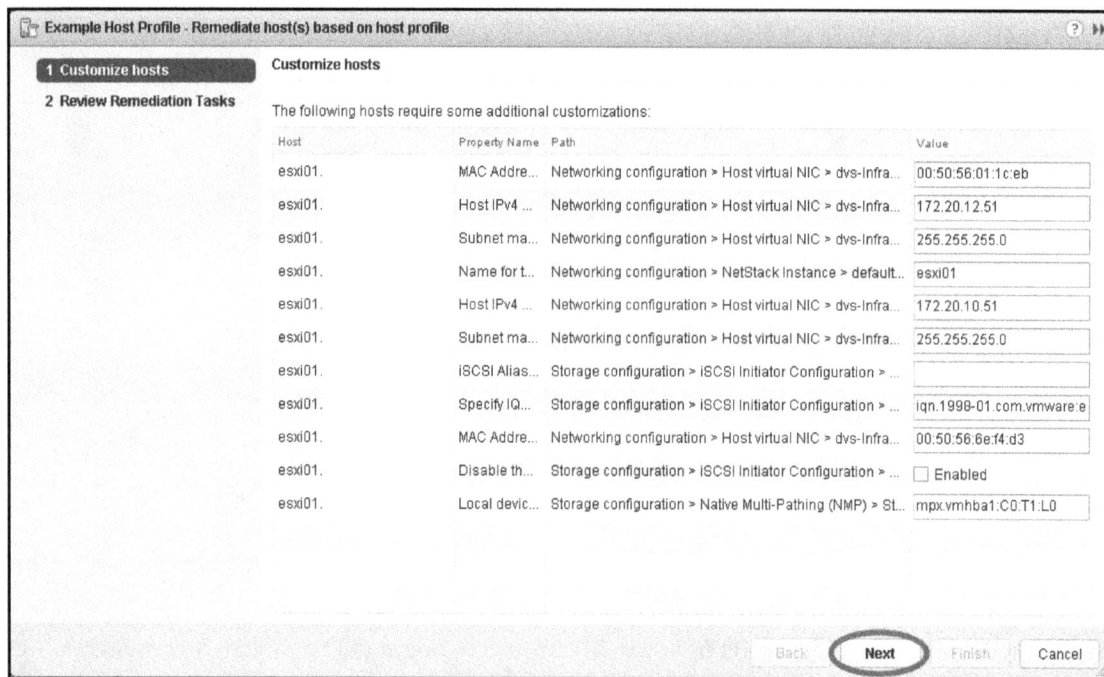

Example Host Profile - Remediate host(s) based on host profile			? ►►

1 Customize hosts

2 Review Remediation Tasks

Customize hosts

The following hosts require some additional customizations:

Host	Property Name	Path	Value
esxi01.	MAC Addre...	Networking configuration > Host virtual NIC > dvs-Infra...	00:50:56:01:1c:eb
esxi01.	Host IPv4 ...	Networking configuration > Host virtual NIC > dvs-Infra...	172.20.12.51
esxi01.	Subnet ma...	Networking configuration > Host virtual NIC > dvs-Infra...	255.255.255.0
esxi01.	Name for t...	Networking configuration > NetStack Instance > default...	esxi01
esxi01.	Host IPv4 ...	Networking configuration > Host virtual NIC > dvs-Infra...	172.20.10.51
esxi01.	Subnet ma...	Networking configuration > Host virtual NIC > dvs-Infra...	255.255.255.0
esxi01.	iSCSI Alias...	Storage configuration > iSCSI Initiator Configuration > ...	
esxi01.	Specify IQ...	Storage configuration > iSCSI Initiator Configuration > ...	iqn.1998-01.com.vmware:e
esxi01.	MAC Addre...	Networking configuration > Host virtual NIC > dvs-Infra...	00:50:56:6e:f4:d3
esxi01.	Disable th...	Storage configuration > iSCSI Initiator Configuration > ...	☐ Enabled
esxi01.	Local devic...	Storage configuration > Native Multi-Pathing (NMP) > St...	mpx.vmhba1:C0:T1:L0

Back **Next** Finish Cancel

The **Review Remediation Tasks** pane allows you an opportunity to take a look at all of the configurations that will be made before pressing **Finish**:

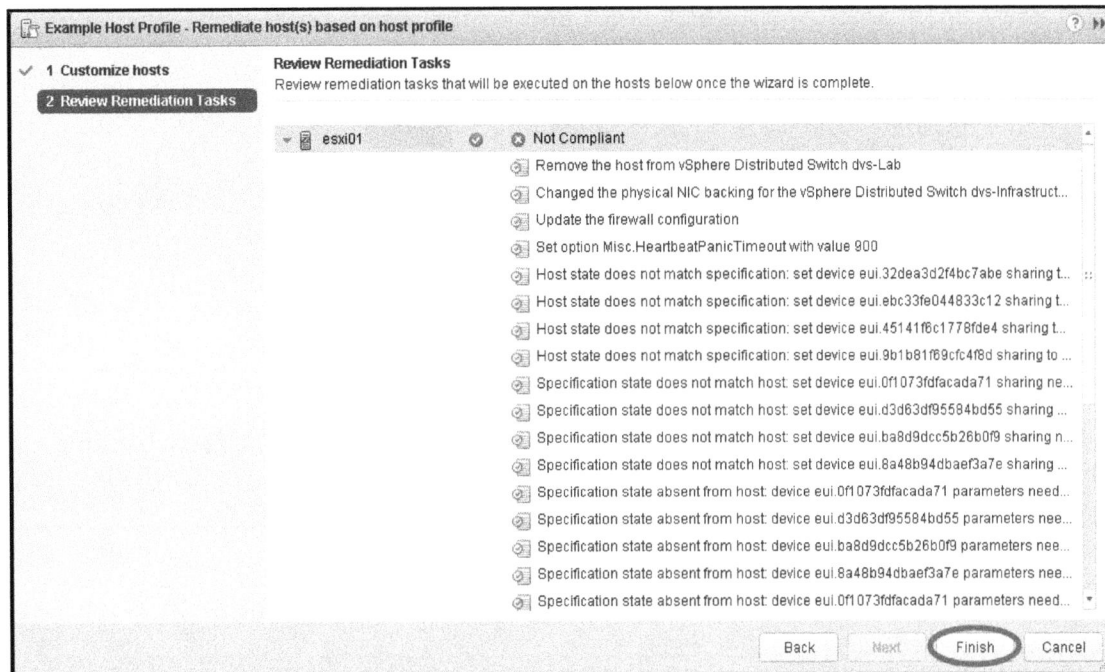

Once you press **Finish**, the remediation process will begin.

Detaching a host profile

Once you are finished using the host profile, you may detach it from the ESXi host or clusters. To do so, press the **Attach/Detach a host profile to hosts and clusters** button, as demonstrated in the following image:

Select the hosts or clusters to detach on the right-hand pane and press the **Detach** button. The hosts or clusters should now appear in the right-hand screen:

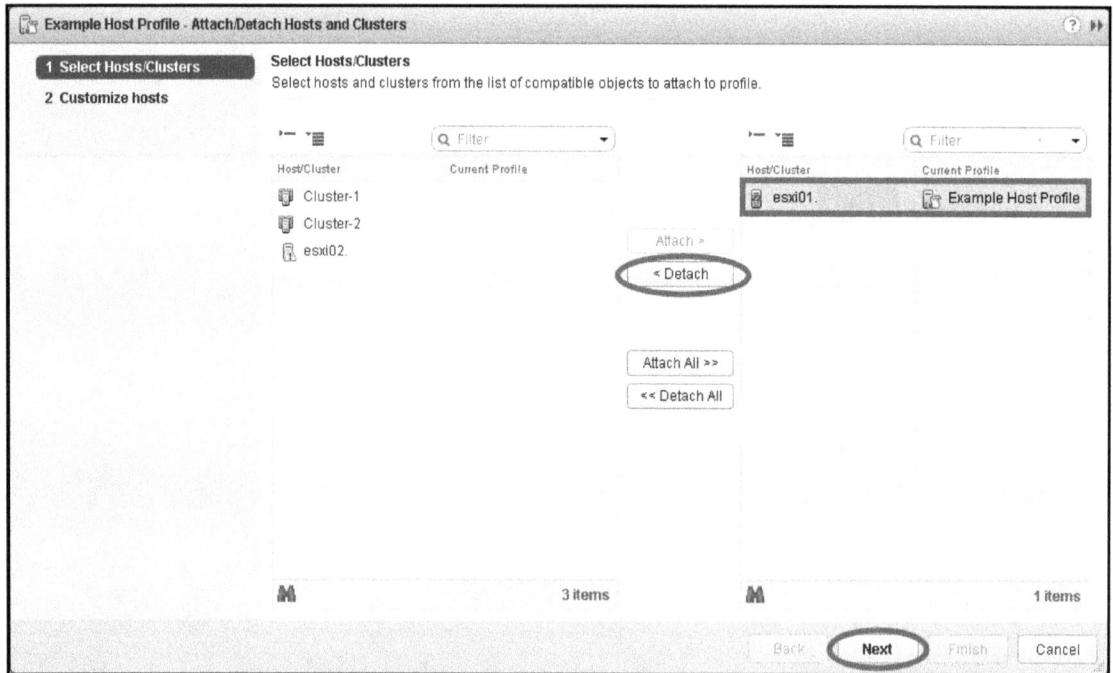

Press **Next** and review all information before hitting the **Finish** button to complete the wizard.

Managing host profiles

We've covered how to attach, check compliance, remediate, and detach a host profile but one of the more time-consuming, never-ending parts of using host profiles is the management piece. Host profiles can be edited, as well as imported and exported.

Editing a host profile

Once you have created a host profile, spend some time going through each of the settings abstracted from the reference ESXi host. You can modify values as well as removing settings from being a part of the compliance check. For example, something that is specific or unique to that reference host, but is not necessarily applicable to the rest of the ESXi host should be something to remove from the profile, like local storage.

To edit a host profile, select the host profile and press the **Action** drop-down menu; from there, select **Edit Settings...**:

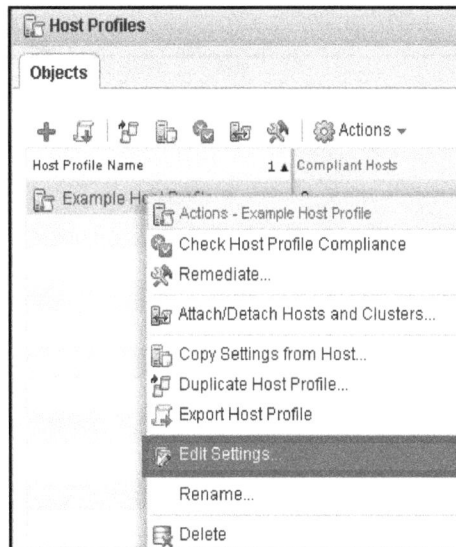

By selecting **Edit Settings**, a dialog box will pop up that allows you to go through each of the settings abstracted from the reference ESXi host and do further customization:

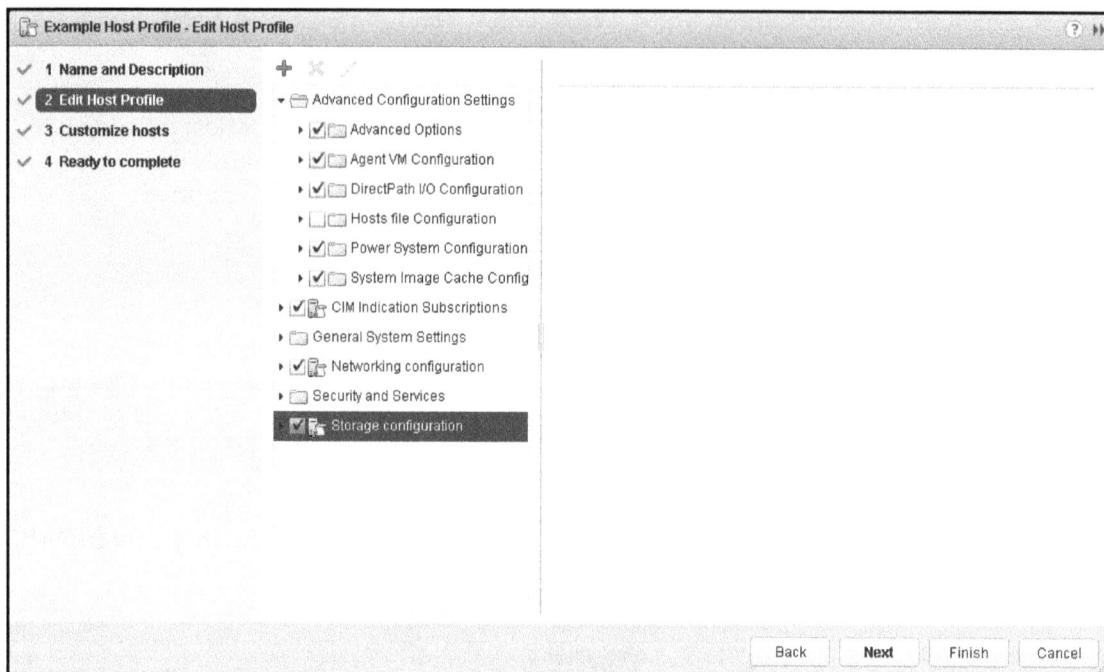

As an example, the following image demonstrates the ability to set configurations for **vSwitch0** that differ from how the reference host was configured. I could choose to modify the **MTU policy** or even specify to not create the vSwitch0 at all. I could even dig further into the **Link configuration** or **Number of ports** by further expanding the virtual switch:

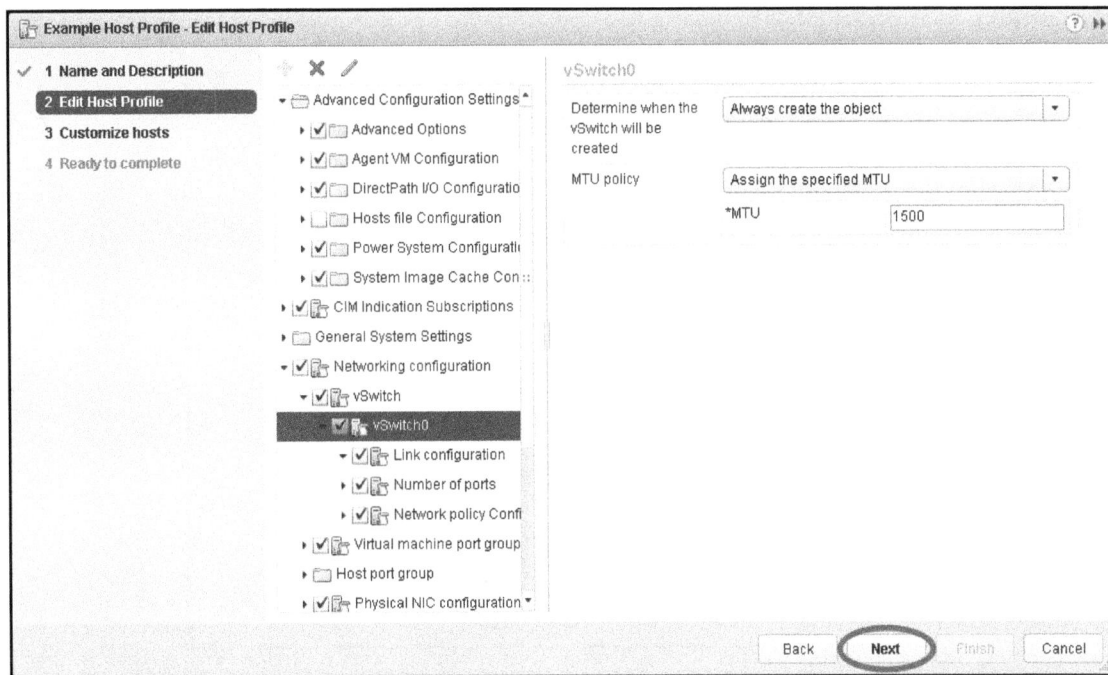

Continue to customize the host profile until it fits your specific needs and then press **Next** and then **Finish**.

Exporting a host profile

At some point you may have the need to share a host profile with another site or with a customer. You have the ability to export a host profile as a `.vpf` file, which can be imported into another vCenter server. The export method could also be used as a way to backup a host profile.

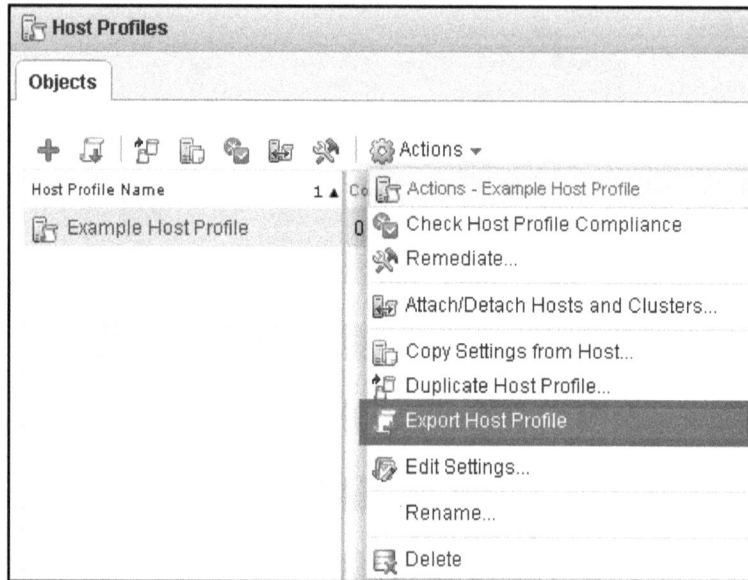

A security warning will pop up alerting you that passwords are not exported as a part of the host profile. Click the **Save** button:

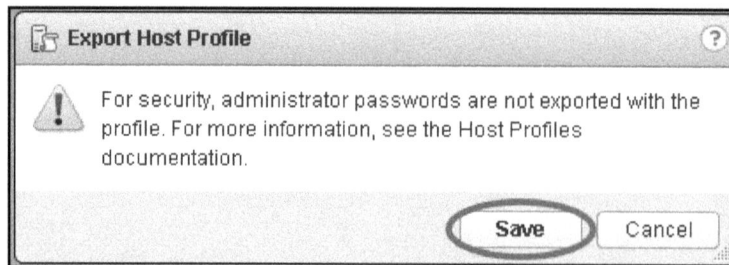

The save dialog will appear to allow you to choose a saved location and the name of the `.vpf` that will be created:

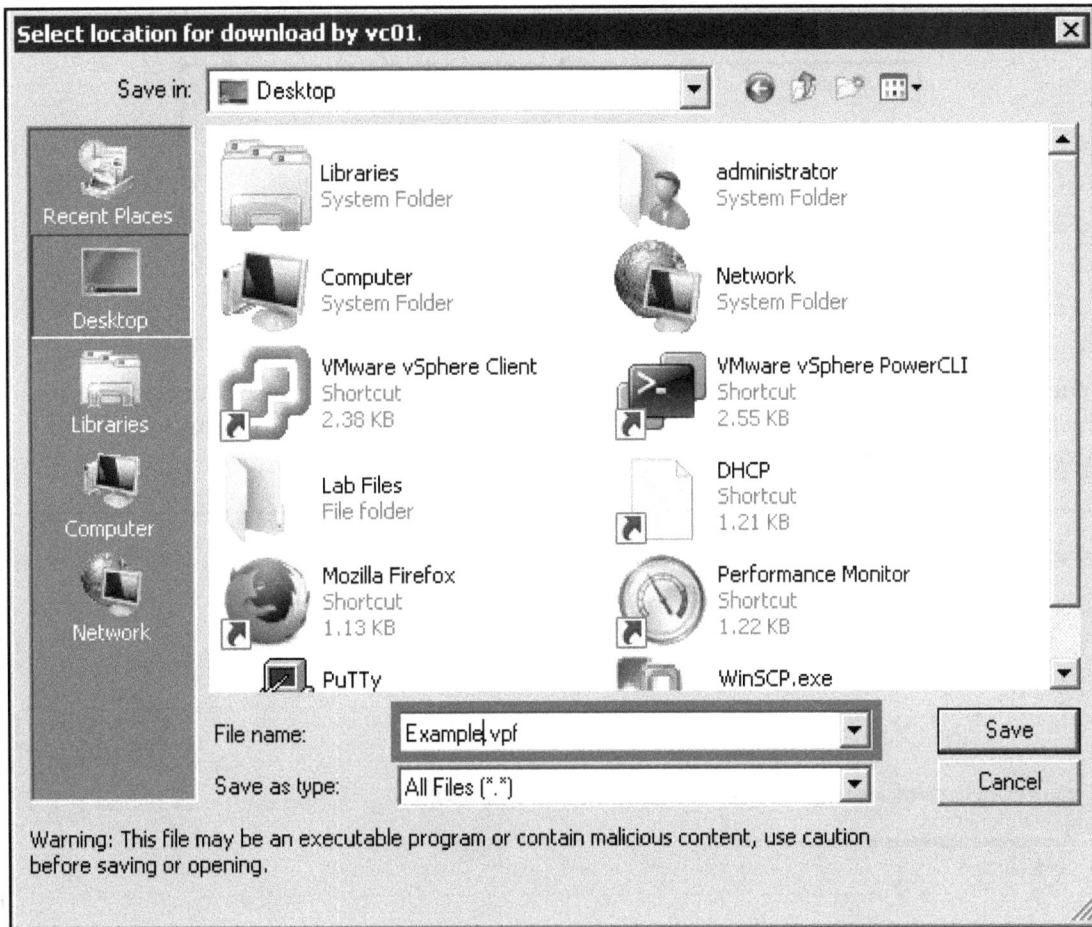

Press **Save** when finished.

Importing a host profile

Once there is a .vpf file, you will be able to press the **Import Host Profile** button and select an available host profile:

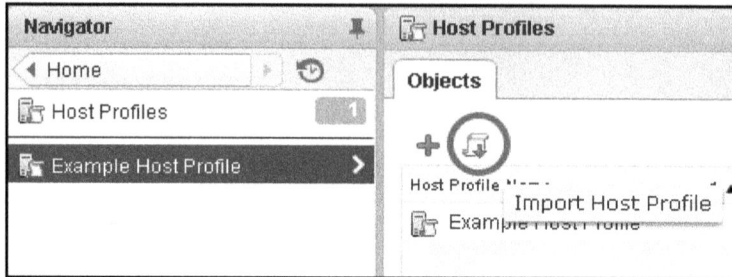

When the **Import Host Profile** dialog appears, select the destination **vCenter Server**, press the **Browse** button and select the desired .vpf file. Name the profile to be imported and add an optional description:

Click **OK** and the host profile will be imported.

Image profiles

vSphere ESXi Image Builder CLI is a command-line interface that allows for the customization and management of image profiles, software depots, and software packages (VIBs).

A quick overview of the vocabulary before we get into details:

- **Image profile**: this is the logical collection of VMware and third-party VIBs required for the installation of ESXi. Image profiles can be exported as a ZIP archive or an ISO file.
- **vSphere Installation Bundle** (**VIB**): the idea is somewhat similar to a tarball or ZIP archive since it is a collection of files packaged into a single archive for distribution. These typically contain drivers and additional software for ESXi from VMware and third-party partners.
- **Software depot**: used to package and distribute VIBs, this can be online (accessed remotely using HTTP) or offline (downloaded and accessed locally).

This is a useful tool if there isn't a third-party ESXi image already made for your hardware. With Image Builder, you could take a base ESXi image and modify it by adding VIBs containing drivers specific to your hardware rather than potentially having to install them after the fact.

Image Builder is available as a snap-in for PowerCLI. PowerCLI is a command-line tool that can be used to automate vSphere management.

Creating an image profile

To begin, first use the `Connect-VIServer` cmdlet to specify a target vCenter Server. In the example we specified **vc01.domain.local** and used the SSO administrator account to authenticate. The command is:

```
Connect-VIServer -Server vc01.domain.local -user
administrator@vsphere.local -Password VMware1!
```

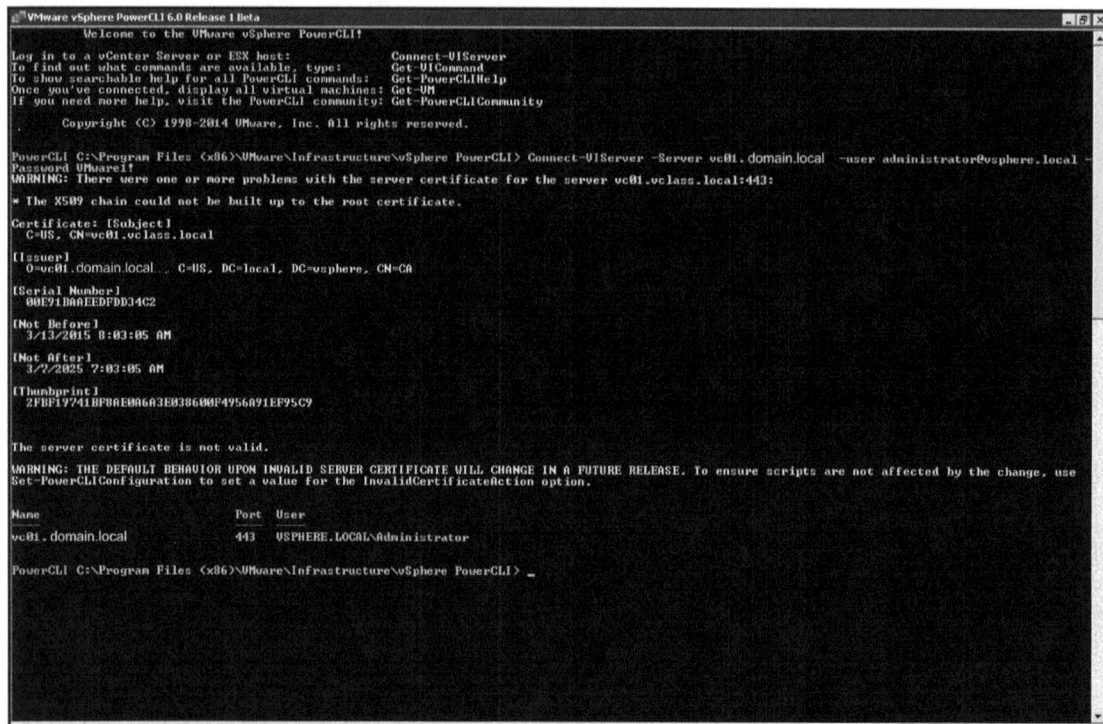

Use `Get-ExecutionPolicy` to determine the execution policies for the current session. We want to set the execution policy to unrestricted so that scripts can be run if necessary. To do so, type `Set-ExecutionPolicy unrestricted`. This is demonstrated in the following screenshot:

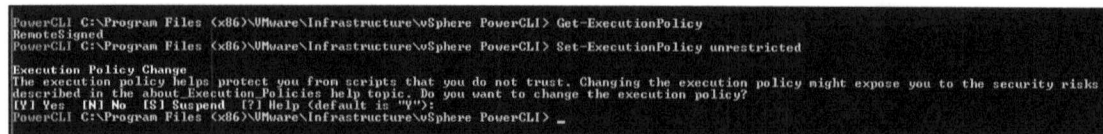

Next, we need to make sure that PowerCLI can access the software depot so that we can modify the image profiles as necessary. The command used was:

Add-EsxSoftwareDepot C:\Depot\VMware-ESXi-6.0.0-2445857-depot.zip

```
PowerCLI C:\Program Files (x86)\VMware\Infrastructure\vSphere PowerCLI> Add-EsxSoftwareDepot C:\Depot\VMware-ESXi-6.0.0-2445857-depot.zip
Depot Url
zip:C:\Depot\VMware-ESXi-6.0.0-2445857-depot.zip?index.xml
```

Once the software depot has been added, ensure that the image profiles are available by entering `Get-EsxImageProfile`. We have two image profiles that are available for use; a standard ESXi image and one with no tools:

```
PowerCLI C:\Program Files (x86)\VMware\Infrastructure\vSphere PowerCLI> Get-EsxImageProfile

Name                          Vendor        Last Modified    Acceptance Level
----                          ------        -------------    ----------------
ESXi-6.0.0-2445857-standard   VMware, Inc.  1/17/2015 9:...  PartnerSupported
ESXi-6.0.0-2445857-no-tools   VMware, Inc.  1/17/2015 9:...  PartnerSupported
```

Once the Software Depot is added and PowerCLI has access to the images, then we are ready to begin modifying our image profiles.

Cloning and customizing an image profile

It's recommended to clone an image profile and modify the cloned copy in case any mistakes are made and you need to start over. To do so, use a command similar to the following:

```
New-EsxImageProfile -CloneProfile ESXi-6.0.0-2445857-no-tools -Name
SampleImage -Vendor "VMware, Inc."
```

```
PowerCLI C:\Program Files (x86)\VMware\Infrastructure\vSphere PowerCLI> New-EsxImageProfile -CloneProfile ESXi-6.0.0-2445857-no-tools -Name SampleImag
e -Vendor "VMware, Inc."
Name            Vendor        Last Modified    Acceptance Level
----            ------        -------------    ----------------
SampleImage     VMware, Inc.  1/17/2015 9:...  PartnerSupported
```

The output of this command will show the newly cloned image profile, in this case called **SampleImage**, created and listed.

Exporting an image profile

Once you have modified the image profile as desired, you may export it as an ISO or ZIP file. To do so, use one or both of the following sample commands:

- ```
  Export-EsxImageProfile –ImageProfile SampleImage –ExportToIso –FilePath C:\Depot\SampleImage.iso
  ```
- ```
  Export-EsxImageProfie –ImageProfile SampleImage –ExportToBundle –FilePath C:\Depot\SampleImage.zip
  ```

```
PowerCLI C:\Program Files (x86)\VMware\Infrastructure\vSphere PowerCLI> Export-EsxImageProfile –ImageProfile SampleImage –ExportToIso –FilePath C:\Depot\SampleImage.iso
PowerCLI C:\Program Files (x86)\VMware\Infrastructure\vSphere PowerCLI> Export-EsxImageProfile –ImageProfile SampleImage –ExportToBundle –FilePat:\Depot\SampleImage.zip
```

When that command completes, we can use `ls` to determine the content of the **C:\depot** directory. The following image shows our newly exported image profiles listed:

```
PowerCLI C:\Program Files (x86)\VMware\Infrastructure\vSphere PowerCLI> ls C:\Depot


    Directory: C:\Depot


Mode                LastWriteTime     Length Name
----                -------------     ------ ----
-a---         3/3/2016   8:59 PM   177729536 SampleImage.iso
-a---         3/3/2016   9:00 PM   167380248 SampleImage.zip
-a---         2/5/2015  11:55 AM   361433069 VMware-ESXi-6.0.0-2445857-depot.zip
```

Now that the image profiles are in an ISO or ZIP format, you can burn that image to disc or even use it for vSphere Auto Deploy.

Auto Deploy

vSphere Auto Deploy is a cool feature that came out with vSphere 5. It allows you the ability to provision hundreds of ESXi hosts at a time. You specify the image to deploy, which hosts to provision, a host profile for the settings, a target vCenter Server, and cluster, and voila, you'll have your ESXi host provisioned in no time! Once Auto Deploy is configured, the ESXi hosts will use a PXE boot infrastructure paired with host profiles to provision and customize the hosts. This can be configured for stateless, stateless caching, or stateful.

Let's take a look at the three types of Auto Deploy setup:

- Stateless – the image resides in the memory; no local disks needed. PXE infrastructure will always be used for boot.
- Stateless caching – introduced in vSphere 5.1, this feature allows you to cache the ESXi host's image locally on a host disk or a USB device. The ESXi host will continue to boot using the PXE infrastructure unless its unavailable, at which point it would boot from the locally cached image.
- Stateful installs – introduced in vSphere 5.1, this feature allows you to install ESXi over the network. After the initial network boot, a stateful ESXi host will boot like any other ESXi host where ESXi is installed locally.

Let's have a look at the advantages of using auto deploy:

- Reduced storage costs since there is no need for a dedicated boot disk for each server using the stateless auto deploy configuration.
- Fast server provisioning; once everything is configured then deploying a new ESXi host is as simple as enabling PXE boot and powering on the new server.
- Simplified patch management as each ESXi host is booted using an ESXi image profile. Therefore, you could do a one-time update to the ESXi image profile and reboot the ESXi hosts and all will contain that update.
- Eliminate configuration drift or image standardization.

Auto Deploy architecture

vSphere Auto Deploy is made up of several moving parts, to include PowerCLI, a PXE environment, vCenter Server and host profiles, image profile, and the Auto Deploy service itself.

The following image demonstrates the vSphere Auto Deploy architecture:

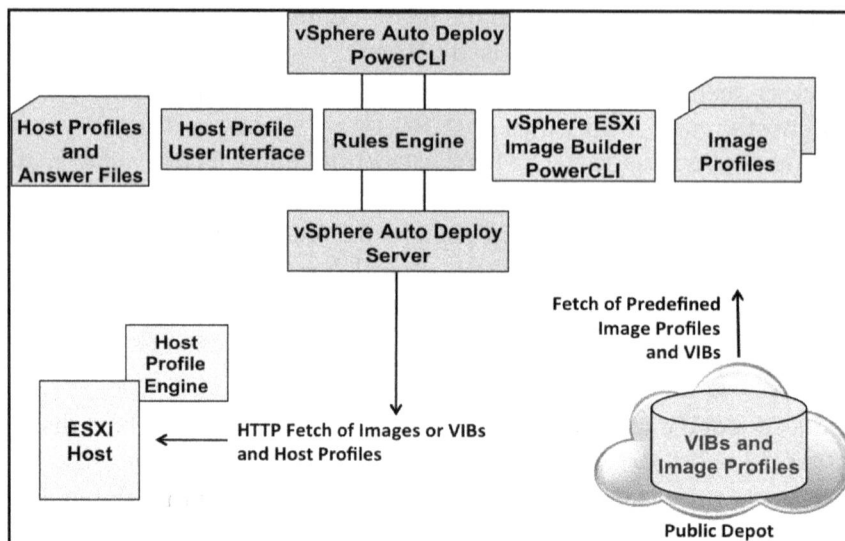

The PXE infrastructure consists of a DHCP server and a TFTP server. As a part of Auto Deploy, you will need to configure DHCP scope and a few DHCP options. DHCP option 66 (Boot Server Host Name) should be set to the TFTP server IP address and the DHCP option 67 (File Name) should be set to the Auto Deploy gPXE filename that the ESXi hosts will be downloading during the PXE boot process from the TFTP server. The Auto Deploy gPXE file is manually copied from the vCenter Server to the home directory of the TFTP server during the Auto Deploy configuration.

The Auto Deploy Server is the core of the infrastructure and it consists of two parts, a server and a rules engine. The server side serves images and host profiles to the ESXi hosts. During the gPXE boot, the ESXi host provides the Auto Deploy server with attributes that identify the host, for example, the MAC address, IP address, and vendor tag information. These attributes are passed on to the rules engine where it will determine which ESXi image profile to use, which host profile to use, and which vCenter Server, as well as where in vCenter's inventory the ESXi host should be placed once it is provisioned. The Auto Deploy service is a part of the vCenter Server component.

The image profile determines the version of ESXi and which VIBs will be used during the boot process.

Host profiles define the configurations and setup of the ESXi host for things like networking and storage.

A host customization file, or answer file, stores the information that you provide when a host profile is applied to an ESXi host. This would contain anything that is unique to that individual host, like an IP address.

The last component needed for Auto Deploy is PowerCLI. You will use PowerCLI to create an image profile, as demonstrated earlier in the chapter, and also to create Auto Deploy rules.

Auto Deploy rules

vSphere Auto Deploy's behavior is determined by the rules specified using PowerCLI. The Auto Deploy rules engine checks the rule set for matches with the host pattern to determine which items (image profile, host profile, vCenter Server location) to use to provision the ESXi host. The rules engine maps these items to the ESXi host, based on the host attributes.

If changes are made to the rules, PowerCLI cmdlets should be used to test and repair rule compliance.

The rules engine includes rules and rule sets.

Rules can assign image profiles and host profiles to individual ESXi hosts, a set of hosts, or a cluster or folder location on a target vCenter Server. Rules reference ESXi hosts based on a unique attribute, such as a boot MAC address, BIOS UUID, SMBIOS information, vendor, model, or even a fixed DHCP IP address. Most rules can apply to multiple hosts. Once a rule is created, it must be added to a rule set. There are only supported rule sets, an active rule set, and the working rule set.

A newly started ESXi host will contact the Auto Deploy service with an image profile request, and Auto Deploy checks the **active rule set** for a matching rule. The matching rule will map the image profile, host profile, and vCenter Server inventory location and use them to boot the host.

The **working rule set** allows for changes to rules to be tested before making these changes active. PowerCLI will be used to test compliance with the working rule set and this test verifies that the vCenter Server-managed ESXi hosts are following the rules in the working rule set.

Auto Deploy boot overview

When a host is booted, vSphere Auto Deploy should provision or reprovision the image profile, host profile, and vCenter Server location.

The first time an ESXi host is provisioned with vSphere Auto Deploy, the process goes as follows:

1. When the host is turned on, it will begin a PXE boot sequence.
2. The DHCP Server will assign an IP address and instruct the host to contact the TFTP server.
3. The host will contact the TFTP server and download the iPXE file (executable boot loader) and iPXE configuration file.
4. iPXE will execute and instruct the host to make an HTTP boot request to the Auto Deploy server. This HTTP request will include hardware and network information.
5. The rules engine will be queried for host information.
6. The image profile, host profile, and vCenter Server location information will be streamed to the host. This is cached on the Auto Deploy server to make subsequent reboots faster.

7. The host will boot using the image profile and the host profile will be applied.
8. The ESXi host will be added to the vCenter Server and placed in the correct inventory location.

A subsequent reboot will follow a similar process.

Auto Deploy configuration

In order to be able to PXE boot an ESXi host using vSphere Auto Deploy, the prerequisite software, including DHCP and TFTP needs to be installed and configured.

Configuring prerequisites

vCenter Server will need to be installed, and the Auto Deploy service started. The following image displays starting the server for the vCenter Server Appliance using the vSphere Web Client. To do so, log into the vCenter Server using the vSphere Web Client, on the home page, click **Administration**. Under **System Configuration**, select **Services**. Select **Auto Deploy**, and near the top of the image, select **Start**. You may also select **Edit Startup Type** and choose to set the service to **Automatic**:

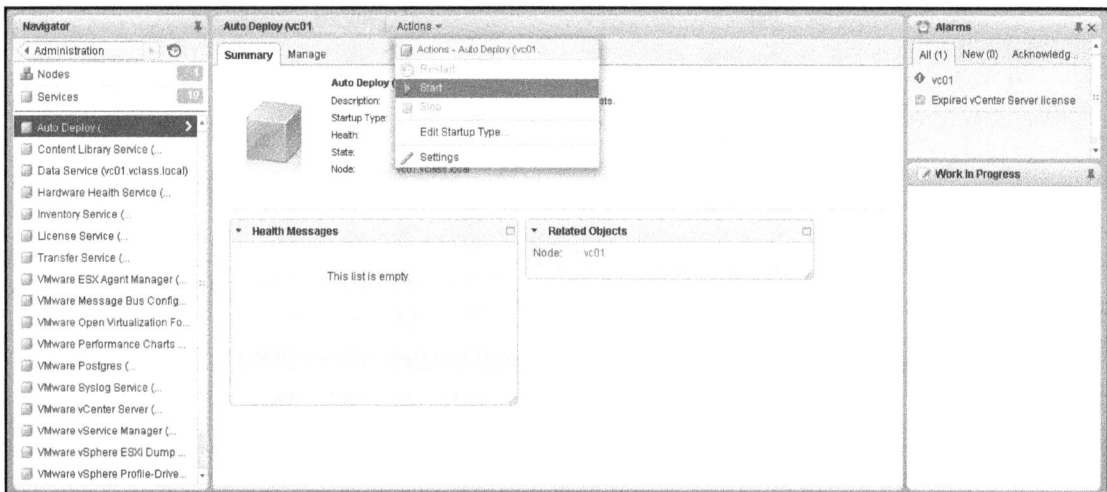

Next you will need to configure the TFTP server. Using the vSphere Web Client, you will need to select your vCenter Server in the inventory, and select the **Manage** tab. Click **Settings** and then **AutoDeploy**. Click on **Download TFTP Boot Zip** to download the TFTP configuration file and then unzip that file in the TFTP server directory that stores files. The TFTP server is included with the vCenter Server Appliance but this is a separately installed component if you're using the Windows vCenter Server.

Create a DHCP reservation for the ESXi hosts to ensure that the same IP address is used consistently for the management network. To do so, open **DHCP**, under the **IPscope**, and select **Reservations**. Right-click **Reservations** and select **New Reservation**. When the dialog box pops up, enter **Reservation name**, **IP address**, **MAC address**, and a **Description**:

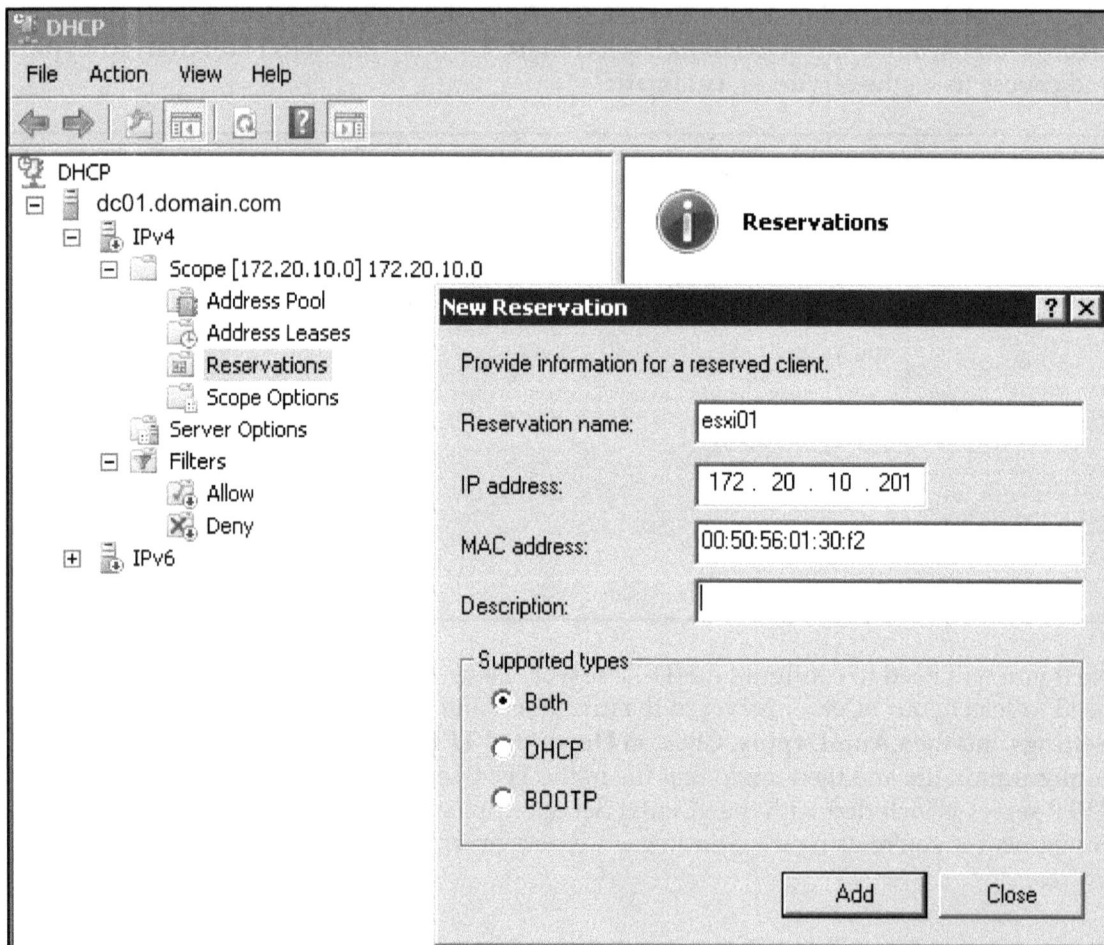

Click **Add** once this is complete.

The next image demonstrates setting the DHCP server to point to the TFTP server where the TFTP ZIP file resides. Choose option **066**, which is **Boot Server Host Name** and in the **String value**, place the **IP address** of the TFTP server. In this case, the TFTP service is also my vCenter Server, **vc01**:

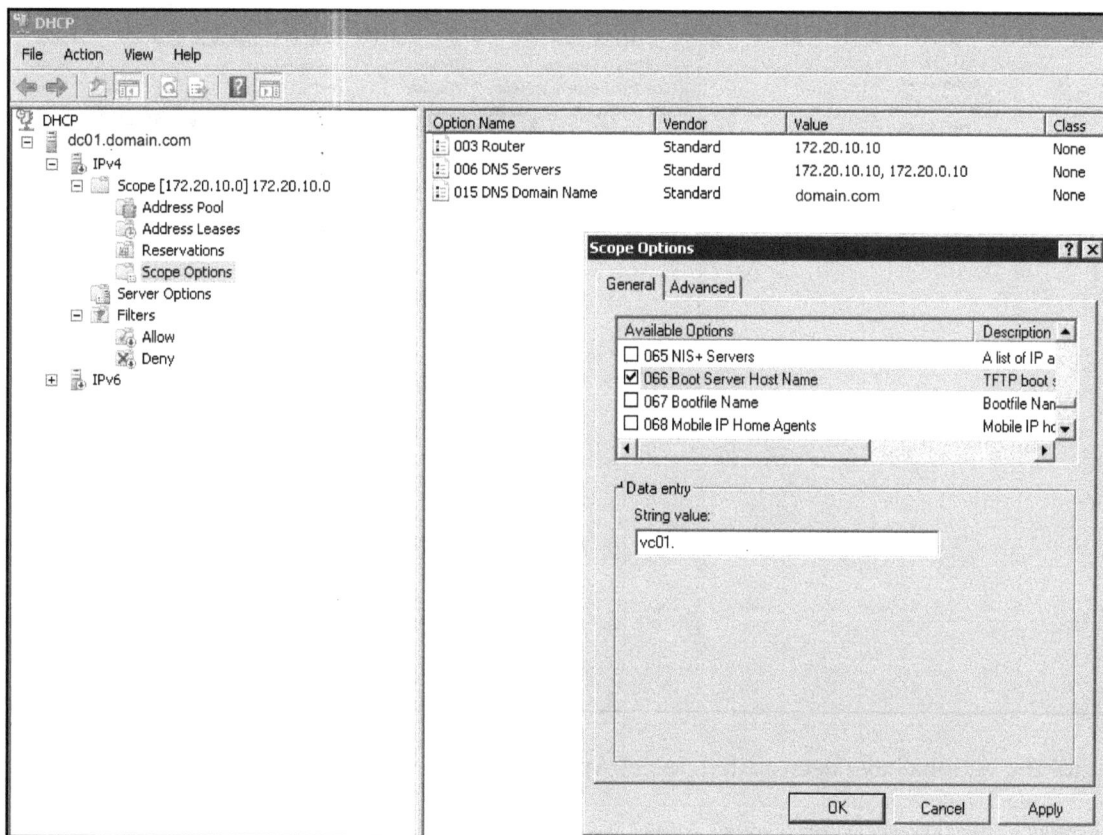

Also, select option **067 Bootfile Name**. Specify the boot file name, which is **undionly.kpxe.vmw-hardwired**:

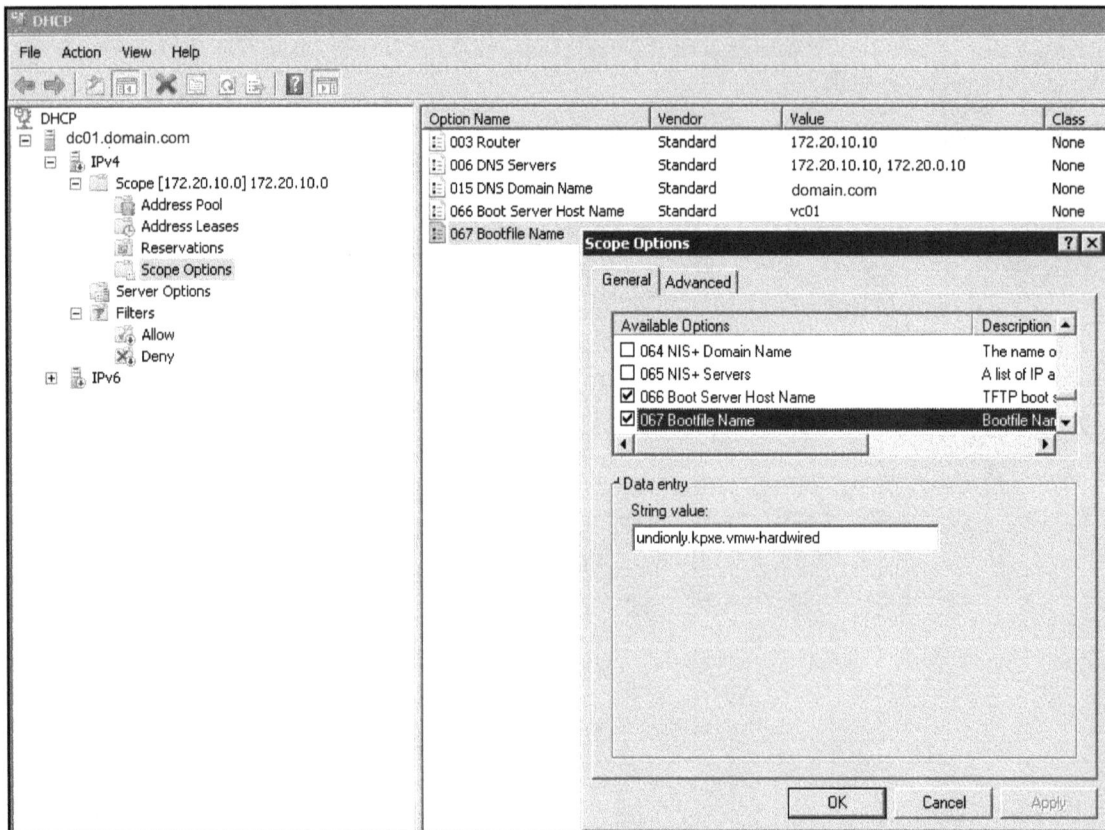

Once the options have been added, select **Apply** and then **OK**.

Creating and assigning a rule

If you haven't yet already, use the `Connect-VIServer` to connect to the vCenter Server to which Auto Deploy is registered. For example, `Connect-VIServer 192.168.10.5` or `Connect-VIServer vc01.domain.com`.

This example will demonstrate creating a rule for PXE booting stateless ESXi hosts.

At the PowerCLI prompt, define a rule where the image profile is assigned to an ESXi host. The following screenshot uses the `New-DeployRule` cmdlet. The example given is `New-DeployRule -Name ImageRule -Item SampleImage -AllHosts`. This assigns the **SampleImage** image profile to all ESXi hosts:

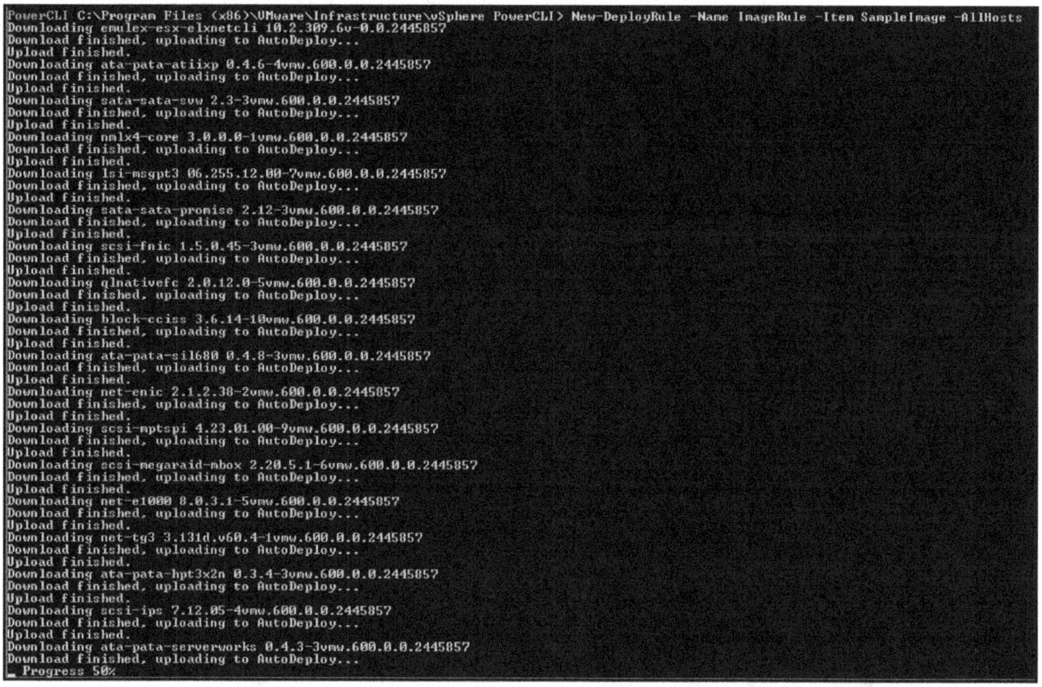

```
PowerCLI C:\Program Files (x86)\VMware\Infrastructure\vSphere PowerCLI> New-DeployRule -Name ImageRule -Item SampleImage -AllHosts
Downloading emulex-esx-elxnetcli 10.2.309.6v-0.0.2445857
Download finished, uploading to AutoDeploy...
Upload finished.
Downloading ata-pata-atiixp 0.4.6-4vmw.600.0.0.2445857
Download finished, uploading to AutoDeploy...
Upload finished.
Downloading sata-sata-svw 2.3-3vmw.600.0.0.2445857
Download finished, uploading to AutoDeploy...
Upload finished.
Downloading nmlx4-core 3.0.0.0-1vmw.600.0.0.2445857
Download finished, uploading to AutoDeploy...
Upload finished.
Downloading lsi-msgpt3 06.255.12.00-7vmw.600.0.0.2445857
Download finished, uploading to AutoDeploy...
Upload finished.
Downloading sata-sata-promise 2.12-3vmw.600.0.0.2445857
Download finished, uploading to AutoDeploy...
Upload finished.
Downloading scsi-fnic 1.5.0.45-3vmw.600.0.0.2445857
Download finished, uploading to AutoDeploy...
Upload finished.
Downloading qlnativefc 2.0.12.0-5vmw.600.0.0.2445857
Download finished, uploading to AutoDeploy...
Upload finished.
Downloading block-cciss 3.6.14-10vmw.600.0.0.2445857
Download finished, uploading to AutoDeploy...
Upload finished.
Downloading ata-pata-sil680 0.4.8-3vmw.600.0.0.2445857
Download finished, uploading to AutoDeploy...
Upload finished.
Downloading net-enic 2.1.2.38-2vmw.600.0.0.2445857
Download finished, uploading to AutoDeploy...
Upload finished.
Downloading scsi-mptspi 4.23.01.00-9vmw.600.0.0.2445857
Download finished, uploading to AutoDeploy...
Upload finished.
Downloading scsi-megaraid-mbox 2.20.5.1-6vmw.600.0.0.2445857
Download finished, uploading to AutoDeploy...
Upload finished.
Downloading net-e1000 8.0.3.1-5vmw.600.0.0.2445857
Download finished, uploading to AutoDeploy...
Upload finished.
Downloading net-tg3 3.131d.v60.4-1vmw.600.0.0.2445857
Download finished, uploading to AutoDeploy...
Upload finished.
Downloading ata-pata-hpt3x2n 0.3.4-3vmw.600.0.0.2445857
Download finished, uploading to AutoDeploy...
Upload finished.
Downloading scsi-ips 7.12.05-4vmw.600.0.0.2445857
Download finished, uploading to AutoDeploy...
Upload finished.
Downloading ata-pata-serverworks 0.4.3-3vmw.600.0.0.2445857
Download finished, uploading to AutoDeploy...
_ Progress 50%
```

This rule may take a few minutes to upload the image to the Auto Deploy server. Be patient and wait until it is complete before proceeding:

```
Download finished, uploading to AutoDeploy...
Upload finished.
Downloading scsi-bnx2fc 1.78.78.v60.8-1vmw.600.0.0.2445857
Download finished, uploading to AutoDeploy...
Upload finished.
Downloading lsu-lsi-mpt2sas-plugin 1.0.0-1vmw.600.0.0.2445857
Download finished, uploading to AutoDeploy...
Upload finished.
Downloading scsi-mpt2sas 19.00.00.00-1vmw.600.0.0.2445857
Download finished, uploading to AutoDeploy...
Upload finished.
Downloading esx-dvfilter-generic-fastpath 6.0.0-0.0.2445857
Download finished, uploading to AutoDeploy...
Upload finished.
Downloading scsi-megaraid-sas 6.603.55.00-2vmw.600.0.0.2445857
Download finished, uploading to AutoDeploy...
Upload finished.
Downloading lpfc 10.2.309.8-2vmw.600.0.0.2445857
Download finished, uploading to AutoDeploy...
Upload finished.
Downloading scsi-aacraid 1.1.5.1-9vmw.600.0.0.2445857
Download finished, uploading to AutoDeploy...
Upload finished.
Downloading ata-pata-amd 0.3.10-3vmw.600.0.0.2445857
Download finished, uploading to AutoDeploy...
Upload finished.
Downloading net-forcedeth 0.61-2vmw.600.0.0.2445857
Download finished, uploading to AutoDeploy...
Upload finished.
Downloading ata-pata-pdc2027x 1.0-3vmw.600.0.0.2445857
Download finished, uploading to AutoDeploy...
Upload finished.
Downloading net-mlx4-en 1.9.7.0-1vmw.600.0.0.2445857
Download finished, uploading to AutoDeploy...
Upload finished.
Downloading ipmi-ipmi-si-drv 39.1-4vmw.600.0.0.2445857
Download finished, uploading to AutoDeploy...
Upload finished.
Downloading rste 2.0.2.0088-4vmw.600.0.0.2445857
Download finished, uploading to AutoDeploy...
Upload finished.
Downloading net-ixgbe 3.7.13.7.14iov-20vmw.600.0.0.2445857
Download finished, uploading to AutoDeploy...
Upload finished.
Downloading uhci-usb-uhci 1.0-3vmw.600.0.0.2445857
Download finished, uploading to AutoDeploy...
Upload finished.
Downloading scsi-mptsas 4.23.01.00-9vmw.600.0.0.2445857
Download finished, uploading to AutoDeploy...
Upload finished.
Downloading ipmi-ipmi-msghandler 39.1-4vmw.600.0.0.2445857
Download finished, uploading to AutoDeploy...
Upload finished.


Name        : ImageRule
PatternList :
ItemList    : {SampleImage}


PowerCLI C:\Program Files (x86)\VMware\Infrastructure\vSphere PowerCLI> _
```

The following image demonstrates creating a rule to assign the host profile called `Host-Profile-Example` to all ESXi hosts. The command used is:

```
New-DeployRule -Name ProfileRule -Item Host-Profile-Example -AllHosts
```

```
PowerCLI C:\Program Files (x86)\VMware\Infrastructure\vSphere PowerCLI> New-DeployRule -Name ProfileRule -Item Host-Profile-Example -AllHosts

Name        : ProfileRule
PatternList :
ItemList    : {Host-Profile-Example}
```

The next command specifies the attribute of the IP range 172.20.10.201 – 172.20.10.220 for the rule. The command used in the following image is:

```
Set-DeployRule ImageRule -Pattern "ipv4=172.20.10.201-172.20.10.220"
```

If you recall, in one of the above images (*creating a DHCP reservation for the ESXi hosts*, in the section, *Configuring Prerequisites*), we created a DHCP reservation that is within this scope:

```
PowerCLI C:\Program Files (x86)\VMware\Infrastructure\vSphere PowerCLI> Set-DeployRule ImageRule -Pattern "ipv4=172.20.10.201-172.20.10.220"

Name        : ImageRule
PatternList : {ipv4=172.20.10.201-172.20.10.220}
ItemList    : {SampleImage}
```

An additional rule is needed to specify the vCenter Server inventory location once the PXE booted ESXi hosts are added. It is specified that all ESXi hosts will be placed in the cluster called **Auto-Deploy-Cluster**. The command used is:

```
New-DeployRule -Name ContainerRule -Item Auto-Deploy-Cluster -allhosts
```

```
PowerCLI C:\Program Files (x86)\VMware\Infrastructure\vSphere PowerCLI> New-DeployRule -Name ContainerRule -Item Auto-Deploy-Cluster -allhosts

Name        : ContainerRule
PatternList :
ItemList    : {Auto-Deploy-Cluster}
```

You can use the `Get-DeployRule` cmdlet to see the rules created. Notice that the **ImageRule** has the IP range attribute that we configured in the image immediately before the above image. We can see the three rules we created in the following image:

```
PowerCLI C:\Program Files (x86)\VMware\Infrastructure\vSphere PowerCLI> Get-DeployRule

Name        : ImageRule
PatternList : {ipv4=172.20.10.201-172.20.10.220}
ItemList    : {SampleImage}

Name        : ProfileRule
PatternList :
ItemList    : {Host-Profile-Example}

Name        : ContainerRule
PatternList :
ItemList    : {Auto-Deploy-Cluster}
```

Now it's time to add our rules to the active rule set, to do so use the `Add-DeployRule` cmdlet. We'll be repeating this for each of our rules created. To add the **ImageRule** to the active rule set, use `Add-DeployRule -DeployRule ImageRule`:

```
PowerCLI C:\Program Files (x86)\VMware\Infrastructure\vSphere PowerCLI> Add-DeployRule -DeployRule IMageRule

Name        : ImageRule
PatternList : {ipv4=172.20.10.201-172.20.10.220}
ItemList    : {SampleImage}
```

To add the **ProfileRule** to the active rule set, enter `Add-DeployRule -DeployRule ProfileRule`:

```
PowerCLI C:\Program Files (x86)\VMware\Infrastructure\vSphere PowerCLI> Add-DeployRule -DeployRule ProfileRule

Name        : ImageRule
PatternList : {ipv4=172.20.10.201-172.20.10.220}
ItemList    : {SampleImage}

Name        : ProfileRule
PatternList :
ItemList    : {Host-Profile-Example}
```

To add the **ContainerRule**, use `Add-DeployRule -DeployRule ContainerRule`:

```
PowerCLI C:\Program Files (x86)\VMware\Infrastructure\vSphere PowerCLI> Add-DeployRule -DeployRule ContainerRule

Name        : ImageRule
PatternList : {ipv4=172.20.10.201-172.20.10.220}
ItemList    : {SampleImage}

Name        : ProfileRule
PatternList :
ItemList    : {Host-Profile-Example}

Name        : ContainerRule
PatternList :
ItemList    : {Auto-Deploy-Cluster}
```

Voila! We're now ready to PXE boot our host for the first time and it will have the image profile, host profile, and be placed into the vCenter Server inventory based on the rules that we created.

Stateless caching and stateful installs

To configure vSphere Auto Deploy for stateless caching or stateful install, you will modify the host profile. Edit the host profile, and under **Advanced Configuration Settings**, expand **System Image Cache Configuration** and select the **System Image Cache Configuration Settings**. This will allow you to select **Enable stateless caching on the host**, **Enable stateful installs on the host**, **Enable Stateless caching to a USB disk on the host**, or **Enable stateful installs to a USB disk on the host**:

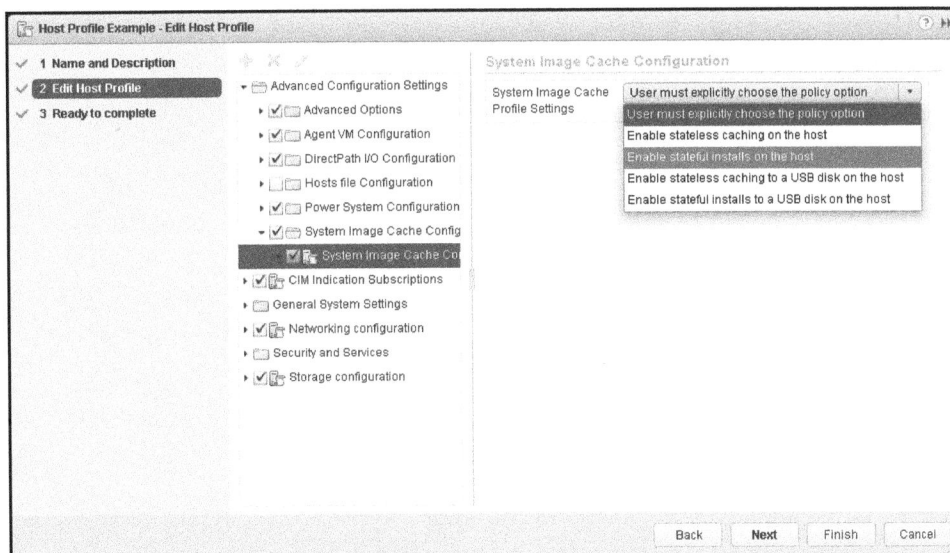

Otherwise, the configuration is similar. PowerCLI rules are used to configure which image profile, host profile, and vCenter Server inventory location will be used.

Summary

This chapter covered the topics of host profiles, vSphere Auto Deploy, and image profiles. Host profiles are like templates for ESXi hosts. A host profile is abstracted from a reference host and can be edited. vSphere Auto Deploy can be used to quickly provision a large number of ESXi hosts using a PXE boot infrastructure. Host profiles can be created independently of vSphere Auto Deploy but are a requirement when Auto Deploy is in use. Each host has an answer or configuration file that contains unique information such as IP addresses. Image Builder is a command line utility that allows you to modify an image profile. Images can be exported as an ISO or a ZIP file. A vSphere Auto Deploy rule should dictate an image profile, a host profile, and an inventory location in the vCenter Server. PowerCLI is used to manage vSphere Auto Deploy rules.

The next chapter will take a deeper look at some of the virtual machine concepts and management.

8

Virtual Machines Concepts and Management

A virtual machine is a set of virtual hardware whose characteristics are determined by a set of encapsulated files; it is this virtual hardware that a guest operating system is installed on. A virtual machine runs an operating system and a set of applications in a similar fashion to a physical server. Essentially, a virtual machine is comprised of configuration files and its physical resources are provided by an ESXi host.

Virtual machines are created within a virtualization layer, and this virtualization layer manages requests from the virtual machine for resources such as CPU or memory. It is this virtualization layer that is responsible for translating these requests to the underlying physical hardware.

Each virtual machine is granted a portion of the physical hardware. All VMs have their own virtual hardware (there are important ones to note, called the *core 4*: CPU, memory, disk, and network). Each VM is isolated from the other and each interacts with the underlying hardware through a thin software layer known as the *hypervisor*. This is different from a physical architecture in which the installed operating system interacts with the installed hardware directly.

With virtualization, there are many benefits in relation to portability, security, and manageability that aren't available in an environment that uses a traditional physical infrastructure. However, once provisioned, virtual machines use many of the same principles that are applied to physical servers.

In this chapter, we will learn:

- The components of a virtual machine
- New vSphere 6 virtual machine features
- How to create a virtual machine
- Virtual machine settings
- vSphere Fault Tolerance

Virtual machine components

A virtual machine needs four core resources: CPU, memory, network, and storage (disk). These resources are granted to the virtual machine through the configuration of the virtual hardware.

Virtual hardware

When a virtual machine is created, a default set of virtual hardware is assigned to it. VMware provides devices and resources that can be added and configured to the virtual machine. Not all virtual hardware devices will be available to every single virtual machine; both the physical hardware of the ESXi host and the VM's guest OS must support these configurations. For example, a virtual machine will not be capable of being configured with more vCPUs than the ESXi host has CPU sockets.

The virtual hardware available includes:

- **BIOS**: Phoenix Technologies 6.00 that functions like a physical server BIOS. Virtual machine administrators are able to enable/disable I/O devices, configure boot order, and so on.
- **DVD/CD-ROM**: NEC VMware IDE CDR10 that is installed by default in new virtual machines created in vSphere. The DVD/CD-ROM can be configured to connect to the client workstation DVD/CD-ROM, an ESXi host DVD/CD-ROM, or even an .iso file located on a datastore. DVD/CD-ROM devices can be added to or removed from a virtual machine.

- **Floppy drive**: They are installed by default with new virtual machines created in vSphere. The floppy drive can be configured to connect to the client device's floppy drive, a floppy device located on the ESXi host, or even a floppy image (`.flp`) located on a datastore. Floppy devices can be added to or removed from a virtual machine.

- **Hard disk**: This stores the guest operating system, program files, and any other data associated with a virtual machine. The virtual disk is a large physical file, or potentially a set of files, that can be easily copied, moved, and backed up.

- **IDE controller**: Intel 82371 AB/EB PCI Bus Master IDE Controller that presents two **Integrated Drive Electronics** (**IDE**) interfaces to the virtual machine by default. This IDE controller is a standard way for storage devices, such as floppy drives and CD-ROM drives, to connect to the virtual machine.

- **Keyboard**: This mirrors the keyboard that is first connected to the virtual machine console upon initial console connection.

- **Memory**: This is the virtual memory size configured for the virtual machine that determines the guest operating system's memory size. A maximum of 4 TB may be configured for a virtual machine.

- **Motherboard/Chipset**: The motherboard uses VMware proprietary devices that are based on the following chips:
    - Intel 440BX AGPset 82443BX Host Bridge/Controller
    - Intel 82093 AA I/O Advanced Programmable Interrupt Controller
    - Intel 82371 AB (PIIX4) PCI ISA IDE Xcelerator
    - National Semiconductor PC87338 ACPI 1.0 and PC98/99 Compliant Super I/O

- **Network adapter**: ESXi networking features provide communication between virtual machines residing on the same ESXi host, between VMs residing on different ESXi hosts, and between VMs and physical machines. When configuring a VM, network adapters (NICs) can be added and the adapter type can be speci

Keep in mind that snapshots are not supported with DirectPath I/O pass-through device configuration. For more information on virtual machine snapshots, see `http://vmware.com/kb/11518`.

- **Pointing device**: This mirrors the pointing device that is first connected to the virtual machine console upon initial console connection.
- **Processor**: This specifies the number of sockets and core for the virtual processor. This will appear as AMD or Intel to the virtual machine guest operating system depending upon the physical hardware. A maximum of 128 vCPUs may be configured.
- **SATA controller**: This provides access to DVD/CD-ROM devices and virtual disks. The SATA virtual controller will appear to the virtual machine as an AHCI SATA controller.
- **Serial port**: This is an interface for connecting peripherals to the virtual machine. The virtual machine can be configured to connect to a physical serial port, a file on the host, or over the network. The serial port can also be used to establish a direct connection between two VMs. Virtual serial ports can be added to or removed from the virtual machine. A maximum of 32 serial ports may be configured.
- **SCSI controller**: This provides access to virtual disks. The virtual SCSI controller may appear as one of several different types of controllers to a virtual machine, depending on the guest operating system of the VM. Editing the VM configuration can modify the SCSI controller type, a SCSI controller can be added, and a virtual controller can be configured to allocate bus sharing.
- **SCSI device**: An SCSI device interface is available to the virtual machine by default. This interface is a typical way to connect storage devices (hard drives, floppy drives, CD-ROMs, and so on) to a VM. SCSI device is a device that can be added to or removed from a virtual machine.
- **SIO controller**: The **Super I/O controller** provides serial and parallel ports, floppy devices, and performs system management activities. A single SIO controller is presented to the virtual machine. This cannot be configured or removed.
- **USB controller**: This provides USB functionality to the USB ports managed. The virtual USB controller is the software virtualization of the USB host controller function in a VM.
- **USB device**: Multiple USB devices may be added to a virtual machine. These can be mass storage devices or security dongles. The USB devices can be connected to a client workstation or to an ESXi host.
- **Video controller**: This is a VMware Standard VGA II Graphics Adapter with 128 MB video memory.

- **VMCI**: The **Virtual Machine Communication Interface** provides high-speed communication between the hypervisor and a virtual machine. VMCI can also be enabled for communication between VMs. VMCI devices cannot be added or removed.
- **Parallel port**: This is an interface for connecting peripherals to the virtual machine. Virtual parallel ports can be added to or removed from the virtual machine.
- **PCI controller**: This is a bus located on the virtual machine motherboard, communicating with components such as a hard disk. A single PCI controller is presented to the virtual machine. This cannot be configured or removed.
- **PCI device**: DirectPath devices can be added to a virtual machine. The devices must be reserved for PCI pass-through on the ESXi host that the virtual machine runs on. You may add up to 16 CPI vSphere DirectPath devices to the virtual machine.

Core 4 resources

Virtualization decouples physical hardware from an operating system. Each virtual machine contains a set of its own virtual hardware and there are four primary resources that a virtual machine needs in order to correctly function. These are CPU, memory, network, and hard disk. These four resources look like physical hardware to the guest operating systems and applications. The virtual machine is granted access to a portion of the resources at creation and can be reconfigured at any time thereafter. If a virtual machine experiences constraint, one of the four *core* resources is where a bottleneck will generally occur.

CPU

The virtualization layer runs CPU instructions to make sure that the virtual machines run as though accessing the physical processor on the ESXi host. Performance is paramount for CPU virtualization, and therefore will use the ESXi host physical resources whenever possible.

A virtual machine can be configured with up to 128 virtual CPUs (vCPUs) as of vSphere 6.0. The maximum vCPUs able to be allocated depends on the underlying logical cores that the physical hardware has. Another factor in the maximum vCPUs is the tier of vSphere licensing; only Enterprise Plus licensing allows for 128 vCPUs. The VMkernel includes a CPU scheduler that dynamically schedules vCPUs on the ESXi host's physical processors.

The VMkernel scheduler, when making scheduling decisions, considers socket-core-thread topology. A *socket* is a single, integrated circuit package that has one or more physical processor cores. Each core has one or more logical processors, also known as threads. If hyperthreading is enabled on the host, then ESXi is capable of executing two threads, or sets of instruction, simultaneously. Effectively, hyperthreading provides more logical CPUs to ESXi on which vCPUs can be scheduled, providing more scheduler throughput. However, keep in mind that hyperthreading does not double the core's power. During times of CPU contention, when VMs are competing for resources, the VMkernel time-slices the physical processor across all virtual machines to ensure that the VMs run as if having a specified number of vCPUs.

VMware **Virtual Symmetric Multiprocessing** (**SMP**) is what allows the virtual machines to be configured with up to 128 virtual CPUs, which allows a larger CPU workload to run on an ESXi host. Though most supported guest operating systems are multiprocessor aware, many guest OSs and applications do not need and are not enhanced by having multiple vCPUs. Check vendor documentation for operating system and application requirements before configuring SMP virtual machines.

Memory

In a physical architecture, an operating system assumes that it owns all physical memory in the server, which is a correct assumption. A guest operating system in a virtual architecture also makes this assumption but it does not, in fact, own all of the physical memory. A guest operating system in a virtual machine uses a contiguous virtual address space that is created by ESXi as its configured memory.

Virtual memory is a well-known technique that creates this contiguous virtual address space, allowing the hardware and operating system to handle the address translation between the physical and virtual address spaces. Since each virtual machine has its own contiguous virtual address space, this allows ESXi to run more than one virtual machine at the same time. The virtual machine's memory is protected against access from other virtual machines.

This effectively results in three layers of virtual memory in ESXi: physical memory, guest operating system physical memory, and guest operating system virtual memory. The VMkernel presents a portion of physical host memory to the virtual machine as its guest operating system physical memory. The guest operating system presents the virtual memory to the applications:

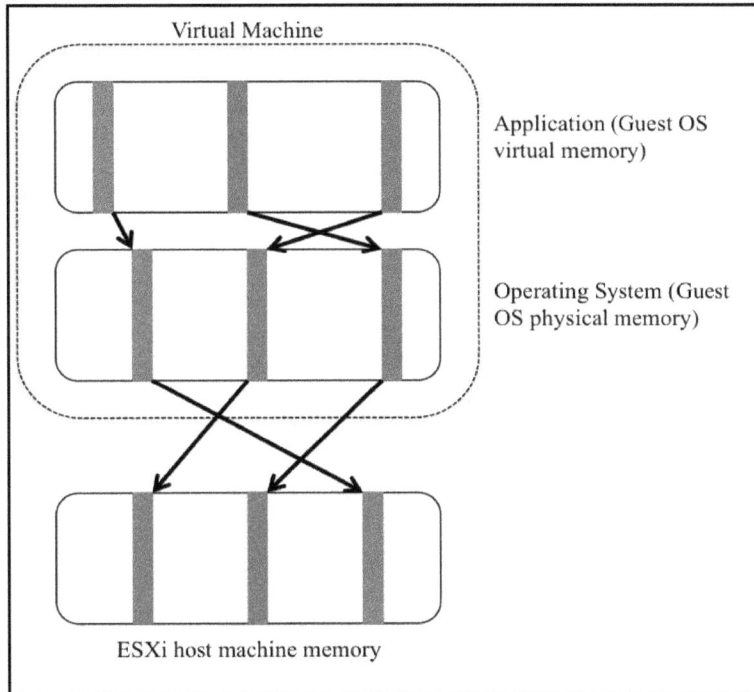

The virtual machine is configured with a set of memory; this is the sum that the guest OS is told it has available to it. A virtual machine will not necessarily use the entire memory size, it only uses what is needed at the time by the guest OS and applications. However, a VM cannot access more memory than the configured memory size. A default memory size is provided by vSphere when creating the virtual machine. It is important to know the memory needs of the application and guest operating system being virtualized so that the virtual machine's memory can be sized accordingly.

Network

There are two key components with virtual networking: the virtual switch and virtual Ethernet adapters. A virtual machine can be configured with up to 10 virtual Ethernet adapters called **vNICs**. A vNIC is the virtual machine's network adapter that connects it to the port group on a virtual switch, whereas a vmnic is the physical NIC acting as an uplink on an ESXi host.

Virtual network switching is software interfacing between virtual machines at the vSwitch level until the frames hit an uplink or a physical adapter, exiting the ESXi host and entering the physical network. Virtual networks exist for virtual devices; all communication between the virtual machines and the external world (physical network) goes through vSphere standard switches or vSphere distributed switches.

Virtual networks operate on layer 2, data link, of the OSI model. A virtual switch is similar to a physical Ethernet switch in many ways. For example, virtual switches support the standard VLAN (802.1Q) implementation and have a forwarding table, like a physical switch. An ESXi host may contain more than one virtual switch. Each virtual switch is capable of binding multiple vmnics together in a **Network Interface Card (NIC)** team, which offers greater availability to the virtual machines using the virtual switch.

There are two connection types available on a virtual switch: a port group and a VMkernel port. Virtual machines are connected to port groups on a virtual switch, allowing access to network resources. VMkernel ports provide a network service to the ESXi host to include IP storage, management, vMotion, and so on. Each VMkernel port must be configured with its own IP address and network mask. The port groups and VMkernel ports reside on a virtual switch and connect to the physical network through the physical Ethernet adapters known as *vmnics*. If uplinks (vmnics) are associated with a virtual switch, then the virtual machines connected to a port group on this virtual switch will be able to access the physical network.

Disk

In a non-virtualized environment, physical servers connect directly to storage, either to an external storage array or to their internal hard disk arrays to the server chassis. The issue with this configuration is that a single server expects total ownership of the physical device, tying an entire disk drive to one server. Sharing storage resources in non-virtualized environments can require complex filesystems and migration to file-based **Network Attached Storage (NAS)** or **Storage Area Networks (SAN)**, or with vSphere 6.0, **Virtual SAN (VSAN)** or **Virtual Volumes (VVOLs)**.

Shared storage is a foundational technology that allows many things to happen in a virtual environment (High Availability, Distributed Resource Scheduler, and so on). Virtual machines are encapsulated in a set of discrete files stored on a datastore. This encapsulation makes the VMs portable and easy to be cloned or backed up. For each virtual machine, there is a directory on the datastore that contains all of the VM's files. A datastore is a generic term for a container that holds files as well as .iso images and floppy images. It can be formatted with VMware's **Virtual Machine File System (VMFS)** or can use NFS. Both datastore types can be accessed across multiple ESXi hosts.

VMFS is a high-performance, clustered filesystem devised for virtual machines, which allows a virtualization-based architecture of multiple physical servers to read and write to the same storage simultaneously. VMFS is designed, constructed, and optimized for virtualization. The newest version, VMFS-5, exclusively uses 1 MB block size, which is good for large files, while also having an 8 KB subblock allocation for writing small files such as logs. VMFS-5 can have datastores as large as 64 TB. The ESXi hosts use a locking mechanism to prevent the other ESXi hosts accessing the same storage from writing to the VMs' files. This helps prevent corruption.

Several storage protocols can be used to access and interface with VMFS datastores. These include Fibre Channel, Fibre Channel over Ethernet, iSCSI, and direct attached storage. The NFS protocol can also be used to create an NFS datastore. The VMFS datastore can be dynamically expanded, allowing the growth of the shared storage pool with no downtime.

vSphere significantly simplifies accessing storage from the guest OS of the VM. The virtual hardware presented to the guest operating system includes a set of familiar SCSI and IDE controllers; this way the guest OS sees a simple physical disk attached via a common controller. Presenting a virtualized storage view to the virtual machine's guest OS has advantages such as expanded support and access, improved efficiency, and easier storage management.

Virtual machine files

vSphere administrators should know the components of virtual machines. There are multiple VMware file types that are associated with and make up a virtual machine. These files are located in the VM's directory on a datastore. The following table will summarize and provide a quick reference and short description of all the files that make up a virtual machine:

File	Example filename	Description
.vmx	<vmname>.vmx	Configuration file
.vmfx	<vmname>.vmfx	Additional configuration file
.vmtx	<vmname>.vmtx	Template file
.nvram	<vmname>.nvram	BIOS/EFI configuration
.vswp	<vmname>.vswp	Swap files
	vmx-<vmname>.vswp	
.log	vmware.log	Current log file
	vmware-##.log	Old log file entries
.vmdk	<vmname>.vmdk	Virtual disk descriptor
-flat.vmdk	<vmname>-flat.vmdk	Data disk
-rdm.vmdk	<vmname>-rdm.vmdk	Raw device map file
-delta.vmdk	<vmname>-delta.vmdk	Snapshot disk
.vmsd	<vmname>.vmsd	Snapshot description data
.vmsn	<vmname>.vmsn	Snapshot state
.vmss	<vmname>.vmss	Suspend file

Depending on the state and configuration of the virtual machine, not all files will be present in the virtual machine directory.

Let's explore these virtual machine files in more detail.

Configuration files

The .vmx file describes the current configuration information and hardware settings for the VM. This can contain a large variety of information regarding the virtual machine, to include its specific virtual hardware configuration (amount of RAM, NIC settings, CD-ROM information, parallel/serial port information, and so on), as well as its advanced resource and power settings, VMware tools options, and so forth. It is possible to make changes and directly edit this file; however, you should only do this at your own risk.

> Generally, it is recommended to have a backup of this file first and to not edit until recommended by VMware support.

The .vmx file is a plain-text file that functions as the structural definition of the VM. The .vmx file can be copied from the datastore and opened using a program that supports the creation and saving of files using UTF-8 encoding, such as WordPad. The following excerpt shows an example of a .vmx file for a virtual machine named ExampleVM:

```
.encoding = "UTF-8"
config.version = "8"
virtualHW.version = "11"
nvram = "ExampleVM.nvram"
pciBridge0.present = "TRUE"
svga.present = "TRUE"
pciBridge4.present = "TRUE"
pciBridge4.virtualDev = "pcieRootPort"
pciBridge4.functions = "8"
pciBridge5.present = "TRUE"
pciBridge5.virtualDev = "pcieRootPort"
pciBridge5.functions = "8"
pciBridge6.present = "TRUE"
pciBridge6.virtualDev = "pcieRootPort"
pciBridge6.functions = "8"
pciBridge7.present = "TRUE"
pciBridge7.virtualDev = "pcieRootPort"
pciBridge7.functions = "8"
vmci0.present = "TRUE"
hpet0.present = "TRUE"
svga.vramSize = "8388608"
memSize = "4096"
```

```
sched.cpu.units = "mhz"
sched.cpu.affinity = "all"
sched.mem.affinity = "all"
powerType.powerOff = "default"
powerType.suspend = "default"
powerType.reset = "default"
scsi0.virtualDev = "lsisas1068"
scsi0.present = "TRUE"
sata0.present = "TRUE"
scsi0:0.deviceType = "scsi-hardDisk"
scsi0:0.fileName = "ExampleVM.vmdk"
sched.scsi0:0.shares = "normal"
sched.scsi0:0.throughputCap = "off"
scsi0:0.present = "TRUE"
ethernet0.virtualDev = "e1000e"
ethernet0.networkName = "VM Network"
ethernet0.addressType = "vpx"
ethernet0.generatedAddress = "00:50:56:ac:e1:a8"
ethernet0.present = "TRUE"
sata0:0.startConnected = "FALSE"
sata0:0.deviceType = "cdrom-raw"
sata0:0.clientDevice = "TRUE"
sata0:0.fileName = "emptyBackingString"
sata0:0.present = "TRUE"
floppy0.startConnected = "FALSE"
floppy0.clientDevice = "TRUE"
floppy0.fileName = "vmware-null-remote-floppy"
displayName = "ExampleVM"
guestOS = "windows8srv-64"
disk.EnableUUID = "TRUE"
toolScripts.afterPowerOn = "TRUE"
toolScripts.afterResume = "TRUE"
toolScripts.beforeSuspend = "TRUE"
toolScripts.beforePowerOff = "TRUE"
uuid.bios = "42 2c 9e f6 48 47 8f 8c-60 2f 5a 66 37 0a 6e 3c"
vc.uuid = "50 2c 81 6b 04 4c 47 19-77 c9 16 97 d0 1b 33 43"
sched.cpu.min = "0"
sched.cpu.shares = "normal"
sched.mem.min = "0"
sched.mem.minSize = "0"
sched.mem.shares = "normal"
```

Reading through this file gives us important information regarding the configuration of the virtual machine. Here are a few examples:

- The VM's configured guest operating system can be derived from the `guestOS` line
- Based upon the `memsize` line, it is known that the VM was configured for 4 GB of memory
- The virtual machine only has one network adapter configured for the *VM Network* port group based on the `ethernet0` lines
- The virtual machine's vNIC has a MAC address of `00:50:56:ac:e1:a8`, specified by the `ethernet0.generatedAddress` line

A virtual machine's `.vmx` file is most commonly edited to modify the MAC address so that it matches the effective MAC address set within the guest operating system. However, this practice is becoming less and less common due to this configuration change being done more easily in the vSphere Web Client.

The `.vmx` file is extremely important to the virtual machine. However, keep in mind that it only structurally defines the VM's virtual hardware composition. It does not hold any actual data from the guest OS running within the VM. The virtual machine's data is stored in its virtual disk file. Here's an overview of the configuration and BIOS files:

- `.vmtx`: When a virtual machine is converted to a template, the virtual machine configuration file (`.vmx`) is replaced by the template configuration file (`.vmtx`).
- `.nvram`: This is generally a fairly small file which contains the BIOS settings that the VM uses upon boot. This is similar to how a physical server that has a BIOS chip allows hardware configuration options. The virtual BIOS settings, contained in the `.nvram` file, can be accessed by pressing F2 when the virtual machine is powered on.

Swap files

The `.vswp` file is created when the virtual machine is powered on. The size of the `.vswp` file is equal to that of a configured memory, unless there is a reservation. When a memory reservation is configured for a VM, then the `.vswp` file size would equal the configured memory size minus the memory reservation. This file is used as a last resort when the hypervisor is reclaiming physical memory from its virtual machines due to contention.

Looking at the previous table, you may have noticed the `vmx-<vmname>.vswp` file. This file is for the overhead memory created for a VM, a new feature in vSphere 5.x. Historically, this memory overhead was not swappable. Though there was a memory reservation to back this, the entire address space did not actually have to reside in memory. This file helps to reduce the reservation requirements for virtual machines.

Virtual disks

The following are some of the virtual disk files:

- `.vmdk`: This is the *Virtual disk descriptor*, which holds information such as the size and disk geometry of the virtual disk, information that makes the VM believe it has a real hard disk and not files on a datastore. Such information includes the virtual disk's adapter type, drive sectors, heads, and cylinders. This descriptor file also contains a pointer to the larger data file for the virtual disk or the `-flat.vmdk` file.

- `-flat.vmdk`: This file actually contains the virtual disk's data. This is created by default when a virtual hard drive is added to a virtual machine that is not using the **Raw Device Mapping** (**RDM**) option. When created as a thick provisioned disk, it will be sized approximately to what was specified in the creation wizard.

- `-rdm.vmdk`: This is the mapping file for the RDM option, managing the RDM device's mapping data. The virtual machine isn't aware of this since the mapping file is presented to the ESXi host as a traditional disk file and is available for normal filesystem operations. The storage virtualization layer presents the mapped device as a virtual SCSI device to the VM. An `-rdm.vmdk` file exists for each RDM configured for the virtual machine.

Snapshot files

The following are the snapshot files:

- `-delta.vmdk`: These files are only used when creating snapshots. When a snapshot is created, the original `-flat.vmdk` file is no being longer written to; it becomes read only. All changes that are written to the virtual disk are now being written to the `-delta.vmdk` files instead. The `-delta.vmdk` file cannot exceed the size of the original `-flat.vmdk` file due to the fact that these `-delta.vmdk` files are bitmaps of changes made to a virtual disk. A `-delta.vmdk` file is created for each snapshot taken. These `-delta.vmdk` files are updated in 16 MB increments as changes are written to the virtual disk.

- .vmsd: This file is a snapshot descriptor that contains information regarding which files are used by each snapshot, description, display name, and any associated UIDs. There is only one .vmsd file per virtual machine, regardless of how many snapshots the virtual machine has. This file is updated each time a new snapshot is created or a snapshot is deleted.
- .vmsn: This file stores the virtual machine's state at the time the snapshot was taken. The size of this file varies depending on whether the option to include the VM's memory state was selected during snapshot creation. A separate .vmsn file will be created for each snapshot and will automatically be removed when the snapshot is deleted.

Other files

Let's take a look at some other files:

- .vmss: This file is used when a virtual machine is suspended so as to preserve the VM's memory contents; it is only present when the VM is suspended. When the virtual machine is resumed from the suspended state, it can start again right from where it left off. The contents of this file are written back to the ESXi host's physical memory when the virtual machine is brought out of a suspended state; however, the file will not be automatically deleted until the VM is powered off. This file will be approximately the same size as the configured memory for the virtual machine, unless memory contention is present.

- .log: Log files are created in order to log information regarding the virtual machine, typically used during troubleshooting efforts. The current log file is always named vmware.log, and by default up to six older log files will be retained. These older log files will have a number appended at the end of their names, which will be updated with each file (vmware-2.log).

New vSphere 6 virtual machine features

vSphere 6 brings a handful of new features with the introduction of a new virtual machine compatibility level. The new enhancements include:

- Support for 128 vCPUs
- Support for 4 TB of RAM
- Serial and parallel port enhancements
- USB 3.0 xHCI controller
- WDDM 1.1 GDI acceleration
- Hot-add RAM enhancements to vNUMA

Prior to vSphere 6.0, when virtual NUMA was in use, all memory was allocated to region 0 in the event of hot-add. Now, when a vNUMA virtual machine has memory hot-added to it, that memory is allocated equally across all NUMA regions.

Serial and parallel ports can be removed from a virtual machine using vSphere 6.0 compatibility (virtual hardware version 11). Also, a virtual machine may now have up to 32 serial ports, which may be beneficial when virtualizing point-of-sale systems.

vSphere 6.0 also includes new support for the following guest operating systems:

- Asianux 4 SP4
- FreeBSD 9.3
- Mac OS X 10.10
- Oracle Linux 7
- Oracle Unbreakable Enterprise Kernel Release 3 Quarterly Update 3
- Solaris 11.2
- Ubuntu 12.04.5
- Ubuntu 14.04.

> For a full list of supported OSes, see: `http://partnerweb.vmware.com/comp_guide2/pdf/VMware_GOS_Compatibility_Guide.pdf`.

Creating a virtual machine

In order to launch the virtual machine creation wizard, open up the vSphere Web Client and navigate to one of the vCenter views. From there, right click a container that a virtual machine can reside in (Cluster, ESXi host, resource pool, and so on). Select **New Virtual Machine**:

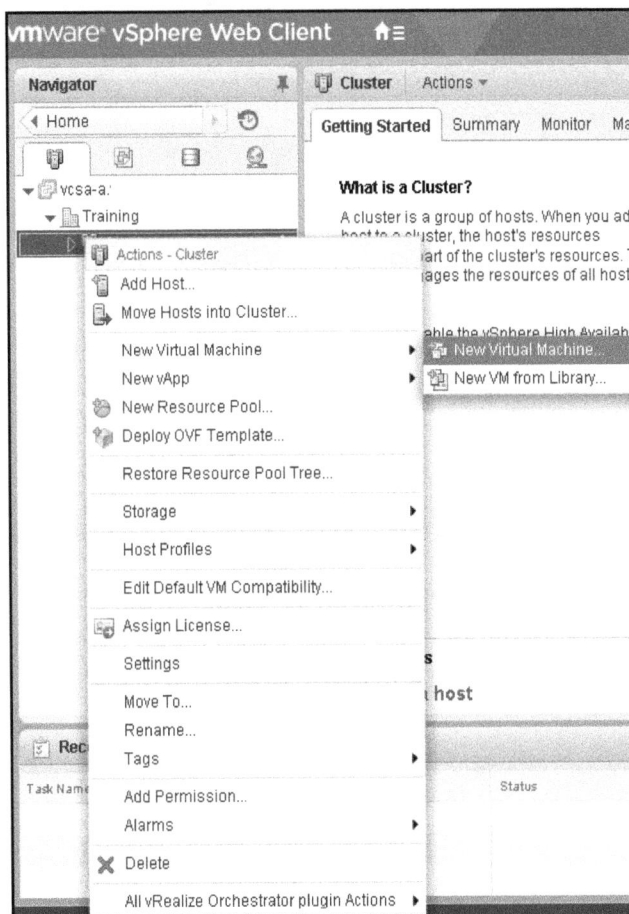

The following image displays the **Select a creation type** pane. There are multiple ways to create a virtual machine, to include cloning, deploying from a template, and so on:

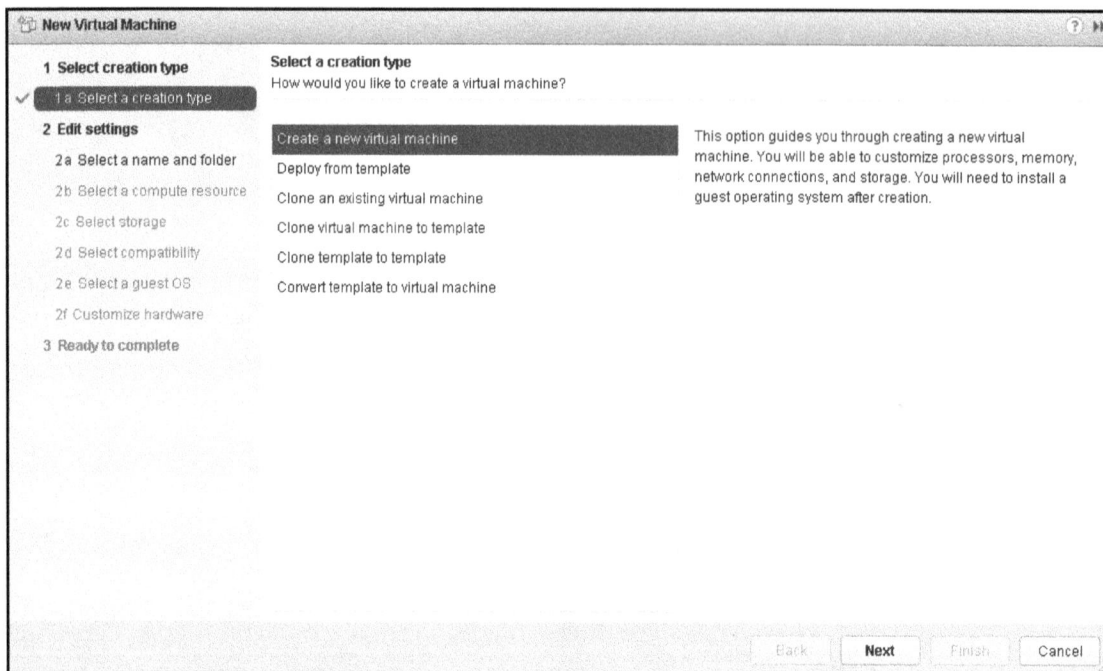

Select **Create a new virtual machine** and press **Next**.

First, **Enter a name for the virtual machine.** being created in the **Select a name and folder** pane. Don't forget that whatever name is specified here will result in all of the virtual machine's files being named the same. Towards the middle of the following image, a folder or datacenter should be selected for the virtual machine's placement in the *VM and Template* view within vCenter:

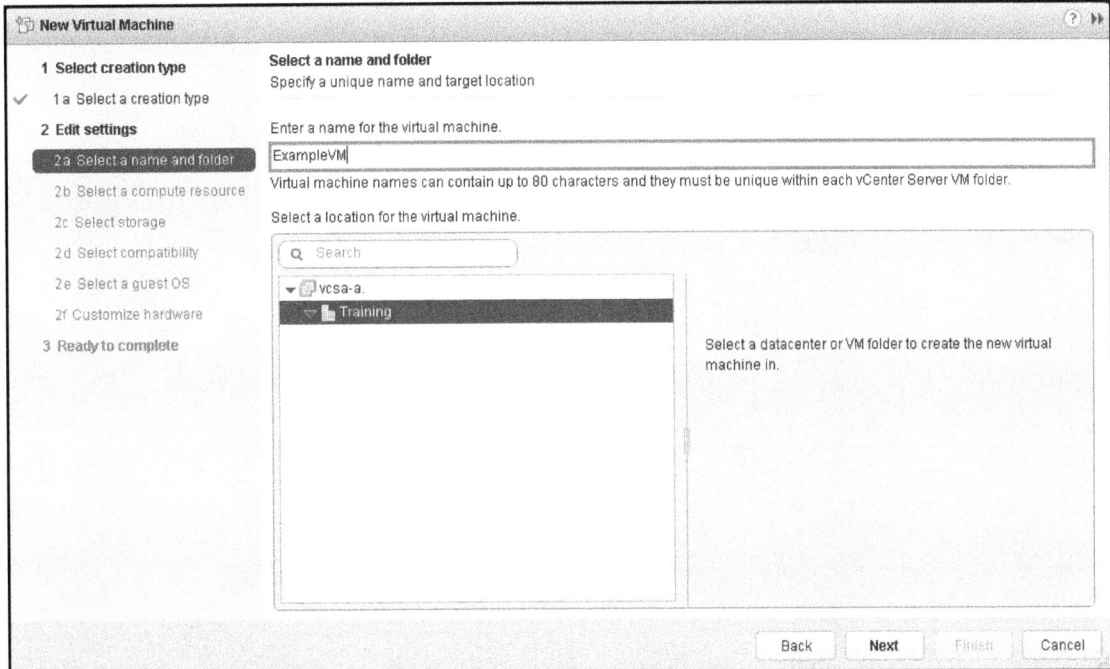

Once the virtual machine's name is specified and its location in the *VM and Template* view is selected, press **Next**.

The following image shows the **Select a compute resource pane**; a cluster (if DRS enabled), ESXi host, resource pool, or vApp should be selected for placement of the virtual machine in the *Hosts and Clusters* view in vCenter:

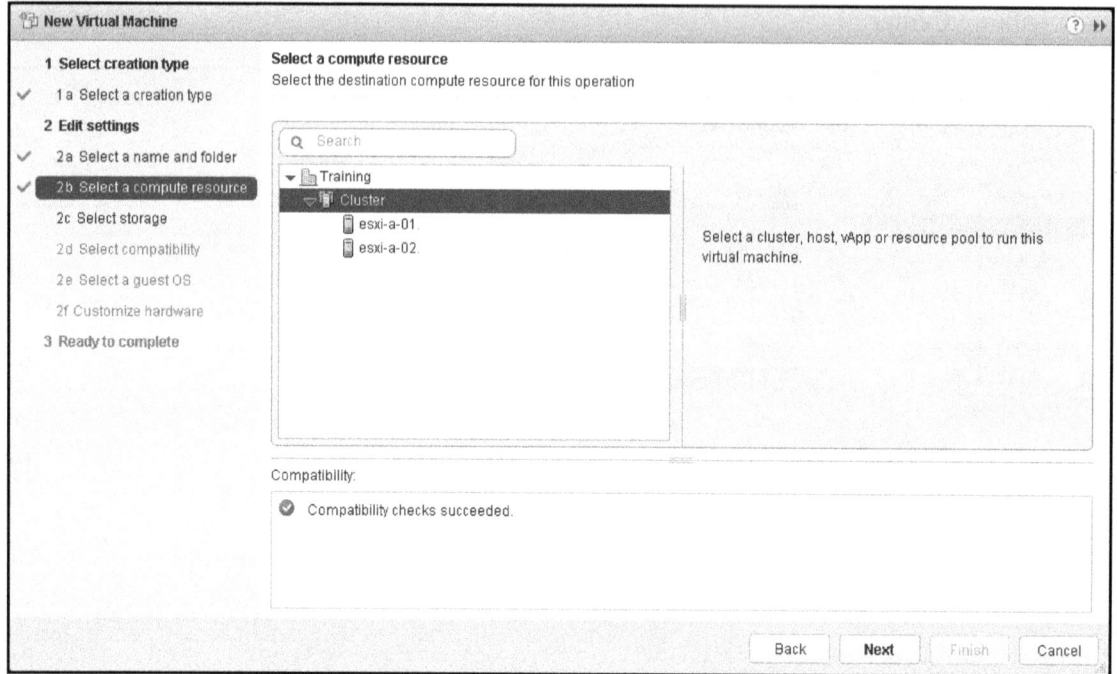

Once the desired compute resource is selected, click on **Next**.

The **Select Storage** pane prompts you to select which datastore the virtual machine's directory and files will be created on. This is not a permanent selection; the VM's files can be migrated to another datastore at any time using Storage vMotion. If VM storage profiles are set up in vCenter, select which storage profile should be associated with the VM being created:

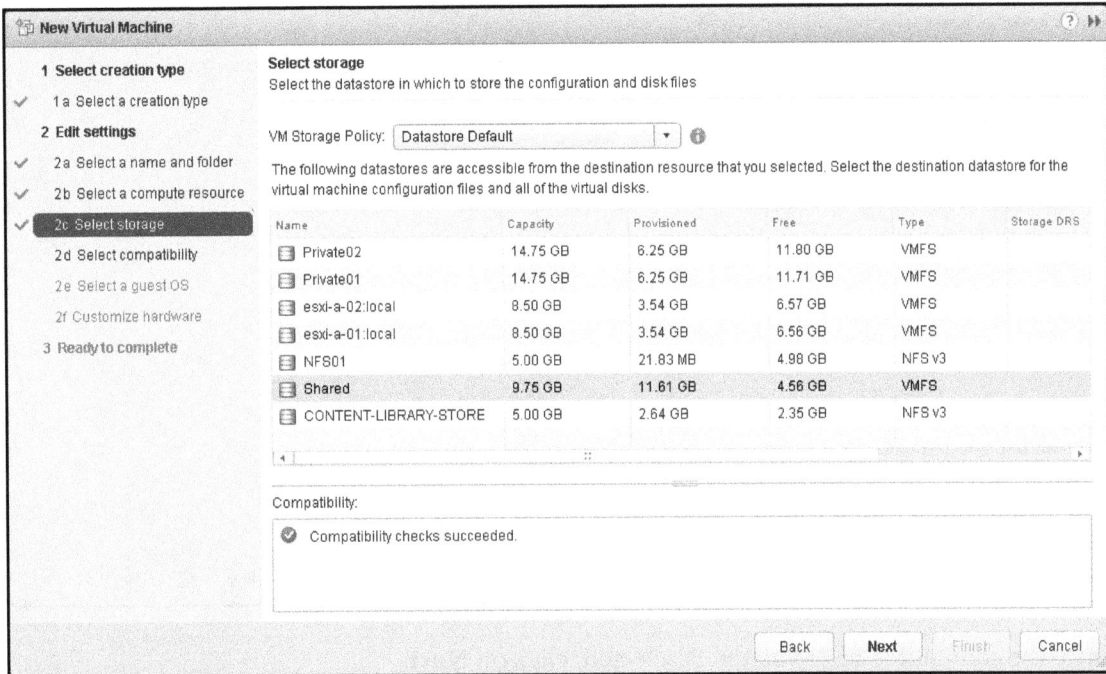

Once the desired datastore is selected, click on **Next**.

The next screenshot presents the **Select compatibility** pane. By selecting a compatible version of ESXi, you are effectively setting the virtual hardware version of the virtual machine being created:

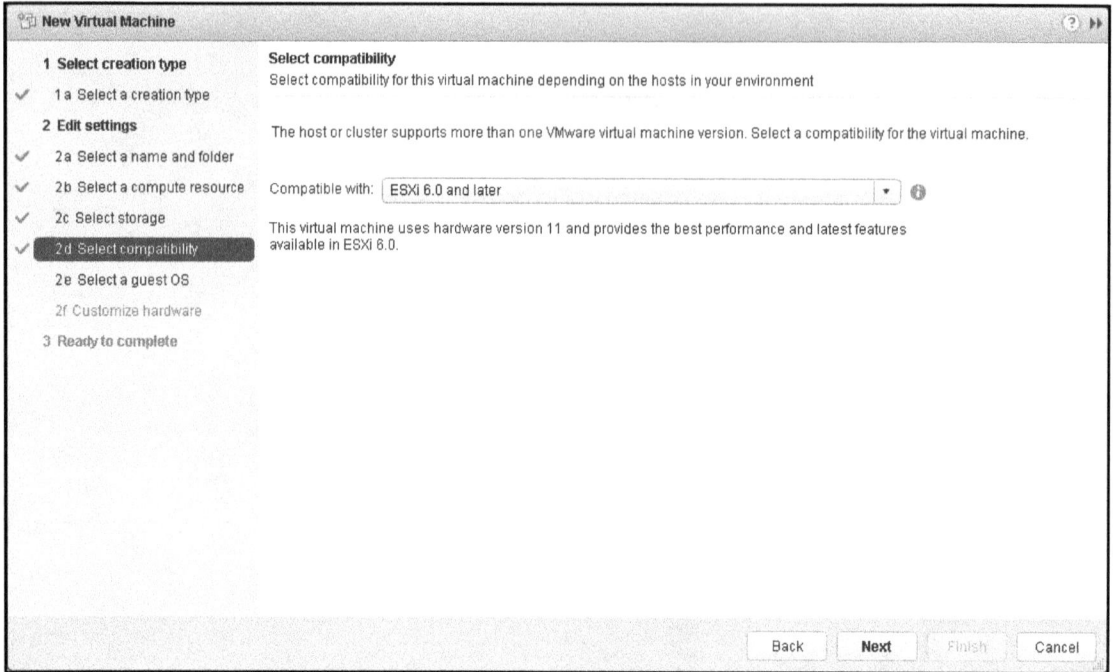

Once the compatible ESXi version is selected, click on **Next**.

Select the **Guest OS Family** and **Guest OS Version** that you plan to install from the list of choices. This is an important selection as it dictates which virtual hardware will be presented to the VM based on its compatibility with the guest OS:

Once the guest operating system has been selected, click on **Next**.

The **Customize hardware** pane allows you to configure the virtual machine appropriately for the requirements of the guest operating system and application that will be installed. Here, you can specify the resource allocation amounts and other options. For example, as shown in the following screenshot, the **New Hard disk** was configured for 10 GB:

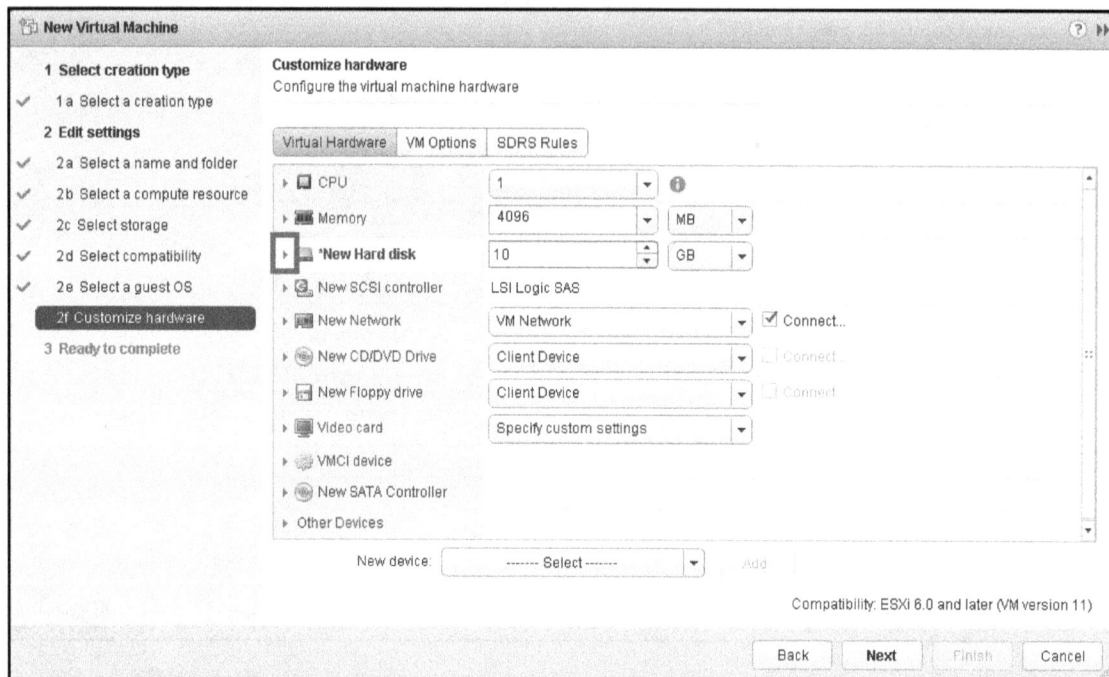

If New Hard Disk is expanded (as shown in the following screenshot), the options to select the **Virtual disk size** and its **Disk provisioning** type are available. The virtual disk can be up to 62 TB as of vSphere 5.5.

ESXi supports the following virtual disk types:

- **Thin Provision**: In this case, the disk is allocated and zeroed on demand, as needed, rather than a full provisioning at creation like thick provisioning. This results in a thin provisioned disk having a shorter creation time. Subsequent writes to the blocks result in the same performance as eager-zeroed thick disks. There can be a more effective usage of the datastore space, but it can result in an over-provisioned datastore.

- **Thick Provision Eager Zeroed**: In this case, the disk space is allocated and zeroed out at disk creation. This increases the time taken to create the disk, but using this type of a disk results in the best performance, even upon first write to each block. This is required for using the Fault Tolerance feature with VMs.
- **Thick Provision Lazy Zeroed**: In this case, the disk space is allocated at disk creation but each block is not zeroed until the first write. Comparatively, this results in a shorter creation time than eager-zeroed. This is the default option in vSphere Client and is good for most cases.

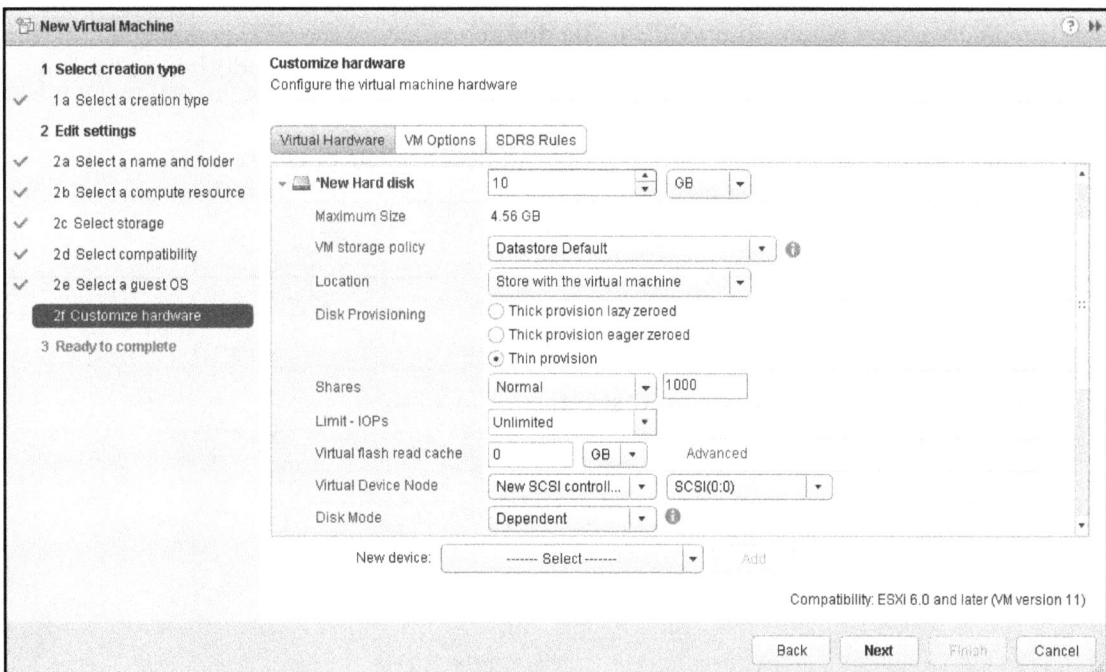

If CPU is expanded, as demonstrated in the following screenshot, choose how many **virtual sockets** and **virtual cores** will be available to the guest operating system.

VMware introduced the ability to configure a multi-core vCPU in vSphere 4.1. This improvement helped avoid socket restrictions from the guest operating systems. The OS vendor generally restricts only the physical CPUs (sockets) and not the logical CPUs (cores). For example, Windows 7 allows a maximum of two sockets, so what if you needed to configure this virtual machine with four vCPUs? A vCPU is presented to the guest OS as a single core within a single socket which limits the number of vCPUs that should be available to an operating system. To assist in solving this limitation, VMware introduced the vCPU configuration options of *virtual sockets* and *cores per socket*.

Four single-core sockets equal four vCPUs. Two dual-core sockets also equal four vCPUs. One quad-core socket equals four vCPUs. The difference is how the CPU is presented to the guest operating system, not how the vCPUs will be scheduled on the underlying physical processors.

Will it make a performance impact when using multiple sockets or one socket? No! There's no performance impact between using virtual sockets or cores other than the usable number of vCPUs:

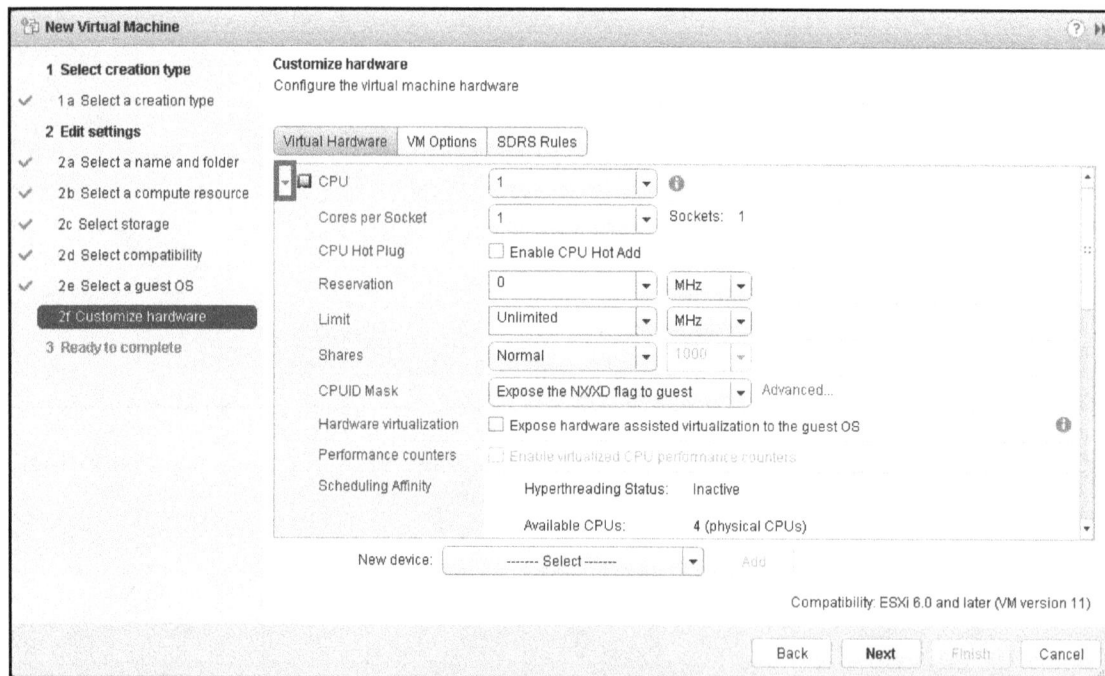

When **New Network** is expanded, you can choose not only the virtual machine port group but also the **Adapter Type**:

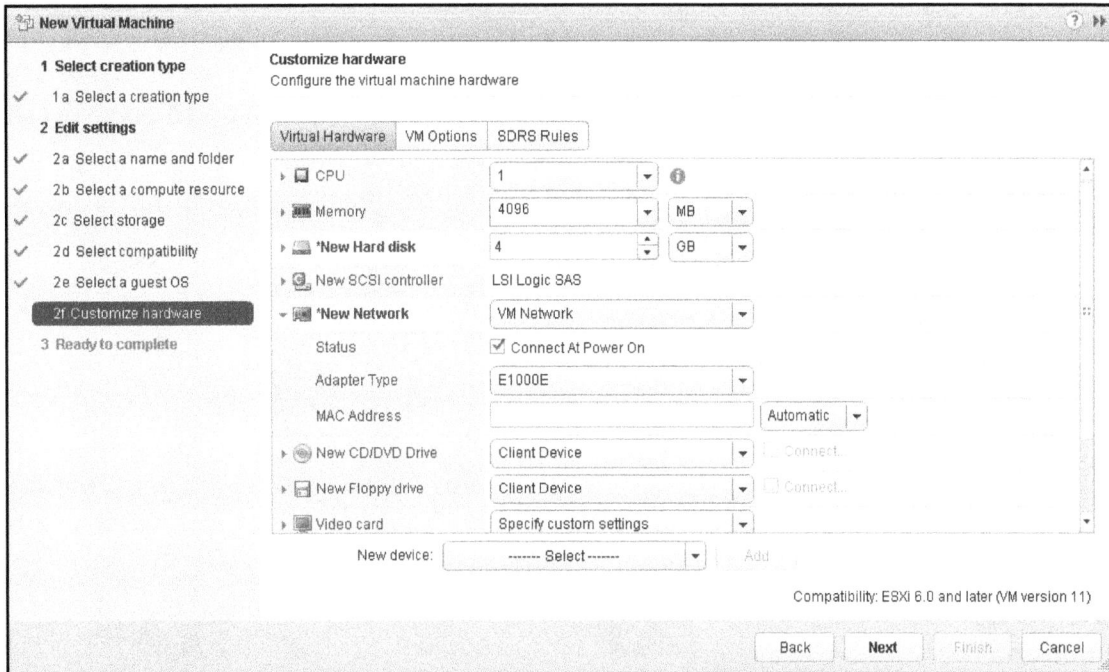

Once all hardware customizations have been made, press **Next**.

The last pane of the **New Virtual Machine** wizard summarizes the virtual machine's configuration for one last review prior to creation of the files. The **Ready to complete** pane is shown in the following screenshot:

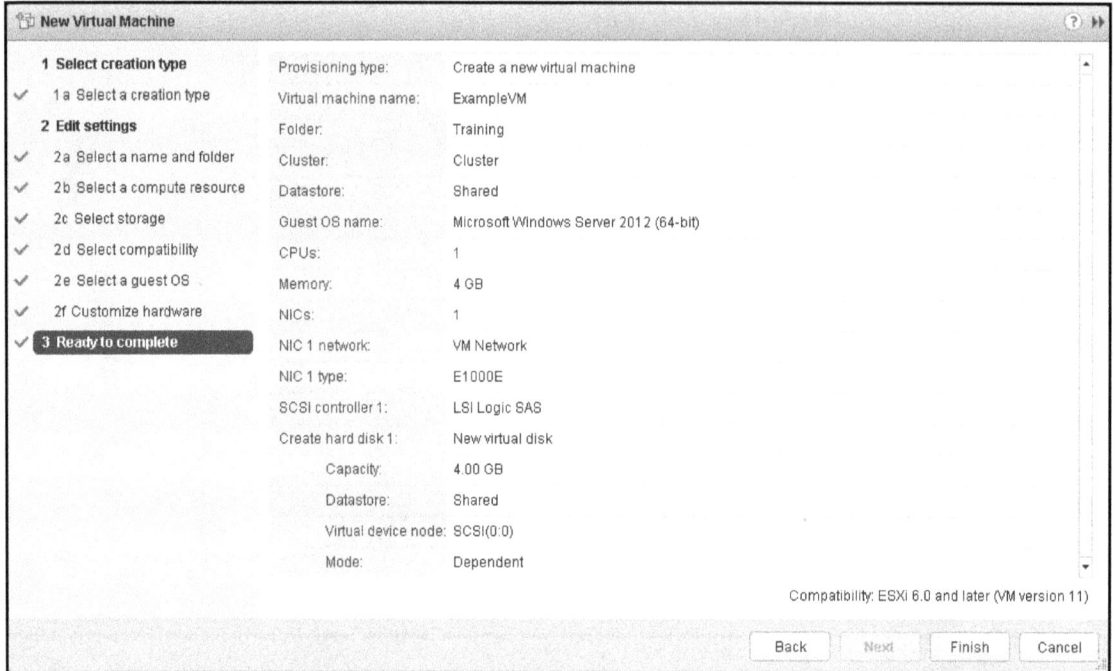

Once satisfied with the virtual machine's configuration, click on **Finish**.

Virtual machine settings

An administrator can modify many advanced configurations of a virtual machine. These advanced configurations will affect the virtual machine's functionality, compatibility, and performance.

To modify the settings of a virtual machine, simply right click the virtual machine and select **Edit Settings**. This is shown in the following screenshot:

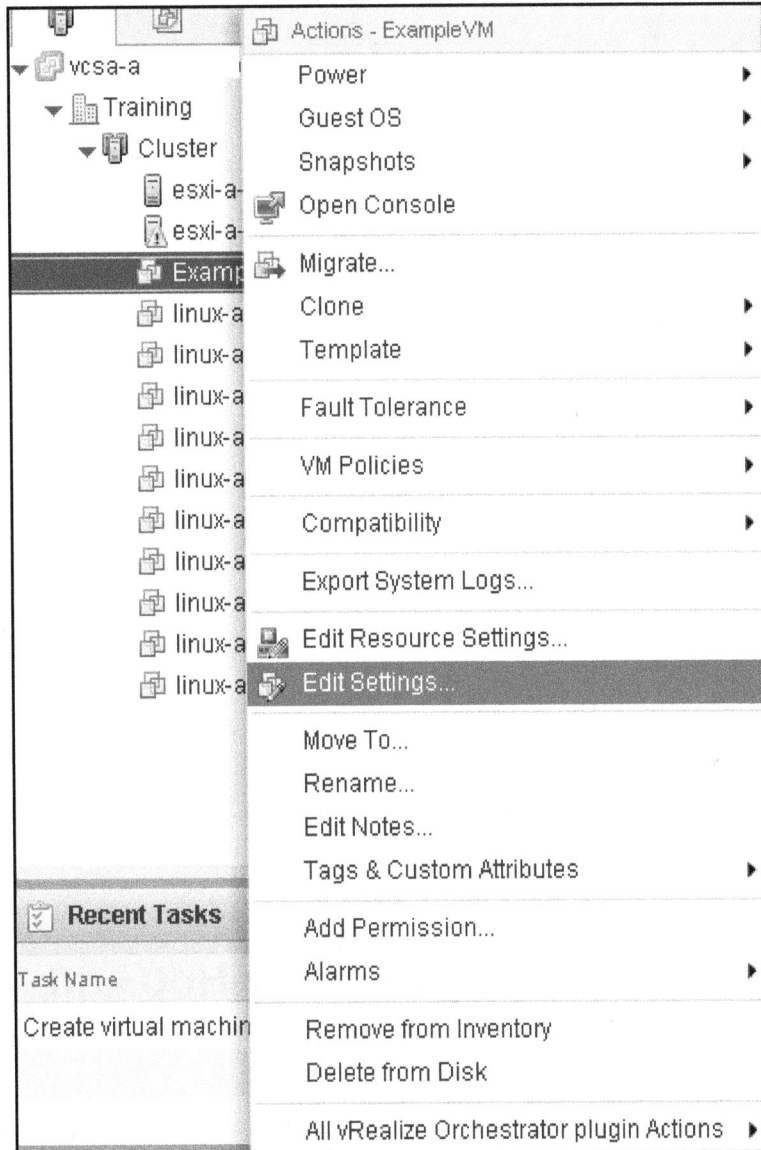

This action will open the virtual machine settings dialog:

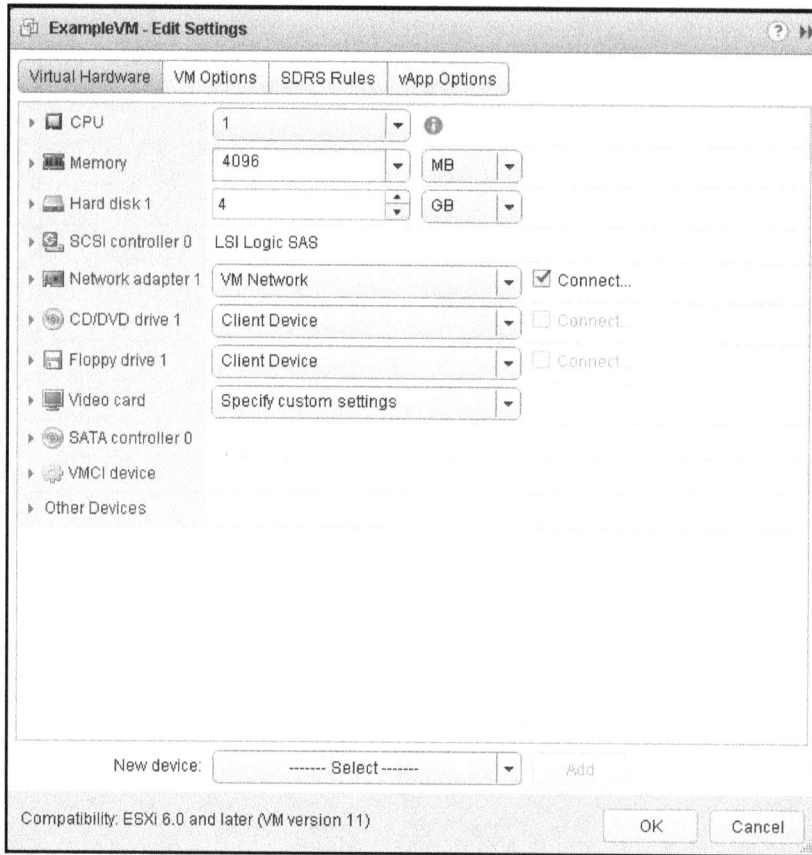

From here, an administrator can modify the settings as required.

Enabling CPU Hot-Plug/Memory Hot-Add

Enabling Hot-Plug and/or Hot-Add allows you to add more CPU or memory resources, respectively, while the virtual machine is powered on.

Virtual machines do not support Hot-Add (adding memory) and Hot-Plug by default. This capability will need to be enabled on a per virtual machine basis in order to utilize it. The virtual hardware version needs to be 7 or greater, so an upgrade may be necessary. Not all guest operating systems support this functionality; make sure to verify compatibility by referring to VMware and the guest operating system documentation before enabling.

To enable this feature, the virtual machine must be shut down. Once powered off, right-click the virtual machine and select **Edit Settings**. On the **Virtual Hardware** tab, expand the **CPU** selection and check the box next to **Enable CPU Hot Add**:

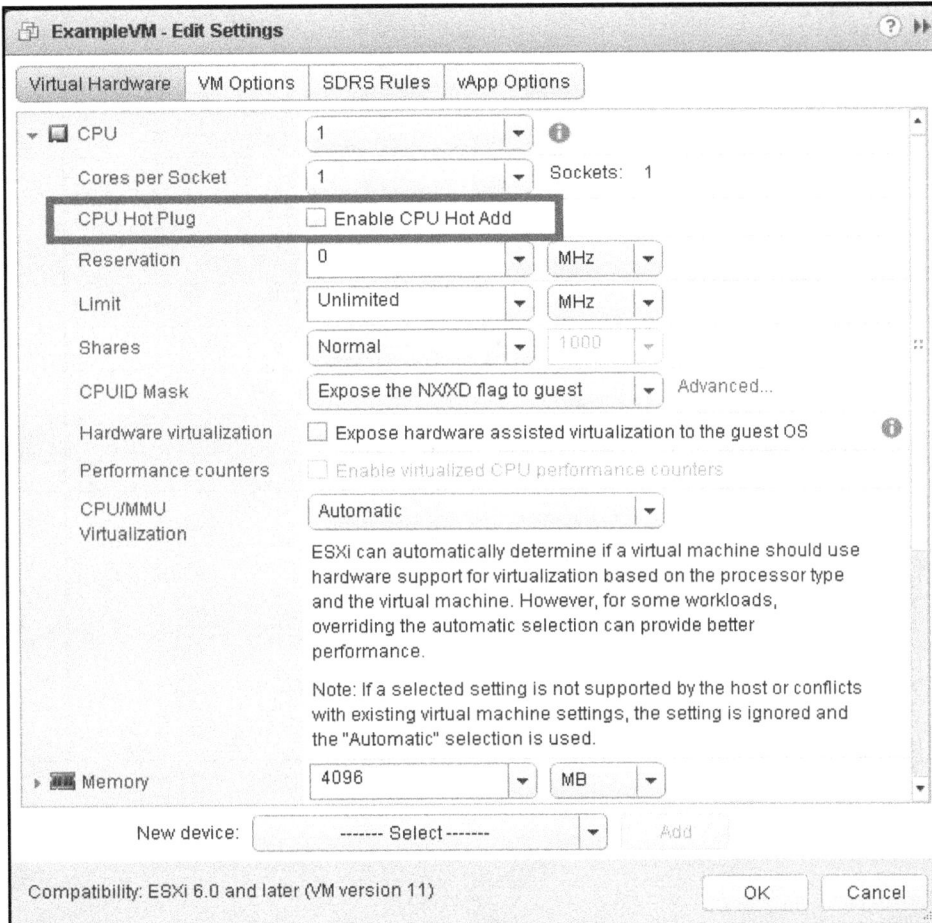

In order to enable this for memory, expand the **Memory** selection and check the box next to **Memory Hot Plug**:

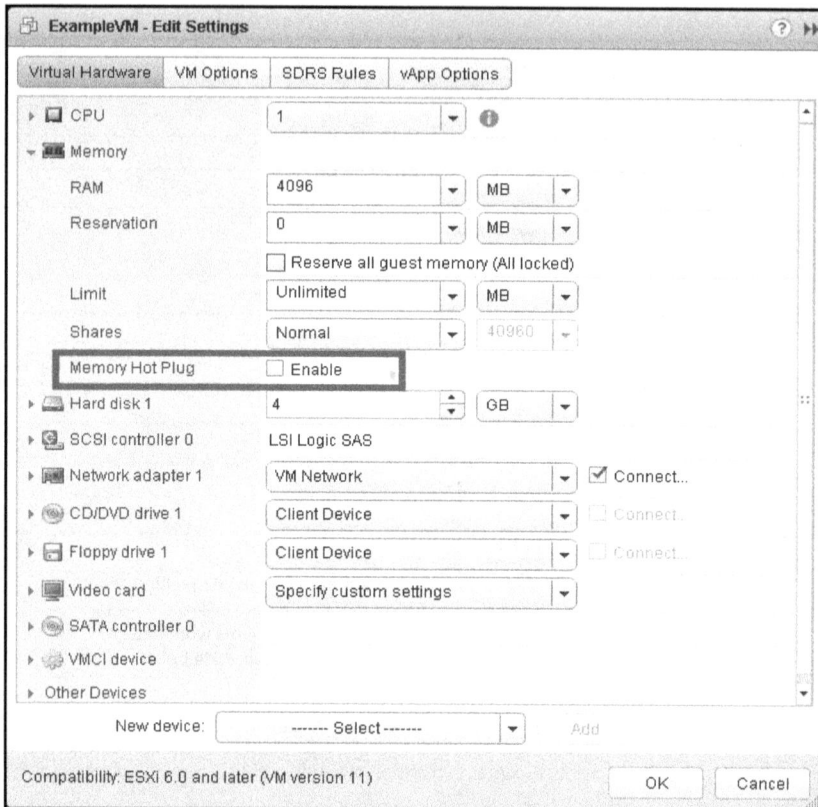

Once enabled, power on the virtual machine. If more resources are needed, simply right-click the virtual machine and select **Edit Settings**. Increase the CPU and/or memory as needed while the virtual machine is powered on.

> Keep in mind that even though you will now be able to add memory or CPU resources, once added resources cannot be reduced while the VM is powered on.

CPUID masks

CPU Identification (CPUID) masks control the CPU features made visible to the guest operating system of the virtual machine. Masking CPU NX/XD bits can make a virtual machine more compatible to migrate to ESXi hosts. Leaving the CPU NX/XD bit exposed serves a security purpose of marking memory pages as data-only to prevent buffer overflow attacks and malicious software exploits.

> See `http://vmware.com/kb/1993` for more information.

The CPU features are compared by vCenter Server to determine whether to allow or disallow a vMotion migration. Masking the AMD**No eXecute** (**NX**) and the Intel **eXecute Disable** (**XD**) bits prevents the virtual machine from using these features, allowing the migration to ESXi hosts that do not have this capability. If the NX/XD bit is visible then the virtual machine can only be migrated to ESXi hosts on which the feature is enabled.

To modify the CPUID mask, shut down the virtual machine and right click, selecting **Edit Settings**. On the **Virtual Hardware** tab, expand **CPU** and make a selection for the **CPUID Mask** configuration:

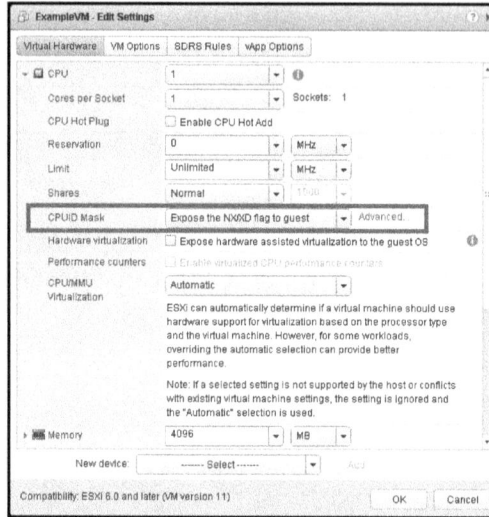

Click **OK** after making the configuration.

CPU affinity setting

The CPU affinity setting allows you to restrict the assignment of the virtual machine to a subset of the available processors. This effectively assigns each virtual machine to the processors in the specified affinity set. CPU affinity not only applies to the virtual machines' vCPUs, but also to all the other worlds associated with the virtual machine. A world is similar to a process in a conventional operating system that can be scheduled on a processor. This can include emulating the screen, keyboard, mouse, CD-ROMs, and so on.

CPU affinity can prevent ESXi systems from performing automatic DRS load balancing across its processors and the host's ability to meet reservations specified for the virtual machine. The CPU scheduler may not be able to manage a virtual machine that is configured using CPU affinity. Use this feature sparingly due to these potential issues.

To configure CPU affinity, power off the virtual machine. Right click the virtual machine in the vCenter Server inventory and select **Edit Settings**. On the **Virtual Hardware** tab, expand **CPU** and in the **Scheduling Affinity** panel, enter a comma-separated list of hyphenated processor ranges. For example, 0,2-4 would be CPUs 0, 2, 3, and 4. You must provide as many processor affinities as you have vCPUs configured. To not use CPU affinity, ensure that nothing is entered in the **Scheduling Affinity** panel, as displayed in the following screenshot:

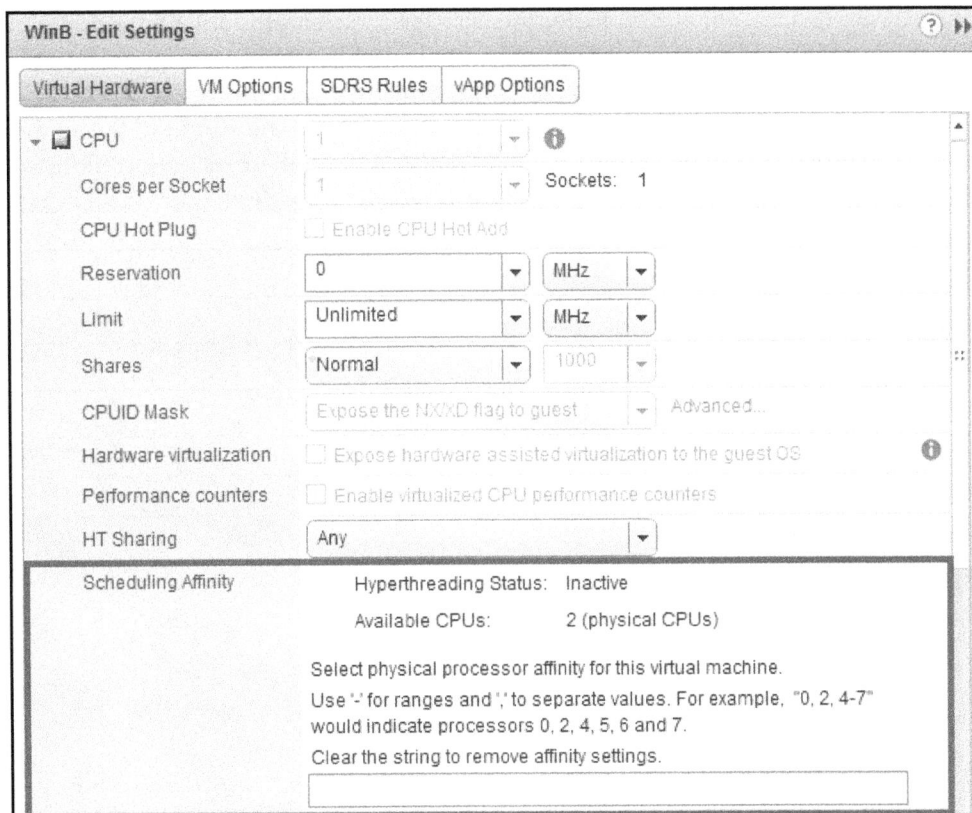

Click **OK** after checking the configuration.

Setting the .vswp location

The .vswp file can be placed on an alternate location besides the datastore where all of the other virtual machine's files are stored. An example of this is a high performance database being stored on a separate datastore to the .vswp file. This configuration could affect vMotion performance because the .vswp files may need to be copied between datastores if this is not taken into consideration for the design.

> Remember, the size of the .vswp file is the configured memory size minus any memory reservation.

To set the .vswp file location at the cluster level, select the cluster in the vSphere Web Client and go to the **Manage** tab. Under the **Settings** tab, click on **General** underneath the **Configuration** section. Select **Edit...** next to **Swap File Location**; this brings up the dialogue displayed in the following image. By default, the .vswp file will be stored in the same directory as the virtual machine. Alternatively, **Datastore specified by host** could be selected, which will allow for the specification of a datastore location at the ESXi host level:

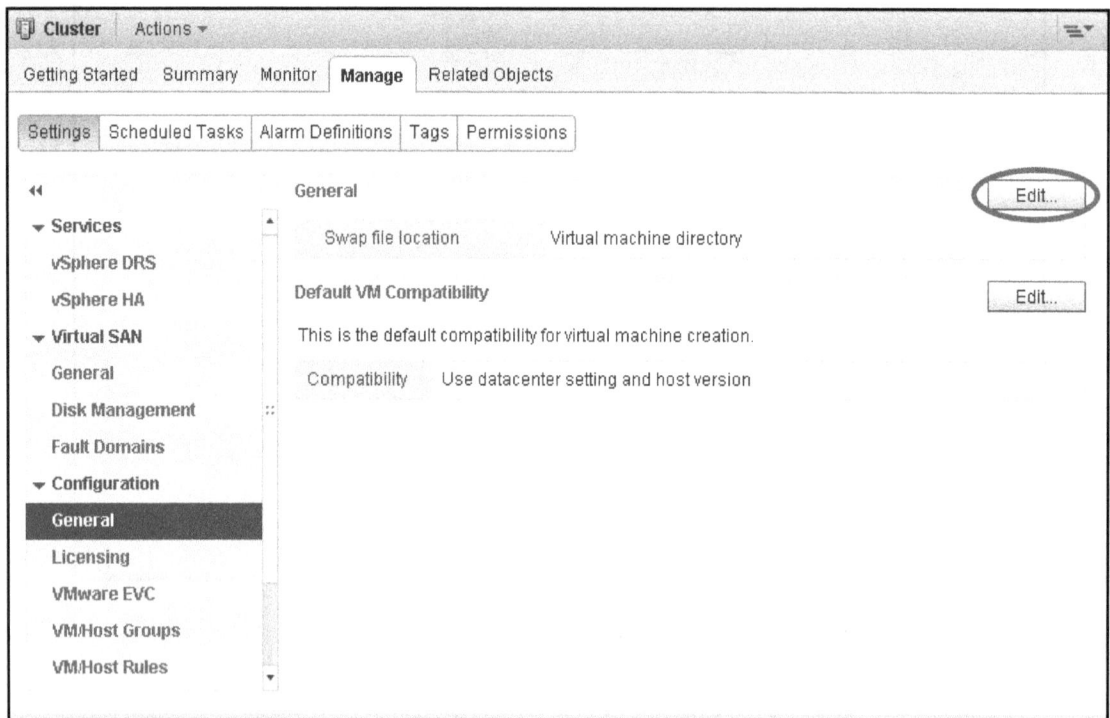

To configure all of the virtual machines on an ESXi host to use an alternate `.vswp` file location other than the datastore on which the rest of the virtual machine files are located, go to the **Manage** tab of the selected ESXi host. Select the **Edit Swap file location** and then choose **Use a specific datastore**:

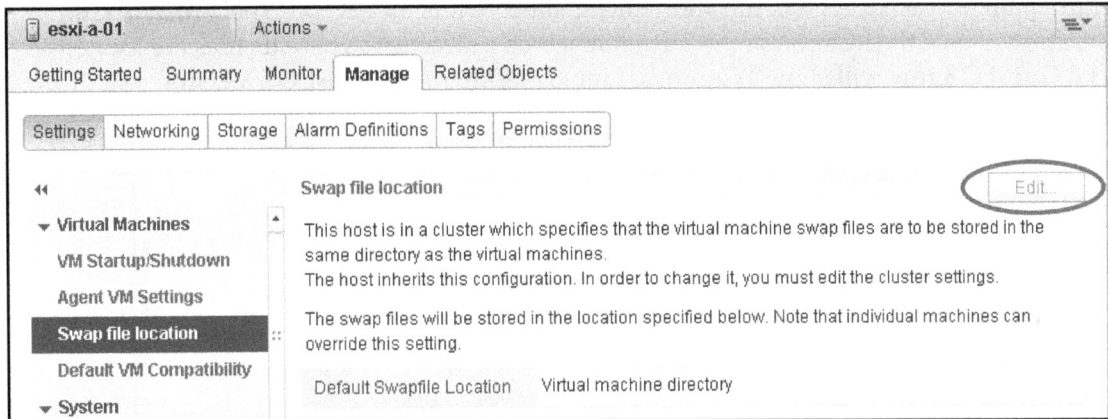

Choose the desired datastore and then click **OK**.

> Note that **Edit** will be greyed out if the ESXi host is in a cluster. Go to the cluster and change the swap file location to **Specified by ESXi host** and then this option will be available.

This setting will take effect once the virtual machines on the ESXi host are power cycled.

This can also be configured at the virtual machine level but can quickly become challenging when managing the different file locations. Use this sparingly.

Viewing other advanced options

There are many advanced virtual machine options available to adjust. This section will go over some of the more common advanced configurations that may be modified.

To modify the virtual machine, right click in the vCenter Server inventory and choose **Edit Settings**.

General Options

On the **VM Options** tab, under **General Options**, you will see the **VM Name**; this specifies what the virtual machine's name appears as in the vCenter Server inventory, not necessarily what the Computer Name in the guest operating system is. The **VM Config File** shows the entire path to reach the `.vmx` file and which datastore it is located on. The **VM Working Location** details the location of the virtual machine's directory where its files are located. The **Guest OS** row will show Windows, Linux, or Other; the **Guest OS Version** will display the exact version within that **Guest OS** type:

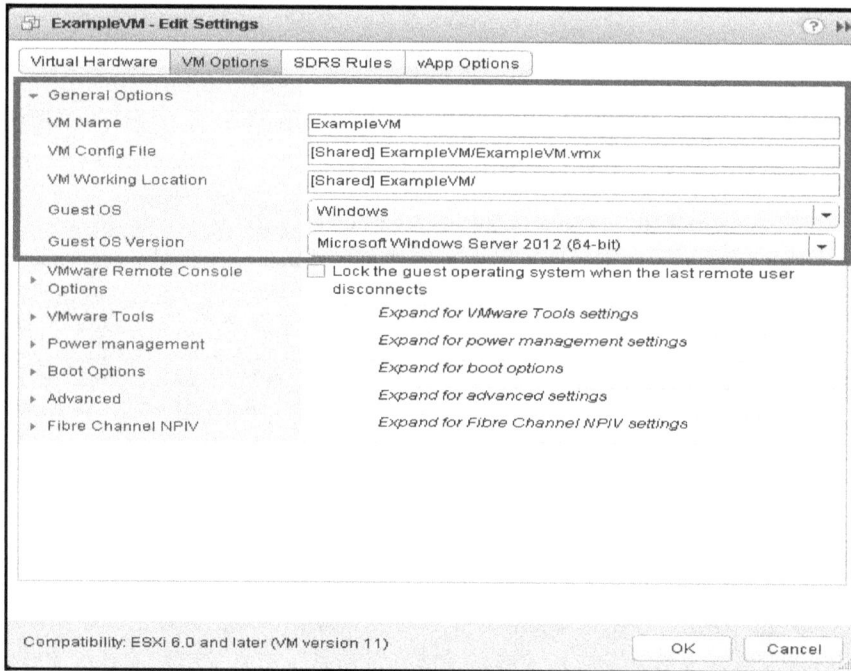

VMware Remote Console Options

Under the **VMware Remote Console Options** section, there are two available options: **Guest OS lock** and **Maximum number of sessions**. **Guest OS lock** locks the guest operating system upon disconnection of the last remote user. The **Maximum number of sessions** option limits the number of simultaneous connections to this virtual machine:

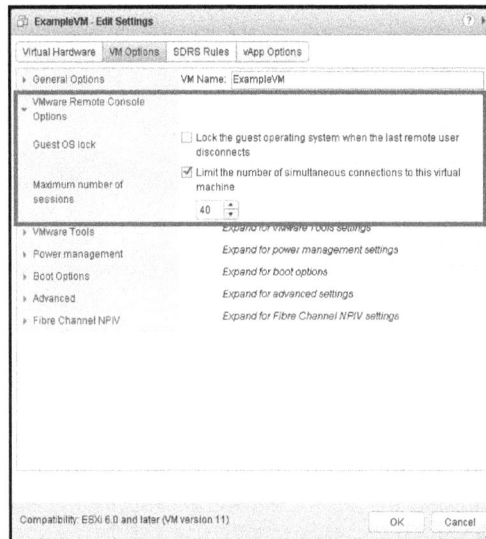

VMware Tools

The **VMware Tools** pane controls how VMware Tools in the VMs respond to certain external events, such as whether a virtual machine will power off or shut down when the stop button is pressed. You can use these controls to customize the different power buttons, determining whether hitting the top button or recycle button will cleanly shut down the guest operating system or a hard power off.

VMware Tools can be set to run certain scripts when specific events occur. Scripts are set in the VMware tools dialog box in the guest OS and then configured when to run under **VM Options**.

There is an option to **Check and upgrade VMware Tools before each power on**. When selected, this will help keep VMware Tools updated so that the virtual machines always have the newest drivers. This requires VMware Tools to already be installed in the guest operating system. The option checks whether the currently installed version is the most recent for the ESXi host version and, if not, will initiate the upgrade. The final VMware Tools option is to **Synchronize guest time with host**, which will use the ESXi host that the virtual machine is residing on for time settings:

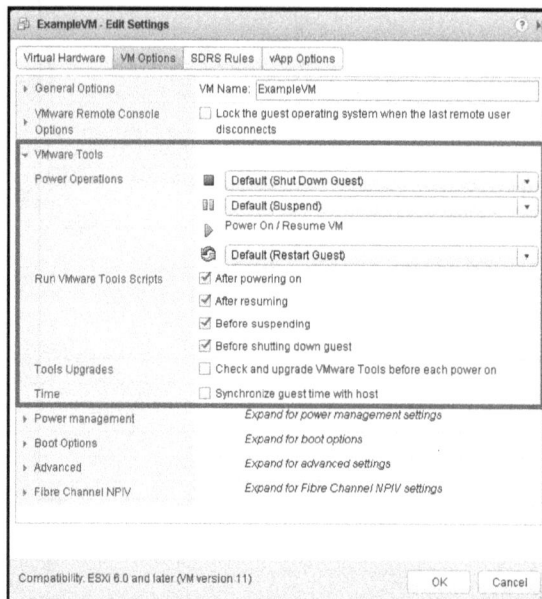

Boot options

When you build a virtual machine and select a guest operating system, a **Firmware** type, BIOS or **Extensible Firmware Interface** (**EFI**), is selected by default (this depends on the firmware supported by the operating system; for example, Mac OS X Server supports only EFI):

- **Boot Delay** allows you to a set a delay before the virtual machine is turned on. This can be useful for staggering VM startups when several VMs are being powered on.

- **Force BIOS Setup** is used to change BIOS settings (like booting from CD). The next time the virtual machine boots up, it goes straight into the BIOS.
- **Failed Boot Recovery** has the virtual machine retry booting after 10 seconds if the virtual machine fails to find a boot device. Checking the box and then entering the number of seconds before retrying boot can adjust this interval.

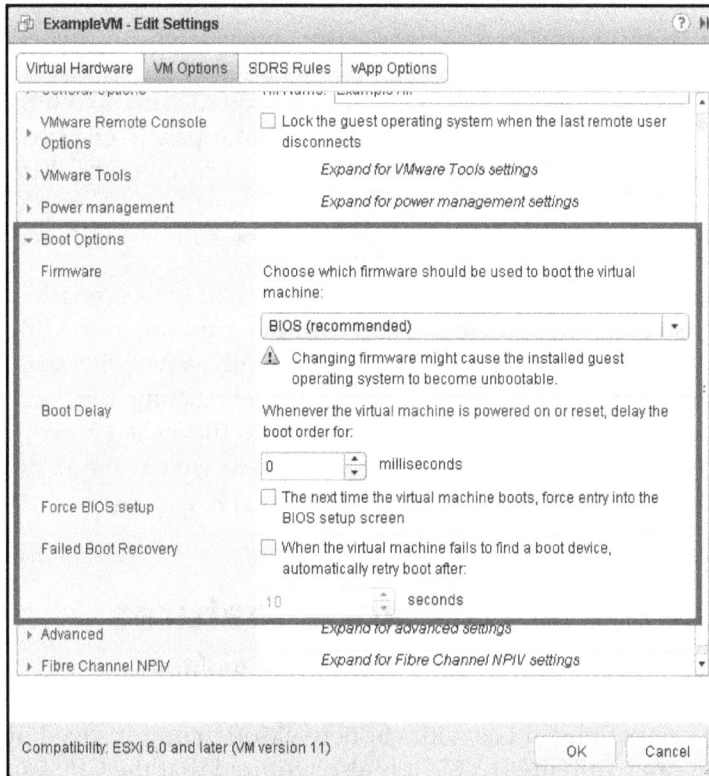

Click **OK** after making all the desired advanced configurations.

Fault Tolerance

vSphere Fault Tolerance can be used to ensure a higher level of availability than what is offered by vSphere HA for your virtual machines. It provides continuous availability by having identical virtual machines running on separate ESXi hosts in a cluster.

A protected virtual machine is known as the primary VM and a duplicate, the secondary VM, is created and runs on another ESXi host within the cluster. A Primary VM and Secondary VM cannot run on the same host. The execution of the Secondary VM is identical to the Primary VM and is capable of taking over at any point with no interruptions. The Primary and Secondary VMs monitor one another continuously to ensure that a Fault Tolerant state is maintained. If a failure occurs on the host running the Primary VM, then the Secondary VM will be activated immediately to replace the Primary VM. A new Secondary VM will be started and Fault Tolerance will be automatically reestablished.

Atomic file locking is used on shared storage to avoid a *split brain* scenario and to coordinate failover so that only one side would continue running as the Primary VM and a new Secondary VM are started automatically. Additionally, a new file, the `.ftgeneration` file, is used to ensure that only one instance of the virtual machine can read from or write to the virtual machine's virtual disks. There is also a second file, called `shared.vmft`, which contains vSphere Fault Tolerance metadata information as well as the `.vmx` paths and UUID information for the Primary and Secondary virtual machines.

vSphere 6.0 Fault Tolerance features

With vSphere 6, Fault Tolerance now allows symmetric multiprocessor (SMP) virtual machines, with up to four vCPUs. The CPUs used in ESXi host for fault tolerant virtual machines must be compatible for use with vSphere vMotion or improved by using Enhanced vMotion Compatibility (EVC). It is also required that the CPUs support Hardware MMU (memory management unit) virtualization (Intel EPT or AMD RVI). A dedicated 10 Gbit Ethernet logging network for FT with low latency should be used.

Another consideration is licensing; the level of vSphere licensing limits the number of vCPUs supported by a virtual machine with Fault Tolerance enabled. Support is as follows:

- vSphere Standard and Enterprise: up to two vCPUs
- vSphere Enterprise Plus: up to four vCPUs
- Fault Tolerance is not supported with vSphere Essentials or vSphere Essentials Plus

The following list provides an overview of the Fault Tolerance enhancements with vSphere 6:

- Support for up to four vCPUs and 64 GB RAM (maximum of 8 FT protected vCPUs per host).
- Support vMotion of both Primary and Secondary virtual machines.
- Supports for vSphere Storage APIs for Data Protection (VADP).
- Secondary copy of virtual machine files like .vmx, .vmdk, and so on, to protect the Primary virtual machine from both host and storage failures. Primary and secondary VM files can be stored on different datastores.
- Support for all virtual disk provisioning types (eager zeroed thick, lazy zeroed thick, and thin).
- Fast checkpointing, a new technology introduced (as a replacement for legacy vLockstep technology) to keep primary and secondary virtual machines synchronized. Historically, with vLockstep, the secondary virtual machine executed the same instruction stream as the Primary and replayed events at exact points logged on primary; this is otherwise known as *record and replay*. Fast checkpointing allows for the continuous copying or checkpointing of the primary virtual machine's state (similar to the idea of a non-stop vMotion).

Also keep in mind that there are quite a few vSphere features not supported when using vSphere Fault Tolerance. These include:

- **Snapshots**: Any snapshot must be removed or committed before Fault Tolerance can be enabled on the VM. Once Fault Tolerance is enabled, snapshots cannot be taken.
- **Storage vMotion**: To migrate storage, Fault Tolerance would need to be temporarily turned off. To do this, conduct the Storage vMotion and then re-enable Fault Tolerance.
- Linked clones.
- **Virtual Machine Component Protection (VMCP)**: If enabled on the cluster, VM overrides are created to turn this feature off for fault tolerant VMs.
- Virtual volumes.
- Storage based policy management.
- Physical RDMs.
- Serial and parallel ports.
- VMDKs exceeding 2 TB.

Configuring Fault Tolerance on a VM

Prior to enabling Fault Tolerance on a virtual machine, ensure that:

- The Fault Tolerance logging network and a vMotion network are configured
- vSphere HA is enabled on the cluster
- You are licensed for Fault Tolerance
- The ESXi host has Hardware Virtualization (HV) enabled in the BIOS
- Virtual machines files are on shared storage

To configure vSphere Fault Tolerance:

1. Right click the virtual machine. Select **Fault Tolerance** and then **Turn On Fault Tolerance**:

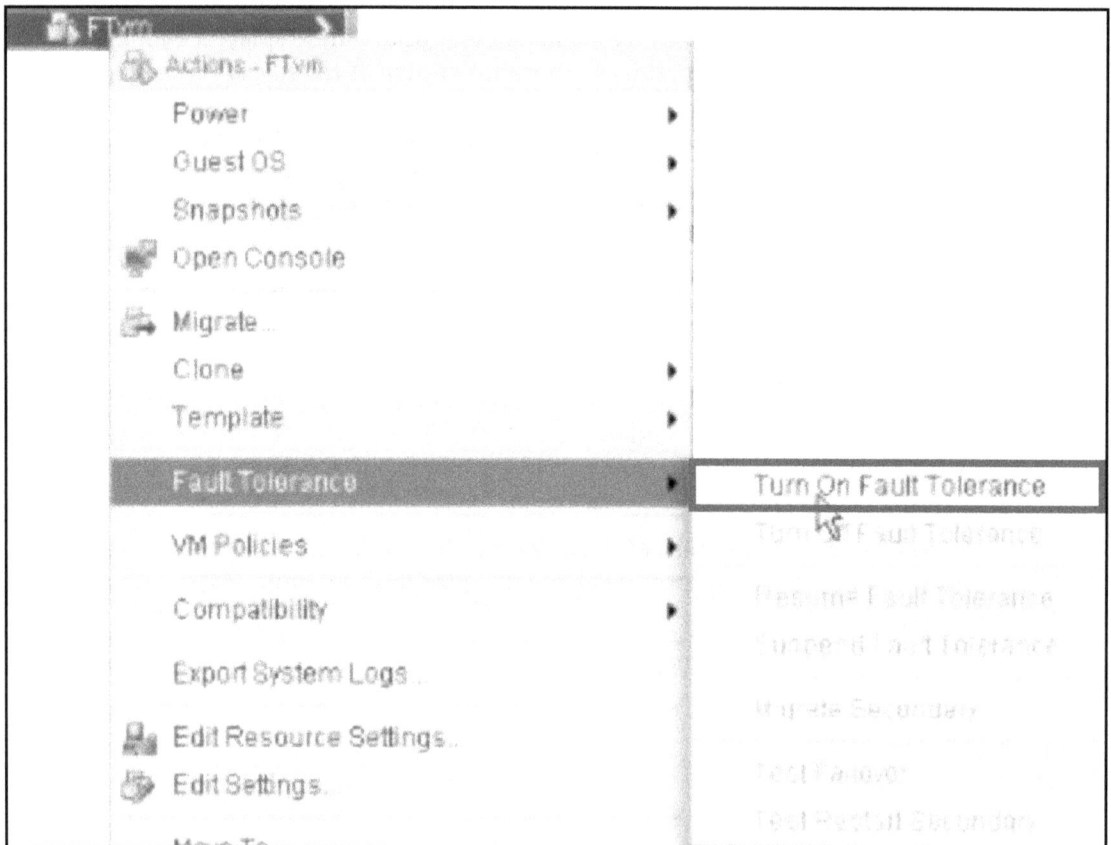

2. The **Turn On Fault Tolerance** wizard will appear. On the **Select datastores** pane, choose the appropriate **Storage** for the **Configuration File**, **Tie BreakerFile**, and **Hard Disk** by pressing the **Browse...** button:

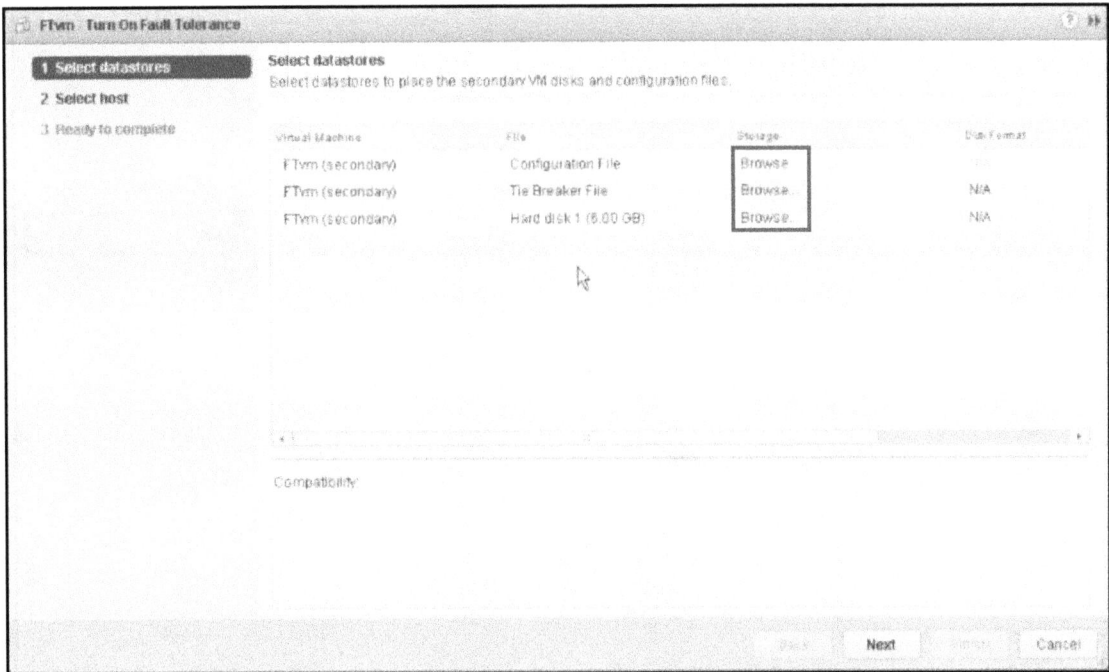

3. On the **Select a datastore cluster or datatore dialog**, select the appropriate datastore on which to store the file(s):

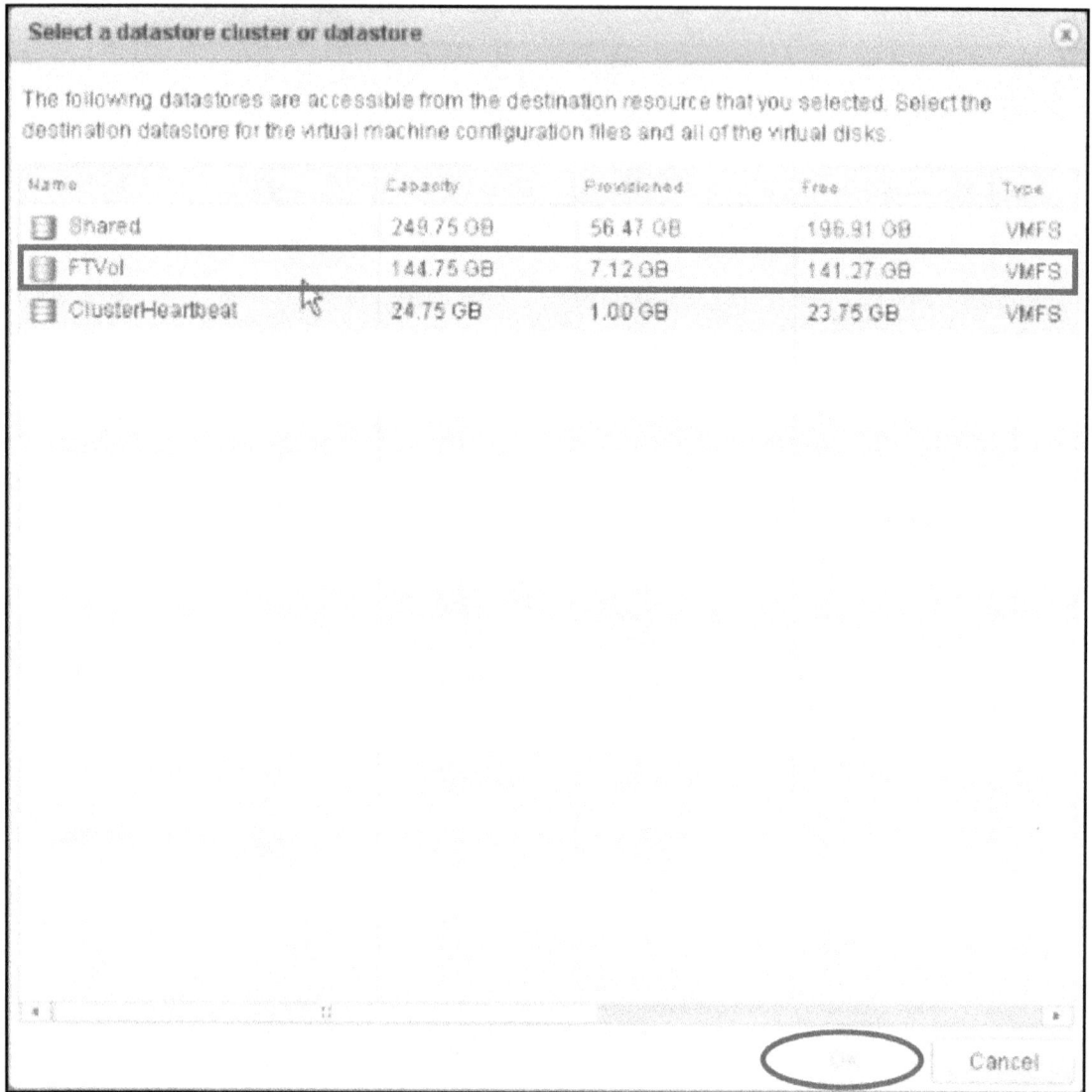

4. Press **OK** to close the dialog.
5. Press **Next** on the **Select datastores** pane.

6. Select an ESXi host on which to place the secondary VM:

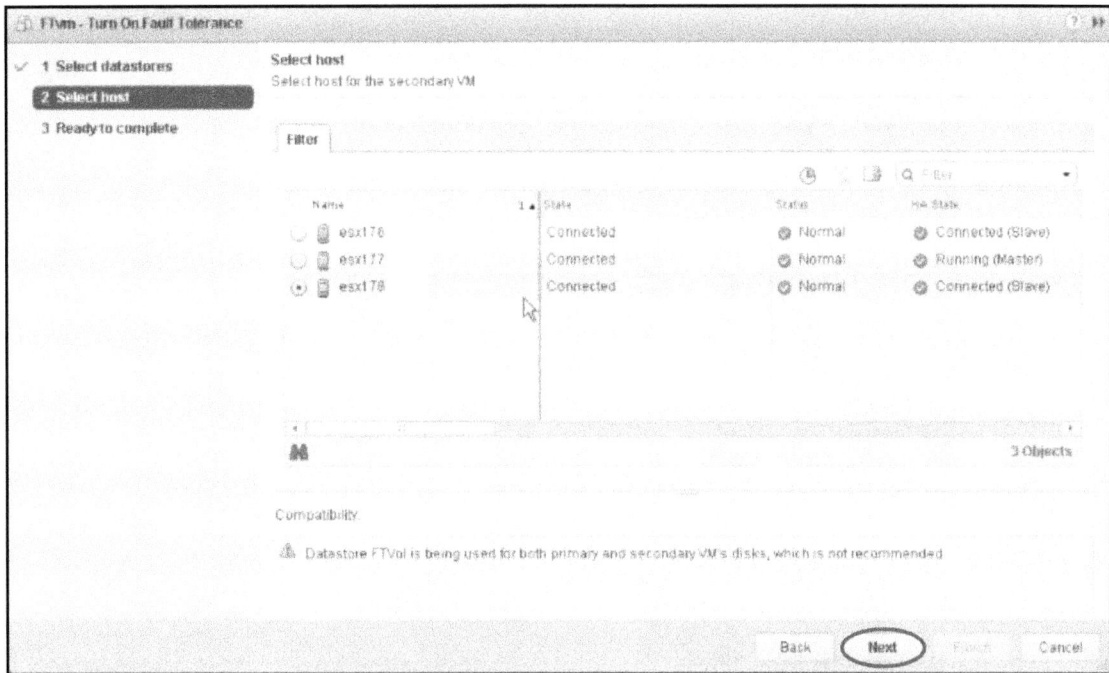

7. Press **Next**.

8. On the **Ready to complete** pane, review the selected options:

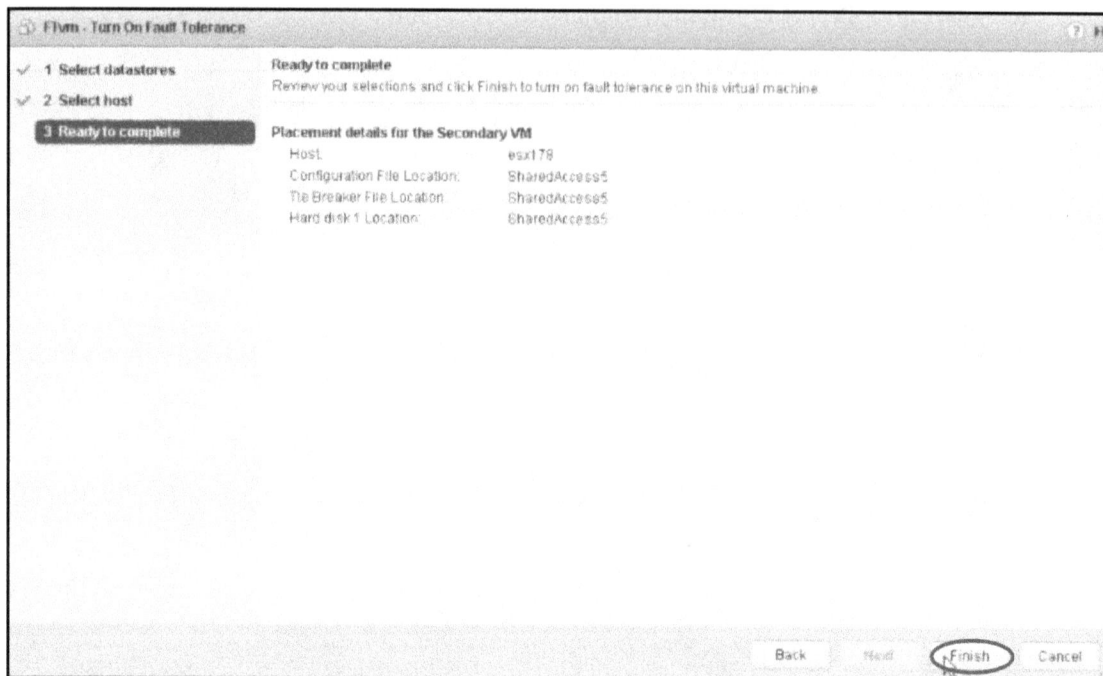

9. Press **Finish** to complete.

Summary

A vSphere administrator needs to understand virtual machine concepts before creating virtual machines. A virtual machine is a set of virtual hardware presented to a guest operating system whose characteristics are determined by a set of files. There are multiple VMware file types that are associated with and make up a virtual machine and are located in the VM's directory on a datastore. These files include the `.vmx`, `.nvram`, `.vswp`, `.vmdk`, `-flat.vmdk`, and `.log` files. Each virtual machine is equipped with virtual hardware and devices, such as one or more virtual CPUs, memory, video cards, IDE devices, SCSI devices, DVD/CD-ROM, parallel and serial ports, and network adapters that provide the same functionality as physical hardware.

CPU Hot-Plug and Memory Hot-Add, when enabled, allow for more CPU and memory resources to be added to virtual machines on demand. CPUID masks control the CPU features made visible to the guest operating system of the virtual machine. The CPU affinity setting allows you to restrict the assignment of the virtual machine to a subset of the available processors. The `.vswp` file can be placed on an alternate location besides the datastore where all of the other virtual machine's files are stored. Generally, this is done for some sort of performance or storage tiering reason.

vSphere Fault Tolerance provides continuous availability by having identical virtual machines running on separate ESXi hosts in a cluster. There is now support for up to four vCPUs and 64 GB RAM (maximum of 8 FT protected vCPUs per host).

The next chapter will discuss monitoring the performance of a vSphere environment.

9
Monitoring Performance of a vSphere Environment

In this chapter, we will discuss performance and discover how vSphere administrators can monitor the resource usage of different inventory objects. It is important to monitor the vSphere infrastructure to determine if there is a resource bottleneck or if a virtual machine or ESXi host is experiencing constraint. There are many tools that are available within vSphere that can assist VMware administrators to monitor resources and detect any potential bottlenecks. Both `esxtop` and performance charts are natively available within vSphere for monitoring. Alarms may also be configured to alert administrators when specific events occur or when thresholds are exceeded. In this chapter, you will learn about:

- CPU performance considerations
- Memory performance considerations
- Network performance considerations
- Storage performance considerations
- Resource controls
- vSphere performance charts
- esxtop
- Alarms

Understanding CPU performance

Performance is emphasized with CPU virtualization, and therefore will run on available processors when possible. The virtual machines use the underlying physical resources and only use the virtualization layer to run instructions when necessary so that the virtual machines continue to run as though directly accessing physical server hardware. A virtual machine can be configured with up to 128 virtual CPUs (vCPUs) as of vSphere 6.

Keep in mind that a virtual machine cannot have more vCPUs than logical CPUs available on the ESXi host. A logical CPU (LCPU) is a physical core, unless hyperthreading is enabled, at which point there are two logical CPUs per core. The VMkernel includes a CPU scheduler that dynamically schedules vCPUs on the ESXi host's physical processor.

The CPU scheduler can use each logical processor independently to execute VMs, providing capabilities similar to traditional **Symmetric Multi-Processing (SMP)** systems. Symmetric multiprocessing is simply the act of having more than one vCPU on a single physical CPU. The VMkernel intelligently manages processor time to guarantee that the load is spread smoothly across processor cores in the system. Every 2-40 milliseconds the VMkernel looks to migrate vCPUs from a logical processor to another to keep the load balanced. If a logical processor has no work, it is put into a halted state. This action frees its execution resources and allows the virtual machines running on the other logical processor on the same core to use the full execution resources of the core.

The VMkernel scheduler considers socket-core-thread topology when making scheduling decisions. Intel and AMD have developed processors that combine two or more processor cores into a single integrated circuit, called a socket in this discussion. A socket is a single package that can have one or more physical processor cores, with each core having one or more logical processors, or threads.

If hyperthreading is enabled on the host system, then ESXi can execute two threads, or sets of instructions, at the same time. The benefit of hyperthreading is that it provides more scheduling options, and effectively more scheduler throughput. However, keep in mind that hyperthreading does not double the core's power. Hyperthreading is enabled by default. To ensure that it is functioning, consult the hardware documentation to see if the BIOS includes support for hyperthreading and then enable hyperthreading in the system BIOS, if necessary.

Co-scheduling allows the execution of a set of threads or processes simultaneously to achieve high performance. Since multiple cooperating threads or processes often synchronize, not allowing for concurrent execution would increase the latency of synchronization. Operating systems require synchronous progress on all CPUs and malfunction may occur if this requirement is not met. When these operating systems are run within a virtual machine, ESXi must maintain this synchronous process on the vCPUs.

Since ESXi 3.x, VMware has been using relaxed co-scheduling to meet the challenge presented. Only vCPUs that are skewed must be co-started, this makes sure that when any vCPU is scheduled, any vCPU that is deemed *behind* will also be scheduled, which reduces skew. Relaxed co-scheduling allows for a subset of a virtual machine's vCPUs to be simultaneously scheduled after the skew is detected.

In many environments, ESXi allows for a significant amount of CPU over commitment, which is effectively just allocating more vCPUs than LCPUs (or cores). CPU over commitment may not affect virtual machine performance. However, if the ESXi host becomes saturated, where the virtual machines and other workloads demand all or more CPU resources than the host has, latency-sensitive virtual machines may experience performance issues. During times of CPU contention, when virtual machines are competing for resources, the VMkernel time-slices the physical processor across all virtual machines to ensure that the virtual machines run as if having the specified number of vCPUs but with fewer resources.

Configuring a virtual machine with more vCPUs than what its workload requires may cause increased resource utilization and could impact performance. For example, you wouldn't configure a single threaded workload with four vCPUs. The same principle applies to vSMP virtual machines; configuring a virtual machine with 16 vCPUs doesn't do any favors if the workload doesn't use more than eight vCPUs. There is still overhead associated with a vCPU, even if the guest operating system of the virtual machine doesn't use it, and this results in CPU consumption on the ESXi host.

It's a good idea to monitor CPU usage of the ESXi host, which can be done using the vSphere Web Client or `esxtop`. Additional management tools, for instance vRealize Operations Manager, may be purchased to monitor a virtual infrastructure.

Understanding memory performance

The virtual machine is configured with a set of memory; this is the sum that the guest OS is told it has available to it. A virtual machine will not necessarily use the entire memory size; it only uses what is needed at the time by the guest OS and applications. However, a VM cannot access more memory than its configured memory size plus overhead. A default memory size is provided by vSphere when creating the virtual machine but can be adjusted by the administrator. It is important to know the memory needs of the application and guest operating system being virtualized so that the virtual machine's memory can be sized accordingly.

Don't forget to factor in memory overhead. Memory overhead can be broken down into two categories, ESXi overhead and virtual machine overhead. The system, or ESXi, overhead is used for the VMkernel and other host agents such as hostd or vpxa. There is also per virtual machine overhead that is used for the **Virtual Machine Monitor** (**VMM**), **Virtual Machine Executable** (**VMX**) process and virtual hardware devices. The amount of virtual machine overhead varies depending on how many vCPUs and other virtual devices are configured.

When configuring a virtual machine, ensure that enough memory has been allocated to hold the working set of applications that will run. Over-allocating memory unnecessarily results in increased memory overhead. Conversely, if not enough memory has been allocated, the virtual machine's performance may suffer from memory starvation.

Memory overcommitment happens when the physical memory installed on an ESXi host is less than the sum of memory allocated to all virtual machines, as well as overhead. The virtual machine's overhead memory is extra host physical memory that is required by the VMkernel beyond the memory allocated to the virtual machine. So why overcommit memory resources? Overcommitment allows for a more effective use of physical resources by raising the consolidation ratio, lowering the total cost of operating virtual machines, and increasing operational efficiency. Memory overcommitment does not necessarily lead to performance loss in a guest OS or its applications, but may when a large portion of a virtual machine's memory has to be reclaimed due to contention.

Memory overcommitment allows the VMkernel to reclaim memory that is not actively used by virtual machines in order to meet the demands of other virtual machines as well as the hypervisor itself. It is important to understand that the VMkernel is not natively aware of the guest operating system's internal memory management and reclamation techniques. Typically, guest operating systems have an allocated memory list and a free memory list. As guest operating systems request memory pages, *virtual* pages are backed by the VMkernel's physical memory. Eventually a page of memory is no longer used within the guest operating system but the data is not removed, instead the guest operating system removes the address space pointer from the allocated memory list and points it to the free memory list. The ESXi host keeps this page in physical memory since the data has not changed.

A virtual machine cannot be powered on if the minimum memory isn't available or the swap file size doesn't equal the difference between allocated and reserved memory. Also, the virtual machine will not power on if the datastore on which the swap files will be created does not have sufficient space.

Transparent Page Sharing

Transparent Page Sharing (TPS) allows pages of memory that are identical to be stored in the same place. This is the only memory reclamation technique that occurs at a regular interval; the other options that will be discussed happen when the ESXi host experiences memory contention. During periods of idle CPU time, the hypervisor looks for identical memory pages located across multiple virtual machines. Once these pages are matched, they are then shared in the physical RAM. ESXi systems use a proprietary page sharing technique to securely eliminate redundant copies of memory pages as to allow for a more efficient support of overcommitment.

Transparent Page Sharing is basically a de-duplication method applied to memory rather than storage. For organizations that tend to use the same operating system or very similar operating systems for many virtual machines, the memory impact can provide substantial savings.

A page of memory is typically 4 KB unless large memory pages are in use. Some operating systems or applications may achieve better performance with the use of large memory pages, which are 2 MB. The likelihood that a 2 MB page of memory will be identical to another is very low; therefore large memory pages are not shared. However, if memory over-commitment is high enough, large memory pages will be broken down into small pages and sharing will be attempted.

The following diagram demonstrates transparent page sharing. The top half of the diagram is indicative of virtual machine memory and the bottom half is the physical host memory. Notice that each virtual machine contains a green page of memory so this is shared by all three virtual machines.

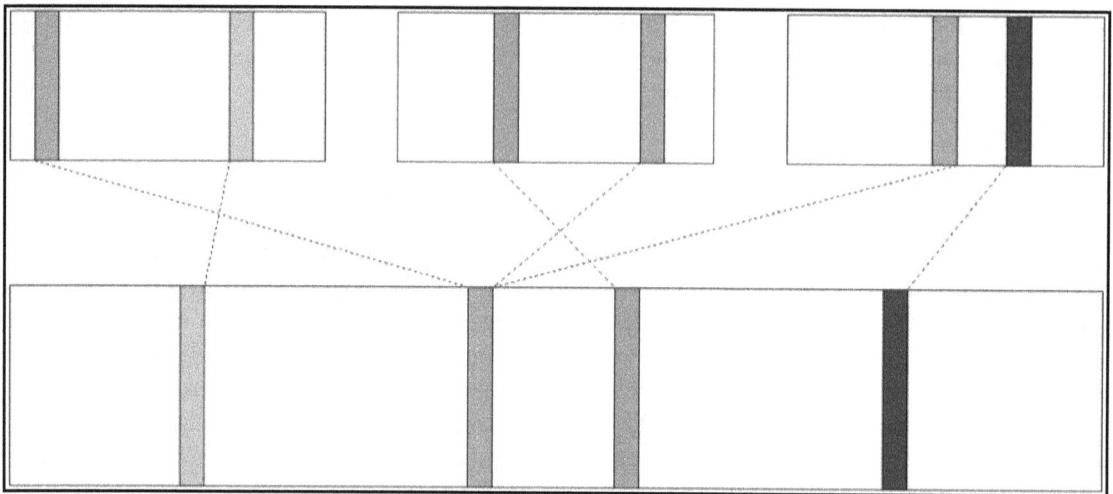

Remember that transparent page sharing always occurs, when enabled, whereas the next topics only occur during memory contention.

As of vSphere 6, *intra-VM sharing* is enabled by default; this is page sharing within a virtual machine. *Inter-VM sharing*, or sharing between virtual machines, only occurs when the virtual machines' salt value matches. This change was made to increase protection of the virtual machine memory contents. See VMware KB 2080735 (`https://kb.vmware.com/kb/28735`) and KB 2097593 (`https://kb.vmware.com/kb/297593`) for more information.

Ballooning

Ballooning occurs during memory contention before using the .vswp file. VMware Tools must be installed for this mechanism to function; part of this driver package is the memory balloon driver (vmmemctl). The memory balloon driver works with the hypervisor to reclaim pages of memory that are considered to be the least valuable to the virtual machine's guest operating system, generally these are page marked as free or idle but can reclaim active pages if absolutely necessary. If the ESXi server begins to run low on physical memory it will communicate with the memory balloon driver to reclaim memory inside the guest operating system that is no longer valuable to the operating system. Essentially, the hypervisor will grow the memory balloon driver within the guest operating system as to increase memory pressure. The pressure caused by the increase of the memory balloon driver will cause the guest operating system to use its own native memory management algorithm. Ballooning will utilize the guest operating system's own virtual disk (for Windows this is the page file, while Linux operating systems use a swap partition).

The real beauty of ballooning is that it is intelligent memory management because it allows the guest operating system to make the hard decision of which pages of memory will be paged out, without any hypervisor involvement. The guest operating system is fully aware of the memory state; therefore, the virtual machine will keep performing well as long as it has idle or free pages of memory to balloon. When ballooning is engaged in a guest operating system, it can only force virtual machines to page up to 65% of their memory and the VMkernel is responsible for determining which virtual machines will be ballooned and which will not. The goal is to balloon idle virtual machines before active virtual machines.

This process reduces the chance that the physical ESXi host will begin to swap, which will cause performance degradation.

Compression

The physical pages of memory can be compressed and then decompressed by the ESXi host. If pages of memory that would normally be swapped can be compressed and stored in the compression cache then the next page access would result in decompression. Decompression is much faster than disk access. If memory compression were taking place, there may be a few non-compressible pages (cannot be compressed to 2 KB or smaller) that may need to be swapped out even if the compression cache is not full. Otherwise pages that would normally be swapped to disk are chosen as candidates for memory compression. This only occurs during memory contention and will not occur if unnecessary.

Compression is preferred to swapping because the page compression technique used is much faster than the normal page swap-out operation, which involves using disk I/O.

Swapping to host cache

If an ESXi host has **Solid-State Drives** (**SSD**), then these can be used for a VMFS datastore where it can be specified for use as a host cache. This cache is created on a low-latency disk used as a write back cache for virtual machine swap files. This cache is shared by all virtual machines running on an ESXi host. Keep in mind that the host will still create regular swap files on a datastore even if a host cache is enabled; the virtual machines will swap to this host cache until the limited SSD space is depleted, at which point the virtual machines will use their regular swap files on the datastore.

In most cases, swapping to an SSD is much faster than swapping to regular swap files on hard disk storage. The idea is that as SSDs come down in price, this is a feature that will be more widely used. Another possibility is that a datastore is backed by a storage array with SSDs and the `.vswp` files are stored on that specific datastore.

To configure a host cache, browse to an ESXi host in the vSphere Web Client. Click on the **Manage** tab, select the **Storage** tab, and select **Host Cache Configuration**. Select the pencil icon to edit this configuration.

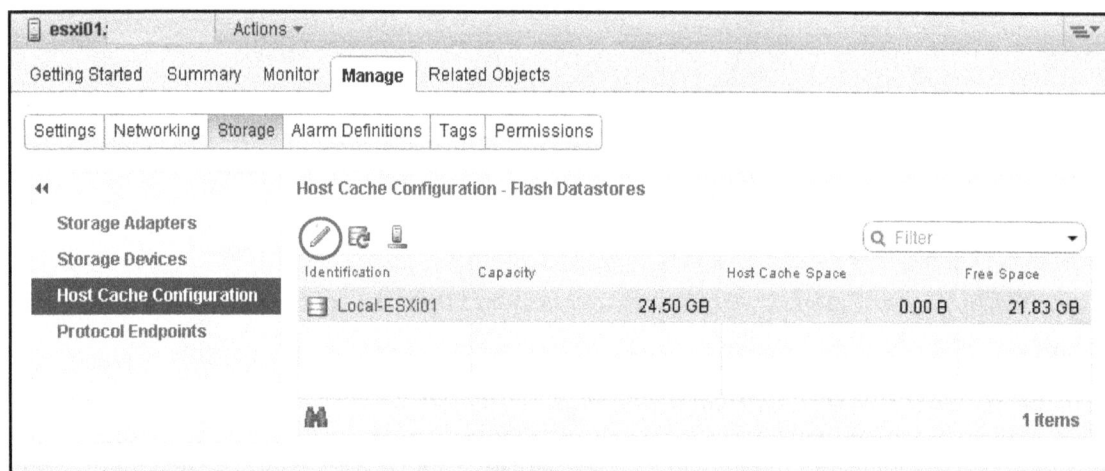

This will open a dialog box. You must have an SSD-backed datastore in the inventory. If this prerequisite is met, then you will select the datastore in this list and select the **Allocate space for host cache** checkbox and configure a size for the allocation. This is demonstrated in the following screenshot that allows you to specify size for the host cache:

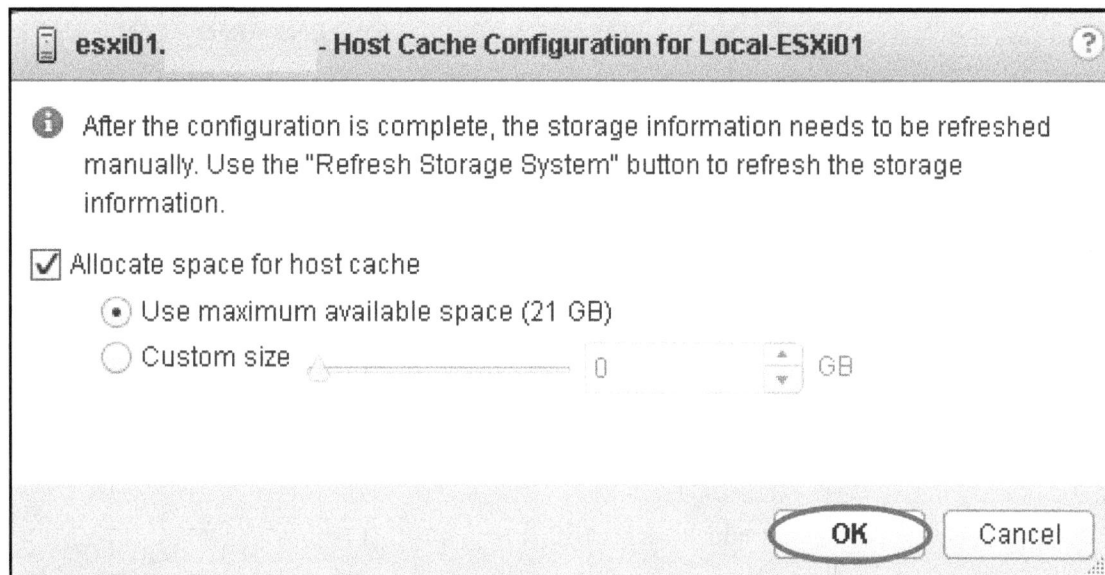

Click on **OK**.

Once the host cache has been configured, click on the **Settings** tab under the **Manage** tab and choose **System Swap**. If the ESXi host is not configured to use the host cache then click on the **Editâ❋⁝** button:

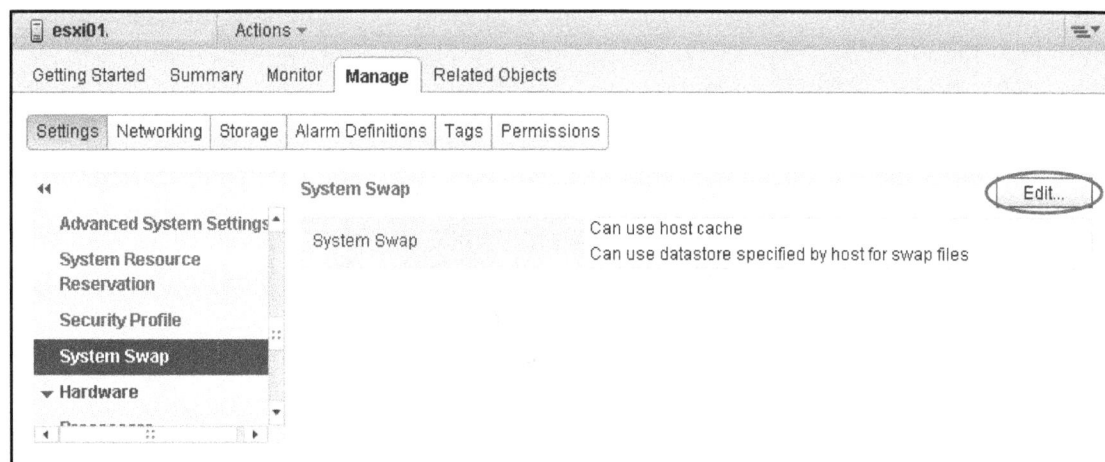

This will bring up a dialog box, which will allow for the selection to check the box for **Can use host cache**:

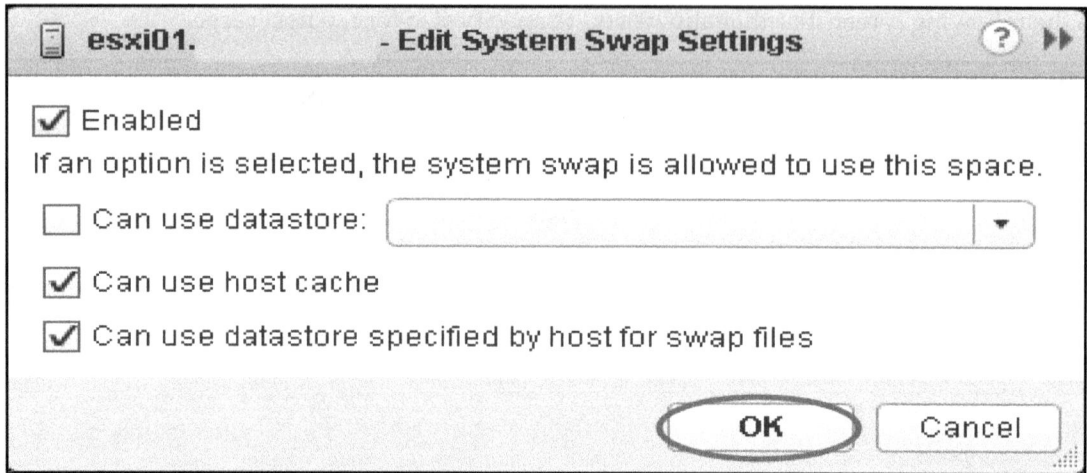

Once this selection has been made, click on **OK**.

Hypervisor swapping

When each virtual machine powers on, a set of swap files (vmname.vswp and vmx-vmname.vswp) is created by the hypervisor. In the event that ballooning, compression, and transparent page sharing are not sufficient to reclaim memory, the hypervisor will swap a virtual machine's memory to its swap file as to free up physical memory for the hypervisor and other virtual machines.

Host level swapping is a guaranteed way to reclaim a large amount of memory in a short time. In comparison, it takes time for transparent page sharing and ballooning to reclaim memory from virtual machines. Page scan rates and opportunity affect transparent page sharing, while ballooning is dependent on the virtual machine guest operating system response time. Additionally, there is a 65% memory size limitation on how much memory ballooning can reclaim.

However, hypervisor swapping is used as a last resort to reclaim memory from the virtual machine due to its impact on performance. During swapping, the hypervisor will arbitrarily steal pages from the guest. It doesn't care what memory it takes, it just forces the guest operating system to go to disk with its remaining sum of memory.

Memory will be forcibly reclaimed using swapping as a last resort unless the virtual machine cannot balloon. Times that swapping would occur before ballooning, include:

- The vmmemctl driver (memory balloon driver), or VMware Tools, was not installed.
- The vmmemctl driver was explicitly disabled.
- VMware Tools is not running. For instance, when a guest operating system is booting up.
- The memory balloon driver is unable to reclaim memory fast enough to satisfy the current system demands.

If the memory balloon driver is properly functioning but the maximum balloon size has been reached, then swapping will occur.

Swap space must be provisioned for any virtual machine memory that is not reserved for each virtual machine's swap files. This means that the size of the virtual machine's .vswp file is equal to the virtual machine's configured memory minus any memory reservations. These files are created at the virtual machine's power on to ensure that ESXi can preserve the virtual machine's memory under any circumstance.

By default, the virtual machine's swap files are created in the same datastore location as the rest of the virtual machine files. If the default configuration is not desired, this can be changed at the virtual machine level or at the ESXi host level.

Here is how to change the datastore used to store the virtual machine swap files at the host level:

1. Using the vSphere Web Client, browse to the ESXi host.
2. Choose the **Manage** tab and select **Swap file location** under **Settings**. By default, the swap file location is the virtual machine's directory where the rest of its files are located.
3. To change this, choose the **Editâ✲┊** button.

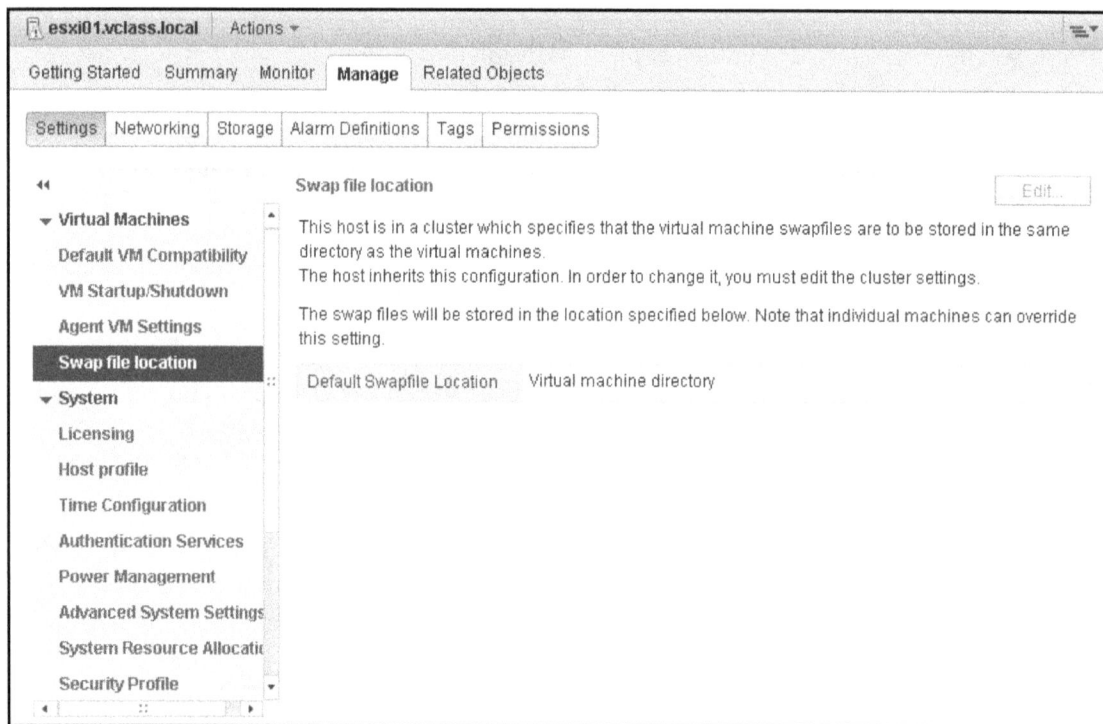

The following screenshot demonstrates the options available for the **Swap file location** dialog box:

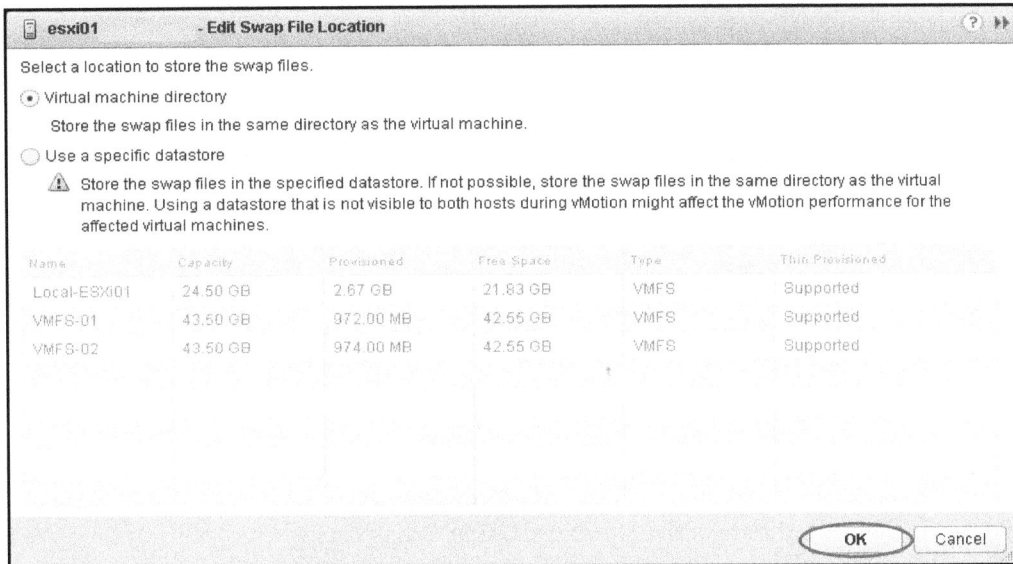

esxi01	- Edit Swap File Location				? ►►

Select a location to store the swap files.

⦿ Virtual machine directory

   Store the swap files in the same directory as the virtual machine.

◯ Use a specific datastore

   ⚠ Store the swap files in the specified datastore. If not possible, store the swap files in the same directory as the virtual machine. Using a datastore that is not visible to both hosts during vMotion might affect the vMotion performance for the affected virtual machines.

Name	Capacity	Provisioned	Free Space	Type	Thin Provisioned
Local-ESXi01	24.50 GB	2.67 GB	21.83 GB	VMFS	Supported
VMFS-01	43.50 GB	972.00 MB	42.55 GB	VMFS	Supported
VMFS-02	43.50 GB	974.00 MB	42.55 GB	VMFS	Supported

OK   Cancel

Once modified, the next time the virtual machines residing on this ESXi host are power cycled their swap files will be created on the specified datastore.

Understanding network performance

CPU utilization plays a major role in network throughput. More CPU resources are needed for processing higher throughput levels. Insufficient CPU resources limit maximum throughput so monitoring CPU is imperative.

Network performance issues are typically caused by the saturation of a network link between the clients and servers. vSphere 6 supports 1 Gigabit, 10 Gigabit Ethernet, and also 40 Gigabit Ethernet. These higher bandwidth networks reduce the chance of having network bottlenecks but it is always a possibility. The network performance will be dependent on application workload as well as the network configurations. Network-intensive applications can result in oversubscribed network links, which may lead to network contention.

Physical NICs (vmnics) are commonly used by multiple consumers (virtual machines and/or VMkernel ports). It's possible that each consumer could impact the performance of another. Consider placing consumers with heavy networking I/O on separate physical NICs than consumers with latency-sensitive workloads.

Ultimately, ensure that the infrastructure bandwidth is sufficient for all traffic types. Network I/O Control, discussed previously in `Chapter 5`, *vSphere Storage Concepts and Management*, can be configured to prioritize network access for the different traffic types.

Understanding storage performance

Saturating the underlying storage hardware often causes storage performance issues. Disk intensive applications could saturate the storage and/or the path. To determine whether your vSphere environment is experiencing storage issues you need to monitor disk latency. Storage I/O Control, discussed in `Chapter 6`, *Advanced vSphere Infrastructure Management*, can be used to determine if a latency threshold is exceeded. Ensure that your storage can meet the I/O demands of the virtual machines. Consider using SSD solutions as a means of removing the disk spindle from the equation. Using a disk cache approach can increase the IOPS that your storage is capable of. **Input/Output Operations Per Second (IOPS)** is a common metric used to judge overall storage performance. Shares may also be used to prioritize virtual machine access to storage resources.

Understanding resource controls

An administrator can customize the amount of resources allocated to a virtual machine or to the resource pool in which those virtual machines reside by modifying resource controls. Each of the primary four resources (CPU, memory, network, and storage) can be controlled, but network and storage require the use of the advanced features of Network I/O Control or Storage I/O Control, respectively. There are three resource controls that are available to determine how resources are provided to a virtual machine, these are: *shares*, *limits*, and *reservations*. When an ESXi host's memory or CPU resources are overcommitted, a virtual machine's allocation target is somewhere between its specified reservation and specified limit, depending on the VM's share and the system load. This is something that we will explore later on in this chapter.

Shares

A *share* is a value that specifies the relative priority or importance of a virtual machine (or resource pool) in regards to its access to a given resource. Keep in mind that shares only operate in times of contention. Meaning that if, for example, a virtual machine has twice the memory share value of another virtual machine it is competing against then that means it is entitled to twice as much memory when those two virtual machines are competing for resources. However, it is important to note that if there is no contention then share values are irrelevant and a virtual machine can consume up to its limit if available.

Share values may be configured as **High**, **Normal**, or **Low** (or customer values may be used) and these values specify a 4:2:1 ratio, respectively, and this is demonstrated in the following screenshot. A **Custom** value can also be selected to assign a specific number of shares, or proportional weight, to the virtual machine if the default values are not desired. Be careful when using Custom values; don't lose track of the ratio because doing so will potentially result in disproportioned resources.

By default, virtual machines are assigned a **Normal** share value. To modify this configuration, right-click on the virtual machine and select **Edit Settings**. Under **Virtual Hardware**, expand either **CPU** or **Memory** and modify the drop-down box next to **Shares**. The following screenshot provides an example of memory resource controls that are available to be configured:

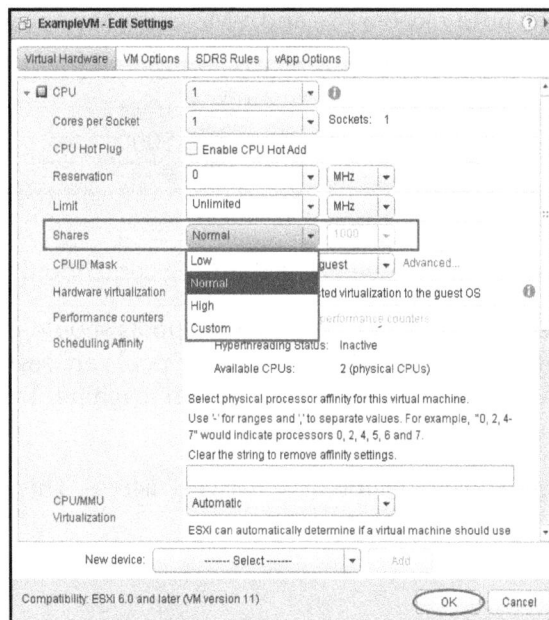

These share values can be assigned individually for memory and CPU resources. For example, a virtual machine may be configured for a **High** share value for CPU but a **Normal** value for memory resources.

Shares make more sense when it is considered that shares work in comparison to other virtual machines or other resources pools at the same level. This means that shares are used to compete against sibling objects (virtual machines or resource pools) while in contention within the same parent in a resource pool hierarchy.

The following figure demonstrates a three virtual machine scenario where share values are being enforced (during contention). The total share values equal 9000 in total; this means that during contention VM1 receives 3000/9000 or 33% of resources, VM2 receives 1000/9000 and gets 11%, and VM3 receives 5000/9000 or 56% of resources.

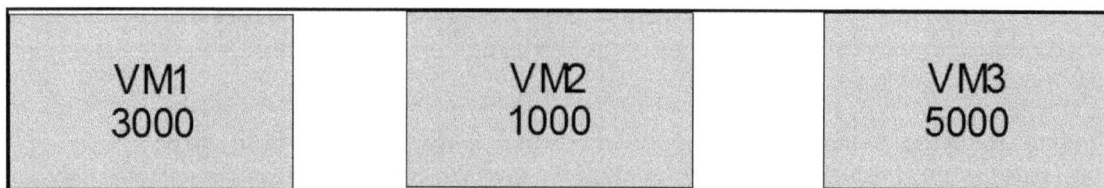

VM1 3000		VM2 1000		VM3 5000

Keep in mind that this is all relative so should another virtual machine power on at this level then the total amount of shares change. Now the share values total to 14000. VM1 would receive 21%, VM2 would receive 7%, and VM3 and VM4 would receive 36% each.

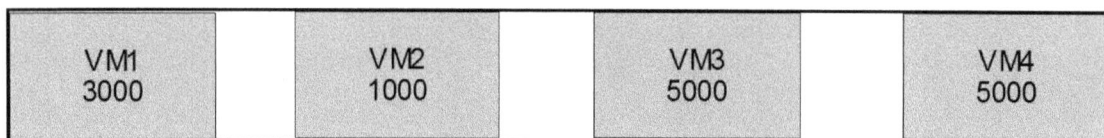

VM1 3000		VM2 1000		VM3 5000		VM4 5000

Do not forget that share values are only enforced during contention!

It is recommended that virtual machines and resource pools should not be made sibling objects within a hierarchy because, by default, resource pools are assigned shares that may not appropriately compare to those assigned to a virtual machine. This can potentially cause performance issues.

Shares can also be configured for datastore and network access. This is discussed later in the chapter.

Limits

A limit specifies the ceiling of CPU cycles or amount of host physical memory that a virtual machine can consume. By default, a virtual machine is set to unlimited for both CPU and memory resources, but this is a bit misleading. A limit is specified in megahertz or megabytes. A virtual machine can only consume up to its configured amount plus overhead; if a virtual machine is configured for 8 GB of memory then it cannot exceed 8 GB plus memory overhead even though the memory limit is set to unlimited. In this scenario, 8 GB plus memory overhead is the virtual machine's inherent and effective limit since that is the configured amount.

Limits can be used to manage user expectation in a small environment and are especially great for use in test environments to continually lower the amount of resources in order to determine how much should be configured in production. The drawback to configuring a limit is that the guest operating system believes that it has the configured amount of the resource but a limit was configured. Let's say a virtual machine is configured for 8 GB of memory and a limit was set at 4 GB. If you look at the system properties of the guest operating system, it will display that 8 GB of memory is available and is unaware that a limit was set and the virtual machine cannot exceed 4 GB of physical host memory. When a limit is reached, the guest operating system can still request new pages of memory, but because of the configured limit, the VMkernel will not allow the guest operating system to consume more physical memory. The virtual machine will be treated as though it were under contention. Memory reclamation techniques will be used to allow the virtual machine to consume more memory resources as requested. First, the VMkernel will inflate the memory balloon driver to let the guest operating system memory manager decide which to page out, then compression will occur, and in a worst-case scenario, swapping can occur. If swapping is possible in your environment, consider placing the .vswp files on Tier 1 storage for better performance when in contention.

If a CPU limit is set on a virtual machine, then the virtual machine is deliberately restrained from being scheduled on a physical processor once the allocated CPU resources are consumed. For a symmetric multiprocessing virtual machine, this means that the sum of all vCPUs cannot exceed the specified limit. For example, a virtual machine with 4 vCPUs and a limit of 1600 MHz with an equal vCPU load cannot exceed more than 400 MHz per vCPU. If only one vCPU is under stress then the load will be distributed across the rest of the vCPUs.

This can cause certain applications to have undesirable behavior and performance degradation. Use limits sparingly.

To set a resource limit for a virtual machine, right-click on the virtual machine in the vSphere Web Client and select **Edit Settings**. Under **Virtual Hardware,** expand the desired resource and modify the **Limit** as needed. An example of this is demonstrated in the following screenshot:

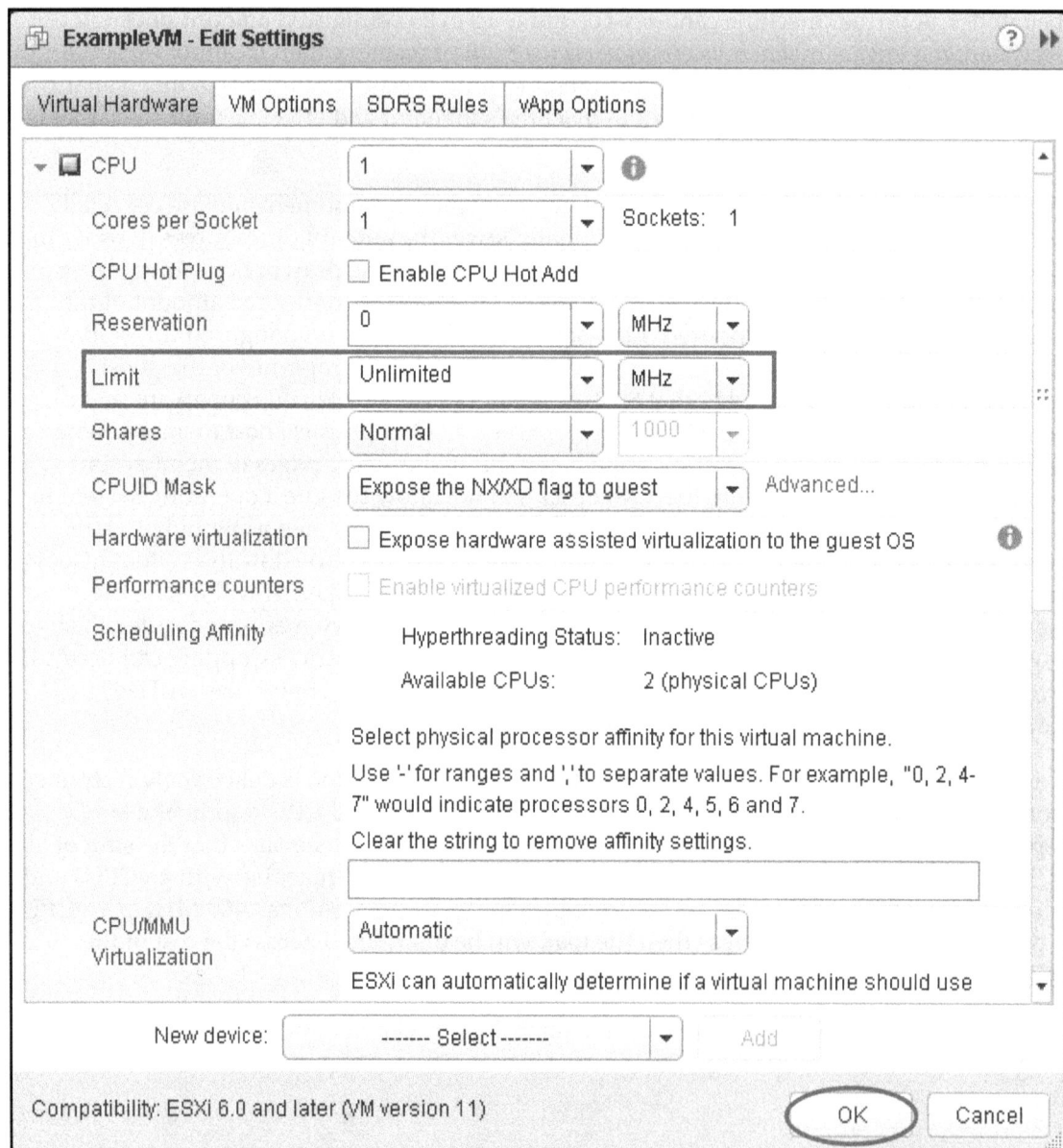

A CPU limit can be configured using the same process outlined above except that the **CPU** will be expanded. Once set, click on **OK**.

Reservations

A reservation specifies the guaranteed minimum resource allocation for a virtual machine. If a virtual machine has a reservation, then the full reservation must be satisfied in order for the virtual machine to power on. A virtual machine will not power on if a reservation is not met. A reservation is specified in megahertz or megabytes. The reservation is guaranteed, even when the server is heavily loaded, meaning that the VMkernel does not reclaim physical memory if it is reserved, even if there is contention. This reserved physical memory will be available to that specific virtual machine at all times, regardless of contention. If a memory reservation is configured for a virtual machine, this is always guaranteed, even when in contention as memory reclamation techniques cannot take away that portion of memory. Since this memory cannot be taken away from a virtual machine during contention then this means that it will not be swapped; a memory reservation changes the size of the .vswp file. Without a reservation, the virtual machine's swap file will be the size of configured memory; however, if a reservation is configured then the swap file will be the size of the configured memory minus any memory reservation. This means if a virtual machine is configured for 4 GB of memory then the .vswp will be 4 GB unless there is a reservation. If a reservation of 1 GB is configured then the .vswp file would be sized at 3 GB.

Reservations should be used for business-critical virtual machines in order to guarantee a specific minimum amount of CPU and/or memory resources.

To set a resource limit for a virtual machine follow these steps:

1. Right-click the virtual machine in the vSphere Web Client and select **Edit Settings**.
2. Under **Virtual Hardware,** expand the desired resource and modify the **Reservation** as needed.

A memory reservation can be configured using the same process outlined above except that **Memory** will be expanded. Once set, click on **OK**.

Monitoring performance

There are many different tools available to monitor the performance of a virtual infrastructure. This section will explicitly cover vSphere performance charts and `esxtop`.

Performance charts

Performance charts can be displayed using the vSphere Client or by using the vSphere Web Client. Throughout this chapter, we will be discussing tools that are natively available within vCenter and ESXi, but keep in mind that vRealize Operations Manager may also be used to monitor the health of your infrastructure. These performance charts can provide a great deal of useful information for an administrator to analyze performance. There are two types of charts available: overview and advanced.

Overview performance charts

Overview performance charts display the performance statistics that are most useful for quickly diagnosing problems and monitoring performance.

To view an overview performance chart:

1. Select a virtual machine or ESXi host in the vCenter inventory pane within the vSphere Web Client.
2. Click on the **Monitor** tab.
3. Choose the **Performance** button and click on the **Overview** link on the left pane.

Depending on what target object is selected from the inventory pane, using this process will provide a quick view of the ESXi host or virtual machine's health and its performance. The following screenshot provides a partial view of the overview performance charts for an ESXi host; to view more you would typically just scroll down in the vSphere Web Client. Overview performance charts should be used when you are just seeking a quick view of the most common metrics for the selected inventory objects.

The following screenshot displays the CPU usage of an ESXi host; notice that the % is very low as there is not much currently running on the selected host. There are many different overview performance charts that may be viewed, such as CPU ready time, memory ballooning, swap activity, and so on. Continue scrolling down to see more charts.

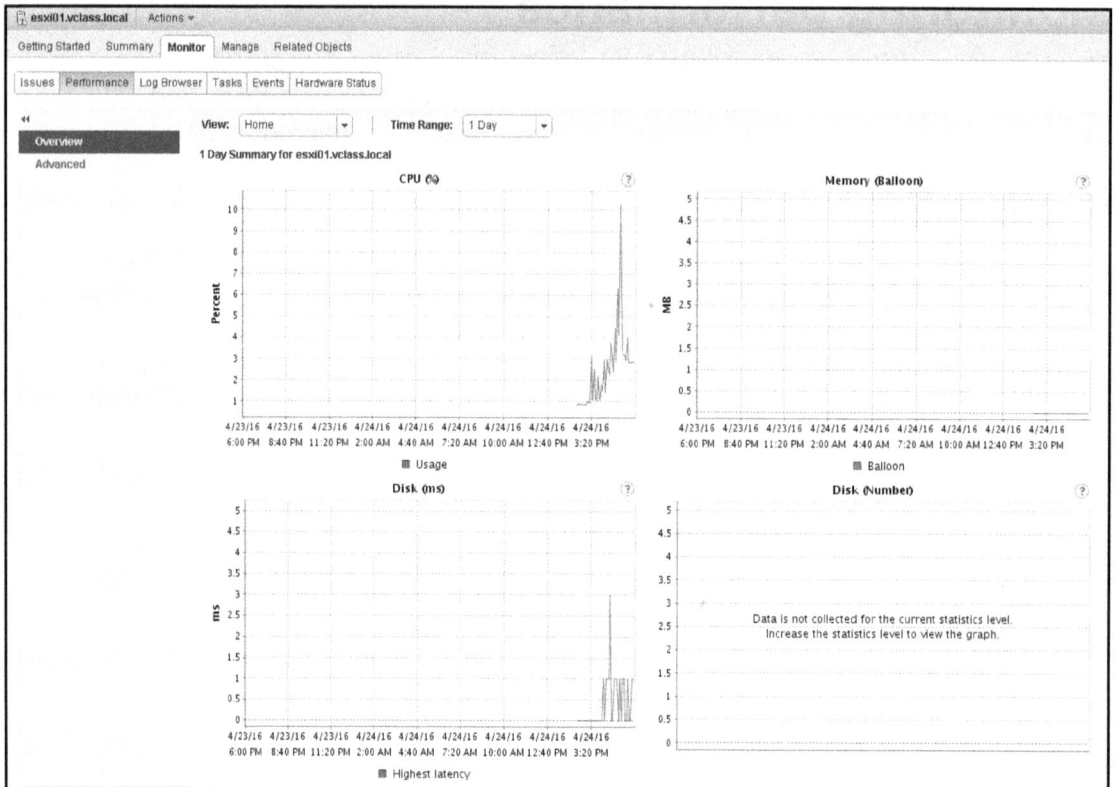

Advanced performance charts

An advanced performance chart provides a more granular graphical display of an object's statistical data. For example, the performance data can be displayed over multiple time periods. You can use an advanced performance chart to examine a variety of objects in more detail, to include:

- Datacenters
- Clusters
- ESXi hosts

- Resource pools
- Virtual machines
- vApps
- Datastores

To view an advanced performance chart:

1. Select an object in the vCenter inventory pane within the vSphere Web Client.
2. Choose the **Monitor** tab.
3. Click on the **Performance** button.
4. Click on the **Advanced** link on the left pane.

The following screenshot provides an example of the advanced performance charts for an ESXi host. To customize the advanced performance chart, select the **Chart Options** hyperlink:

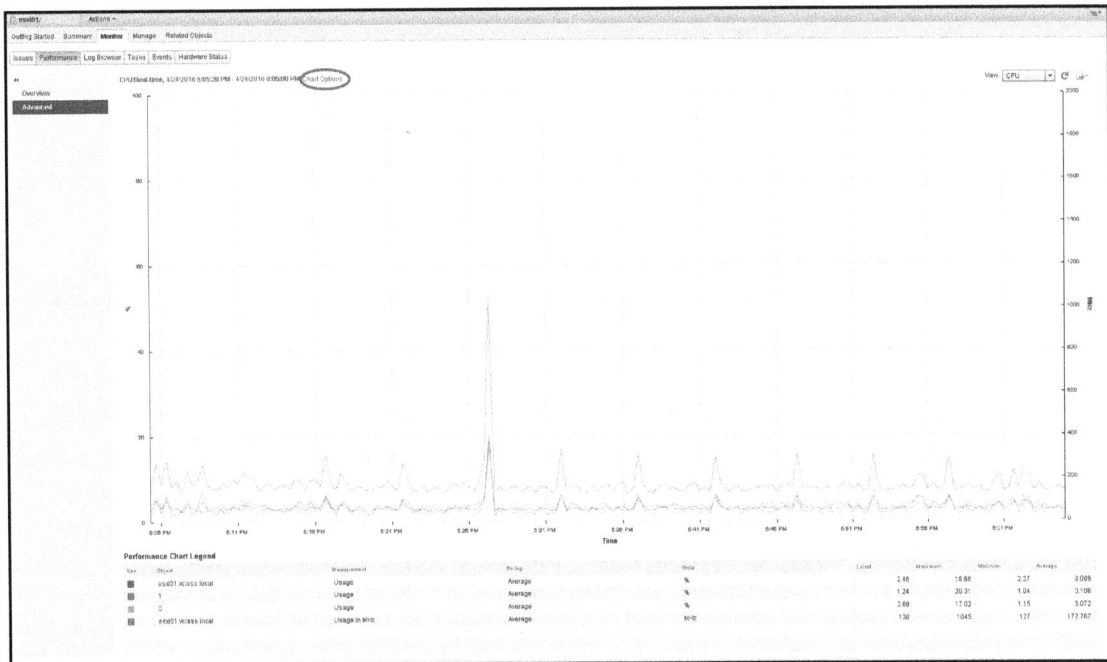

There are many options that are available using an advanced performance chart. Selecting the **Chart Options** hyperlink will present a dialog allowing the administrator to customize the advanced performance chart. The following screenshot displays the many chart options available when using this type of chart:

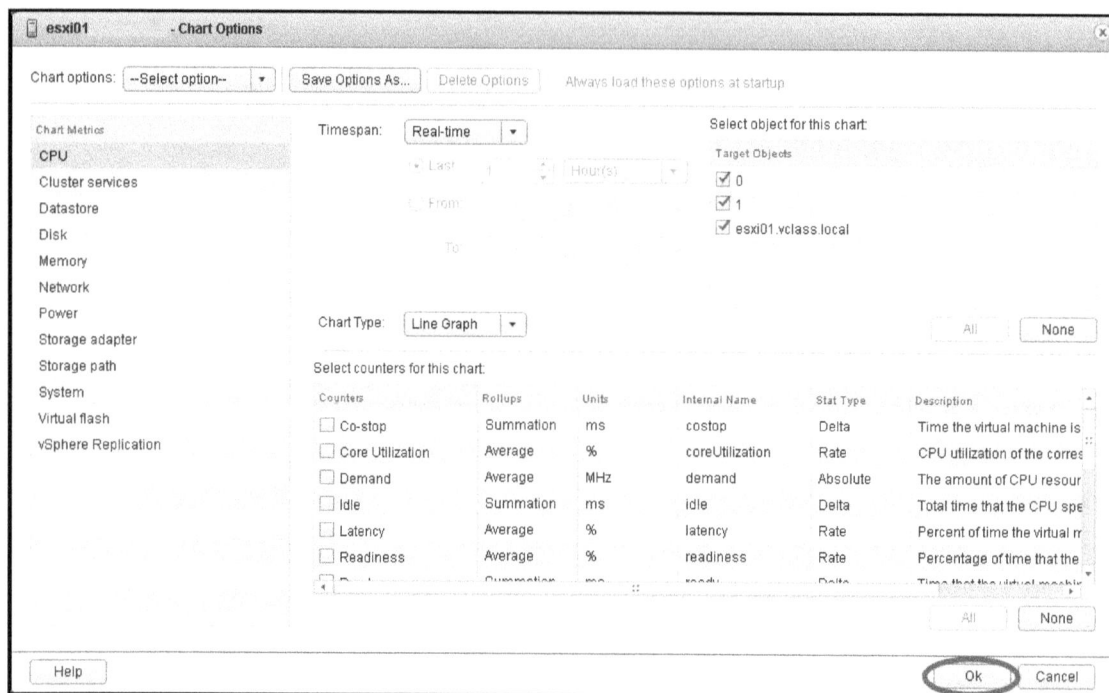

The options available using the advanced performance chart include:

- **Chart Metrics** – select which resource or object to view the available metrics for.
- **Timespan** – historical information can be used to see the past day, week, month, and year at a varying granularity. There is no option for true real-time results; real time is generated at a 20 second interval for a period of an hour. After an hour, those values get stored into 5-minute rollups. The weekly results get rolled up into 30-minute samples. Monthly results are rolled up into 2-hour samples. Annual samples are rolled up into daily intervals so the charts don't inundate the vCenter Server database.
- **Select objects for this chart** – objects are instances or aggregations of devices such as physical cores, vCPUs, HBAs, NICs, and so on.

- **Chart Type** – can choose line graphs or stacked graphs. A line graph shows the monitored instances independently, each plotted on a separate line in the chart. The stacked graph option shows each monitored instance stacked on top of each other for comparison purposes.
- **Select counters for this chart** – counters identify which statistics to collect with regard to the selected objects. For example, ready time for the selected vCPUs or packets dropped for the selected NIC. If unsure which counter to select, a description is provided in order to assist in this process. Consult the vSphere Monitoring and Performance guide for more information regarding available counters.

The selection of the counter determines what the unit of measurement is, the rollup, and the statistic type. Depending on which counter is selected, there are a few different statistic types that may be used:

- Rate – a value over a current interval, for example CPU usage
- Delta – a change from a previous interval, for example CPU ready
- Absolute – a value that is a completely independent value, for example, active memory

The unit of measurements dictates the standard in which the statistic quantity is measured. Another value that is determined by the counter select is the rollup. Rollup is the conversion between our statistic intervals. The past hour statistics are shown at a 20 second granularity, for instance. The rollup is the type of statistical values returned for that particular counter. There are a few different ways that the data can be rolled up:

- Average – collected data during an interval that is gathered and averaged
- Latest – represents the current value
- Minimum – minimum value is rolled up
- Maximum – maximum value is rolled up
- Summation – the data that is collected is summed and the measurement displayed is the sum of the data collected during the set interval

After this advanced performance chart has been customized as desired, the options can be preserved for future use by clicking on the **Save Options As** button.

Use advanced performance charts to gain a more granular view of an object's performance. An overview performance chart gives very limited information for common counters. If anything appears abnormal when viewing the overview performance chart then use an advanced performance chart to gain more insight with what is occurring. Once a bottleneck or constraint is identified, a solution can be formulated to resolve the issue.

For information regarding data collection intervals and levels, view the *vSphere Monitoring and Performance* guide.

Using esxtop

The `esxtop` and `resxtop` commands enable command-line monitoring for real-time ESXi host resource usage for each of the core four resources: CPU, memory, network, and disk. When this tool is used interactively, the data is viewed on different types of screens, one for each of the resources. The data presented includes some metrics that are not accessible using the overview or advanced performance charts. The only difference between `resxtop` and `esxtop` is that `esxtop` can only be started through the local shell of the ESXi host (using the DCUI or SSH) whereas `resxtop` can be used remotely.

There are three modes of execution for `esxtop` and `resxtop` available:

- Interactive mode – the default mode. This option provides real-time statistics that can be viewed by navigating throughout the different resource screens.
- Batch mode – this mode allows the collection of data in order to save the resource utilization statistics in a file. To do this, use the command `esxtop -b > filename.csv`. Alternatively, `resxtop` may be used.
- Replay mode – this mode uses data collected by the `vm-support` command and interprets and plays it back as `esxtop` statistics.

The `resxtop` utility is a vSphere CLI command; it therefore requires the vSphere CLI package or the **vSphere Management Assistant (vMA)**.

The following screenshot displays an example of running the `esxtop` utility directly in the ESXi Shell. First, open an SSH application, for example PuTTY, and connect to an ESXi host. SSH would need to be enabled for the target ESXi host prior to beginning this process.

If connecting to the ESXi Shell using an SSH application, ensure SSH is enabled on the desired ESXi host. For steps on how to enable SSH, check `http://vmware.com/kb/11791`.

Once authenticated, type `esxtop` to begin running this utility.

There are several statistics that appear on all the available views within `esxtop` (or `resxtop`) while running in interactive mode:

- The top line is the Uptime line; this displays the current time, the time since the last time ESXi was restarted, the number of worlds currently running, and CPU load averages. A world is a component that is schedulable, just like a process on a guest operating system. Worlds, just like processes, are scheduled by the VMkernel.

- Underneath that, the load averages over different time samples of the past one-minute, 5 minutes, and 15 minutes are displayed. These load averages take the running as well as the ready-to-run worlds into consideration. A load average of 1.00 means that there is full utilization of all physical CPUs; likewise, a load average of 2.00 means that the ESXi host system may need double as many physical CPUs as are currently available. A 0.50 load average would mean that the physical CPUs are half-utilized.

These are demonstrated at the top of the following screenshot:

```
esxi01.          - PuTTY                                                   _ □ ×
11:21:07pm up 1 day 19:12,  453 worlds,  0 VMs,  0 vCPUs; CPU load average: 0.02, 0.02, 0.01
PCPU USED(%):  0.8 2.4 AVG: 1.6
PCPU UTIL(%):  1.0 2.5 AVG: 1.7

      ID       GID NAME                NWLD   %USED    %RUN    %SYS     %WAIT %VMWAIT     %RDY
  755584    755584 esxtop.135053          1    2.01    2.00    0.00     97.86       -     0.01
       2         2 system               104    0.35    0.37    0.00  10386.24       -     0.48
     805       805 vmsyslogd.32998        3    0.12    0.12    0.00    299.42       -     0.02
       8         8 helper               162    0.10    0.10    0.00  16178.92       -     0.04
   15321     15321 vmtoolsd.35064         2    0.07    0.07    0.00    199.62       -     0.01
    5438      5438 sdrsInjector.33        2    0.04    0.04    0.00    108.84       -     0.00
   11834     11834 vpxa.34616            14    0.03    0.03    0.01   1397.64       -     0.02
    1702      1702 net-lacp.33181         3    0.03    0.03    0.00    299.55       -     0.01
    7365      7365 hostd.34039           18    0.02    0.02    0.00   1797.15       -     0.02
  747152    747152 vmkiscsid.13377        2    0.02    0.02    0.00    199.71       -     0.00
    2042      2042 nfsgssd.33314          1    0.02    0.02    0.00     99.84       -     0.00
  755543    755543 sshd.135048            1    0.02    0.02    0.00     99.84       -     0.00
   14003     14003 openwsmand.3489        3    0.01    0.01    0.00    299.58       -     0.00
    5013      5013 storageRM.33738        1    0.01    0.01    0.00     99.85       -     0.00
   16329     16329 sfcb-ProviderMa       10    0.01    0.01    0.00    998.37       -     0.00
    3135      3135 swapobjd.33504         1    0.00    0.00    0.00     99.84       -     0.00
    9116      9116 dcbd.34265             1    0.00    0.00    0.00     99.85       -     0.00
    5058      5058 rhttpproxy.3374        8    0.00    0.00    0.00    798.88       -     0.00
       9         9 drivers               12    0.00    0.00    0.00   1198.44       -     0.02
```

Monitoring CPU

The default view in esxtop is the CPU pane. In this utility, a group refers to a running virtual machine, a non-virtual machine, or a resource pool world. These groups will be assigned a group ID (GID).

Some of the common CPU statistics are:

- **%USED** – percentage of physical CPU core cycles used
- **%SYS** – percentage of time spent in the VMkernel to process interrupts and other system activities
- **%WAIT** – percentage of time spent in the block or busy wait state; includes idle
- **%RDY** – percentage of time ready to run, but not provided CPU resources on which to execute
- **%CSTP** – percentage of time spent in a ready, co-schedule state
- **%MLMTD** – percentage of time not running due to a limit
- **NWLD** – the number of worlds that are associated with a given group

The CPU pane is demonstrated in the previous screenshot.

Monitoring memory

To view the memory statistics, press the m key (upper or lowercase). This panel will display host-wide and group memory utilization information. The top line is the Uptime line; this displays the current time, the time since the last time ESXi was restarted, and the number of currently running worlds consuming memory and over-commitment averages. Underneath this line are multiple useful lines regarding ESXi host memory utilization; these are all displayed in megabytes (MB):

- **PMEM** – memory information for the server
- **VMKMEM** – memory statistics for the ESXi VMkernel
- **PSHARE** – amount of memory being shared using transparent page sharing
- **SWAP** – swap usage statistics
- **ZIP** – memory compression information
- **MEMCTL** – memory balloon data

The following screenshot displays `esxtop` in the memory view:

```
esxi01            - PuTTY                                                    _ □ X
11:25:11pm up 1 day 19:16, 449 worlds, 0 VMs, 0 vCPUs; MEM overcommit avg: 0.00, 0.00, 0.00  ▲
PMEM   /MB: 6143    total: 1242     vmk,120 other, 4779 free
VMKMEM/MB:  6114 managed:   326 minfree,  3348 rsvd,    2766 ursvd,  high state
PSHARE/MB:      21  shared,      21  common:      0 saving
SWAP  /MB:       0     curr,       0 rclmtgt:                 0.00 r/s,   0.00 w/s
ZIP   /MB:       0   zipped,       0   saved
MEMCTL/MB:       0     curr,       0  target,        0 max
  E:   NWLD = Num Members

     GID NAME                 MEMSZ     GRANT      CNSM     SZTGT      TCHD    TCHD W     SWCUR
    7365 hostd.34039          59.16     33.56     33.56     36.92      5.84      5.84      0.00
   11834 vpxa.34616           25.12     16.30     16.30     17.93      2.47      2.47      0.00
   16320 sfcb-ProviderMa      18.02     14.64     14.64     16.10      3.05      3.05      0.00
    5438 sdrsInjector.33      17.58      1.93      1.93      2.12      0.40      0.40      0.00
  747152 vmkiscsid.13377      16.84      2.63      2.63      2.89      0.12      0.12      0.00
   16329 sfcb-ProviderMa      16.21      7.07      7.07      7.78      2.21      2.21      0.00
     942 vobd.33017           12.17      2.03      2.03      2.23      0.14      0.14      0.00
   16083 dcui.35160           10.44      2.42      2.42      2.66      0.52      0.52      0.00
    5058 rhttpproxy.3374       8.80      3.78      3.78      4.16      0.57      0.57      0.00
     805 vmsyslogd.32998       7.71      5.36      5.36      5.89      4.93      4.93      0.00
    9238 smartd.34280          7.38      2.05      2.05      2.26      0.45      0.45      0.00
    9287 nscd.34286            6.05      0.20      0.20      0.22      0.04      0.04      0.00
     781 vmsyslogd.32995       5.65      4.56      4.56      5.01      4.22      4.22      0.00
   16614 sfcb-ProviderMa       5.02      1.98      1.98      2.18      0.58      0.58      0.00  ▼
```

There are a few more notable memory counters, which include:

- **MEMSZ** – amount of memory allocated to the group.
- **GRANT** – amount of memory actually mapped to the group.
- **CNSM** – amount of consumed memory.
- **SZTGT** – amount of memory that the ESXi VMkernel wants to allocate to the group.
- **MCTL?** – whether or not the memory balloon driver is installed. Y means yes, N means no.
- **MCTLSZ** – memory amount reclaimed by ballooning.
- **SWCUR** – current swap usage.
- **SWR/s** – swap reads per second, or the rate that ESXi swaps memory in from disk.
- **SWW/s** – swap writes per second, or the rate that ESXi swaps memory out to disk.
- **ZIP/s** – compressed memory per second.
- **UNZIP/s** – decompressed memory per second.

`esxtop` often shows more information than what is needed to troubleshoot a specific problem. To display only virtual machine instances, type V (uppercase V) and this will shift the view to only virtual machine resource utilization. The following screenshot demonstrates the memory view but filters the information to only virtual machines:

```
esxi01          - PuTTY                                                    _ □ ×
11:40:31pm up 1 day 19:31, 460 worlds, 1 VMs, 1 vCPUs; MEM overcommit avg: 0.00, 0.00, 0.00
PMEM   /MB: 6143    total: 1254     vmk,556 other, 4332 free
VMKMEM/MB:  6114 managed:   326 minfree,  3381 rsvd,   2733 ursvd,   high state
PSHARE/MB:     631 shared,      21 common:      610 saving
SWAP   /MB:       0    curr,       0 rclmtgt:             0.00 r/s,   0.00 w/s
ZIP    /MB:       0 zipped,       0   saved
MEMCTL/MB:        0    curr,       0 target,      665 max
  E:   NWLD = Num Members

    GID NAME             MEMSZ     GRANT      CNSM     SZTGT      TCHD   TCHD W    SWCUR
 761467 ExampleVM      1024.00   1024.00    414.12    437.86    983.04   860.16    0.00
```

Monitoring network

The network panel will display server-wide network utilization statistics. To view the network pane, press the n key (upper or lower-case). The statistical information for each configured virtual network device is arranged by port ID.

```
esxi01          - PuTTY                                                    _ □ ×
11:41:15pm up 1 day 19:32, 460 worlds, 1 VMs, 1 vCPUs; CPU load average: 0.01, 0.02, 0.01

  PORT-ID         USED-BY  TEAM-PNIC DNAME        PKTTX/s   MbTX/s    PSZTX   PKTRX/s  MbRX/
  33554433     Management       n/a vSwitch0         0.00     0.00     0.00      0.00    0.0
  33554434         vmnic0         - vSwitch0       134.28     0.28   268.00     48.83    0.0
  33554435 Shadow of vmnic0      n/a vSwitch0         0.00     0.00     0.00      0.00    0.0
  33554436           vmk0  vmnic0 vSwitch0         134.28     0.28   268.00     36.62    0.0
  33554437           vmk1  vmnic0 vSwitch0           0.00     0.00     0.00      0.00    0.0
  50331649     Management       n/a vSwitch1         0.00     0.00     0.00      0.00    0.0
  50331650         vmnic1         - vSwitch1         0.00     0.00     0.00      0.00    0.0
  50331651 Shadow of vmnic1      n/a vSwitch1         0.00     0.00     0.00      0.00    0.0
  50331652         vmnic3         - vSwitch1         0.00     0.00     0.00      0.00    0.0
  50331653 Shadow of vmnic3      n/a vSwitch1         0.00     0.00     0.00      0.00    0.0
  50331654 135996:ExampleVM vmnic3 vSwitch1         0.00     0.00     0.00      0.00    0.0
  67108865     Management       n/a vSwitch2         0.00     0.00     0.00      0.00    0.0
  67108866         vmnic2         - vSwitch2         0.00     0.00     0.00      0.00    0.0
  67108867 Shadow of vmnic2      n/a vSwitch2         0.00     0.00     0.00      0.00    0.0
  67108868           vmk2  vmnic2 vSwitch2           0.00     0.00     0.00      0.00    0.0
```

Some helpful network statistics are:

- **PORT-ID** – virtual network device port ID
- **USED-BY** – user for virtual network device
- **TEAM-PNIC** – physical NIC used for the team uplink
- **PKTTX/s** – packets transmitted per second
- **PKTRX/s** – packets received per second
- **MbTX/s** – MegaBits transmitted per second
- **MbRX/s** – MegaBits received per second
- **%DRPTX** – transmit packets dropped percentage
- **%DRPRX** – receive packets dropped percentage

More network counters can be added by pressing the f key (upper or lower case).

Monitoring storage

The next image displays the statistics that are available in the storage adapter view. Press *D* (upper or lowercase) to see the disk adapter information.

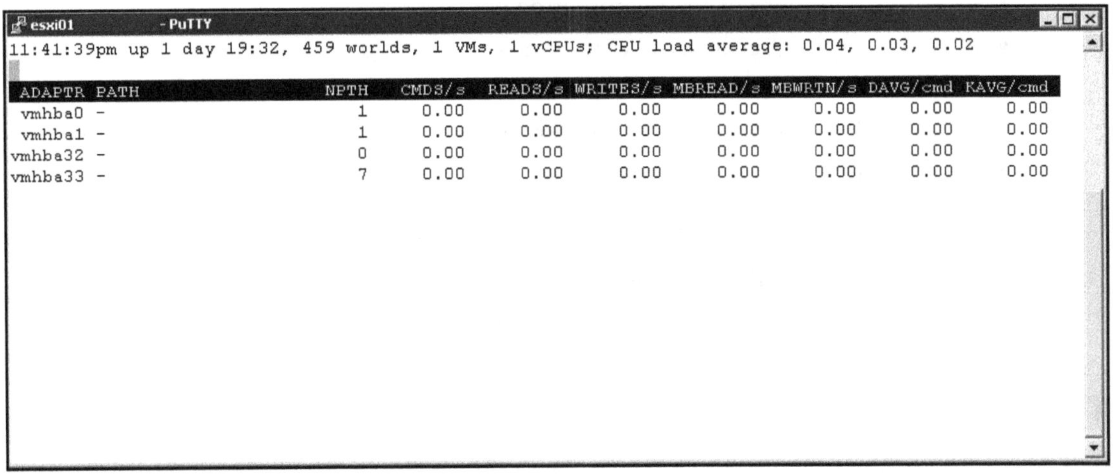

```
esxi01              - PuTTY                                                    _ □ ×
11:41:39pm up 1 day 19:32, 459 worlds, 1 VMs, 1 vCPUs; CPU load average: 0.04, 0.03, 0.02

ADAPTR PATH                 NPTH    CMDS/s   READS/s WRITES/s MBREAD/s MBWRTN/s DAVG/cmd KAVG/cmd
 vmhba0 -                     1      0.00     0.00     0.00     0.00     0.00     0.00     0.00
 vmhba1 -                     1      0.00     0.00     0.00     0.00     0.00     0.00     0.00
vmhba32 -                     0      0.00     0.00     0.00     0.00     0.00     0.00     0.00
vmhba33 -                     7      0.00     0.00     0.00     0.00     0.00     0.00     0.00
```

Pressing the *U* key (upper or lowercase) will display the storage device view. This view displays server-wide storage device information, demonstrated by the following screenshot:

```
esxi01          - PuTTY                                                    _ □ ×
11:42:24pm up 1 day 19:33, 460 worlds, 1 VMs, 1 vCPUs; CPU load average: 0.04, 0.03, 0.02

DEVICE                           CMDS/s  READS/s WRITES/s MBREAD/s MBWRTN/s
eui.28cc9920557ad9d5              0.00    0.00    0.00     0.00     0.00
eui.523873014aa8aaed              0.00    0.00    0.00     0.00     0.00
eui.68162383505096af              0.00    0.00    0.00     0.00     0.00
eui.8c851a79beb5b6b2              0.00    0.00    0.00     0.00     0.00
eui.b0465b2d00000000              0.00    0.00    0.00     0.00     0.00
eui.c234ca4000000000              0.00    0.00    0.00     0.00     0.00
eui.eb46ba2b92fb5ccb              0.00    0.00    0.00     0.00     0.00
mpx.vmhba0:C0:T0:L0               0.00    0.00    0.00     0.00     0.00
mpx.vmhba1:C0:T0:L0               0.00    0.00    0.00     0.00     0.00
```

A few common storage statistics include:

- **CMDS/s** – number of commands per second
- **READS/s** – number of read commands per second
- **WRITES/s** – number of write commands per second
- **MBREAD/s** – Megabytes ready per second
- **MBWRTN/s** – Megabytes written per second
- **DAVG/cmd** – average device read latency per command (in milliseconds)
- **KAVG/cmd** – average ESXi VMkernel latency per command (in milliseconds)

Once again, don't forget that the storage information for the virtual machines can be displayed by pressing *V* (uppercase *V*) in the disk device view.

The esxtop options

If at any point you are unsure of which options are available to you, press either *H* (upper or lowercase) or ? to print out all available interactive mode commands. The following screenshot demonstrates how the help option can be used and gives a brief summary of available choices and lists the esxtop displays:

```
┌─ esxi01.        - PuTTY                                                    _□×
│                                                                            ▲
│Interactive commands are:
│
│fF        Add or remove fields
│oO        Change the order of displayed fields
│s         Set the delay in seconds between updates
│#         Set the number of instances to display
│W         Write configuration file ~/.esxtop60rc
│k         Kill a world
│e         Expand/Rollup Disk World Statistics
│P         Expand/Rollup Disk Path Statistics
│t         Expand/Rollup Disk Partition Statistics
│L         Change the length of the DEVICE field
│
│Sort by:
│        r:READS/s        w:WRITES/s
│        R:MBREAD/s       T:MBWRTN/s
│        N:Default
│Switch display:
│        c:cpu            i:interrupt     m:memory      n:network
│        d:disk adapter   u:disk device   v:disk VM      p:power mgmt
│        x:vsan
├─────────────────────────────────────────────────────────────────────────
│Hit any key to continue:                                                    ▼
```

To change views simply press the key listed in the help menu.

Press *F* (upper or lowercase) to display all available statistics that can be added or removed from the current view. The following screenshot displays pressing f and viewing all statistics available in the memory pane:

```
┌─ esxi01.        - PuTTY                                                    _□×
│                                                                            ▲
│Current Field order: AbcdefghIjklmnop
│
│ * A:   DEVICE = Device Name
│   B:   ID = Path/World/Partition Id
│   C:   NUM = Num of Objects
│   D:   SHARES = Shares
│   E:   BLKSZ = Block Size (bytes)
│   F:   QSTATS = Queue Stats
│   G:   IOSTATS = I/O Stats
│   H:   RESVSTATS = Reserve Stats
│ * I:   LATSTATS/cmd = Overall Latency Stats (ms)
│   J:   LATSTATS/rd = Read Latency Stats (ms)
│   K:   LATSTATS/wr = Write Latency Stats (ms)
│   L:   ERRSTATS/s = Error Stats
│   M:   PAESTATS/s = PAE Stats
│   N:   SPLTSTATS/s = SPLIT Stats
│   O:   VAAISTATS= VAAI Stats
│   P:   VAAILATSTATS/cmd = VAAI Latency Stats (ms)
│
│Toggle fields with a-p, any other key to return: ▓
│                                                                            ▼
```

To add or remove fields, simply press the specified letter.

For information on all counters available within `esxtop` and `resxtop`, consult the *vSphere 6 Monitoring and Performance guide*.

Using alarms

An alarm is a notification in response to a selected condition or event for an object in the vCenter Server inventory. There are many predefined alarms for most objects within the vCenter Server inventory. The predefined alarms are configurable to an extent but if the alarm doesn't address a specific event or condition that you want to monitor then a custom alarm can be defined.

Custom alarms can be created as either condition-based or event-based. *Condition-based alarms* monitor the current condition or state of an object, whereas *event-based alarms* monitor for events that occur within vCenter.

Some examples of condition-based alarms include:

* An ESXi host becomes disconnected from vCenter
* A virtual machine is using 90% of its total memory
* A datastore's total space is 85% provisioned

Some examples of event-based alarms include:

* A vSphere license has expired
* SSH was enabled on an ESXi host
* A virtual machine was migrated

Depending on what you are trying to monitor for will dictate which type of alarm should be chosen.

Creating condition-based alarms

Use condition-based alarms to monitor a specific state or condition of an object.

To create an alarm:

1. Using the vSphere Web Client, browse to an object in the vCenter Server inventory.
2. Go to the **Manage** tab.
3. Select the **Alarm Definitions** button.
4. To create a new custom alarm, click on the green + icon.

This process is demonstrated in the following screenshot:

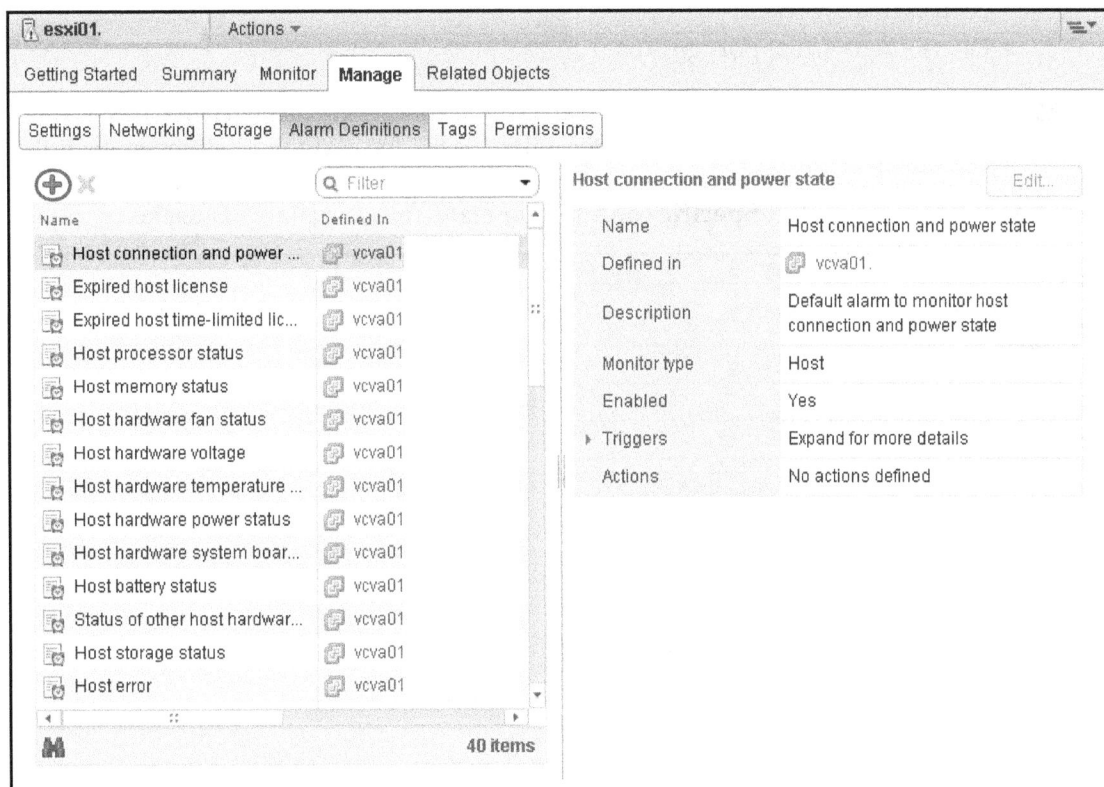

Clicking on the green + icon will result in a dialog allowing the creation of a custom alarm.

Enter a **Name** and **Description** for this alarm. On the **Monitor** choice, select what object should be monitored by this alarm. The available choices are:

- Datacenters
- Clusters
- ESXi hosts
- Virtual machines
- Datastores
- Networks
- Distributed switches
- Distributed virtual port groups

The **Monitor for** choice allows for the specification of a condition-based alarm or an event-based alarm. A condition-based alarm trigger will monitor the current condition state of the object and will notify when the threshold has been exceeded. To create this alarm as a condition-based alarm, select **Specific condition or state, for example CPU usage**.

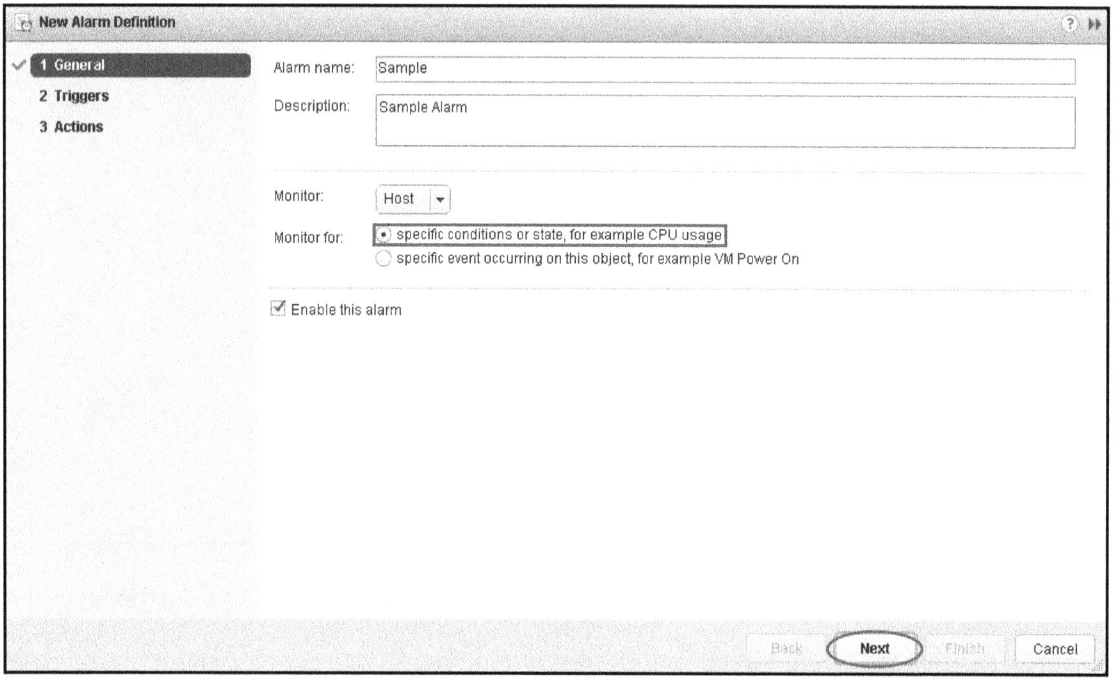

Leave the box checked for the alarm to be enabled. Click on **Next**.

Alarms do not have triggers configured by default. To configure a trigger, click on the + button. Specify what the **Trigger** will be, whether to monitor for a state above, below, or equal to a **Warning Condition** and/or **Critical Condition**. Specify what the **Warning Condition**, **Critical Condition**, and the condition length will be. Warnings mean getting concerned, whereas critical signifies that you need to take action immediately. The length should be set to an appropriate amount so that you are not notified of very temporary issues, such as a short CPU spike.

Towards the top of the screen, specify whether all conditions should be met (in a case where multiple triggers are specified) or any condition met will be met to generate an alarm. Once configured, click on **Next**.

An action can be configured in response to an alarm. There are three configurable actions available:

- Notification e-mails
- SNMP notification trap
- Run a command within vCenter

These colors and shapes signify an alarm's severity: a red diamond is a critical alert, a yellow triangle is a warning, and a green circle is normal.

These actions can be triggered when the state changes:

- From green circle to yellow triangle
- From yellow triangle to red diamond
- From red diamond to yellow triangle
- From yellow triangle to green circle

For each action, it can be specified to do nothing (leave empty), have vCenter Server do the action only one time (specify **Once**), or have vCenter Server repeat the action until a state change occurs (specify **Repeat**).

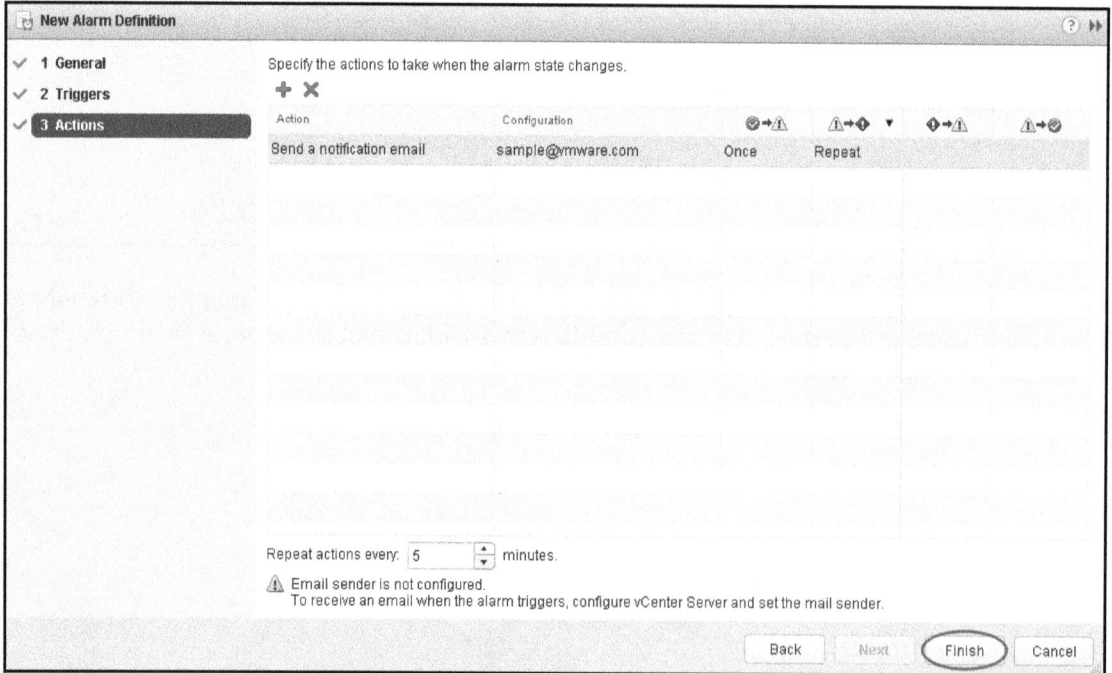

Specify the minutes desired for **Repeat actions every...**, which is 5 minutes by default. For the notification e-mail or SNMP trap, this must be set up in the advanced vCenter Server settings prior to configuring an alarm action.

Click on **Next** after configuration.

Creating event-based alarms

The process for creating an event-based alarm is similar, except that on the **General** pane, under **Monitor for**, select **specific event occurring on this object, for example VM Power On**.

Click on **Next**.

Event-based alarms do not rely on any kind of threshold or duration. This type of alarm uses **arguments**, **values**, and **operators** to identify a triggering event. The **Event** specified on the following screenshot is vSphere HA detecting a host failure. The **Argument** and **Operator** specifies that the datacenter name should be equal to the **Value** of *West*. So for this alarm to be triggered, any host residing in the *West* datacenter would have to be detected as failed by vSphere HA.

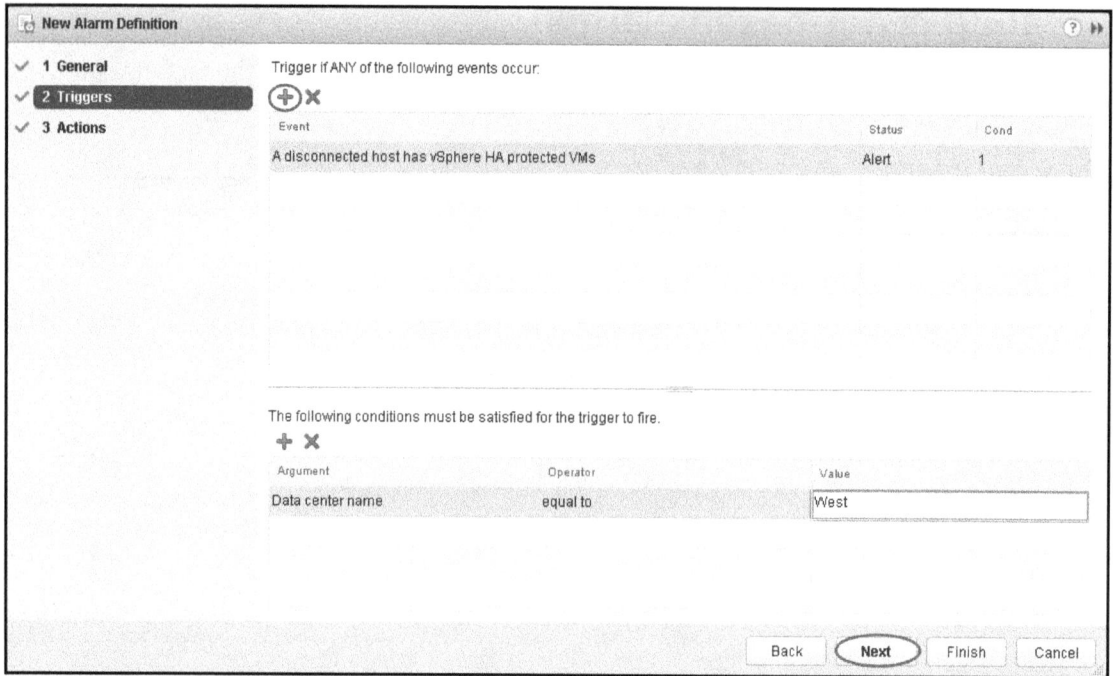

Upon configuring the triggers, click on **Next**. After specifying the Actions, click on **Finish**.

Other places to find information

There are many places that you can find performance and resource usage information besides the places we've discussed so far.

For example, consider using a guest operating system such as Perfmon. VMware Tools includes a Perfmon DLL providing additional counters, which gives the guest operating system some visibility into the ESXi host memory and CPU usage. Perfmon is an SNMP-based tool for Windows operating systems that is used for performance monitoring. Using these new counters available, such as VM Processor and VM Memory, enables the administrator to view actual use, which can be compared to the statistics viewed in the vSphere Web Client.

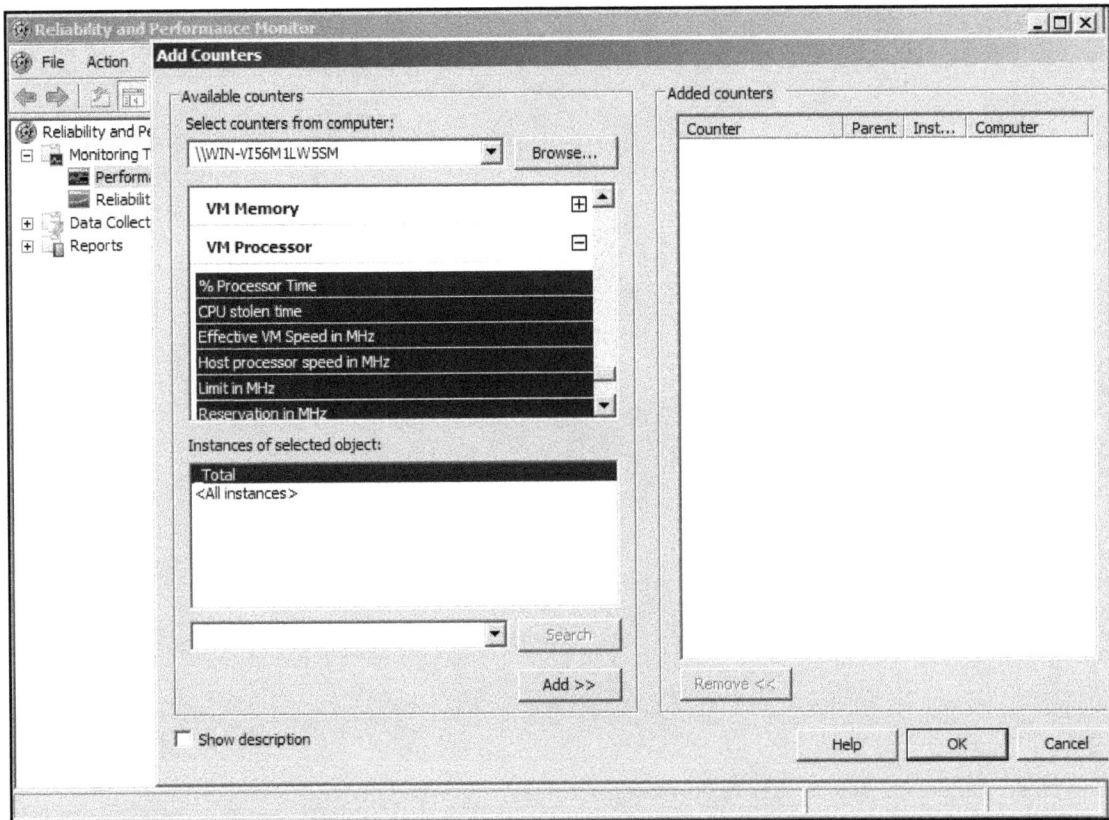

Without VMware Tools, the Perfmon counters are inaccurate because the guest operating system is unaware of virtualization.

Also consider using an object's **Summary** tab. The **Summary** tab can provide useful information for objects such as an ESXi host (demonstrated in the following screenshot), a virtual machine, resource pool, or a vApp. At the top-right of the screenshot, there are a few bars signifying the **Capacity**, **Free** amount, and **Used** amount of the **CPU**, **Memory**, and **Storage** resources.

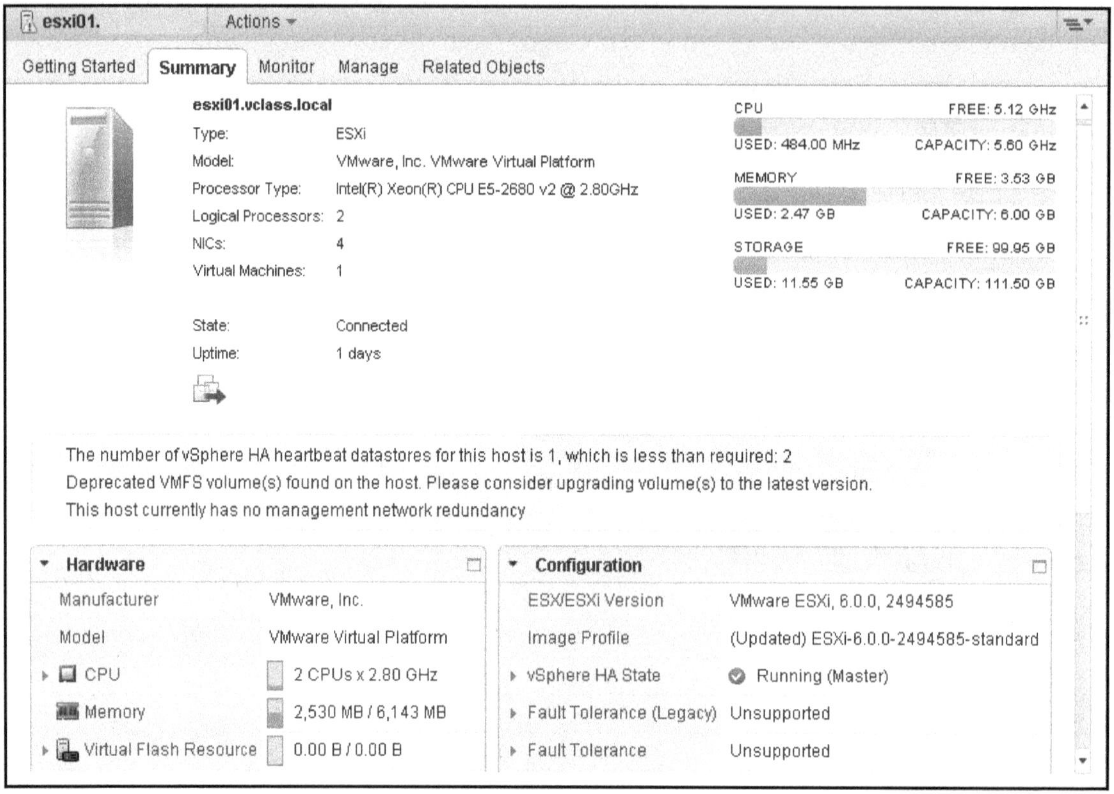

The **Hardware** pane shows the ESXi host information for the physical server. The **Configuration** pane provides the software information regarding the ESXi configuration. For example, the **ESXi Version** and **Image Profile** specify the specific ESXi build that is currently installed.

Another good place to view information is the **Monitor** tab. The following screenshot demonstrates the **Utilization** button on a resource pool. One of the more useful pieces of information is the **Guest Memory** pane. This demonstrates the amount of **Private** and **Shared** guest memory, which shows transparent page sharing in action. The **Shared** memory is the amount of memory currently being shared using TPS.

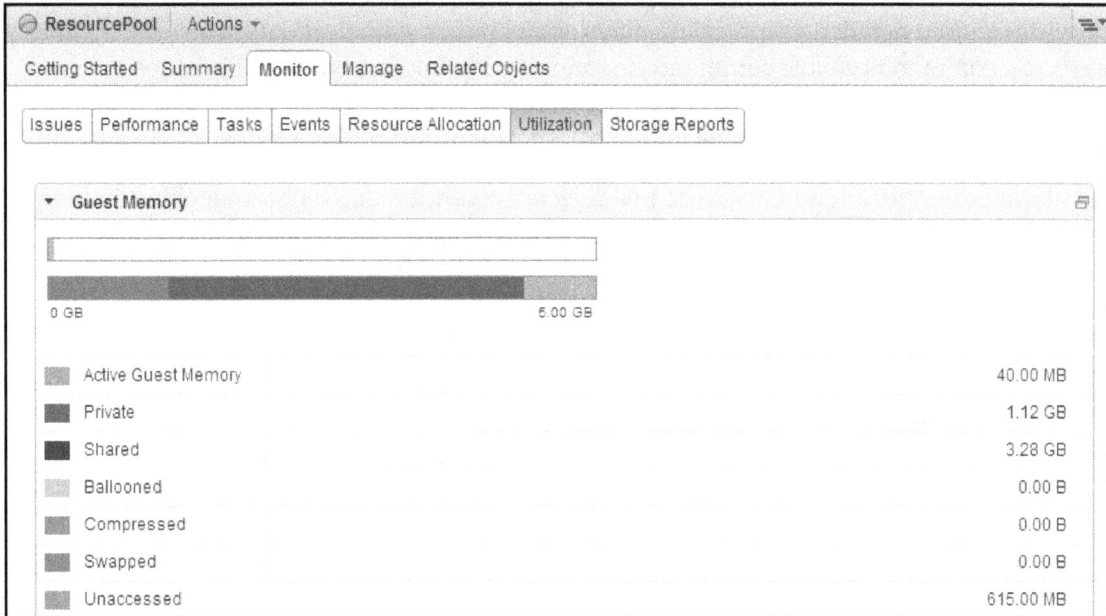

Here you can also see the amount of memory within this resource pool being **Ballooned**, **Compressed**, and **Swapped** during memory reclamation.

Summary

Performance charts can be displayed using the vSphere Client directly connected to an ESXi host directly, to a vCenter Server, or by using the vSphere Web Client. Overview performance charts display the performance statistics that are most useful for quickly diagnosing problems and monitoring performance. An advanced performance chart provides a more detailed graphical display for an object's statistical data. The esxtop and resxtop commands enable command-line monitoring for real-time ESXi host resource usage for each of the core four resources: CPU, memory, network, and disk. The esxtop and resxtop utilities are available in interactive, batch, and replay modes.

An alarm is a notification in response to a selected condition or event for an object in the vCenter Server inventory. A condition-based alarm trigger will monitor the current condition state of the object and will notify when the threshold has been exceeded. Event-based alarms use arguments, values, and operators to identify a triggering event. Alarms can be configured to perform an action of either running a command, sending a notification e-mail, or an SNMP notification trap.

The next chapter will discuss certificate management.

10
Certificate Management for a vSphere Environment

Secure Socket Layer (SSL) certificates are used to keep sensitive information sent between vSphere components encrypted so that only the intended recipient can decrypt it. When SSL certificates are used, the information is unreadable to anything other than the recipient that the information is sent to. This protects the information from being intercepted, thereby decreasing the possibility of a man-in-the-middle attack. vSphere 6 changes the way that SSL certificates are managed for vSphere components.

In this chapter, you will learn:

- SSL certificate concepts
- How VMware products use SSL certificates
- Using the SSL Certificate Manager Utility
- Installing the default root certificate
- Managing ESXi SSL certificates

SSL certificate concepts

Public Key Infrastructure (PKI) is based on digital certificates used for encrypting or signing data. These digital certificates are known as X.509 certificates. A certificate could be equated to having a virtual ID card. In the real world, we use IDs, like a passport or a driver's license, to prove our identities. The difference here is that certificates are not issued to people, but to computers or software packages.

PKI provides functions such as authenticating users, signing and distributing certificates, and managing and revoking certificates.

SSL certificates are used for establishing secure communication between vSphere components. By default, vSphere components use self-signed certificates and keys that are created during installation.

The main reason that the self-signed SSL certificates are replaced by **Certificate Authority (CA)** signed certificates is to prevent or reduce the risk of man-in-the-middle attacks. A man-in-the-middle attack is where a valid system is impersonated by using an untrusted or self- signed SSL certificate, and in this process is able to intercept encrypted traffic.

How VMware products use SSL certificates

vSphere 6 introduces a new component called the **Platform Services Controller (PSC)**, which is foundational to vCenter and its services. The PSC contains multiple services, which include:

- License service
- Single Sign-On (Secure Token Service, Identity Management Server)
- VMware Directory Service
- Lookup Service
- VMware Certificate Authority
- VMware Endpoint Certificate Store

The new **VMware Certificate Authority (VMCA)** and **VMware Endpoint Certificate Store (VECS)** change the way that certificates are deployed and managed in a vSphere environment.

vSphere components, such as vCenter Server, Single Sign-On, and the vSphere Web Client, use SSL certificates to securely communicate with each other and with ESXi hosts.

As of vSphere 6, the VMCA provisioned a signed certificate for each vCenter service and each ESXi host. There are several options for certificate management in vSphere 6: replace existing certificates with VMCA signed certificates, make VMCA a subordinate CA, or replace with custom certificates.

VMware Certificate Authority

Communication between components in a vSphere environment is secured with SSL certificates in order to ensure integrity and confidentiality. The VMCA is a complete certificate authority that is configured primarily via command lines. Luckily, once it is configured, there's not much required maintenance. The VMCA may be used to automatically issue SSL certificates to all vCenter Server components and the ESXi hosts.

Certificate deployment options

Historically, there have only been two options: use self-signed certificates or replace with CA signed certificates. With vSphere 6, there are four certificate deployment options: VMCA as a root CA, a subordinate CA, use of an external CA, or a hybrid configuration. These options will be discussed in the next few sections. Ultimately, the organization's level of security consciousness and regulation will determine which option should be used.

VMCA root CA

This option relies on the new VMCA component to provision and manage certificates for vCenter Server components and the ESXi hosts. The VMCA is available once the PSC is installed and it needs no additional configuration. Keep in mind that with any browser-based services, for example, the vSphere Web Client, an SSL warning will still appear until the VMCA root certificate is trusted in the browser.

This functionality is similar to the self-signed certificate option from prior releases, but in this case, it is a central CA that manages the certificates and certificate life cycle. This is the simplest deployment and is the default option. This is ideal for an infrastructure that currently does not replace the default certificates.

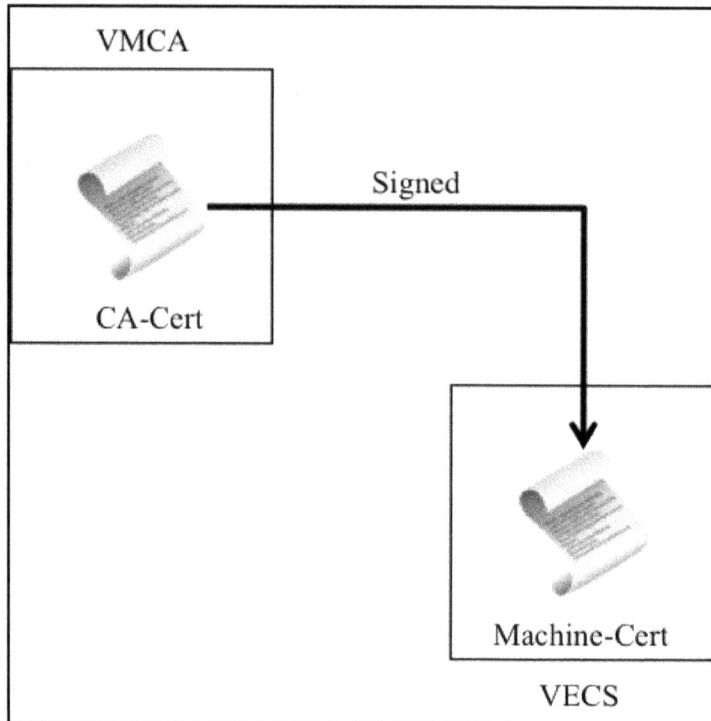

Subordinate VMCA

In this case, the VMCA imports a root signing certificate from a trusted enterprise root CA, making the VMCA a subordinate CA to the enterprise root CA. Any VMCA-aware component that is deployed will be issued a trusted SSL certificate. This includes the ESXi hosts being issued trusted certificates without additional manual configuration since the ESXi hosts are managed by the VMCA. Keep in mind that the vSphere 5.5 certificate replacement tool cannot be used with vSphere 6. A new command-line replacement utility, called vSphere Certificate Manager, is available.

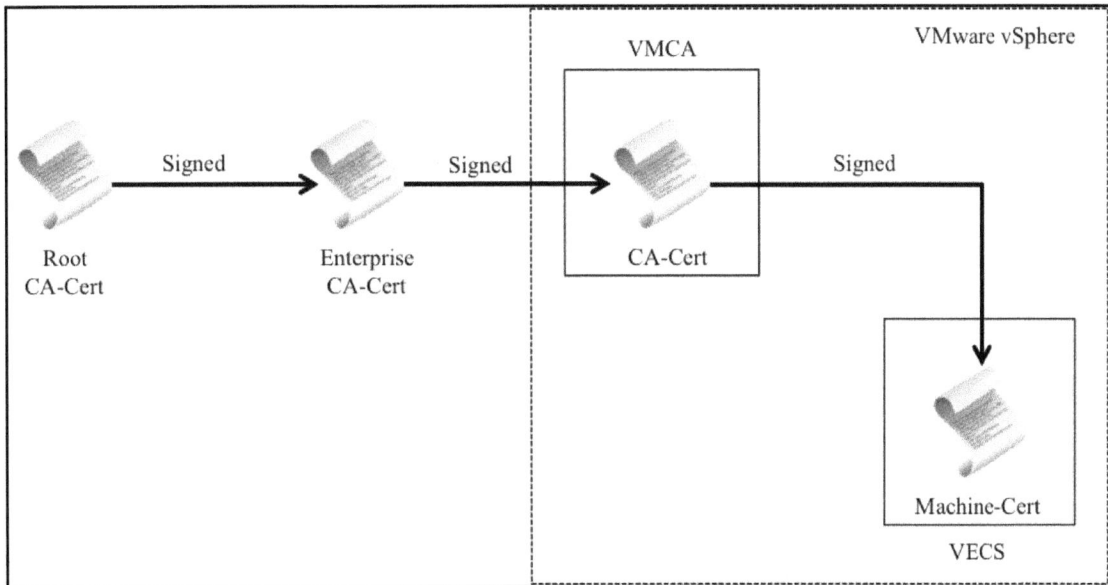

External CA

Using an external CA has always been a vSphere option. This option means that the VMCA is bypassed and the certificates are manually replaced by certificates from a trusted CA. This option is arguably the most secure but it is also the most tedious process of the certificate options.

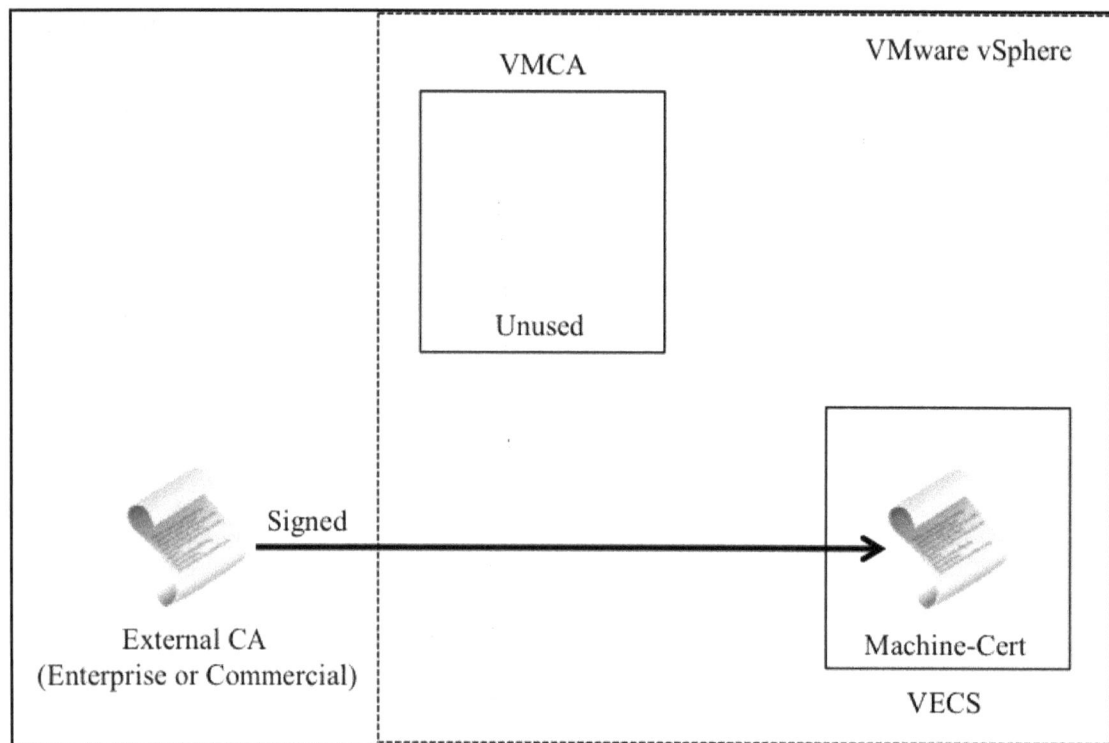

Hybrid

The last option is a hybrid scenario, which uses the VMCA as well as an external CA. This combination could, for example, have the VMCA issue certificates for internal-facing components (such as Single Sign-On and the ESXi hosts) and the other CA replace external-facing components (such as the vSphere Web Client).

VMware Endpoint Certificate Store

The VECS is a local keystore repository for private keys, certificates, and other certificate information. The VMCA may not be used as the certificate authority in your infrastructure, but it is mandatory that the VECS is used to store the certificates and other information. The only exception is the ESXi certificates, which are stored locally on the ESXi host.

Types and locations of certificates

The scope of certificates changed between vSphere 5.5 and vSphere 6. In vSphere 5.5, seven different services, each a solution user, required a certificate. A certificate was installed for each service individually. When scaling, this one-to-one relationship between service and solution user is not ideal. This relationship is demonstrated in the following diagram:

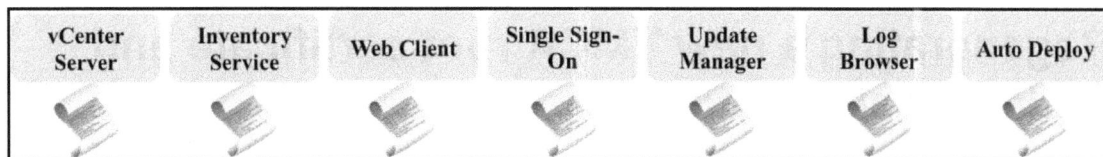

vCenter Server	Inventory Service	Web Client	Single Sign-On	Update Manager	Log Browser	Auto Deploy

This one-to-one relationship does not persist in vSphere 6 as it would be unmanageable because there are more than 20 services requiring a certificate with this release. To address this issue, the services are consolidated under a set of four solution users with only the solution users requiring a certificate. The following diagram demonstrates this:

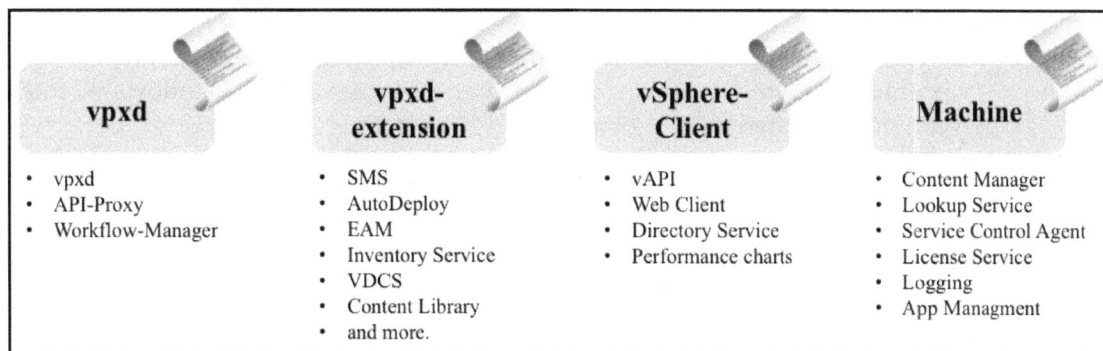

vpxd	**vpxd-extension**	**vSphere-Client**	**Machine**
• vpxd	• SMS	• vAPI	• Content Manager
• API-Proxy	• AutoDeploy	• Web Client	• Lookup Service
• Workflow-Manager	• EAM	• Directory Service	• Service Control Agent
	• Inventory Service	• Performance charts	• License Service
	• VDCS		• Logging
	• Content Library		• App Managment
	• and more.		

A solution user encapsulates the vCenter Server services, using the certificates to authenticate against vCenter Single Sign-On through a **Security Assertion Markup Language (SAML)** token exchange. Authentication against Single Sign-On must happen for each individual solution user.

Certificate revocation

In the event that there is suspected compromise of a certificate, all (including the VMCA root certificate) certificates should be replaced. vSphere 6 does not enforce certificate revocation. Revocation is a manual process.

Using the vSphere Certificate Manager Utility

The vSphere Certificate Manager Utility is a command-line utility that allows for most certificate management tasks to be performed interactively by the administrator. The utility prompts for which task to perform, for any additional information, and then automatically stops and starts services, ultimately replacing the certificates.

Regenerating a new VMCA root certificate and replacing all certificates

Regenerating a new VMCA root certificate and replacing all certificates is useful in the event that the certificates have expired or compromised and new certificates need to be issued to the different vSphere components.

To begin:

1. Console to the PSC virtual machine (in this case, it is an embedded deployment, meaning that the vCenter Server virtual machine is also the PSC virtual machine).
2. Enable and launch BASH. To launch the Certificate Manager Utility enter `/usr/lib/vmware-vmca/bin/certificate-manager` (for a Windows vCenter Server, this is located at `C:\Program Files\VMware\vCenter Server\vmcad\certificate-manager`) and press *Enter*.

3. Now that the Certificate Manager Utility has launched, select `4.` `Regenerate` `a` `new` `VMCA` `Root` `Certificate` `and` `replace` `all` `certificates` by pressing *4* and then *Enter*. (Optionally, option `8.` `Reset` `all` `Certificates` may also be chosen.)

```
Last login: Thu May 26 00:00:25 UTC 2016 from student-a.vclass.local on pts/0
Last login: Thu May 26 03:43:16 2016 from student-a.vclass.local
vcsa-a:~ # /usr/lib/vmware-vmca/bin/certificate-manager
 _ _ _ _ _ _ _ _ _ _ _ _ _ _ _ _ _ _ _ _ _ _ _ _ _ _ _ _ _ _ _ _ _
|                                                                   |
|        *** Welcome to the vSphere 6.0 Certificate Manager  ***    |
|                                                                   |
|                   -- Select Operation --                          |
|                                                                   |
|        1. Replace Machine SSL certificate with Custom Certificate |
|                                                                   |
|        2. Replace VMCA Root certificate with Custom Signing       |
|           Certificate and replace all Certificates                |
|                                                                   |
|        3. Replace Machine SSL certificate with VMCA Certificate   |
|                                                                   |
|        4. Regenerate a new VMCA Root Certificate and              |
|           replace all certificates                                |
|                                                                   |
|        5. Replace Solution user certificates with                 |
|           Custom Certificate                                      |
|                                                                   |
|        6. Replace Solution user certificates with VMCA certificates|
|                                                                   |
|        7. Revert last performed operation by re-publishing old    |
|           certificates                                            |
|                                                                   |
|        8. Reset all Certificates                                  |
|_ _ _ _ _ _ _ _ _ _ _ _ _ _ _ _ _ _ _ _ _ _ _ _ _ _ _ _ _ _ _ _ _|
Note : Use Ctrl-D to exit.
Option[1 to 8]: 4
```

4. Enter the SSO administrator (`administrator@vsphere.local`) password (this is defined during installation).

5. Press *Y* to reconfigure the `certool.cfg` file.

6. Enter the values as prompted:

- Enter proper value for 'Country' [Previous value: US]:
- Enter proper value for 'Name' [Previous value: Acme]:
- Enter proper value for 'Organization' [Previous value: AcmeOrg]:
- Enter proper value for 'OrgUnit' [Previous value: AcmeOrg Engineering]:
- Enter proper value for 'State' [Previous value: California]:
- Enter proper value for 'Locality' [Previous value: Palo Alto]:
- Enter proper value for 'IPAddress' [optional]:
- Enter proper value for 'Email' [Previous value: email@acme.com]:
- Enter proper value for 'Hostname' [Enter valid Fully Qualified Domain Name (FQDN), For Example : example.domain.com]:

```
Please provide valid SSO password to perform certificate operations.
Password:
Certool.cfg file exists, Do you wish to reconfigure : Option[Y/N] ? : y

Press Enter key to skip optional parameters or use Previous value.

Enter proper value for 'Country' [Previous value : US] :

Enter proper value for 'Name' [Previous value : Acme] :

Enter proper value for 'Organization' [Previous value : AcmeOrg] :

Enter proper value for 'OrgUnit' [Previous value : AcmeOrg Engineering] :

Enter proper value for 'State' [Previous value : California] :

Enter proper value for 'Locality' [Previous value : Palo Alto] :

Enter proper value for 'IPAddress' [optional] :

Enter proper value for 'Email' [Previous value : email@acme.com] :

Enter proper value for 'Hostname' [Enter valid Fully Qualified Domain Name(FQDN), For Example : example.domain.com] : vc
sa-a.vclass.local

You are going to regenerate Root Certificate and all other certificates using VMCA
Continue operation : Option[Y/N] ? : y
```

7. As shown in the following screeenshot, type Y to confirm the request in order to proceed.

```
You are going to regenerate Solution User Certificates using VMCA
Continue operation : Option[Y/N] ? : y
Status : 100% Completed [All tasks completed successfully]
```

8. This will take several minutes to complete.

The completion of this task will result in a replacement of the VMCA root certificate with a new certificate and newly issued replacement certificates for each of the solution users.

Configuring VMCA as a subordinate CA

This section will cover configuring the VMCA as a subordinate certificate authority. The procedure entails the VMCA importing a root signing certificate from a trusted enterprise root CA, therefore making the VMCA a subordinate CA to the enterprise root CA.

To begin this process:

1. Console to the PSC virtual machine (in this case, it is an embedded deployment, meaning that the vCenter Server virtual machine is also the PSC virtual machine).

2. Enable and launch BASH. To launch the Certificate Manager Utility enter
   `/usr/lib/vmware-vmca/bin/certificate-manager` (for a Windows vCenter
   Server, this is located at `C:\Program Files\VMware\vCenter`
   `Server\vmcad\certificate-manager`) and press *Enter*.

```
VMware vCenter Server Appliance 6.0.0

Type: vCenter Server with an embedded Platform Services Controller

root@vcsa-a.vclass.local's password:
Last login: Tue May 24 22:18:01 2016 from student-a.vclass.local
Connected to service

    * List APIs: "help api list"
    * List Plugins: "help pi list"
    * Enable BASH access: "shell.set --enabled True"
    * Launch BASH: "shell"

Command> shell.set --enabled True
Command> shell
        ---------- !!!! WARNING WARNING WARNING !!!! ----------

Your use of "pi shell" has been logged!

The "pi shell" is intended for advanced troubleshooting operations and while
supported in this release, is a deprecated interface, and may be removed in a
future version of the product.  For alternative commands, exit the "pi shell"
and run the "help" command.

The "pi shell" command launches a root bash shell.  Commands within the shell
are not audited, and improper use of this command can severely harm the
system.

Help us improve the product!  If your scenario requires "pi shell," please
submit a Service Request, or post your scenario to the
communities.vmware.com/community/vmtn/server/vcenter/cloudvm forum.

vcsa-a:~ # /usr/lib/vmware-vmca/bin/certificate-manager
```

3. Now that the Certificate Manager Utility has launched, select 2. Replace VMCA Root certificate with Custom Signing Certificate and replace all Certificates by pressing *2* and then *Enter*.

```
vcsa-a:~ # /usr/lib/vmware-vmca/bin/certificate-manager
- - - - - - - - - - - - - - - - - - - - - - - - - - - - - - - - - - - -
|                                                                       |
|         *** Welcome to the vSphere 6.0 Certificate Manager  ***       |
|                                                                       |
|                      -- Select Operation --                           |
|                                                                       |
|       1. Replace Machine SSL certificate with Custom Certificate      |
|                                                                       |
|       2. Replace VMCA Root certificate with Custom Signing            |
|          Certificate and replace all Certificates                     |
|                                                                       |
|       3. Replace Machine SSL certificate with VMCA Certificate        |
|                                                                       |
|       4. Regenerate a new VMCA Root Certificate and                   |
|          replace all certificates                                     |
|                                                                       |
|       5. Replace Solution user certificates with                      |
|          Custom Certificate                                           |
|                                                                       |
|       6. Replace Solution user certificates with VMCA certificates    |
|                                                                       |
|       7. Revert last performed operation by re-publishing old         |
|          certificates                                                 |
|                                                                       |
|       8. Reset all Certificates                                       |
|                                                                       |
- - - - - - - - - - - - - - - - - - - - - - - - - - - - - - - - - - - -
Note : Use Ctrl-D to exit.
Option[1 to 8]: 2
```

4. Enter the password for the SSO account (administrator@vsphere.local).

```
Please provide valid SSO password to perform certificate operations.
Password:
```

5. Press *1* to select `1. Generate Certificate Signing Request(s) and Key(s) for VMCA Root Signing certificate`. This will generate the private key (the `.key` file) and the certificate signing request (the `.csr` file). The `.csr` file is needed for the certificate authority to grant a certificate.

```
Please provide valid SSO password to perform certificate operations.
Password:
        1. Generate Certificate Signing Request(s) and Key(s) for VMCA Root Signing certificate

        2. Import custom certificate(s) and key(s) to replace existing VMCA Root Signing certificate

Option [1 or 2]: 1
```

6. You will be prompted to enter an **Output directory path**. The example uses `/cert/` (a custom-made directory for this specific purpose).

```
Please provide valid SSO password to perform certificate operations.
Password:
        1. Generate Certificate Signing Request(s) and Key(s) for VMCA Root Signing certificate

        2. Import custom certificate(s) and key(s) to replace existing VMCA Root Signing certificate

Option [1 or 2]: 1

Please provide a directory location to write the CSR(s) and PrivateKey(s) to:
Output directory path: /cert/
2016-05-24T22:46:17.279Z   Running command: ['/usr/lib/vmware-vmca/bin/certool', '--genkey', '--privkey', '/cert/root_si
gning_cert.key', '--pubkey', '/tmp/pubkey.pub']
2016-05-24T22:46:17.472Z   Done running command
2016-05-24T22:46:17.472Z   Running command: ['/usr/lib/vmware-vmca/bin/certool', '--gencsrfromcert', '--privkey', '/cert
/root_signing_cert.key', '--cert', '/var/lib/vmware/vmca/root.cer', '--csrfile', '/cert/root_signing_cert.csr']
2016-05-24T22:46:17.514Z   Done running command

CSR generated at: /cert/root_signing_cert.csr
        1. Continue to importing Custom certificate(s) and key(s) for VMCA Root Signing certificate

        2. Exit certificate-manager

Option [1 or 2]: 
```

7. Once finished, it will say `Done running command`, as demonstrated in the previous screenshot. Minimize, but do not close, this session as it will be used again later.

8. Open a similar tool, WinSCP, connect to the PSC (in this case, the embedded vCenter Server appliance), and navigate to the directory that was used for the output of the `.csr` and `.key` files. Copy the `.csr` file to a directory on your desktop. Leave the `.key` file as it will be needed later on.

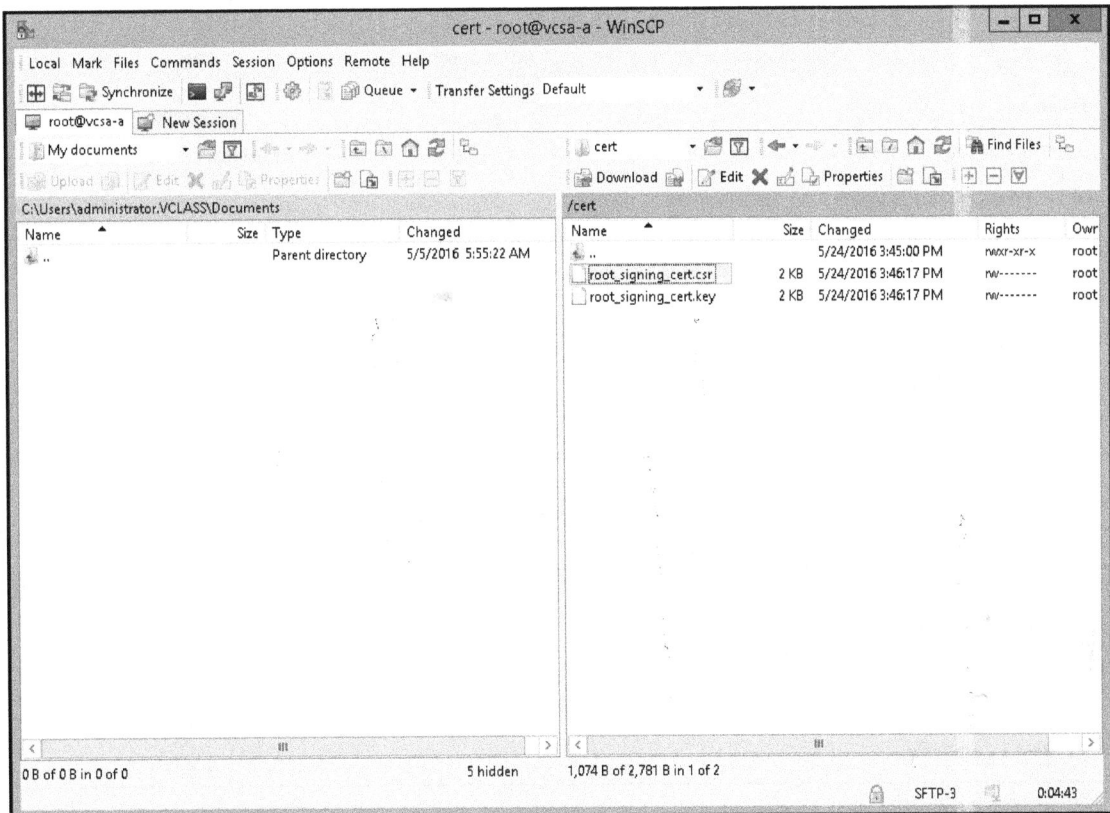

9. Next, open up a web browser. Go to `https://<CA FQDN>/certsrv` and click on the **Request a certificate** link.

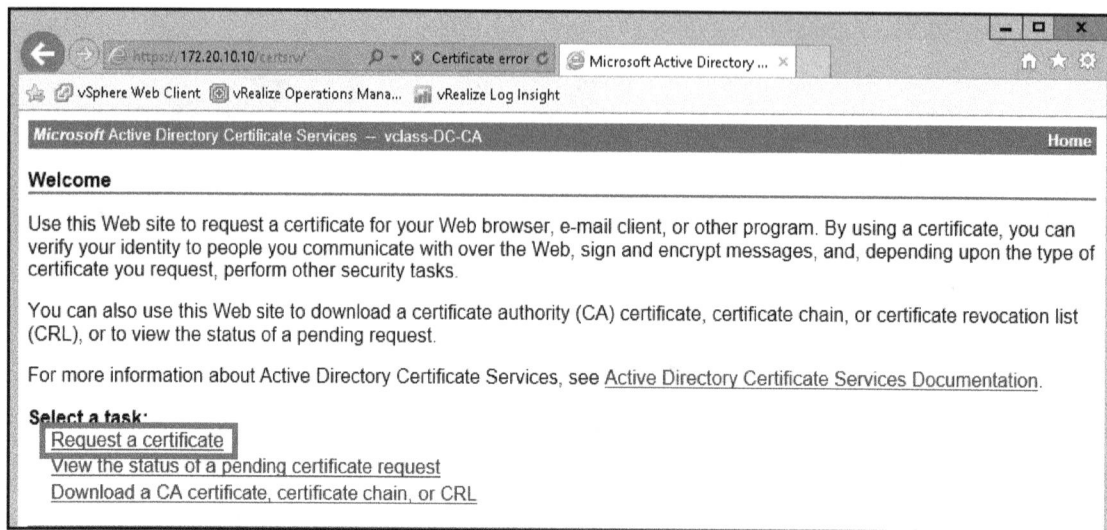

10. Select **Or, submit an advanced certificate request**.

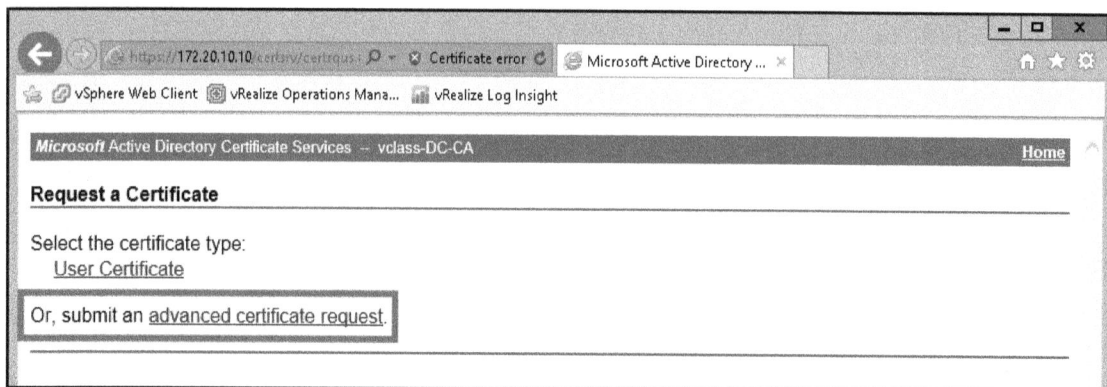

11. This brings up the **Submit a Certificate Request or Renewal Request** form. The next few steps will describe filling this form out.

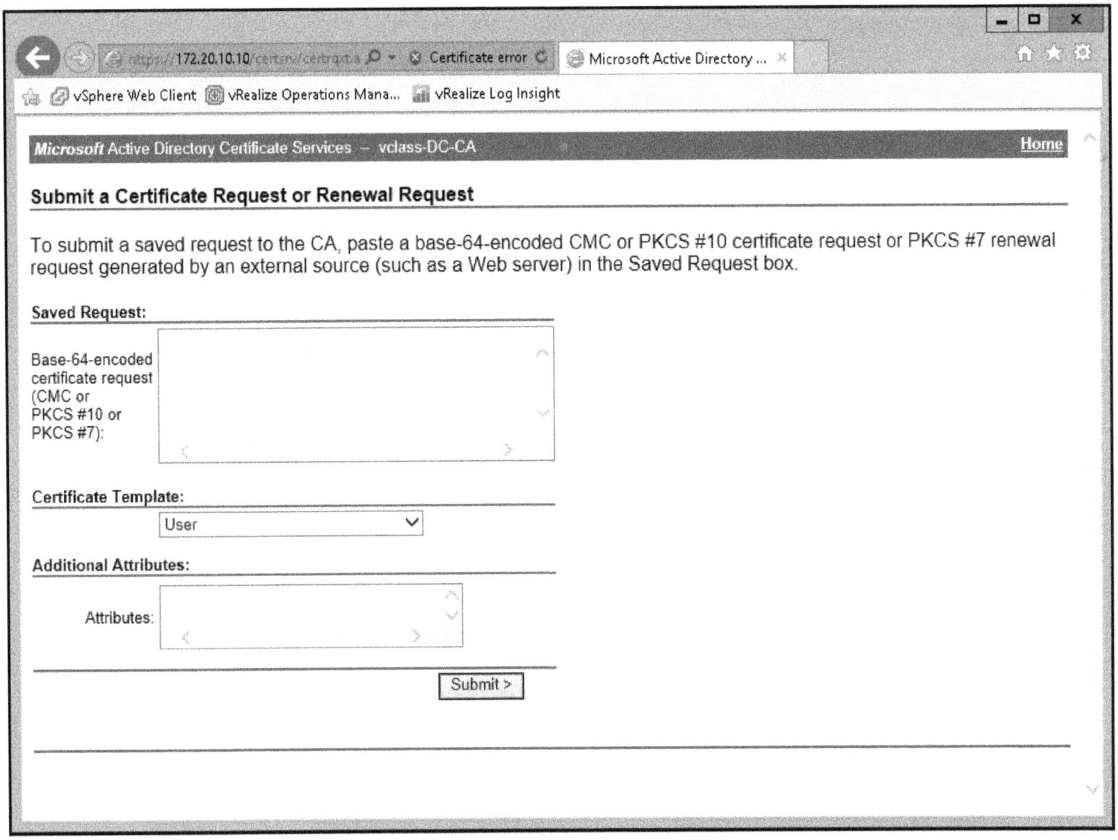

12. To start, open up the `.csr` file using Notepad or a similar application. Copy the contents of the `.csr` file. The contents of a `.csr` file are demonstrated in the following screenshot:

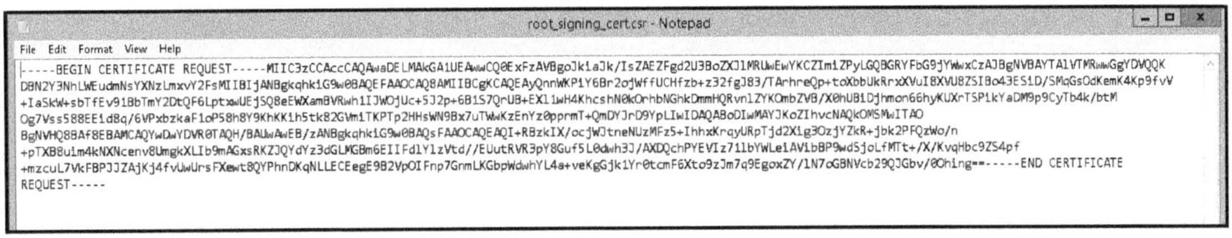

13. Paste the contents of the `.csr` file into the **Base-64-encoded certificate request (CMC or PKCS #10 or PKCS #7)** section. Under the **Certificate Template** section, select the dropdown and choose the **Subordinate Certification Authority** option. No attributes should be added. Click on the **Submit** button when finished.

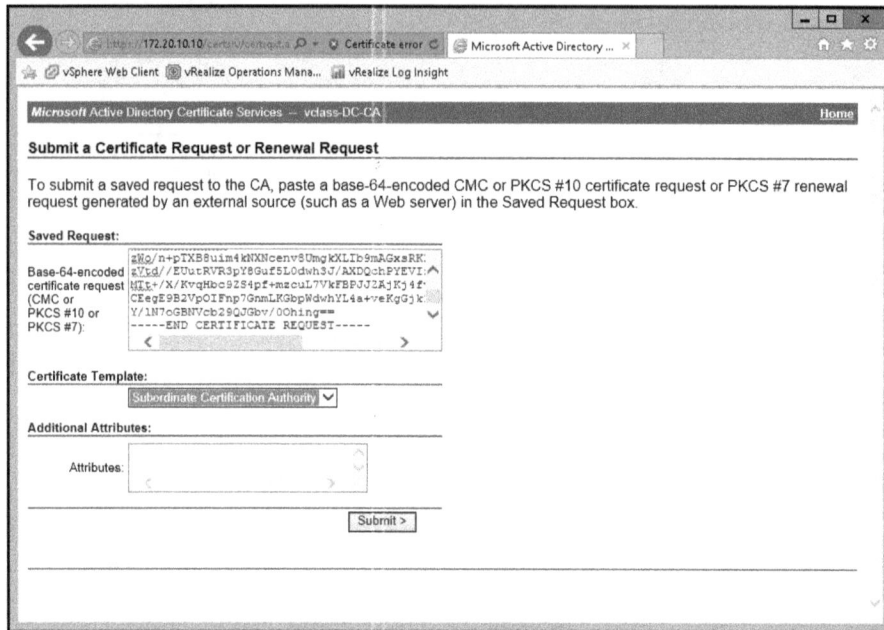

14. The certificate authority will issue a certificate that is available for download. Ensure that you select **Base 64 encoded** and click on **Download certificate**.

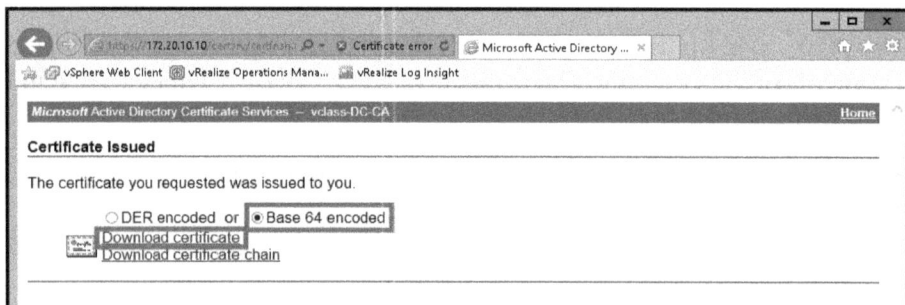

15. The next part is a little bit tricky; you need to concatenate the certificate that was just generated and downloaded with the certificate authority's root CA into a single `.cer` file. First, copy the contents of the certificate that was just downloaded and then follow it with the root CA certificate contents. Save this file as `root_signing_chain.cer` or something similar, just ensure that `.cer` is the file extension. An example of this is demonstrated in the following screenshot:

16. Switch back to the **Certificate Manager Utility** window where we left off in step 7. Press *1* to choose the `1. Continue to importing Custom certification(s) and key(s) for VMCA Root Signing certificate` option and hit *Enter*.

```
CSR generated at: /cert/root_signing_cert.csr
        1. Continue to importing Custom certificate(s) and key(s) for VMCA Root Signing certificate

        2. Exit certificate-manager

Option [1 or 2]: 1

Please provide valid custom certificate for Root.
File : /cert/intermediate.cer
```

17. Enter the path for the `.cer` and `.key` files. Enter *Y* to replace the certificates.

```
CSR generated at: /cert/root_signing_cert.csr
        1. Continue to importing Custom certificate(s) and key(s) for VMCA Root Signing certificate

        2. Exit certificate-manager

Option [1 or 2]: 1

Please provide valid custom certificate for Root.
File : /cert/intermediate.cer

Please provide valid custom key for Root.
File : /cert/root_signing_cert.key

You are going to replace Root Certificate with custom certificate and regenerate all other certificates
Continue operation : Option[Y/N] ? : y
```

18. The following screenshot demonstrates the required values for the `certool.cfg` file:

```
You are going to replace Root Certificate with custom certificate and regenerate all other certificates
Continue operation : Option[Y/N] ? : y
Status : 35% Completed [Replaced Root Cert...]
Please configure certool.cfg file with proper values before proceeding to next step.

Press Enter key to skip optional parameters or use Default value.

Enter proper value for 'Country' [Default value : US] :

Enter proper value for 'Name' [Default value : Acme] :

Enter proper value for 'Organization' [Default value : AcmeOrg] :

Enter proper value for 'OrgUnit' [Default value : AcmeOrg Engineering] :

Enter proper value for 'State' [Default value : California] :

Enter proper value for 'Locality' [Default value : Palo Alto] :

Enter proper value for 'IPAddress' [optional] :

Enter proper value for 'Email' [Default value : email@acme.com] :

Enter proper value for 'Hostname' [Enter valid Fully Qualified Domain Name(FQDN), For Example : example.domain.com] : vc
sa-a.vclass.local
Status : 70% Completed [stopping services...]
```

19. It will take several minutes for the services to restart.

20. To validate that the SSL certificate installation has completed, open a web browser and go to `https://<PSC FQDN>/websso/`. From here, open the certificate properties for the site by clicking on the lock icon at the top of the navigation bar.

21. Once the Certificate dialog pops up, select the **Certificate Path** tab. Verify that all enterprise CAs are listed. If only a single entry is on the list, this means that the VMCA subordinate CA is not trusted. The following screenshot shows the certificate chain:

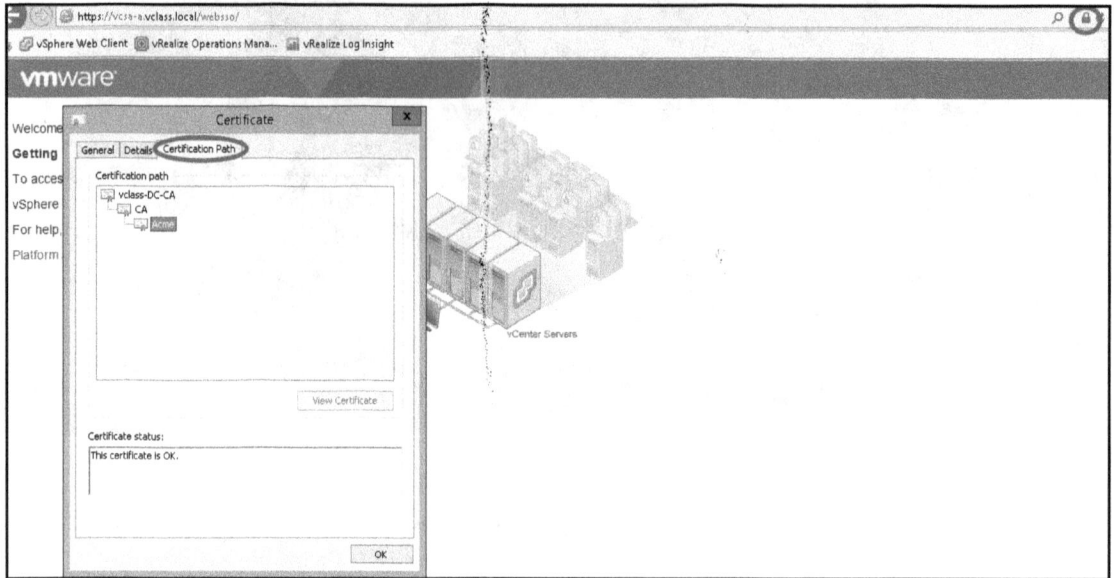

Replacing all certificates with custom certificates

It may be required by security policy to use CA (other than VMCA) signed certificates for the vSphere components. The Certificate Manager Utility can be used to replace the solution user certificates.

To get started:

1. Console to the PSC virtual machine (in this case, it is an embedded deployment, meaning that the vCenter Server virtual machine is also the PSC virtual machine).
2. Enable and launch BASH. To launch the Certificate Manager Utility enter `/usr/lib/vmware-vmca/bin/certificate-manager` (for a Windows vCenter Server, this is located at `C:\Program Files\VMware\vCenter Server\vmcad\certificate-manager`) and press *Enter*.

3. Now that the Certificate Manager Utility has launched, select 5. `Replace Solution user certificates Custom Certificate` by pressing *5* and then *Enter.*

```
vcsa-a:~ # /usr/lib/vmware-vmca/bin/certificate-manager
  _ _ _ _ _ _ _ _ _ _ _ _ _ _ _ _ _ _ _ _ _ _ _ _ _ _ _ _ _
 |                                                                          |
 |         *** Welcome to the vSphere 6.0 Certificate Manager  ***          |
 |                                                                          |
 |                        -- Select Operation --                            |
 |                                                                          |
 |         1. Replace Machine SSL certificate with Custom Certificate       |
 |                                                                          |
 |         2. Replace VMCA Root certificate with Custom Signing             |
 |            Certificate and replace all Certificates                      |
 |                                                                          |
 |         3. Replace Machine SSL certificate with VMCA Certificate         |
 |                                                                          |
 |         4. Regenerate a new VMCA Root Certificate and                    |
 |            replace all certificates                                      |
 |                                                                          |
 |         5. Replace Solution user certificates with                       |
 |            Custom Certificate                                            |
 |                                                                          |
 |         6. Replace Solution user certificates with VMCA certificates     |
 |                                                                          |
 |         7. Revert last performed operation by re-publishing old          |
 |            certificates                                                  |
 |                                                                          |
 |         8. Reset all Certificates                                        |
 |  _ _ _ _ _ _ _ _ _ _ _ _ _ _ _ _ _ _ _ _ _ _ _ _ _ _ _ _ _ _ _ _ _ _ _ |
Note : Use Ctrl-D to exit.
Option[1 to 8]: 5

Please provide valid SSO password to perform certificate operations.
Password: 
```

4. Enter the SSO administrator (`administrator@vsphere.local`) password. Select 1. `Generate Certificate Signing Request(s) and Key(s) for Solution User Certificates` by pressing *1* and pressing *Enter.*

```
Please provide valid SSO password to perform certificate operations.
Password:
         1. Generate Certificate Signing Request(s) and Key(s) for Solution User Certificates

         2. Import custom certificate(s) and key(s) to replace existing Solution User Certificates

Option [1 or 2]: 1
```

5. Provide an output directory to place the certificate signing requests and keys. The example uses a custom-made directory `/cert/`.

6. Once the certificate signing requests and keys have been copied to the output directory, the tool should specify `Done running command`.

```
Option [1 or 2]: 1

Please provide a directory location to write the CSR(s) and PrivateKey(s) to:
Output directory path: /cert/
2016-05-25T22:10:41.311Z    Running command: ['/usr/lib/vmware-vmca/bin/certool', '--genkey', '--privkey', '/cert/machine
.key', '--pubkey', '/tmp/pubkey.pub']
2016-05-25T22:10:41.354Z    Done running command
2016-05-25T22:10:41.355Z    Running command: ['/usr/lib/vmware-vmca/bin/certool', '--gencsrfromcert', '--privkey', '/cert
/machine.key', '--cert', '/tmp/vecs_crt.crt', '--csrfile', '/cert/machine.csr']
2016-05-25T22:10:41.373Z    Done running command

CSR generated at: /cert/machine.csr
2016-05-25T22:10:41.384Z    Running command: ['/usr/lib/vmware-vmca/bin/certool', '--genkey', '--privkey', '/cert/vpxd.ke
y', '--pubkey', '/tmp/pubkey.pub']
2016-05-25T22:10:41.576Z    Done running command
2016-05-25T22:10:41.577Z    Running command: ['/usr/lib/vmware-vmca/bin/certool', '--gencsrfromcert', '--privkey', '/cert
/vpxd.key', '--cert', '/tmp/vecs_crt.crt', '--csrfile', '/cert/vpxd.csr']
2016-05-25T22:10:41.594Z    Done running command

CSR generated at: /cert/vpxd.csr
2016-05-25T22:10:41.606Z    Running command: ['/usr/lib/vmware-vmca/bin/certool', '--genkey', '--privkey', '/cert/vpxd-ex
tension.key', '--pubkey', '/tmp/pubkey.pub']
2016-05-25T22:10:41.759Z    Done running command
2016-05-25T22:10:41.759Z    Running command: ['/usr/lib/vmware-vmca/bin/certool', '--gencsrfromcert', '--privkey', '/cert
/vpxd-extension.key', '--cert', '/tmp/vecs_crt.crt', '--csrfile', '/cert/vpxd-extension.csr']
2016-05-25T22:10:41.796Z    Done running command

CSR generated at: /cert/vpxd-extension.csr
2016-05-25T22:10:41.806Z    Running command: ['/usr/lib/vmware-vmca/bin/certool', '--genkey', '--privkey', '/cert/vsphere
-webclient.key', '--pubkey', '/tmp/pubkey.pub']
2016-05-25T22:10:42.052Z    Done running command
2016-05-25T22:10:42.053Z    Running command: ['/usr/lib/vmware-vmca/bin/certool', '--gencsrfromcert', '--privkey', '/cert
/vsphere-webclient.key', '--cert', '/tmp/vecs_crt.crt', '--csrfile', '/cert/vsphere-webclient.csr']
2016-05-25T22:10:42.106Z    Done running command

CSR generated at: /cert/vsphere-webclient.csr
        1. Continue to importing Custom certificate(s) and key(s) for Solution User Certificates

        2. Exit certificate-manager
```

7. Once the keys are exported, minimize (but don't close) the Certificate Manager Utility as it will be used again later.

8. Use a utility similar to WinSCP to copy the certificate signing requests and keys to a desktop that can access the certificate authority.

9. The certificate signing requests should be used to request a certificate. In this example, Microsoft Active Directory Certificate Services is used to generate certificates (open up a web browser and go to `https://<CA FQDN>/certsrv`). To begin, select `Or, submit an advanced certificate request`.

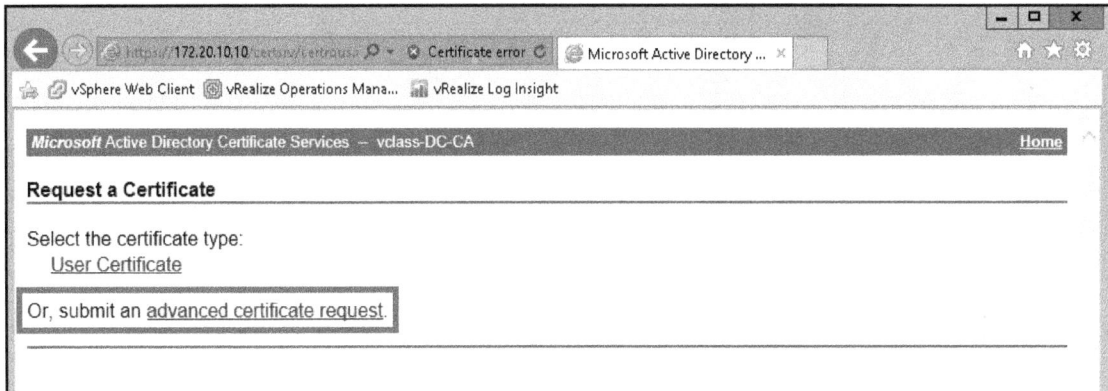

10. Next, select **Submit a certificate request by using a base-64-encoded CMC or PKCS #10 file, or submit a renewal request by using a base-64-encoded PKCS #7 file**.

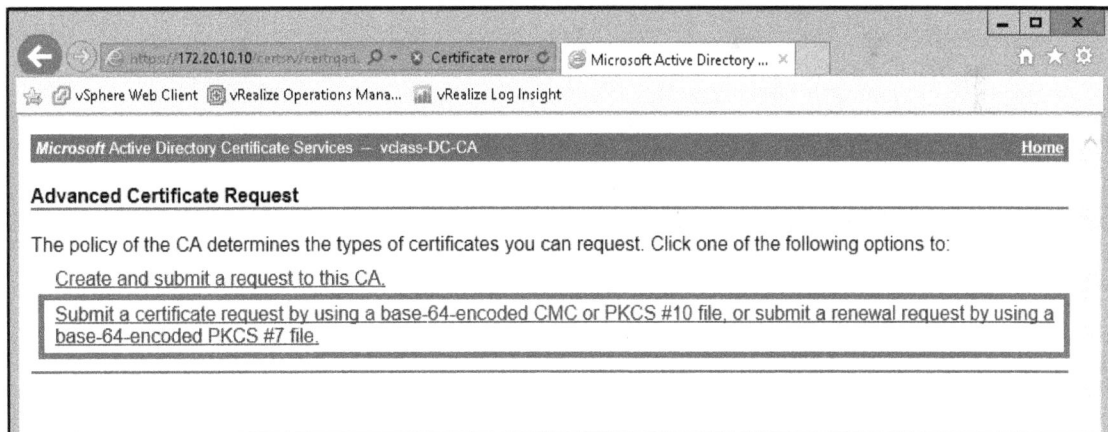

11. At this point, open the first `.csr` file. In the following example, `machine.csr` was opened in Notepad. Select all and copy the contents of this file as it will be used in the certificate request.

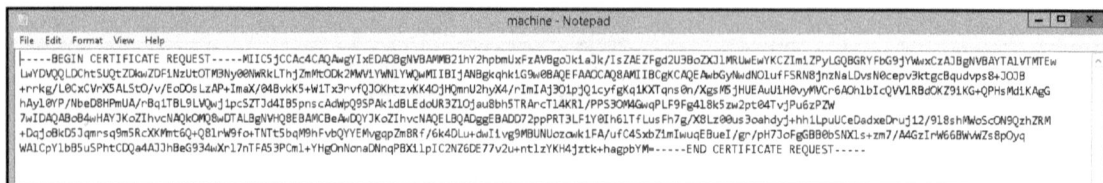

12. Paste the contents of the `.csr` file into the section labeled **Base-64-encoded certificate request (CMC or PKCS #10 or PKCS #7)**. Leave all attributes as default.

13. Click on the **Submit** button.

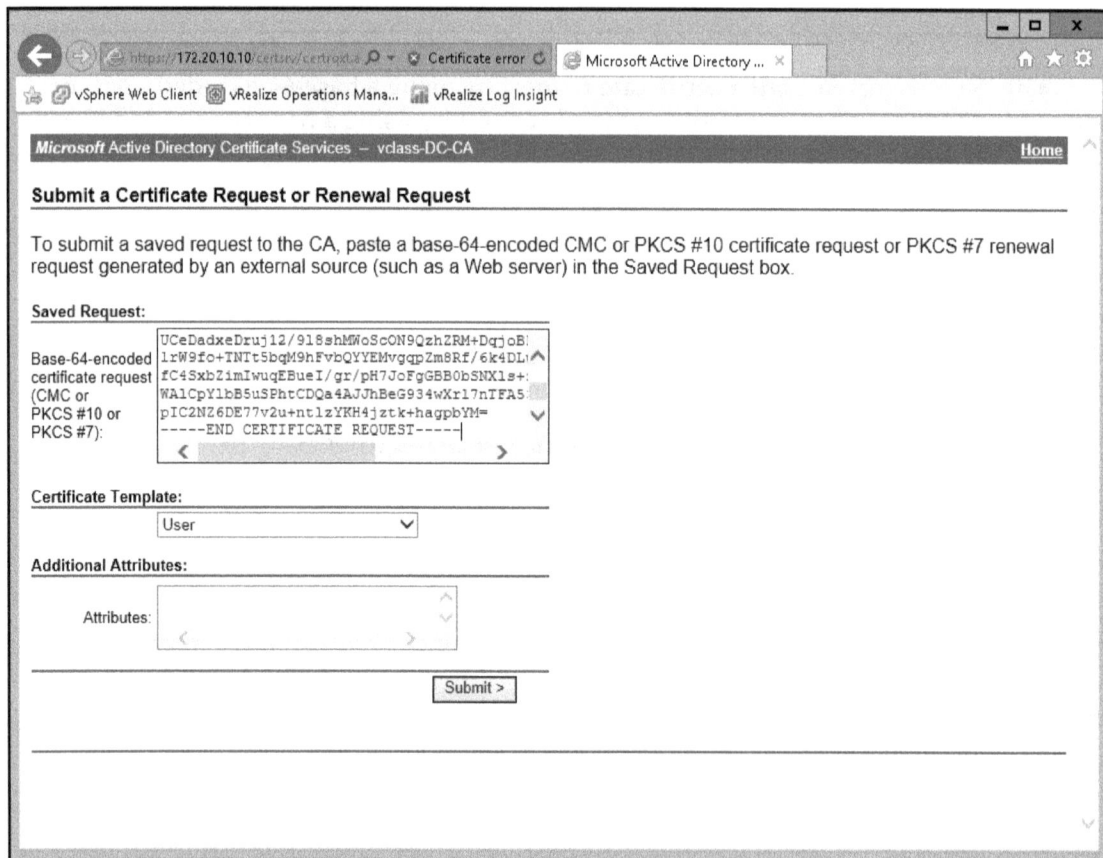

14. Select **Base 64 encoded** and then the **Download certificate** hyperlink. You will be prompted to save the certificate; save it as the solution username using the `.cer` extension.

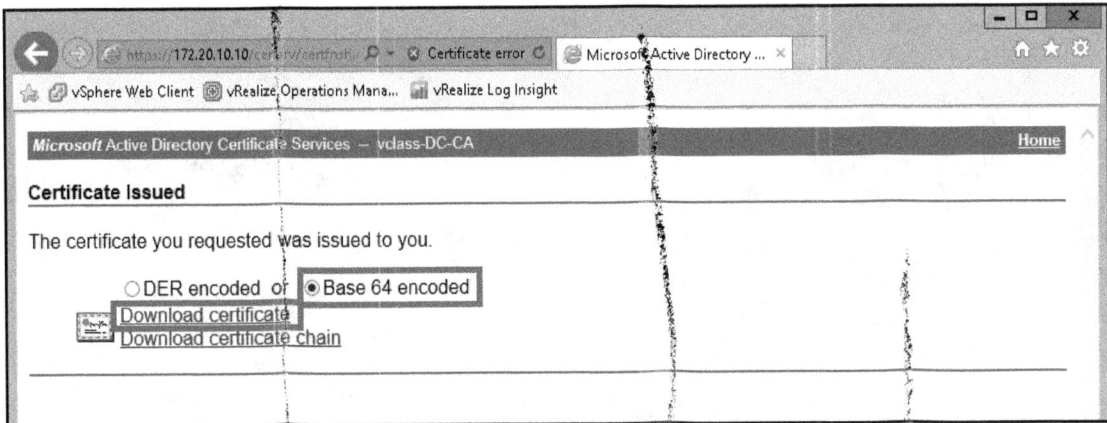

15. Repeat steps 9-14 for all solution users (machine, vpxd, vpxd-extension, and vsphere-webclient).
16. Once this process is completely finished, use a tool similar to WinSCP to copy these `.cer` files into a directory accessible by the PSC.
17. Return to the minimized Certificate Manager Utility.

18. **Picking up, select** `1. Continue to importing Custom certificate(s) and key(s) for Solution User Certificates` **by pressing** *1* **and then** *Enter*.

```
Please provide a directory location to write the CSR(s) and PrivateKey(s) to:
Output directory path: /tmp/
2016-05-25T22:17:20.754Z   Running command: ['/usr/lib/vmware-vmca/bin/certool', '--genkey', '--privkey', '/tmp/machine.
key', '--pubkey', '/tmp/pubkey.pub']
2016-05-25T22:17:20.934Z   Done running command
2016-05-25T22:17:20.935Z   Running command: ['/usr/lib/vmware-vmca/bin/certool', '--gencsrfromcert', '--privkey', '/tmp/
machine.key', '--cert', '/tmp/vecs_crt.crt', '--csrfile', '/tmp/machine.csr']
2016-05-25T22:17:20.950Z   Done running command

CSR generated at: /tmp/machine.csr
2016-05-25T22:17:20.960Z   Running command: ['/usr/lib/vmware-vmca/bin/certool', '--genkey', '--privkey', '/tmp/vpxd.key
', '--pubkey', '/tmp/pubkey.pub']
2016-05-25T22:17:21.069Z   Done running command
2016-05-25T22:17:21.069Z   Running command: ['/usr/lib/vmware-vmca/bin/certool', '--gencsrfromcert', '--privkey', '/tmp/
vpxd.key', '--cert', '/tmp/vecs_crt.crt', '--csrfile', '/tmp/vpxd.csr']
2016-05-25T22:17:21.086Z   Done running command

CSR generated at: /tmp/vpxd.csr
2016-05-25T22:17:21.096Z   Running command: ['/usr/lib/vmware-vmca/bin/certool', '--genkey', '--privkey', '/tmp/vpxd-ext
ension.key', '--pubkey', '/tmp/pubkey.pub']
2016-05-25T22:17:21.265Z   Done running command
2016-05-25T22:17:21.266Z   Running command: ['/usr/lib/vmware-vmca/bin/certool', '--gencsrfromcert', '--privkey', '/tmp/
vpxd-extension.key', '--cert', '/tmp/vecs_crt.crt', '--csrfile', '/tmp/vpxd-extension.csr']
2016-05-25T22:17:21.282Z   Done running command

CSR generated at: /tmp/vpxd-extension.csr
2016-05-25T22:17:21.292Z   Running command: ['/usr/lib/vmware-vmca/bin/certool', '--genkey', '--privkey', '/tmp/vsphere-
webclient.key', '--pubkey', '/tmp/pubkey.pub']
2016-05-25T22:17:21.506Z   Done running command
2016-05-25T22:17:21.507Z   Running command: ['/usr/lib/vmware-vmca/bin/certool', '--gencsrfromcert', '--privkey', '/tmp/
vsphere-webclient.key', '--cert', '/tmp/vecs_crt.crt', '--csrfile', '/tmp/vsphere-webclient.csr']
2016-05-25T22:17:21.524Z   Done running command

CSR generated at: /tmp/vsphere-webclient.csr
        1. Continue to importing Custom certificate(s) and key(s) for Solution User Certificates

        2. Exit certificate-manager

Option [1 or 2]: 1
```

19. Provide the path to each solution user certificate and key. The utility will prompt for:

- Please provide valid custom certificate for solution user store: machine
- File: /tmp/ssl/machine.cer
- Please provide valid custom key for solution user store: machine
- File: /tmp/ssl/machine.key
- Please provide valid custom certificate for solution user store: vpxd
- File: /tmp/ssl/vpxd.cer
- Please provide valid custom key for solution user store: vpxd
- File: /tmp/ssl/vpxd.key
- Please provide valid custom certificate for solution user store: vpxd-extension
- File: /tmp/ssl/vpxd-extension.cer
- Please provide valid custom key for solution user store: vpxd-extension
- File: /tmp/ssl/vpxd-extension.key
- Please provide valid custom certificate for solution user store: vsphere-webclient
- File: /tmp/ssl/vsphere-webclient.cer
- Please provide valid custom key for solution user store: vsphere-webclient
- File: /tmp/ssl/vsphere-webclient.key
- Please provide the signing certificate of the Solution User Certificates
- File: /tmp/ssl/Root64.cer

20. This process will take several minutes to finish once all of the directories have been input.

```
        1. Continue to importing Custom certificate(s) and key(s) for Solution User Certificates

        2. Exit certificate-manager

Option [1 or 2]: 1

Please provide valid custom certificate for solution user store : machine
File : /cert/machine.cer

Please provide valid custom key for solution user store : machine
File : /cert/machine.key

Please provide valid custom certificate for solution user store : vpxd
File : /cert/vpxd.cer

Please provide valid custom key for solution user store : vpxd
File : /cert/vpxd.key

Please provide valid custom certificate for solution user store : vpxd-extension
File : /cert/vpxd-extension.cer

Please provide valid custom key for solution user store : vpxd-extension
File : /cert/vpxd-extension.key

Please provide valid custom certificate for solution user store : vsphere-webclient
File : /cert/vsphere-webclient.cer

Please provide valid custom key for solution user store : vsphere-webclient
File : /cert/vsphere-webclient.key

Please provide the signing certificate of the Solution User Certificates
File : /cert/signing.cer

You are going to replace all Solution User Certificates using custom cert
Continue operation : Option[Y/N] ? : y
Status : 0% Completed [Publishing Root cert...]
```

Once this has finished, the ESX agent manager must be updated.

For more information see VMware KB 2112577 at `http://bit.ly/2cN8SX` s.

Installing the default root certificate

If using the default VMCA certificates is chosen, then the root certificate should be retrieved and deployed as a trusted root certificate. While this is not a requirement, the annoying untrusted security notices would always appear when accessing the vSphere Web Client if not done. This is seen in the following screenshot:

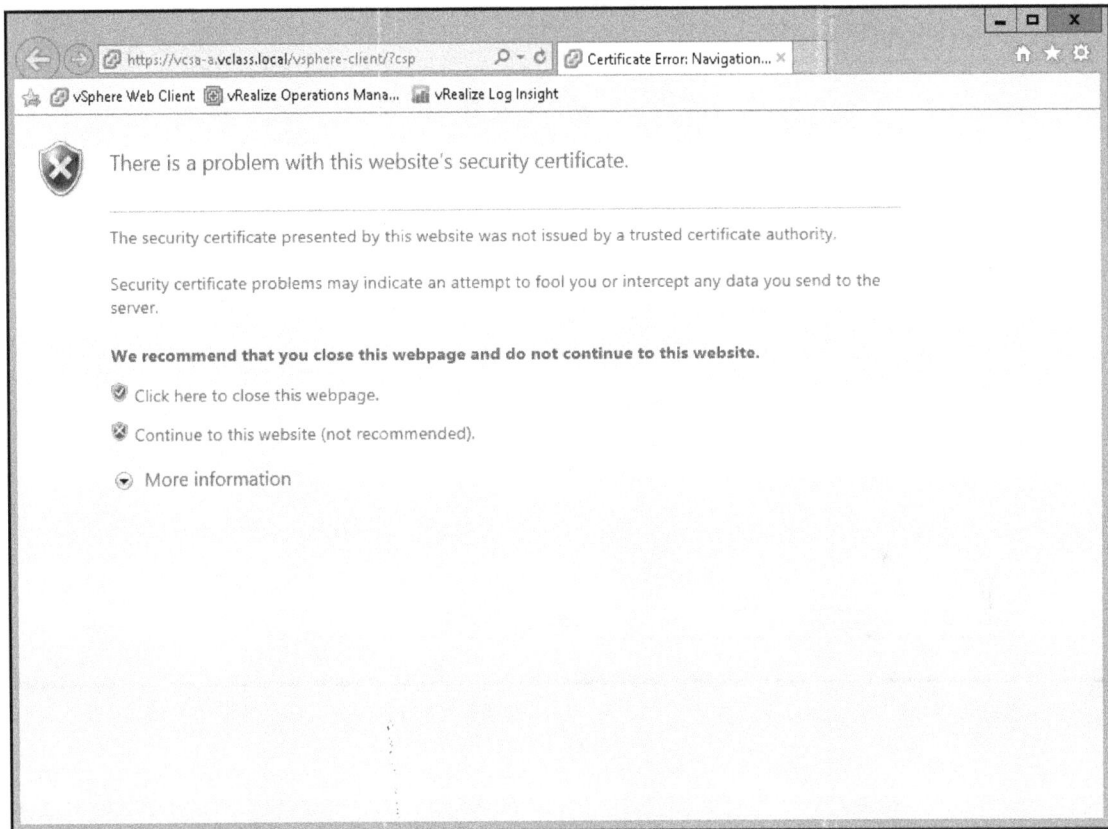

This is a multistep process that will include retrieving the root certificate from vCenter Server, converting it to a .cer format, and then deploying it as a trusted root certificate. Typically, the easiest way to do this is by using Group Policy.

To begin this process:

1. Open a web browser and navigate to the vCenter Server page: `<https://<vCenter FQDN>`.

2. In the lower-right corner of the page, select the **Download trusted root CA certificates** link.

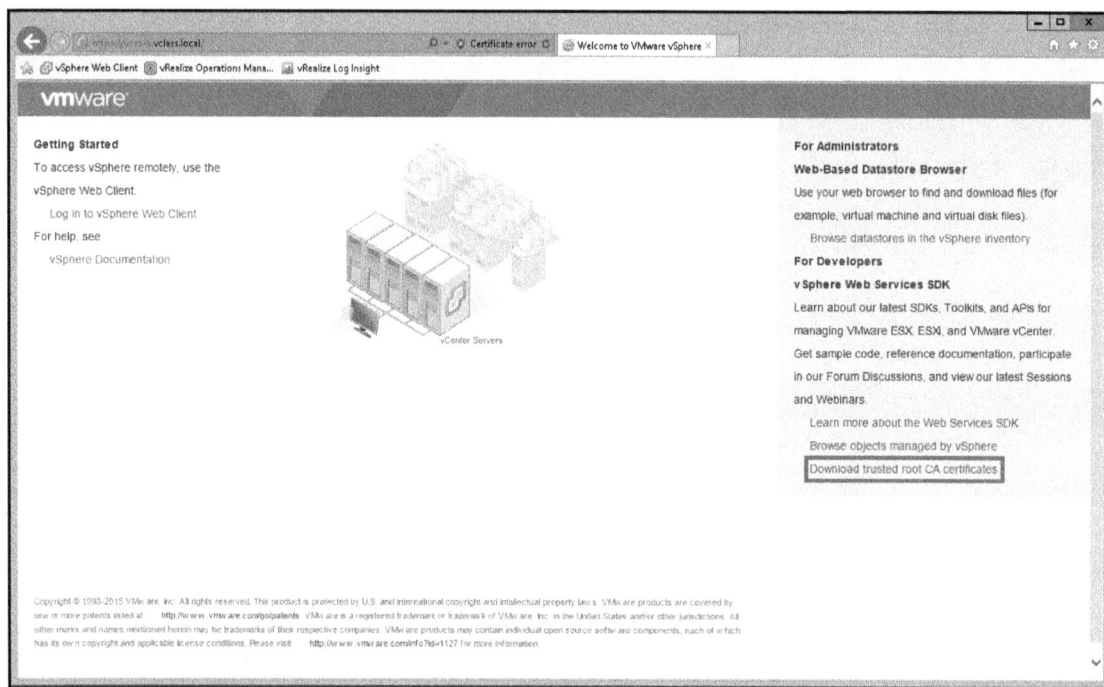

3. Selecting this link will prompt you to save the root certificate. Choose where to save and what to call the file. Ensure that the file is in a `.zip` format. Click on the **Save** button when finished.

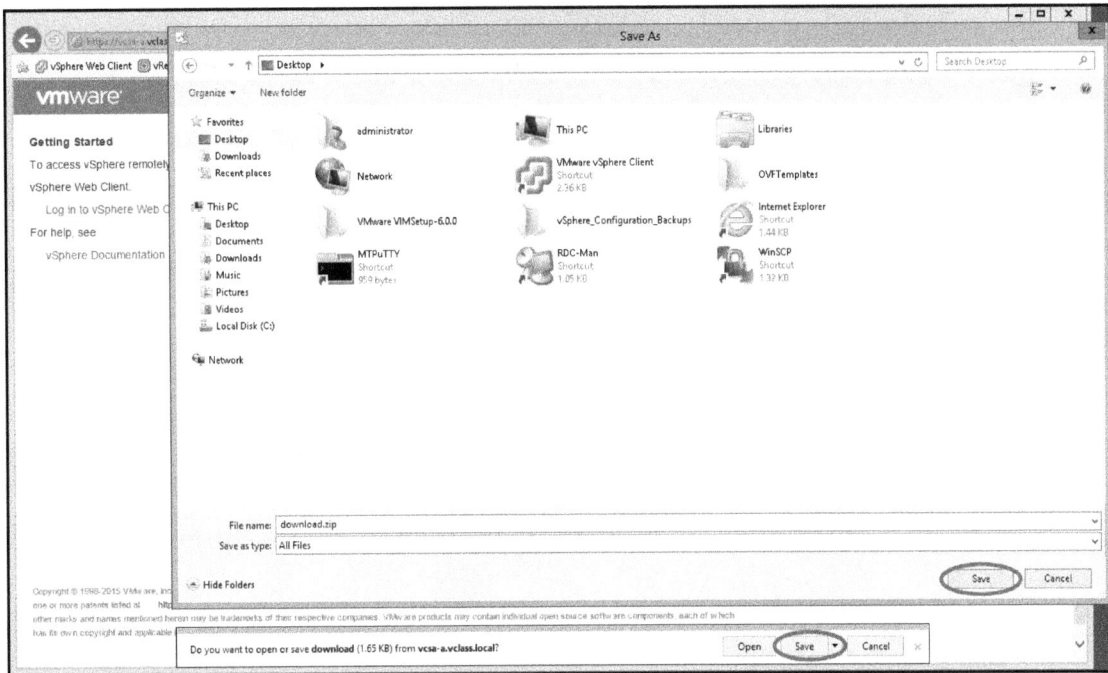

4. Once the `.zip` file has successfully saved, right-click on it and select **Extract All…** .

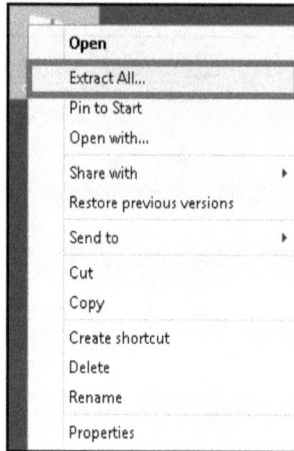

5. Choose where to extract the files from the `.zip` file. Click on the **Extract** button.

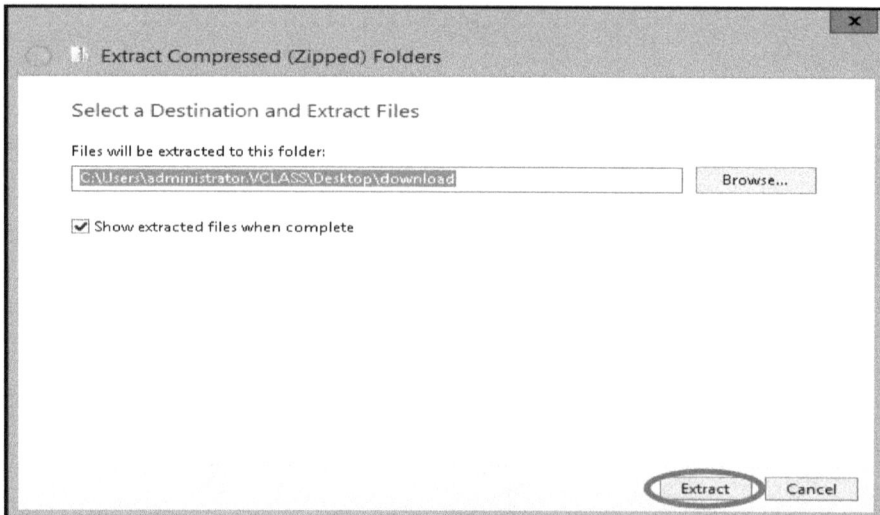

6. Once extracted, open this folder. There will be a folder called `cert`, open this folder as well. There will be two files. The `.0` file is a **Privacy Enhanced Mail (PEM)** encoded certificate file, while the `.r0` file is the certificate revocation list.

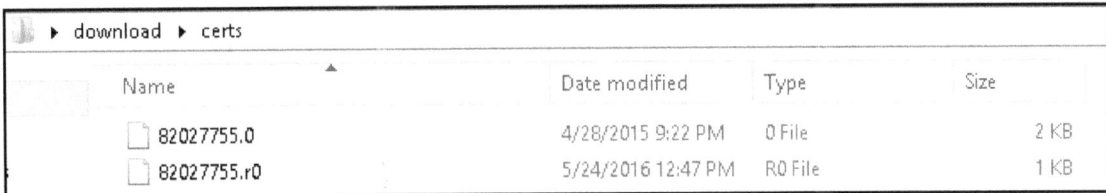

download ▸ certs			
Name ▲	Date modified	Type	Size
82027755.0	4/28/2015 9:22 PM	0 File	2 KB
82027755.r0	5/24/2016 12:47 PM	R0 File	1 KB

7. Rename the `.0` file to a `.cer` file extension.

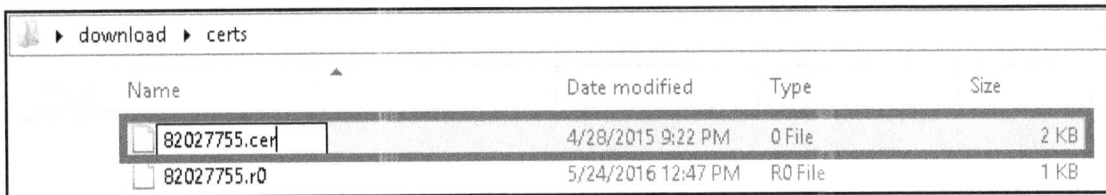

download ▸ certs			
Name ▲	Date modified	Type	Size
82027755.cer	4/28/2015 9:22 PM	0 File	2 KB
82027755.r0	5/24/2016 12:47 PM	R0 File	1 KB

8. A message will appear stating that the changed file extension could make the file unstable. Click on **Yes**.

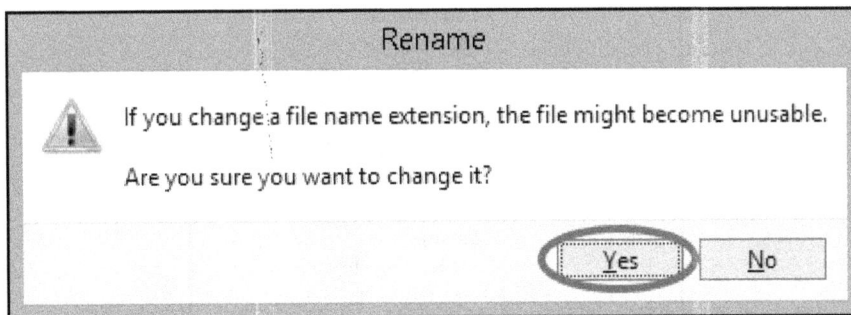

Rename

If you change a file name extension, the file might become unusable.

Are you sure you want to change it?

Yes   No

9. Once you have a `.cer` file, open up the **Group Policy Management Console** and select an existing GPO to edit, a new GPO could be created for deploying the certificate. Once a GPO has been selected, navigate to **Computer Configuration** | **Policies** | **Windows Settings** | **Security Settings** | **Public Key Policies** | **Trusted Root Certificate Authorities**. Right-click on **Trusted Root Certificate Authorities** and select **Importâ✤**.This is demonstrated in the following screenshot:

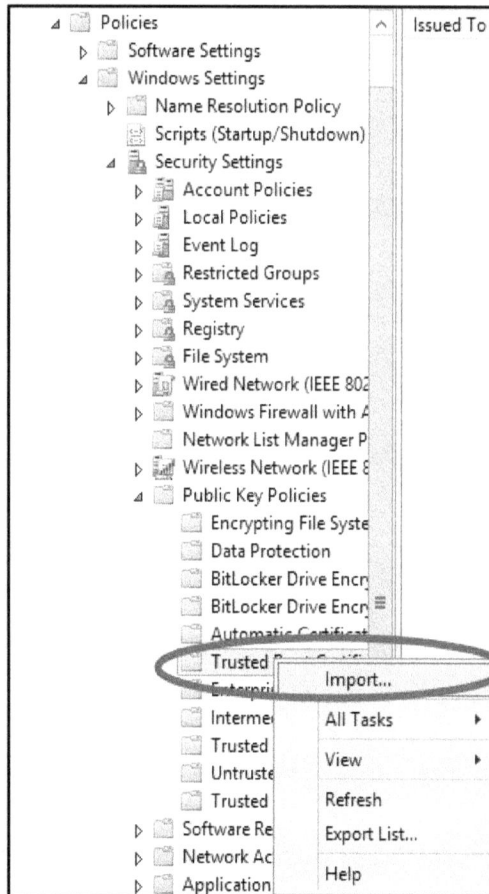

10. This will bring up the **Certificate Import Wizard**. Select the **Browseâ✱⁞** button to choose the `.cer` file. Click on **Next**.

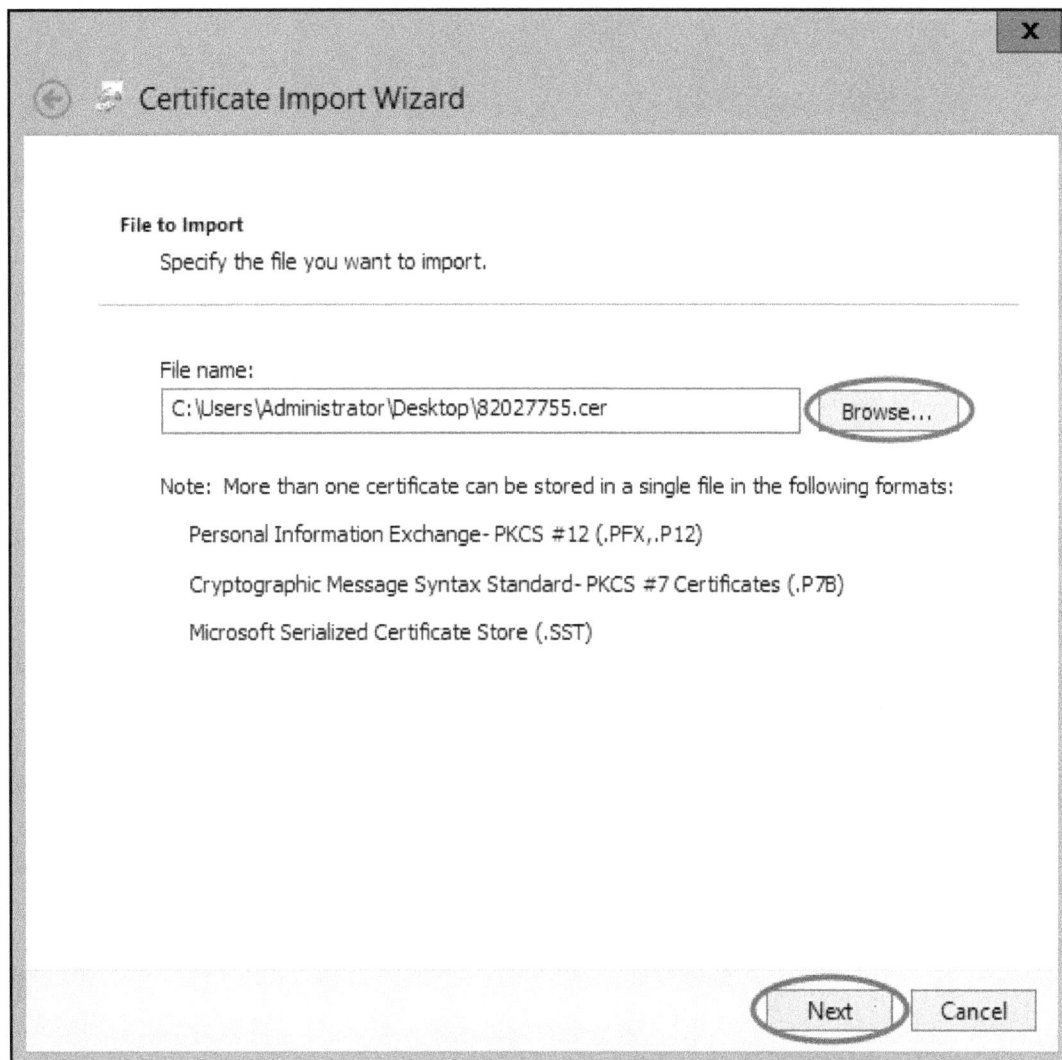

11. Validate that the certificate is to be placed in **Trusted Root Certificate Authorities**. Click on **Next**.

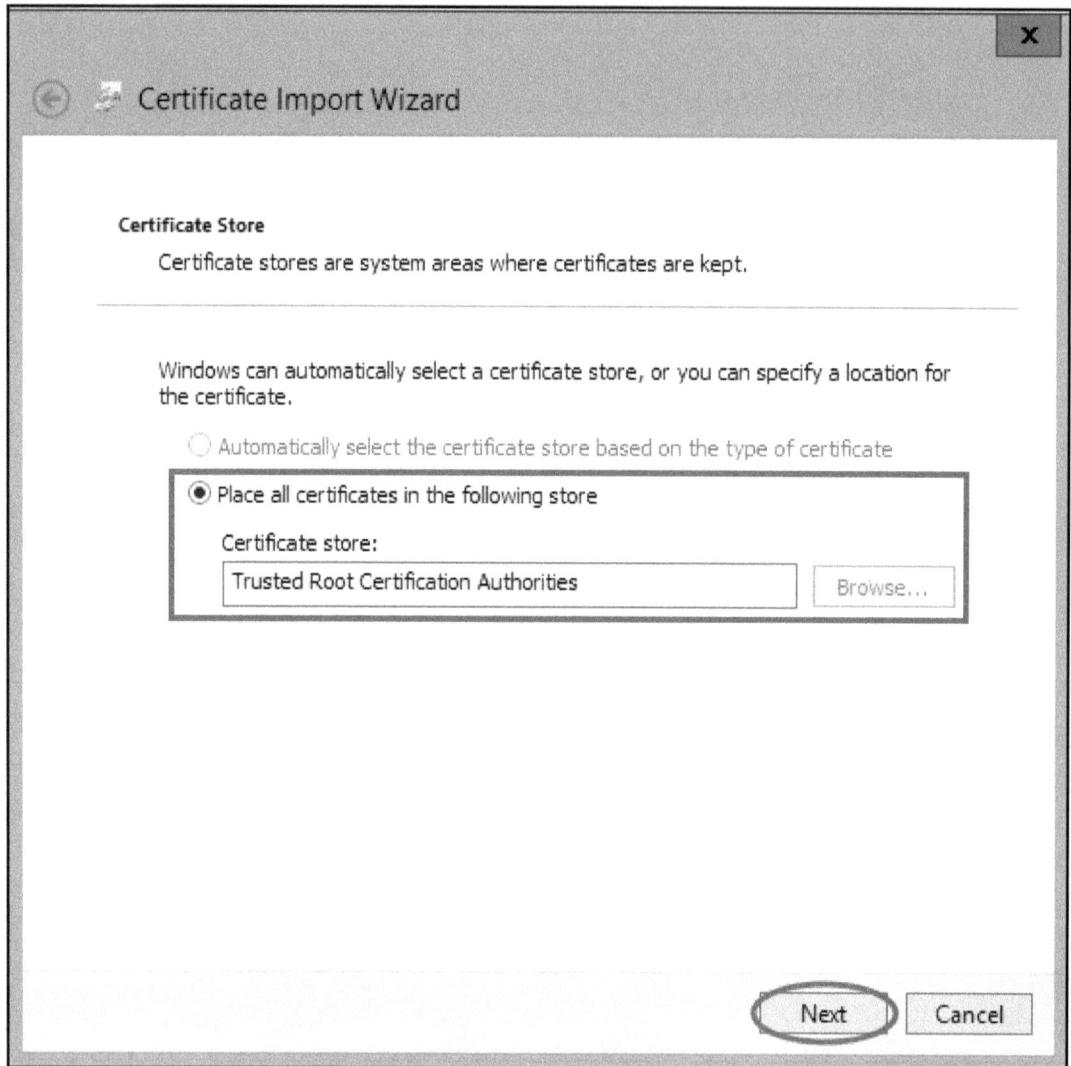

12. Review the information in the **Certificate Import Wizard** and click on **Finish**.

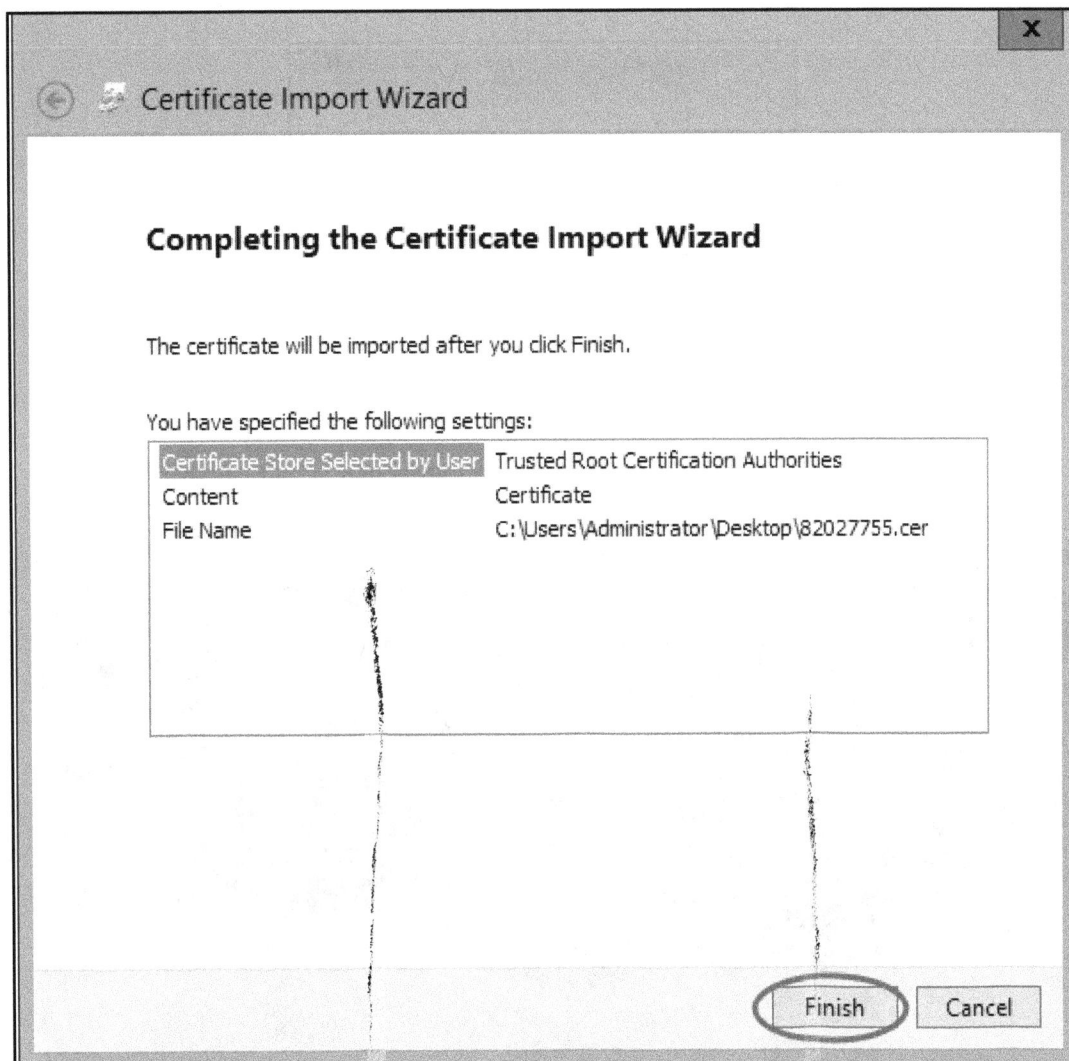

13. A popup message should appear that specifies that the import was successful. Click on **OK**.

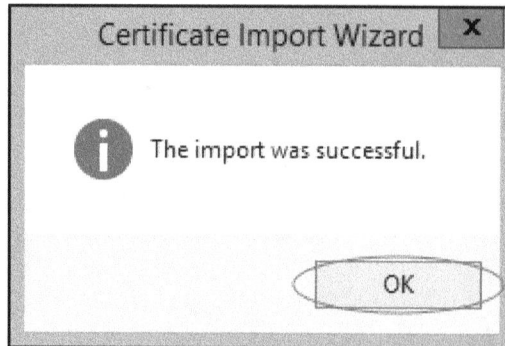

14. To expedite the GPO process, open Command Prompt. Enter `GPUpdate /force`. This updates all group policies on the computer.

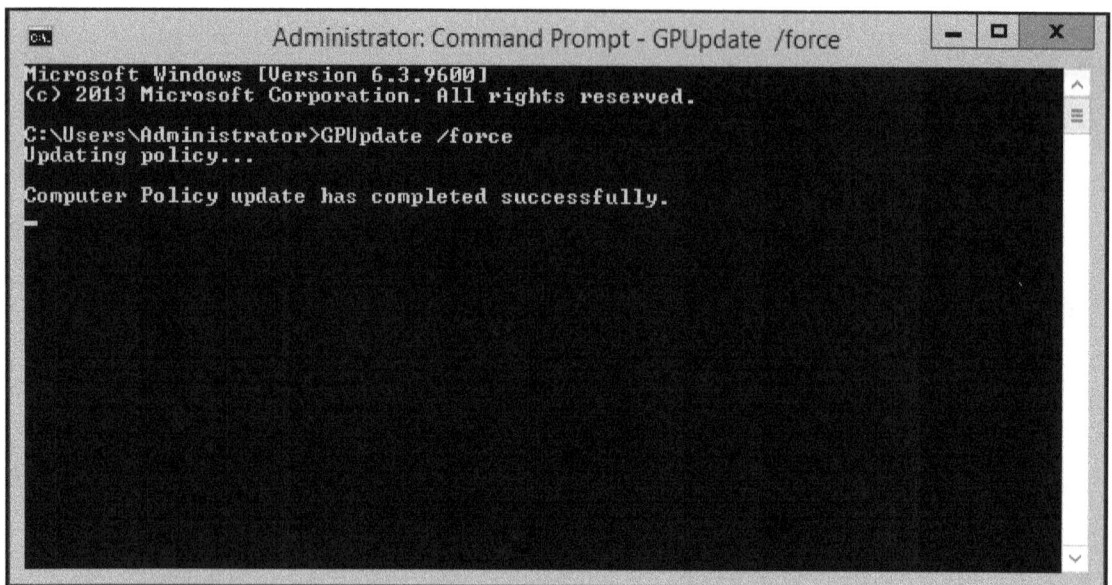

15. Once the group policies have updated, open up a web browser and navigate to the vSphere Web Client. There should no longer be a certificate trust error, as shown in the following screenshot:

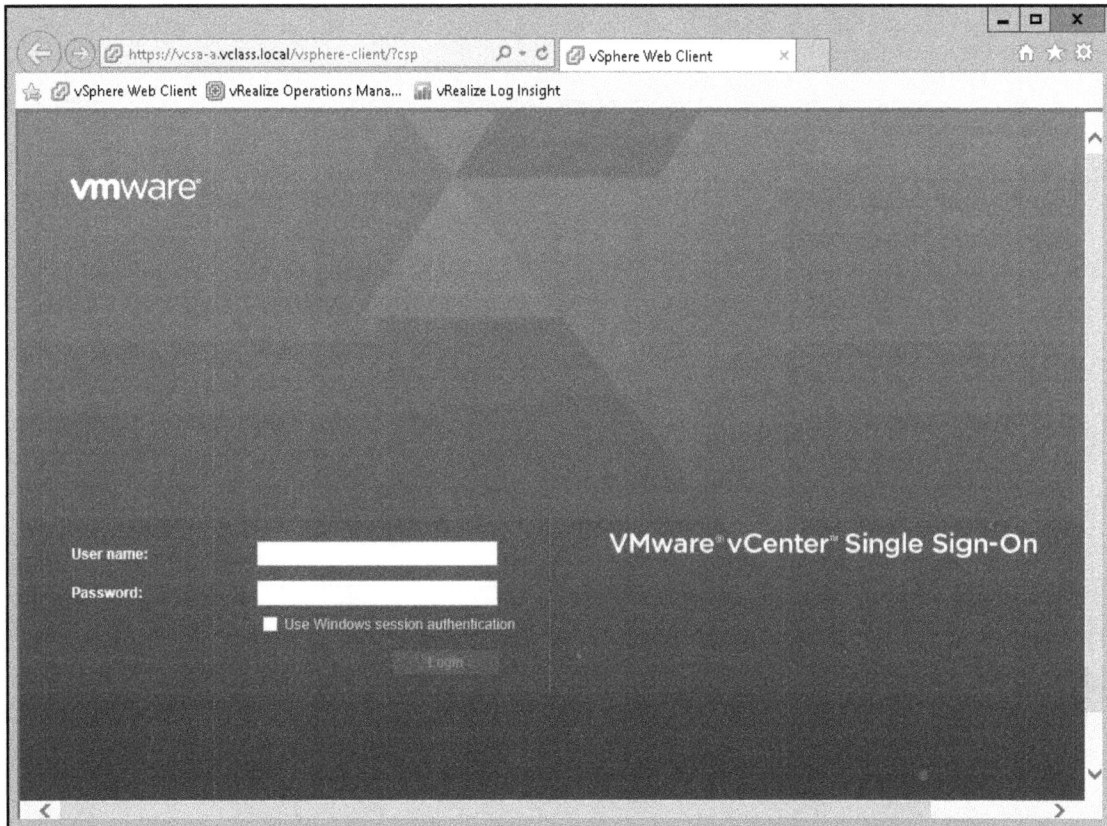

Managing ESXi SSL certificates

The VMCA, in vSphere 6, provisions a signed certificate to each ESXi host. The certificate specifies the VMCA as the root certificate authority by default. The certificate is provisioned when the ESXi host is added to vCenter Server, or installed or upgraded to ESXi 6.0 or later.

Renewing VMCA certificates

If the VMCA is a subordinate certificate authority, it is allowed to sign certificates for the ESXi hosts. This can be done using the vSphere Web Client. To do so, log into the vSphere Web Client and navigate to the Hosts and Cluster inventory view. Right-click on the ESXi host, and select **Certificates I Renew Certificate**.

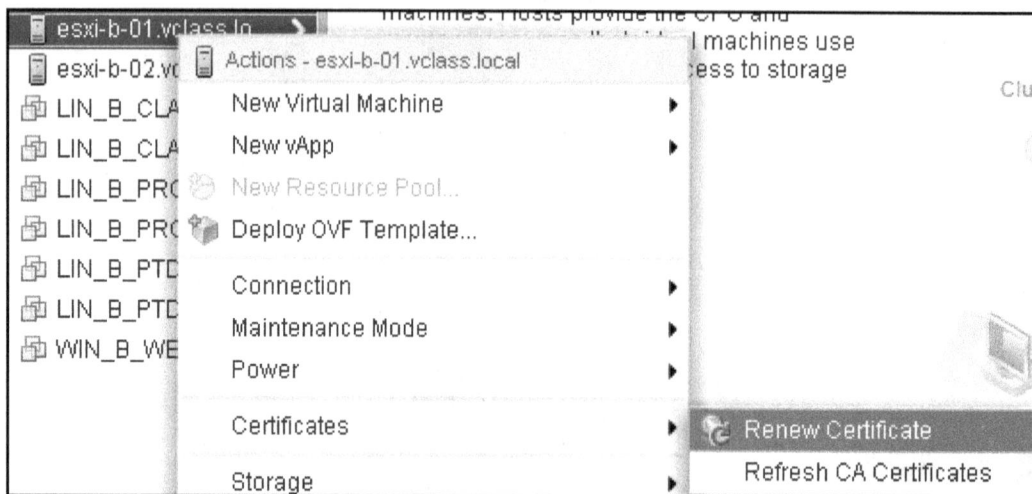

This will bring up the **Renew Certificate** dialog; click on the **Yes** button.

This can also be done without making the VMCA a subordinate certificate authority. This process would need to be before the certificate expires or if the hostname is changed. However, if the certificate has already expired, just disconnect and remove the ESXi host from the inventory and then reconnect it. The vCenter Server will renew an expired certificate when a host is added to the inventory.

Custom CA certificates

By default, the ESXi host uses the automatically generated certificates that were created at installation. If required by security policy, these certificates may be replaced.

To begin this process:

1. Log into the ESXi shell with root privileges.
2. Navigate to the /etc/vmware/ssl directory and use the ls command to view the contents of this location. The .crt file and the .key file will be listed.

```
login as: root
Using keyboard-interactive authentication.
Password:
The time and date of this login have been sent to the system logs.

VMware offers supported, powerful system administration tools.  Please
see www.vmware.com/go/sysadmintools for details.

The ESXi Shell can be disabled by an administrative user. See the
vSphere Security documentation for more information.
[root@esxi-a-01:~] cd /etc/vmware/ssl
[root@esxi-a-01:/etc/vmware/ssl] ls
castore.pem         rui.bak            rui.crt            rui.key            vsanvp_castore.pem
[root@esxi-a-01:/etc/vmware/ssl] 
```

3. It's a good idea to keep the old .crt and .key file in case of any issues. To rename those files, use the mv command, as shown:

```
mv rui.crt old.rui.crt
mv rui.key old.rui.key
```

```
[root@esxi-a-01:~] cd /etc/vmware/ssl
[root@esxi-a-01:/etc/vmware/ssl] ls
castore.pem         rui.bak            rui.crt            rui.key            vsanvp_castore.pem
[root@esxi-a-01:/etc/vmware/ssl] mv rui.crt old.rui.crt
[root@esxi-a-01:/etc/vmware/ssl] mv rui.key old.rui.key
[root@esxi-a-01:/etc/vmware/ssl] ls
castore.pem         old.rui.crt        old.rui.key        rui.bak            vsanvp_castore.pem
[root@esxi-a-01:/etc/vmware/ssl] 
```

4. Next, copy the new certificate and key to /etc/vmware/ssl. Any file transfer application that uses an HTTPS session may be used, however, the following screenshot demonstrates using WinSCP.

5. If the certificate and key are not currently named `rui.crt` and `rui.key` (respectively) then rename the files to match the aforementioned names.

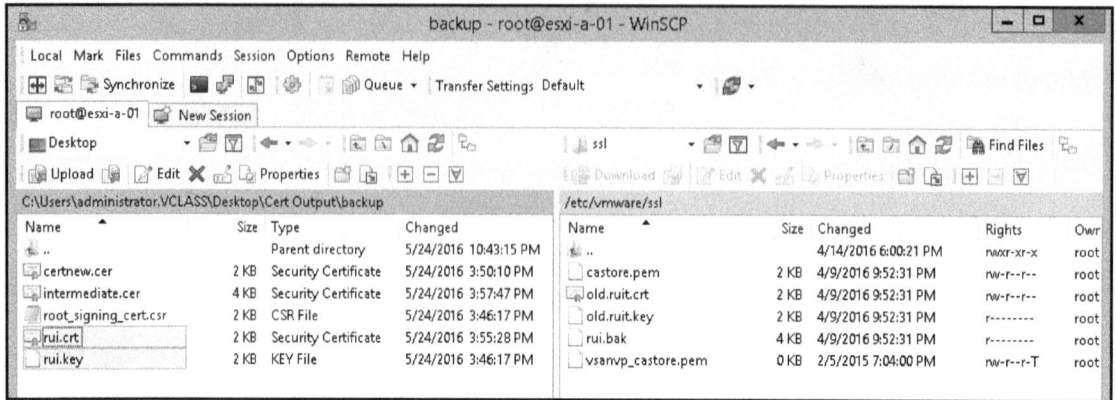

6. Once the certificates are in place in the `/etc/vmware/ssl` directory, restart the ESXi host. (Or the host could be put into maintenance mode, the new certificates installed and the management agents restarted).

Viewing certificates using the vSphere Web Client

The vSphere Web Client may be used to view certificates known to the VCMA to determine whether certificates will expire soon, see the root certificate status, as well as to view expired certificates.

To view certificates in the vSphere Web Client:

1. Log into the vSphere Web Client as the SSO administrator (`administrator@vsphere.local`).

2. Navigate to **Administration**, then **Deployment**, and select **System Configuration**. Choose **Nodes** and then select the appropriate node to view certificate information.

3. Click on the **Manage** tab, and then select **Certificate Authority**. From there, choose which certificate type to view. The following screenshot demonstrates **Active Certificates**:

- **Active Certificates** show the active certificates along with the validation information
- **Revoked Certificates** display the certificates that have been revoked
- **Expired Certificates** list the certificates that have expired
- **Root Certificates** provide information regarding the root certificates available to the VMCA

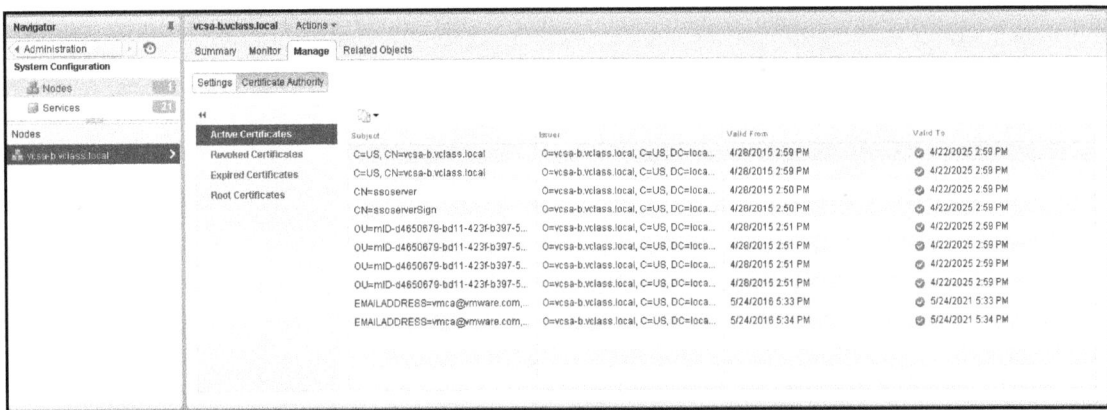

The following screenshot demonstrates the **Root Certificates** information:

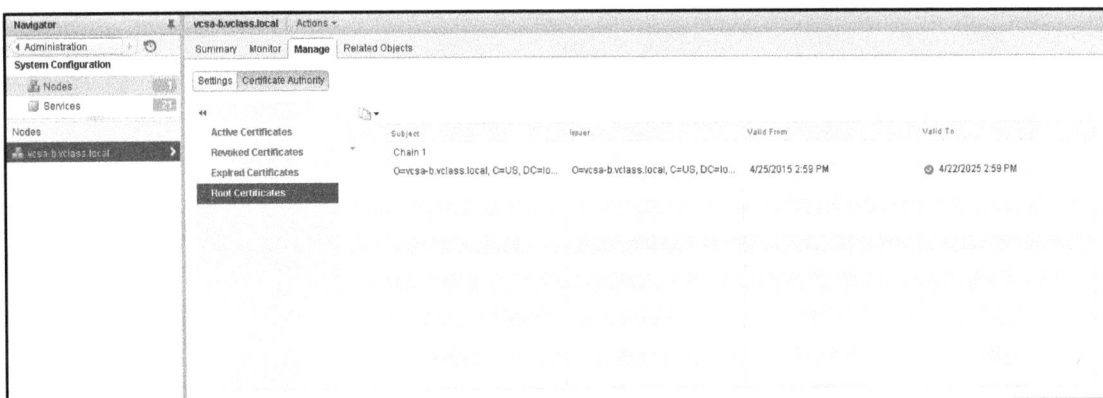

Summary

PKI is based on digital certificates used for encrypting or signing data. SSL certificates are used to keep sensitive information sent between vSphere components encrypted so that only the intended recipient can decrypt it. CA signed certificates are used to prevent or reduce the risk of man-in-the-middle attacks. This chapter introduced vSphere 6's new VMCA and discussed how it could be used to alleviate some of the headache surrounding certificate management. We looked at multiple configurations, which include using VMCA signed certificates, using VMCA as an intermediate certificate authority, and using external certificate authority signed certificates, or a hybrid configuration. The Certificate Manager Utility is a command-line utility that assists with the certificate configuration process.

In the next chapter, we will further discuss securing a vSphere environment.

11
Securing a vSphere Environment

Security is a major consideration in many environments, typically acting as a major design quality. Some environments sacrifice availability and/or performance for the sake of security. vSphere is relatively secure out of the box with its default configuration. However, there are some configurations that can be made to ESXi, vCenter Server, and virtual machines to further enhance an infrastructure's security configuration.

In this chapter, you will learn about:

- Securing ESXi
- Securing vCenter
- Single Sign-On
- vSphere permissions
- Syslog
- Virtual machine hardening

VMware provides Security Hardening Guides as a means for further guidance regarding how to secure vSphere components. More information may be found at `http://www.vmwar e.com/security/hardening-guides.html`.

Securing ESXi

Securing vSphere components is an aspect of any design and implementation. Components should be secured to minimize vulnerabilities that could be maliciously exploited. Though ESXi is secure post-installation, there are a few configurations that could be made to further harden the hypervisor. Consider using a host profile (discussed previously in `Chapter 7`, *Understanding Host Profiles, Image Profiles, and Auto Deploy*) to create a baseline and make these changes across all ESXi hosts.

Joining ESXi to an Active Directory domain

ESXi hosts may be configured to use Active Directory to manage user access. Using local user accounts on each host would be tedious, and may potentially involve having to create and manage account names and passwords across many ESXi hosts. Using a directory service, like Active Directory, can help reduce ESXi host configuration, simplifying management, and reducing the chance that a configuration issue may lead to unintended unauthorized access.

To configure an ESXi host to use Active Directory:

1. Verify time synchronization between the directory system using NTP and the ESXi host.
2. Verify that ESXi's configured DNS server is able to resolve the hostname of the domain controllers.
3. Navigate to the ESXi host in the vSphere Web Client inventory.
4. Select the **Manage** tab and then click on the button for **Settings**.
5. Choose **Authentication Services** under **System**.
6. Once at the **Authentication Services** menu, click on the **Join Domain...** button:

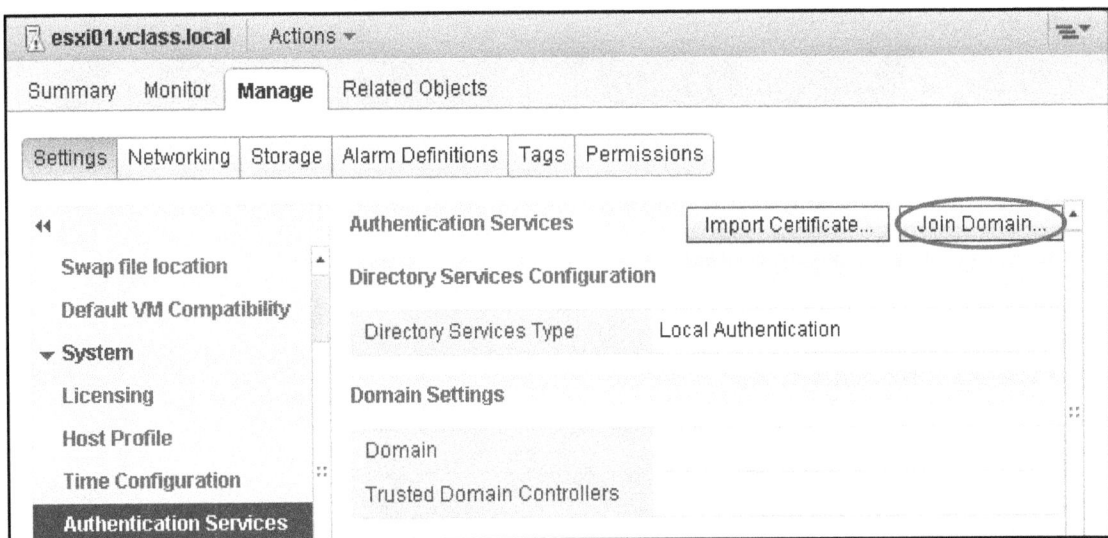

7. This will bring up the **Join Domain** dialog box. Enter the **Domain** name as well as the **User name** and **Password** of an Active Directory user with permissions to join ESXi to the domain:

8. Click on **OK** once finished.

Using lockdown mode

Lockdown mode can be enabled to increase the security of the ESXi hosts. When the ESXi hosts are in lockdown mode, all operations must be made using vCenter Server. vSphere 6 introduces the ability to select normal or strict lockdown modes as well as the exception user list. Any user on the exception user list does not lose their privileges when a host is configured for lockdown mode.

To configure an ESXi host for lockdown mode:

1. Using the vSphere Web Client, navigate to an ESXi host in the inventory.
2. Select the **Manage** tab, then the **Settings** button, and lastly choose **Security Profile**.
3. To modify the **Lockdown Mode** settings, click on the **Edit** button:

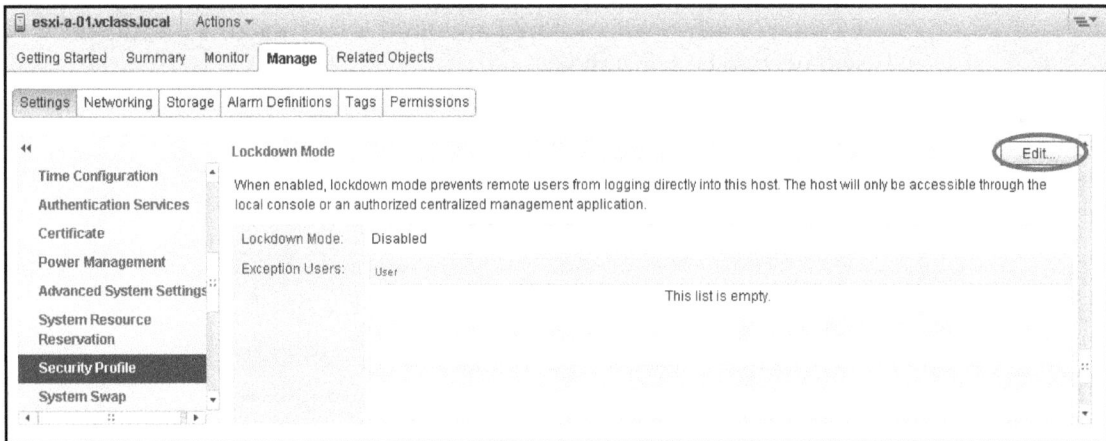

4. This will bring up the **Lockdown Mode** dialog. Choose one of the following settings:

- **Disabled**: This setting specifies to not use lockdown mode. There are no restrictions when accessing ESXi. This is the default.
- **Normal**: This setting specifies that the ESXi host is only accessible through the vCenter Server; however, the DCUI service is not stopped. Therefore, should vCenter Server be inaccessible for any reason, a user in the exception user list (DCUI.Access advanced option) can access the ESXi host using the DCUI.
- **Strict**: This setting specifies that the ESXi host is only accessible through the vCenter Server and the DCUI service is stopped. In the event that vCenter Server is unavailable, the ESXi host is also unable to be accessed unless ESXi Shell and SSH services are enabled and users are defined in the Exception Users list. Should the connection to vCenter Server not be restored and ESXi is still inaccessible, the host will need to be reinstalled:

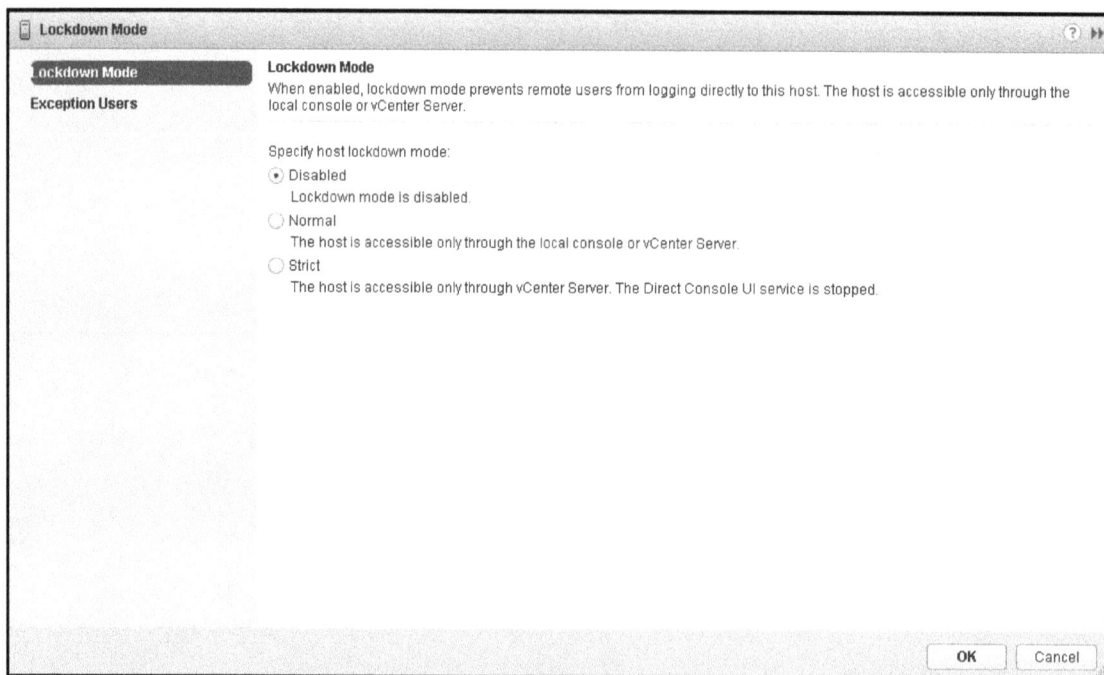

5. Once a Lockdown Mode configuration has been made, select **Exception Users** in the left-hand pane.

6. To add a user to the **Exception Users** list, click on the add button (+):

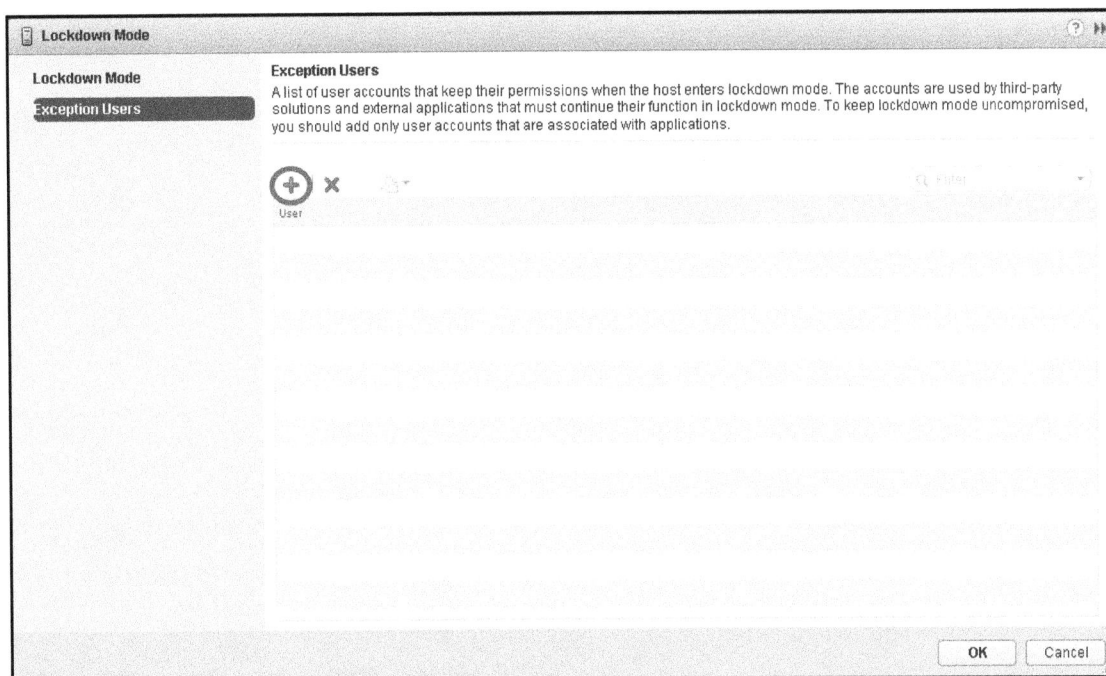

7. This will bring up the **Add User** dialog. Select the appropriate **Domain** and the user. Click on the **Add** button and click on **OK** once finished:

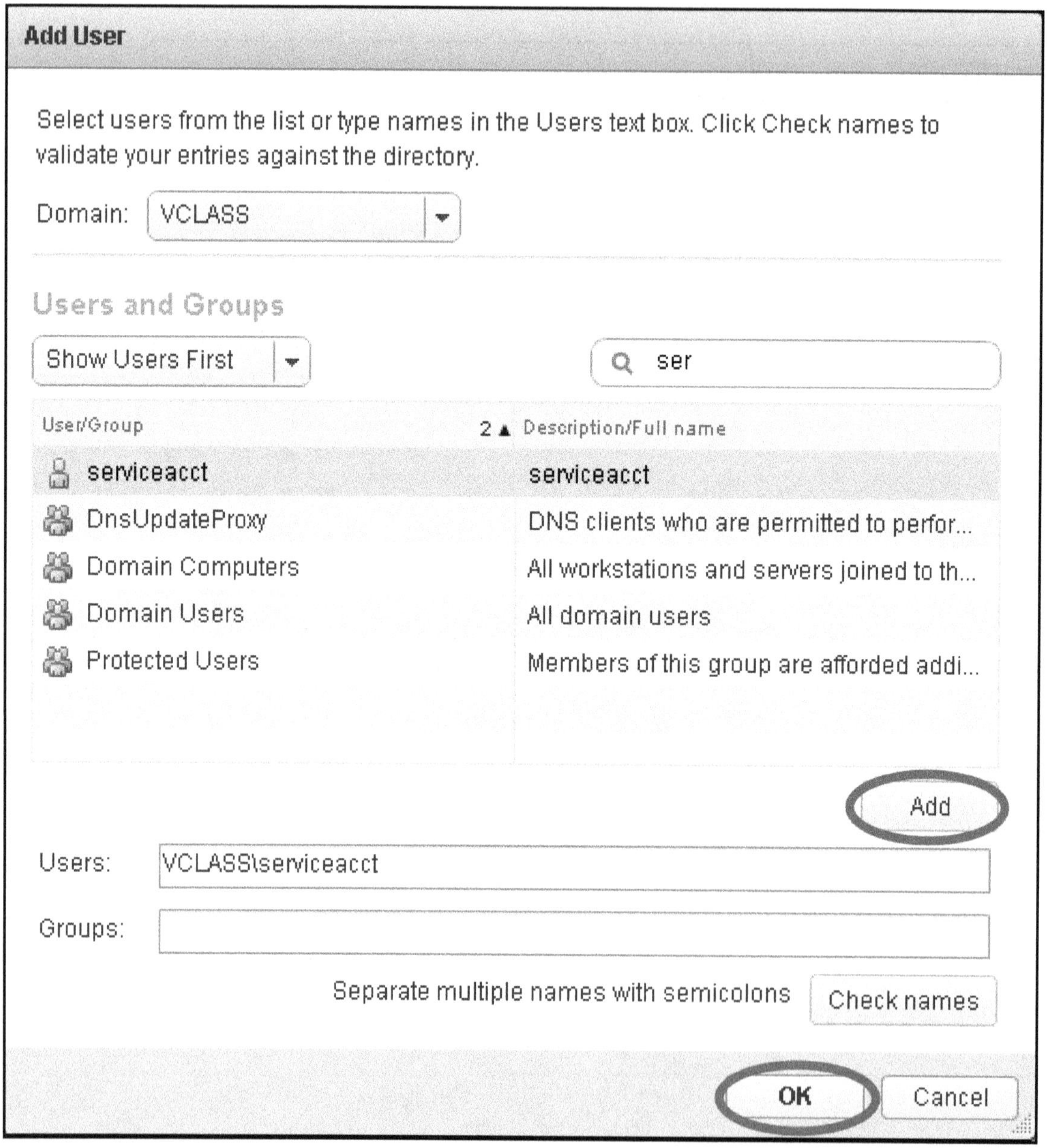

Add User

Select users from the list or type names in the Users text box. Click Check names to validate your entries against the directory.

Domain: VCLASS ▼

Users and Groups

Show Users First ▼   Q ser

User/Group	2 ▲ Description/Full name
🔒 serviceacct	serviceacct
👥 DnsUpdateProxy	DNS clients who are permitted to perfor...
👥 Domain Computers	All workstations and servers joined to th...
👥 Domain Users	All domain users
👥 Protected Users	Members of this group are afforded addi...

Add

Users: VCLASS\serviceacct

Groups:

Separate multiple names with semicolons   Check names

OK   Cancel

8. The user(s) selected should appear in the **Exception Users** pane in the **Lockdown Mode** dialog:

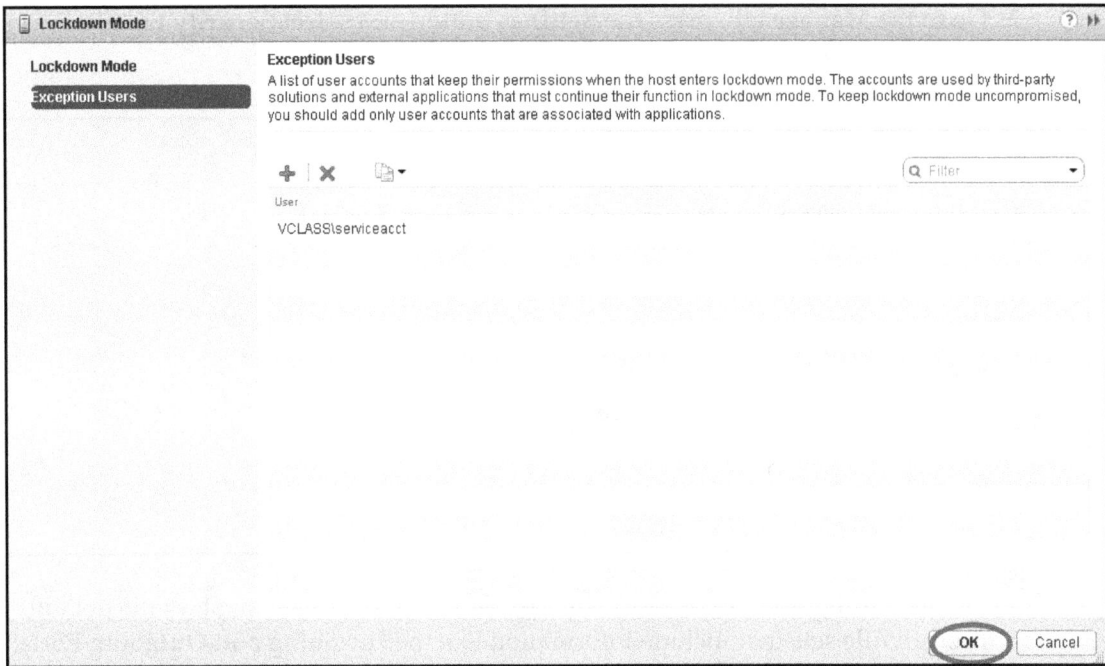

9. Review this information and if all is correct, click on **OK**.

ESXi firewall

The ESXi hosts have a built-in firewall (as part of the security profile) that is enabled by default. The firewall is configured to block inbound and outbound traffic, with the exception of services enabled as a part of the ESXi hosts' security profile.

To manage the ESXi firewall:

1. Navigate to an ESXi host in the inventory using the vSphere Web Client.
2. Go to the **Manage** tab, press the **Settings** button and select **Security Profile**.
3. Find the **Firewall** section and click on **Editâ⁎⁞** :

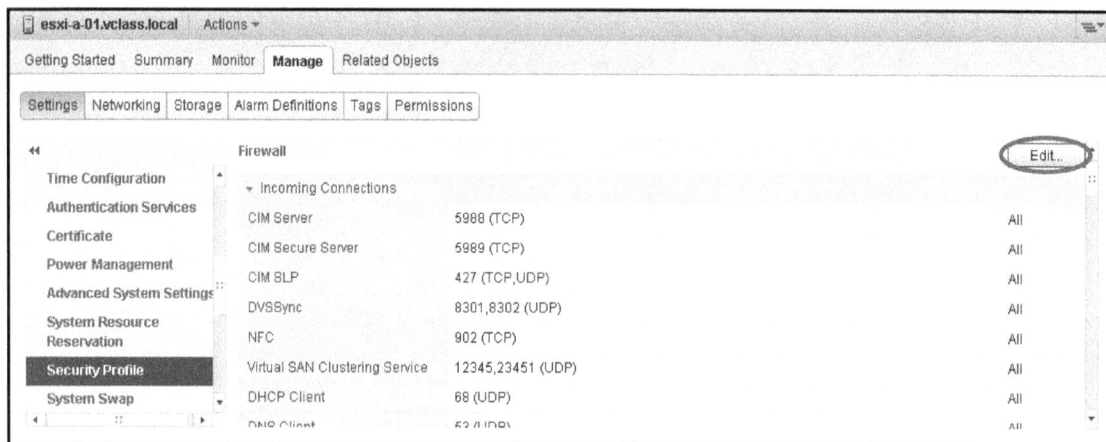

4. This will bring up the **Edit Security Profile** dialog box. This displays the default firewall rule sets that include information like the **Incoming** and **Outgoing Ports**, **Protocols**, and **Daemon**.

5. Some services can be configured to explicitly specify IP addresses or subnets from which connections are allowed. The following image displays the default setting of **Allow connections from any IP address**:

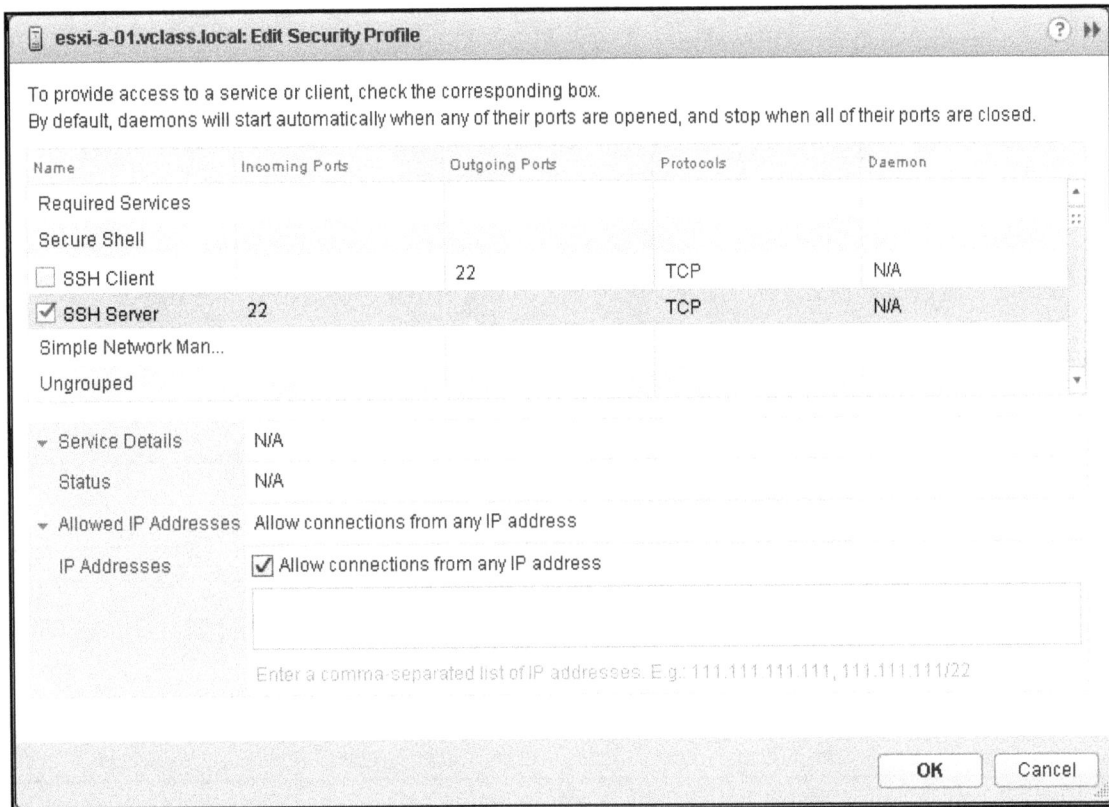

6. To explicitly define an IP address or subnet for allowed connections, deselect the checkbox next to **Allow connections from any IP address**. This is demonstrated in the following screenshot.

7. Enter the IP address(es) and/or subnet(s) from which connections should be allowed. Connections from anywhere else will be denied:

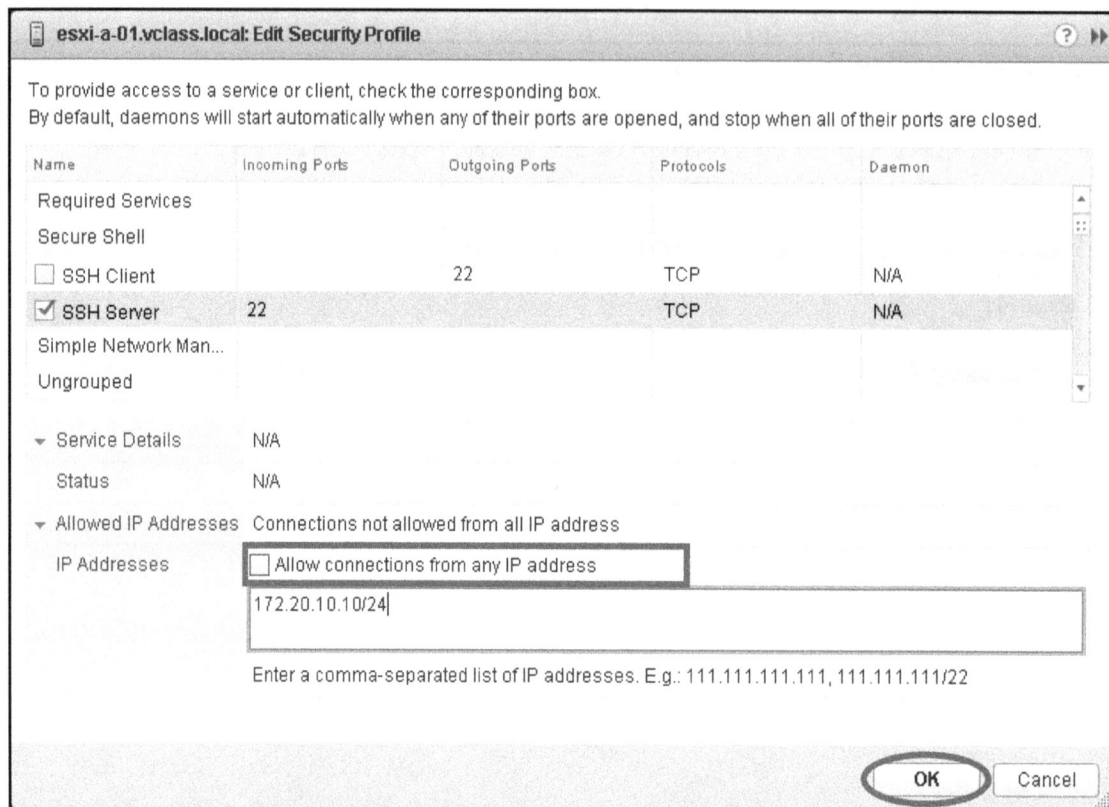

8. Click on **OK** once finished.

Securing vCenter Server

A big part of securing vCenter Server is limiting access. Ensure that permissions are given only as necessary and that the roles used to specify privileges explicitly give what is necessaryâ⊚⊚nothing more and nothing less. For more information on permissions, see the section on vSphere permissions later in this chapter.

Joining vCenter Server Appliance to an Active Directory domain

The vCenter Server Appliance may be joined to an Active Directory domain so that Active Directory accounts can be used to authenticate directly to the virtual machine.

To join the vCenter Server Appliance to an Active Directory domain:

1. Navigate to **Administration** and go to **System Configuration** using the vSphere Web Client.
2. Choose **Nodes** and select the vCenter Server.
3. Go to the **Manage** tab and click on the **Settings** button.
4. Select **Active Directory** under **Advanced**.
5. Click on the **Join...** button:

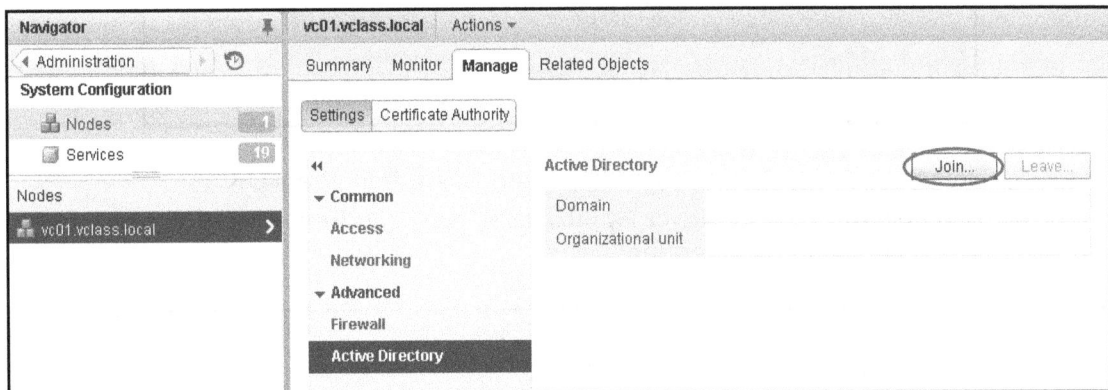

6. The **Join Active Directory** dialog box will appear. Enter the domain, as well as the **User name** and **Password** of an account that has permissions to join vCenter Server to the domain:

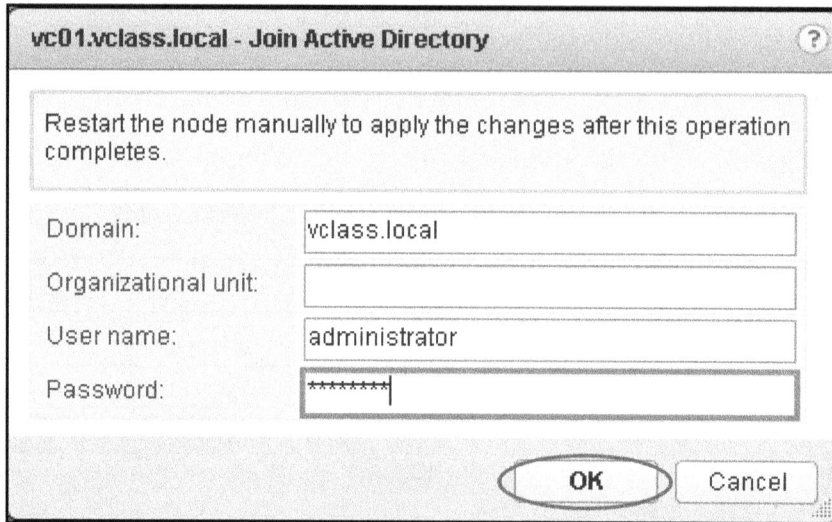

7. Note the message specifying that a restart is required. Press **OK**.
8. To reboot the vCenter Server Appliance, select the **Actions** drop-down box and click on the **Rebootâ✽ ¦** option:

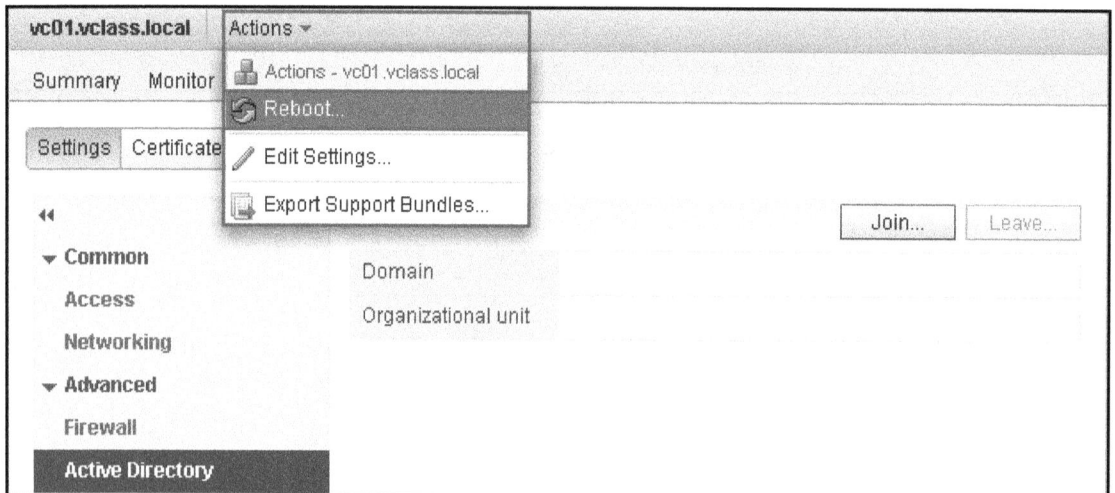

9. The **Reboot** dialog box will appear. Enter a reason for rebooting the vCenter Server Appliance:

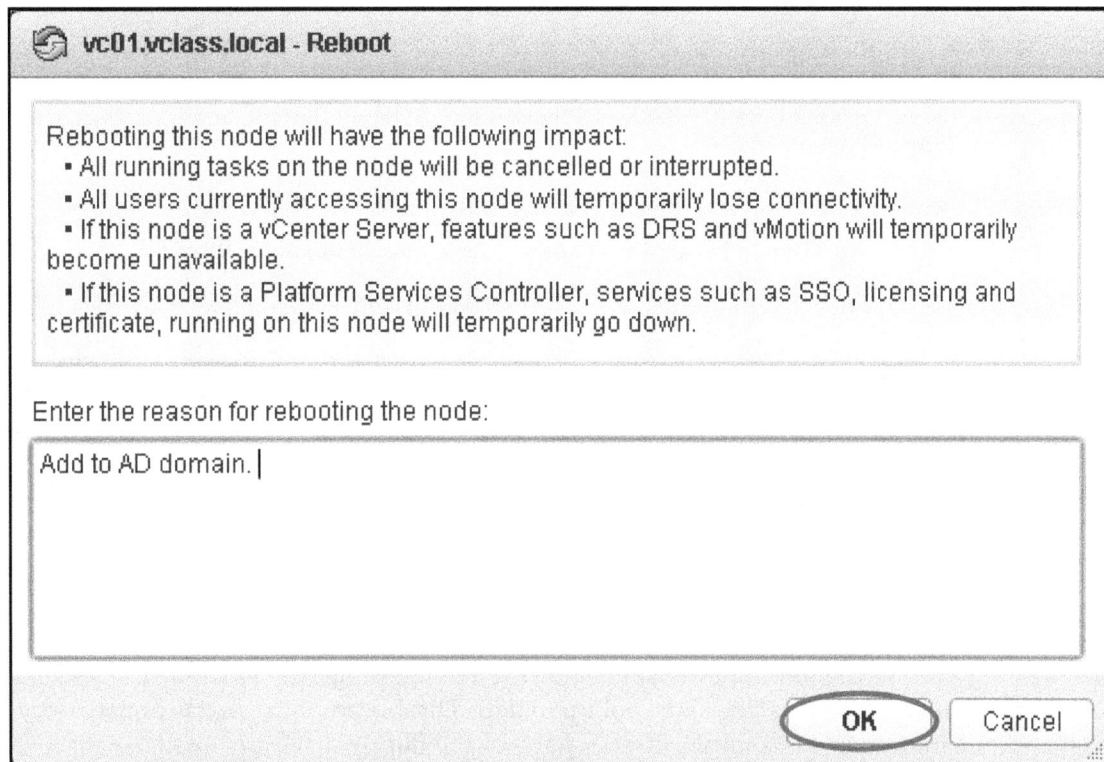

---

vc01.vclass.local - Reboot

Rebooting this node will have the following impact:
- All running tasks on the node will be cancelled or interrupted.
- All users currently accessing this node will temporarily lose connectivity.
- If this node is a vCenter Server, features such as DRS and vMotion will temporarily become unavailable.
- If this node is a Platform Services Controller, services such as SSO, licensing and certificate, running on this node will temporarily go down.

Enter the reason for rebooting the node:

Add to AD domain.

OK   Cancel

---

10. Click on **OK** to reboot.

Alternatively, the vCenter Server Appliance may be joined to Active Directory via the command line. This may be required if the vCenter Server is using an external platform services controller. This is a known issue; see KB 2118543 for more information.

To join a vCenter Server to Active Directory via the command line:

1. Open a console to the vCenter Server Appliance and log in using root and its password.
2. Run the following command:

```
/opt/likewise/bin/domainjoin-cli join domain.com
domainuser password
```

For example:

```
/opt/likewise/bin/domainjoin-cli vclass.local administrator VMware1!
```

The following screenshot demonstrates what the command will look like when successful:

```
vcsa-a:~ # /opt/likewise/bin/domainjoin-cli join vclass.local administrator VMware1!
Joining to AD Domain:   vclass.local
With Computer DNS Name: vcsa-a.vclass.local

SUCCESS
```

Securing virtual machines

For the most part, virtual machines should be secured in the same way as a physical server. Ensure that anti-virus and patches are kept up to date. Disable anything that is unnecessary on the virtual machine. For example, if serial ports or the floppy drive are not in use for a virtual machine, disable those interfaces or remove those devices. Unused interfaces could potentially be used for direct access to a virtual machine. Ideally, these configurations are made once on a virtual machine that is converted to a template, thereby reducing the risk of misconfiguration.

There are several advanced configurations that can be made to help harden the virtual machines. To do so:

1. Navigate to a virtual machine in the inventory using the vSphere Web Client.
2. Right-click on the virtual machine and select **Edit Settingsâ€¦** :

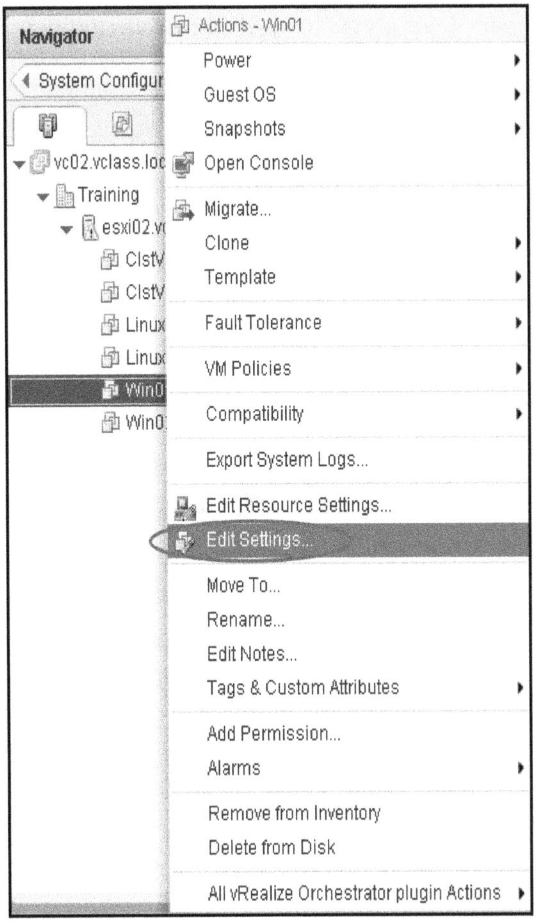

3. Click on the **VM Options** tab and expand **VMware Remote Console Options**.

4. Modify the **VMware Remote Console Options** as needed:

- **Guest OS lock**: This setting specifies to lock the guest operating system once the last remote console session is disconnected

- **Maximum number of sessions**: This setting specifies the maximum number of sessions allowed to this virtual machine concurrently:

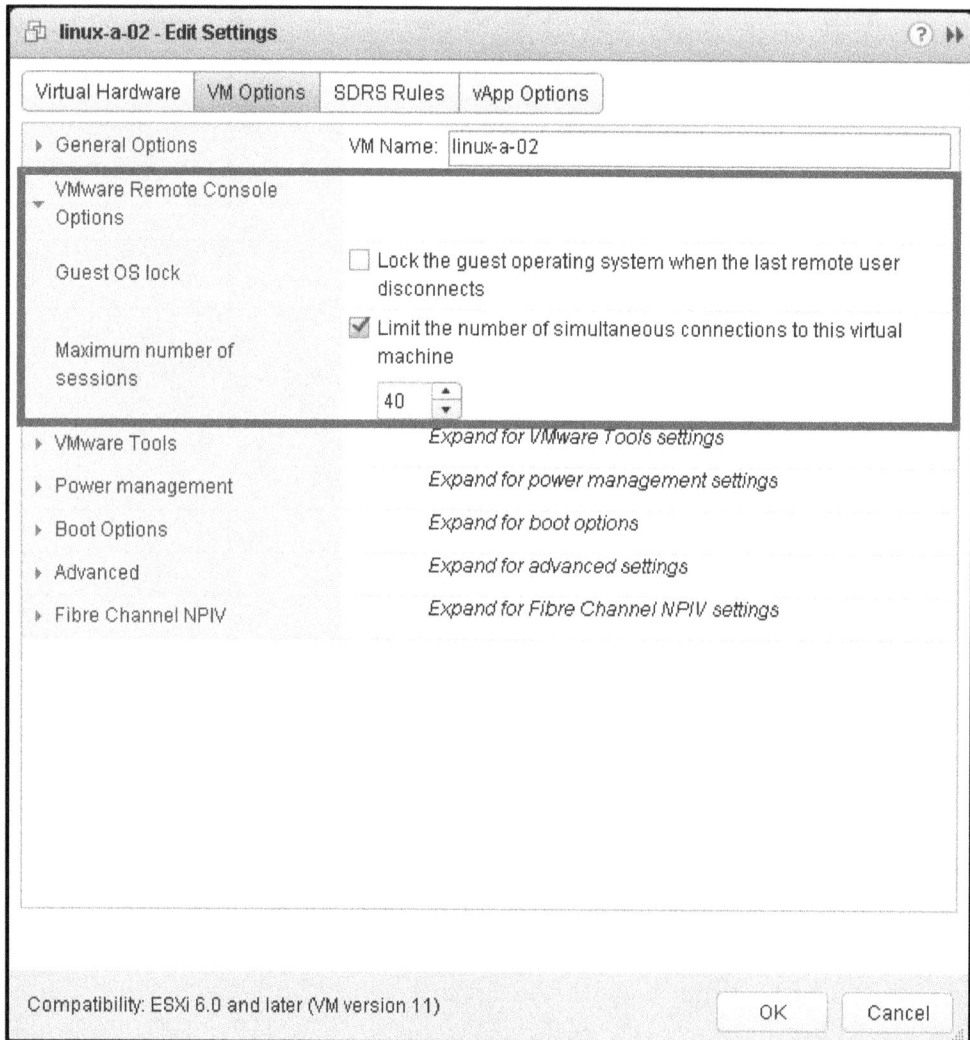

5. Additional security configurations may be made by modifying the virtual machine's advanced configuration; to do so, expand **Advanced** under the **VMOptions** tab.

6. Click on the **Edit Configurationâ✻!** button. This is demonstrated in the following screenshot:

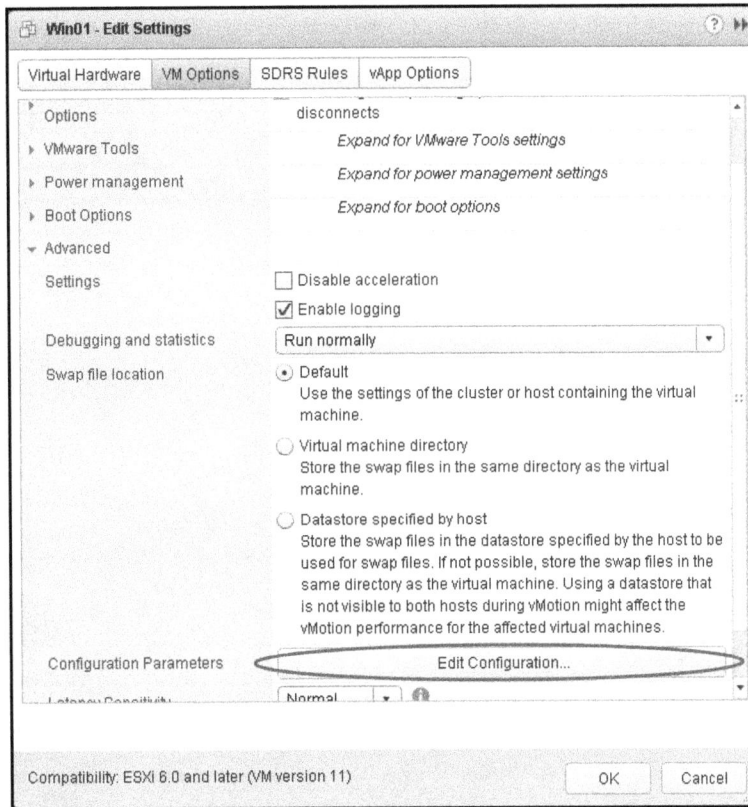

7. This will open the **Configuration Parameters** dialog, allowing for advanced options to be entered.
8. As an example, an attacker could use unused display features as an attack point for inserting malicious code. Features can be disabled if not in use. The following screenshot shows clicking on the **Add Row** button and entering the option of `svga.vgaonly` with a value of `TRUE`. When this value is set to `TRUE`, any advanced graphics will no longer function, allowing only the character-cell console mode:

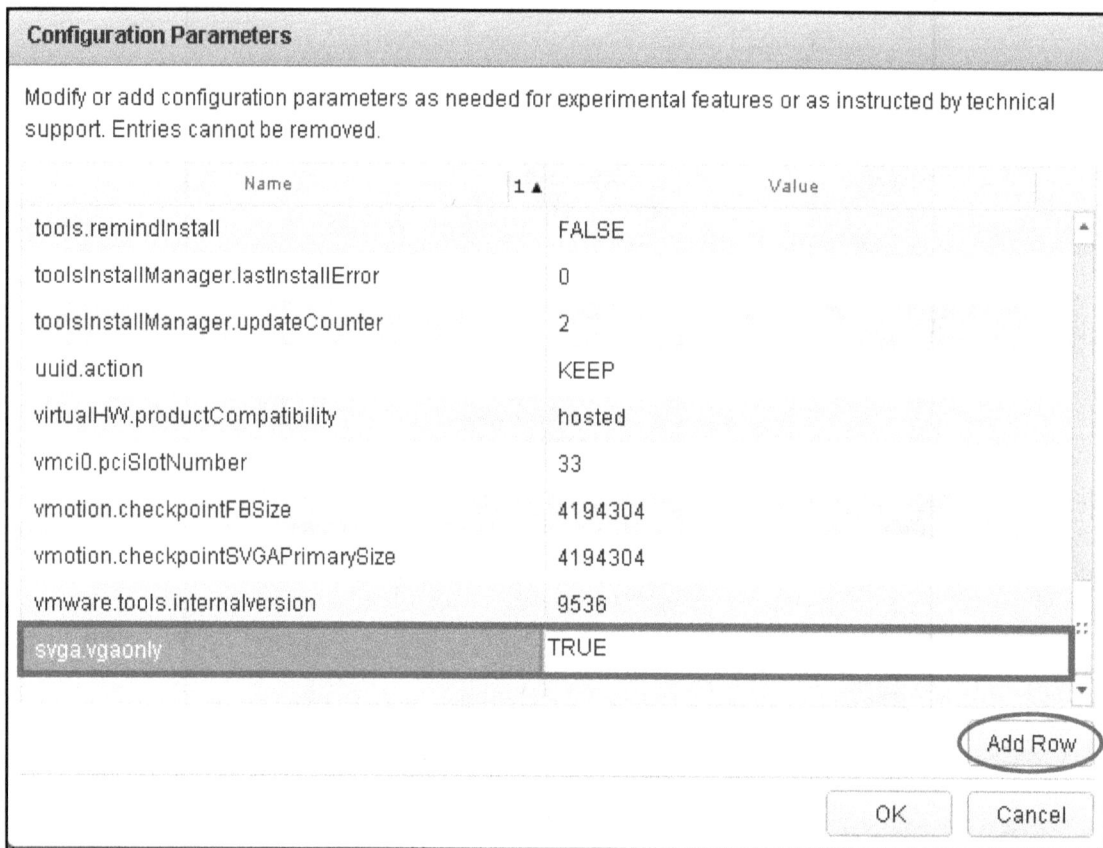

Configuration Parameters

Modify or add configuration parameters as needed for experimental features or as instructed by technical support. Entries cannot be removed.

Name	1 ▲	Value
tools.remindInstall	FALSE	
toolsInstallManager.lastInstallError	0	
toolsInstallManager.updateCounter	2	
uuid.action	KEEP	
virtualHW.productCompatibility	hosted	
vmci0.pciSlotNumber	33	
vmotion.checkpointFBSize	4194304	
vmotion.checkpointSVGAPrimarySize	4194304	
vmware.tools.internalversion	9536	
svga.vgaonly	TRUE	

Add Row

OK   Cancel

9. Another example, in the following image, shows the option of `mks.enable3d`; when the value is set to `FALSE`, virtual machines will not use 3D functionality:

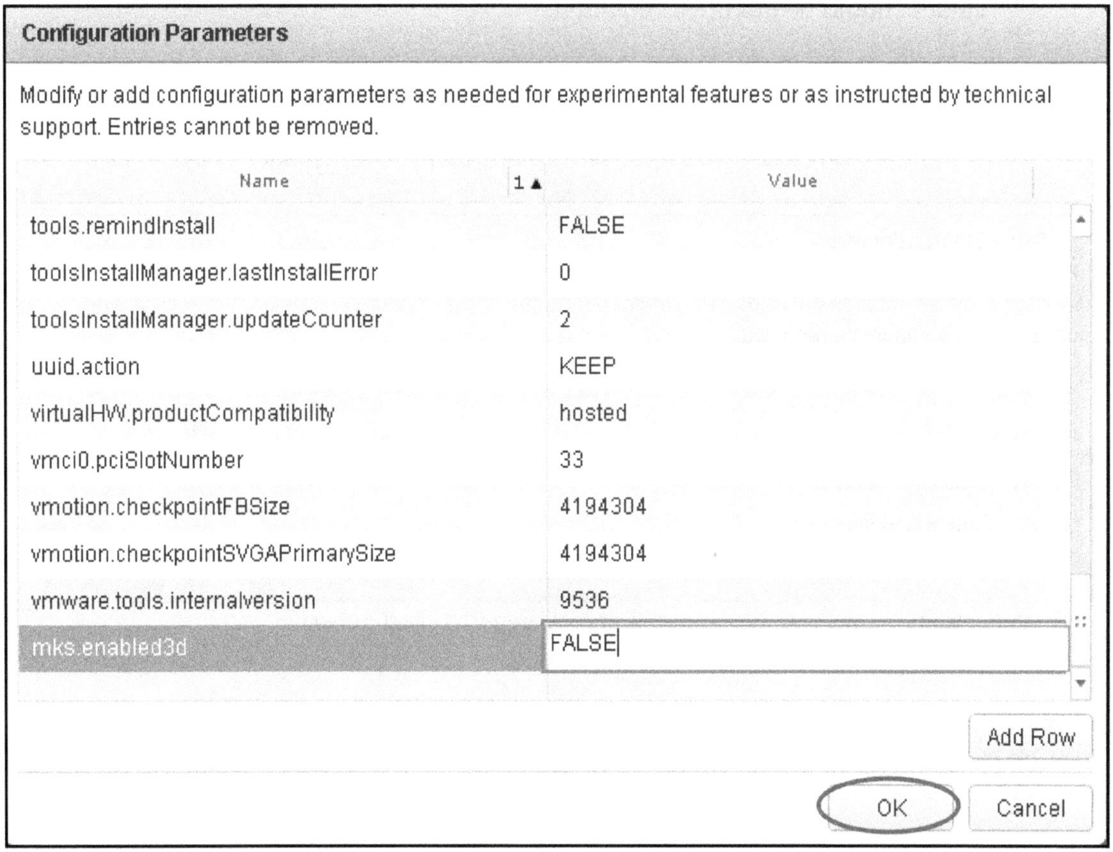

Configuration Parameters

Modify or add configuration parameters as needed for experimental features or as instructed by technical support. Entries cannot be removed.

Name	1 ▲	Value
tools.remindInstall		FALSE
toolsInstallManager.lastInstallError		0
toolsInstallManager.updateCounter		2
uuid.action		KEEP
virtualHW.productCompatibility		hosted
vmci0.pciSlotNumber		33
vmotion.checkpointFBSize		4194304
vmotion.checkpointSVGAPrimarySize		4194304
vmware.tools.internalversion		9536
mks.enabled3d		FALSE

Add Row

OK   Cancel

10. For a more common example, copy and paste is enabled whenever VMware Tools is installed. This allows copying and pasting between the guest operating system and the remote client. This functionality may be disabled. The following values should be modified or added:

- `isolation.tools.copy.disable` should be set to `true`
- `isolation.tools.paste.disable` should be set to `true`
- `isolation.tools.setGUIOptions.enable` should be set to `false`

Configuration Parameters

Modify or add configuration parameters as needed for experimental features or as instructed by technical support. Entries cannot be removed.

Name	1 ▲	Value
hpet0.present		true
isolation.tools.copy.disable		true
isolation.tools.paste.disable		true
isolation.tools.setGUIOptions.enable		false
migrate.hostLog		linux-a-02-179ad053.hlog
migrate.hostLogState		none
migrate.migrationId		0
monitor.phys_bits_used		42
nvram		linux-a-02.nvram
pciBridge0.pciSlotNumber		17
pciBridge0.present		TRUE

Add Row

OK   Cancel

11. The preceding screenshot demonstrates disabling copy and paste between the console session and the guest operating system. Once finished modifying advanced values, click on **OK**.

For more information regarding virtual machine hardening, see the vSphere Hardening Guide and the vSphere Security Guide.

vSphere authentication

vSphere uses Single Sign-On as its authentication broker and for exchanging security tokens. Authentication is separated from permissions. Single Sign-On authorizes users to authenticate once the user has been validated; however, this does not necessarily mean that the authenticated user has permissions within a vCenter Server. Permissions must be granted within the vCenter Server, separately from Single Sign-On. This section will cover Single Sign-On and its configuration. See the vSphere Permissions section for granting privileges to users.

vCenter Single Sign-On overview

Single Sign-On is a vSphere component that acts as an authentication broker and is an infrastructure for security token exchange. vCenter Single Sign-On is one of the components that the vSphere 6 **Platform Services Controller (PSC)** consists of.

Configuring Single Sign-On

Single Sign-On is a required component of the vSphere Platforms Controller (on which the vCenter Server is dependent). This section covers how to configure Single Sign-On identity sources and policies.

Identity sources

Identity sources are collections of user and group data and may be used to attach one or more domains to Single Sign-On. This user and group data is typically stored locally in the Single Sign-On machine's operating system, OpenLDAP, or Active Directory. Single Sign-On also contains an internal security domain, commonly called `vsphere.local`. This local security domain may also be used for authentication.

To configure a Single Sign-On identity source:

1. Navigate to **Administration** and then select **Configuration** underneath **Single Sign-On**. Choose the **Identity Sources** tab.
2. To add an identity source, select the add (+) button:

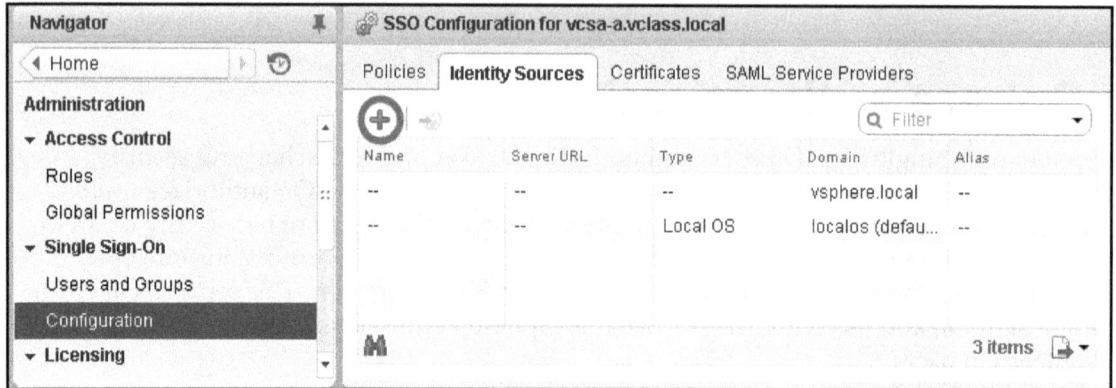

3. The **Add identity source** dialog box will appear. Select an **Identity source type** and enter the **Identity source settings** as required. There are several types of identity sources:

   - **Active Directory (Integrated Windows Authentication)**: This is ideal for Active Directory 2003 or later. A single domain may be specified as an identity source, though this domain may be a forest root domain or have child domains.
   - **Active Directory as an LDAP Server:** This option is primarily for backwards compatibility for vSphere 5.1 Single Sign-On.
   - **OpenLDAP**: This supports for OpenLDAP 2.4 or later; there is support for multiple OpenLDAP identity sources.

- **Local OS**: Only a single local operating system identity source may be configured. This option only exists with a simple Single Sign-On deployment, meaning that it is not available if multiple Single Sign-On instances (PSCs) are deployed:

4. Once the settings information has been entered, click on the **Test Connection** button to ensure that Single Sign-On can bind successfully to the identity source.

5. A popup will appear, as shown in the following screenshot, to notify you whether the connection was successfully established or not.

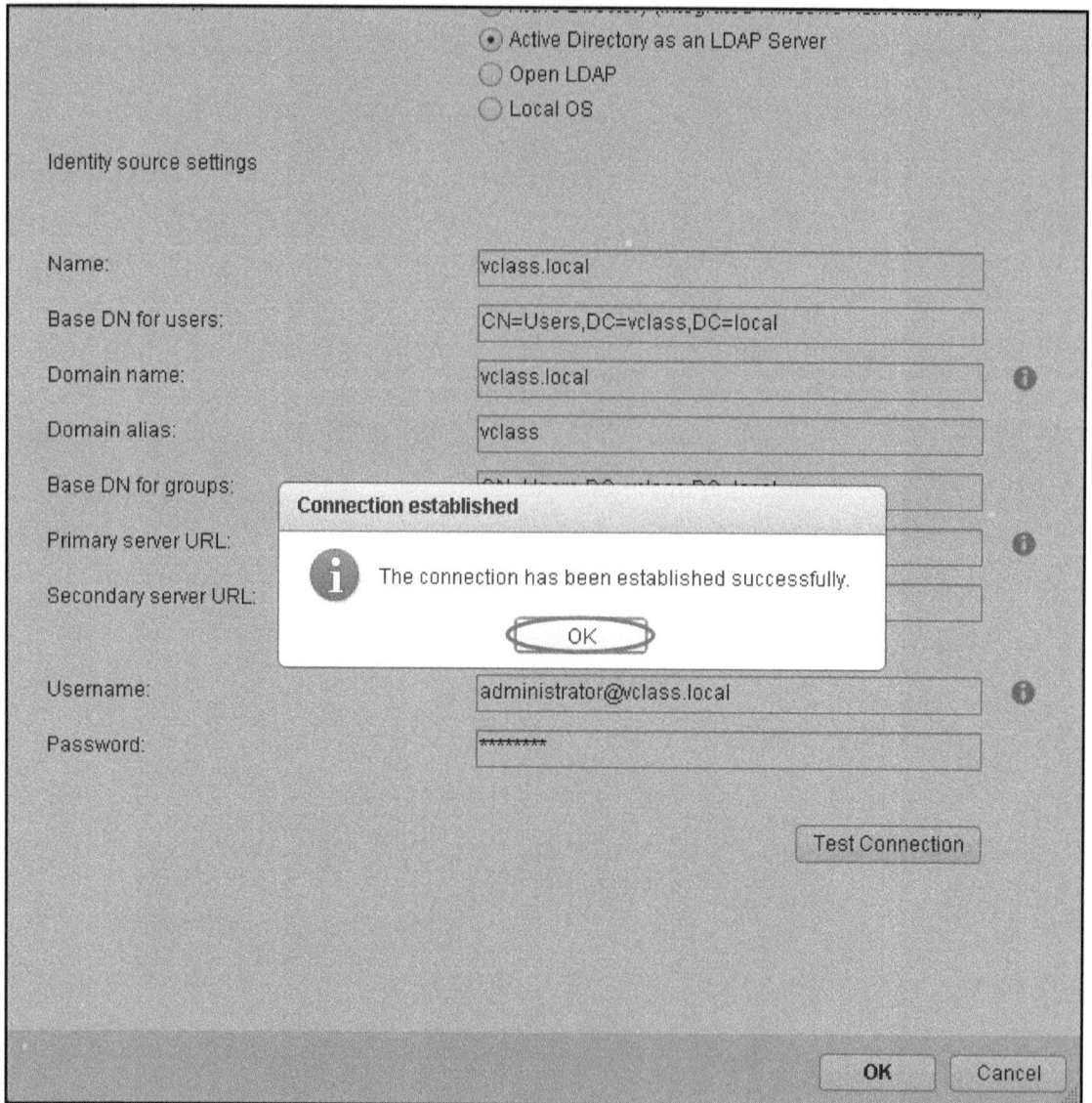

⦿ Active Directory as an LDAP Server
○ Open LDAP
○ Local OS

Identity source settings

Name:	vclass.local
Base DN for users:	CN=Users,DC=vclass,DC=local
Domain name:	vclass.local
Domain alias:	vclass
Base DN for groups:	
Primary server URL:	
Secondary server URL:	
Username:	administrator@vclass.local
Password:	********

Connection established

ⓘ The connection has been established successfully.

OK

Test Connection

OK   Cancel

6. Once successfully established, click on **OK**:

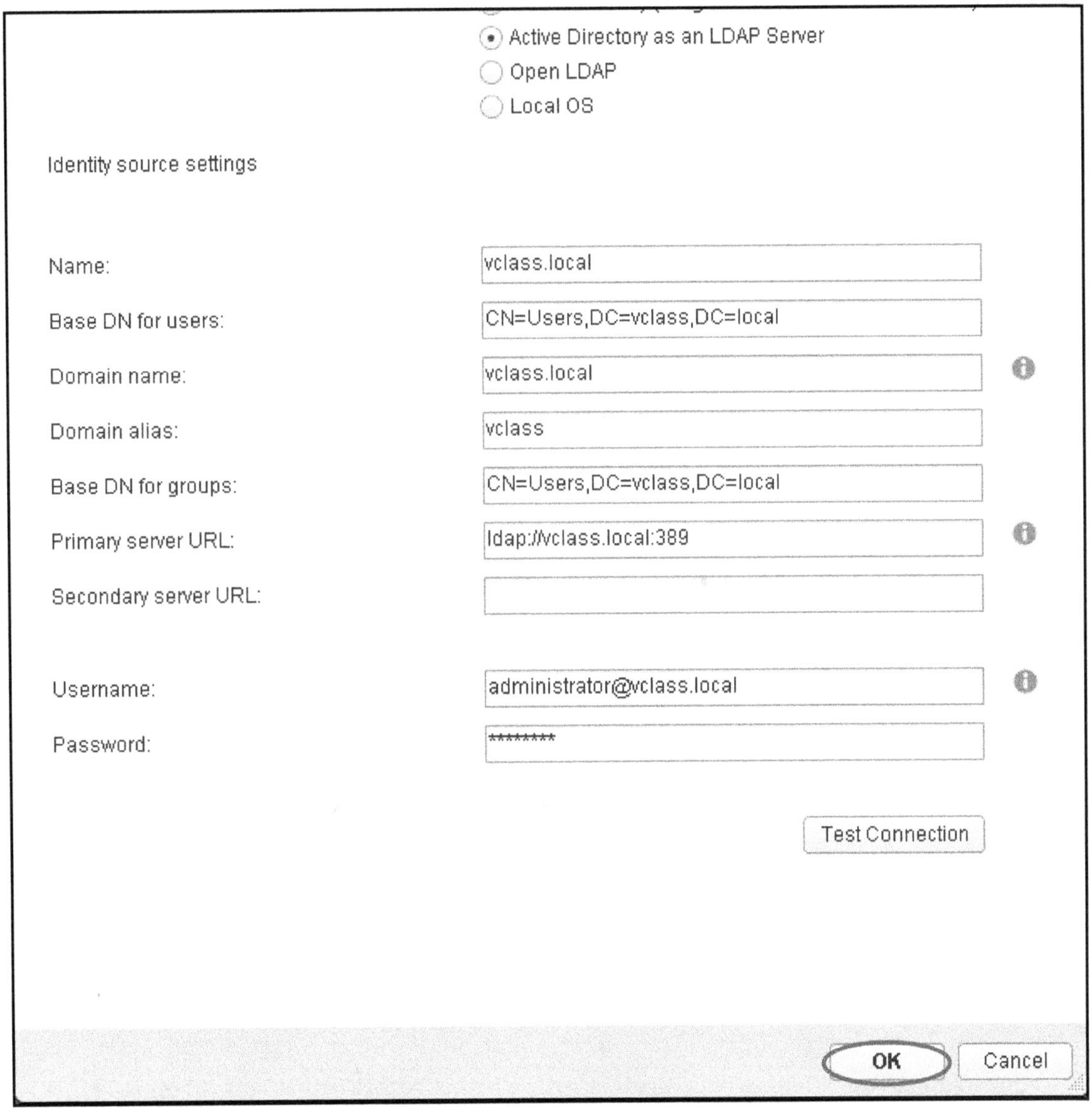

○ Active Directory as an LDAP Server
○ Open LDAP
○ Local OS

Identity source settings

Name: `vclass.local`

Base DN for users: `CN=Users,DC=vclass,DC=local`

Domain name: `vclass.local`

Domain alias: `vclass`

Base DN for groups: `CN=Users,DC=vclass,DC=local`

Primary server URL: `ldap://vclass.local:389`

Secondary server URL:

Username: `administrator@vclass.local`

Password: `********`

Test Connection

OK   Cancel

7. Once the connection has been established successfully, click on **OK** in the **Add identity source** dialog box.

Setting the default domain

The default domain specifies which domain is used for authentication when a user attempts to log in using Single Sign-On. After installing the Platform Services Controller, the default domain is set to the Single Sign-On security domain `vsphere.local`. A user signing in from any other domain would have to specify the domain at each login.

To change the default domain:

1. Log into the vSphere Web Client as a Single Sign-On administrator.
2. Navigate to Administration and then select **Configuration** under **Single Sign-On.** Choose the **Identity Sources** tab.
3. Select the desired domain. Click on the default domain button (circled in the following screenshot):

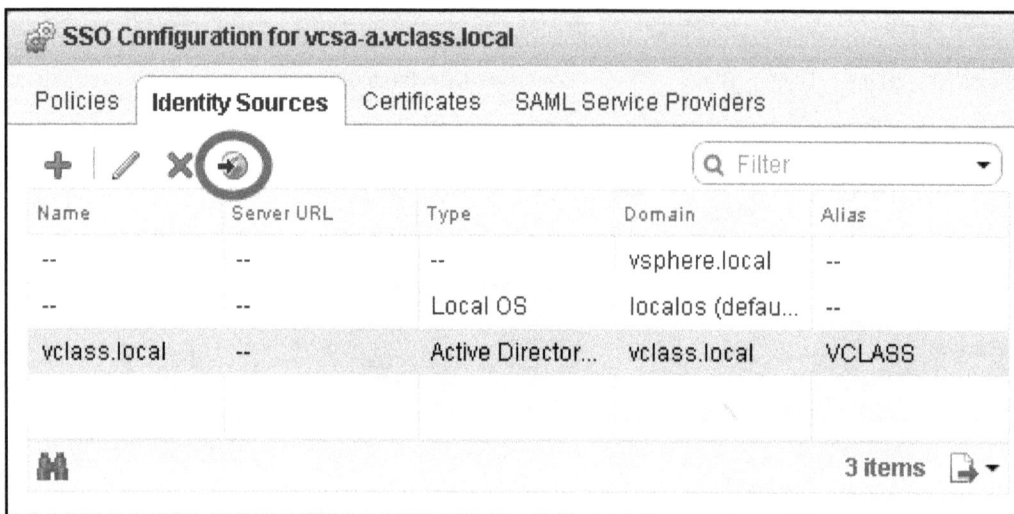

4. A **Warning** dialog will appear:

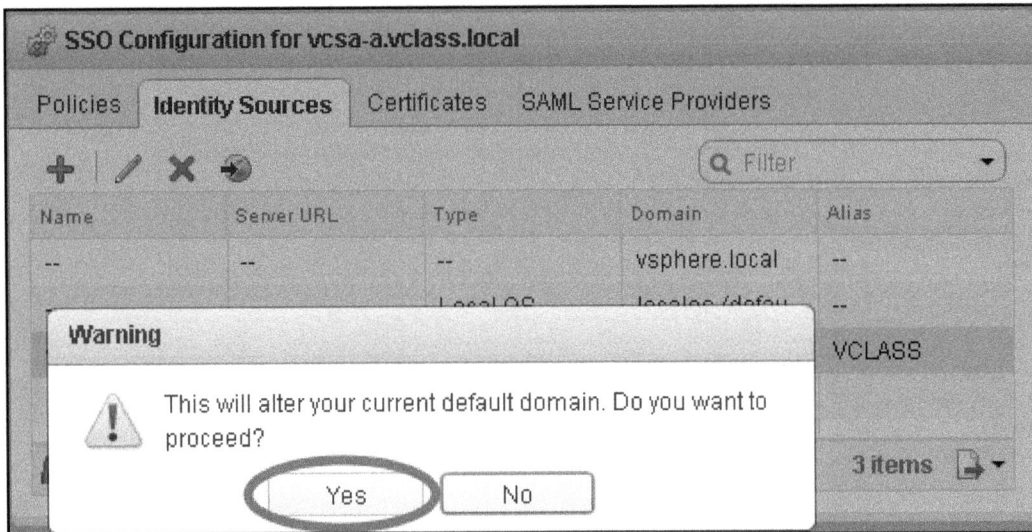

5. Click on **Yes** to change the default domain for authentication.

Single Sign-On policies

There are several different Single Sign-On policies that may be configured to enforce various security rules in a vSphere environment. This section will cover password policies, lockout policies, and token policies.

Password policies

Password policies are a set of restrictions and rules on password expiration and password format for Single Sign-On users. Keep in mind that this policy only applies to built-in Single Sign-On security domain (vsphere.local) users. To modify the password policies:

1. Log into the vSphere Web Client as a Single Sign-On administrator and navigate to **Administration**, and choose **Configuration** under **Single Sign-On**.
2. Select the **Policies** tab and then click on the **Password Policy** button.

3. Review the policies and click on **Editâ**¦ to modify:

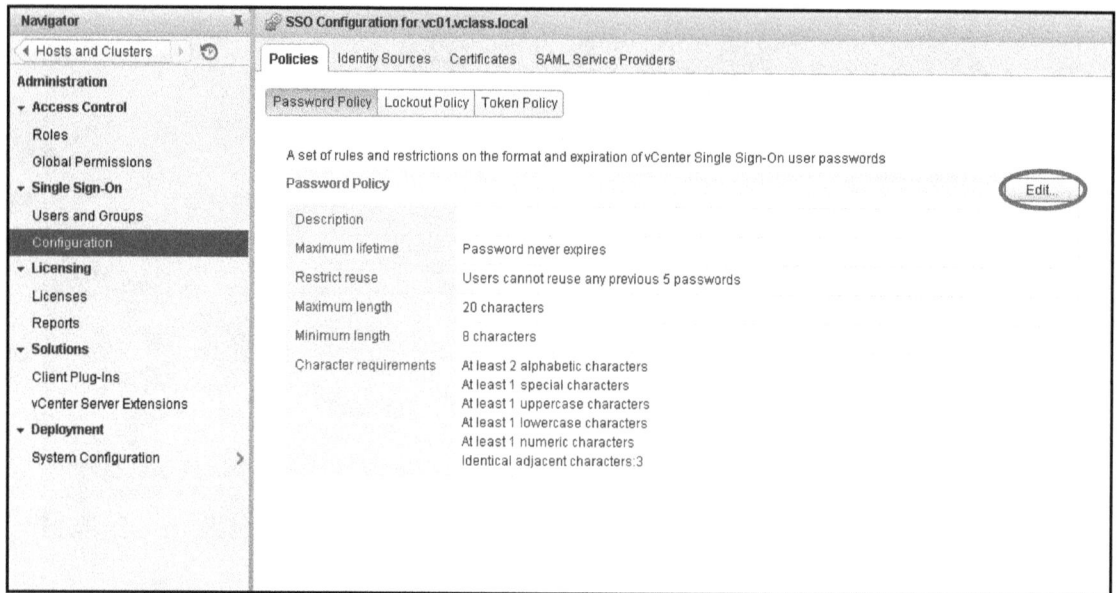

4. The **Edit Password Policies** dialog box will appear. Modify the settings as needed.

- **Maximum lifetime**: This setting specifies the maximum number of days before a password must be changed
- **Restrict reuse**: This setting specifies whether a password can be reused
- **Maximum length**: This setting specifies the maximum number of characters in a password
- **Minimum length**: This setting specifies the minimum number of characters in a password
- **Character requirements**: This setting specifies the minimum number of each character type required in a password

- **Identical adjacent characters**: This specifies the maximum number of identical characters that are consecutively allowed

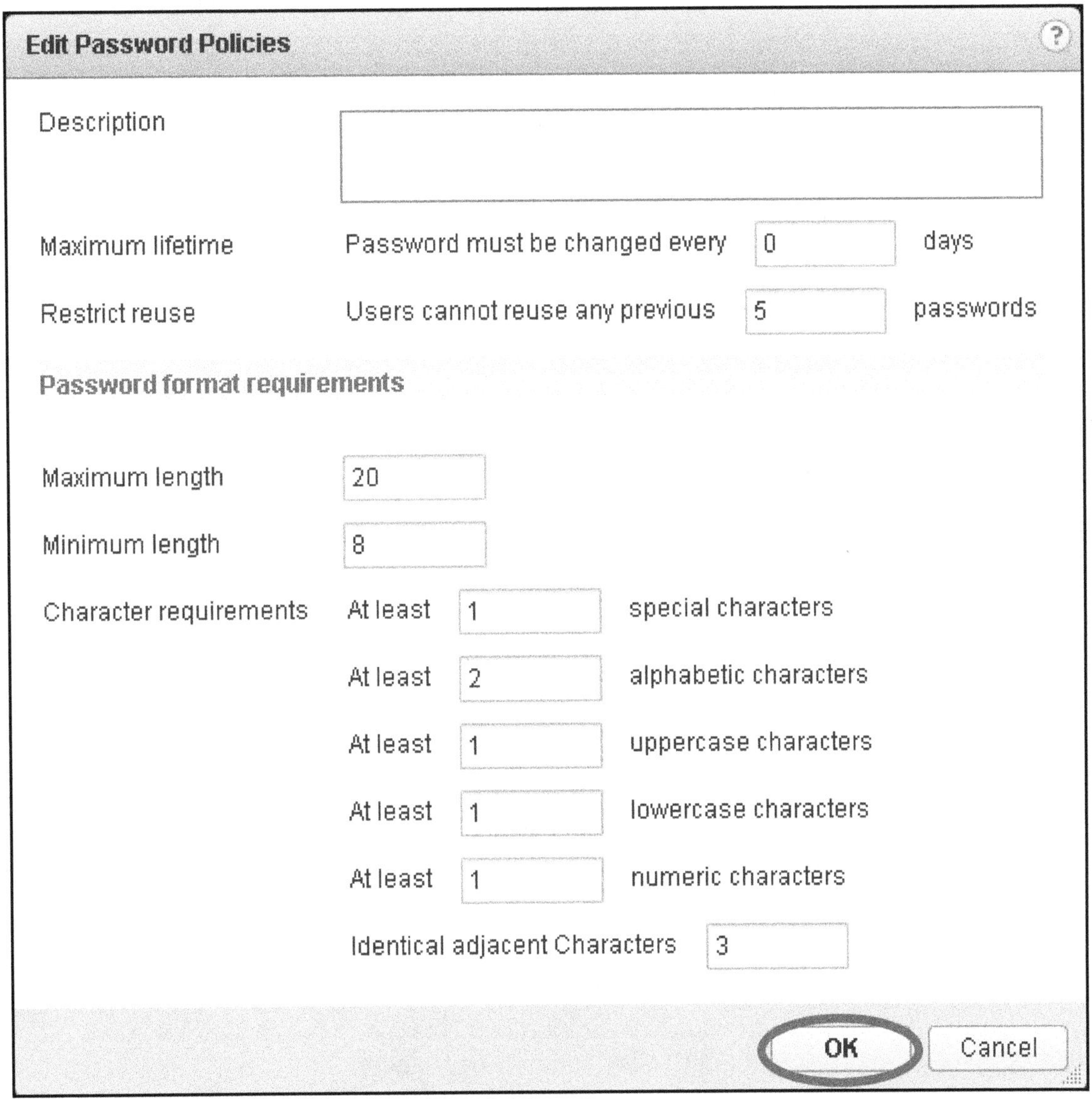

Edit Password Policies		?

Description

Maximum lifetime — Password must be changed every `0` days

Restrict reuse — Users cannot reuse any previous `5` passwords

Password format requirements

Maximum length `20`

Minimum length `8`

Character requirements — At least `1` special characters

At least `2` alphabetic characters

At least `1` uppercase characters

At least `1` lowercase characters

At least `1` numeric characters

Identical adjacent Characters `3`

[OK] [Cancel]

5. Once the password policy has been set as desired, click on the **OK** button.

Lockout policy

The Single Sign-On lockout policy specifies the settings surrounding what happens when a `vsphere.local` user enters the wrong password multiple times. To modify the lockout policy:

1. Log into the vSphere Web Client as a Single Sign-On administrator and navigate to **Administration**, and choose **Configuration** under **Single Sign-On**.
2. Select the **Policies** tab and then click on the **Lockout Policy** button.
3. Review the policies and click on the **Editâ*** button if modifying the policies is desired:

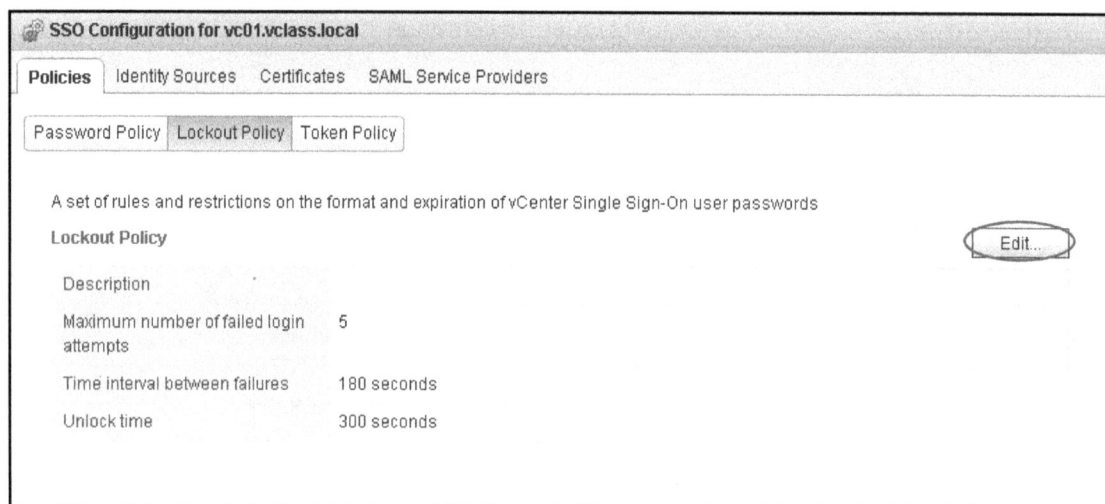

SSO Configuration for vc01.vclass.local

Policies   Identity Sources   Certificates   SAML Service Providers

Password Policy   Lockout Policy   Token Policy

A set of rules and restrictions on the format and expiration of vCenter Single Sign-On user passwords

Lockout Policy   Edit...

Description

Maximum number of failed login   5
attempts

Time interval between failures   180 seconds

Unlock time   300 seconds

---

4. The **Edit Lockout Policy** dialog will appear, allowing modifications to the policy. The following policies may be changed:

   - **Maximum number of failed login attempts**: This specifies the maximum number of times that an account may fail to log in before it is locked.
   - **Time interval between failures**: This specifies the allowable time period in which a lockout may be triggered.

- **Unlock time**: This specifies the length of time in which the lock remains. If set to 0, administration will be required to unlock the account:

5. Once finished editing the policy, click on **OK**.

Token policy

The token policy for Single Sign-On specifies such token properties as clock tolerance and renewal count. Like the other Single Sign-On policies, this may be configured to meet different infrastructure requirements. To modify the token policies:

1. Log into the vSphere Web Client as a Single Sign-On administrator and navigate to **Administration**, and choose **Configuration** under **Single Sign-On**.
2. Select the **Policies** tab and then click on the **Token Policy** button.

3. If modifying the policies is desired, click on the **Edit** button:

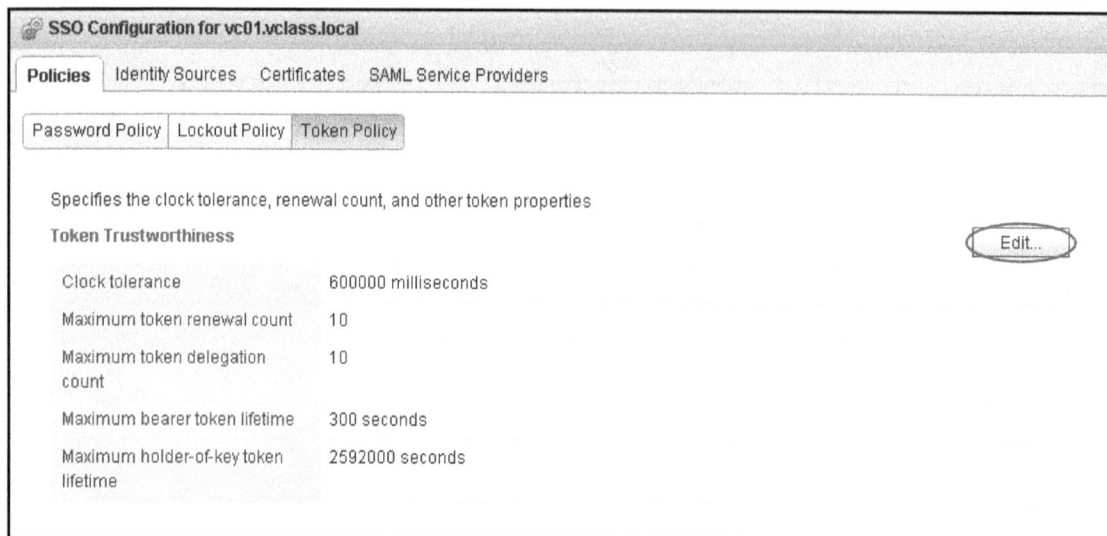

```
 SSO Configuration for vc01.vclass.local

 Policies   Identity Sources   Certificates   SAML Service Providers

  Password Policy | Lockout Policy | Token Policy


   Specifies the clock tolerance, renewal count, and other token properties
   Token Trustworthiness                                                    ( Edit... )

     Clock tolerance                   600000 milliseconds

     Maximum token renewal count       10

     Maximum token delegation          10
     count

     Maximum bearer token lifetime     300 seconds

     Maximum holder-of-key token       2592000 seconds
     lifetime
```

4. This will bring up the **Edit Token Policy** dialog box. The following variables may be modified:

   - **Clock tolerance**: This setting specifies the allowable time difference between the client and the domain controller clock. If the time difference exceeds the configured value then Single Sign-On will declare the token invalid.

   - **Maximum token renewal count**: This setting specifies the maximum allowable times that a token may be renewed. A new security token will be required once the maximum number of renewal attempts is exceeded.

   - **Maximum token delegation count**: This setting specifies the maximum allowable times that a single holder-of-key may be delegated. Holder-of-key tokens may be delegated to vSphere services. A token request may specify a DelegateTo identity, specifying a service that will perform on behalf of the principle that provided the token.

- **Maximum bearer token lifetime**: This setting specifies the maximum allowable lifetime of the bearer token before reissue is required. A bearer token provides authentication based on its possession. It is meant to be a single use, short-term operation.
- **Maximum holder-of-key token lifetime**: This setting specifies the maximum allowable lifetime of the holder-of-key token before it is marked as invalid. A holder-of-key token provides security artifact-based authentication that is embedded in the token. These are used for delegation.

Edit Token Policy			?
Clock tolerance	600000	Milliseconds	▾
Maximum token renewal count	10		
Maximum token delegation count	10		
Maximum bearer token lifetime	300	Seconds	▾
Maximum holder-of-key token lifetime	2592000	Seconds	▾
		OK	Cancel

5. Once finished modifying the values, click on **OK**.

Users and groups

Users and groups that are internal to the Single Sign-On security domain may be reviewed and additional users may be created on vsphere.local. While it is not possible to add users to other domains using the vSphere Web Client, you may add users to Single Sign-On groups.

Reviewing and creating Single Sign-On users

To view and create Single Sign-On users:

1. Log into the vSphere Web Client as a Single Sign-On administrator.
2. Navigate to **Administration** and then select **Users and Groups** underneath **Single Sign-On**.
3. Choose the **Users** tab to view the users within the vsphere.local domain. To view users in different domains, select the drop-down box next to **Domain**. (Keep in mind that users may not be created in any domain other than `vsphere.local`.)
4. A new user may be created in the Single Sign-On security domain by clicking on the plus sign (+).

Navigator								
◀ Hosts and Clusters ▶								
Administration								
▼ Access Control								
Roles								
Global Permissions								
▼ Single Sign-On								
Users and Groups								
Configuration								

vCenter Users and Groups

Users | Solution Users | Groups

Domain: vsphere.local ▾

⊕   Q Filter

Username	First Name	Last Name	Email	,	Description	Locked	Disabled	Domain
krbtgt/VSPH...						No	No	vsphere.local
Administrator	Administrator	vsphere.local				No	No	vsphere.local
waiter-6679...	waiter	6679d9ae-c...				No	No	vsphere.local
K/M						No	No	vsphere.local

5. This will bring up the **New User** dialog box. Enter a **User name**, **Password**, and optionally **First name**, **Last name**, and **Email address**.

6. Once finished, click on **OK**.

Single Sign-On user management

Single Sign-On users can be disabled, enabled, or unlocked if necessary.

To disable an account:

1. Go to the **Users** tab in Single Sign-On configuration.
2. Select the desired user account and then click on the **Disable** button (circled in the following screenshot):

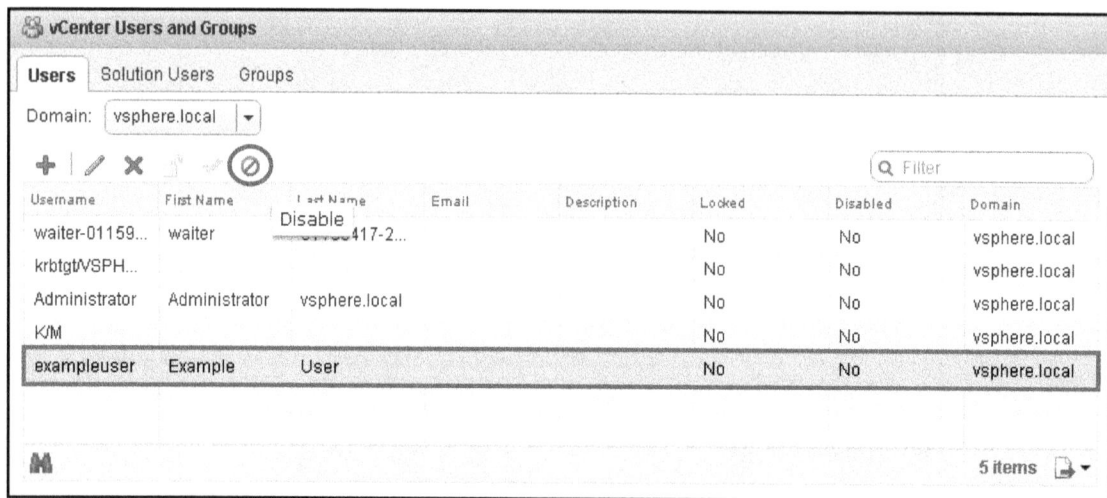

3. The **Disable user** dialog will appear. Click on **Yes** to disable the account.

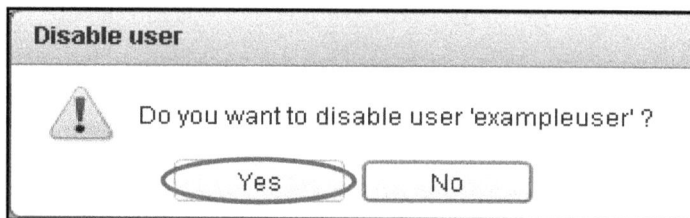

To re-enable a user account:

1. Go to the **Users** tab in Single Sign-On configuration.
2. Select the desired user account and then click on the Enable button (circled in the following screenshot).

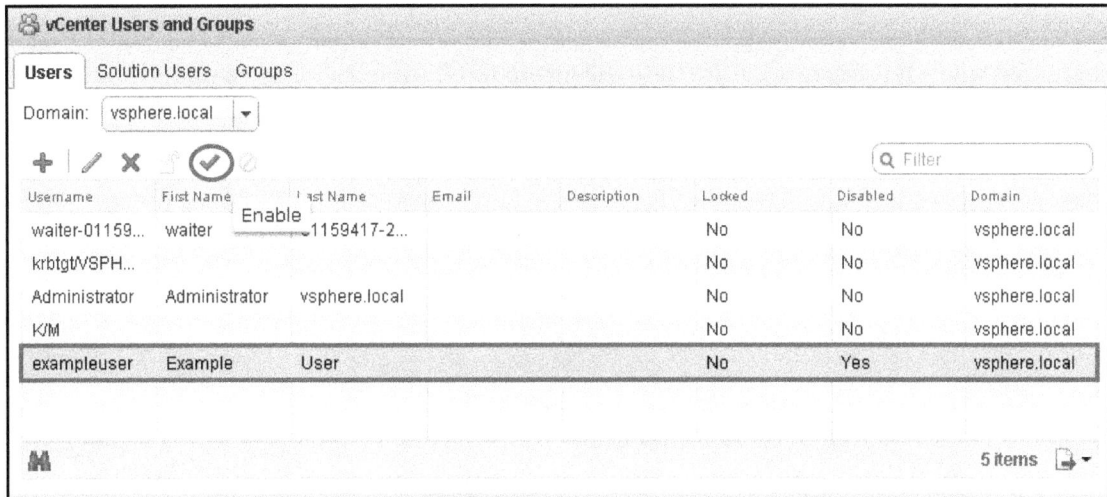

Username	First Name	Last Name	Email	Description	Locked	Disabled	Domain
waiter-01159...	waiter	-1159417-2...			No	No	vsphere.local
krbtgt/VSPH...					No	No	vsphere.local
Administrator	Administrator	vsphere.local			No	No	vsphere.local
K/M					No	No	vsphere.local
exampleuser	Example	User			No	Yes	vsphere.local

3. To re-enable the account, click on **Yes**.

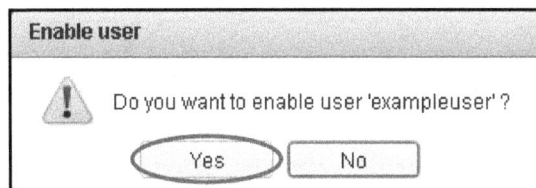

An account may also be unlocked by clicking on the lock button after selecting a user.

Managing group membership

Single Sign-On groups may have members that are users of other groups, and these may come from multiple identity sources. To add a user to a Single Sign-On group:

1. Log into the vSphere Web Client as a Single Sign-On administrator account.
2. Navigate to **Administration** and then choose **Users and Groups** under Single Sign-On.
3. Select the **Groups** tab. Choose the group to which a user will be added.
4. Click on the **Add Members** button under the **Group Members** area.

5. The **Add Principals** dialog box will appear. Select the **Domain** and then select the user that should be a group member.

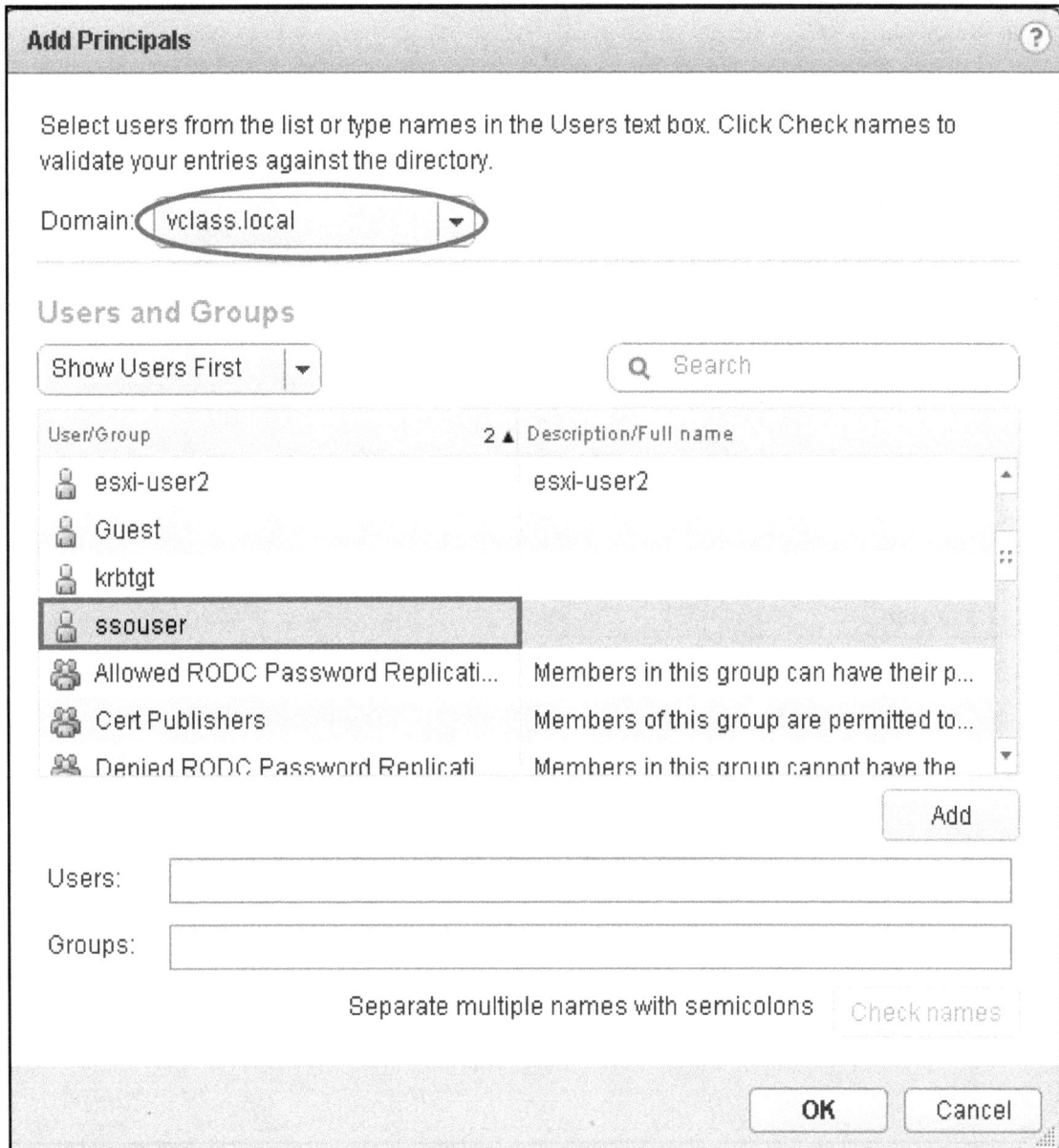

6. Once the user has been selected, click on the **Add** button. Click on the **Check names** button.

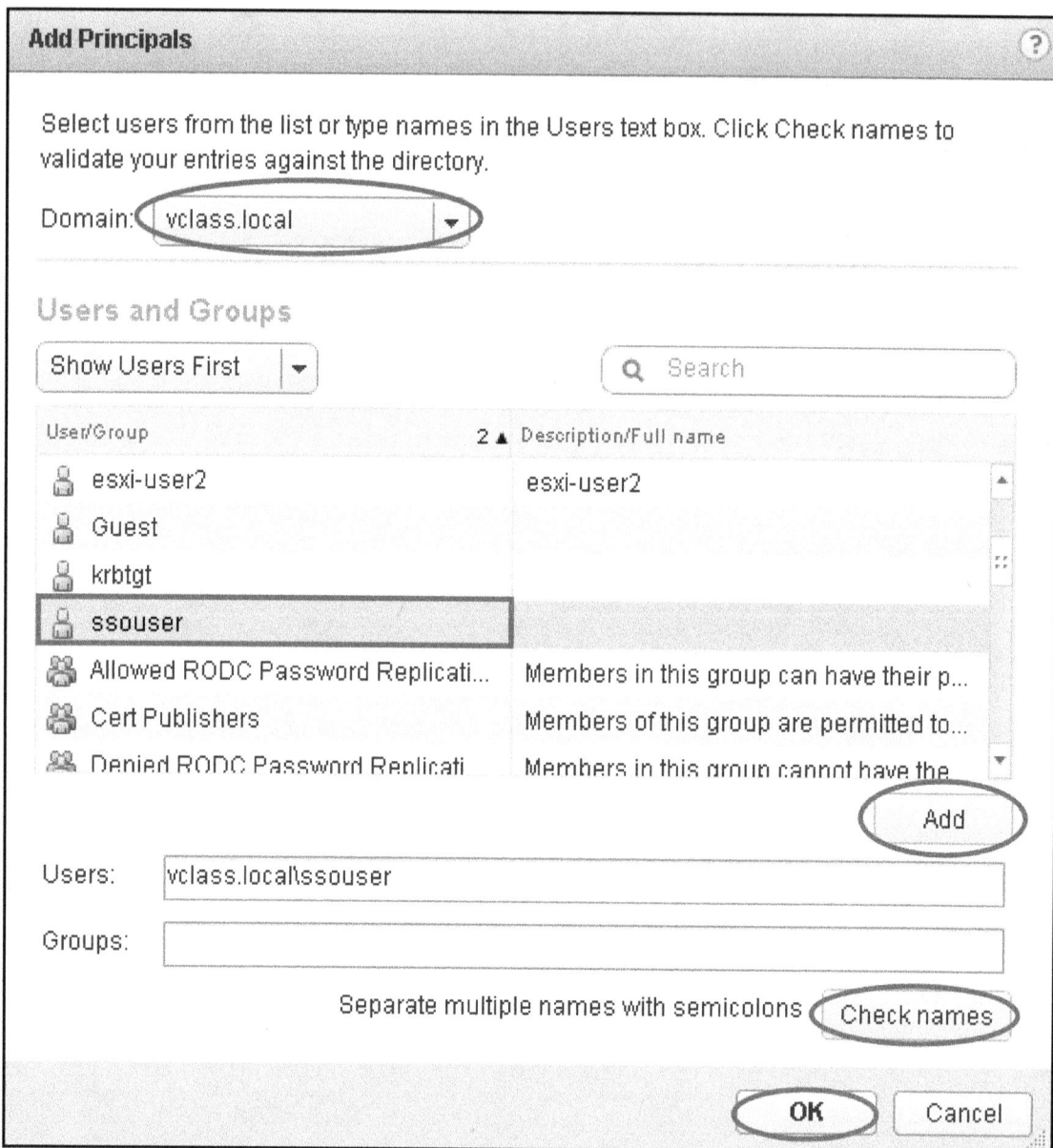

Add Principals

Select users from the list or type names in the Users text box. Click Check names to validate your entries against the directory.

Domain: vclass.local

Users and Groups

Show Users First

Q Search

User/Group	2 ▲	Description/Full name
👤 esxi-user2		esxi-user2
👤 Guest		
👤 krbtgt		
👤 ssouser		
👥 Allowed RODC Password Replicati...		Members in this group can have their p...
👥 Cert Publishers		Members of this group are permitted to...
👥 Denied RODC Password Replicati		Members in this group cannot have the

Add

Users: vclass.local\ssouser

Groups:

Separate multiple names with semicolons   Check names

OK   Cancel

7. Click on **OK** once finished.

vSphere permissions

Single Sign-On provides authentication, but once authenticated vCenter Server defines the scope of access. Permissions are defined within the vCenter Server inventory hierarchy and consist of three things:

- **User/Group**: This specifies who has access
- **Role:** This specifies the user or group's privileges
- **Object:** This specifies where the user or group can execute their privileges

In order to have permissions, all three of these must be defined.

Defining a custom role

There are three built-in roles: administrator, no access, and read-only. Quite a few sample roles have also been created and are available for use. Custom roles may also be created to fit an organization's needs. To create a custom role:

1. Log into the vSphere Web Client as an administrator.
2. Navigate to **Administration** and select **Roles** under **Access Control**.
3. To create a custom role, click on the Add button (+).

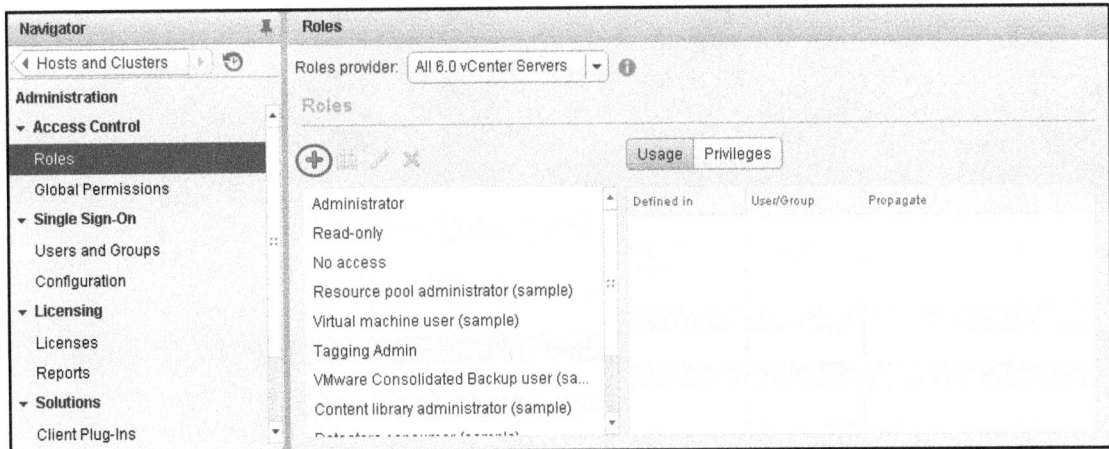

4. The **Create Role** dialog will appear. Go through and select the desired privileges for the role. The example is called **Virtual Machine Creator** and consists of the following privileges:

- Allocate space, under **Datastore**
- Assign network, under **Network**
- Assign virtual machine to resource pool, under **Resource**
- Add new disk, Add or remove device, and Memory under **Virtual machine** | **Configuration**
- All privileges within Interaction, under **Virtual machine**
- Create new, under **Virtual machine** | **Inventory**

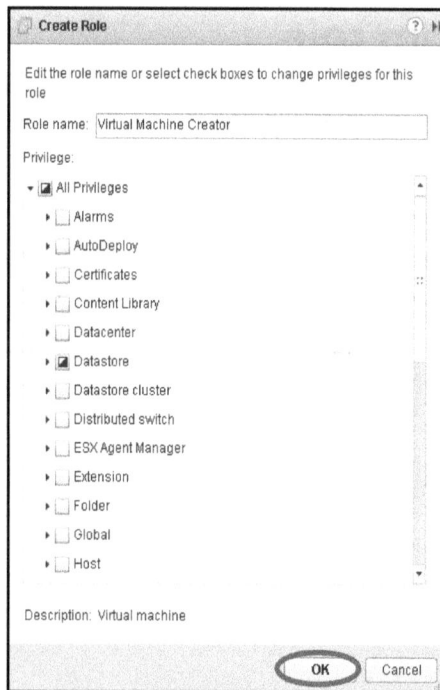

5. Click on **OK** once the privileges are assigned.

Appling permissions

1. To assign a newly created role as a permission, go to an inventory object (in this case, the training data center) and select the **Manage** tab. Choose the **Permissions** button.
2. Click on the Add (+) button.

3. This will bring up the **Add Permission** dialog box. On the right-hand pane, select the drop-down box and choose the desired role with the correct set of privileges.

4. To select which users and/or groups should be assigned to the role on this object, click on the **Addâ✤¦** button.

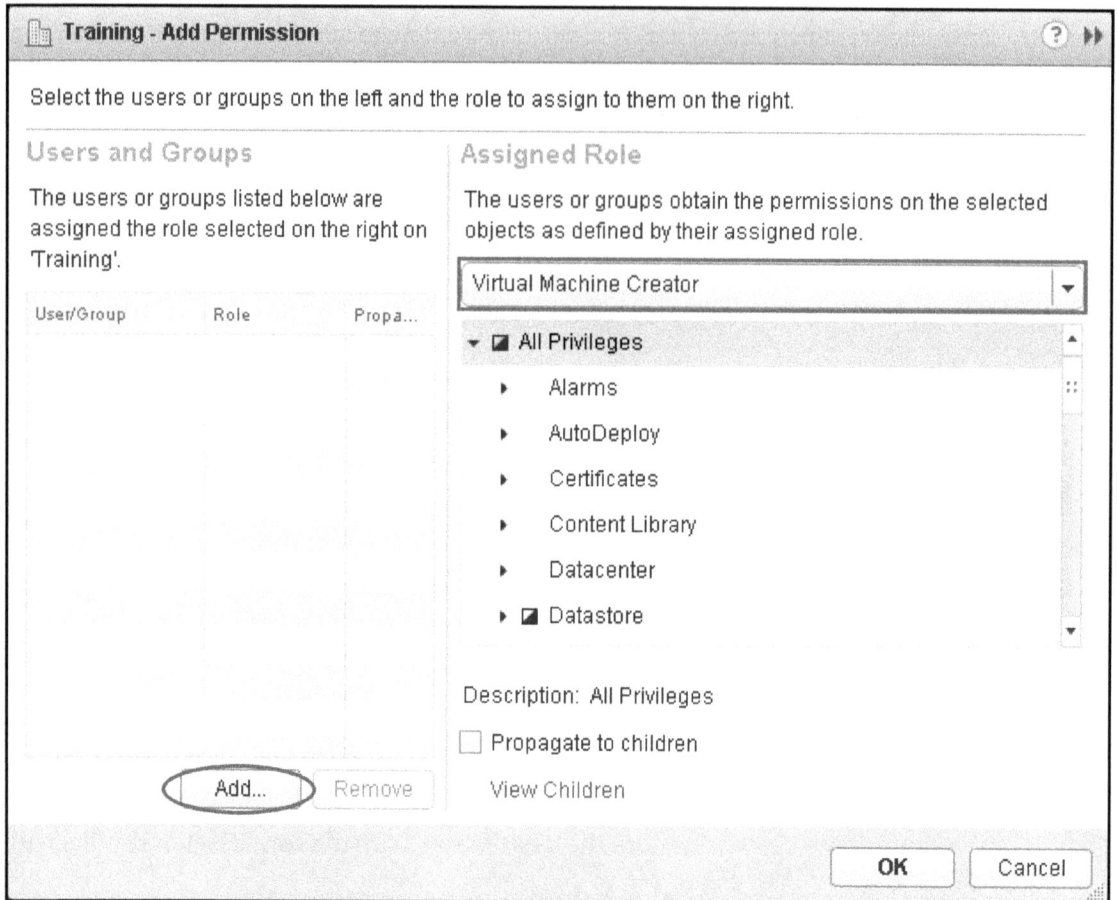

5. The **Select Users/Groups** will bring up the dialog box. Choose the **Domain** and select which user or group should be given granted permissions.

6. Once the user and/or group has been selected, click on **Add** and then **Check names**.

7. Click on **OK** once finished.

8. Review the selections made.

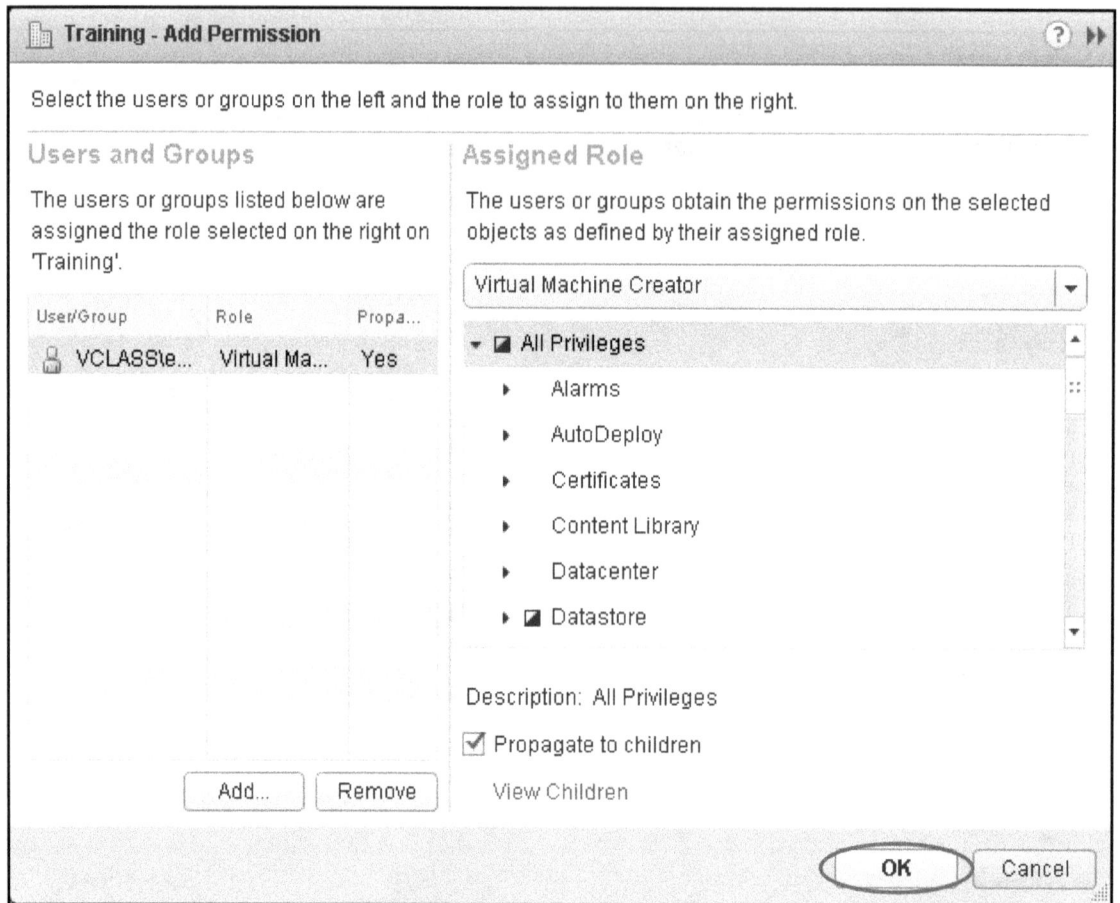

9. Click on **OK** once finished.
10. Repeat steps 1 through 9 as necessary to ensure that permissions have been placed on all the required inventory objects.

Reviewing permissions

Once permissions are assigned, it is possible to review the role's application. To do so:

1. Log into the vSphere Web Client as an administrator.
2. Navigate to **Administration** and select **Roles** under **Access Control**.
3. Select a role from the list and click on the **Usage** button.

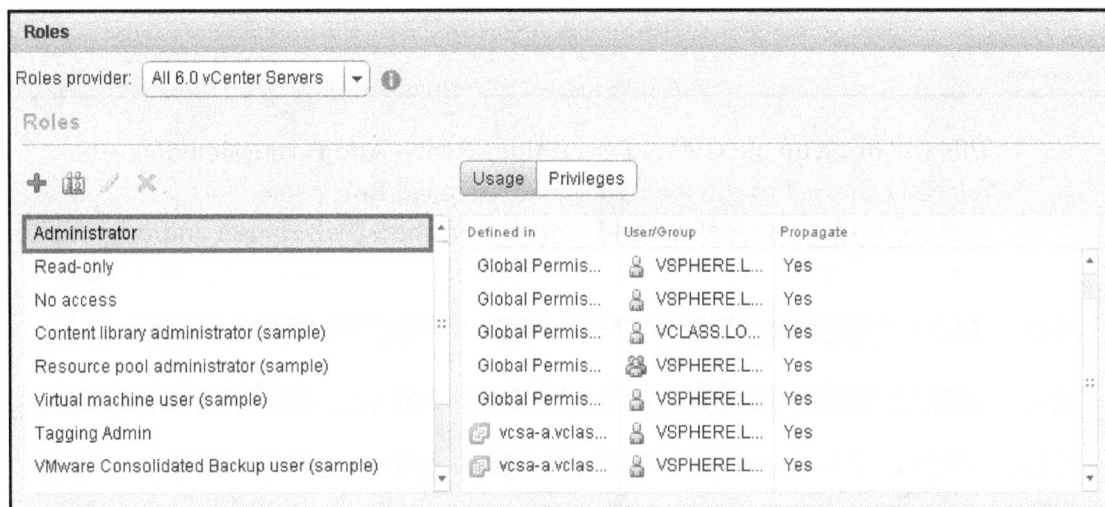

This shows where the permissions have been applied. This is useful for troubleshooting when permissions do not work as desired.

Global permissions

Global permissions are applied at a global root level and span multiple VMware solutions. Global permissions can be used to assign privileges to users or groups across all objects in all hierarchies. Use global permissions only as needed.

To add a global permission:

1. Log into the vSphere Web Client as an administrator.
2. Navigate to **Administration** and select **Global Permissions** under **Access Control**.

3. To add a permission, click on the Add button (+).

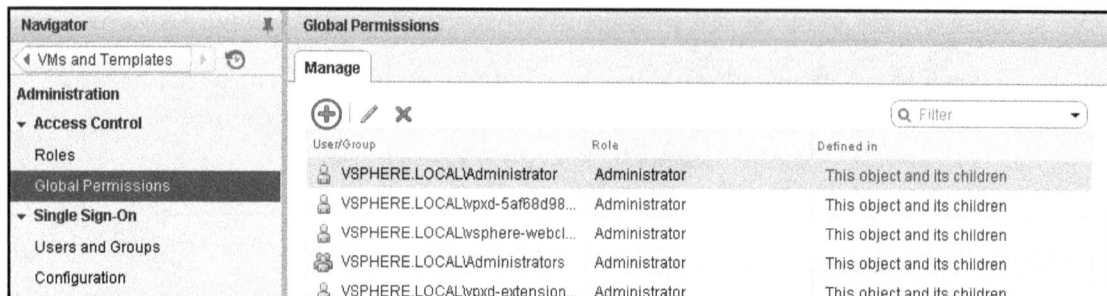

4. This will bring up the **Global Permissions Root – Add Permission** dialog box.
5. Select the desired role in the right-hand **Assigned Role** pane.
6. Click on **Add...** under **Users and Groups** and choose which user and/or group to assign privileges to.

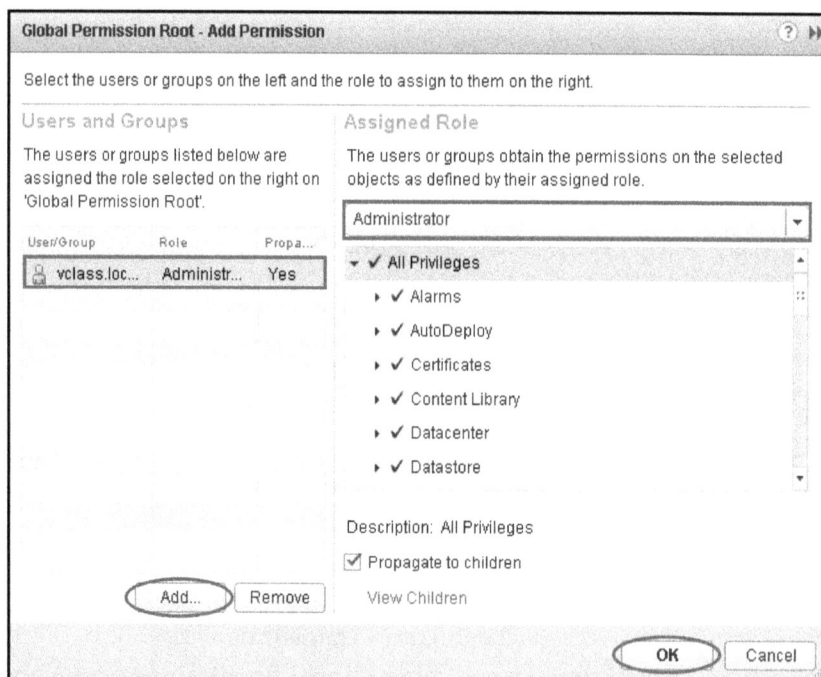

7. Click on **OK** once finished.

Syslog

Each ESXi host runs a syslog service that is used to log VMkernel messages, as well as messages from other system components, to a set of log files.

Syslog settings may be modified using the vSphere Web Client.

To do so:

1. Using the vSphere Web Client, navigate to an ESXi host in the inventory.
2. Go to the **Manage** tab and select the **Settings** button.
3. Choose **Advanced System Settings** underneath the **System** section.
4. Search `syslog` in the query section, as demonstrated in the following screenshot:

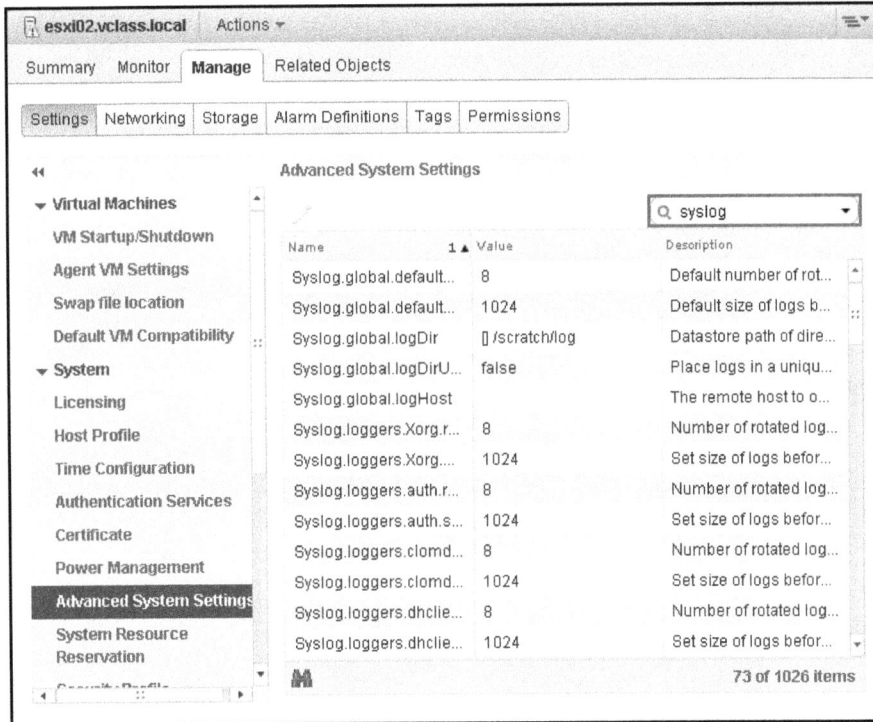

5. The following syslog values may be changed:

- `Syslog.global.defaultRotate`: This setting specifies the maximum number of logs to keep.
- `Syslog.global.defaultSize`: This setting specifies the default size of a log, in KB, before a log is rotated by the system.
- `Syslog.global.LogDir`: This setting specifies the directory in which logs are stored. This can be an NFS or VMFS datastore.
- `Syslog.global.logDirUnique`: This setting creates a unique subdirectory with the name of the ESXi host.
- `Syslog.global.LogHost`: This setting specifies the remote host and port where syslog messages are forwarded.

6. To modify a syslog value, select the **Name** in the list and click on the Modify (pencil) button.

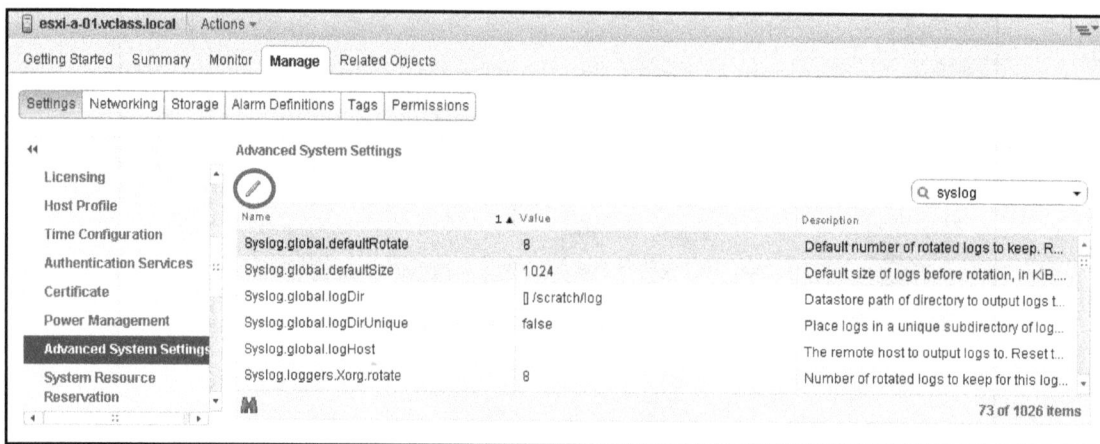

7. The following screenshot demonstrates modifying the
   `Syslog.global.defaultRotate` option.

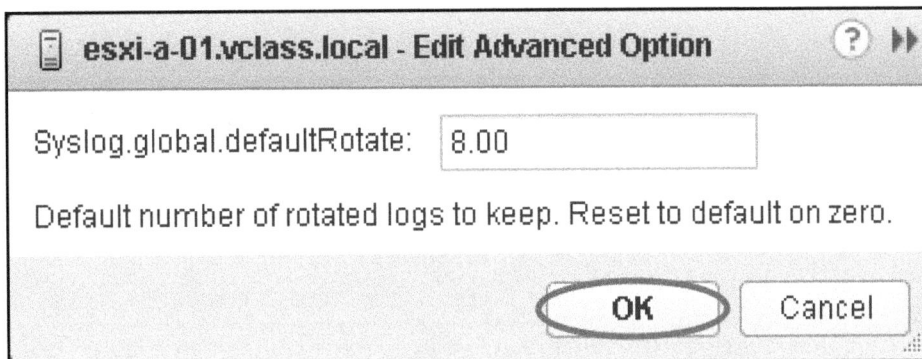

> **esxi-a-01.vclass.local - Edit Advanced Option**
>
> Syslog.global.defaultRotate: 8.00
>
> Default number of rotated logs to keep. Reset to default on zero.
>
> **OK**   Cancel

8. Once the value has been modified as desired, click on **OK**.
9. Repeat steps 5-8 as needed.

Summary

In this chapter, the importance of securing a vSphere environment was discussed. Also covered was how to secure ESXi, vCenter Server, and virtual machines. Virtual machines should typically be secured just like a physical server, and anything unused can be disabled. ESXi has a built-in firewall that can be modified, as well as a lockdown mode that can be enabled. vSphere permissions can be used to limit access to the infrastructure by creating custom roles and only applying permissions where needed. Single Sign-On provides an authentication framework for vSphere by creating its own security domain.

The next chapter will discuss vSphere life cycle management, covering the upgrade of vSphere components from vSphere 5.x to vSphere 6.

12
Life Cycle Management of a vSphere Environment

Proper management and maintenance of a vSphere environment requires a comprehensive understanding of vSphere components and the order in which they are to be updated. This process should always begin with reading the vSphere release notes and the installation guide for the latest version. Generally this process will begin with upgrading vCenter Server, followed by vSphere Update Manager, ESXi, then vSphere Distributed Switches and lastly the virtual machines (VMware Tools and then virtual hardware).

In this chapter, you will learn about:

- Planning an upgrade
- Upgrading vCenter Server
- Upgrading vSphere Update Manager
- Upgrading ESXi
- Upgrading Virtual machines

Planning an upgrade

There are many options for upgrading a vSphere environment to vSphere 6.0. It is imperative that the upgrade options, task sequence, and configuration details are understood. The vCenter Server architecture has changed as a part of this vSphere release, introducing the Platform Services Controller. Be sure to review new architecture prior to beginning an upgrade.

The following provides an overview for upgrading to vSphere 6.0:

1. Review the vSphere release notes.
2. Ensure that the system to be upgraded meets the hardware and software requirements for vSphere 6.0 (See the vSphere Upgrade guide `https://pubs.vmw are.com/vsphere-6/topic/com.vmware.ICbase/PDF/vsphere-esxi-vcenter-s erver-6-upgrade-guide.pdf` and Hardware Compatibility List `http://www.vmw are.com/resources/compatibility/search.php`).
3. Verify that any plug-ins or additional VMware solutions are compatible with vSphere 6.0.
4. Back up the current configuration.
5. Upgrade vCenter Server.
6. Upgrade the vSphere Client.
7. Upgrade vSphere Update Manager.
8. Upgrade ESXi hosts.
9. Upgrade VMware Tools in virtual machines.
10. Upgrade virtual machine hardware version.

Upgrading vCenter Server

Keep in mind that the vCenter Server architecture has changed in vSphere 6. Refer back to `Chapter 3`, *The Management Layer – VMware vCenter* for more information.

Upgrade Paths

An infrastructure's vCenter Server 5.1/5.5 configuration will determine its configuration post-upgrade. If the outcome is not desired, consider installing a new vCenter Server rather than completing an in-place upgrade. However, if the vCenter Server is 5.0, there is no Single Sign-On installed and configured, therefore an option will be presented to choose whether the vCenter Server 6.0 configuration should be embedded or external.

The following image demonstrates a vCenter Server 5.1 or 5.5 simple installation, where all components were installed on the same system. When upgrading to vCenter Server 6.0, the outcome will result in an embedded configuration (with the vCenter Server and Platform Service Controller components co-installed on the same system).

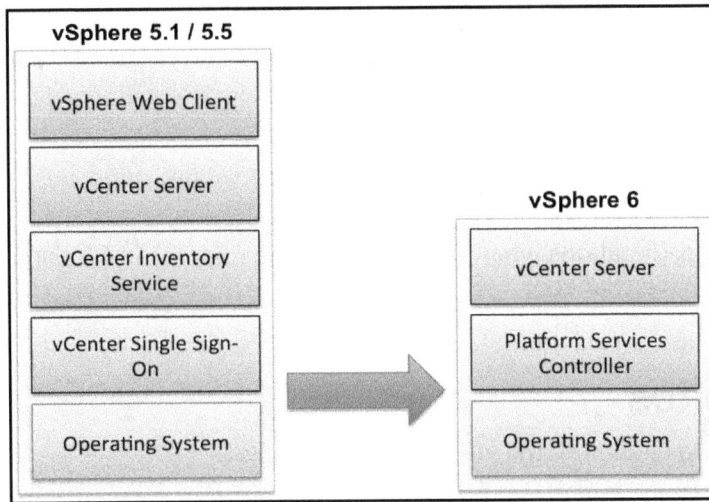

On the other hand, if the vCenter Server 5.1/5.5 is a custom installation with the vCenter Single Sign-On services installed on a separate system, then the vCenter Server 6.0 upgrade will result in a deployment with vCenter Server and the Platform Services Controller on separate systems (external configuration). This is demonstrated with the following image:

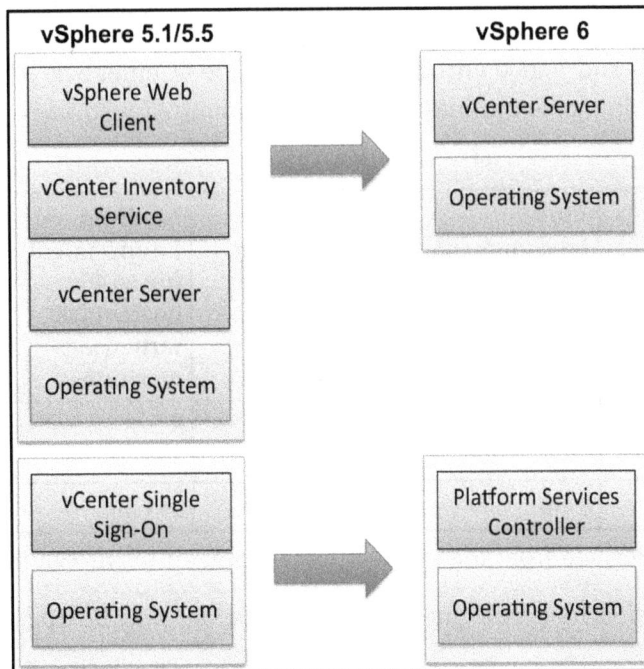

Any variation of the aforementioned configuration where vCenter Single Sign-On is installed separately from the vCenter Server, will result in an external vCenter Server 6.0 deployment.

Upgrading vCenter Server

There are many considerations when upgrading vCenter Server to 6.0 as the architecture and requirements have changed.

Prerequisites

A few notes prior to beginning the vCenter Server upgrade:

- vCenter Server 6.0 is able to manage ESXi 5.x and 6.x hosts but not 4.x.
- vCenter Server's clock must be synchronized.
- If deploying the Windows vCenter Server, a 64-bit operating system is required, along with a 64-bit system DSN for database connectivity.
- Each vCenter Server instance is required to have its own database.
- The Windows vCenter Server is bundled with a PostgreSQL database that may be used for an environment with up to 20 hosts and 200 virtual machines (Up to 1,000 hosts and 10,000 virtual machines for the vCenter Server Appliance).
- The following table outlines the minimum required resources for vCenter Server 6.0:

	Platform Services Controller	Tiny Environment (up to 10 hosts, 100 virtual machines)	Small Environment (up to 100 hosts, 1,000 virtual machines)	Medium Environment (up to 400 hosts, 4,000 virtual machines)	Large Environment (up to 1,000 hosts, 10,000 virtual machines)
Number of CPUs	2	2	4	8	16
Memory	2 GB	8 GB	16 GB	24 GB	32 GB

This information is derived from the vSphere Installation and Setup Guide.

Once these prerequisites have been met, the vCenter Server may be upgraded to 6.0.

More information may be found at: `http://www.vmware.com/content/dam/digitalmarke` `ting/vmware/en/pdf/techpaper/vmware-vcenter-server6-deployment-guide-white-p` `aper.pdf`

Upgrading Windows vCenter Server

To begin the Windows vCenter Server upgrade:

1. Log into the vCenter Server system as an administrator.
2. Launch the **VMware vCenter Installer**.
3. Select **vCenter Server for Windows** and press **Install**:

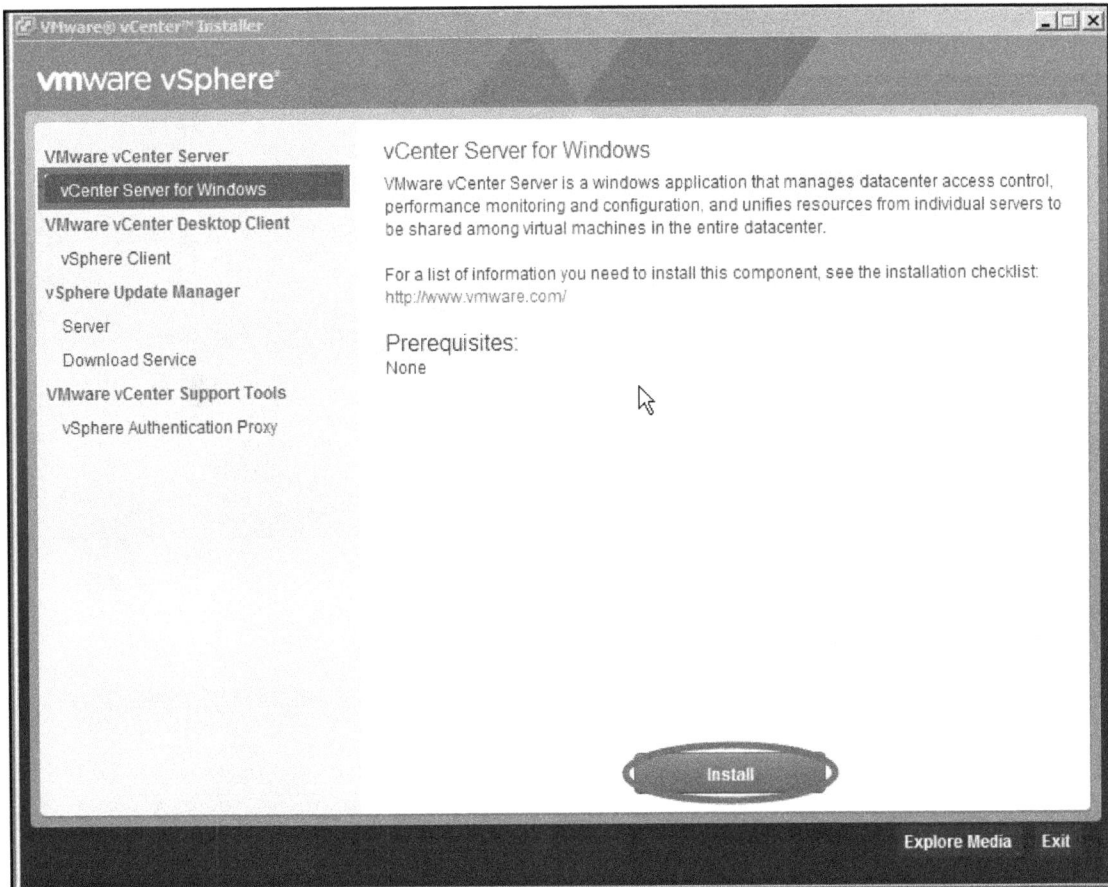

4. Once the installer launches, press **Next**:

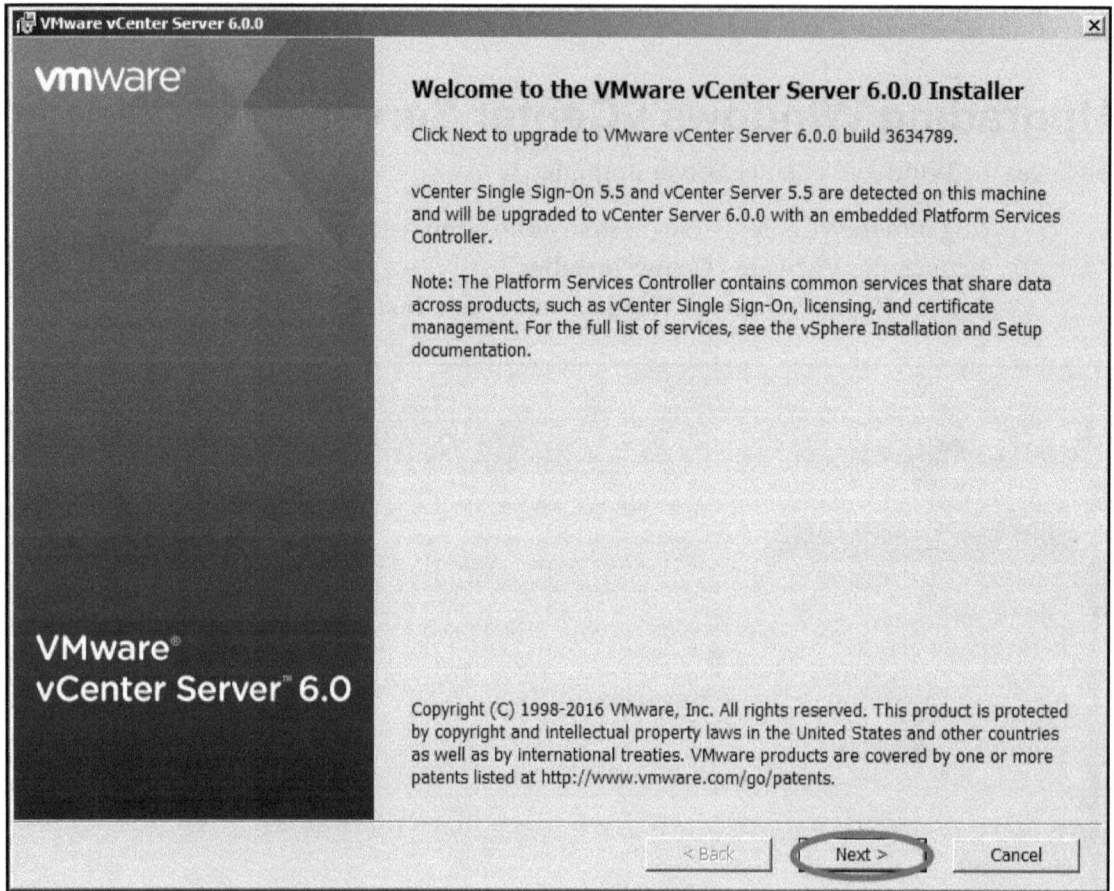

5. Review the **End User License Agreement**. Ensure to tick the checkbox next to **I accept the terms of the license agreement** so that the **Next** button is available:

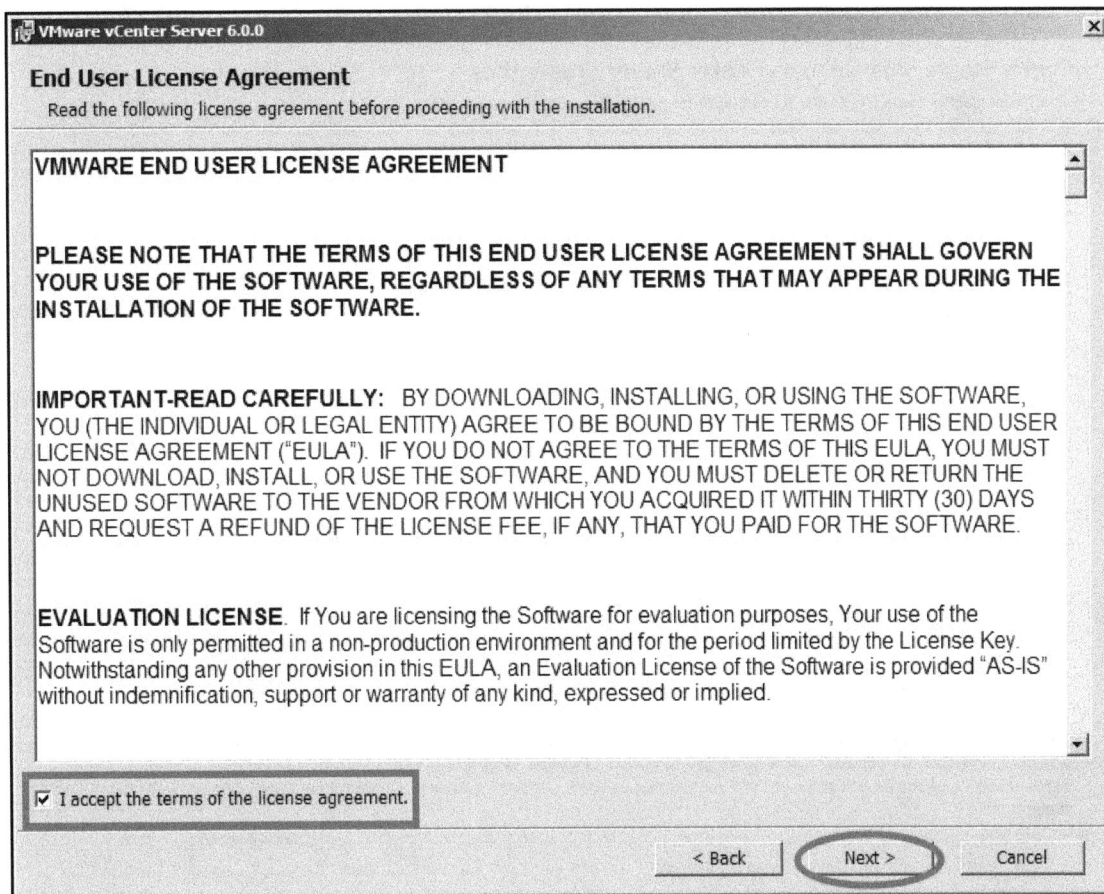

6. Press **Next**.

7. Enter the password for **vCenter Single Sign-On** and select whether or not to **Use the same credentials for vCenter Server:**

8. Press **Next**.

9. A notification dialog will appear (demonstrated in the following screenshot) specifying that pre-upgrade checks are in progress:

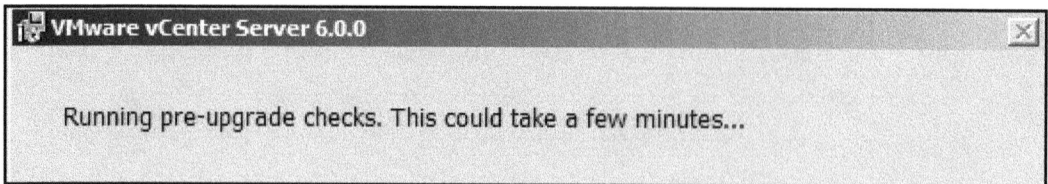

10. If the embedded Microsoft SQL Express database is in used, a warning will appear as a notification that its contents will be migrated to vPostgreSQL.

Microsoft SQL Express is not a supported database in vSphere 6.0.

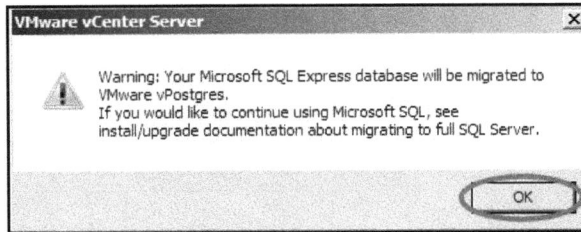

11. Press **OK**.
12. On the **Configure Ports** screen, verify that the default ports will be used:

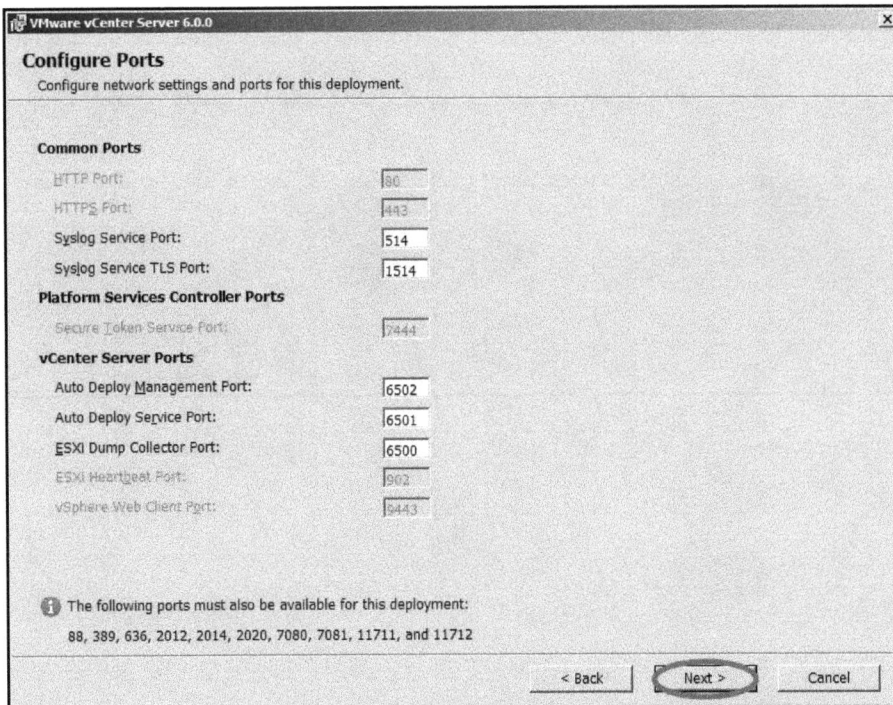

13. Press **Next**.

14. The **Destination Directory** screen will allow modifications to the installation directories and the directory for the 5.x data, if desired:

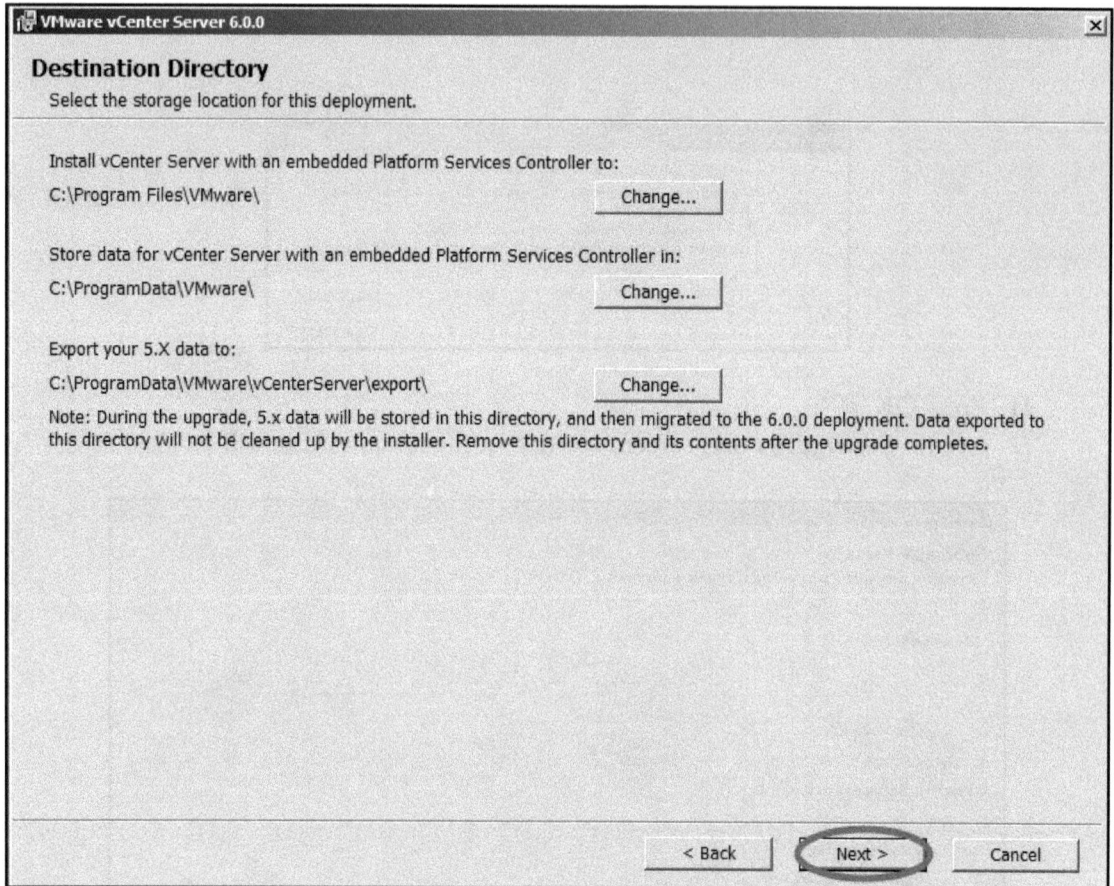

15. Press **Next**.

16. Choose whether or not to **Join the VMware Customer Experience Improvement Program** by ticking the checkbox:

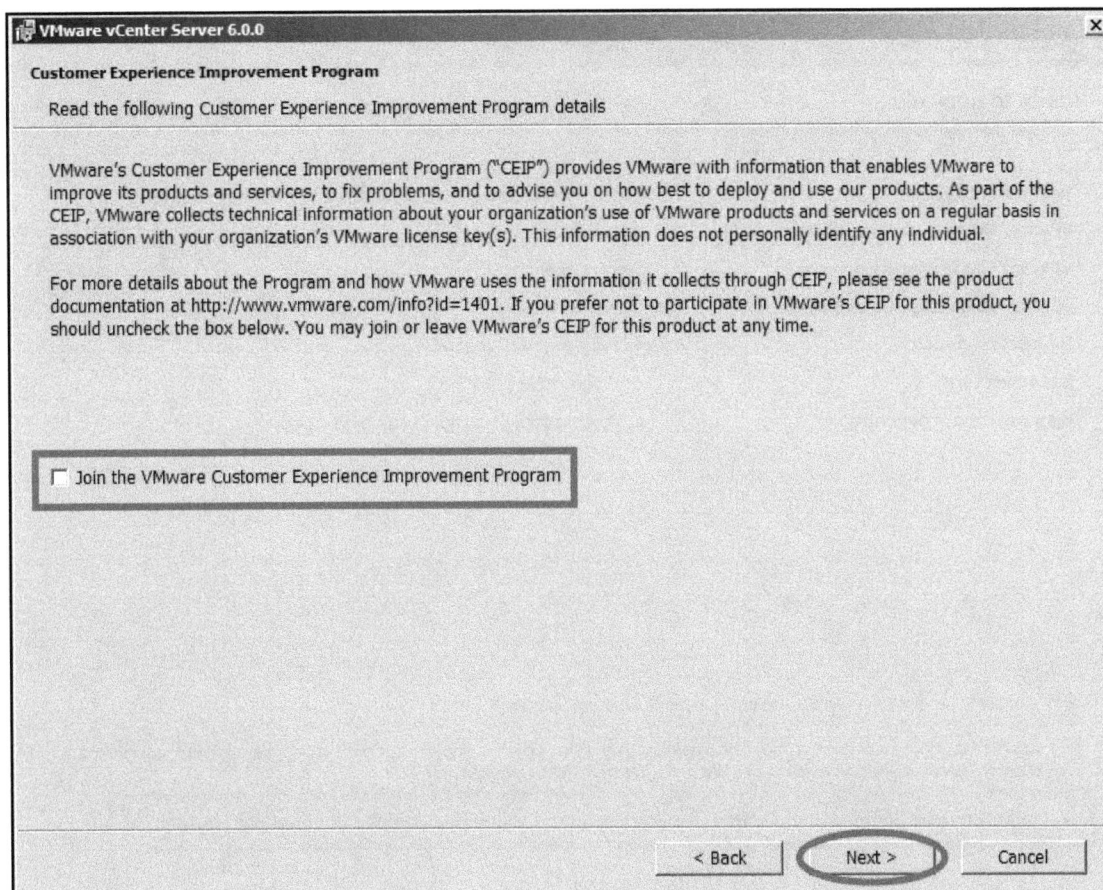

17. Press **Next**.
18. The **Ready to upgrade** screen allows for the review of all upgrade selections.

19. Before the upgrade can begin, ensure to tick the checkbox that specifies **I verify that I have backed up the vCenter Server machine and the embedded Microsoft SQL Server Express database**:

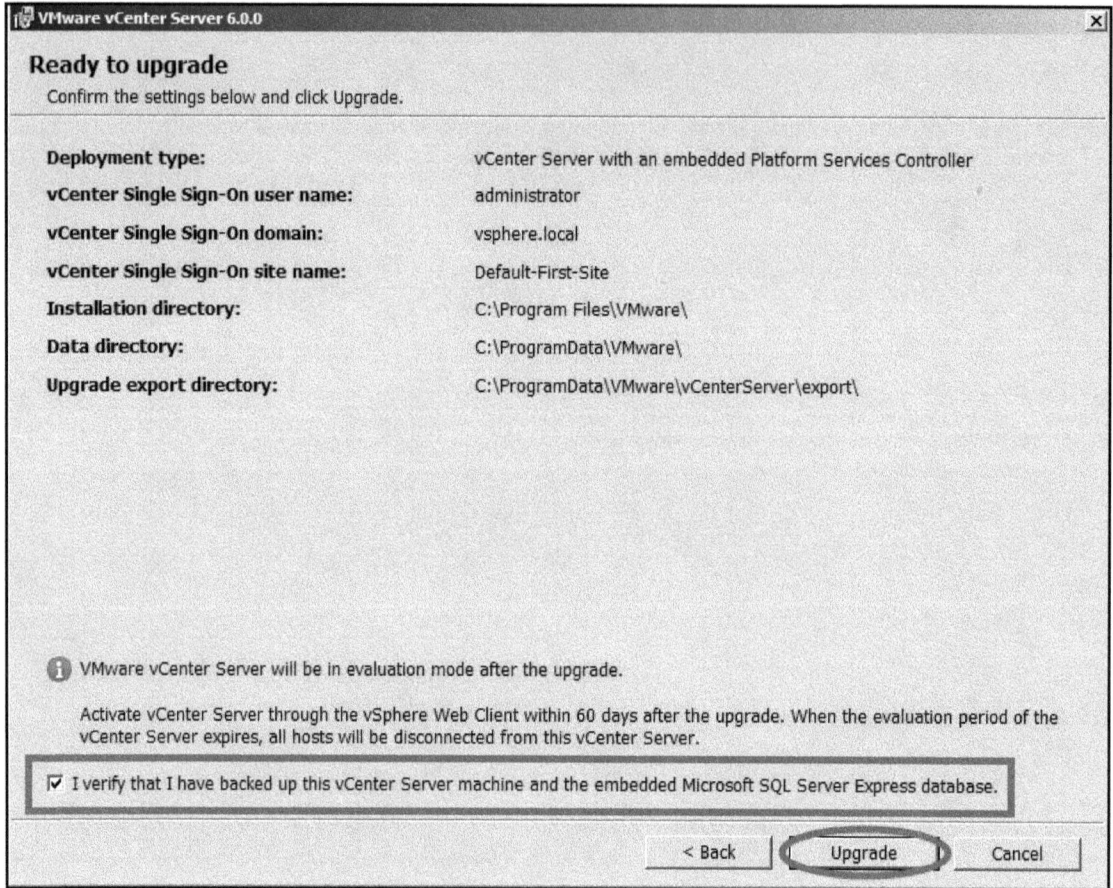

20. Press the **Upgrade** button to proceed.

21. The following image demonstrates the **Installation progress** screen that keeps track of the upgrade status:

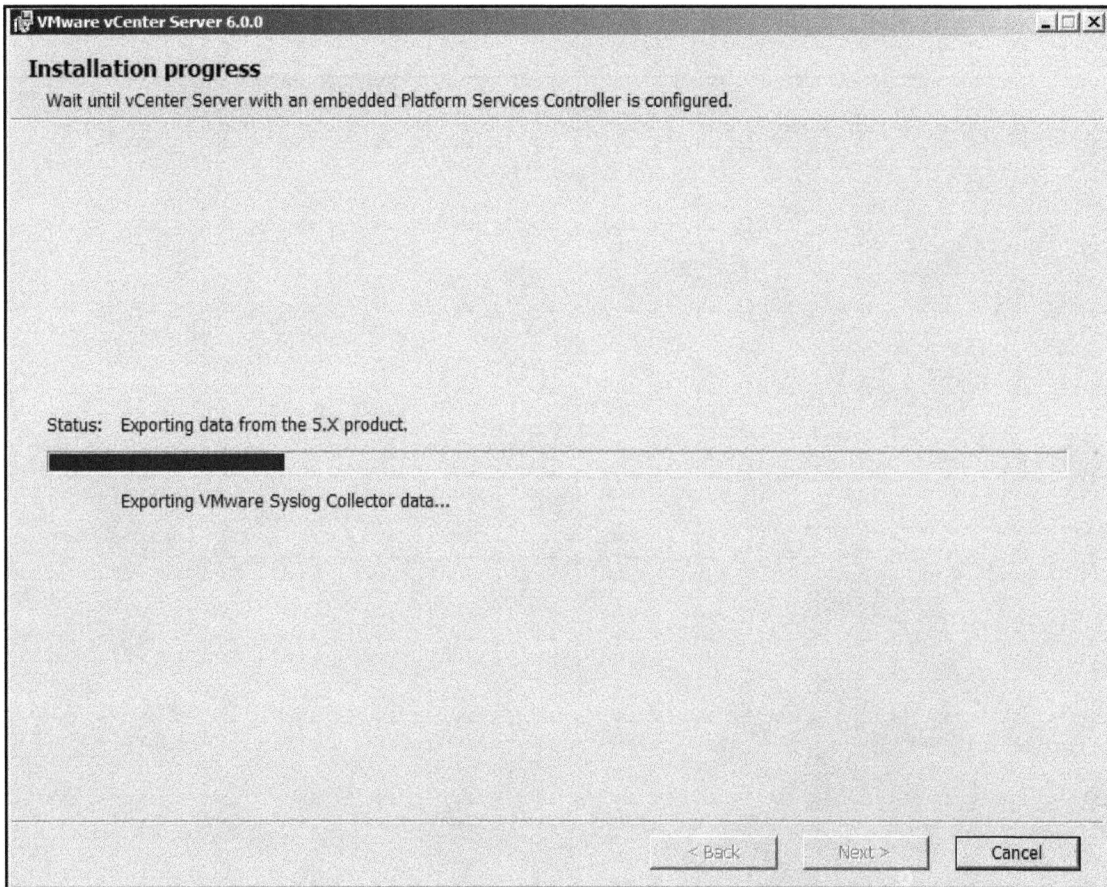

22. Once the upgrade has completed, the **Setup Completed** screen will appear. It notifies you of the required post-installation steps. Note that vCenter Server 6.0 is in evaluation mode post-upgrade. Ensure to log in and assign valid vSphere 6 licenses:

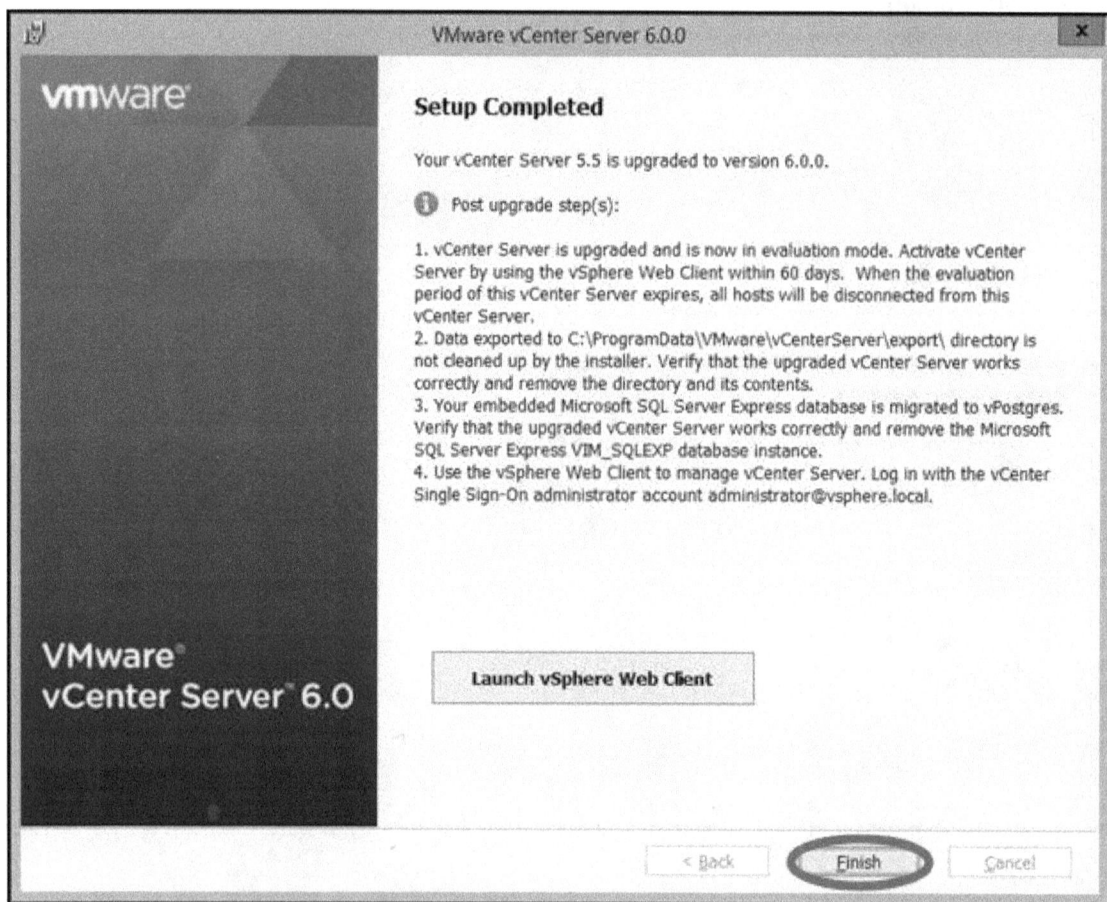

23. Press **Finish**.

Upgrading vCenter Server Appliance

Something to keep in mind regarding upgrading the vCenter Server Appliance is that it's only version 5.1 update 3 or later may be upgraded to vCenter Server Appliance 6.0. In order to upgrade vCenter Server Appliance 5.0, it first has to be upgraded to version 5.1 update 3 or 5.5 update 2. Only then can it be upgraded to vCenter Server Appliance 6.0.

Client Integration Plug-in

In order to upgrade to vCenter Server Appliance 6.0, the Client Integration Plug-in must be installed. This is included in the installation media for the vCenter Server Appliance. Before installing the Client Integration Plug-in, ensure that at least one of the supported browsers is installed:

- Microsoft Internet Explorer, version 10 and 11
- Mozilla Firefox, version 30 or later
- Google Chrome, version 35 or later

To install the Client Integration plug-in:

1. Mount the installation .iso to a Windows machine.
2. Browse to the /vcsa directory and launch the **VMware-ClientIntegrationPlugin-6.0.0.exe** file to begin:

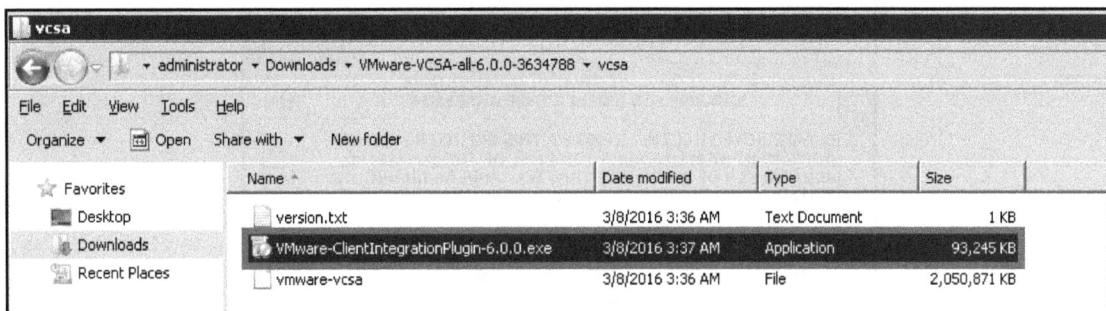

3. The installer will launch. Press **Next** to start this process.

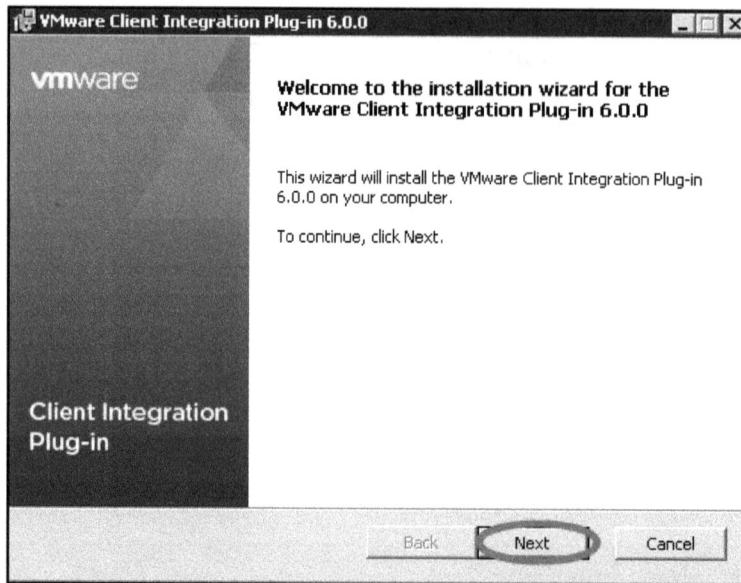

4. On the **End-User License Agreement** screen, select **I accept the terms in the License Agreement** option:

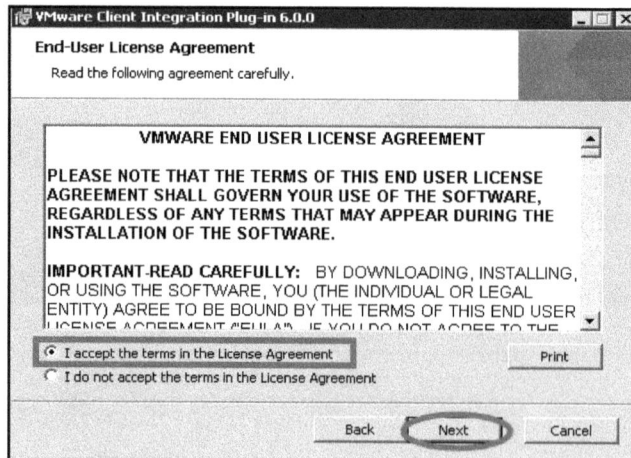

5. Press **Next**.

6. Verify the installation directory on the **Destination Folder** screen:

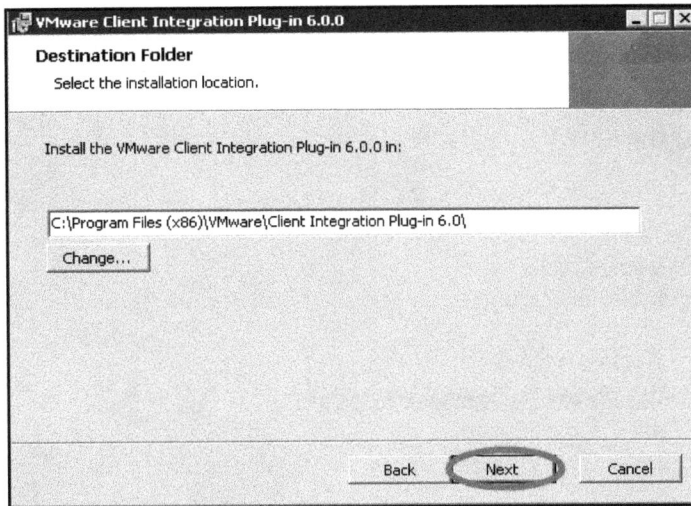

7. Press **Next** as highlighted in preceding screenshot.

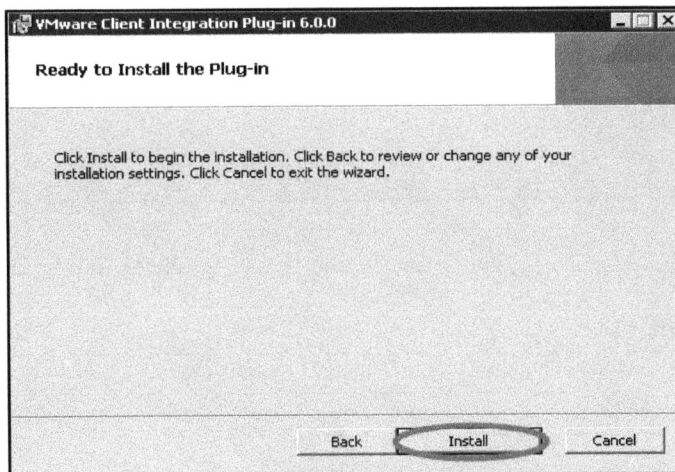

8. Press **Install** as highlighted in the preceding screenshot.
9. The following screen demonstrates the installation process. This will take a few minutes.

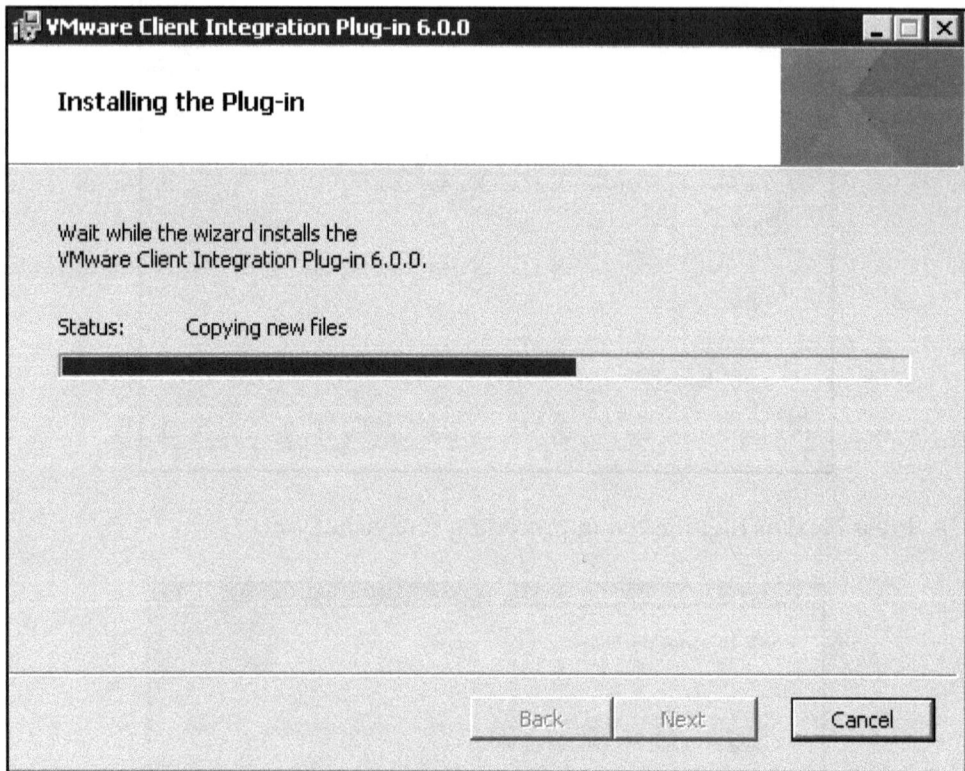

10. Press **Finish** once the installation has completed.

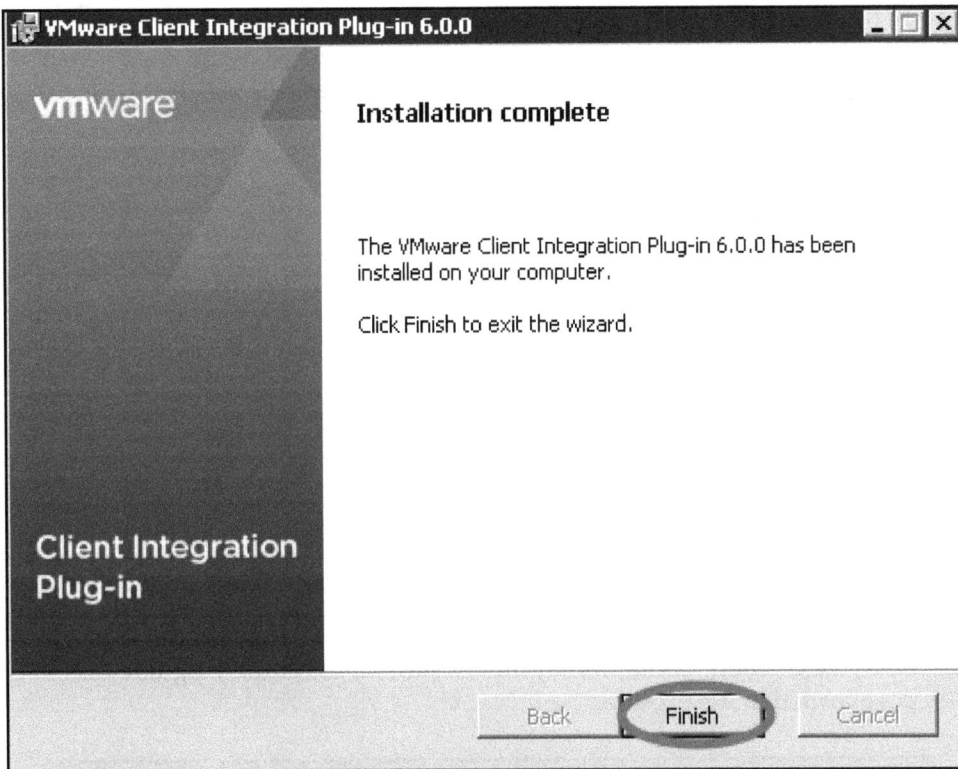

Upgrading vCenter Server Appliance

Once the client integration plug-in has been installed, the vCenter Server Appliance may be upgraded. Of note, the vCenter Server Appliance is always upgraded to an embedded vCenter Server Appliance; this means that the Platform Services Controller will be co-installed with the vCenter Server software. If an external Platform is desired, a new vCenter Server Appliance should be deployed.

To begin:

1. In the root directory of the software installer, select `vcsa-setup.html`:

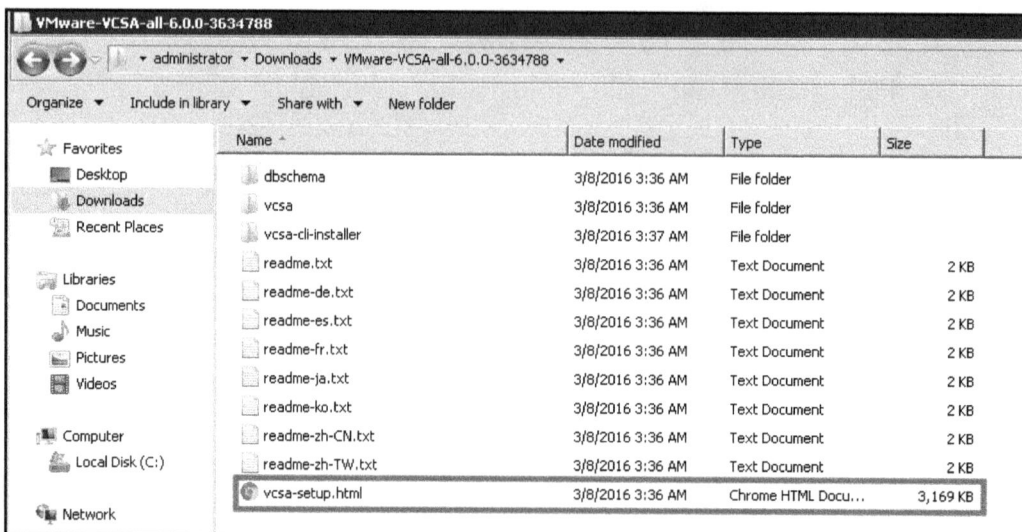

2. Once the Client Integration Plug-In has started, select the **Upgrade** button on the page loaded in the browser:

3. Review the **Supported Upgrades** dialog box. Press **OK** to continue to upgrade:

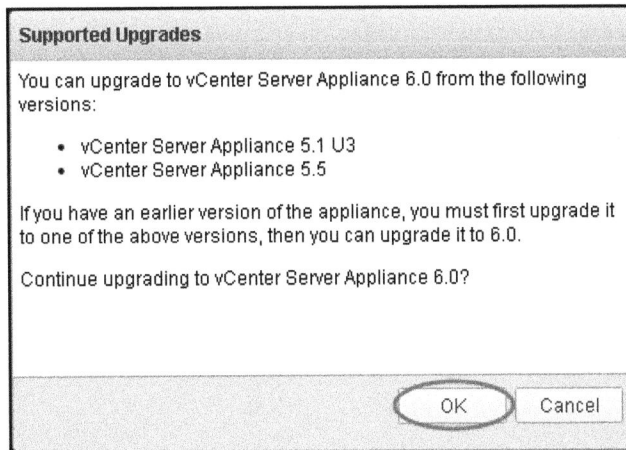

Supported Upgrades

You can upgrade to vCenter Server Appliance 6.0 from the following versions:

- vCenter Server Appliance 5.1 U3
- vCenter Server Appliance 5.5

If you have an earlier version of the appliance, you must first upgrade it to one of the above versions, then you can upgrade it to 6.0.

Continue upgrading to vCenter Server Appliance 6.0?

OK   Cancel

4. Review the **End User License Agreement**. Tick the checkbox next to **I accept the terms of the license agreement:**

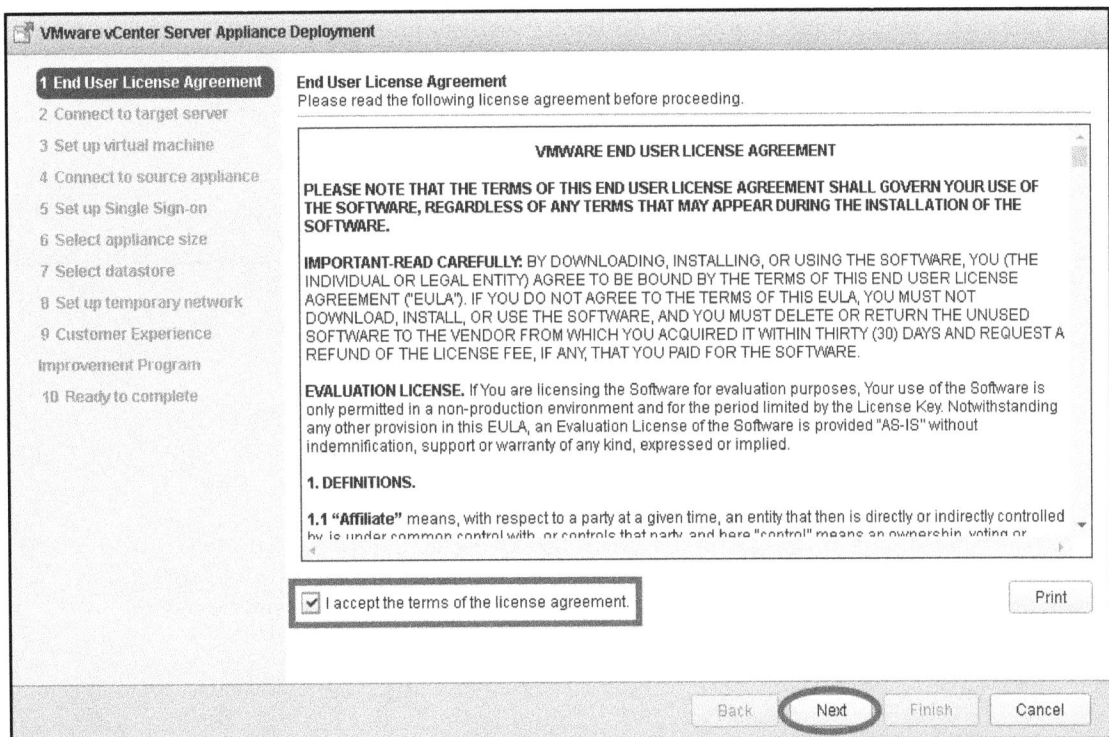

VMware vCenter Server Appliance Deployment

1 End User License Agreement
2 Connect to target server
3 Set up virtual machine
4 Connect to source appliance
5 Set up Single Sign-on
6 Select appliance size
7 Select datastore
8 Set up temporary network
9 Customer Experience Improvement Program
10 Ready to complete

End User License Agreement
Please read the following license agreement before proceeding.

VMWARE END USER LICENSE AGREEMENT

PLEASE NOTE THAT THE TERMS OF THIS END USER LICENSE AGREEMENT SHALL GOVERN YOUR USE OF THE SOFTWARE, REGARDLESS OF ANY TERMS THAT MAY APPEAR DURING THE INSTALLATION OF THE SOFTWARE.

IMPORTANT-READ CAREFULLY: BY DOWNLOADING, INSTALLING, OR USING THE SOFTWARE, YOU (THE INDIVIDUAL OR LEGAL ENTITY) AGREE TO BE BOUND BY THE TERMS OF THIS END USER LICENSE AGREEMENT ("EULA"). IF YOU DO NOT AGREE TO THE TERMS OF THIS EULA, YOU MUST NOT DOWNLOAD, INSTALL, OR USE THE SOFTWARE, AND YOU MUST DELETE OR RETURN THE UNUSED SOFTWARE TO THE VENDOR FROM WHICH YOU ACQUIRED IT WITHIN THIRTY (30) DAYS AND REQUEST A REFUND OF THE LICENSE FEE, IF ANY, THAT YOU PAID FOR THE SOFTWARE.

EVALUATION LICENSE. If You are licensing the Software for evaluation purposes, Your use of the Software is only permitted in a non-production environment and for the period limited by the License Key. Notwithstanding any other provision in this EULA, an Evaluation License of the Software is provided "AS-IS" without indemnification, support or warranty of any kind, expressed or implied.

1. DEFINITIONS.

1.1 "Affiliate" means, with respect to a party at a given time, an entity that then is directly or indirectly controlled by is under common control with, or controls that party and here "control" means an ownership, voting or

☑ I accept the terms of the license agreement.

Print

Back   Next   Finish   Cancel

5. Press **Next**.

6. On the **Connect to target server** screen, input the **FQDN or IP address**, **Username**, and **Password** of the ESXi host on which the vCenter Server Appliance should be deployed:

7. Press **Next**.

8. A **Certificate Warning** dialog will appear. Press **Yes** to continue:

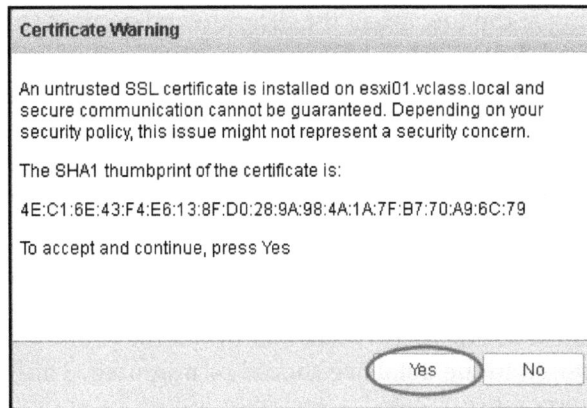

Certificate Warning

An untrusted SSL certificate is installed on esxi01.vclass.local and secure communication cannot be guaranteed. Depending on your security policy, this issue might not represent a security concern.

The SHA1 thumbprint of the certificate is:

4E:C1:6E:43:F4:E6:13:8F:D0:28:9A:98:4A:1A:7F:B7:70:A9:6C:79

To accept and continue, press Yes

Yes   No

9. Enter the desired **Appliance name** of the vCenter Server on the **Set up virtual machine** screen. Select the checkbox to determine whether or not SSH is enabled:

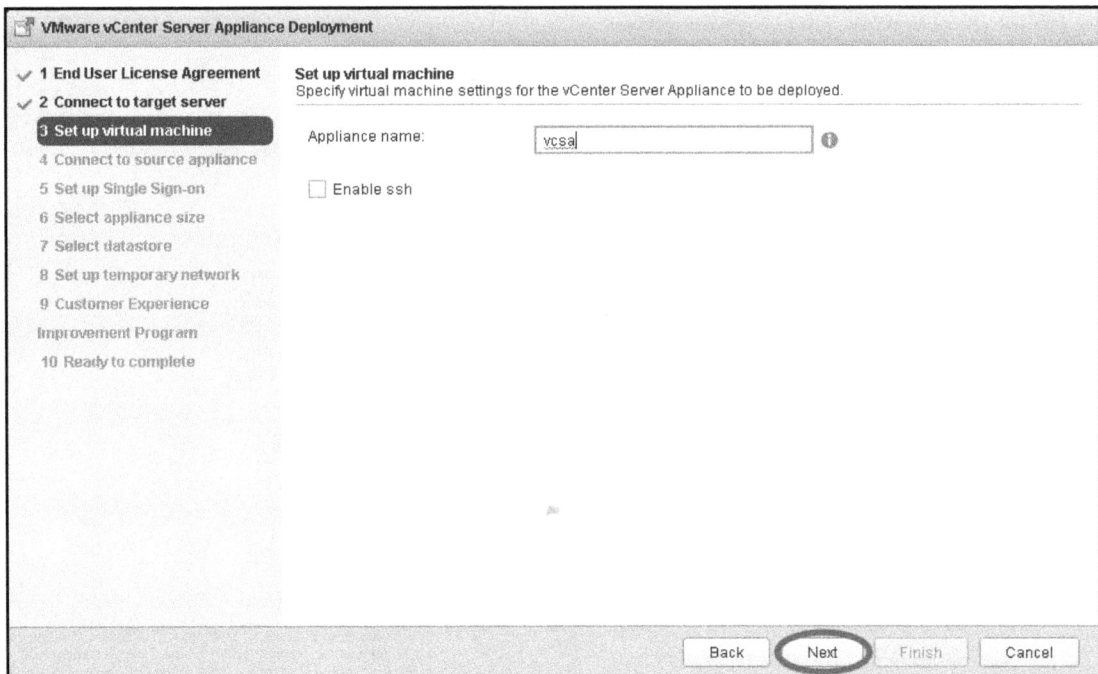

VMware vCenter Server Appliance Deployment

✓ 1 End User License Agreement
✓ 2 Connect to target server
3 Set up virtual machine
4 Connect to source appliance
5 Set up Single Sign-on
6 Select appliance size
7 Select datastore
8 Set up temporary network
9 Customer Experience Improvement Program
10 Ready to complete

Set up virtual machine
Specify virtual machine settings for the vCenter Server Appliance to be deployed.

Appliance name: vcsa   ⓘ

☐ Enable ssh

Back   Next   Finish   Cancel

10. Press **Next**.

11. There's quite a bit of information to enter on the **Connect to source appliance** screen. Starting at the top, select the drop-down box next to **Existing appliance version**. **vCSA 5.5 or vCSA 5.1 U3** may be chosen.

12. Under the **vCenter Server Appliance** section, enter the **vCenter Server IP Address/FQDN** and set the **vCenter administrator password**. The default **vCenter HTTPS Port** is **443** but may optionally be modified. Enter the **Appliance (OS) root password**.

13. The **Temporary Upgrade Files Path** is /tmp/vmware/cis-export-folder by default. This path specifies the directory to temporarily store the configuration data. Optionally, the checkbox to enable **Migrate performance & other historical data** may be ticked. This selects whether or not the performance and historical data that is stored in the database should be migrated. This migration may slow the upgrade process.

14. Scroll down in the screen to complete the rest of the required information:

15. Underneath the **Source ESXi host** section, enter the **ESXi host IP address/FQDN**, **ESXi host user name**, and **ESXi host password**. The source ESXi host is the host that the vCenter Server Appliance to be upgraded is currently located at:

16. Press **Next**.

17. A **Warning** dialog will appear. Press **Yes** to accept and continue the upgrade process:

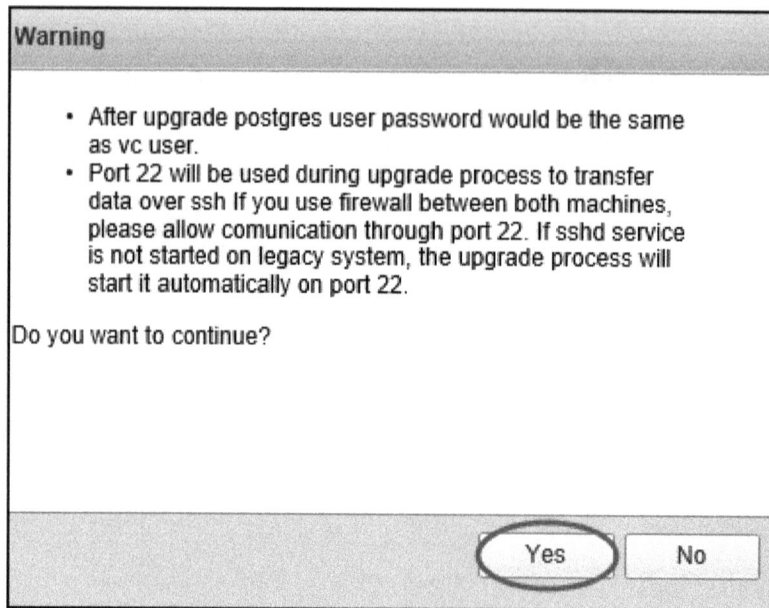

Warning

- After upgrade postgres user password would be the same as vc user.
- Port 22 will be used during upgrade process to transfer data over ssh If you use firewall between both machines, please allow comunication through port 22. If sshd service is not started on legacy system, the upgrade process will start it automatically on port 22.

Do you want to continue?

Yes   No

18. If upgrading from vCenter Server Appliance 5.1 U3, an additional screen will appear to configure the Single Sign-On settings. If upgrading from vCenter Server Appliance 5.5 these settings will be automatically migrated.

19. On the **Select appliance size** screen, choose the drop-down box to select the **Appliance size**. In the following screenshot, **Tiny (up to 10 hosts, 100 VMs)** has been chosen. Be aware that this selection dictates the virtual hardware configuration of the appliance. In this case, a Tiny vCenter Server Appliance results in the appliance being deployed with 2 vCPUs and 8 GB of memory:

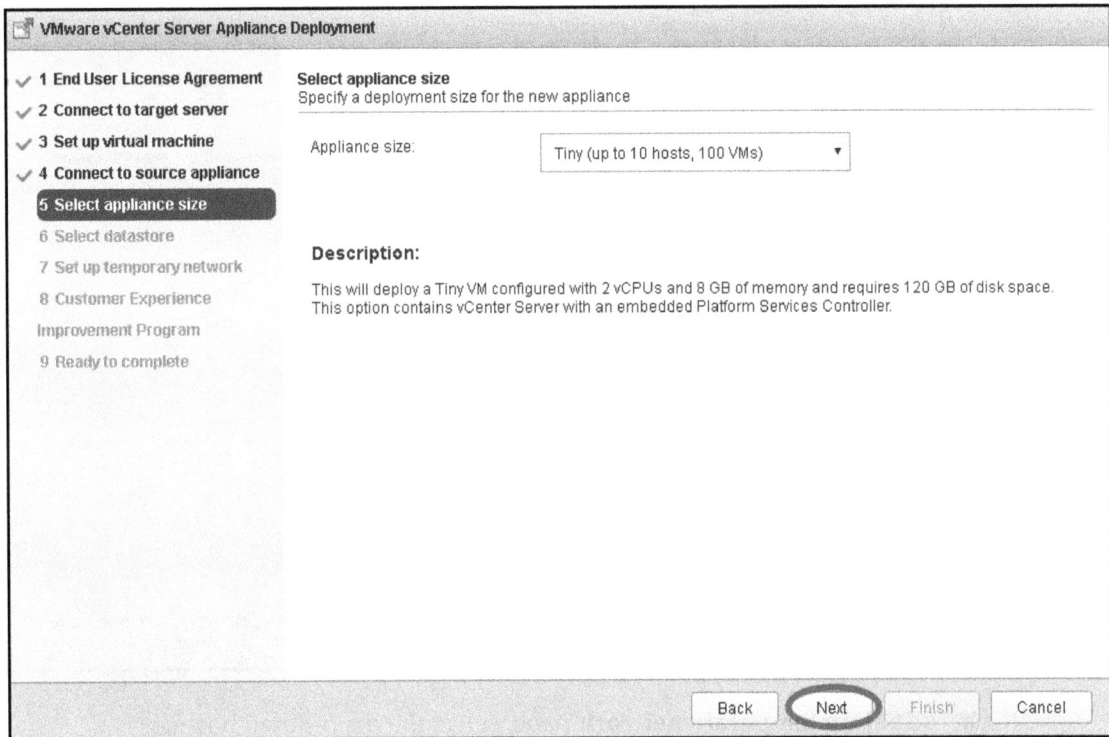

20. Press **Next**.

21. Select the appropriate datastore on which to store the virtual machine files. Choose whether or not to **Enable Thin Disk Mode** (thin provisioning) by ticking the checkbox:

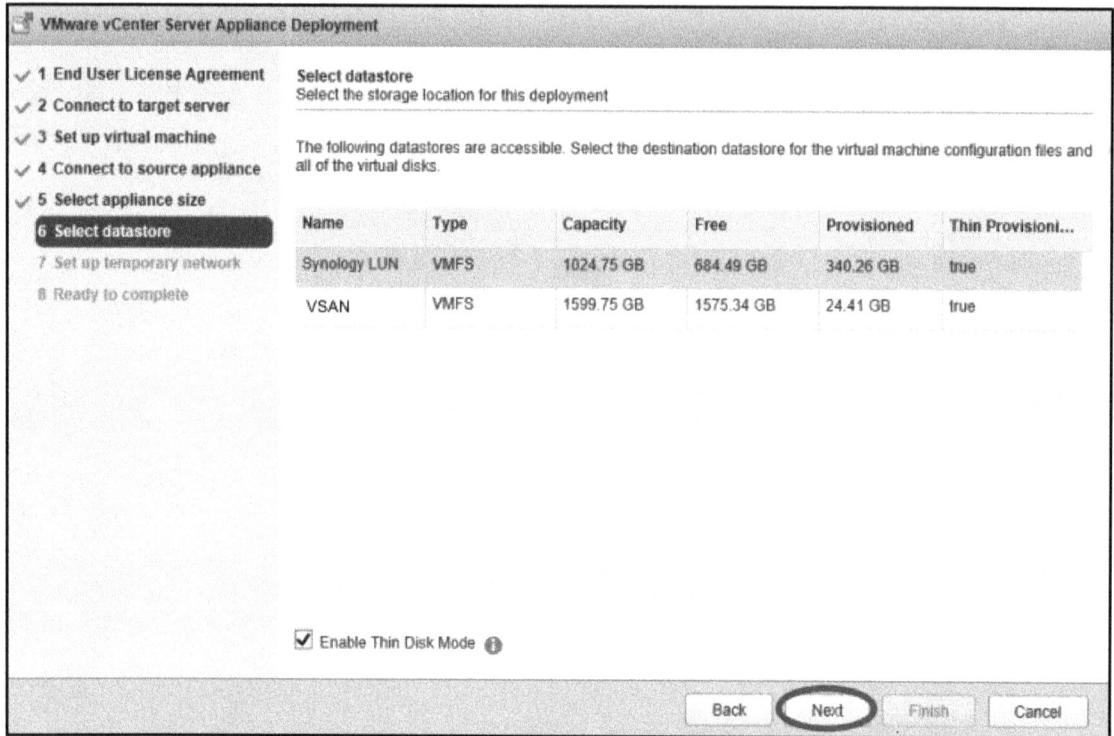

VMware vCenter Server Appliance Deployment						

✓ 1 End User License Agreement
✓ 2 Connect to target server
✓ 3 Set up virtual machine
✓ 4 Connect to source appliance
✓ 5 Select appliance size
  6 Select datastore
  7 Set up temporary network
  8 Ready to complete

Select datastore
Select the storage location for this deployment

The following datastores are accessible. Select the destination datastore for the virtual machine configuration files and all of the virtual disks.

Name	Type	Capacity	Free	Provisioned	Thin Provisioni...
Synology LUN	VMFS	1024.75 GB	684.49 GB	340.26 GB	true
VSAN	VMFS	1599.75 GB	1575.34 GB	24.41 GB	true

☑ Enable Thin Disk Mode ⓘ

Back Next Finish Cancel

22. On the **Set up temporary network** pane, select the drop-down box for **Temporary network** and choose a portgroup. This network is used for communication between the vCenter Server Appliance being deployed and the vCenter Server Appliance to be upgraded.

23. For **Network type**, select **DHCP** or **static**. If **static** is chosen, enter the **Network address**, **Subnet mask**, **Network gateway**, and **Network DNS Servers**:

24. Press **Next**.

25. Review all of the settings on **the Ready to complete** screen.

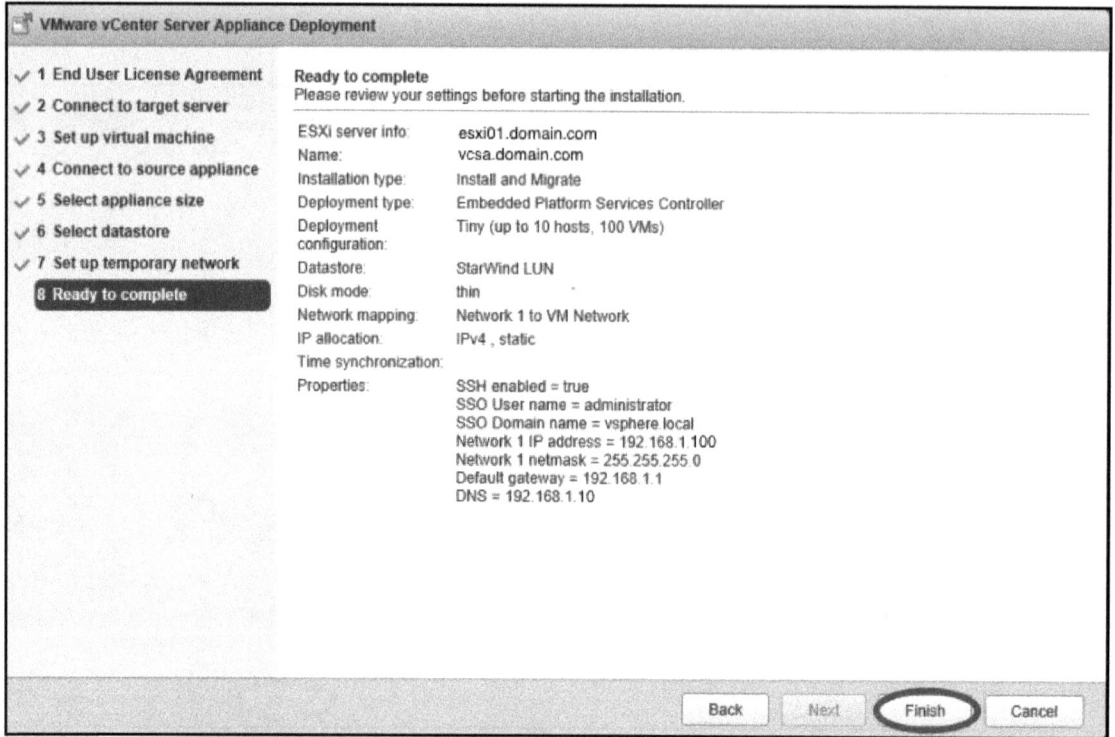

26. Press **Finish** to begin the upgrade process.

27. This process will take several minutes. Progress may be monitored, as demonstrated by the following screenshot:

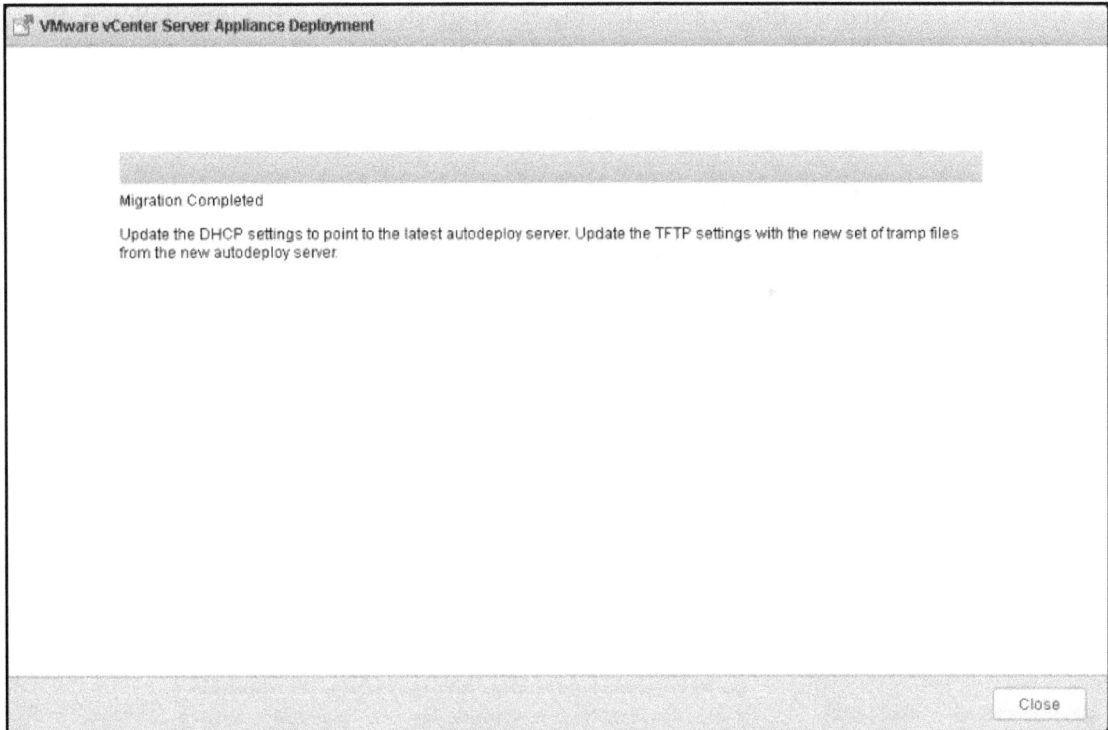

28. Once the upgrade is complete click **Close**.

At the end of the upgrade, the old vCenter Server Appliance is powered off and the new vCenter Server Appliance is started.

Upgrading vSphere Update Manager (VUM)

Upgrading to Update Manager 6.0 may only be done from Upgrade Manager 5.x installed on a Windows 64-bit operating system. During the upgrade process, the installation path and patch download location cannot be changed. If it is desired to modify these settings, Update Manager should be re-installed instead of upgraded.

To begin the upgrade process:

1. Open the Window vSphere installer and select the **Server** option underneath **vSphere Update Manager**. Choose whether to **Use Microsoft SQL Server 2012 Express as the embedded database**:

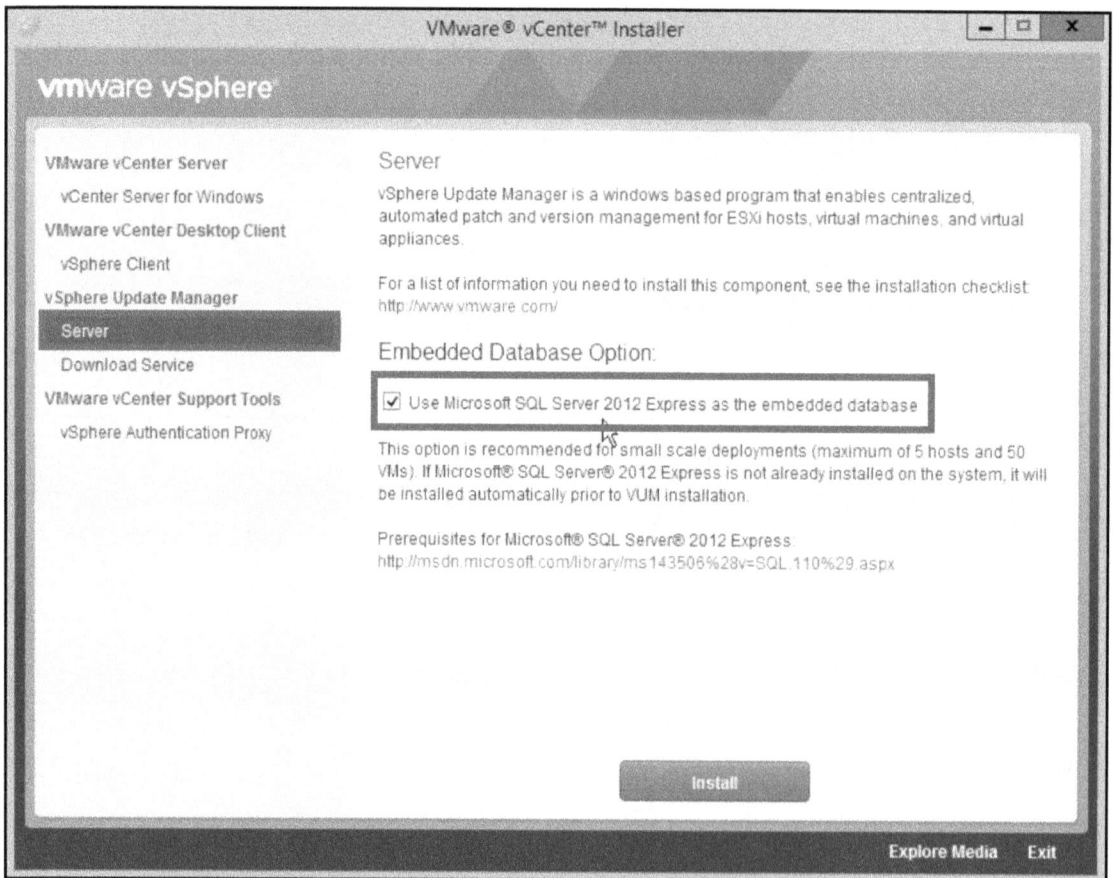

2. Press **Install**.

3. Select the installation language:

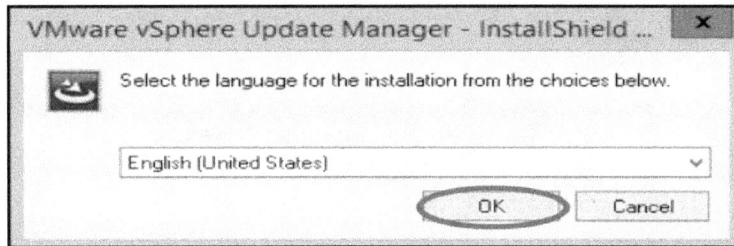

4. Select **OK**.

5. It may take a minute to load the Update Manager installer for the upgrade:

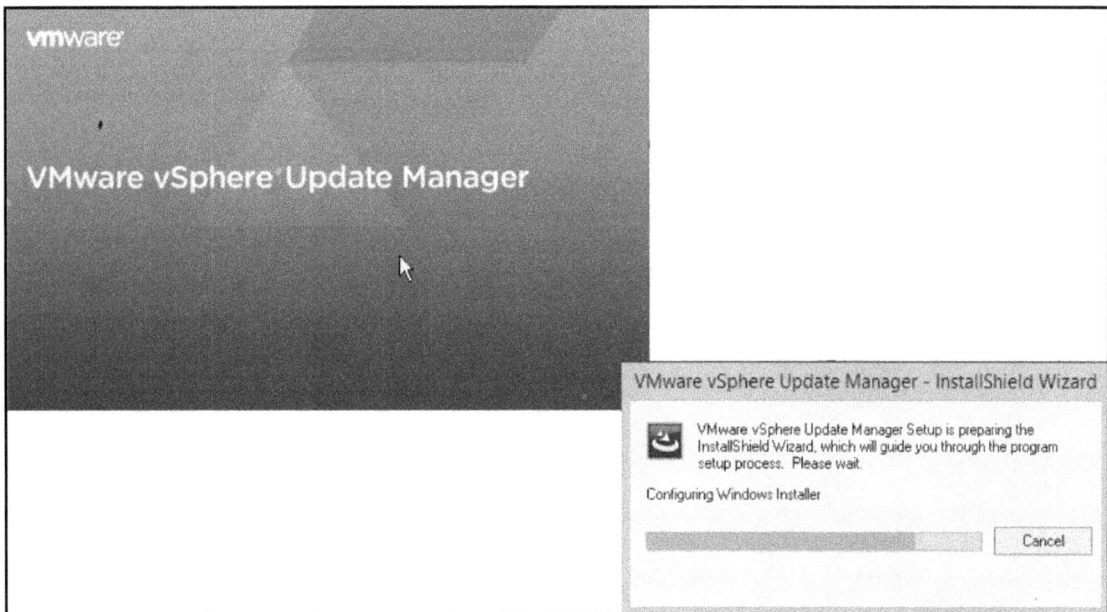

6. A dialog will appear as a notification regarding Update Manager already installed. The installer will continue as an upgrade:

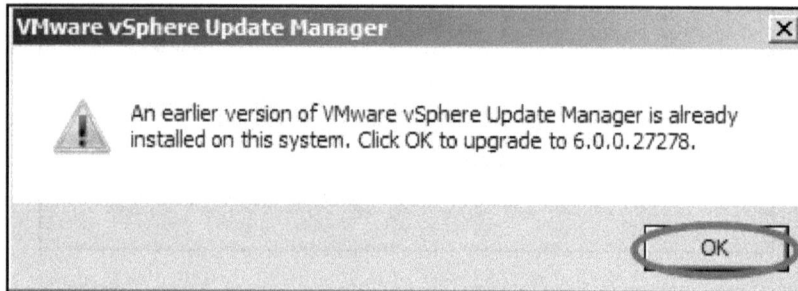

7. Press **OK**.
8. Once the upgrade wizard appears, press **Next**:

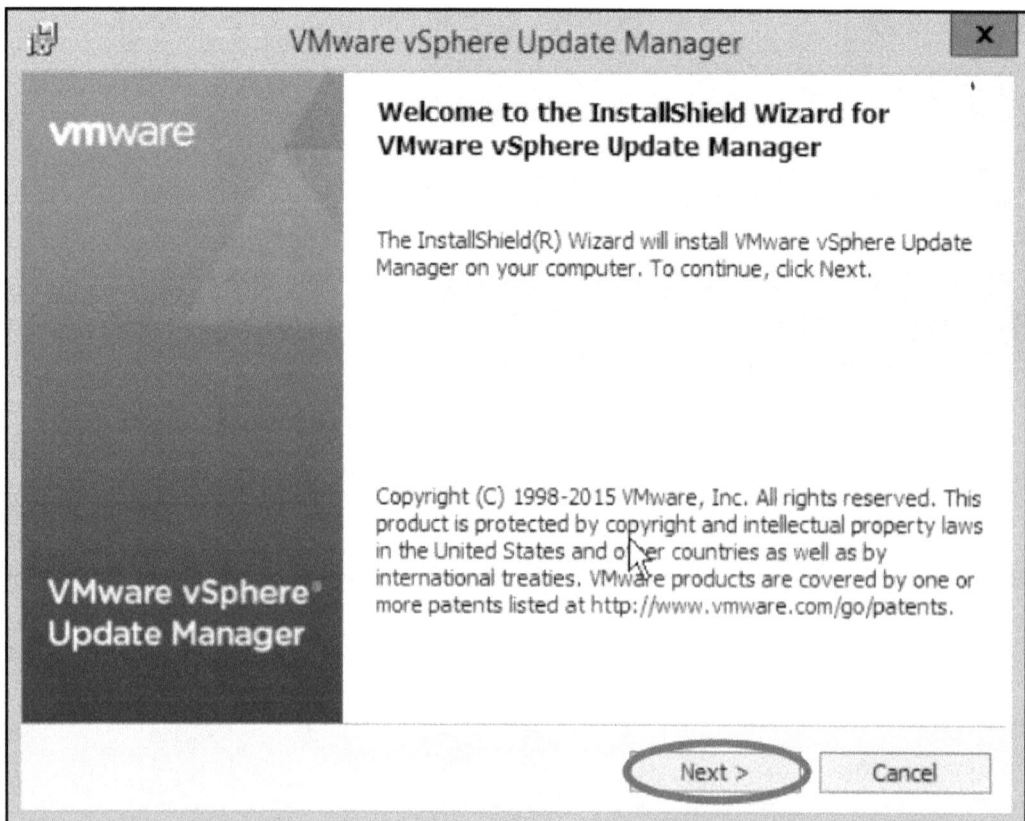

9. On the **License Agreement** screen, select **I accept the terms in the license agreement** to continue:

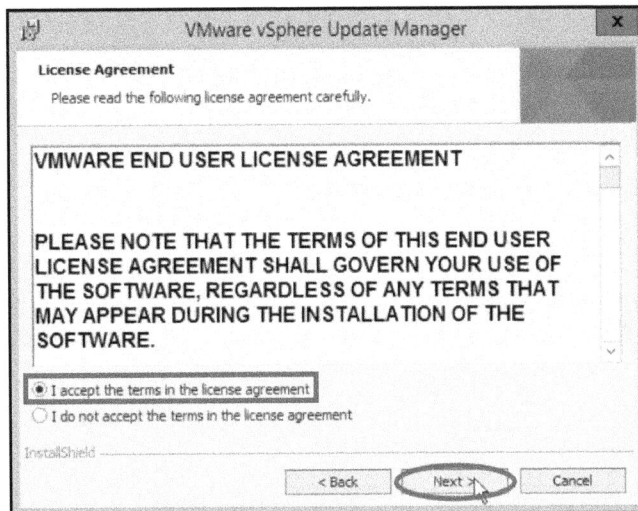

10. Press **Next**.
11. Select whether to **Download updates from default sources immediately after installation**:

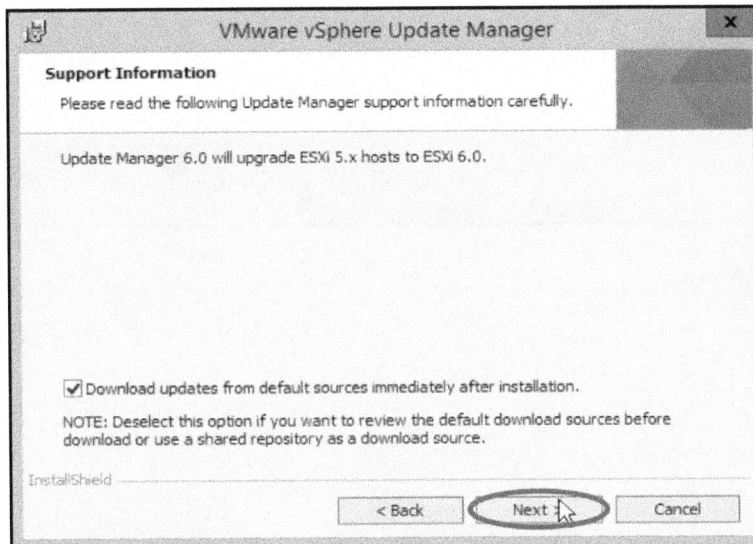

12. Press **Next**.

13. On the **vCenter Server Information** pane, enter the **IP Address/Name**, **Username**, and **Password**. The **HTTP Port** is 80 by default but may be changed:

14. Press **Next**.

15. On the **Database Information** pane, a password may need to be entered:

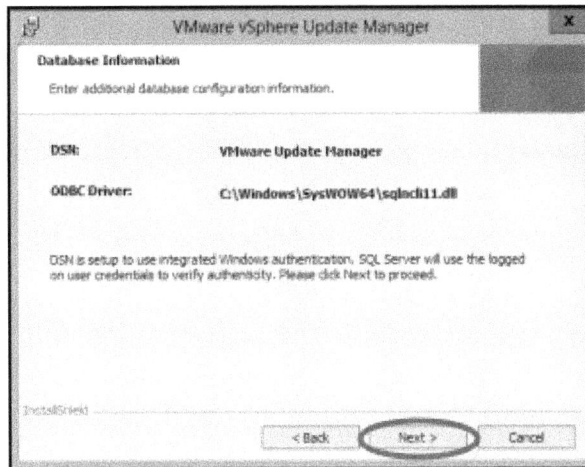

16. Press **Next**.

17. Select **Yes, I want to upgrade my Update Manager database** and tick the checkbox designating that **I have taken a backup of the existing Update Manager database**:

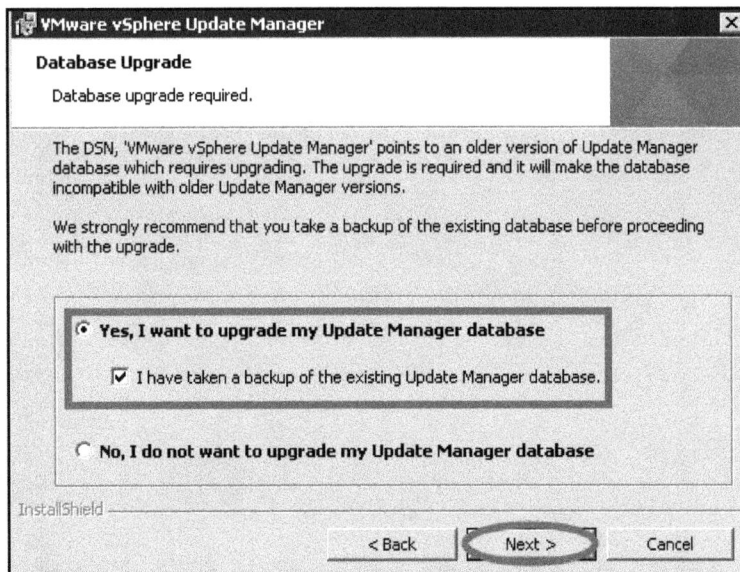

18. Press **Next**.

19. On the **Port Settings** pane, accept the default ports for communication to vCenter Server or change as necessary.

20. Optionally, select **Yes, I have Internet connection and I want to configure proxy settings now if a proxy** is required to access the internet:

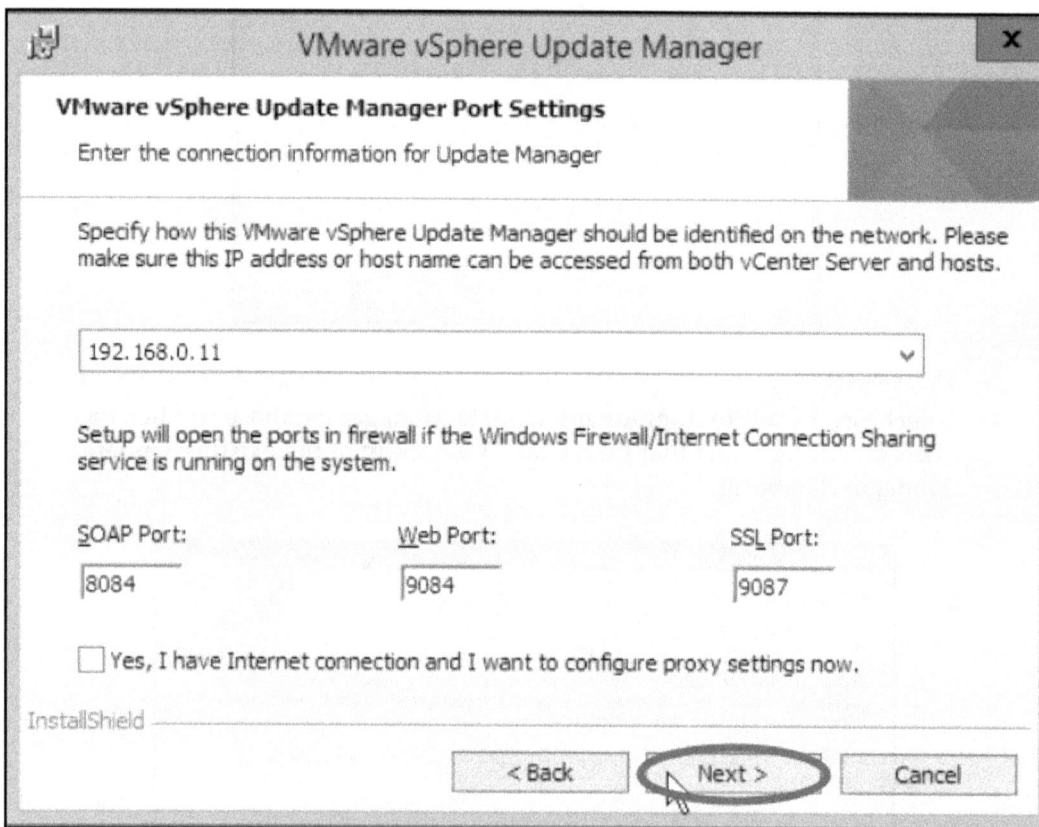

21. Press **Install** to begin the upgrade process:

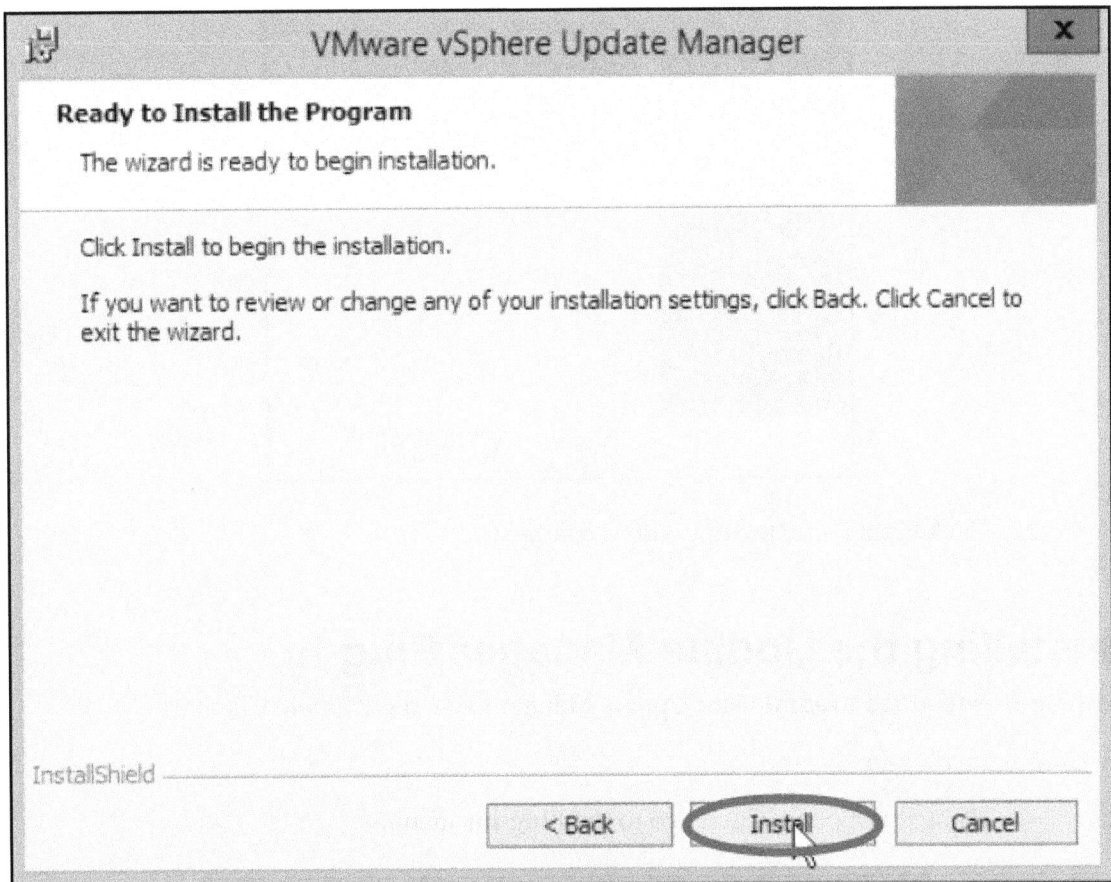

22. It may take several minutes to complete the upgrade process.

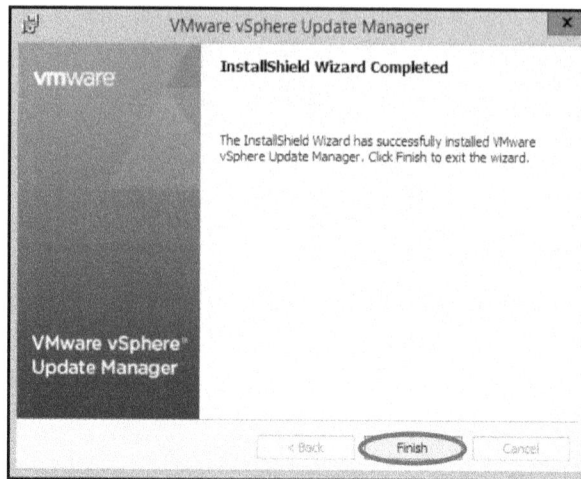

23. Click **Finish** once the upgrade is complete.

Installing the Update Manager Plug-in

A plug-in is required to administer Update Manger using the vSphere Client.

To install the plug-in:

1. Using the vSphere Client, go to the **Plug-ins** menu:

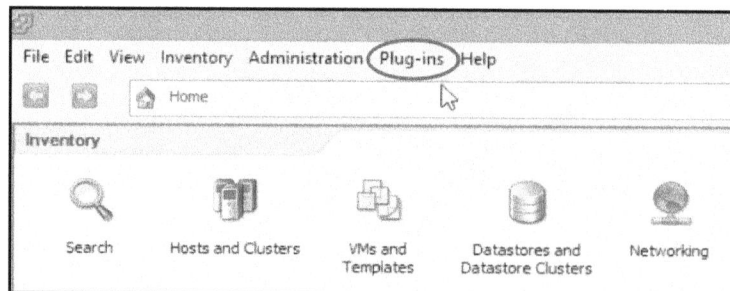

2. The **Plug-in Manager** dialog will appear; select **Download and Install** for the VMware vSphere Update Manager server:

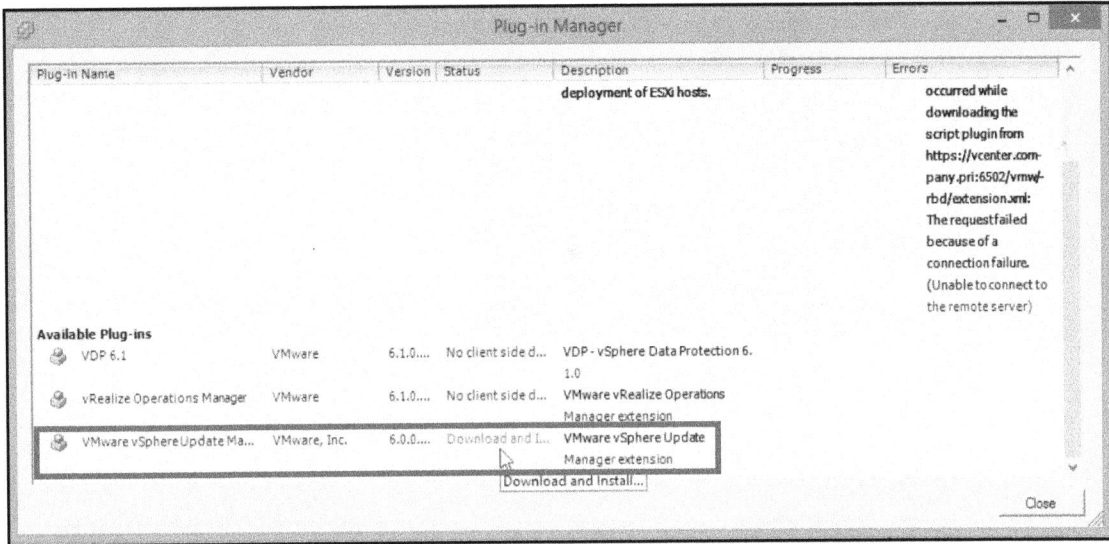

3. Select the language for the installer:

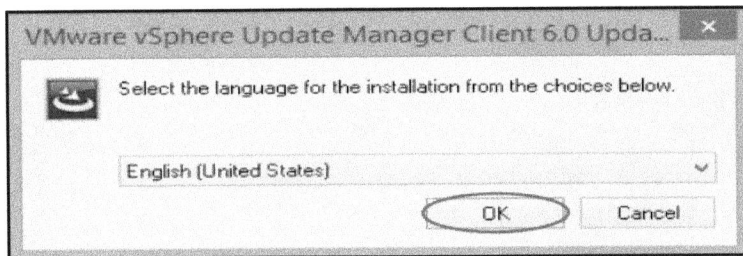

4. Click **OK**.

5. It may take a minute for the installer to launch:

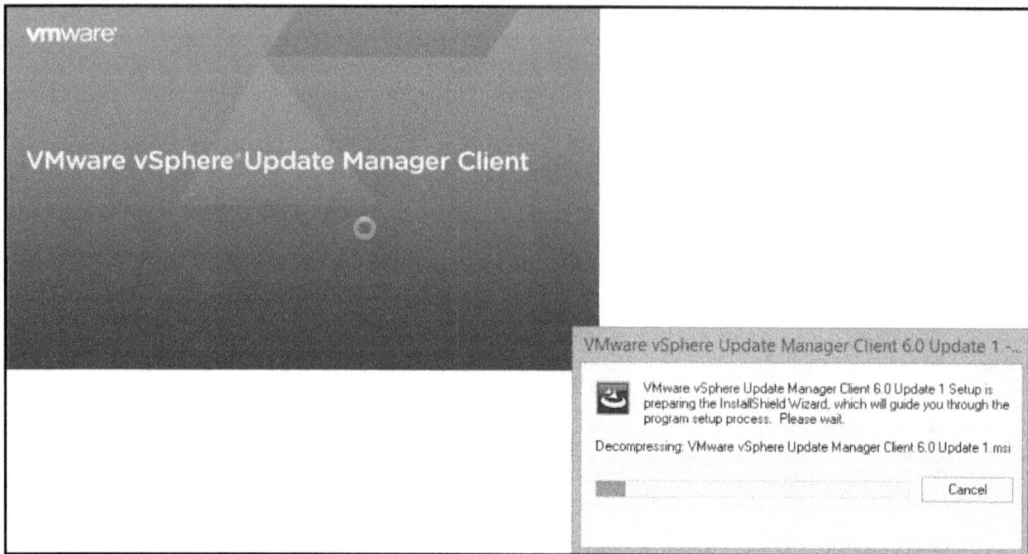

6. Click **Next** to start the installer:

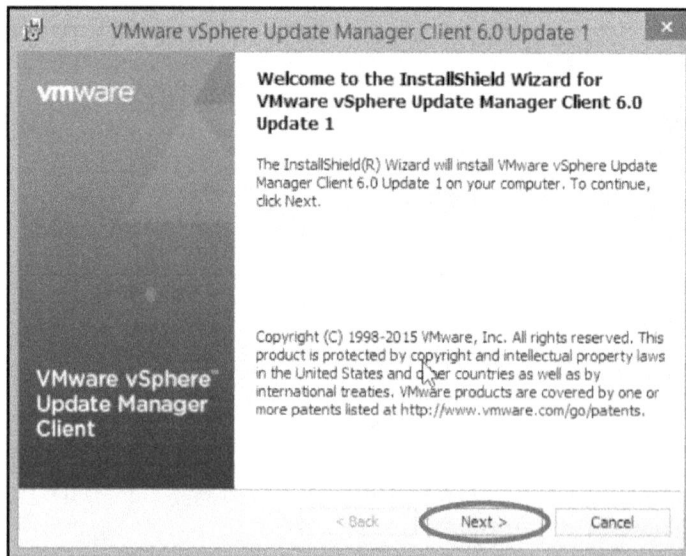

7. On the **End User License Agreement**, select **I accept the terms in the license agreement** to continue:

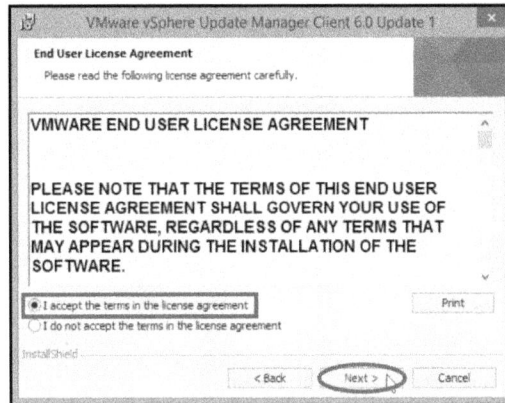

8. Press **Next**.
9. Press **Install**:

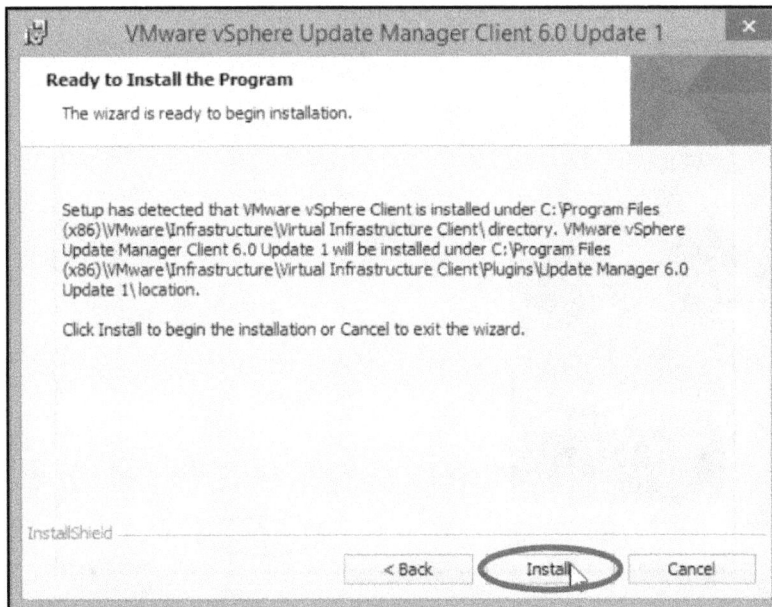

10. It may take a minute for the installation to complete:

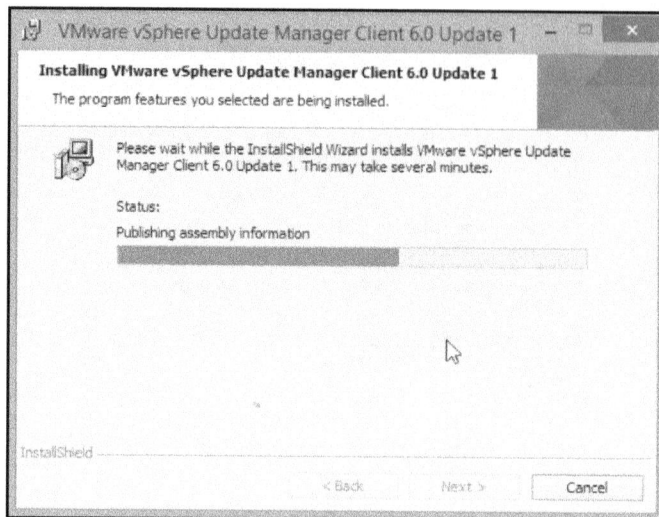

11. Press **Finish** once complete:

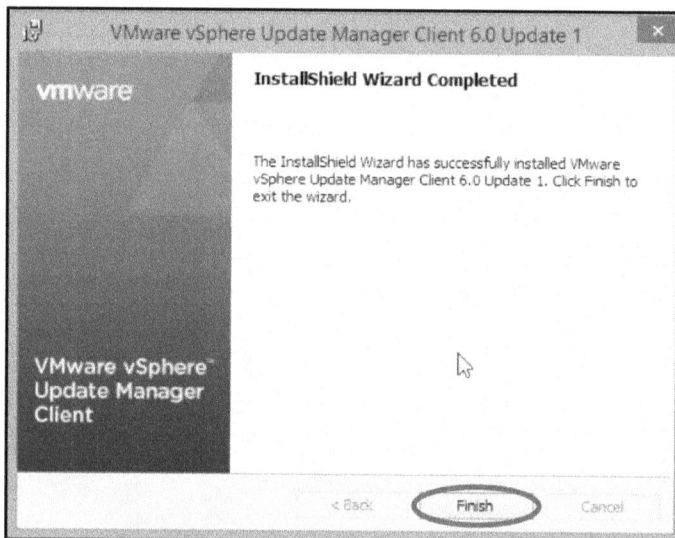

The vSphere Web Client may also be used to administer **Update Manager**:

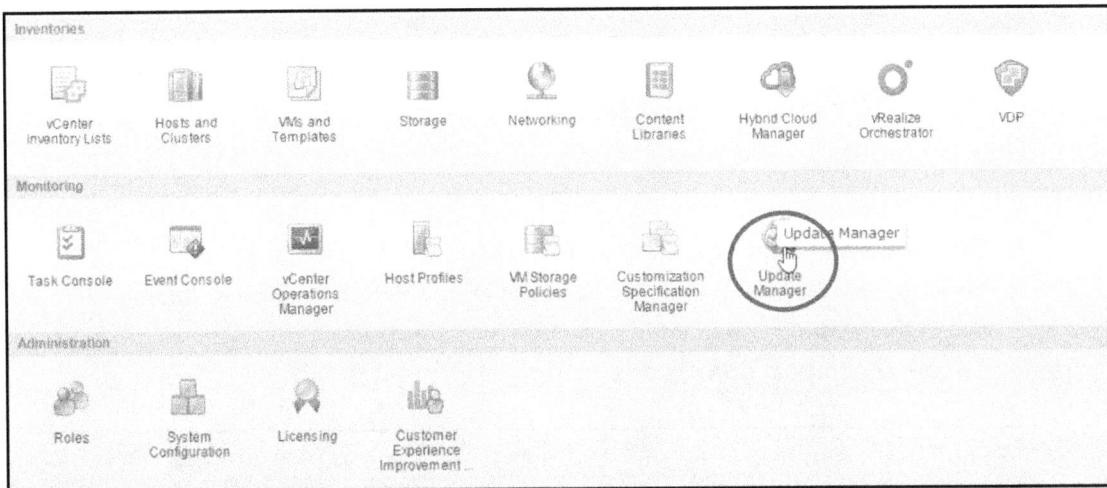

As of vSphere 6 U1, vSphere Update Manager is fully integrated into the vSphere Web Client. Check `http://blogs.vmware.com/vsphere/215/9/vsphere-update-manager-fully-integrated-interface-with-the-vsphere-web-client.html` for more information.

Upgrading ESXi

Prior to beginning an ESXi upgrade, ensure to read the release notes and back up the host configuration. ESXi can be upgraded in one of several ways:

- vSphere Update Manager
- Interactive upgrade using ESXi installer
- Scripted upgrade
- vSphere Auto Deploy
- esxcli

Determine which method is most appropriate for upgrading your infrastructure. This section will cover using vSphere Update Manager.

Importing a Host Image

Before creating an upgrade baseline for ESXi hosts, a host image must first be imported. To import a host image:

1. Download an ESXi image in `.iso` format from VMware's website.
2. Log into the vSphere Web Client and navigate to vSphere Update Manager.
3. Select the **Manage** tab and click the **ESXi Images** button.
4. Choose the **Import ESXi Image** button:

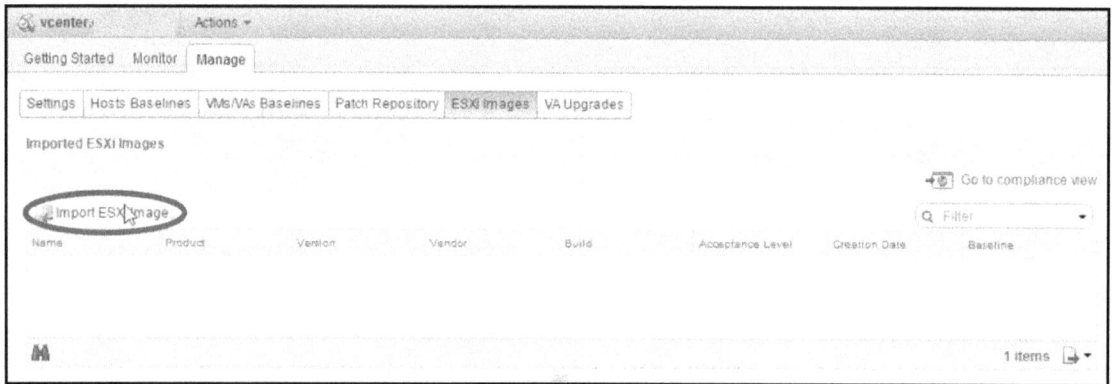

5. A dialog will appear. Press the **Browse...** button to navigate the client desktop:

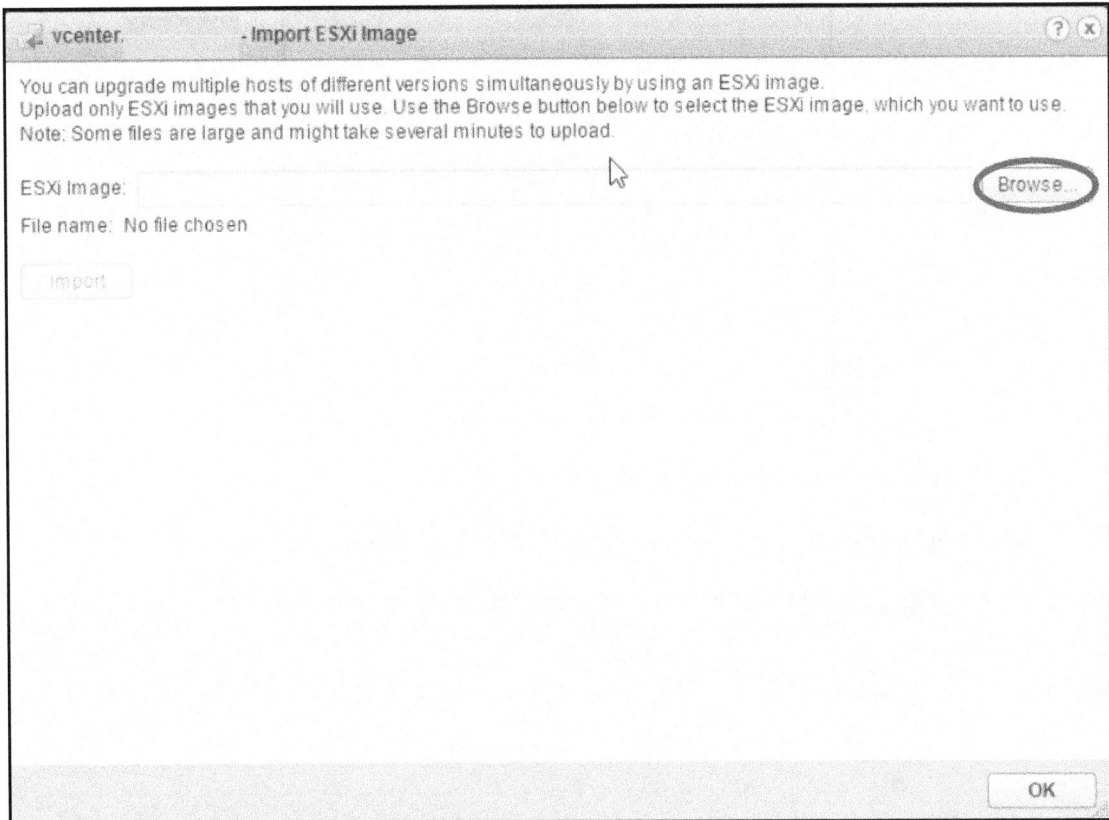

6. Select the ESXi image that is to be uploaded. Press **Open**:

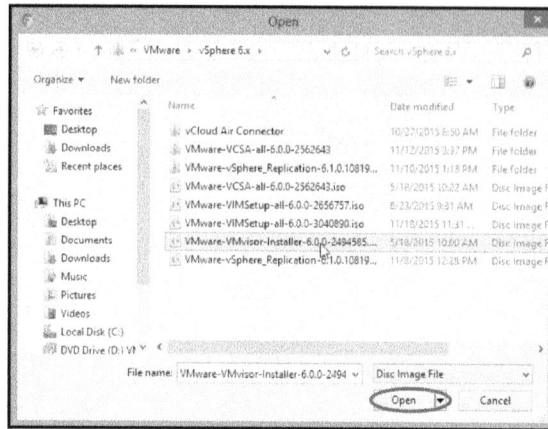

7. In the previous screen, press **OK** to upload.

8. A certificate warning may appear. Select to accept the certificate.

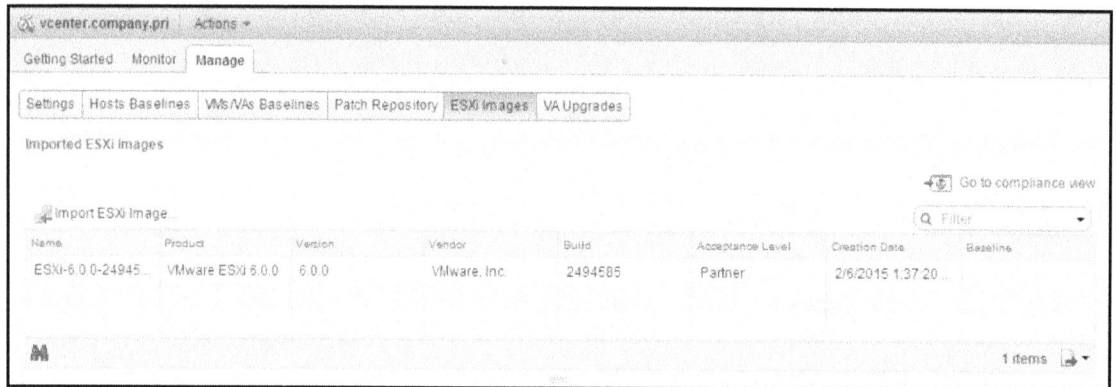

The ESXi image should appear in the list of Imported ESXi Images. This is demonstrated in the above screenshot.

Create an ESXi Upgrade Baseline

The next step in the process is to create an ESXi upgrade baseline containing the imported ESXi image. To begin:

1. Right click the imported ESXi image and choose **Create baseline**:

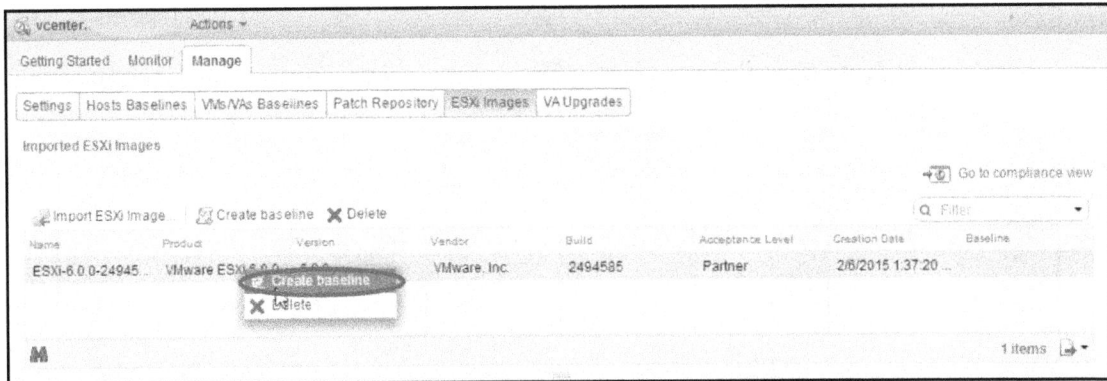

2. The **Create Host Upgrade Baseline** dialog will appear. Enter the **Name** and **Description** for the baseline. Verify the **ESXi image details**:

3. Press **OK** once finished.

Attach an ESXi Upgrade Baseline

Baselines are attached to objects in the vCenter Server inventory in order to scan and determine compliance. Once compliance is determined, baselines are used to remediate inventory objects. A baseline may be attached to a variety of objects. This example shows the baseline being attached to an individual ESXi host.

To do so:

1. Right click an ESXi host in the vSphere Web Client inventory. Select **Update Manager** ǀ **Attach Baseline**:

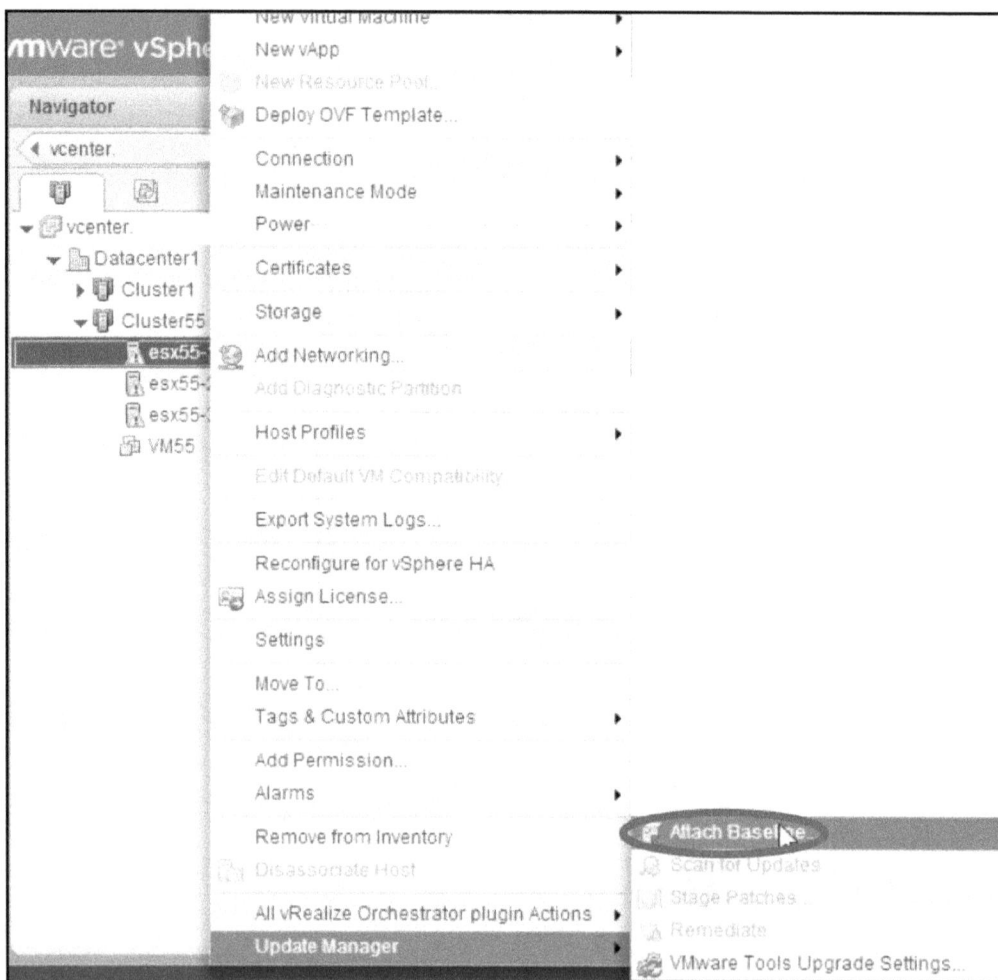

2. The **Attach Baseline or Baseline Group** dialog will appear. Select the appropriate option under **Upgrade Baseline**:

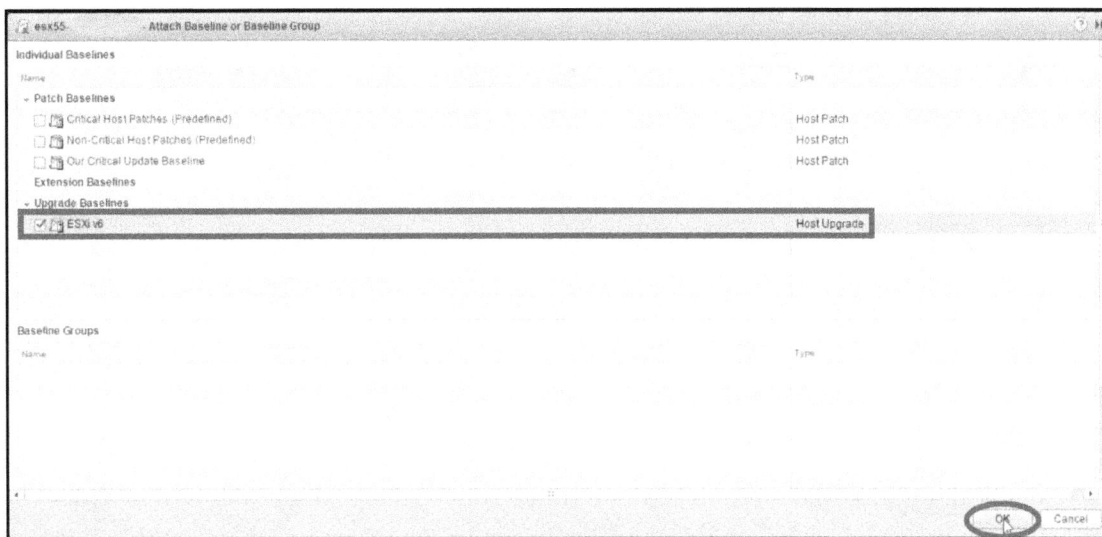

3. Press **OK**.

Remediate an ESXi Host to Upgrade

An ESXi host can be remediated against an upgrade baseline to upgrade its version to vSphere 6.0. Using vSphere Update Manager, an ESXi host may be upgraded from vSphere 5.x to vSphere 6.x. This example demonstrates upgrading a single ESXi host.

To upgrade an ESXi host:

1. Right click the ESXi host in the vSphere Web Client inventory. Select **Update Manager** | **Remediate**:

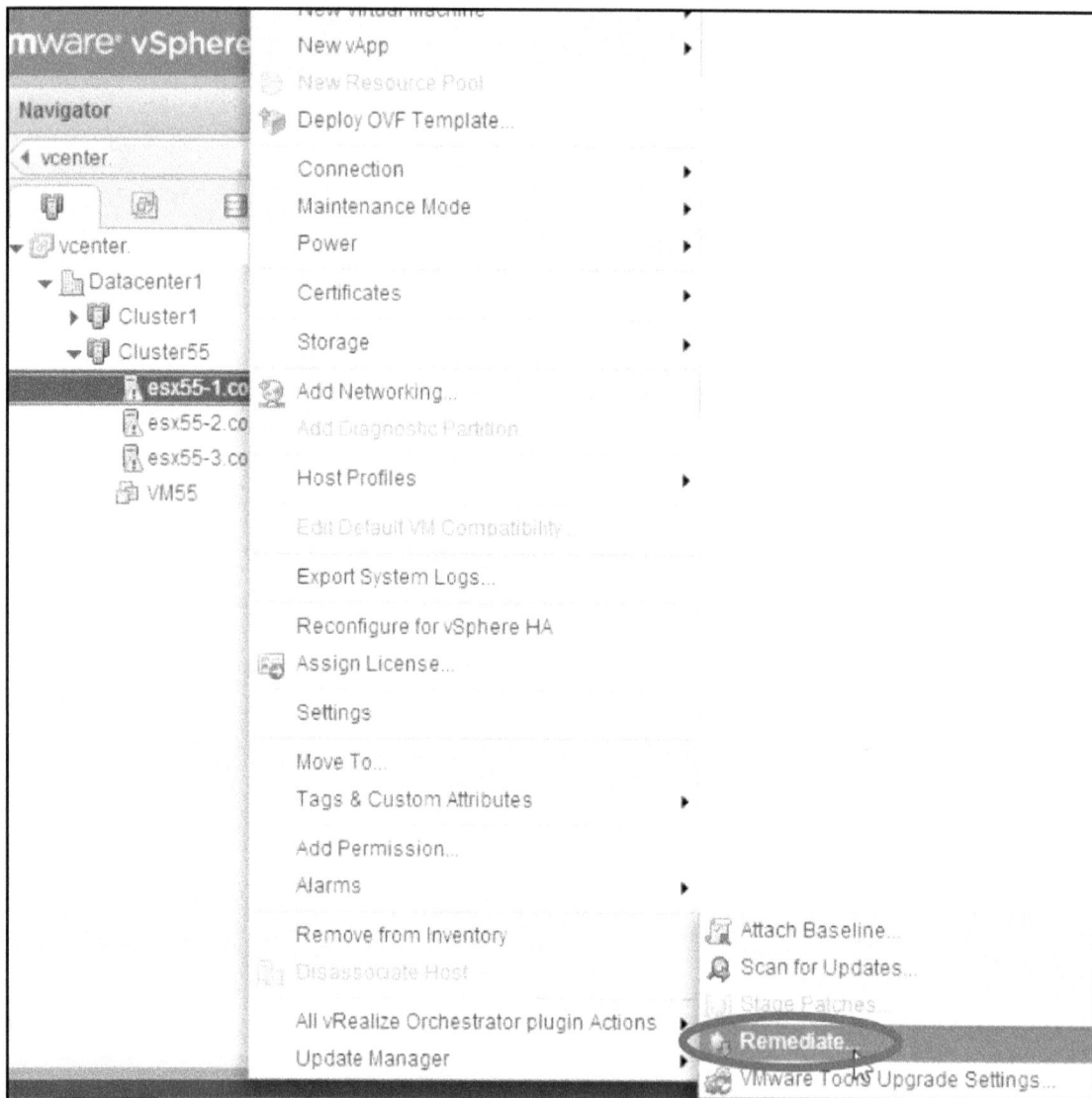

2. The **Remediate** dialog will appear. On the **Select Baselines** pane, choose **Upgrade Baselines** and then the appropriate baseline:

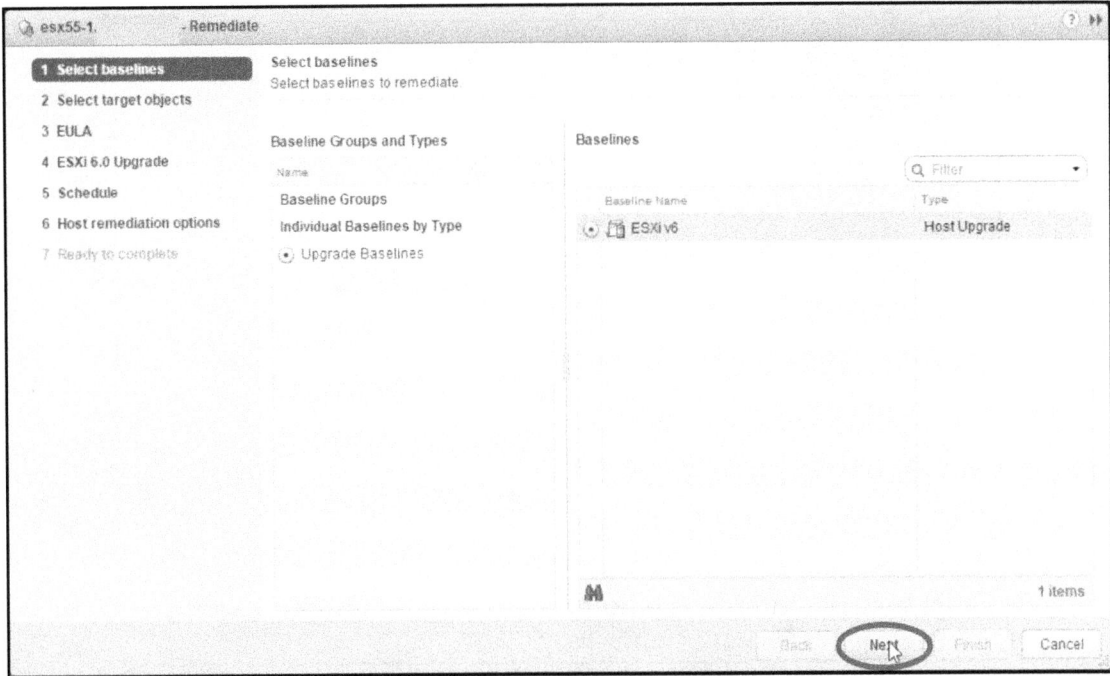

3. Press **Next**.

4. For the **Select target objects** pane, choose the ESXi host(s) to be upgraded:

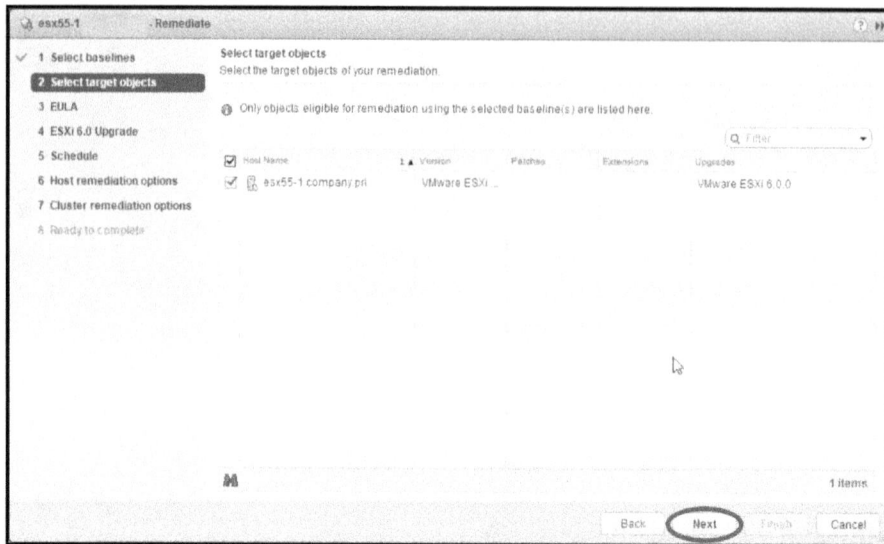

5. Press **Next**.

6. Select **I accept the terms and license agreement** on the EULA screen:

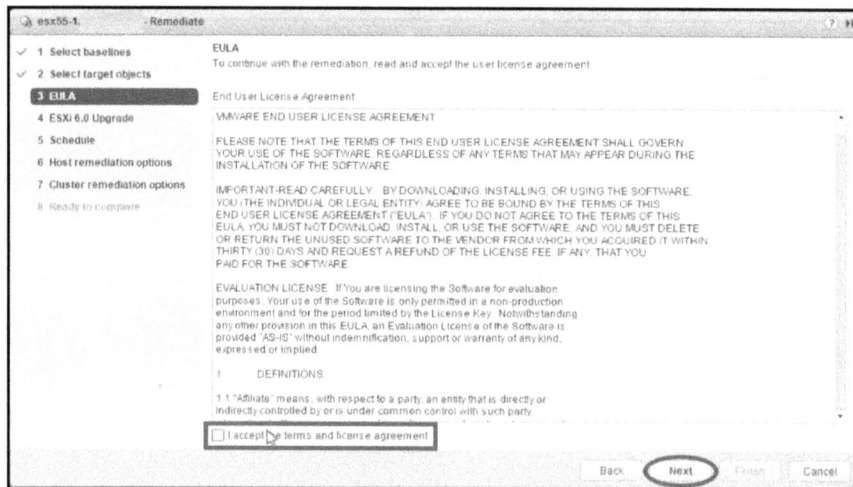

7. Press **Next**.

8. Optionally, select **Ignore warnings and unsupported hardware devices and no longer supported VMFS datastores**, and continue with the remediation:

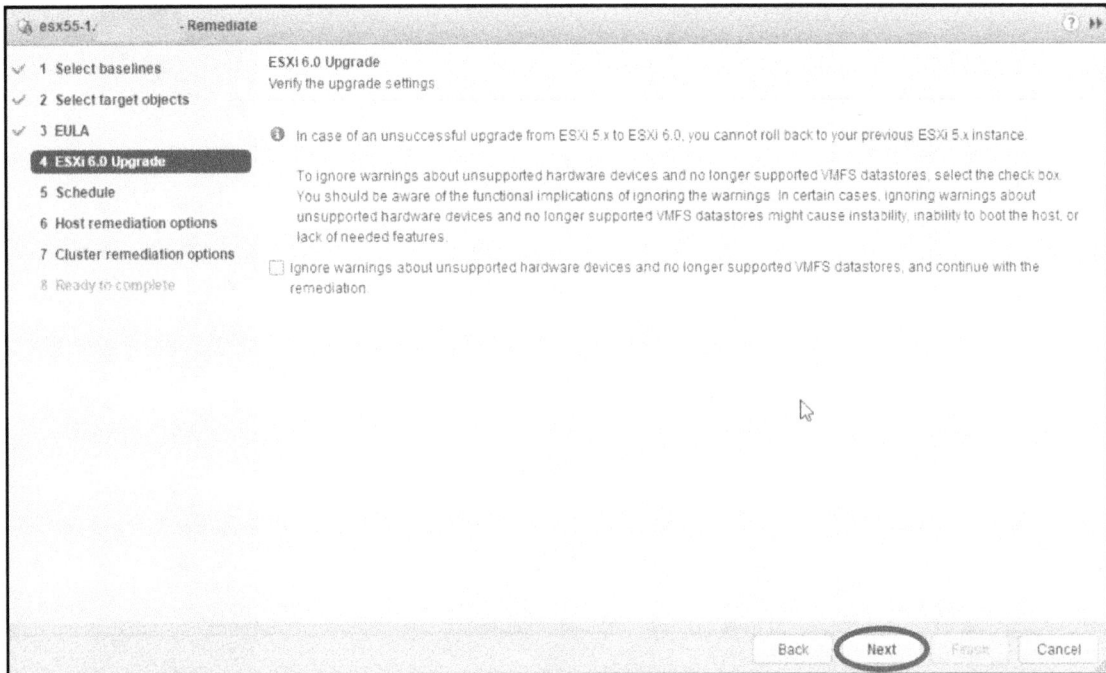

9. Press **Next**.

10. On the **Schedule** pane, choose whether to **Run this action now** or to **Schedule this action to run later**:

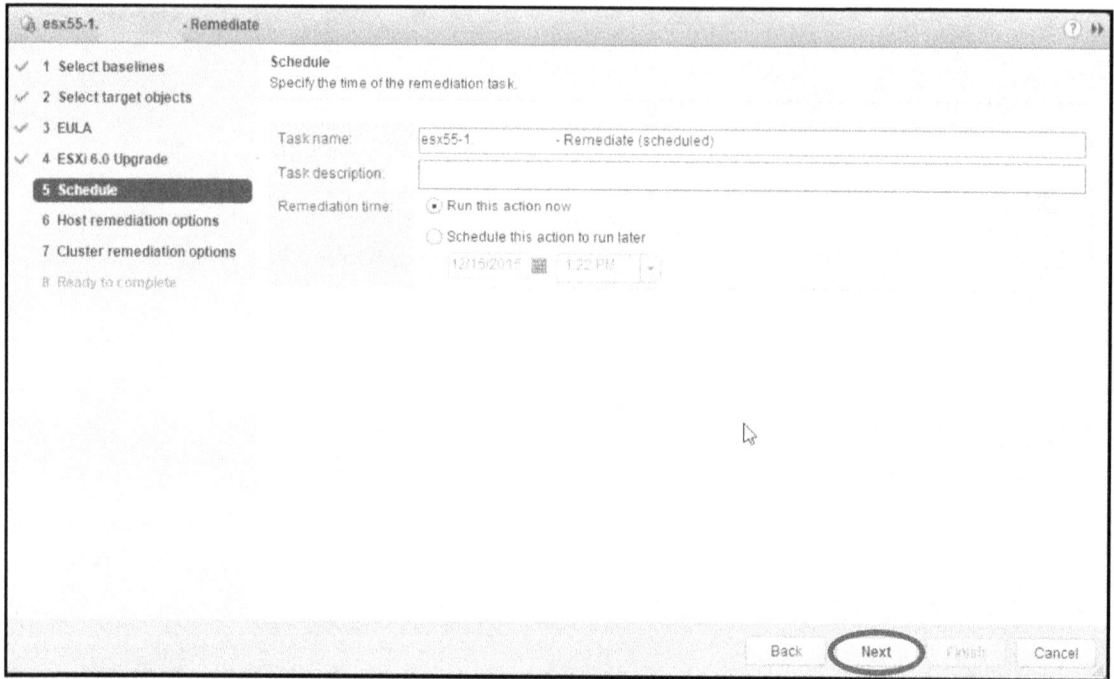

11. Press **Next**.

12. The **Host remediation options** allows for the modification to **VM Power state** (the virtual machines must be migrated off the ESXi host to be upgraded or shut down for the upgrade to complete). It is optional to select whether to **Disable any removable media devices connected to the virtual machines on the host**:

13. Optionally choose whether to **Retry entering maintenance mode in base of failure**. If selected, choose **Retry delay** and **Number of retries**:

14. Press **Next**.
15. On the **Cluster remediation options** screen, choose whether to **Disable Distributed Power Management (DPM)**, **Disabled Fault Tolerance (FT)**, and/or to **Disable High Availability admission control** if enabled. These may be disabled if the enablement of the feature will interfere with vSphere Update Manager evacuating an ESXi host to complete an upgrade.

16. Optionally, **Enable parallel remediation for the hosts in the selected clusters** may be chosen so that more than one ESXi host may be upgraded at one time. This is useful in larger clusters. Another option is to **Migrate powered off and suspended VMs to other hosts in the cluster**, if a host must enter maintenance mode:

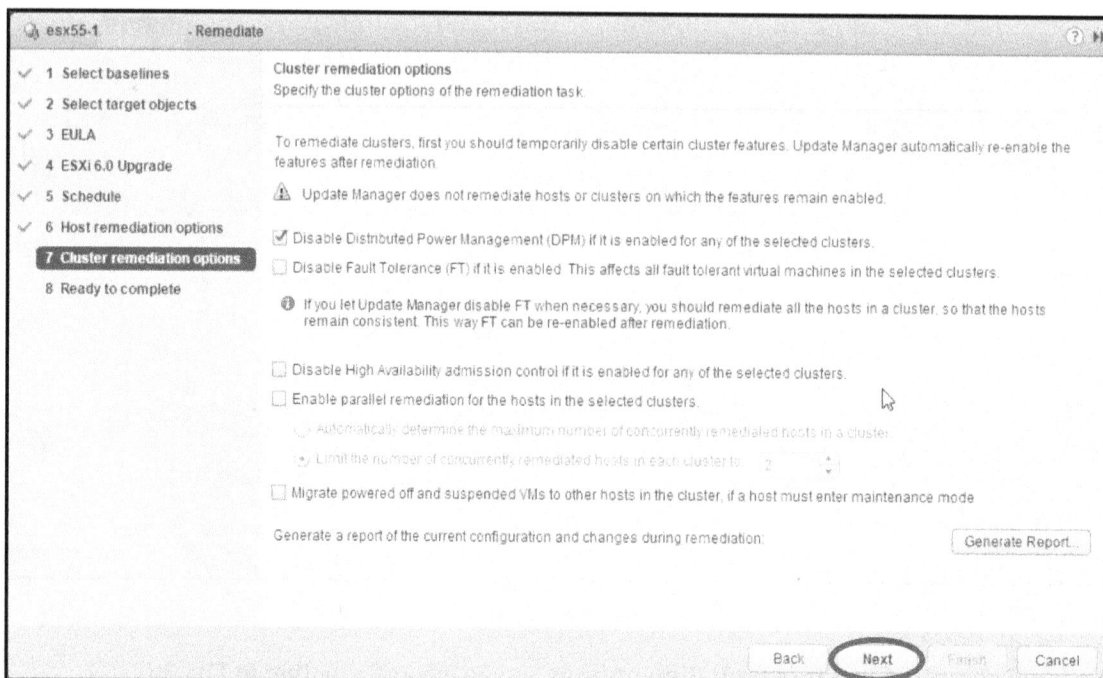

17. Press **Next**.
18. Review the configured options and press **Finish** to begin the upgrade.

Upgrades for ESXi may also be done at a higher level, for example, a cluster, in order to avoid upgrading each ESXi host individually.

Upgrading Distributed Switch

Once the vCenter Server and the ESXi hosts have been upgraded, the vSphere Distributed Switch should be upgraded.

To do so:

1. Select the distributed virtual switch in the vSphere Web Client inventory. Right click and select **Upgrade** | **Upgrade Distributed Switch**:

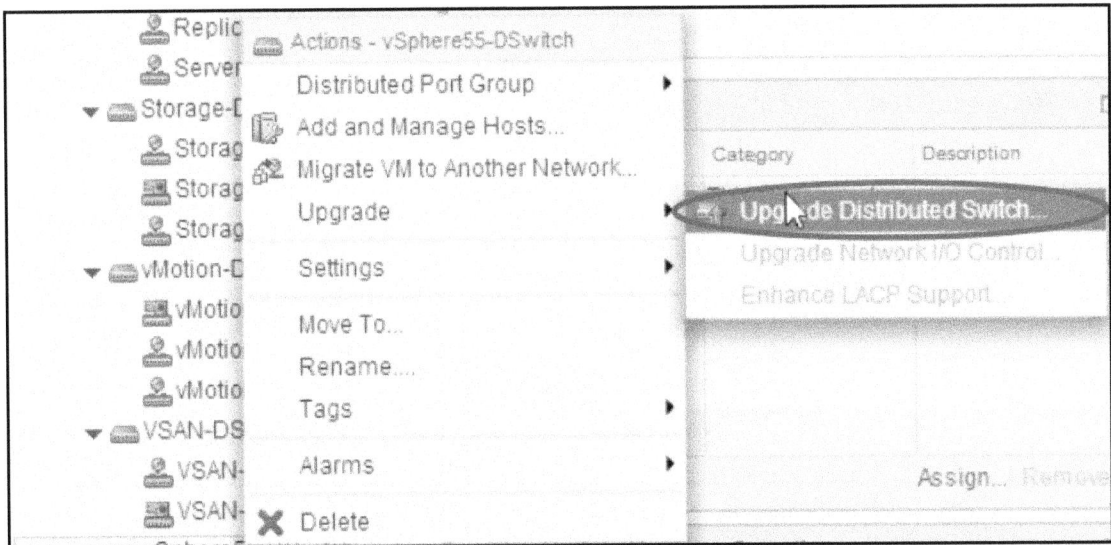

2. The **Upgrade Distributed Switch** dialog will appear. If upgrading from Version 5.5.0 to Version 6.0.0 there is no selection on the **Configure upgrade** pane. However, if an older distributed switch exists, select to which version to upgrade:

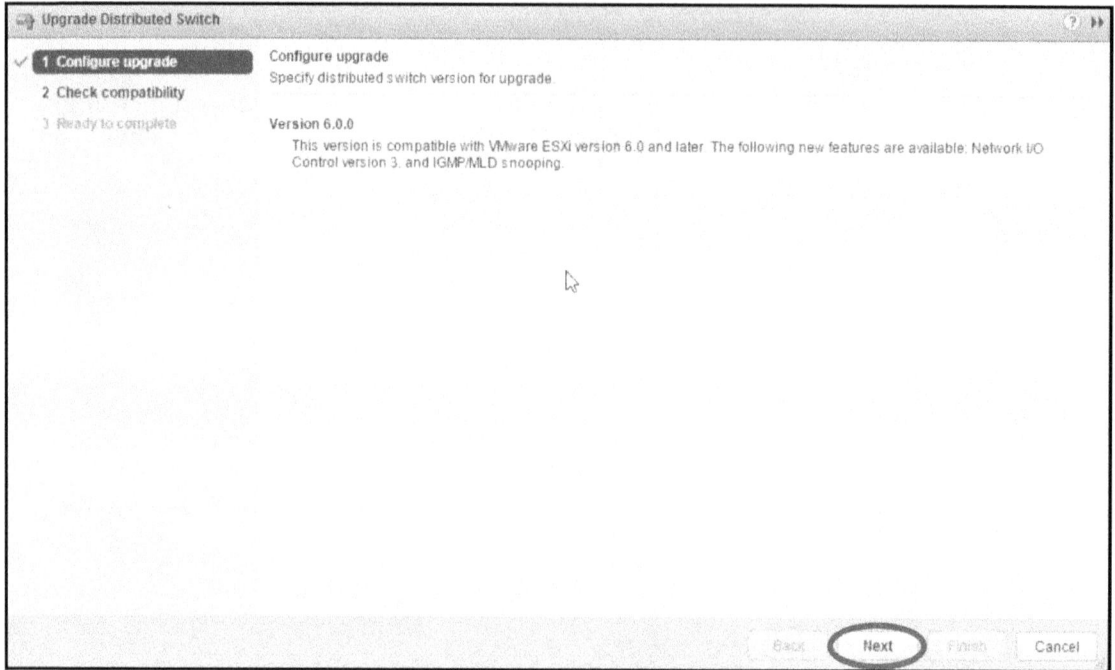

3. Press **Next**.

4. The **Check compatibility** pane will determine compatibility with the connected ESXi hosts. Notice that the following screenshot example shows ESXi hosts that are not yet upgraded to vSphere 6.0, therefore the distributed switch cannot be upgraded. Once all of the ESXi hosts are upgraded to vSphere 6.0 then the distributed switch may be upgraded:

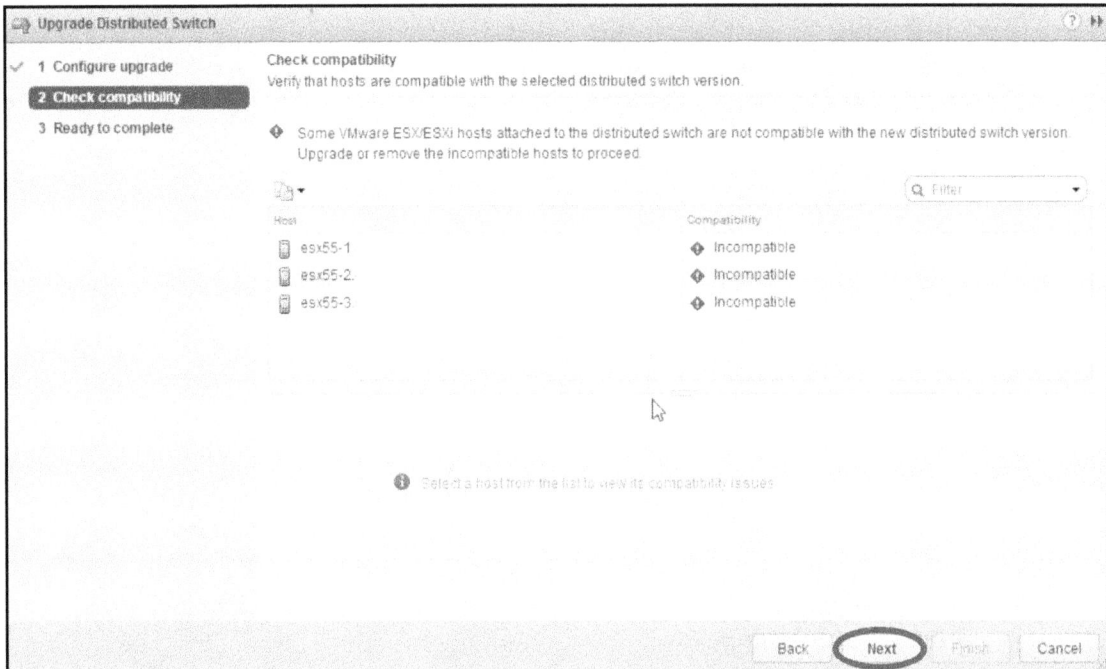

5. Press **Next**.
6. Review settings and press **Finish**.

Upgrading Virtual Machines

Once the vCenter Server and the ESXi hosts have been upgraded, the virtual machines may be upgrade so that they can use the new features that the release brings.

VMware Tools

VMware Tools should be upgraded prior to upgrading the virtual hardware version so that the drivers for any new virtual hardware are available. This can be done using a vSphere Update Manager predefined baseline or manually upgrading the virtual machines.

To manually upgrade a virtual machine's VMware Tools:

1. Using the vSphere Web Client, right click a powered-on virtual machine.
2. Select **Guest OS | Upgrade VMware Tools**:

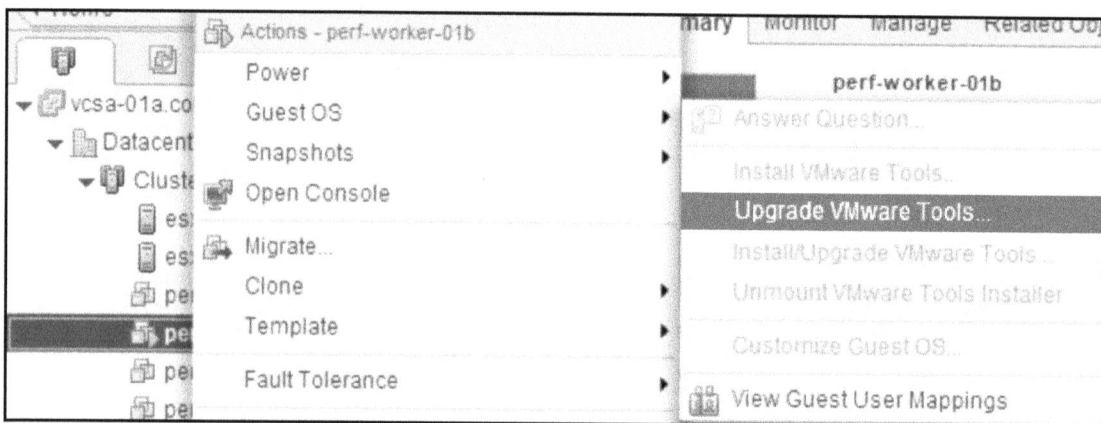

3. Log into the guest operating system of the virtual machine and follow any prompts that may appear.

Keep in mind that a restart may be required.

Virtual Hardware

Once VMware Tools has been upgraded then the virtual hardware version may be upgraded to the newest version. This process may be done on a single virtual machine (as demonstrated in this section) or may be done on multiple virtual machines using vSphere Update Manager.

To upgrade a virtual machine's virtual hardware version:

1. Right click a powered off virtual machine, select **Compatibility | Upgrade VM Compatibility**:

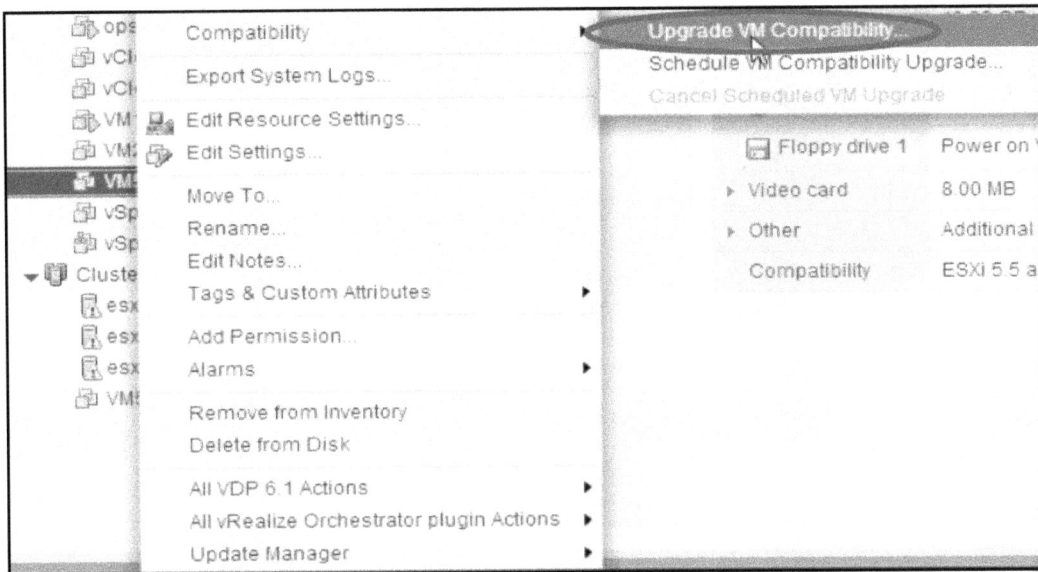

2. The **Confirm VM Compatibility Upgrade** dialog will appear. Press **Yes** to continue.

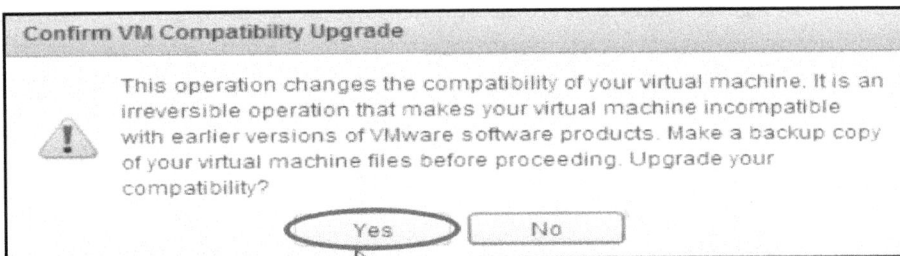

3. **Select a compatibility for the virtual machine upgrade** by choosing **ESXi 6.0 and later** in the drop-down dialog:

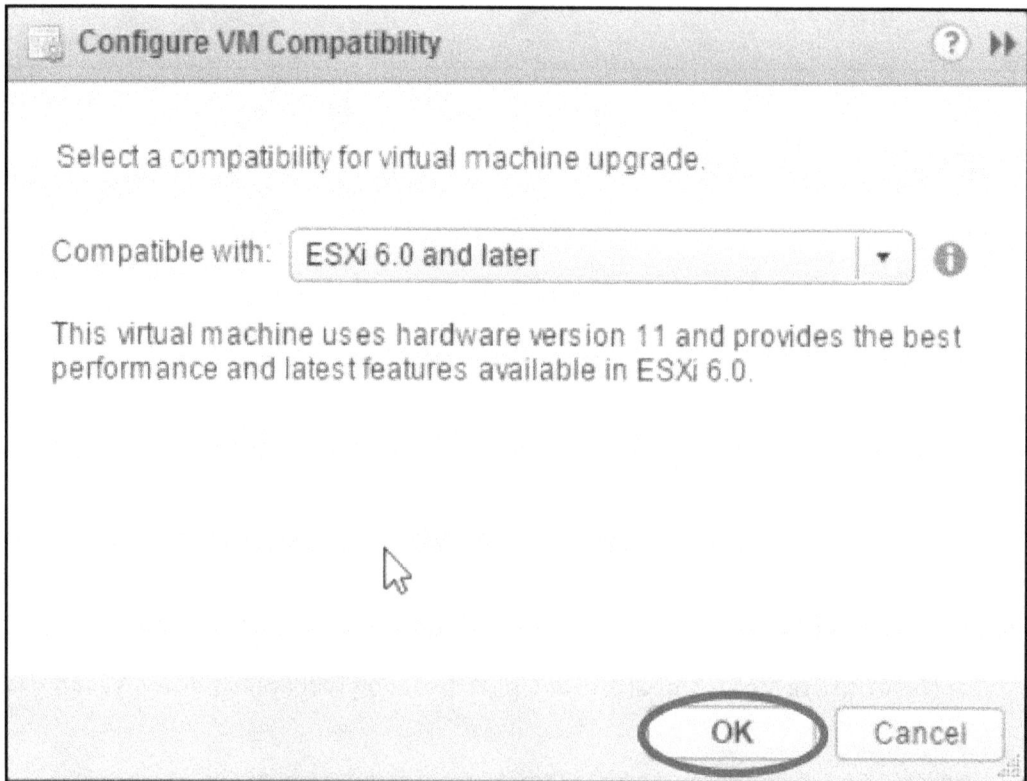

4. Press **OK**.

Summary

Keeping a vSphere environment up to date ensures that access to new features is available. Begin this process by reviewing the vSphere release notes. In this chapter you learned step-by-step how to upgrade vCenter Server, vSphere Update Manager, ESXi, vSphere Distributed Switches, and virtual machines. Remember that the upgrade order is paramount to its success!

Index

access, configuring 213
NFS shares, mounting 213, 214, 215
NFS shares, mounting on multiple hosts 216
prerequisites 213
Node Port IDs 198

O

Organizationally Unique Identifiers (OUI) 109

P

performance charts
  about 389
  advanced performance charts 390, 391, 392,
    393, 394
  overview 389, 390
performance monitoring
  about 389
  alarms, using 402
  esxtop, using 394, 395
  performance charts 389
  resources 408, 409, 410, 411
Permanent Device Loss (PDL) 275
physical NIC enumeration 106
physical switch
  versus virtual switch 105
Platform Services Controller (PSC) 414, 481
  about 63
  VMCA 64
  VMware Licensing Service 67
  VMware SSO 65
Pluggable Storage Architecture (PSA) 186, 187
port allocation, dvPortGroup
  about 131
  elastic allocation 132
  fixed allocation 132
port binding 202
port binding configuration
  NIC teaming, configuring 209, 210
  performing 209
  vmkernel interfaces, binding to iSCSI adapter
    210, 211, 212
port binding, dvPortGroup
  about 129
  dynamic binding 130
  ephemeral binding 131

static binding 130
port groups, vSwitch
  about 111
  virtual machine port group 112
  VMkernel port group 112
port mirroring
  about 169
  distributed port mirroring 169
  distributed port mirroring, configuring 169
  encapsulated remote mirroring (L3) source 169
  remote mirroring destination 169
  remote mirroring source 169
PostgreSQL database 62
prefix-based allocation scheme 109
Primary Node 66
promiscuous VLAN 145
Public Key Infrastructure (PKI) 413
PVLAN support, on VDS
  about 145
  community VLAN 146
  isolated VLAN 146
  promiscuous VLAN 145

Q

Quality of Service (QoS) 28

R

RAID groups
  about 184
  mirroring 185
  RAID-0 185
  RAID-1 185
  RAID-10 185
  RAID-5 185
  striping 185
range-based allocation scheme 109
Rapid Virtualization Index (RVI) 22, 38
Redundant array of independent disks (RAID) 184
replication 32
resource controls
  about 382
  limits 385, 386, 387
  reservations 387, 388
  shares 383, 384
root resource pool 249